MW00770936

Elaisha
Spring 2007

BALKAN IDOLS

RELIGION AND GLOBAL POLITICS

SERIES EDITOR
John L. Esposito
University Professor and Director
Center for Muslim-Christian Understanding
Georgetown University

ISLAMIC LEVIATHAN
Islam and the Making of State Power
Seyyed Vali Reza Nasr

RACHID GHANNOUCHI
A Democrat Within Islamism
Azzam S. Tamimi

BALKAN IDOLS
Religion and Nationalism in Yugoslav States
Vjekoslav Perica

Balkan Idols

Religion and Nationalism in Yugoslav States

Vjekoslav Perica

OXFORD

UNIVERSITY PRESS

2002

OXFORD

UNIVERSITY PRESS

Oxford   New York
Auckland   Bangkok   Buenos Aires   Cape Town   Chennai
Dar es Salaam   Delhi   Hong Kong   Istanbul   Karachi   Kolkata
Kuala Lumpur   Madrid   Melbourne   Mexico City   Mumbai   Nairobi
São Paulo   Shanghai   Singapore   Taipei   Tokyo   Toronto

and an associated company in Berlin

Library of Congress Cataloging-in-Publication Data
Perica, Vjekoslav.
Balkan idols : religion and nationalism in Yugoslav states / Vjekoslav Perica.
p. cm.—(Religion and global politics)
Includes bibliographical references and index.
ISBN 0-19-514856-8
1. Yugoslavia—Religion.   2. Nationalism—Yugoslavia—History—20th century.
3. Nationalism—Religious aspects—Srpska pravoslavna crkva—20th century.
4. Nationalism—Religious aspects—Catholic Church—History—20th century.
5. Nationalism—Religious aspects—Islam—History—20th century.   I. Title.   II. Series.
BL980.Y83 P47 2002
322'.1'094970904—dc21   2001036604

2 4 6 8 9 7 5 3 1
Printed in the United States of America
on acid-free paper

PREFACE

Yugoslavia, that ethnically diverse country . . . began the 1990s
with the brightest future in Eastern Europe. It boasted a
literate, well-trained population that traveled frequently abroad,
and had an unusually large number of companies that had
evaded the inefficiencies of the communist economy and could
compete on the international market . . . food shortages and lines
at stores commonplace in the rest of the Eastern bloc were
virtually unknown in a land blessed with fertile soil and a
breathtaking coastline that attracted billions of dollars in foreign
tourism.

New York Times, 13 April 1992

If you take all guns out of Yugoslavia, they would kill
themselves with knives. Then they would use their teeth. . . .
The historic controversies that Europe thought it had put behind
it—nationalism, religious hatred—have blossomed and now
drive the fighting. . . . Some Europeans fear that the war in
Yugoslavia may represent the beginning of a new division of
Europe—this time along religious lines.

Boston Globe, 28 October 1991

Religion is one of the major forces of conflict in our world today.
Six months after Islamic radicals' deadly terrorist attacks on
New York and Washington, D.C.; as Hindus and Muslims clash anew in
India; Jews and Muslims fight a bloody civil war in Palestine; and religion
fuels conflicts and wars elsewhere in Asia and Eurasia, in Africa, in the
Balkans and Northern Ireland; as religious organizations thwart democratic

transitions in many former communist countries; while religious fundamentalism accompanied with bigotry and xenophobia grows in the "Christian West," religion causes concern more often than hope. Putting the Marxist "opium" metaphor in even stronger terms, the iconoclastic author Salman Rushdie has recently referred to religion as a "poison" for the people. Yet only a decade ago, the dominant global public discourse on religion portrayed it a force of peace, catalyst of the remarkable triumph of democracy over totalitarianism, and hallmark of a new ideal world order.

In the late 1980s, the end of the communist reign in Eastern Europe was approaching. The great change was accompanied by signs of what seemed a religious renaissance. In the multinational Yugoslav federation founded by the communists during World War II, the most visible opposition, the country's religious institutions, celebrated what they perceived as a religious revival. Church attendance visibly increased. Large crowds turned out at massive liturgical events held in shrines, in the streets, in stadiums, and at historic sites. Like Eastern European clergy, the Western media cheered a "return of God" after the fall of the Marxist utopia. Churches were viewed as locomotives of democratization and as proven anticommunists, natural allies of the West (as they had been during the Cold War). Writing my column "Religion and Politics" in the Croatian weekly newspaper *Nedjeljna Dalmacija* from 1988 to 1991, I also repeatedly expressed the belief that religious institutions would contribute to the consolidation of liberal democracy in former communist countries. At that time, in addition to writing my "religious" column, I was also a public activist trying to contribute to democratization of church–state relations by serving on the state commission for relations with religious communities in Croatia. I believed that changes should have occurred swiftly and often could not grasp the sources of difficulties. I also hoped that multiethnic Yugoslavia would remain united and, thanks to her relative prosperity, rich resources, human capital, softer communism, and independence from the USSR, enter a full-fledged democratic transition before any other East European country. I was taught the lesson of history according to which the peoples of the Yugoslav federation could attain prosperity, liberty, and international reputation only through unity and multiethnic equality and cooperation. One does not need Marxist philosophy to understand and espouse such a lesson in Balkan history. Both common sense and a fair use of genuinely religious perspectives would reveal the same truth.

Optimism, like pessimism, is contagious. Communist regimes were collapsing throughout Eastern Europe, and the obnoxious Soviet Union ceased to be a global superpower. The American scholar Francis Fukuyama published his optimistic essay "The End of History?" celebrating contemporary Western states and societies as ideal-types of government. Another influential social scientist, Samuel P. Huntington, argued that at this moment, religion, notably Christianity (both Catholic and Protestant and possibly even Eastern Orthodox), had become increasingly and actively supportive of liberal democracy worldwide.[1] In a similar vein, religious scholars and apologists of faith published books about the mythic "final revolution" unfolding through the 1980s and 1990s, in which virtuous forces, notably churches, were ultimately triumphing over forces of evil.[2] Such theses even seemed to receive some kind of divine support. At Medjugorje in Bosnia-Herzegovina, visionaries and pilgrims allegedly received a message from the Virgin Mary that the current Balkan Marian apparitions would be the last such apparitions on Earth because Mary had completed her historic struggle for peace and justice on Earth![3] In the spring of 1992, a group of jubilant Catholics, mostly from western Europe and the United States, even went to Russia and marched in Red Square carrying the Virgin Mary's statue, celebrating what they perceived as a great, final, godly triumph in history.

At least for a moment, many (including me) believed in the advent of a "golden era" of peace and prosperity for all. The moment of truth, however, came soon. Starting in 1991 and at this writing, 2001, still continuing, the Balkan wars brought the quickly forgotten human practices of warfare, mass murder, torture, concentration camps, and genocide. Triggered by the breakdown of the former Yugoslavia in the early 1990s, the Balkan wars dominated international news and world politics for most of the last decade of the twentieth century. What initially seemed to be a "distant local war," a reminder of the Balkans wars of 1912–13 became the century's marker.[4] The Yugoslav wars exceeded the dimensions of local or regional conflicts and evolved (like the Spanish Civil War or the conflict in the Middle East) into a "world war" of sorts. The technology of the communication revolution brought Balkan horrors into every home in the west. Western audiences and political establishments were shocked by the quick spread of hatred and the galloping war that so quickly tore apart the multiethnic and multiconfessional Yugoslav society. The Balkan malady, from which a nation was dying before Western cameras, especially worried leaders and citizens in every similarly structured and vulnerable multiethnic society. The fact that Yugoslavia was communist was cold comfort. After all, Yugoslav communism since the 1960s had been open to the world and softer than any similar regime. Notwithstanding, neither the crude communist multiethnic USSR nor the rigid communist regime in multiethnic Czechoslovakia disintegrated via genocide and massive human suffering as did the Balkans.

First casualties and artillery barrages in the Balkans were accompanied by Western political analysts' efforts to explain the "roots" and "causes" of the conflict. Religion, the usual suspect in the long history of human conflict and suffering, became one of the primary suspects. In September 1992, the *New York Times* reported from Bosnia as follows: "[N]ew specters of ancient religious fervor are driving the ferocity of the fighting. They are accompanied by equally menacing memories and myths, which are fomenting the hatred among Muslims, Catholic Croats and Orthodox Serbs. These feelings have transformed the fighting in Bosnia into a religious conflict marked by zealotry and brutal extremism."[5] At first glance, the religious war perspective sounded appealing to the Western audience. Yugoslavia's multiethnic and multireligious structure could foster group rivalry that the communist system had failed to manage.

During the 1990s, books on Yugoslavia flooded bookstores and libraries. Most of this literature made no mention of religious institutions as a crucial factor in the conflict.[6] Among authors of several studies[7] that took religion seriously, the agile journalist and author Robert Kaplan, who specialized in reporting from conflict zones worldwide, became very influential.[8] In consequence, between the 1999 Kosovo War and the fall 2000 renewal of violence in Palestine, the Balkans and the Middle East, despite considerable differences, began to look like twin cases in world affairs.[9] During the media focus on the Balkan crisis, the West faced the risk of being both confused and afraid while also getting tired of "all those faraway places of which we know little," to rephrase the notorious dictum of Neville Chamberlain's in 1938. Another paradox was that two American scholars, presumably the most knowledgeable about religion in the Balkans, namely Sabrina Petra Ramet of the University of Washington and the Methodist scholar Paul Mojzes from Pennsylvania, although both published invaluable books,[10] still exerted only a minor influence that was confined to academic circles and experts like them who had no power to influence a broad audience or decision-making in Washington, D.C. What has been missing in the recent scholarship on Yugoslavia is a study explaining the uniqueness of the Yugoslav case and the concrete, active history-making forces, such as religious institutions. A documented history of religion and its interaction with ideologies, nations, and states has not been published. Consequently, the grand debate on the Yugoslav case in the West induced by the media focus on the Balkan wars in the 1990s ended up with the same preexisting popular misconception that religion per se, that is, the different beliefs and styles of worship, suffice to cause (out of the blue) serious conflicts. This misconception is especially harmful for countries like the United States, because in this multiethnic country, no less vulnerable than similar societies, some people have been seriously frightened by the Yugoslav disaster, while others have downplayed it, attributing to the United States some kind of immunity to what had befallen the allegedly "uncivilized" Yugoslavia.

The religious connotations of the Yugoslav wars also reignited the never-ending global scholarly debates about religion in a modern and changing world and about secularization, revival, and "new" religious fundamentalism. Some analysts argued that Yugoslavia is simply another case to sustain the hypothesis that the world is experiencing a surge in extraordinary religious activism (desecularization and revival). According to this argument, the ideological strife of the Cold War era was replaced by a conflict of cultures and religions or, as Samuel P. Huntington referred to it, a "clash of civilizations."[11] Opponents of the "desecularization" argument saw nothing sacred in Yugoslavia-like conflicts.[12] At any rate, recent comparative and general studies dealing with the new politics of religion worldwide, the "new" fundamentalism, and "religious nationalism" have lacked a case study on religion in Yugoslavia.[13]

This study is not only on outgrowth of the Balkan crisis and debate of the 1990s but also the result of a several-decades-long scholarly inquiry about religion in Yugoslav states. Studies published between the 1960s and 1980s, predominantly works of sociology and political science, examined popular belief, secularization, and church-state relations.[14] Historians were especially interested in the interaction between religion and the crucial question of nationalism. As the communist era was nearing its end, religion became an increasingly interesting topic for historians of nationalism, at this time viewed as particularly important by the Serbian school of historiography.[15] In the 1980s, two landmark historical studies of nationalism in Yugoslav lands, written by Ivo Banac and Milorad Ekmečić, discussed the involvement of the Serbian Orthodox Church and Croatian Catholicism in nationalist politics and in ethnic strife.[16] Ivo Banac argued that religious relations among Yugoslav peoples "never occasioned religious wars on the scale of those fought in Western Europe after the Reformation."[17] Banac, followed by other Croat historians, designated the ideology of Great Serbian nationalism, to which the Serbian Orthodox Church paid lip service, as the principal cause of the failure of the interwar Yugoslav kingdom, ill famed for its continuous ethnic strife.[18] A member of the Serbian Academy of Sciences and Arts, Milorad Ekmečić argued that religions and clergy divided several similar Slavic peoples, turned them against one another, and prevented them from forming a viable and influential European nation-state.[19] Ekmečić criticized all clergy as backward, sectarian, and conflict prone but singled out the Catholic Church as a "state within a state" that undermines every state, as it allegedly did in the South Slavic country with an Orthodox majority.[20] With the advent of war and rise of new patriotic historiographies in the successor states of the former Yugoslavia, the unfinished Banac-Ekmečić debate was expanded into a Serbo-Croatian-Muslim dispute over religion and church in history of the Yugoslav peoples.[21]

This study aims at becoming the first political history of religion in modern Yugoslav states. It combines a narrative and analysis. The narrative presents chronologically the process of the making, decay, and collapse of several regimes and nation-states, highlighting the role of religion in the process under consideration while also presenting a history of several religious institutions. The analysis, to put it most succinctly, deals with the role of religious institutions, symbols, and practices in state-formation and state-destruction. The largest portion of this study examines the largest Yugoslav religious organizations, namely the Serbian Orthodox Church, the Roman Catholic Church in Croatia and Bosnia-Herzegovina, and the Islamic religious organization (Islamic Community). In this study I write what religious scholars ordinarily avoid: a political history of religion. Finally, there are in later chapters several topics neglected by previously published works on religion and nationalism in Yugoslav lands, such as interfaith relations (observed at an institutional level), church-state relations (analyzed on the basis of documentation from state archives and government agencies of the communist era previously inaccessible for research), the phenomenon of civil religion, the role of the mainstream religious organizations in landmark ethnic nationalist movements, exile politics and churches abroad, the international dimension of religious organizations' activity, and a number of other themes that have been either altogether omitted or insufficiently studied earlier.[22]

Religion is a highly complex phenomenon. I have been conscious of its nature but as a historian of nationalism, I had to narrow my analysis to religion's social and political dimensions in relation to that topic. For readers with a stronger interest in spiritual and cultural than political aspects of Balkan religions, I refer to works by religious scholars such as Paul Mojzes, Miroslav Volf, Mirko Djordjević, and Michael A. Sells.[23] Consequently, I looked at religion above all as the important source of political legitimacy and agency of nation-formation, especially relevant in an environment such as the Balkans. I was particularly interested in the impact of religion on the formation of multiethnic and multiconfessional nations—"nations of many nations" and nations of many faiths. Furthermore, I have espoused two important general assumptions about the role of faith in the formation of nation-states that came from a religious scholar and a sociologist of religion. The first is Reinhold Niebuhr's statement that "nations are held together largely by force and by emotion," where the emotional precondition for nationhood is provided by religion, and the second is Robert Bellah's argument that "a nation cannot be forged or changed by rational politics alone, without the appeal to the nation's soul."[24] Consequently, I also examined the phenomenon that I have termed "the Yugoslav civil religion of brotherhood and unity." This "invisible religion" (to borrow Peter Berger's phrase applied to a different discourse) has been ignored by earlier analyses of Yugoslavia, which viewed it as a communist trickery or at best mere rhetoric although millions of people sincerely embraced it and accomplished important things inspired by it. Brotherhood and unity was the faith of Yugoslavia's golden age. Faiths that preceeded and succeded it are faiths of this country's dark ages.

Finally, a note about the scope of this study may be in order. In the process of research and writing, an initially modest scope has become quite broad and ambitious. This has occurred, so to speak, "out of necessity" rather than my own design. Although this book is mostly about what used to be the multiethnic nation of South Slavs, it is more than a case study, country study, or regional history. The first reason for this is the nature and complexity of religion. Second, hardly any book dealing seriously with the Balkans can remain within regional limits because of the crucial mutual impact between the region under consideration and the world, that is, because of the interaction between local and global history and politics. Small wonder one of the most valuable volumes emerging from the vast literature produced in the wake of the global focus on the Yugoslav wars in the 1990s—Misha Glenny's *The Balkans, 1804–1999: Nationalism, War and the Great Powers*—underscores that the understanding of Yugoslavia requires a broad perspective as much as European, and international histories of the modern era cannot afford to overlook Yugoslavia.[25] It must be acknowledged that Glenny is one of the few western Balkan analysts who realized two critically important things about the region under consideration. The first is that one of the major causes of the Balkan peoples' "eternal" troubles is their inability to cooperate with each other and attain some degree of unity for the sake of common good and liberty. For that matter, the lesson of Yugoslavia should be both about a remarkable failure and promise of success (i.e., potential through cooperation). The second is that the Balkan peoples shed their blood in order to master their own destiny only to realize after every cycle of massacres and wars that outsiders—the great powers—would decide their fate. Consequently this book cannot remain a case study even if it were designed as such because it examines a country of an extraordinary cultural heterogeneity that happened to be located in a region which, analogous, for example, to the Middle East, is the world in a microcosm. No less important, this is the region where Rome and Byzantium and later Ottoman Turkey and Habsburg Austria challenged each other and vied for souls and loyalties of the local peoples; where the notorious "Eastern Question" originated; where the 1914 Sarajevo assassination led toward World War I; where the first large heresy within the communist block was born; where the first large-scale post–Cold War conflict took place; and so forth. Consequently, a book like this one indispensably had to exceed boundaries of a country and even regional studies and, in addition to contributing to the Yugoslav scholarship, draw several broader generalizations concerning nationalism, religion, secularization, communism, and the world after Yugoslavia's collapse.

ACKNOWLEDGMENTS

This is a historical research monograph, so a few notes on sources seem indispensable. The documentation on which this study is based includes some Yugoslav communist-era documents, mostly obtained through municipal and regional commissions for relations with religious communities (called earlier "commissions for religious affairs"), as well as documents from government and party (the League of Communists) organs and agencies in the republics and the federation, obtained through the local commissions. Commissions for relations with religious communities were the only specialized agencies for church-state relations that harbored some data about religious institutions and occasionally produced good analyses and information—usually for a restricted audience (that is, confidential or semiconfidential material for state and party officials). One of a few valuable sources not produced by these commissions but still available to me during the research and writing of this book, was the bimonthly bulletin *Religija, politika, društvo* (*Religion, Politics, Society*—cited later in this English translation) published by the analytical department of the Yugoslav government's news agency TANJUG. Thanks to my experience in the archives, a great deal of previously unpublished information is to be revealed in this book. The bulk of the research and fieldwork was carried out between 1985 and 1991, and most cited and examined documents originated between the 1960s and the late 1980s. Initially I intended to write a typical journalistic book on religion, communism, and the Balkan conflict. In 1993 I had completed such a book in Croatian. That unpublished manuscript became the key source of information for my doctoral dissertation, as well as this book.

During my doctoral and postdoctoral work in the United States (1995–2000) I consulted secondary as well as some primary sources. I was also able to acquire a new perspective and familiarize myself with the new art of conflict management developing in the United States. After completing the dissertation at the University of Minnesota, the research and writing of this book was accomplished in Washington, D.C., above all thanks to the splendid resources of the Library of Congress. The period in Washington included my appointments as a Peace Scholar in residence at the United States Institute of Peace, Research Scholar at East European Studies division of the Woodrow Wilson International Center for Scholars, and a research analyst affiliated with the Federal Research Division of the Library of Congress. When I began to teach history in the winter of 2000, I realized that I had had a privilege available to only a few lucky scholars, that is, to complete a major book-length work free from the teaching burden.

As noted in the preface, one reason why a coherent historical study in church-state relations and the religious dimension of nationalism in the Yugoslav states has been hitherto unwritten, was the restriction of access to both state and church archives during the communist era, as well as the near impossibility of document-based scholarly research under the postcommunist regimes. Nevertheless, scholars and journalists with good connections in the government, as well as some government officials, were able to publish a number of more or less well-documented analyses, doctoral dissertations, master's theses, and monographs based on documentation from government agencies, police archives, commissions for religious affairs, embassies, and other state organs. I had the privilege to work both as a Croatian government official and as a journalist with good contacts in religious institutions.

The documentation utilized here is relatively limited in scope and number. Most interesting documents I had a chance to read were communist-era confidential analyses of church-state relations and correspondence between government and church officials. Unfortunately I had no chance to reexamine archival material and expand my research after the fall of communism. According to the current situation, future researchers will be facing numerous difficulties, especially in the two largest successor states of the former Yugoslavia. In Croatia, for example, the Tudjman regime politically exploited communist-era archives and secret police files. The regime favored the Catholic Church to an extent that, according to unconfirmed information I received from private sources, an unknown amount of communist-era police files and documents from commissions for relations with religious communities had been transferred to private clerical possession and to the Vatican archives. It is noteworthy, however, that some documents about the Catholic Church in Croatia during World War II and under communism are kept in the Museum of the Victims of Genocide in Belgrade. In addition, the United States Holocaust Museum in Washington, D.C., has recently acquired some material about the Croatian wartime state and the Catholic Church that came largely from U.S. sources and Serbian sources (always eager to discredit Croatia and the Catholic Church), with some coming from Croatia and Bosnia-Herzegovina. In November 2001 the Croatian government turned over to the state archives 38,000 communist-era secret police files plus some six hundred new files from the Tudjman era (1990–2000) and allowed affected citizens to familiarize themselves with these files' content. On this occasion commentators and editorials again noted that many files had earlier been destroyed or stolen, and some affected citizens rejected the right to read their files because they did not wish to take part what seemed to be another compromise between powerholders rather than a service to democratic transition. (See *Slobodna Dalmacija*, 6 November 2001, and *Feral Tribune*, no. 843, 10 November 2001.)

A vast amount of material on the Catholic Church in Yugoslavia and other religious institutions is still kept in former government agencies, government archives, and other institutions in of Belgrade. The Belgrade bi-weekly *Republika* wrote in May 2000 about Yugoslav president Milošević's use of secret police files and archival documents against political opponents. Unfortunately for researchers on communist Yugoslavia, the Serbian government also controlled the former Yugoslavia's government archives. In Bosnia-Herzegovina, much documentation was lost in the 1992–95 war. Still, some encouraging news came from researchers affiliated with Woodrow Wilson International Center for Scholars in Washington, D.C., who visited Sarajevo in 1999 looking for archival sources for the Cold War International History Project. They reported that a massive communist-era archive was saved and will be open to Western researchers. Similar news may soon come from the former Yugoslav republic of Macedonia.

My autumn 1999 visit to Europe, the first after eight years in America, was filled with good sentiments only during my week-long stay in Berlin. As I traveled southward, I thought about a motto I found in a Bosnian "alternative" newspaper: *Što južnije, to tužnije* (the more you're moving to the South, the more it looks sad). After two weeks I gave up my efforts to conduct a "ten years after" set of interviews, because no one seems as open and ready to talk as during the prewar crisis (when none of us really expected such a war). Eventually I realized that my most effective tool is my experience and my research and fieldwork, carried on from 1985 to 1991 and updated with the hindsight of 1991–2000 and my Washington research.

In the bibliographical section of this book I list a number of documents in my personal archive from offices of commissions for relations with religious communities. None of those documents has been cited in similar studies on Yugoslavia published either in English or local languages. These documents are cited in the notes using their original titles, with a free translation by me in parentheses. Quotations from these documents and other sources in Serbo-Croatian also appear in my translation unless otherwise noted. Documents are classified and cited according to the institution of their origin rather than the location where they were kept (this includes almost all of the documents I have obtained through the municipal or regional commissions for relations with religious communities in Split, Croatia, between 1985 and 1991).

Finally, I would like to acknowledge support without which this book would have not been possible. I am indebted to several institutions and individuals for support, guidance, and encouragement that I received during the making of this book. First of all I remember with appreciation all those who were my friends, coworkers, and interviewees during the prewar crisis in former Yugoslavia and Croatia, when I worked for the weekly *Nedjeljna Dalmacija* and for the regional commission for church-state relations in Split, Croatia. My personal experience of the late 1980s and early 1990s eventually became what is usually called "fieldwork" and "area studies" that generated both my dissertation and this book. From this period I remember with special gratitude Marin Kuzmić, Vito Unković, Radovan Samardžić, Kruno Kljaković, Srdjan Vrcan, Tomislav Šagi-Bunić, and Ševko Omerbašić.

To Roko Andričević, Efi Foufulla-Gheorgiu, and my wife Sanja's NASA fellowship in hydrological research I owe my coming to America. I also feel obliged to thank the United States for receiving me and many other members of my generation after the disintegration of our homeland. Furthermore, let me thank the University of Minnesota for admitting a Balkan latecomer to its Graduate School. Special thanks to my dissertation adviser, Professor Theofanis G. Stavrou, and all the teachers I met during my studies in Minneapolis. Furthermore, I acknowledge with gratitude dissertation fellowship awards that I received from the Jennings Randolph Program for International Peace of United States Institute of Peace and the Harry Frank Guggenheim Foundation. I am especially grateful to Joseph Klaits of the United States Institute of Peace for his support and encouragement beyond the dissertation. Many thanks also to the United States Institute of Peace Grant Program. And the Woodrow Wilson International Center for Scholars–East European Studies has been supportive and invaluable to me during my doctoral as well as postdoctoral research. I would also like to thank the academic journals *East European Societies* and *Religion, State and Society* for permission to reprint in this book my earlier published articles or sections in published articles. I am also more than grateful for the precious advice as well as benevolent criticism I got from Sabrina Petra Ramet. Many thanks also to Zoran Mandić, Diana Roglić, Dražen Gudić, Pero Jurišin, Boris Orcev, and Momčilo Markuš for illustrations, various materials, and information they sent me from the Balkans during the late 1990s. I also very much appreciate the invaluable contribution to this book of the anonymous readers for Oxford University Press, Oxford's editors Cynthia Read, Bob Milks, and Theo Calderara, copyeditor Martha Ramsey, and the series editor John Esposito. Finally, my gratitude to my family goes beyond words. I wish to acknowledge the concrete and invaluable service with editing, maps, and bibliography I got from my wife, Sanja, and our son, Karlo, as well as immeasurable support and encouragement I have received from Sanja, her mother, Nada, and our daughter, Maria.

CONTENTS

NOTE ON PRONUNCIATION AND FOREIGN LANGUAGE TERMS

Most foreign language terms and personal, institutional, and place names in this book come from the Serbo-Croatian, Serbian, and Croatian languages. The written languages are phonetical, which means that each letter of the alphabet represents a separate sound. Basic rules for pronunciation are as follows. The letter *c* is pronounced as "ts" or "tz" and is never pronounced as "k" (for example, *Stepinac* should be "Stepinats," not "Stepinak" or "Stepäïnek"; *Jasenovac* is "Jasenovats," not "Jasenovak," and *Srebrenica* is "Srebrenitsa"). The letter *j* is always pronounced as a *y* (*Jugoslavija* is "Yugoslavia" or "Yugoslaviya"). The most common diacritical marks are:

ć is pronounced "ch" (*Kuharić* is "Kuharich");

č is pronounced "tch" (*Gračanica* is "Gratchanitsa")

š is pronounced "sch" (*Milošević* is "Miloschevich").

ž is pronounced "zh" (*Žanić* is "Zhanich").

Toponyms appear in anglicized form only, as in "Belgrade" and "Yugoslavia" (the native language forms are "Beograd" and "Jugoslavija"), but only if the anglicized form is in general use in international news and literature. Otherwise the native language form is maintained (e.g., "Peć" instead of the historic "Ipek," and "Marija Bistrica," not "Maria Bistrica"). Most names appear in their native-language form, such as "Pavle," not "Paul"; "Franjo," not "Francis"; and "Alojzije," not "Aloysius."

CHRONOLOGY

1935–1939

The Kingdom of Yugoslavia and the Holy See sign a concordat regulating the status of the Catholic Church in the multinational country. The largest nation's religious organization, Serbian Orthodox Church, opposes the treaty. On 19 July 1937 the "Bloody Liturgy" incident takes place in Belgrade, when the Serbian Orthodox Church stages demonstrations against the concordat and prevents its ratification by the National Assembly. The "Concordat Crisis" fuels hostility between the Serbian Orthodox Church and the Catholic Church of Croatia, aggravating crisis in the national turn.

1939

The Serbian Orthodox Church celebrates the 550th anniversary of the battle of Kosovo and improves relations with the royal government. Ratification of the concordat is canceled. The Croatian episcopate mobilizes Croatian Catholics for a nine-year celebration of the jubilee "Thirteen Centuries of Christianity in the Croat People."

1941–1945

Civil war along ethnic lines is fought in a Yugoslavia dismembered by Axis Powers. The Communist Party of Yugoslavia, led by Croat Tito, organizes the "People's Anti-fascist Liberation Struggle"—a successful multiethnic resistance to both for-

eign invaders and domestic ethnic
factions. Tito is backed by the Allies.

1941–1945   The Independent States of Croatia (NDH),
allied with the Axis, brutally persecutes
the Serbian Orthodox Church and the
Serb population in Croatia and Bosnia-
Herzegovina. The Serb nationalist militia,
the Četniks, massacre Croats in southeastern Croatia and Muslims in Bosnia-
Herzegovina. The Catholic Church hierarchy supports the NDH.

1946   The victorious communist government
condemns religious leaders for collaboration with ethnic wartime regimes and
foreign invaders. Many clerics and religious leaders are executed, jailed, or exiled. The Archbishop of Zagreb, Alojzije
Stepinac, is sentenced to 16 years in
prison. The Serbian bishop Nikolaj Velimirović goes into exile, and the theologian Justin Popović is sent into long-term
confinement. Numerous anti-Yugoslav
ethnic nationalistic organizations are
founded in the West. Some religious leaders and diaspora churches support these
émigré groups and organizations.

1948   Yugoslavia breaks from the Soviet Union
but preserves independence. The Serbian
Orthodox Bishop Nikolaj Velimirović, ex-
iled in the United States, urges Serbs in
America to petition the United Nations
for recognition of Croat massacres of
Serbs during World War II as genocide
he compares to the Inquisition and the
Holocaust. The Tito regime sentences to
long prison terms a group of Bosnian
Muslims who fight for an independent
Muslim state.

1952–1953   Yugoslavia and Italy are involved in a
heated border dispute. The Italian anticommunist pope, Pius XII, makes the
jailed Archbishop Stepinac a cardinal and
excommunicates the Croat communist
Tito from the Catholic Church.

1960   Cardinal Stepinac dies in confinement.
Germanus Djorić becomes head of the
Serbian Orthodox Church with the con-

	sent of the regime and initially refrains from championing ethnic nationalism through the Church.
1962	Branches of the Serbian Orthodox Church in North America secede from the Serbian patriarchate in Belgrade, and the Macedonian Orthodox clergy announce a similar intentions. The Serbian Orthodox church is weakened while Yugoslav Catholicism and Islam recover and expand.
25 January 1966	In the aftermath of the Second Vatican Council, the first historic Catholic-Orthodox interfaith prayer service is held in the city cathedral in Split, Croatia; a Croatian bishop and Serb-Orthodox prelate worship together. Interfaith cooperation spreads throughout country, including Protestants and Muslims as well as Catholics and Orthodox. The regime cautiously supports this new ecumenism, which helps to stabilize the country's ethnic relations.
1966	A protocol on talks between the Holy See and government of the Socialist Federal Republic of Yugoslavia is signed in Rome, leading to the establishment of diplomatic relations between the two states.
1967	The orthodox clergy in the Yugoslav Republic of Macedonia, with local communists' backing, secedes from the Serbian patriarchate in Belgrade. The Serbian Orthodox Church does not recognize the new national Orthodox church and blames the regime for inciting the schism.
1968	The Serbian Orthodox Church, defying the authorities' ban, organizes a commemoration of Serb medieval ruler Dušan in downtown Belgrade. Patriarch Germanus returns the Church to a nationalist course.
1968–1969	Bosnian Slavs of Muslim faith are recognized by the regime as a nationality under the religious label. The Islamic Religious Community changes its name to

	"Islamic Community" but rejects ethnic nationalism and supports Tito's federation.
1969	Patriarch Germanus writes to Tito seeking government protection against Albanian attacks on church property, clergy, and faithful in the province of Kosovo. In September, the Serbian Orthodox Church celebrates the 750th anniversary of ecclesiastical independence. The 1969 jubilee is the first such massive religious event publicly celebrated in the communist country since 1945.
1970	In Sarajevo, the Bosnian Muslim nationalist Alija Izetbegović publishes a document entitled "The Islamic Declaration— A Program for the Islamization of Muslims and the Muslim Peoples." Izetbegović uses Islam to mobilize Bosnian Muslims in a struggle for nationhood and statehood. A few Muslim clerics join him at this point.
1975–1984	The Croatian Catholic episcopate organizes the "Great Novena," a nine-year jubilee entitled "Thirteen Centuries of Christianity in the Croat People." After the Polish "Great Novena of the Millennium," in the 1950s, the Croat Novena is the most grandiose religious event freely celebrated in the communist countries of Eastern Europe.
1979	The Catholic Church in Croatia begins annual commemorations of Cardinal Alojzije Stepinac, persecuted by the communists. The regime protests but does not ban the commemoration.
1980	Tito dies in Belgrade. The two largest churches send condolences to the government. The Islamic Community and the Macedonian Orthodox Church hold commemorations in churches and mosques.
1981	Unknown arsonists, suspected to be Kosovo Albanian separatists, set ablaze the residential section of the Serbian medieval patriarchate at Peć, near the Albanian border. Serbian bishops seek govern-

	ment protection of Serbs in Kosovo. Belgrade media focus on Kosovo.
1981	At the Croatian village of Medjugorje in western Herzegovina, a group of children announces through Franciscan priests that they see daily a Croatian-speaking Virgin Mary. The Medjugorje apparitions draw crowds of pilgrims from whole world to take part in what will become the longest and one of most massive series of Marian apparitions in history of Catholicism. The Serbian Orthodox Church perceives Medjugorje apparitions as the work of Croat nationalists and as a desecration of the mass graves of Serbs killed in the vicinity of Medjugorje by the Independent State of Croatia in World War II.
1983	In Sarajevo, Alija Izetbegović and a group of Muslim nationalists are tried in state criminal court for "hostile propaganda" and "spreading religious and ethnic hatred" and sentenced to long prison terms.
September 1984	The Croatian Great Novena concludes with a "National Eucharistic Congress." At the same time, the Serbian Orthodox Church organizes a pilgrimage and liturgy at the Jasenovac concentration camp. The event commemorates Serbs killed by the regime of the Independent State of Croatia during World War II.
May 1985	A groundbreaking ceremony and worship service is held at the Vračar hill in Belgrade after Serbia's government allows the construction of the Saint Sava's memorial temple, commenced in 1935.
987	Slobodan Milošević rises to power in Serbia. The Serbian Orthodox Church publishes a volume containing maps and pictures of medieval monasteries and churches in Kosovo to repel Albanian separatists and prove Serbia's claims. Church's newspaper, *Pravoslavlje*, publishes an editorial that urges the partition of Yugoslavia into Catholic and Orthodox parts.

1989	Celebrations of the 600th anniversary of the Kosovo Battle are held throughout Yugoslavia. Slobodan Milošević speaks at the historic battlefield but does not attend the holy liturgy.
1989–1991	Serbian and Croatian bishops argue through the media and top-level correspondence over various issues in church history, most vehemently over the role of the Catholic Church in the Independent State of Croatia during World War II. By 1991 all forms of interfaith cooperation cease.
1990	Ethnic nationalist parties come to power in Serbia, Montenegro, Croatia, and Bosnia-Herzegovina. Religious institutions back them.
1990	A Belgrade newspaper publishes an interview with the head of the Serbian Orthodox Church, Patriarch Germanus, in which this church leader says that the partition of Yugoslavia is inevitable and Serbs should establish a homogenous state of their own. He believes that peaceful partition is possible through Serbo-Croat negotiations that would also involve leaders of the Serbian Orthodox and Catholic churches. Several other Serb bishops echo the idea in interviews with secular and church media.
1990–1991	The Serbian Orthodox Church in Croatia and Bosnia-Herzegovina calls local Serbs to arm themselves and rise to prevent genocide in order to avoid new massacres of Serbs as occurred in the Independent State of Croatia during World War II. Serb uprisings spread through Croatia and later occur in Bosnia-Herzegovina.
1991	Serb and Croat bishops meet to call for a peaceful resolution of the crisis, but no church supports Yugoslavia's unity. On these meetings Serb bishops propose the partition of Bosnia and Herzegovina and changes of borders of Croatia. Talks collapse.
1991–1992	The Yugoslav federation, established by the communists in World War II, col-

lapses. The Milošević regime in Serbia appropriates the Yugoslav name, under which it pursues Serbian nationalist politics.

1991–1995   Large-scale bloody wars are fought in Croatia and Bosnia-Herzegovina. Ethnic militia conduct genocidal "ethnic cleansing" practices. Thousands of churches and mosques are destroyed. Religious institutions support ethnic nationalist factions, blaming each other for the war.

1998–1999   War in Kosovo. In retaliation for the Milošević regime's persecution and the Serbian Church's role as the ally of Serb nationalism, Albanians attack Serb churches and expel the Serb population. The Orthodox Church remains in the province, with a few Serbs as guardian of Serb sacred sites.

1992–2000   International religious organizations and foreign religious leaders provide humanitarian aid and labor to reconcile hostile religious institutions in the successor states of the former Yugoslavia.

2000   The Milošević regime is ousted in Serbia, and the Orthodox Church improves relations with the state. The Tudjman regime is voted out of power in Croatia, but the Catholic Church continues to support the radical ethnic nationalist opposition. Ethnic nationalist parties, backed by religious organizations, remain strong in Bosnia and Herzegovina, now a multiethnic country with a highly uncertain future.

2001   Slobodan Milošević is put under arrest and brought before the International War Crimes Tribunal for the Former Yugoslavia at the Hague, Netherlands. A war between Slavic Macedonians and ethnic Albanians breaks out in the former Yugoslav republic of Macedonia.

February 2002   The Milošević trial at the Hague begins. The former Serb leader is charged with genocide and crimes against humanity.

● Croat Catholic
■ Serb Orthodox
☾ Bosnian Muslim
★ Communist Era Civil Religion
✳ Macedonian
◆ Montenegrin
✦ Jewish
● Capital

CROATIA

Marija Bistrica
Zagreb
Vukovar
Jasenovac
★ ■ ✦

Nin
Knin
■ ●

Solin

SLOVENIA
CROATIA
BOSNIA AND HERZEGOVINA
SERBIA
MACEDONIA

BOSNIA AND HERZEGOVINA

☾ Ajvatovica
★ ■ Kozara
Srebrenica ☾
Jajce ★

Sarajevo
☾ ● Foča
Čapijina ■
☾ ★
● Medjugorje
Neretva-Jablanica ★
★ Sutjeska

Sites of memory, martyrdom, and contesting myths

- ⬢ Croat Catholic
- ■ Serb Orthodox
- ☾ Bosnian Muslim
- ★ Communist Era Civil Religion
- ✳ Macedonian
- ◆ Montenegrin
- ✸ Jewish
- ● Capital

SERBIA, MONTENEGRO, AND KOSOVO

● Belgrade

■ Žića   ■ Studenica

★ Užice

Kosovo Battlefield
■ Gračanica

Cetinje
◆ ■

■ Patriarchate of Peć

Lovćen
◆ ■

■ Dečani

SLOVENIA

CROATIA

BOSNIA AND
HERZEGOVINA

SERBIA

MACEDONIA

MACEDONIA

✳ ■
Prokhor
Pčinjski

● Skopje

✳ Ohrid

BALKAN IDOLS

1

RELIGION, ETHNICITY, AND
NATIONHOOD

Symbols

On 8 June 2000, as the war between the NATO alliance and the Federal
Republic of Yugoslavia was concluding, the cover page of the Belgrade
weekly *NIN* featured a blue-helmeted UN soldier (apparently from an African
country) on guard duty in front of the fourteenth-century Byzantine church
of Gračanica near the Kosovo battlefield of 1989. As the defeated Serb army
left the Kosovo province, Albanian militants (mostly Muslims by religion)
attacked dozens of Serb medieval churches and monasteries with arson and
explosives. Young educated English-speaking Serb monks rushed to publicize
these attacks via the internet, and Church authorities, by September, published a monograph about the destruction.[1] The Serbian Church deliberately
forgot a massive destruction of Albanian villages and cultural centers and
expulsions and killings of Albanian civilians committed by Serbs during the
1998–2000 Serbo-Albanian War.[2] Even more important, the Serbian Church
did not take advantage of modern communication and publishing to tell the
world about the destruction of thousands of Croat Catholic Churches and
Bosnian Muslim mosques carried out by Serb militants during the wars in
Croatia and Bosnia-Herzegovina in 1991–95. The Catholic Church published
monographs about these "religious wars."[3] The Bosnian Islamic Community
informed the international community about the destruction of mosques.[4]
Speaking of the religious dimension of the wars in Croatia and Bosnia-
Herzegovina, the Serbian patriarchate cried out about what they called a
"spiritual genocide against the Serb people," listing hundreds of ancient and
modern sacred places destroyed by Croats and Muslims.[5] It must be also
noted that during the brief Croat-Muslim war in 1993–94, the two parties
attacked each other's sacred heritage and cultural landmarks. The decade
of wars in the Balkans during the 1990s thus highlighted the crucial,
centuries-old problem in the area: a mixed population of diverse ethnic and

3

religious descent and vague cultural boundaries that makes the creation of culturally homogenous nation-states via partition of land and peaceful drawing of state borders virtually impossible, or "possible" only at the expense of destructive perpetual wars. Sacred landmarks, as border guards and visible material cultural markers, were built for millennia by various empires, native regimes, and foreign invaders. Other monuments, as symbols of changes in history and guardians of memory, stood by sacred places in a region pregnant with one of heaviest burdens of history in the world.[6]

Reporting from the heartland of Yugoslavia in the 1970s, the *Washington Post* correspondent Dusko Doder described Yugoslavia as a "vague country" with a problematic identity and for an American visitor an especially confusing "landscape of Gothic spires, Islamic mosques and Byzantine domes."[7] The local groups, however, know well who is who. "The ethnic group is defined by exclusion," John Armstrong points out, and he emphasizes that "one ethnic group often constituted an antithetical duality with the opposed ethnic group. . . . [I]n the process of drawing inter-ethnic boundaries, the symbolic border guards such as peculiar architecture are critically important."[8] The age of modern nations expanded the function of preserved ancient sacred symbols as material evidence of a the nation's long tradition and continuity. "Sacred sites," wrote Peter van der Veer, "are . . . the physical evidence of the perennial existence of the religious community and, by nationalist expansion, of the nation. . . . The history of shrines, as told in religious tales, and established by archeological evidence, is the history of the nation."[9]

Myth

In the modern era, forms of spiritual life have changed. Patriotic sentiments and national identities seem to have been by far more powerful as social forces, as well as individual emotions, than the beliefs in a heavenly God, angels, theologies, and religious myths that modern societies organized as nation-states inherited from antiquity. George L. Mosse referred to nationalism as a "secular religion" and implied that this kind of religion overpowered ancient forms of spirituality.[10] Enlightened thinkers such as Rousseau and Tocqueville, as well as contemporaries such as Robert Bellah and others, have spoken about the fusion and interaction between religious symbols, rituals, myths, and other similar practices and the new secular, profane forms of national identity and state worship, calling this phenomenon "civil religion."[11] In regimes generally hostile toward traditional religion, such as communism and Nazism, various forms of secular worship of the state and political leaders and peculiar "secular religions" were engineered by power holders.[12] Yet traditional religious institutions found it hard to legitimize such regimes, so the term "civil religion" actually refers to more benign systems tolerant of all faiths as well as of nonbelief.

Regarding the phenomenon of the nation-state: it consists of territories with borders, peoples, armies, and bureaucracies, but that is not enough: the nation-state cannot exist without an adequate system of public patriotic worship, symbol, myth, and ritual. Nation-states require of their citizens not only that they be governed and they govern but also that they love their "country" and be prepared to kill, die, and lie for it. As in the case of religion, an individual or group's disrespect of this requirement calls for some kind of excommunication, punishment, and sometimes even death.

Nation-states also cannot exist without history and myth, which also require a worshipful acceptance. Myth is a narrative about the origin, that is, "birth," of the community. This narrative, often historically inaccurate, becomes *sacred*; that is to say, historical narrative becomes *religion* rather than history based on evidence.[13] According to functionalist explanations of myth, myth explains and justifies the existence and distribution of political power under current circumstances.[14] Myths make nations, and nations make myths. The crucial difference among the three Slavic Serbo-Croatian–speaking Yugoslav ethnic nations and the Serbs, Croats, and Bosnian Muslims who constitute two-thirds of the population in the two common Yugoslav states is not religion (Serb Orthodoxy, Croatian Catholicism, or Bosnian Islam) but the *myth of national origin*, which is consecrated by native religious institutions. Hypothetically, in spite of the three religions involved, a different mythmaking, in which religious institutions could have collaborated, could have made the three a single nation, provided they agreed to espoused common faith, not in a single heavenly God but in a *common myth of national origin as a single nation*.

"No serious historian of nations and nationalism can be a committed political nationalist," wrote Eric Hobsbawm, because "nationalism requires too much belief in what is patently not so."[15] Nationalist historiographies are usual suspect—for being "mythical" and therefore, strictly speaking, false, created not by history but by scholars in service of power-holders and ideologies. Ernest Renan considered "deliberate forgetting" of certain events in history, such as crimes, moments of shame and defeat, bad things about heroes and leaders, and so forth, as important as the preservation of the historical memory of noble struggle, glory, and martyrdom that is the essence of national identity.[16] "Men calculate and compute with memory and forgetting," wrote Friedrich Nietzsche.[17]

Institutions

For the Yugoslav peoples, Michael B. Petrovich pointed out, "religion was not so much a matter of *private* conscience as of one's *public* identity. In some cases, the identification between religion and nationality was so great that a religious conversion automatically entailed a change of nationality, in the eyes of others if not in those of the convert himself."[18] In the second

Yugoslav state, Tito's Yugoslavia (so called, after the country's communist leader, Josip Broz Tito, 1892–1980), the census of 1953 registered both religious affiliation and nationality and confirmed that ethnic, national, and religious identities commingled, creating the three "ethnic nations"[19] The census data and ensuing empirical research confirmed that

> there exists a rather strong correlation between religious affiliation, commitment to religion and involvement in the church on one side and nationality on the other. It is obvious that the Slovenes and Croatians would be predominantly or exclusively Roman Catholic and Serbians and Montenegrins Orthodox and, consequently, that there would be a strong correlation between the national identity of the Slovenes and Croatians and their religious affiliation with the Roman Catholic Church.[20]

In Yugoslavia

The major religious institutions worked together with modern secular nationalistic intellectuals on the task of creating the nations and nationalities of Yugoslavia by means of mythmaking, linguistic efforts, commemorations, and holidays and through the creation of "national saints" and calculations involving history and memory.

The Serbian Orthodox Church

In his memoirs a Serbian archpriest recollects the following verses he was taught in his family as a child: "Srpsko je nebo plave boje; na njemu stoluje Srbin bog; a oko njega Srbi andjeli stoje; i dvore Srbina boga svog" ("The Serbian heaven is blue; the Serb God reigns in heaven; angel Serbs stand around him; and serve their Serb God").[21] "More so than in the rest of Catholic or Protestant Western Europe," wrote Michael Radu, "the Orthodox churches of Eastern Europe have long been openly and actively involved in national politics and are intimately and historically connected with the region's dominant postcommunist ideology—nationalism."[22] The Orthodox church in Eastern Europe was perceived as "the historic repository of nationhood, national values, and quite often, as the savior of a nation's very existence."[23] The historian of modern Serbia Michael B. Petrovich pointed out that "the Serbian Orthodox church was a cultural and quasi-political institution, which embodied and expressed the ethos of the Serbian people to such a degree that nationality and religion fused into a distinct 'Serbian faith.' This role of the Serbian church had little to do with religion either as theology or as a set of personal beliefs and convictions."[24]

Serb rulers and bishops of the Serbian Orthodox Church built shrines, monuments, and cemeteries as places of worship and markers along state borders and communal boundaries. Ancient landmarks show how the medieval Serbian kingdom was established and how it expanded, was destroyed, and was renewed in modern times. The oldest sacred landmarks are Žiča

about the Serbian Orthodox church

→ how propagated religion, how used it to create self identity

(where Saint Sava founded the Church and was enthroned as its first archbishop), Studenica, Sopoćani, Ravanica, Resava, Manasija, and Mileševo (located across the Drina in today's Bosnia-Herzegovina).[25] The church and
state then expanded into what is today the Kosovo province and Yugoslav
Macedonia, while also moving westward after the Ottoman conquest.[26]

In the Orthodox world, the Church, ethnic community, and state grow
together. From 1217 (the coronation of a king) and 1219 (the recognition
of *autocephaly, that is, ecclesiastical autonomy* under Saint Sava as first archbishop) to 1331 (the coronation of a king-emperor) and 1346 (when the
emperor-king established a patriarchate), medieval Serbian state took shape.
Under the long Ottoman rule, Serb clergy actively participated in popular
uprisings and wars for the restoration of statehood.[27] Serbian Orthodox
Church became a warrior-church devoted to the preservation of ethnic identity and the struggle for statehood and nationhood. A British scholar who
traveled to the Balkans in the mid–nineteenth century wrote about the Orthodox "warrior-priest Yovan," who allegedly "had defended the convent of
Morača with 200 men, against 20,000 Albanians."[28] In a similar vein the
same author described the prince-bishop (*vladika*) of Montenegro, Petar I
Petrović-Nejgoš, as a bishop "of majestic height, of about six feet eight
inches, who can hit with a rifle a lemon thrown into the air by one of his
attendants."[29]

The key element of Serbian religion and nationalism (i.e., "Serbian faith")
is the Kosovo myth. It commemorates the 28 June 1389 battle at the Kosovo
field in which Turks defeated the Serbs and continued the successful conquest of the Balkan peninsula.[30] Fused with another mythical historic event,
the 1690 Great Migration of Serbs to northern Habsburg lands when Serbs
left Kosovo under guidance of the Church, as well as the reconquests of the
province in 1912 and in 1918, the Kosovo myth energized numerous efforts
aimed at the restoration of Serbian nation-state.[31] The Serbian Orthodox
Church was founded at Ipek (or Peć or Peje) in what today is Kosovo (or
Kosova) by the Serb emperor Stephen Dušan the Mighty in 1346. The patriarchate of Peć (*Pećka parijaršija*) in present-day Kosovo embodies the continuity of the Serbian state. During Ottoman rule, from 1557 to 1766, the
Peć patriarchate, that is, present-day Kosovo, became a "capital" of the Serbian "state." The patriarch and clergy took the place of secular authority
that did not exist and organized courts, foreign affairs, and the collection of
taxes. Patriarchs from Peć led the first massive migration of Serbs to the
north in 1690 and several subsequent migrations to the areas under Habsburg rule. Gradually the Serbs abandoned Kosovo, Metohija, and Macedonia.
The non-Slavic people, ethnic Albanians, who had converted from Christianity to Islam, populated some of the areas earlier settled by Serbs.[32] However, the Serbian Orthodox Church preserved the memory of the Serbian
state with Kosovo as its major sacred center. Kosovo is the central myth and
symbol of Serbian Orthodoxy. It is also a sacred center, the nation's rallying

point and its lost paradise. Kosovo is often referred to as "Serbian Zion" or "Serbian Jerusalem." Parallels between Kosovo and Jerusalem and between the Serbs and the people of Israel appeared as early as the fifteenth century in folk poetry and have been passed by the Serbian church's liturgy down to this day.[33] The phrase "Serbian Jerusalem" reverberated in political discourse in Yugoslavia in the 1930s, in the 1960s and 1970s, and most strikingly during the crisis of the 1980s and 1990s.

In addition to the Kosovo myth, the cult of ethnic saints, rather than Orthodox theology, helped the creation of the Serbian nation. The Serbian Church commemorated Serbian medieval rulers as saints. Eric Hobsbawm noted that "religion and Orthodox church would not have distinguished the Serbs from say, Bulgarians, but . . . the memory of the old kingdom defeated by the Turks was preserved in song and heroic story, and, perhaps more to the point, in the daily liturgy of the Serbian church which had canonized most of its kings."[34] The cult of native saints is one of the hallmarks of Serbian Orthodoxy, but it is also an important element of Serbian national identity. According to church historian Radoslav M. Grujić, "beginning in the late sixteenth and through the seventeenth century, leaders of our church had inaugurated a wise and far-reaching practice, by supporting the faith and national pride through the worship of our national saints and martyrs."[35] According to the secular historian Milorad Ekmečić, the church councils, held from 1769 to 1787 (dealing with restructuring of Church calendar), marked the beginning of the Church's relevant contribution to modern Serbian nationalism.[36] In the interwar kingdom, the Serbian Church worshiped over 30 national saints. In communist Yugoslavia, the number of saints more than doubled; new saints were inaugurated by the assembly of bishops in 1962, 1965, 1973, and most recently in 1998. From the beginning of the systematic worship of the national saints in the late sixteenth century to the present, the Serbian Orthodox Church canonized 76 saints who were all ethnic Serbs. Most Serbian national saints are Church leaders and clergy, with 22 rulers and statesmen, several peasants and artisans, and six women.[37]

At least since the eighteenth century (according to Milorad Ekmečić), the Church turned ethnic nationalism into a religion and fused *pravoslavlje* (the Orthodox faith) with the ideology of the restored nationhood.[38] Religion, wrote the Serb bishop and theologian Nikolaj Velimirović, gave "to this nationalism its aura, revolutionary fervor, prophetic vision, and justification."[39] For Nikolaj, "the healthy nationalism of the Gospel is the only right path."[40] The day of the Kosovo battle—Saint Vitus' Day (or *Vidovdan*, 15 or 28 June) became a main Serbian state holiday in 1903, and the Serb army, as the avenger of Prince Lazar, occupied Kosovo in 1912. In the Yugoslav monarchy, all Orthodox believers from Macedonia, Montenegro, Serbia, Bosnia-Herzegovina, and Croatia were brought under the jurisdiction of the Serbian patriarchate (*Srpska patrijaršija*); hence the patriarch's seat was relocated from Srijemski Karlovci to the capital city of Belgrade. The Church was governed by an assembly of bishops, the Sveti Arhijerejski Sabor (Holy Assembly of Bishops). This body meets regularly once a year in May and, if necessary, more often. The Sabor elects a patriarch for lifelong tenure and in addition the Church's executive body, the Sveti arhijerejski sinod (Holy Synod of Bishops), which consists of four bishops elected every two years and is chaired by the patriarch. The patriarch also appoints new bishops, and bishops decide about appointments of lower clergy. Bishops are normally selected from the ranks of prominent monks and monk-theologians. The central Church's administration is called the *patrijaršija* (patriarchate). Local church units are dioceses, archdioceses, monastic communities, and *parohije* (parishes). The same church organization was preserved in the second Yugoslavia, with some changes in the procedure of patriarch's election. During communist rule, the united Serbian Orthodox Church in Yugoslavia (especially prior to the Macedonian schism in 1967) achieved its largest size ever and until the end of communist Yugoslavia was expanding and rebuilding its facilities nationwide. In 1986 the Serbian Church (without three dioceses in Macedonia) had 3 Metropolitan dioceses; 28 dioceses (8 of them abroad); 27 active bishops; 2,553 parishes and 2,298 churches and chapels; 2,019 ordained priests; 29 deacons; 179 monasteries with 231 monks (8 novices) and 744 nuns (61 candidates); a central Orthodox theological school in Belgrade (Pravoslavni bogoslovski fakultet) with 8 faculty members and about 100 students; and four theological seminaries with 538 candidates for priesthood. The Hilandar monastery at Mount Athos in Greece had 130 monks in 1902. In 1930 the number had decreased to 70 and in 1991 had dropped to 25. Publishing activity, however, was steadily expanding. Having started with only a few newsletters in the 1930s, the Church published, in the 1980s, more than 60 newspapers, periodicals, and other bulletins.[41] While expanding and flourishing under the liberal phase of communism since the 1960s, the Serbian Church, like other religious institutions in Yugoslavia whose leaders could freely travel abroad, was also receiving Western financial aid as one of the churches persecuted by the communists (see more on this in the next chapter).

Croatian Catholicism

In contrast to the development of the Serbian "ethnic" church, always tied to the Serbian states, the process of "ethnicization" or "nativization" of Catholicism in Croatia and the Croat-populated areas of Bosnia-Herzegovina began and steadily advanced only in the second half of the nineteenth century.

A number of Croat native priests excelled as patriots, even though most bishops were foreigners. For example, Croat native priests, or *glagoljaši*, used the Glagolitic alphabet and Church Slavonic language in worship services; the founder of Croatian literature, Marko Marulić (1450–1524), wrote and published both in Latin and in the vernacular; Jesuit Bartol Kašić in 1604 published the first Croatian morphology and the Dominican Rajmund Damjanić created in 1639 the first Croatian orthography; the Franciscan Andrija Kačić-Miošić wrote poetry in vernacular in 1756; and the remarkable Franciscan monk-priests were guardians of Croat ethnic communities in Bosnia-Herzegovina under Ottoman rule; anti-Turkish fighters such priest Marko Mesić and Luka Ibrišimović nineteenth-century patriotic clerics such as Strossmayer, Dobrila, and Pavlinović, who defended Croatian identity and championed South Sea Unity, and so on. Finally, as Serbs honor their shrines in Serbia, Kosovo, and Macedonia, the Croats take pride in monuments and artifacts from the era of Croatian native rulers located in Dalmatia around ancient cities such as Solin, Nin, and Knin.[42] The founders of Croatian archeology were Catholic priests and scholars such as Lujo Marun and Frane Bulić, who carried out excavations not only in old Croatia but also in areas later populated by Serb Orthodox settlers.[43]

Croatian nationalistic movements in the nineteenth century urged the Holy See to appoint more native Croat church leaders as well as native saints and blessed martyrs. The popes were generally receptive to this, and the numbers of ethnic Croat bishops had steadily risen, but the Croats, in contrast to other Catholic nations of Europe, had to wait much longer for their native saints. The first blessed martyr of Croat ethnic background (Bishop Augustin Kažotić, 1260–1323) was beatified in 1702. The first native Croat saint of the Roman Catholic Church came as late as 1970. At that time, for example, the Roman Catholic Church in Poland had commemorated 249 saints and blessed martyrs, all ethnic Poles and Polish Catholics, including 108 saints and saintly candidates martyred during World War II by German invaders.[44] The rival neighboring Orthodox Church of Serbia then worshiped 60 saints, all ethnic Serbs.[45] In order to mitigate the Croatian frustration over the lack of native saints (while both rival Orthodox Serbs and Western Catholic nations worshiped numerous saints of their own), Pope Paul VI changed several centuries-old regulations for the canonization of saints. As a result in 1970 the Dalmatian Franciscan missionary and crusader Nikola Tavelić (1340–91) was canonized in Rome. Croatian clergy put pressure on the popes for more native saints. Between 1970 and 1998 the so-called Church in the Croat People (Crkva u Hrvata), as it came to be referred to by church leaders and church press, had acquired three saints of Croat ethnic background, two more blessed martyrs, and four "servants of God" (future sainthood candidates). The Slavic pope John Paul II awarded to the Croats two saints, one blessed martyr, and three cardinals. Croatian Catholicism, unofficially calling itself the Church in the Croat People, experienced an unprecedented growth and success during late communism and in postcommunism. Croatian Catholicism attained its largest size in history in communist Yugoslavia between the 1960s and 1980s. Most of the bishops, including the chairman and vice-chairman of the Conference of Bishops of Yugoslavia (BKJ) were ethnic Croats. Three metropolitan-archbishops were based in Croatia and one in Bosnia-Herzegovina. The Church maintained seminaries, theological schools, colleges, publishing houses, and so forth. In communist Yugoslavia the Catholic Church (including its Croatian and Slovene branches) was organized into 5 ecclesiastical provinces, 8 archdioceses, 13 dioceses, and 4 apostolic *administraturae*, with a total of 2,702 parishes, 182 monasteries, and 415 convents. Bishops communicated with state authorities through the BKJ, headquartered in Zagreb. The BKJ regularly cooperated with the papal nuncio in Belgrade, and this official would attend all conference sessions by invitation (not by his "higher authority"). The Church had 32 bishops, 4,121 diocesan priests, 1,416 monks, and 6,587 nuns. There was also an influential Church unit abroad, with 181 parishes and missions with 250 priests. The Catholic Church in Yugoslavia had 2 Catholic universities in Ljubljana (Slovenia) and Zagreb, with theological schools in Zagreb and Split; and 7 Catholic colleges and 19 seminaries for preparation of priests were attended in the 1980s by some 1,300 students. There are also two institutes for Croats and Slovenes in Rome who attend Catholic universities. The Catholic Church in Yugoslavia maintained two publishing houses and 32 book publishers, in addition to some 180 periodicals and religious newspapers with a circulation of over seven hundred thousand.[46]

The Muslim Religious Organization (The Islamic Community)

Prior to the Austrian rule established in Bosnia-Herzegovina between 1878 and 1908, Bosnian Muslim religious leaders, clergy, and other learned men trained in Islamic law and theology (*ulema*) did not have an autonomous religious organization. These South Slavs of Christian (Serbian and Croatian) ancestry operated under Ottoman religious authority (the *Meshihat*) in Istanbul. During the Austrian rule, Bosnian Muslim clergy showed more enthusiasm toward the establishment of a self-administered religious institution.[47] In the interwar Yugoslav kingdom, the Muslim Religious Organization, headquartered first at Belgrade and then in Sarajevo, became autonomous but close to the Bosnian Muslim political party, the Yugoslav Muslim Organization (YMO). The Belgrade regime supported both the Muslim Religious Organization and the YMO and used them as checks against the two major domestic nationalisms. In both Yugoslavias, the Muslim religious organization supported the common state and viewed it as an acceptable political framework for Slavic as well as non-Slavic Muslims scattered across Bosnia, Herzegovina, Serbia, Sandjak, Montenegro, Kosovo, Macedonia, and Croatia. During World War II, most of the lower clergy and lay Muslim leaders, including many beys, sided with the partisan movement. The Muslim religious organization (the Islamic Religious Community, later renamed into Islamic Community) rebuilt itself in socialist Yugoslavia. In the early 1980s, the Islamic Community (IZ) was an organization of Muslim clerical and lay officials headquartered in Sarajevo, Bosnia, and Herzegovina. During the communist era, the unified Muslim religious organization was established in all six Yugoslav republics and two provinces. The supreme religious authority was the *reis-ul-ulema* (head of the ulema). There was also an assembly of prominent laymen and clerics called the Supreme Islamic Assembly of Elders, which was elected by another larger assembly called the Supreme Council of the Islamic Community in Yugoslavia. The Community had four administrative units and reached its relatively largest size, with the greatest number of mosques and religious schools in the history of the organization. The Islamic Community in the Socialist Federal Republic of Yugoslavia was divided into four territorial units administered through regional assemblies—in Sarajevo for Bosnia-Herzegovina; in Priština (Kosovo) for Serbia; in Skopje for Macedonia; and in Titograd for Montenegro, with a meshihat (an executive authority) in Zagreb for Croatia-Slovenia and three *muftis* in Mostar, Tuzla, and Belgrade. The Community employed over 1,400 professional officials and men of the clergy (imams). More than 3,000 mosques and mosques without a minaret (*mesdjid*) were open for worship in the 1970s. In the mid-1980s, the Islamic Theological School and the Oriental Institute in Sarajevo had 16 faculty members and researchers and 35 students. There were two middle religious schools or seminaries (*medresa*) with 366 seminarists, a *medresa* for women in Sarajevo with 62 students, and a newly opened *medresa* in Skopje. The Sarajevo headquarters issued a semiofficial biweekly newspaper, *Preporod* (Renewal) in 27,000 copies and several dozen other periodicals.[48] After the disintegration of the Yugoslav communist federation, the Yugoslav Muslim religious organization was abolished and the autonomous Islamic Community of Bosnia-Herzegovina was founded in Sarajevo.

The Church and Nation
of Macedonia

The Macedonian Orthodox Church is de facto an independent national Orthodox church in what is at this writing the Republic of Macedonia (or, as in some international documents, the Former Yugoslav Republic of Macedonia—FYROM). The church came into life with the regime's support between 1958 and 1967. In order to bolster a distinct nationality for Yugoslav Macedonians, Yugoslav communists encouraged a group of Orthodox priests in Macedonia to secede from the Belgrade Patriarchate. The Macedonian Church and the Macedonian nation were designed by Yugoslav communists as checks against Serbian, Bulgarian, and Greek appropriations of land and people in the southernmost pocket of the former Yugoslavia. In Tito's Yugoslavia, the Macedonian Orthodox Church was the most patriotic religious organization in the country. During the communist era in united Yugoslavia, the Macedonian Church, like other mainstream churches, expanded and rebuilt, witnessing its golden age in spite of a Marxist regime. Like the Serbian Church, the Church of Macedonia was governed by an assembly of bishops but had no patriarch. The Church's administration, located in Skopje and Ohrid, consisted of the archbishop-metropolitan of Ohrid as head of the Church, an assembly of bishops, and the Holy Synod as the Church's executive body of several elected bishops, chaired by the archbishop-metropolitan of Ohrid. In 1981, the following were under the jurisdiction of the Church of Macedonia: 6 dioceses in Yugoslavia, one in Australia, and one in Canada; 225 parishes, 102 monasteries, about 250 priests, and some 15 monks. In the 1970s, a seminary and theological school were opened in Skopje, and there were about one hundred students in each at the beginning of the 1980s.[49]

Religious Minorities

In addition to the four mainstream religious institutions, Yugoslavia was also the homestead of around 40 religious minority groups, organized in religious communities and recognized by the state under the names they referred to themselves. They are worth mentioning not merely to complete the presentation of the ethnoreligious mosaic of Yugoslavia but also to contrast them to the mainstream religious organizations with regard to the crucial interaction between religion and nationalism. In contrast to the four major denominations, in which religion and nationality commingle and religious leaders carry out a "national mission" in the political sphere and through mutual competition, the religious minorities, though not altogether apolitical, are definitely less nationalistic. Most religious minorities are multiethnic (only two are ethnically based: the Slovak Evangelical Christian Church of the Augsburg Confession and the Romanian Orthodox Church).

In the early 1980s, the Federal Commission for Relations with Religious Communities in Yugoslavia, listed the following as the largest among the minor religious communities: (1) The Evangelical Church, headquartered in Zagreb, is an association of several evangelical denominations; it had several dozen places of worship and more than 40 ministers throughout the country. (2) The Federation of Jewish Communities in Yugoslavia embraced 29 Jewish communes and 5 commissariats, with headquarters in Belgrade. There were two professional rabbis in Zagreb and Belgrade. According to the census of 1953, the number of Jews by nationality was 2,307 and by religion 2,565; (3) The Calvinist Reformed Church had 43 parishes in Vojvodina and northern Croatia; (4) The Baptist Church, with its seat in Zagreb, had 20 professional preachers and 54 parishes; (5) The Methodist Church, headquartered in Novi Sad, Vojvodina, had 40 preachers and four church districts in the eastern part of the country; (6) The Christian Community of Jehovah's Witnesses had its seat in Belgrade and more than 130 communities in all Yugoslav republics; (7) The Pentecostal Church of Christ maintained its main administration and its Theological Institute, for the training of preachers, in Zagreb and in regional communities in all the Yugoslav republics; (8) There were Seventh-Day Adventist churches in Vojvodina and in northern Croatia: (9) The Christian Community of the Nazarene and (10) the Church of the Brethren were both in Vojvodina: (11) The Church of Jesus Christ of Latter-Day Saints was in Zadar, Croatia: (12) The Old Catholic Church had five autonomous local church communities, 11 parishes, 10 priests, and 7 places of worship: (13) The Vicariate of the Rumanian Orthodox Church, in Banat, was the only Orthodox church among significant minor religious communities. (14) The Rufai Dervish Order and other independent Sufi monastic communities, associated with the Community of Islamic Ali Dervish Orders (ZIDRA), was based in Prizren (Kosovo).[50]

In the mid-1980s, the first scholarly study on minor religious communities in Yugoslavia surveyed 16 denominations.[51] According to this study,

> the minor Christian religious communities seem to be spared from the tensions along ethnic lines that are growing in our society. . . . Their congregations are multiethnic and believers who, although they declare their ethnic background without hesitation, have abandoned the familial tradition of religionational identification. . . . Members of the minor religious communities cannot even imagine that their religious organization could be a progenitor or pillar of a nation and see no reason to get involved in current disputes among the ethnic nations and mainstream religious organizations.[52]

The study concludes that in the minor Christian communities in Yugoslavia, "as a formative factor, the national element is of no great importance, as is often case in the world, and at least partly in Yugoslavia.] . . . Members are devoted to salvation, to which nationality is of no importance, [and] belonging to the idea of salvation makes the national idea less important, lowering it to the place it has in the revealed hierarchy of values."[53]

Although Western studies concerned with religious affairs in Yugoslav lands overlooked religious minorities, familiarity with this form of religious life might be crucial for understanding the history of religious relations in the Yugoslavias and their successor states in the twentieth century. Not only did these religious minorities have nothing to do with nationalism, ethnic conflict, genocide, and ethnic cleansing, but they by and large supported the six-republic federation as a common house for all. Many minor religious communities were multiethnic. A confidential communist-era federal government document judged minor religious communities as by and large patriotic, insofar as they did not espouse ethnic nationalisms and were not involved in the fratricidal strife during the Second World War II. The only exceptions to such positive evaluation were the Jehovah's Witnesses and the Nazaranes, who refused to serve in the armed forces.[54] A number of new faiths were established freely. Thus, for example, the administration in Croatia did not obstruct the foundation of the Church of Jesus Christ of Latter-Day Saints in 1974 in Zadar. Upon his return from Utah, the basketball star *at cempts to spread*

Krešimir Ćosić organized church life and a base for missionary work in Eastern Europe and obtained a place of worship, thus making possible the first established community of this rapidly expanding American church in the communist world. A number of other minor faiths (e.g., the Transcendental Meditation movement and several gurus and swamis operating in the East and West) were also allowed to establish themselves without restrictions. Paradoxically, after the fall of communism, as I will show chapters 10 and 11, the major local religions and ethnic nationalistic regimes considered domestic religious minorities and foreign missionaries a gross threat, harassed their leaders, obstructed their development of new places of worship, attacked them in the media, and sometimes even persecuted their members.

change earlier Croati are more benign

Interfaith Relations

In the history of the two peoples and churches, Serb Orthodox and Croatian Catholic clergy recorded best results in interchurch cooperation when both ethnic communities found themselves facing a foreign threat. Thus, a common enemy made the two churches allies *occasionally* (definitely not always) under Turkish Ottoman rule or, remarkably, in the European revolutionary year 1848, when Serbs and Croats, including their native clergy in the Habsburg monarchy, forged a "fraternal" South Slavic alliance in order to resist an aggressive nationalism from Hungary. In this fascinating and unique case, even top church leaders and official hierarchies supported the interethnic and interchurch alliance. Otherwise, interfaith cooperation between Croatian Catholicism and Serbian Orthodoxy or good relations of the two churches with Slavic Muslim clergy was a sporadic practice and, by and large, a result of individual enthusiasm.

The religious history of South Slavs records conversions, tensions, and interfaith incidents, although as Ivo Banac pointed out no large-scale religious wars ever occurred in the region as in western and central Europe.[55] Examples of amity as well enmity were recorded among various religious denominations. Thus, the Serb Orthodox bishop Nikodim Milaš views the religious history of Dalmatia and Croatia as a history of hatred and intolerance of ethnic Serbs under Venetian and Austria rule.[56] The Ottoman conquest of the Balkans also worsened religious relations.[57] Although Christians of Catholic and Orthodox faith occasionally cooperated in the struggle against the Turks and served in Christian armies, Christian clergy in the Ottoman zone fought for survival and often at the expense of each other. After the massive Serb migration from Kosovo to Habsburg lands, church struggles escalated and aggravated Catholic-Orthodox relations in the seventeenth and eighteenth centuries. In 1611 in Marča (present-day northern Croatia), a group of Orthodox bishops founded a "Uniate" diocese, thus bringing local Orthodox population (of various ethnic origins, including Serbs, Romanian Vlachs, and Ukrainians) under papal authority. After the great migration of Serbs from Kosovo to Habsburg lands in 1690, Serb bishops launched several anti-Uniate campaigns that resulted in the ravaging of the Marča monastery by Serbs in 1739. In 1785, Croatian Uniates of Serb, Vlach, and Ukrainian descent founded a new diocese in Križevci.

In the nineteenth century, as Drago Roksandić pointed out, the first conflicts among Orthodox Serbs and Catholic Croats occurred as a consequence of "building religious identity into the foundation of national identity and the development of mass (secular) nationalism."[58] During this period, secular liberal nationalism was predominant in nationalist movements and often in dispute with antiliberal "clericalism." The nineteenth century and early twentieth century also witnessed the first "ecumenical" movements seeking unity of Christians Serb and Croat clergy united in 1848 against Hungarian nationalism. Catholic Croats and Orthodox Serbs were called on for cooperation and possible unification in a South Slav federation by the eminent Austrian philanthropist and church leader of Croatian descent, Bishop Josip Juraj Strossmayer (1815–1905). Strossmayer sympathized with Pan-Slavism, as did his precursor, the Croat Jesuit theologian Juraj Križanić (1618–83), and both prelates considered the rapprochement between Roman Catholicism and the Orthodox church a key precondition for the fulfilment of Pan-Slavic ideals. From 1896 to 1903, Croatian and Slovene ecumenical enthusiasts, backed by the archbishop of Sarajevo, Josip Stadler, published the ecumenical journal *Balkan* in Zagreb and Sarajevo. The most important ecumenical organization in interwar period was the St. Cyril and St. Method Movement, active in Zagreb and Ljubljana. In the 1920s, Protestant ecumenical advocates founded the ecumenical associations known as "Life and Work" and "Faith and Order." These enjoyed support from the then influential Serbian Orthodox Church. In communist Yugoslavia, ecumenical-oriented clergy were considered patriotic, and Bishop Strossmayer was appropriated by the nation's patriotic ideology of "brotherhood and unity." The most notable ecumenical activities (perhaps the most dynamic and extensive, if not the most successful in history) had been accomplished under communism in the aftermath of the Second Vatican Council (1962–65).

2

THE FIRST STRIFE

The Crisis of the 1930s, War, and the Cease-Fire of the 1960s

O n Sunday, 19 July 1937, the Cathedral of the Serbian Patriarchate in Belgrade was packed. The holy liturgy was presided over by Patriarch Varnava, with all the bishop members of the Holy
Bishops' Assembly. After the service, the patriarch, with members of the
hierarchy, clergy, monks, nuns, and seminarists, left the church to march
at the head of what quickly grew into a massive, tens of thousands–strong
column heading down the avenues of Yugoslavia's capital. As had been
announced earlier, the Church took the people to the streets to protest the
Popular Assembly's expected ratification of an international treaty, a
concordat signed in 1935 between the royal Yugoslavia government and the
Holy See. The long-negotiated concordat aimed at regulating the legal
status of the Catholic Church in the Yugoslav kingdom with an Orthodox
majority and numerous other faiths. Concurrently, the bishops' assembly
of the Serbian Orthodox Church had passed its "Instructions for Imple-
mentation of Sanctions," threatening excommunication from the Church
for all Serb delegates who voted for the ratification of the concordat.
The procession turned into massive riots that were labeled "Bloody Liturgy"
by the press. A few days later, the sudden death of the patriarch further
destabilized the situation in the capital, and riots spread throughout the
country.

From the signing of the concordat in 1935 to the "Bloody Liturgy," Serbian Orthodox Church leaders vehemently opposed the treaty. They argued
that the concordat provided a privileged status for the Catholic Church at
the expense of other faiths. As early as November 1936, the Holy Assembly
of Orthodox Bishops sent a protest letter to Prime Minister Milan Stojadi-
nović in which the bishops warned that the concordat "would upset the
interconfessional equilibrium in the country" and put the Orthodox Church
and other non-Catholic religions "in a difficult and unfavorable position. . . .

The concordat . . . would eventually make our country and state subordi-
nated to the Roman Curia," they wrote.

Nikolaj Velimirović, a prominent Serb theologian and bishop of Žiča, was
the leading outspoken opponent of the concordat and one of the organizers
of the protest liturgy of 1937. In his letter to all senators of Serb Orthodox
background, as a follow-up to the proclamation in which the Church threatened excommunication for a vote to ratify the concordat, Velimirović warned
that the concordat "gives enormous rights and privileges to an international
organization at the expense of our national Saint Sava's Church."[2] In a
sermon before 30,000 faithful in Valjevo on 26 September 1937, Bishop
Nikolaj argued that modern principles of separation of church and state
cannot be applied to Serbia. On this occasion, Nikolaj exclaimed:

> Rise three fingers Orthodox Serbs! This popular rebellion does not under-
> mine, it will fortify our homeland. Down with all antinational elements:
> parasites and bloodsuckers, capitalists, godless, and communists! The Ser-
> bian faith is awakened because it is hurt. Serbian national consciousness
> is awakened because it resists the attack from all internationalists and
> those who build bridges for the pope of Rome and his Church—the oldest
> international, the oldest fascism, the oldest dictatorship in Europe![3]

The Catholic Church, especially its Croatian branch, was embittered.
Church leaders resented the Serbian Orthodox Church's status of a privileged state religion because equality of religions had been agreed on by the
founders of the Yugoslav state. That is why the interwar Yugoslav kingdom
(1918–41) never secured legitimation from either of the two largest religious
institutions. The Serbian Church, as early as the mid-1920s, obtained a
special law by which it became the de facto state religion.[4] For Serbian
Church leaders, the Yugoslav state was "a Serbian state born in the blood
of the victorious Serbian Army" in World War I.[5] The major state holiday
in the interwar kingdom was *Vidovdan* (Saint Vitus' Day), commemorating
the 1389 Kosovo battle. Most of the patriotic myths commemorated the
Serbian medieval kingdom, the battle of Kosovo, the subsequent Serbo-
Turkish wars, and Serbia's martyrdom and glory in World War I. In con-
sequence, the Catholic Church, especially its Croatian branch, was upset.
Church leaders never granted legitimation to the Serb-dominated kingdom.
Catholicism conditioned legitimation by concordat. For the Catholic Church
and ethnic Croats, the new state was initially a necessity because Catholic
Croats and Slovenes would have become minorities in several states: Italy,
Austria, and Serbia. Nevertheless, the new state was also an opportunity for
the expansion of Catholicism. The Croatian historian Mužić pointed out that
the Vatican welcomed the chance to "expand eastward and brought Orthodox 'schismatics' into union with the papacy."[6] Back then, conversion of the
Orthodox was official Vatican policy, not to be changed prior to 1965.

Facing the conspicuous showing of the Serbian Orthodox Church, Croat bishops and prominent laymen labored on developing a secular political force, namely, the Croatian Catholic (Lay) Movement, inaugurated as early as 1903 under the leadership of the bishop of Krk, Anton Mahnič. It would be part of the global "Catholic Action," initiated by Pope Pius XI in 1922 and established in the Kingdom in 1927. In the 1920s, Catholic youth, student, and sport organizations proliferated in western parts of the kingdom. The umbrella youth organization, the "Croatian Brotherhood of the Cross," was founded in 1930, and "King Domagoj's Movement" became a Croat national cultural association close to the Catholic Church. In the same year that the Serbian Church obtained the "special law" whereby it became state religion, Croatian bishops organized the largest Croatian church-ethnic jubilee in Yugoslavia, the one-thousand-year anniversary of the foundation of the kingdom of Croatia under the native ruler Tomislav (925–928).

For churches, symbols matter as much as or even more than for political parties and movements. In the 1920s, the Serbian Church launched an ambitious rebuilding program. In 1935 atop the Vračar Hill in the capital city of Belgrade, the Church began construction of the largest church in Yugoslavia and one of the largest Orthodox cathedrals in the world, the Saint Sava Memorial Church (see more on this church hereafter). New Orthodox places of worship mushroomed in all areas of the country, including those areas where earlier Orthodox temple had not existed or had been destroyed under foreign rule.

Furthermore, the two largest churches were in discord over a number of specific issues concerning interfaith relations and Church-state relations. Thus, Catholic clergy complained over alleged pressure on Catholic civil servants to convert to Orthodoxy.[8] Incidentally, between the first census of 1921 and the second census of 1931, the number of the Orthodox church members increased by 2.1 percent, while the number of Catholics dwindled by 2 percent.[9] Furthermore, the Serbian Orthodox Church received a relatively larger amount of financial aid from the state than the other faiths.[10] The Serbian Church and the government also backed the so-called Croatian Old Catholic Church, considered by Croatian Catholic episcopate a schismatic church. There were a number of other specific issues (concerning religious instruction, mixed marriages, spiritual assistance in the armed forces, etc.) that thwarted interfaith relations.

During the concordat crisis of 1937, two important figures in recent Yugoslav history, both ethnic Croats and both opponents of Serbian nationalism, seeing it as the major threat to the country's stability, came to the fore. Josip Broz Tito (1892–1980) became general secretary of the Communist Party of Yugoslavia. The young Catholic prelate Alojzije Stepinac (1898–1960), became the archbishop of the largest Croatian diocese of Zagreb. Stepinac began to abhor the ecumenical Yugoslavism invented in the nineteenth century by the Croat-Austrian Bishop Strossmayer. After the Serbian Church's "rebellion" of 1937, the Vatican was angered, too. According to a Serb historian, in a 1937 consistory, Pope Pius XI allegedly said that "many in Yugoslavia would regret the missing generous opportunity provided by the Church, the opportunity that could have helped the stabilizing of the unity of Yugoslavia."[11] Finally, the royal dictatorship of 1929 and growing Serbian nationalism of the 1930s played into the hands of Croatian nationalist extremists. The crisis was simmering after the 1928 shooting by the Serb deputy at Croat deputies in the Belgrade parliament. The Croat radical nationalist *Ustaša* (plural: *Ustaše*) movement was founded and carried out terrorist activities (King Alexander I was assassinated in 1934). A Croat nationalist friar wrote: "The Catholic Church was discriminated against in a number of ways, but nothing so gravely embittered Catholics as did the Serbian regime and Orthodox church's blockade of the concordat."[12]

The concordat was never ratified. The dispute of the 1930s, the Catholic historian Mužić argues, accelerated the domestic crisis that led to the disintegration of the Kingdom of Yugoslavia in 1941.[13] From 1937 to 1941, both major Yugoslav churches carried out ethnic nationalist mobilization of their respective ethnic and religious communities. In June 1939, the Serbian Orthodox Church commemorated the 550th anniversary of the Kosovo Battle with massive outbursts of ethnic nationalist euphoria. At that same time, the Croatian Catholic episcopate announced the commencement of the grand jubilee of the 1300th anniversary of the evangelization of the Croats in 641. (Thirteen Centuries of Christianity in the Croat People). The Croatian jubilee was conceived as a nine-year-long sequence of commemorations, liturgical events, and pilgrimages to landmark historical sites that would fortify the tradition and continuity of nationhood and church-nation symbiosis. The grand jubilee was symbolically announced in the tumultuous year of 1937, when Archbishop Alojzije Stepinac led a "Croatian pilgrimage" in Jerusalem and other biblical sites in Palestine.

On 28 June 1939, on Saint Vitus' Day, thousands of Serbs gathered at the Ravanica monastery to commemorate the 550th anniversary of the Kosovo battle. In his sermon, Bishop Nikolaj Velimirović spoke about the spirit of commemoration and the liberation and redemption of the Kosovo province with its shrines and historic sites as the dominant form of religious and national consciousness and national identity of the Serbs. This spirit, the Bishop pointed out, knows no compromise; the choice is always between freedom or death. There cannot be a partial freedom, only full and complete freedom or death.[14] Velimirović also appealed to the restless Croats to reunite with Serbs, because, in his words: "Isn't it better to live together as brothers in our common and free homeland, instead of, divided and weakened, to succumb again to foreign imperial domination?"[15] Yet he did not reverse his stance on the concordat issue. During the official state-sponsored celebration of the 550th anniversary of the Kosovo battle in 1939, the government, fearing German invasion, made an attempt to "reinvent" the Kosovo myth as a patriotic myth common to all Yugoslav peoples. A proregime newspaper appealed to Catholic Croats and Slovenes to espouse the Kosovo myth as a "source of strength" and example of integrated national and religious ideals. In a similar vein, General Milan Nedić, soon to become the "Serbian Petain"—head of the World War II Serbian pro-Nazi puppet regime at Belgrade—wrote in a Belgrade newspaper about Yugoslav peoples' "return to Kosovo—the Serbian Jerusalem."[16] Yet, as far as the Croats are concerned, their religious leaders had already made the decision to develop a Croatian equivalent to the Kosovo myth. In 1939, the Catholic Church in Croatia announced the beginning of the nine-year jubilee entitled "Great Novena—Thirteen Centuries of Christianity in the Croat People."

The Catholic episcopate responded to the grand Serbian jubilee by showing Croat pride via commemoration of the evangelization of the Croats, which took place, according to Church historians, in 641, that is, much earlier than the Serbs became Christians. The Croat jubilee-in-preparation featured large parish and diocesan "Eucharistic congresses," emphasizing the role of the Church in the preservation of Croatian ethnic identity and desire for statehood-nationhood. The nine-year sequence of Croat Church festivals and pilgrimages was solemnly opened in September 1941 but soon halted by the collapse of the Yugoslav kingdom the Axis occupation, and a civil war.[17]

Civil War and Communist Revolution, 1941–1950

After the April 1941 invasion and occupation of Yugoslavia by the Axis powers and their allies (Bulgaria, Hungary, Albania, etc.), Yugoslavia was divided into several occupational zones and pro-Axis satellites states. The civil war that soon erupted was accompanied with massive massacres of the civilian population, first started in spring of 1941 by Croat Ustašas and later also carried out by other ethnic factions. This first Yugoslav civil war was a proof that the Yugoslav question could not be managed either by a centralized state or by partition. In fact, partition seemed to be worse than any form of unity. Initially the strongest among domestic warring factions were the Croatian radical nationalists or native fascists, the Ustašas. These were led by the lawyer Ante Pavelić, an admirer of Hitler and Mussolini. The Ustašas, backed by the Axis powers, founded a state in Croatia and Bosnia-Herzegovina named "the Independent State of Croatia" (NDH). Mussolini's Italy, which aspired to annexation of the northern tier of the Adriatic coast and weakening of the Yugoslav state, wholeheartedly sponsored the NDH.[18] In return, Pavelić ceded Istria, Dalmatia, and the isles to Italy. As a consequence, many Croats hated the NDH, formed resistance combat units together with Serbs, and joined the communists who fought against fascism for a Croat republic within a Yugoslav federation.

The second strongest among the domestic warring factions was the communist-led multiethnic "Anti-fascist People's Liberation Front" (also known as the *Partizani*, or Partisans), led by Josip Broz Tito, who assumed the title of "supreme commander of the People's Liberation Army–Partisans and general secretary of the Communist Party of Yugoslavia." This "People's Liberation Struggle" emphasized equality of all national groups and minorities, defeat of domestic and foreign fascism, and the halt of ethnic massacres by the force of a multiethnic army. The communist leaders did not yet insist on what was presumably their chief goal: communist revolution. The Yugoslav Partisan movement ideology can be described in Eric Hobsbawm's terms as "antifascist *nationalism* of the late 1930s and 1940s," that is, "remarriage of social revolution and patriotic sentiment."[19] The ethnic nationalists' massacres reinforced the Partisan ranks, first with the most endangered Croatian and Bosnian Serbs. After the fall of Mussolini, a significant number of Croats fighting for the formerly Italian-occupied and predominantly Croat-populated littoral joined the Partisan army. When the Allies recognized Tito's movement in 1943 and began sending massive aid to Tito, the Partisans' victory became imminent.

The third major warring faction was a Serb nationalist-royalist guerilla organization, the Četniks, under the royal general staff officer Dragoljub Draža Mihajlović. The Četniks were formed in Spring 1941 in Serbia and even joined forces with the communists in several attacks on Germans. Many Croatian and Bosnian Serbs joined them to escape the NDH terror. At the end of 1941, the Četniks broke up with the communists, halted antiinvaders' activities, and even collaborated with Germans and Italians against the Partisans in the hope of forming an independent Serbian state. The Četniks committed massive crimes against non-Serbs in Croatia and Bosnia-Herzegovina.[20] In Serbia's towns and cities, the quisling regime under general Milan Nedić and the Serbian native fascist Dimitrije Ljotić collaborated with the Germans. There was also a quisling regime in Slovenia, led by the Catholic bishop Gregorij Rožman, and pro-Axis Bosnian Muslim and Kosovo Albanian groups. The foreign invaders and native nationalist factions carried out massive genocidal atrocities, bloody reprisals, torture, deportations, and executions of civilians. The native ethnic nationalist factions all committed what today is known as the crime of "ethnic cleansing." They would repeat it 50 years later.

The Ustašas maintained several dozen concentration camps and large prisons. The largest concentration camp was located near the town of Jasenovac on the Sava river.[21] Most of prisoners in these camps were Partisan fighters and members of their families, members of urban guerilla squads of the Communist Party and Communist Youth, and all who belonged to and/or supported the Partisans. The killings at Jasenovac also indicate the NDH regime's intention to "cleanse" all Serbs, Jews, and Gypsies from the NDH. At any rate the Pavelić regime in the NDH pro-Axis state was perhaps the most brutal among the quisling regimes in Axis-occupied Europe.[22]

Much has been written about these Ustaša and Četnik massacres of the civilian population in Yugoslavia, but the problem still invites new analyses.

Although contemporary historians focus on statistics seeking to determine exact numbers of victims identified by ethnoreligious background, one of the most remarkable characteristic of World War II in Yugoslavia is Ustaša and Četnik brutality, torture, and sadism targeting men, women, children, and elderly alike. For that matter, the two local ethnic nationalistic factions differed both from German invaders and the communist Partisan resistance because these executed most of their victims by shooting. Torture of civilians and rape and murder of women and children were rare, particularly on the part of the Partisans (Germans did execute thousands of women and children in retaliation for Partisan actions, and during the last months of the war Partisans retaliated against their enemies' families, too, but there was no systematic torture and rape). In his recent relation of Balkan history, Misha Glenny has correctly pointed out that brutality was a remarkable feature of all Balkan wars, and World War II in Yugoslavia saw presumably the worst kind of inhuman atrocity. Although Glenny, like many before him, partly described some of these atrocities, he noted that a more detailed account would be "pornographic," suggesting the pathological nature of the hatred generated by the local history, religion, ethnicity, and myths.[23] The nature and scope of Balkan ethnic nationalistic massacres needs to be further analyzed in the context of the post–Cold War reconsideration of nationalism, communism, fascism, and Nazism. In the context of the "what was worse: communism or fascism?" debate, an analysis of the actions of the Yugoslav Partisans compared to those of the Ustašas and Četniks is missing, although it would be illuminating. Only by keeping in mind not only the statistics about victims' profile according to ethnicity and religion but also the "pornographic" details about Ustaša and Četnik massacres of civilians and prisoners of war can one properly understood the secret of the communist success in Yugoslavia and the origins of the communist-era civil religion of brotherhood and unity (see chapter 6).

While clergy either remained passive or supported various factions, including the Partisans, leaders of religious organizations backed the nationalist factions directly or indirectly. The Serb Orthodox hierarchy, lacking two of its leading prelates (patriarch Gavrilo and Bishop Nikolaj Velimirović were both sent into confinement by German military authorities in order to weaken national homogeneity of the Serbs) backed the quisling general Nedić. A large number of Orthodox priests in Serbia, Montenegro, Croatia, and Bosnia-Herzegovina supported the Četniks, and some joined their military formations. The Serb Orthodox priest Momčilo Djujić became commander-in-chief ("duke") of the Četnik "Dynaric division," which carried out ethnic cleansing of the Muslim and Catholic population in Croatia and Bosnia. Some Orthodox clergy in Croatia and Bosnia joined the Partisans or supported them because they defended ethnic Serbs from the Ustašas. A number of Muslim clerics from Croatia and Bosnia-Herzegovina were associated with the Ustaša regime or served as recruiters and military chaplains with the so-called Handžar legion, which was an SS unit staffed by

Bosnian Muslim men. Nonetheless, the Partisans won over many lower clergy and a few religious leaders, particularly among the Orthodox clergy in Macedonia, Croatia, Bosnia-Herzegovina, Kosovo, and Montenegro, as well as a number of Muslim imams and members of the ulema, and relatively the fewest but still in the hundreds, Croat and Slovene Catholic clergy from Italian and German-occupied regions.[24]

In contrast to the stateless Serb Četniks, who remained the replica of traditional Balkan banditry, the NDH was well equipped by the Axis and used state resources to eliminate from its territory the communists (of all ethnic backgrounds), Serbs who refused to convert into "Orthodox Croats," the Jews, and the Gypsies (Roma). Serb and Jewish cultural and other institutions in the NDH had to be destroyed. Consequently, the Serbian Orthodox Church in Croatia and Bosnia-Herzegovina lost 217 priests and 3 bishops, killed by the Ustašas, and 334 priests, expelled to Serbia. In addition, 350–400 Orthodox churches were destroyed.[25] A large number of Orthodox Serbs were forcibly converted to Catholicism as part of the Ustaša regime's policy to turn them into ethnic Croats of the "Eastern-Greek Christian faith."[26] In 1942 the Ustaša regime founded a "Croatian Orthodox Church." Concurrently, the Ustašas carried out massacres and deportations of Jews and (Gypsies) people. According to a Croat historian of Jewish descent, out of 39,000 prewar Jews, the Ustašas executed and deported to concentration camps almost 30,000, destroyed almost all synagogues, and killed 47 rabbis and other Jewish religious officials.[27] According to the independent scholar Žerjavić, 57,000 Yugoslav Jews perished during World War II, 33,000 were killed in the country (mostly in Croatia and in Serbia) and 24,000 in Nazi concentration camps in Europe.[28]

How was it possible that some two hundred Ustaša militants who returned to Croatia in 1941 and were never popular as a party or took part in any elections, could establish some kind of a "state" and even earn some popular support for the NDH? The answer is, first, thanks to the foreign support from Italy and Germany, which provided the material support and armed the NDH military forces; second, thanks to domestic support by the Roman Catholic Church. Historians Eric Hobsbawm and Peter Sugar, among other analysts of fascism in Europe, have argued that relatively small and unpopular native fascist regimes such as that in Croatia and Slovakia would have not been able to establish and legitimize their government without the decisive role of the local Catholic churches.[29] The Church's support for the NDH is well sustained by evidence. The regime emphasized its adherence to Roman Catholicism by passing appropriate laws. Abortion was a crime in some cases punishable by death. Likewise, pornography, blasphemy, cursing in public, and disrespect for the diet on Friday and work on Sunday were serious offenses. The Catholic hierarchy maintained a number of institutionalized links with the Ustaša regime. Church leaders viewed the NDH as a legitimate Croatian nation-state. Thousands of clerics and laymen became members of the Ustaša movement (i.e., the political party so entitled). The archbishop of Sarajevo, Ivan Šarić, and his general vicar Krunoslav Draganović sought to fuse Roman Catholic faith and Ustaša ideology. The bishop of Banja, Luka Josip Garić, was a member of the Ustaša organization. For them and many other clerical and lay Catholics who in 1941 began the church-national celebration of the thirteen centuries of the evangelization of the Croats, the NDH had accomplished a historic breakthrough, that is, the return of the ancient Western nation of the Croats (oppressed by Orthodox Serbs in the Yugoslav state) into the sphere of Western civilization.[30] The Catholic Church supplied the new regime with crucial components of statehood, such as a founding myth, patriotic ritual, and state bureaucracy. According to the myth, the NDH was the outgrowth of the thirteen centuries-old tradition. Concerning state-building, tens of thousands of members of Catholic lay organizations served the NDH. The new state recruited a large number of its officials from the Catholic lay movement and from graduates of Catholic seminaries and gymnasia. Most of Catholic clergy outside Italian-occupied zones were Ustaša supporters. A number of Catholic clerics wore Ustaša uniforms, and some served as the regime's officials. According to the Croatian historian Fikreta Jelić-Butić, 25 Catholic priests held offices in the Ustaša state and 11 clerics took part in massacres of civilian population.[31] A Croat Catholic survivor of the Jasenovac concentration camp recalls that camp guards, most of whom were murderers and torturers, would regularly attend mass and receive holy sacraments, only to return to their murderous business.[32] A Yugoslav government analysis of clergy exiled after 1945 designated 16 priests (12 Catholic and 4 Serb Orthodox) as war criminals.[33] A study published in 1991 in the United States, drawing on newly opened secret Allied archives, alleged that a number of internationally wanted Ustašas war crimes suspects escaped justice through the Vatican.[34]

The Church in Croatia, of course, is not the same as the Croatian people. Serb and Croat clergy could not cooperate, but the people could. During World War II, the Serbs in Croatia and Bosnia-Herzegovina—together with divisions of Croat Partisan fighters, including the highest ranked Partisan leader, Josip Broz Tito, and at least several dozen Catholic clerics who were supporters of the Partisans—defeated the Ustašas and destroyed the NDH.[35] It is plausible to argue that the NDH was an aberration in the long history of the Croat people. In the interwar kingdom, the Croat people widely supported the influential interwar Croat Peasant Party. The Communist Party of Croatia (including its youth wing and communist-led labor unions) enjoyed by far larger support than the Ustašas ever did. The peculiarity in the Croatian political history is a struggle for autonomy by legal means under existing political authority, through institutions such as the Sabor (diet) and the Ban (viceroy) and via linguistic-cultural campaigning. As summarized in the 1990 Constitution's preamble, the long history of the Croats has been a long political-legal and largely peaceful cultural struggle.[36] The Croatian Constitution of 1990 says in its preamble that a Croatian authority established in 1944 by the antifascist Partisan movement reasserted Croatian "rights to statehood in opposition to the Independent State of Croatia."[37]

Yet neither during the Cold War nor after 1989 could the Catholic Church legitimize the communist-led Partisans, even if hundreds of thousands of them had been ethnic Croats. In Yugoslavia, there was no Charles De Gaulle or effective noncommunist resistance as there was, for example, in France. Yugoslav communists organized a large army and massive popular resistance. The party allowed only a few significant noncommunist figures to play a part in this and "communized" them after the war through the new patriotic mythology. After the war the victory was ascribed completely to the Party, communist leaders' heroism, and their leadership skills. This kind of history became the new official nationalism (see chapter 6).

In addition, the end of the war and the Partisan military triumph brought about a massive post–civil-war retaliation, followed by a Bolshevik-styled revolution and dictatorship of the Communist Party. From 1945 to approximately 1953, a crude Balkan variant of Bolshevism waged a war against class enemies, "kulaks," and wartime collaborators (the so-called domestic traitors). Tens of thousands of Yugoslavs of all nationalities were killed by the communists. Persecution of clergy was an earmark of this period.[38] As Milovan Djilas testified, top Partisan leaders knew of these atrocities.[39] The party itself sought revenge: over 70 percent of the total prewar party membership of 12,000 and more than half of the 30,000 prewar members of the Communist Youth lost their lives. A part of this persecution was the Partisan army's May 1945 massacre and persecution of nearly 30,000 retreating members of various domestic pro-Axis factions, mostly the Croat Ustašas at Bleiburg on the Austrian border. However, the most massive form of repression during this period of Yugoslav Bolshevism was the persecution of some 30,000 to 50,000 members of the Communist Party, who, after the Yugoslav-Soviet conflict in 1948, sided with Stalin against Tito. Tito jailed many of these hard-line Stalinists on the Adriatic Naked Island concentration camp, where many lost their lives. This is considered by a group of comparative historians of communism the most severe and massive manifestation of the repressive character of communism in Yugoslavia.[40]

From 1945 to 1953, church-state relations were tense. The Islamic Community and the Orthodox Church in Macedonia legitimized the regime and the state and were financially supported by the state and free to worship as other religious institutions were, provided, of course, that the worship was devoid of excessive ethnic nationalist content. Yet the two largest churches resisted the communist intention to impose state control upon clergy through clerical associations. The Serb Orthodox theologian and bishop Nikolaj Velimirović agitated against the Tito regime from exile in the United States. Velimirović urged the clergy to fight both the regime and Croatian Catholicism and was the first to charge that genocide was committed by Croats against Serbs. Another prominent Serb Orthodox theologian, the archimandrite Justin Popović, carried on an antiregime struggle at home and spent 17 years in jail and in monastery confinement. In 1946 in Zagreb, a 16-year sentence was given to the Catholic archbishop of Zagreb, Alojzije Stepinac. Stepinac angered the regime when he rejected the idea of clerical associations, declined Tito's demands that Catholicism in Yugoslavia loosen its ties with the Vatican, and, in September 1945, convened a bishops' conference and released a pastoral letter against the regime's brutal policies, which included executions and imprisonment of clergy, and confiscation of property. Stepinac also secretly kept NDH archival documents in his palace (entrusted to him by NDH leaders), until the Croat communist leader Bakarić convinced him to turn them over in exchange for a promise to ease the persecution of clergy, and secretly met with high-ranking Ustaša officers who returned to the country to organize sabotage and terrorism. The communists, at the time urged by Stalin to rig the elections and consolidate power in all of Eastern Europe, took this chance to discredit Archbishop Stepinac and the noncooperative clergy and put Stepinac on trial along with these Ustaša officers war criminals and terrorists. These officers and some other internationally wanted war criminals sought by the Allies and by some Jewish organizations, were captured, put on trial, and executed. The prosecutor, Jakov Blažević, expanded the indictment against Stepinac, trying and not quite succeeding to prove by arguing that he indeed had contacts with the accused terrorists and knew about escapes of other Ustaša leaders to the West, thanks to the Church's help—his collaboration with the NDH and the Germans and the Church's contribution to the persecution of Serbs and Jews. The prosecutor ignored documents in the possession of Western intelligence sources that reported that Stepinac a few times protested against the worst NDH massacres and even sympathized with the Allies after 1943, trying to bring the NDH over to the winners' side.[41] Eventually, Stepinac spent five years in jail and was released, because of poor health, to his native village, where he died in 1960. In any case, though several religious leaders were jailed at the time in Eastern European countries after Stalinist show trials, there was no such a thing as "the Stepinac Trial" in Yugoslavia; there was a trial of a group of Ustaša conspirators, and Stepinac was deftly included among them by the prosecutor. However, Stepinac took the opportunity to protest at the trial against the regime's execution of more than two hundred Catholic priests (some of whom were innocent people killed by a mob and the communist police but most of whom were active Ustaša) as well as against the closing of religious schools and nationalization of Church property. In this way the myth of Stepinac's martyrdom was created in the West during the anticommunist momentum of the 1950s. Pope Pius XII contributed to this myth by making Stepinac a cardinal in 1953, after which Belgrade broke off diplomatic ties with the Vatican.

In the new Yugoslavia, the communists sought legitimacy as guardians of ethnic harmony and guarantors that the genocidal massacres of World War II would not be repeated. In 1945, the Yugoslav People's Assembly, upon Tito's initiative, passed the "law prohibiting the incitement and advocacy of ethnic, religious, and racial hatred." Yugoslav communists had gone so far as to declare and put in school textbooks that the Partisans, socialism, and federalism had "solved" the notorious Yugoslav National Question once and for all. In reality, the opposition remained alive and the country vulnerable. In the first Yugoslavia, only one of the two largest churches did not grant legitimacy to the state; in the second Yugoslavia, both the largest churches thought of the communist regime as illegitimate and sought revenge. In the first Yugoslavia, the regime was challenged by only two revolutionary terrorist organizations (the communists and the Ustaša). In the second Yugoslavia, several dozen terrorist organizations, as I will show, worked against the Belgrade regime.

War Continues: Exile Politics and Warring Myths

After 1945, the Yugoslav government designated 3,764 persons, from over 30,000 exiled members of defeated factions, war crimes suspects, but only a few of these were transferred to Yugoslavia and sentenced for war crimes.[42] According to Yugoslav sources, in the 1960s, there were several hundred active anti-Yugoslav exile organizations publishing around 120 periodicals, newsletters, and other propaganda material.[43] According to U.S. sources published in the 1990s, at least several dozen anti-Yugoslav organizations operated in the United States and Canada alone and were assisted by Western intelligence services.[44] Some anti-Yugoslav groups carried out assassinations, kidnapings, highjackings, sabotage, guerilla raids, bombings, and attacks on Yugoslav embassies, consulates, and cultural outposts abroad. A number of Yugoslav and foreign citizens lost their lives in those acts of terrorism.[45] In the summer of 1972, a 19-strong Croatian guerilla force, formed and trained in Australia and western Europe, penetrated into Bosnia but was destroyed by the Yugoslav Army and police.[46] The Yugoslav secret police, known under several different names (UDBA, or Bureau for State Security, or SDB or SDS, Service of State Security), waged a perpetual war against exile organizations and was most effective by turning them against each other. Anti-Yugoslav nationalist organizations in exile were divided along ethnic lines, linked with organized crime, and distrustful of one another to such an extent that their leaders never succeeded in forming a united anti-Yugoslav and anticommunist opposition front.[47] Yet several groups occasionally succeeded in organizing terrorist attacks. During the regime's liberalization in the 1960s and 1970s, anti-Yugoslav groups intensified deadly terrorist attacks or attempted such attacks.[48]

Some foreign branches of Yugoslav religious institutions and individual clergy abroad provided assistance to anti-Yugoslav exile organizations. According to Western intelligence sources made public in the late 1980s, the Croatian führer Pavelić, along with many prominent Ustaša leaders, escaped justice through the Vatican's Illyrian Institute of St. Girolamo (today the Croatian Institute of Sveti Jeronim).[49] A number of Croatian and Serbian clerics joined émigré organizations and even took part in terrorist activities.[50] Prominent officials of the Ustaša regime, the priests Vilim Cecelja and Krunoslav Draganović, and the uniformed Ustaša officer-priest Dragutin Kamber after 1945 remained members of the Church entrusted with important administrative and even humanitarian tasks.[51] In 1966, the Tito government succeeded in inserting an "antiterrorist" clause into the Protocol, a document on normalization of relations with the Vatican.[52] Although anti-Yugoslav terrorist actions carried out by exiled groups caused numerous deaths and injuries of innocent people, no domestic religious authority in the Croat Catholic or Serb Orthodox Churches (most of the acts of terrorism were carried out by Croats and Serbs) ever released an official statement of condemnation.

While terrorism discredited the anti-Yugoslav opposition in exile, these groups were still quite successful in the spread of ethnic hatred, the manufacturing of myths, and propaganda. Serbian exile groups charged that genocide was allegedly committed by the Ustaša, aided by the Catholic Church. In 1950, on the occasion of the inauguration of the Genocide Convention by the United Nations General Assembly, Serb exile organizations submitted to the United Nations a "Memorandum on Crimes of Genocide Committed against the Serbian People by the Government of the 'Independent State of Croatia' during World War II."[53] In the 1950s and 1960s, several books by Serb authors elaborating the genocide argument, with an emphasis on the role of the Catholic Church as allegedly the principal instigator of genocide, appeared in the West. These books drew the data (citing 40,000 Serbs killed at Jasenovac camp, 700,000 Serb victims in the territory of the Independent State of Croatia, and one million Serbs killed in the whole of Yugoslavia) from the Četnik General Mihajlović's sources, published first in 1943 by the Serbian Orthodox Church diocese in Chicago, Illinois.[54] The Serbian Church espoused a view of World War II in which Yugoslavia committed genocide against the Serbian people. The exiled bishop Nikolaj Velimirović (1888–1956), from Libertyville, Illinois, in his numerous writings and sermons (banned by the communist regime in Yugoslavia and published as late as 1988–92), argued that the Croatian genocide of Serbs was incited by the Catholic Church. In the mid-1950s, Velimirović wrote a pamphlet in which he predicted that soon after Tito's death, the Croats, inspired by the pope, would rush to arm themselves, secede again from Yugoslavia, and commit another genocide of Serbs.[55]

Croat émigrés glorified Cardinal Alojzije Stepinac as a patriot and anti-communist fighter. His 1946 joint trial with a group of terrorists and war criminals became a "Stalinist show trial," a term that might have been applied, partly, to Stepinac but not to other accused on that trial. Émigré Croats also developed the so-called Bleiburg–Way of the Cross myth by exaggerating the number of the dead and jailed among the surrounded retreating pro-Axis groups in May 1945 at the town of Bleiburg on the Yugoslav-Austrian border. Architects of this myth, such as the former Ustaša high officials Ivo Omrčanin and Vinko Nikolić, argued that 550,000 Croats (including soldiers' families) were massacred at Bleiburg and tortured to death on long marches through Yugoslavia (i.e., the Way of the Cross), which Omrčanin called the "Holocaust of Croatians."[56] Yet, according to the independent Croat analyst the demographer Vladimir Žerjavić, the total number of all quisling troops (including Ustašas, Četniks, and others) in the retreat 1945 was around 50,000, and far fewer than that number were captured or killed in May 1945.[57]

The Bleiburg myth (the "Bleiburg Tragedy of the Croatian People") became a Croatian equivalent to the Kosovo myth. The myth built a martyr aura around the NDH and fueled self-pity and a lust for revenge among nationalistic Croats. In the 1960s, exile Croat organizations founded the so-called Bleiburg Platoon of Honor, a paramilitary unit that paraded at annual commemorations at Bleiburg. In July 1972, a 19-man-strong Ustaša guerilla unit, the Croatian Revolutionary Brotherhood (HRB) penetrated Bosnia-Herzegovina and launched a popular uprising of the oppressed Croats against the "Serbo-communists." The group believed that the time was ripe for Croatian rebellion in the aftermath of Tito's crackdown on the massive post-1945 nationalist movement (the so-called Croatian Spring of 1971). The leader of the group, Adolf Andrić, wrote a booklet, the manual for Croatian revolutionary struggle (which included instructions for making explosive devices), entitled "Avengers of Bleiburg." The booklet was found with Andrić, who was killed by Yugoslav military police at Mount Raduša in southwestern Bosnia.[58]

Thanks to the anticommunist mobilization in the West in the 1950s and the active Catholic Church's role in it, perhaps the most effective among the Croatian nationalist myths was a new history presented as martyrdom of the Archbishop of Zagreb, Alojzije Cardinal Stepinac. On the occasion of the papal promotion of the jailed Stepinac to a cardinal in 1953, Croatian émigrés published the first apology of the cardinal, written by a Catholic priest who had been close to the wartime Ustaša state.[59] Croatian exile propaganda centers in Buenos Aires, Rome, London, Melbourne, and elsewhere issued numerous volumes on Stepinac. These publications allegedly cited authentic Stepinac wartime sermons that testified to his humanitarian work and condemnation of repression.[60]

All in all, the Yugoslav ethnic strife unfolding in the interwar kingdom and escalating during World War II continued both at home and through the new exile politics. The communists, in fact, imposed a cease-fire or merely limited the scope and intensity of the struggle. Yugoslavia remained vulnerable and imperiled by the domestic and exiled opposition. If there had not been communism but some other system, the conflict would have probably continued, too. If the common Yugoslav state had not been restored and several new states had emerged via partition, the conflict would have even more probably escalated into another civil war. Peace came because unity and multiethnic communism came and were enforced by the state and party.

Years of Renewal and Peaceful Coexistence

After the Tito-Stalin split of 1948, the country quickly modernized and abandoned crude Leninist-Stalinist politics. In contrast to other East European communist countries, Yugoslavia opened its borders in 1960. The Yugoslavs were better off than ever. Small wonder—Church-state relations had improved. In the aftermath of the Second Vatican Council (1962–65), Belgrade and the Holy See restored diplomatic relations. In 1970, Tito met with Pope Paul VI. The Council, among other things, urged an interfaith dialogue and dialogue with nonbelievers. According to a U.S. Christian analyst of religious affairs in the communist part of Europe, the post-Council dialogue between Christians and domestic Yugoslav Marxists (which involved mostly intellectuals and scholars but only a few religious leaders) was relatively the most open and successful in Europe.[61] Some clerics, such as the Slovene bishop Vekoslav Grmič and the archbishop of Split-Makarska, Frane Franić, even discovered good things in the system's "socialist self-management" and praised it in their writings, sermons, and interviews. The reputable Catholic theologian Tomislav Šagi-Bunić also praised the "self-managed system" but argued that Christians should be granted unrestricted religious liberty, including the right to establish church-sponsored political organizations because the state still remained under a Marxist government.[62] The Dominican Tomo Vereš and the friar minor conventual Špiro Marasović argued that the Church cannot legitimize any form of government under Communist Party leadership.[63] There was much ambiguity about the Christian-Marxist dialogue, but according to postcommunist Church assessments of it, the Church devised the dialogue tactics in the struggle against the Communist enemy. In the pope's words, the dialogue urged the faithful to pursue this struggle not by means of "violent confrontation"; rather, "Christians persisted in trying every avenue of negotiation, dialogue, and witnessing of the truth, appealing to the conscience of the adversary and seeking to reawaken in him a sense of shared human dignity."[64]

The Interfaith Dialogue

In the 1960s, the Vatican also made an attempt to improve relations with the Orthodox Church and other denominations. In January 1966, the Catholic Church in all dioceses in Yugoslavia inaugurated a series of annual interfaith prayers and vigils, the "Octave of Prayer for Christian Unity." The first "concrete" ecumenical Catholic-Orthodox public prayer service was a spontaneous informal move at local level. The prayer involved a Croatian Catholic bishop and Serb Orthodox archpriest and took place in the Croatian coastal city of Split on 25 January 1966. The bishop of Split-Makarska, Frane Franić, invited the local Serb Orthodox archpriest, Marko Plavša, to pray together and hold a joint worship service in a Catholic cathedral. Nothing similar had occurred in history in thousand years. Plavša accepted the invitation in spite of the opposition of the local Serbian bishop Stefan Boca and many Orthodox clerics. Bishop Franić also faced opposition among Catholic clergy. Franić's aides argued that only another bishop or the head of a monastic order would be an appropriate partner for such an occasion.[65]

At any rate, thanks to the Council and Bishop Franić, Catholic Croats and Orthodox Serbs came together to worship in the same Church as united Christians and two Yugoslav nationalities who spoke similar languages and were pillars of the country's unity. Franić recalled the historic 25 January prayer in an interview with the author as follows:

Before the Council, it was unthinkable that we Catholics could invite the Orthodox to our church except to convert them. Likewise, we Catholics never set foot into a "schismatic" church. Yet after the Council, it was no longer a schismatic, but a sister-church. My old friend Marko representing the Serbian Orthodox Church, read the Gospel in Serbian, pronouncing the Scripture in the ekavian dialect otherwise regularly in use in Serbia (even though he, as a native of the nearby city of Sinj, here in our Dalmatia, did not speak that way). Yet on this occasion the Serb priest wanted to assert his Serbian identity. At any rate, two churches worshiped together and the congregation applauded several times, which was, back then, an unusual practice in churches. After the prayer the fraternal hug, and I saw the faithful were deeply moved and many were tearful.[66]

According to the Croatian Catholic historian Juraj Kolarić, the Catholic Church welcomed the Split prayer, but the Serbian Orthodox Church authorities did not.[67] Consequently, contrary to Bishop Franić's desire, the ecumenical prayer at Split was discontinued. In January 1967, it was canceled because Archpriest Plavša was ill. As Archbishop Franić recalled in our conversation in 1989, Plavša, seriously ill, confessed that Bishop Stefan had criticized him for naivete and foolishness. Plavša also received phone threats and angry letters from exiled Serbian nationalist organizations. Some monk zealots called Plavša a traitor of Serbia. Not very long after the historic prayer, the ecumenical pioneer Marko Plavša died of cancer.

Yet the ice was broken, and something that could be labeled an ecumenical movement spread across the country. It brought together Catholics, Protestants, Jews, Orthodox, and Muslims and featured many religious events, mutual visitations of clergy, tolerant debates among theologians, friendly ecumenical articles in religious literature and press, and so forth.[68] According to a Yugoslav government expert on interconfessional relations, ecumenical cooperation was especially cordial in Bosnia-Herzegovina.[69]

However, while this "ecumenism from below" was making progress, relations between church leaders remained cold. The Serbian Church hierarchy called for a public apology from Croat leaders of the Catholic Church for Ustašas' World War II crimes against the Serbian civilian population and specifically against the Serbian Orthodox Church. Only one Croat churchman accepted the apology idea. Alfred Pichler, the Catholic bishop of Banja Luka in Bosnia-Herzegovina, released on 20 December 1963 a Christmas message that contained the following paragraph:

> It was precisely in this country, that, in the past war, many of our brothers of the Orthodox faith were killed because they were Orthodox Christians. Those who killed them called themselves Catholics. And those Christians killed other people, also Christians, because they were not Croats and Catholics. We painfully admit the terrible self-deceit of those strayed people and we beg our brothers of the Orthodox faith to forgive us, just as Christ had forgiven us all from the cross. At the same time, we forgive everyone, if they perhaps hated us or did us injustice.[70]

In contrast to Bishop Pichler, a majority of Croatian clerics voiced countercharges against the Serbian Orthodox Church for the backing the interwar regime that discriminated against Catholics and for supporting the Serbian Četniks who, during World War II, committed massive atrocities against the Catholic civilian population in Croatia and Bosnia. The Catholics proposed either mutual apologies or common interfaith prayers for all victims of World War II (implicitly referring to many victims of the communist terror, too).

The Serbian Church did not positively respond to the ecumenical initiative launched by the Second Vatican Council. In 1968, the Serbian Church became a member of the World Council of Churches (WCC) in Geneva, led by Protestant Christians, of which the Catholic Church was not a member. Protestant denominations, through the WCC, allocated significant financial aid to the Serbian Church—otherwise relatively the most impoverished of all Yugoslav denominations.[71] In addition, antiecumenical theologians in the Orthodox Church were very influential. In 1974, the archimandrite Justin Popović published, in Greece, a radical antiecumenical book.[72] In 1975, the leading Serbian theologian, the archimandrite Atanasije Jevtić, a pupil of the archimandrite Popović and an admirer of Bishop Velimirović, argued, at an ecumenical conference, against interfaith prayers. In a similar vein, the distinguished professor of the Belgrade Orthodox theological school, Dimitrije Bogdanović, wrote as follows:

> I am afraid that the Roman Catholic Church's strategy of dialogue is but another way to achieve re-assertion and rejuvenation of Roman Catholi-

cism as the leading social and political force in the world. That is why we Orthodox cannot espouse this ecumenical dialogue as it is conceived by the Catholic Church. We must not help making a room for political maneuvering. One religious organization cannot be above others. No Church can put itself in the center of social and political power. No Church can be equal partner to the state. If one religious organization acquires for itself such a decisive influence in political life, it would soon demand a special status and privileges that other churches do not ask for themselves. That would disrupt the religious equilibrium in our multi-confessional society, with possible serious political implications. Consequently, the fundamental precondition for a serious and open dialogue will be that the Roman Catholic church as well as other churches become thoroughly apolitical.[73]

The Churches still maintained some ecumenical events, hoping that the ruling communists would expand religious liberties once they noted improved interfaith relations. Bishop Franić argued that "ecumenism should be critically important for our state and society, because it operates as an effective instrument for promoting tolerance, better understanding, and a spirit of liberty among Christians and non-Christians and among peoples of different nationalities in this society."[74] A Serb Orthodox scholar echoed with a similar argument: "Catholic-Orthodox ecumenical dialogue in Yugoslavia can keep in check conflicts between the two largest Yugoslav nationalities, Serbs and Croats. The Church maintains a special role to mitigate nationalist tensions and passions and educate a mature Christian individual fostering Christian consciousness at the base of the national consciousness."[75]

The regime cautiously supported the new ecumenism. A confidential federal government document I had a chance to read contained a section on ecumenical dialogue, as follows:

Ecumenical currents in our country continue through various contacts among clergy and believers of different faiths. Overall, the practice is positive. The clerical cooperation is a counterweight to the traditional religious intolerance and earlier quarrels among the high clergy. When priests and bishops of different religious organizations attend public events and celebrations together (which has been frequently observed, especially in Bosnia-Herzegovina) it creates a favorable political climate. However, the ecumenical ideas are coming into a conflict with conservative orientation inside certain church circles. Thus, top leaders in the Serbian Orthodox Church prohibit its clergy to take part in the interfaith dialogue with Catholic priests. Some Serb church leaders insist that the Catholic Church, as a precondition for the dialogue, condemns publicly Second World War Ustaša crimes against the Serb-Orthodox population in Croatia and Bosnia-Herzegovina. The Catholics say that the Orthodox Church must apologize for the Četnik massacres over Croats and Muslims. Finally, it is our assessment that, mistrust and intolerance between churches is so deeply rooted, that ecumenical cooperation and religious leaders' effort aimed at building an ideological alliance against organized socialist political forces, will not succeed.[76]

Church-State Relations in the Sixties

In 1958, the League of Communists of Yugoslavia released a new program. It sanctioned the legacy of Titoist anti-Stalinism and laid out an ideological base for Yugoslav "self-managed" socialism. Paradoxically, this apparently most liberal of all the programs and documents released by Yugoslav communists since the party's foundation in 1920 inaugurated an antireligious clause not found in previous programs.[77] Hypothetically all power was in the hands of atheistic Marxists, but religious citizens could manifest their patriotic outlook through activism in the Socialist Alliance of Working People, labor unions, and various voluntary associations. All in all, there were only a few noncommunists on significant positions in government, business, and other key segments of societies.

Nevertheless, the social climate had changed, and the regime almost completely halted persecution of clergy and attacks on religion in public. Between 1966 and 1971, Yugoslavia normalized relations with the Vatican by signing a protocol on joint talks and exchanging diplomatic representatives.[78] Both parties made concessions. The regime let churches be built and religious press circulate freely, and the Vatican agreed (without consulting Croatian clergy) not to reopen the case of Alojzije Cardinal Stepinac. The Vatican also discouraged Croatian clergy from collaboration with exiled nationalistic organizations. As part of a secret protocol's agenda, the Vatican let Yugoslavia arrest the Ustaša priest Krunoslav Draganović, who had organized the 1945 escape of Pavelić and other Ustaša leaders with the assistance of the Vatican. In 1967, Draganović came to Yugoslavia and became a collaborator of the communist secret police, the UDBA.[79]

After Tito's purge of the hardliner Alexander Ranković in 1966, the secret police halted systematic spying on domestic clergy. At a conference in November 1969, the chief secretary of Croatia's commission for religious affairs, Ivan Lazić, complained that the secret police had stopped supplying the commissions with confidential information.[80] This conference advised commissions to abandon the old practice of using intelligence obtained through secret police methods and to develop "research and expertise in religious affairs through coverage of religious events, reading the church press, scholarly study of religion, exchange of information through conferences and seminars, and frequent tolerant and kindly communication with religious dignitaries and church representatives."[81] At the same time, the commissioners for religious affairs were deprived of their own funds and lost the status of autonomous agencies of the state. The federal commission for religious affairs stopped providing direct financial assistance to religious communities in 1970. According to 1969 government material, the following religious communities received financial assistance from the state: the Serbian Orthodox Church, the Islamic Community, the Macedonian Orthodox Church, the Union of Old Catholic Churches of Yugoslavia, and the Slovak Evangelical Church.[82] The Serbian Orthodox Church remained the major recipient of financial assistance from the state, followed by the Macedonian Orthodox Church (in Macedonia), the Islamic Community (in Bosnia-Herzegovina), and some minor religious communities. A federal commission report lists financial aid allocated to the Serbian Church in all republics except Macedonia (even there some clergy received payments through the clerical association) and also to other religious communities, with only two modest contributions given to the Catholic Church in Croatia for museums and repair of historic monuments.[83] In its annual report for the years 1979–80, the Commission for Relations with Religious Communities of Croatia had systematized the financial aid paid to religious communities in the republics. Out of 24 religious communities, 6 were awarded government financial aid. Of the total sum allocated by the government for this purpose (37,760,000,000 Yugoslav dinars), 75 percent was given to the Serbian Orthodox Church (mostly for the proregime clergy association's pension fund, the rest for repair and construction of places of worship and monasteries) and the rest was allocated to smaller religious groups like the Evangelical, Baptist, and Pentecostal churches.[84] The commissions had no control over the churches' revenues. The 1969 government report said that information about the churches' financial status was not available and estimated that the Catholic Church in Slovenia annually raised around 1.5 to 2.0 billion "old" dinars (the currency valid before the financial reform of 1965), mostly from donations collected at home and abroad.[85] The report also pointed out that donations went chiefly for construction of places of worship and that some religious communities occasionally evaded paying taxes. The same source concluded that religious communities "have become more economically self-sufficient and overall better off."[86]

According to the 1969 government report cited earlier, "good relations between church and state must be maintained and further improved, provided the churches's activity does not support nationalism and chauvinism and is not overtly antisocialist." The report urges officials in charge of religious affairs:

We must not carry out antichurch and antireligious campaigns. . . . [I]nstead, it will be our concern to secure for citizen believers the free expression of their beliefs, as well as freedom of church activity, provided it is strictly religious, [but] we must work on reducing further the room for church politics and manifestation of the churches' political ambitions. Here we need to bear in mind that it is often quite difficult to determine the factual boundaries between strictly religious, and therefore legal, and political, that is, illegal, activity of the churches. For instance, the whole range of activities the churches traditionally carry out in spheres of cultural and charitable work, although they do not belong narrowly in the sphere of worship and undoubtedly convey some political weight, nevertheless will be difficult to classify as illegal. . . . [I]deological bias and bureaucratic blunders will only make the churches turn inward again and become increasingly zealous and fundamentalist. Hence the attitude of the state and our society toward religious sentiments and religious worship must be highly tolerant.[87]

Nonetheless, institutions demanded more freedom. In 1966, and again in 1968, the Bishops' Conference of Yugoslavia proposed to the federal government that every employee be granted the right to paid absence on the occasion of major religious holidays. The bishops also questioned the legality of restrictions on the priests in providing religious services for patients in hospitals and prison inmates, as well as regulations prohibiting military servicemen from attending churches and receiving religious literature. The bishops also complained about difficulties in finding appropriate locations for church construction in large cities. The regime urged the commissions for religious affairs to facilitate expedited church construction; slow development was, in reality, caused by bad urban planning, massive migration from rural areas into cities, and illegal construction of private homes by these migrants.[88] In 1965, the Yugoslav government (SIV) released an instruction for the republics saying that all religious facilities destroyed or damaged during World War II should have priority in renovation and rebuilding. It was recommended that the state provide financial assistance to religious communities in these cases. The state also took care of some 2,000 damaged buildings listed as monuments of cultural heritage and historic sites.[89]

The government praised the relation with the Holy See and urged local administrations in the republics and provinces to provide a stronger "support for progressive, pro-council forces in the Church."[90] However, relations between the government and the Serbian Orthodox Church had declined after the 1968 rebellion of Kosovo Albanians. Speaking about new tendencies in the Serbian Church at the regime's seminar conference, "Our Policy Toward the Newest Currents in the Religious Communities in the Socialist Republic of Croatia," in November 1969 at Zagreb, the chairman of Serbia's commission for religious affairs, Vitomir Petković, said that "the Serbian church leadership abandoned the earlier course of cooperation, seeking a church-state conflict and showing nationalist and chauvinist tendencies."[91] In response to local ethnic nationalistic movements in Croatia (1967–71) and in Kosovo (1968–71), the Holy Assembly of Bishops released in 1971 and 1973 two official statements expressing the bishop's concern over "growing ethnic and religious intolerance, including attacks on church property in some areas of our country."[92] In the same period, *Pravoslavlje*, the newspaper of the Serbian Patriarchate, was fined twice for allegedly inciting ethnic and religious hatred.[93]

Religion Erodes, Churches Grow

In the sixties and seventies, sociological surveys of religiosity showed a decline in the number of people who declared religious affiliation and attended worship services.[94] Research showed that the number of Orthodox believers had decreased from 41.2 percent to 28.9 percent. The number of Catholics had also declined from 31.7 percent to 21.9 percent.[95] A 1970 international survey of religious consciousness that also included Yugoslavia among 53 countries, found that 63 percent of the population were self-declared atheists in the capital of Yugoslavia (with 23 percent who said they were religious). This survey placed Yugoslavia in second place in terms of the number of self-declared atheists.[96] A survey conducted among high school students in Serbia had found that "all respondents had noticeable antireligious attitudes: 68.7 percent expressed an antireligious attitude toward God, 74.4 percent expressed an antireligious attitude toward the church, 87.5 percent never prayed, and 89.6 percent never went to church."[97] According to several independent polls, the total number of believers in Yugoslavia was steadily decreasing from 90 percent in 1953 to 70.3 percent in 1964 and 53.1 percent in 1969, reaching the lowest point in 1984 (45 percent).[98]

While religious consciousness was eroding, religious institutions took advantage of the liberalization in the communist methods of rule to rebuild and expand their resources. In the second half of the 1960s, the churches of Yugoslavia were relatively better off than religious institutions in Eastern Europe and the Soviet Union. According to the official statistics for 1969, religious communities regularly operated over 14,000 churches, monasteries, mosques, and other facilities.[99] By comparison, in the ten times more populous USSR, the total number of places of worship open for regular service was 11,636.[100] According to a federal government official in charge of religious affairs, 2,800 sacred buildings were registered as cultural monuments and historic sites and maintained by the state.[101] According to the same source, in 1965, over 13.5 million copies of various religious publications were in circulation in Yugoslavia. By the end of the decade, some 50 theological schools and seminaries were open, with 4,224 enrolled students.[102]

According to Serbian Orthodox Church sources, between 1945 and 1970, the Church acquired 181 newly built temples and restored 841.[103] In addition, the Church built 115 new chapels and 8 monasteries and repaired 126 chapels and 48 monasteries.[104] Another source indicates that Patriarch Germanus Djorić, upon his enthronement in 1960, set up a permanent team of architects and designers affiliated with the Patriarchate's Construction Office in Belgrade.[105] Based on blueprints and ideas developed by the designers of the Patriarchate's Construction Office, "around 200 new temples and the same number of other church facilities (chapels, belfries, parish homes, and other), with repairs and reconstruction, had been accomplished before Patriarch Germanus' death in 1990."[106] Furthermore, between 1945 and

1966, the Serbian Church expanded its educational institutions, starting with only one seminary in 1949; by 1966, the Church had four seminaries and a theological school. New buildings for the theological school in Belgrade and a seminary in Krka, Croatia, opened in the eighties. Church publishing activity soared from a single newsletter in the 1950s to hundreds of thousands of copies of newspapers, journals, periodicals, and books in the late 1960s.[107] Also in the sixties, the Serbian Church was busy consecrating newly opened churches and chapels. In the first half of 1966 alone, for example, Orthodox dignitaries celebrated consecration of 27 new churches, temples, and chapels; 4 belfries, 2 monastic houses, and 2 new altars.[108] In the seventies the dynamic of construction and renewal continued. According to the Serbian patriarchate's biweekly newspaper *Pravoslavlje*, from 1972 to 1984, 30 new Orthodox churches had been built in Serbia proper alone.[109]

In Croatia, the Serbian Orthodox Church, which had been the target of genocidal assault by Croatian fascists during World War II, was treated with special care and regularly assisted with government funds. A Croatian government document shows that the Serbian Orthodox Church in 55 counties and municipalities of Croatia (about 80 percent of the republic) had, in the early 1980s, the following facilities: 257 churches and temples in use for regular worship services; 62 chapels; 148 parish houses; 9 monasteries; 1 seminary; 12 residential buildings for clergy; 4 church museums, 4 bishop's palaces, and 1 patriarchal palace; and 63 churches were renewed and repaired, as well as 7 chapels, 12 parish houses, 2 monasteries, and 4 clerical homes. In the period of 1945–82 the Serbian Orthodox Church in Croatia opened 12 new churches, 2 chapels, and 8 clerical houses, while 14 new churches, 2 chapels, and 6 other buildings were under construction. By comparison, the Catholic Church in Croatia built 71 new churches, 69 chapels, 16 parish houses, 42 parish offices, 1 monastery, 8 residential buildings for monks and nuns, 1 seminary, 13 classrooms for religious instruction, and 1 house for retired priests in the same period.[110]

In 1958, the state backed the election of the moderate Bishop Germanus to the patriarchal throne. Hranislav Djorić-Germanus (1899–1990) had served as a parish priest in the Morava region and had a wife and children before he entered the monastery. The government allocated 7,600,000 dinars and granted to the patriarch 11 luxury cars and a police escort during his inaugural ceremonies in Belgrade and in the Kosovo province.[111] The new patriarch praised Tito's foreign policy of nonalignment during his foreign travels and avoided contacts with exiled anti-Yugoslav groups. Yet shortly after his enthronement Germanus held a requiem service at the Tomb of the Unknown Hero in the Avala hills near Belgrade. It would become a traditional annual event, never publicized in the state-controlled media but always attended by a large crowd. The commemorations were aimed at raising the awareness of the suppressed memory of World War I, which the church considered one of the most glorious moments in national history. The moving "March on the Drina," rarely heard in public, was performed as part of Germanus' Avala commemorations. After 1966, Germanus focused his attention on worsening Serbo-Albanian ethnic relations in Kosovo.

Patriarch Germanus was amiable with state officials, used the official rhetoric of socialism, brotherhood, and unity, and, in contrast to the Catholic Church, officially accepted financial aid from the state, including pensions for the clergy. Annual reports of the governmental commission for relations with the religious communities of Croatia contain sections on financial aid given to religious organizations. In its annual report for the year 1980–81, the commission reported that out of 24 religious communities in the republic, 6 were awarded governmental financial aid. Out of total sum of 37,760,000,000 Yugoslav dinars (in 1980 a new Yugoslav-made car could be purchased for 5 million dinars) allocated by the government for this purpose, 75 percent was given to the Serbian Orthodox Church.[112] According to a federal government report from the same period, in Bosnia-Herzegovina and Macedonia republican authorities assisted the Serbian Orthodox Church, the Islamic Community, the Macedonian Orthodox Church, and some minor groups; no assistance to the Catholic Church was shown.[113]

Even without government support, the Catholic Church's relative wealth grew, thanks to a large Croat diaspora. In addition to traditional Croatian migrations overseas, between the 1960s and 1970s, western Europe had employed and uprooted over 500,000 native Croatians.[114] The total number of Yugoslav guest-workers with their families in western Europe reached an all-time record in 1973, with 1,110,000 people registered, plus 160,000 who migrated overseas; again, Croat Catholics were predominant among the migrants.[115] In order to serve these guest-workers in western Europe and provide supportive spiritual assistance to numerous Croatian migrants worldwide, the Bishops' Conference of Yugoslavia (BKJ) began, in 1969, systematically administering an emerging church abroad.

The Croatian export-church benefitted from Vatican II's emphasis on ethnicity. The Council noticed a revival of ethnicity worldwide as well as the phenomenon of global-scale migration. The Church sought to deploy priests of the same ethnic background to serve their ethnic communities abroad.[116] In November 1969, the Bishops' Conference established a new permanent Conference body: the Council for Croatian Migrants, with the National Office for Pastoral Care of Croat Migrants located in Zagreb with an outpost in Rome. This was the inception of the popular idea of the "Croatian foreign flock." Throughout the period 1970–80, a total of 180 Croatian Catholic Missions with 250 priests (let alone monks, nuns, and laypeople employed with the missions) operated worldwide.[117] According to Monsignor Vladimir Stanković, the head of the National Office for Pastoral Work among Croats Abroad, the Church deployed, after 1969, a total of 515 pastoral workers and their assistants abroad, including 252 priests and 263 nuns and laypersons, to work in 192 Croatian missions and parish centers (114 in western Europe and 78 in the Americas, Australia, and South Africa).[118] Croatian

Catholic missions became the foci of social, cultural, and religious life among Croatian ethnic communities abroad. Missions brought people together; organized religious instruction, native-language schooling, libraries, and legal assistance; published newspapers, guides, calendars, and other publications; and organized cultural and athletic events.[119]

Missions abroad helped the domestic Church financially. Croatian Catholic clergy in Dalmatia coined terms such as "hard currency areas" and "Deutschemark parishes," referring to regions from which large number of men went to work in the West and regularly sent back donations and financial contributions for the rebuilding of churches.[120] The Imotska Krajina (along the border of Dalmatian Croatia and western Herzegovina), once one of poorest regions of Yugoslavia, was booming in the 1970s, with about 10,000 out of a total population of 48,000 employed in western Europe.[121] *Washington Post* correspondent Dusko Doder visited the area and reported that since 1968 more than 7,000 villas had been built, while guest-workers pumped hard currency into state banks in Zagreb, Split, and Sarajevo and caused the opening of banking branches in Imotski; "as the county began absorbing West German marks, Swedish crowns and French francs, visions of wealth and comfort replaced the traditional austerity."[122] Clergy from the Split-Makarska diocese craved appointments in the "hard currency parishes" as well as in the missions abroad. With the influx of foreign revenue, many priests endeavored to construct new churches. After the late sixties, the church began building parish "pastoral centers" that included not only a church or chapel but also classrooms for parish catechism, comfortable residences and offices for the clergy, entertainment halls, sport facilities, and other amenities.

In the meantime, the state, which was fighting exiled politicos (including occasional terrorism), viewed Catholic missions as the foci of the exile groups' mobilization and propaganda. In 1980, Yugoslav authorities banned the monograph *Katolička Crkva i Hrvati izvan domovine*, published by the Council for Croatian Migrants. The basis of the censure was the listing of names, photos, and information about a number of exiled priests and laymen affiliated with the Church abroad. Croatia's government officials in charge of religious affairs berated church dignitaries for their alleged boycott of Yugoslav foreign agencies and contacts with anti-Yugoslav exile agitators.[123] The country's official name and the Yugoslav state flag were not to be found in Croatian Catholic missions; domestic secular newspapers were a rarity in the missions' reading rooms. Church dignitaries on frequent pastoral trips abroad avoided Yugoslav consulates, embassies, and cultural information centers. The director of the Bishops' Conference's National Office for Pastoral Work among Croats Abroad, Monsignor Stanković, argued, in an interview with me, that "predominantly Serbian Yugoslav diplomats and foreign servicemen, mostly communists, harbored an a priori hostile attitude toward the Croats and the Catholic Church."[124]

The Croatian Church's foreign branch became the envy of the Serbian

Orthodox Church, whose foreign branches not only were fewer but tended to exceed the control of the Belgrade patriarchate; and finally, the Serbian Church in North America went into a schism. While in the 1970s Catholic priests in some parts of Yugoslavia drove luxury western European cars, the impoverished Serbian Orthodox Church was, according to a patriarchate's report, trying to boost sales of candles in order to maintain core institutions such as the patriarchate and religious schools.[125] In 1973, the Holy Assembly of Bishops of the Serbian Church established a new diocese of Australia-New Zealand, headquartered in Melbourne, Australia.

By all accounts, the Catholic Church in Yugoslavia became, during the 1970s, the relatively wealthiest and overall most highly organized among mainstream Yugoslav religious organizations.[126] Despite problems with enrollment in seminaries, Catholic colleges and seminaries were, by far, the best schools of this type in the country. Religious instruction was organized over weekends and after school, initially in the sacristies and parish houses, with a network of adjunct classrooms gradually developing into "pastoral centers" in the sixties.[127] According to the Slovene sociologist Zdenko Roter,

> Catholicism was the most vital force, with the best developed and widely expanded organizational structure and the most visibly developed universal character. . . . [B]esides, the Church's hierarchical structure operates more efficiently than any other religious organization's leadership, the clergy is the best educated, and the Church as social institution has demonstrated the highest degree of flexibility and adaptability to social change.[128]

To summarize, from the 1930s to the 1960s, one Yugoslav state collapsed and another came into life, but neither secured legitimation from its two largest churches. The two churches posed as guardians of their respective ethnic communities and as such have been always more or less suspicious of any multinational state. In addition, the Yugoslav civil war, the ethnic massacres, and the communist revolution further widened the church-state chasm. The enmity between Croatian Catholicism and Serbian Orthodox ran even deeper. The conflict, without reconciliation continued, after a brief pause imposed by the force of a revolutionary regime. New Yugoslavia had strong opposition at home and abroad, and the churches were pillars of the domestic opposition. The 1960s brought about a renewal and promises of stability. Yet the new liberalization also created opportunities for ethnonationalist and anticommunist activities. On the religious front interdenominational dialogue made some promises, but interconfessional rivalry was growing even faster. The Serbian Orthodox Church lost the short-lived advantage it had enjoyed in the Serbian-dominated kingdom. Roman Catholicism was emerging as relatively the strongest competitor in the Yugoslav religious arena, while Islam was also growing in numbers and in material wealth.

3

THE OTHER SERBIA

The Serbian Church in the Communist Federation

After the mid-1930s, when the Comintern appointed Tito, a professional communist revolutionary of Croat-Slovene ancestry, head of the Communist Party of Yugoslavia, Yugoslav communists labored for the destruction of the centralized Serb-dominated kingdom. The Communist Party of Yugoslavia considered Great Serbian nationalism the principal enemy of the revolution. The Party would follow this course all along until Tito's death in 1980. Tito's successful struggle with domestic nationalist opposition involved the political and military defeat of the Serb militia Četniks during World War II and the suppression of Serbian nationalism during the liberalization of the sixties.[1] After Tito's purge of the Serb communist leader Aleksandar Ranković in 1966 and the dissent of Dobrica Ćosić in 1968, organized domestic carriers of Serbian ethnic nationalism were silenced—all except one: the Serbian Orthodox Church. In the sixties, all religious institutions recovered from the postwar communist terror, but the Serbian Church seemed relatively the weakest among the three main denominations. Catholicism and Islam were expanding and rebuilding relatively faster. Yet, in contrast to the time of the concordat crisis, when the Serbian Church met only one, albeit serious, challenge from Catholicism, in the 1960s, the list of troubles and challenges for the Serbian Church and Serbian ethnic nationalism had multiplied. Albanian ethnic nationalism erupted in Kosovo, the Macedonian branch of the Orthodox Church sought independence, and the Serbian Church's branch in north America went into a schism.

Kosovo Embattled

In 1966, after a power struggle in top party circles, Tito purged the leading Serb communist, Aleksandar Ranković, an advocate of a centralist, Soviet-styled system who had used police repression to extend the Serb minority rule in the predominantly Albanian-populated Kosovo and Metohija. From 1968 to 1973, ethnic Albanians of Kosovo rebelled several times. An underground resistance movement was formed, backed by communist Albania. Tito suppressed extreme nationalists but boosted the cultural rights of ethnic Albanians and urged the republics and federation to invest in modernization of that most backward part of the country. The Albanians acquired a flag for their autonomous province of Kosovo (nearly a replica of the flag of Albania) and were allowed to celebrate their national hero, Skenderbey, also a national icon in neighboring Albania. In the province's capital, Priština, modern sport facilities were built, and an Albanian-language university was opened in the early 1970s. New schools, hospitals, and factories were built across the province. A Croatian newspaper reveled in the 1980s in the fact that the Albanian-language university in Priština had produced relatively the largest number of Ph.D. holders per one thousand residents in Europe![2] The fact that those doctorates were mostly in the humanities, history, and social sciences and that textbooks were obtained through academic and cultural exchange with communist Albania indicates that the university became an epicenter of Albanian ethnic nationalistic ideas and sentiments. The province became virtually exempt from the jurisdiction of the Republic of Serbia. Tito even let the historic name, *Metohija* (designating church property, that is, land owned by the monasteries), be dropped from the province's official title. In the meantime, the portion of the Albanians in the total population of Yugoslavia increased from 4.7 percent in 1953 to 7.7 percent in 1981.[3]

In monastery and parish chronicles the Serbian Orthodox Church noted growing tensions between Serbs and Albanians in Kosovo. In May 1968, the Church staged a public protest in Belgrade. Despite the regime's ban, the Church came out in the streets of the capital city of the Yugoslav federation to hold a liturgy in honor of the emperor Dušan the Mighty (1331–55), the Serb ruler who established the patriarchate of Peć in Metohija. On Sunday, 19 May 1968, after the opening of the regular spring session of the Holy Assembly of Bishops and the liturgy was performed at the patriarchate's church, Dušan's relics were carried down the streets of Belgrade to the city's largest church, the church of Saint Marko. The Serbian Church historian Sljepčević described the transfer of the tzar's relics as "the resurrection of the vision of the glorious Serbian past before the physical and spiritual eyes of the people."[4] In front of Saint Marko's Church (an enlarged replica of the historic Gračanica on the Kosovo battlefield), Patriarch Germanus said:

The Saint Marko church is designated by our Church as the sanctuary for saintly emperor Dušan's holy relics. We could not further delay the transfer of the relics here. What we have accomplished today was God's will. The spirit of Saint Sava has inspired us, and the spirit of Dušan besought us to expose the sacred relics in the largest Belgrade church before the eyes of our faithful people. Now the people see their holy tzar, who was a defender of our Orthodox Serbian faith and our national identity.[5]

The regime described the liturgy as a "nationalistic provocation and the Church's protest march against our government policies of national equality in Kosovo and Macedonia."[6] At the fourteenth session of the League of Communists of Serbs, held in Belgrade a week later, the author Dobrica Ćosić warned Serb communists that if they fail to curb Albanian nationalism and if Serb leaders missed the chance to side with the Serbian people, the Church and other, in Ćosić's words, "primitive nationalists" would take advantage of the situation to become defenders of national interests of the Serbian people.[7] Ćosić was criticized as a nationalist, remained isolated, and soon resigned from the Party.

In November 1968, after massive Albanian riots, the Serbian Orthodox Church stepped up its pressure on the regime through petitions, complaints, and appeals for protection of the Serbian sacred heritage in Kosovo and Metohija, allegedly assaulted by ethnic Albanians. The Raška-Prizren diocese also complained to the Holy Synod and commissions for religious affairs in Belgrade that the province authorities had been ineffective: some petitions had been ignored and no perpetrator of alleged Albanian assaults on church property and clergy had been brought to justice.[8] On 19 May 1969, the Holy Assembly of Bishops send a letter-appeal, written in a kind tone, to President Tito. The letter specified nearly a dozen Albanian attacks on the faithful, on clergy, and on Church property.[9] Within a week Tito replied and promised to investigate the problem through the republic and provincial authorities.[10] A few months later, *Pravoslavlje* expressed disappointment and concluded that the government was unwilling to "halt the savagery."[11] After 1968, *Pravoslavlje* occasionally published reports and listed violent assaults, including rape, murder, theft, arson, intimidation, threats, discriminatory policies, desecration of cemeteries and holy places, and other aggressive activities allegedly committed by nationalist Albanians against the Serbs, the Serbian Church, and Serbian property in Kosovo.[12] However, only a few of these allegations had been sustained by legal prosecution. In response to this, the Church argued that the Albanian-dominated Kosovo state apparatus was biased.[13] Yet, according to research carried out by the Serbian scholar Vesna Pešić, rapes of Serbian women by Albanians (which the Church underscored in its reports), were rare in the history of the region.[14]

Nevertheless, Kosovo Serb migration accelerated to the northern homogeneously Serbian parts of the largest Yugoslav republic. Between 1971 and 1981, more than 30,000 Serbs and Montenegrins left the troubled and most backward Yugoslav province, heading to the big cities and the fertile, wealthy northern province of Vojvodina.[15] The decline of the Orthodox population in the province over a three-decade period showed an alarming tendency:

in 1953, the Serbs and Montenegrins combined had accounted for some 27.9 percent of the province's population; in 1987 this figure had dropped to 10 percent.[16]

Schism and Disunity

Between 1958 and 1967, Patriarch Germanus tried to maintain some forms of ecclesiastical union between the patriarchate at Belgrade and the Macedonian Archdiocese of Skopje-Ohrid. The Serbian patriarchate also recognized the Macedonian nationality. Nevertheless, in 1967, Macedonian-speaking Orthodox clergy, as well as some Serbian priests in Macedonia, proclaimed independence of all Orthodox church units in the territory of the Socialist Republic of Macedonia and appealed for international recognition to foreign Orthodox churches and the Ecumenical Patriarch at Istanbul. The Serbian Church declared this secession uncanonical.[17]

The schismatic church of Macedonia was, however, backed by local Macedonian communists, who had acquired statehood and nationhood in 1945 and sought as much support for them as possible (a national church served the purpose). The federal communist authorities, notably Tito and Kardelj, did not encourage the schism (not to mention the leading Serb communist Aleksandar Ranković, who opposed the idea until his fall from power in 1966). Kardelj even headed a state commission seeking a solution through mediation between schismatic clerics of Macedonia and the Serbian patriarchate at Belgrade. Tito, who never forgot that Macedonian communists had not promptly organized the antifascist struggle in 1941, was not very enthusiastic about any kind of expanding appetites of local bureaucracies, although he did little to discourage them except in cases of excessive ethnonationalism. Macedonian historians, most of them proregime and pronationhood, argued that there had always been an "independent Orthodox church in Macedonia," epitomized in an alleged continuity between the new church and the ancient archdiocese of Ohrid.[18] When the Macedonians applied for membership in the World Council of Churches (WCC) in Geneva, Germanus, as one of the six WCC chairmen, vetoed the admission. The Serbian patriarchate's semiofficial 1969 financial report emphasizes that the Serbian Church expected the state to negotiate the price for the Macedonian ecclesiastical independence, the communist state did not indicate any intention to do so, but the Belgrade patriarchate expected an offer and might have even been prepared to take it into consideration.[19] Instead of any intelligent approach to the Macedonian ecclesiastical dispute, the communist regime sought to resolve the problem by putting political pressure on the Serbian Church. Thus a government document said that the Serbian Church's attitude toward the Macedonian schism was "nationalist, chauvinist, extremely conservative—detrimental to ethnic relations and common social interest."[20]

The Macedonian Church crisis worsened as the Holy See restored pastoral life in several Uniate parishes in southeastern Macedonia that had been founded in the mid–nineteenth century and later abolished by Serbia and Bulgaria. In 1962, the pope installed a Uniate bishop at Skopje. In the meantime, the Macedonian church expanded and consolidated. New churches were built, and in 1977 a new theological school was opened in Skopje. Thus, in the eyes of the Serbian Church, the new Church of Macedonia, developing friendly relations with the Vatican, was viewed as a continuation of the 1859 Union of Kukuš (Macedonia). Indeed, the Vatican sympathized with the schism and arranged for Macedonian Church representatives to attend international religious meetings and advocate their cause abroad. Serb Church leaders blamed the communists while anti-Catholic sentiments also grew among Serb clergy.[21]

In response to the schism, the Serbian Church launched a struggle for church property in Macedonia.[22] Special importance was attributed to the monastery of Saint Prokhor Pčinjski.[23] This nineteenth-century monastery had become a national museum of the Republic of Macedonia, commemorating the foundation of the republic. On Saint Elijah's Day (2 August) in 1944, the communist-led Partisan liberation movement had held a general session of the so-called Anti-Fascist Assembly of the People's Liberation of Macedonia (ASNOM), in the compound of this monastery. The session, according to the Macedonian historian Slavko Dimevski, "had been the highest achievement in the history of the Macedonian people—it was a final phase of the centennial struggle for the legal-constitutional foundation of the Macedonian nation."[24] After the schism, Serbian monks at Saint Prokhor and the Serb Bishop of the nearby Vranje, filed lawsuits demanding the eviction of the museum. The Macedonian Church and state closed ranks, opposing the Serbian pressure. Macedonian clergy also intensified the rebuilding of their own new churches. A modern cathedral dedicated to Saint Kliment and located in the center of the capital city of Skopje was to succeed the church of Holy Martyr Mina, demolished in the catastrophic earthquake of 1963. The magnificent new cathedral opening in 1990, symbolically marked the emancipation of the independent Macedonian Orthodox Church.

The Serbian Church, shaken by the Macedonian schism at home, was in the meantime hit by another schism abroad. The new schism alienated from the Belgrade patriarchate its North American branch, with 3 dioceses, 72 parishes, and 129 temples in the United States and Canada. Since the early 1950s, the Serbian Church in North America had vehemently opposed the normalization of church-state relations in Yugoslavia, demanding of the patriarch that he carry out an overt anticommunist struggle.[25] The discord was aggravated by a number of other issues concerning administration of parishes, appointments of bishops, and the distribution of Western aid for anticommunist activities. Finally, the so-called Free Serbian Orthodox Church of America broke ties with the Belgrade patriarchate in 1962. The conflict had begun during the World War II, when the head of the American branch of the Church, Bishop Dionisije, in spite of the Allies' support for the communist-led antifascist resistance, remained supportive of King Peter Karadjordjević and General Mihajlović's Četniks, who collaborated with the Axis. According to the memoirs of a Serb priest in America, the U.S. State Department criticized Bishop Dionisije and the nationalist Serbs for extending support to the collaborator Mihajlović.[26] After 1945, Bishop Dionisije and the exiled Bishop Nikolaj Velimirović labored for the unification of the Serbian diaspora, reinforced with exiled Četniks, around King Peter and the Church, with the aim of organizing an opposition front to the communist regime in Yugoslavia and the new federal Yugoslav republic. Dionisije, Nikolaj, and the king urged the Church at home to boycott the regime or even to mobilize people against it. Church leaders at home, however, particularly when Germanus became the patriarch, chose a strategy of cautious cooperation with the regime, combined with the gradual ethnic and religious mobilization of Serbs. In response to Dionisije's unilateral acts of proclamation of the "Free Orthodox Church," the Holy Assembly of Bishops on its session of 27 July 1963 excommunicated him. He rejected the decision and, using Bishop Velimirović's arguments, accused Germanus and the domestic bishops of collaboration with the communists and disregarding the sacred task of the commemoration of the Ustaša genocide of Serbs. The Church historian Djoko Slijepčević has speculated that the Yugoslav communist secret police, UDBA, masterminded the schism in order to undermine the alliance of Serb exile organizations and King Peter with the Church.[27]

The list of troubles for Serb Church leaders was not exhausted. Ever since 1945, Serb bishops had been frustrated about the proregime clerical association that had grown strong and independent from bishops' authority. Owing to the fact that Orthodox clergy had been persecuted severely in Macedonia by the Bulgarians and in Croatia and Bosnia-Herzegovina by the Ustašas, the Orthodox churches of Serbia and Macedonia had had relatively the largest number of Partisan war veterans and sympathizers of Tito, compared to a few clerical allies Tito recruited in other churches. The regime granted these patriotic priests pensions through the clerical association, which publicly supported brotherhood and unity and was active in interfaith dialogue. According to documents from the archive of the Federated Republic of Croatia's commission for relations with religious communities, nearly 80 percent of all state money allocated for improving church-state relations went to the clerical associations (Orthodox and Muslim) for their offices, newsletters, regular activity, and priests' pensions and health care.[28] Clerical associations were managed by priests who had taken part in the antifascist resistance movement. An almanac published by the Association of Orthodox Clergy of Croatia in 1971 proudly declared: "our Association . . . made a valuable and dignified effort in building our common homeland, in particular by consolidating our peoples' and nationalities' brotherhood and unity and advocating religious tolerance."[29] Although some bishops prohibited clerical membership in these associations, two-thirds of all Orthodox clergy in Yugoslavia were members of them.]

In Montenegro, the Serbian Church encountered problems similar to those in Macedonia as the regime encouraged Montenegrins to develop a distinct nationality. Thus ethnic Montenegrins were becoming estranged from their ethnic relatives, the Serbs, with whom they once shared the same kings and church leaders. The Titoist-communist Montenegrin leadership, emulating their colleagues in Macedonia, went to extremes in emphasizing their cultural differences from Serbs and Serbia. The one-time close Tito aide Milovan Djilas, who was ethnic Montenegrin, argued that this Titoist "exaggerated Montenegrism" would only increase Serbian as well as Montenegrin odium toward the Yugoslav state. In reality, Serbs and Montenegrins were bound by strong ties of memory, history, culture, and ethnic kinship, much stronger than the ties between Serbs and the Macedonian-speaking Slavs. The nineteenth-century British scholar who visited Montenegro noted that Montenegrins' "feelings of attachment to Servia seem never to have been forgotten."[30] It is worth noting that the incorporation of the metropolitan of Cetinje under the Serbian patriarchate in 1920 was the key act of ecclesiastical unification during the foundation of the Yugoslav state. All these accomplishments had been undone by the communists. In June 1945, a group of Orthodox priests led by Partisan war veteran Petar Kapičić held an assembly in Nikšić and on behalf of this assembly requested from state authorities and from the Holy Synod of the Serbian Church to recognize an independent Orthodox church of Montenegro. The establishment of such church was delayed only because of disunity on this issue among Montenegrin communist cadres.

The regime also changed the image of the main symbol of Montenegro, Prince-Bishop Njegoš. Njegoš was "secularized" and commemorated as a statesman who had allegedly anticipated the Yugoslav unification, although in reality he had wanted to mobilize all Christian nations to expel the Turks from Europe once and for all. In the fifties, state authorities decided to destroy the old memorial chapel that was built by Njegoš himself and renovated in the interwar kingdom by the Orthodox church at the summit of Mount Lovćen (1,700 meters).[31] In place of the chapel, the regime set out to erect a monumental mausoleum without religious symbols. In 1950, on the occasion of the one hundredth anniversary of the death of Njegoš, the government of the People's Republic of Montenegro initiated the construction of a new Njegoš memorial, designed by the Croatian sculptor Ivan Meštrović (who then lived in the United States). The regime's committee for construction of the new Njegoš mausoleum announced in a public statement that "present-day generations of the Montenegrin people are building this magnificent monument atop the Lovćen mountain, to pay tribute to the great Montenegrin poet and thinker and also to symbolize brotherhood and unity of all Yugoslav peoples, thus leaving a lasting memorial to this generation's values and truths."[32]

The Holy Assembly of Bishops vehemently protested the "desecration of the prince-bishop's relics."[33] Eventually, in spite of the Church's resistance, the old chapel was brought down in 1972, after the Serbian Orthodox Church lost a long legal battle. Also in 1972, the League of Communists of Serbia fought back by saying in an analysis that the Serbian Orthodox Church, "through the current campaign over Njegoš's mausoleum at Lovćen, again is showing political ambitions and tendencies aimed at opposing the politics of decentralization and national emancipation in our country."[34] The newly built mausoleum was the pride of the Federated Socialist Republic of Montenegro. Visitors could access the mausoleum from a mountain road through a 120-meter-long tunnel and 372 stairs. The main hall was 11 meters high, with a 65-by-37-meter plateau from which visitors could see the magnificent Bay of Kotor in the distance. The mausoleum occupied the entire peak of the mountain, which had been leveled to create room for this monumental structure. The new symbol attracted tourists and excursions and promoted a sense of the distinct Montenegrin national identity as well as Yugoslav socialism and brotherhood and unity.

Commemorations and Renewal

Surveys of religiosity in 1960, 1965, and 1968 carried out by the Institute of Social Sciences in Belgrade showed that the greatest number of those who declared themselves to be religious, despite the general trends of decline of religiosity, were Catholics and Muslims.[35] A 1966 survey of 2,528 students at the universities of Belgrade, Zagreb, and Sarajevo found that "Catholicism had maintained itself to a much higher extent than Orthodoxy."[36] Polls conducted in the 1970s and early 1980s showed similar trends.[37] The sociologist Srdjan Vrcan concluded that "the Serbian Orthodox Church, due to [a] convergence of social, political, and cultural changes with secularizing consequences, seems to be the least resistant to erosion of religious affiliation."[38] Vrcan's research, completed in 1985–86, showed that

> 62.3 percent of all respondents, having identified themselves as Roman Catholics, declared themselves to be personally religious and 31.4 percent were not religious. At the same time 43 percent of all respondents who identified themselves as Moslems declared themselves religious, and 45.3 percent as nonreligious. Only 26.2 percent of all respondents, having identified themselves as Orthodox believers by religious affiliation, considered themselves religious, and 64 percent not so.[39]

In a 1970 homily, Patriarch Germanus lamented: "Our own statistics show that only an insignificant part of Orthodox population welcomes the priest to their homes, read religious publications, and actively participate in church's life."[40] However, the church historian Milan Kašanin, in a September 1969 lecture on the occasion of the 750th anniversary of the Serbian Orthodox Church's autocephaly, did not agonize over the problems pointed out by the patriarch. Kašanin argued that religious revival in Serbia would be induced through a revival of ethnic and historical consciousness. Kašanin noticed encouraging phenomena:

Popular interest in Serbian medieval culture, especially strong in our youth, is evidently growing. Our ancient monuments—churches, monasteries, our icons and frescoes, illustrations and musical compositions—are well cared about and studied with a lot of interest. The works of our medieval writers—poems, books, biographies—are widely read and translated, and many scholarly works have been published. It is clear that a dialogue among generations of Serbs is continuing and that ancestors and descendants understand each other.[41]

The patriarch traveled abroad, raised funds, and encouraged construction and repair of new churches and monasteries, especially in rural areas. Germanus personally supervised construction of a new monastery in the Ovčar-Kablar Canyon, the Church of Saint Luke and Monastery of Saint Stephen, both near Belgrade.[42] Germanus took particular pride in the new church dedicated to the holy Lazar of Kosovo in his native Velika Drenova at the Morava River. While rebuilding churches, the patriarch developed a dynamic program of religious jubilees, festivals, and pilgrimages. After the groundbreaking Tzar Dušan liturgy of May 1968, the Serbian Church the next year celebrated the 750th anniversary of Church independence. On 14 September 1969 in Belgrade a crowd of 10,000 attended the jubilee, and the next day the jubilee continued at the Žiča monastery (founded by King Steven and Saint Sava in 1202) in the heartland of Serbia, about 4 miles southwest of Kraljevo. At Žiča the historic Church council of 1219 proclaimed autocephaly and installed Saint Sava as the archbishop. In his Žiča address, Patriarch Germanus said that the church is not against dialogue with the non-Orthodox, but "the bishops know how far they can go."[43] Germanus also said the following:

All who live with us here in our common home, in our common fatherland of Yugoslavia, we want to live in concord with all, in brotherhood, in love, in community. We have in our present homeland many different nationalities and religious communities and we keep good relations with all of them. We want to live with all as with brothers and sisters in one single house."[44]

The series of jubilees had continued in September and October 1970 as the Serbian Church celebrated the 50th anniversary of the restoration of the Serbian patriarchate (1920–70). In 1971 the Serbian Church marked the three hundredth anniversary of the hermitage of Saint Basil of Ostrog (Montenegro). The Holy Assembly of Bishops met at the historic Ostrog monastery to stress the unity of Serbia and Montenegro. In the mid-seventies the Serbian Orthodox Church marked three jubilees: the centenary of the Herzegovina uprising of 1875–76 (celebrated in Bosnia-Herzegovina and Serbia in 1976); the eight hundredth anniversary of Saint Sava's birth; and the 375th anniversary of the monastery Gomirje in Croatia—the westernmost outpost of Orthodoxy in the Yugoslav lands. The Gomirje jubilee came after the Tito crackdown on the Croatian nationalist movement, so that Croatian authorities helped with the renovation of the Gomirje monastery and utilized the jubilee to reassert their commitment to brotherhood and unity between Serbs and Croats.[45]

The main Serbian Orthodox church jubilee in the 1970s was the eight hundredth anniversary of the birth of Saint Sava. The final celebration was held in Belgrade and Žiča on 4–5 October 1975. In his Žiča address, the patriarch stressed the Church's role as a mediator among the Serbs and guardian of national unity. The patriarch again extended his call for unity to other Yugoslav nationalities:

> This call for concord and unity does not apply to Orthodox Serbs alone, but also to all who live side by side with us in this our common social community—the Socialist Federal Republic of Yugoslavia. . . . Let us all live in concord and peace which will provide tranquility and prosperity to our Serbian Orthodox Church and our fatherland. This is my message of today to all of you here and to all Serbs in the world.[46]

Concurrently with rebuilding and commemorations, Germanus pursued a dynamic foreign policy aimed at upgrading relations with other Orthodox churches and states. Germanus had a rich experience in foreign affairs. As a general secretary of the Holy synod and later bishop of Žiča, Germanus traveled to America, Canada, England, France, Germany, Italy, and Switzerland. In 1955, he accompanied Patriarch Vikentije to Greece and visited Mount Athos and Serbian monks at the Hilandar monastery. Before his election in 1958, Germanus was a delegate of the Serbian Church at a jubilee of the patriarchate of Moscow. After his enthronement in 1960, Germanus visited Jerusalem and the Holy Land. Before Germanus, the only patriarch who had visited Palestine was Arsenius III Crnojević, who conducted the Great Migration of Serbs. Germanus also paid official visits to the ancient patriarchates of Jerusalem, Alexandria, and Antioch and the Ecumenical patriarchate at Phanar and, again, went to the Mount Athos and visited Athens, where he had met with leaders of the Orthodox Church of Greece. In 1968 Germanus traveled to Moscow to attend the celebration of the 50th anniversary of the restoration of the Moscow patriarchate.

He also visited the archbishop of Canterbury and established cordial relations with the Anglican Church and with the churches of Greece, Finland, Poland, and Czechoslovakia. Germanus met twice with the Ecumenical patriarch at Istanbul. Especially important were Germanus' meetings with the patriarch of all Russia, Pimen, in 1972 and 1974.

The 1972 summit meeting of the Russian and Serbian Orthodox churches was encouraged by the regimes in Moscow and Belgrade to help another Yugoslav-Soviet rapprochement following cold relations caused by Tito's criticism of the 1968 Soviet invasion of Czechoslovakia. In October 1972, the newly enthroned patriarch of Moscow and all Russia, Pimen, came to Belgrade. The two patriarchs held talks in Belgrade, Novi Sad, and the historic Resava-Manasija monastery. In his Novi Sad address, Patriarch Pimen pointed out that

in addition to the Orthodox faith and culture, Russians and Serbs, as brothers of one same blood, are also united by the memory of the heroic struggle against fascism in the Second World War, and the Yugoslav and Soviet governments' commitment to the noble goal of building socialism as a truly just and better society, in which our two countries show an example to the humankind.[47]

Germanus in Russia

Germanus replied that the visitation affirms "good relations between the two sister-churches, never impaired over centuries to the present."[48] Yugoslav regime officials and representatives of the Soviet embassy in Belgrade accompanied the patriarchs and the delegations of the two churches on their tour through Serbia and Vojvodina. Yugoslav officials, according to a report by the government commission for religious affairs, sought to familiarize the Russian churchmen and diplomats with the Yugoslav system of self-management and foreign policy of nonalignment.[49] The chairman of the Commission for Religious Affairs of Serbia, Vitomir Petković, in his speech at Resava on 16 October 1972, pointed out that "mutual respect and cooperation between the Serbian Orthodox Church and Russian Orthodox Church mirror relations between our two countries. We hold that aggression on any country is also a threat to our own freedom [and] independence and the common cause of world peace."[50]

Germanus returned a visit to the patriarch of Moscow and all Russia in October 1974. Meanwhile, Yugoslav-Soviet relations had substantially improved. During ceremonies and talks in Moscow, Leningrad, and Pskov, the church leaders fraternized and declared, in Germanus' words, "that we are indeed like one."[51] Germanus proclaimed: "our international initiatives and views are identical" and "fraternal relations between the two sister-churches can give an example not only to believers but also to statesmen."[52] The two patriarchs also talked confidentially about the worries of the two Orthodox churches in the two multiethnic countries under communist rule. In a later interview, Patriarch Germanus revealed that the two churchmen had agreed that both major nationalities (Russians and Serbs) were envied and hated by religious and ethnic minorities and encircled by hostile neighbors.[53]

In spite of Germanus' patriotic rhetoric and foreign policy services, the regime noticed nationalistic tendencies in the Serbian Church. The Central Committee of the League of Communists of Serbia (LCS) put on the agenda of its forty-first regular session, held on 30 June 1972 in Belgrade, new currents in Serbian nationalism. Along with addressing other themes, the conference designated the Serbian Orthodox Church one of the carriers of the new nationalism. The following is a summary of the LCS findings and policy guidelines:

> The Orthodox Church opposes our policy aimed at reducing the power of the central state authority. The Church also resents the policy of a greater equality among Yugoslav nationalities and ethnic minorities. Church leaders also favor the constitutional model of a federation similar to the Soviet model as opposed to the Yugoslav decentralized system. Church leaders work cautiously but persistently to revive the Great Serbian idea. In the domain of interchurch relations, it is obvious that the Serbian Church is distrustful and unreceptive toward reforms of the Second Vatican Council in the Catholic Church. Instead of embracing the Catholic ecumenical initiative, the Serbian Church began questioning the status of the Serb minority in Croatia and opened the explosive issue of the Second World War massacres at Jasenovac and other Ustaša crimes while making no reference to Četnik crimes. The Serbian Orthodox Church is also becoming more active abroad among Serbian exiles and migrants. The strength of the Serbian Church is neither in the doctrine (theology) nor in a strictly religious sphere, and church leaders are aware of this. Backed by the powerful tradition, the Serbian Church targets the Serbian people's ethnic pride and most sensitive emotions pertaining to the Kosovo myth. The crisis in ethnic relations in Kosovo has worked to the Church's advantage. The Church is dramatizing and lamenting what it views as the "disintegration of Serbdom." But there is nothing like a disintegration of Serbdom. There only is a disintegration of statist and centralist politics. . . . Now, the Serbian Orthodox Church claims that it has been for centuries not only a religious but also a political organization and is being called upon, one more time in the history of the Serbs, to defend and lead its people, because no one else seems to be capable of defending Serbian national interest. The Church argues that Serbia has no patriotic leaders at this moment. The Church actually wants to lead, that is, to assume political leadership based on the Great Serbian nationalistic platform in order to mobilize Serb masses in defense of what the Church defines as the Serbian national interest.[54]

As the Kosovo problem grew more complicated, Serbian communists had to face the dilemma that Dobrica Ćosić was talking about in 1968: either the communists will defend the Serbian national cause or anticommunist nationalists (the Church being one of most prominent) will come to the fore as defenders of Serbian national interest. The young Serb communist leaders Latinka Perović and Marko Nikezić were purged as nationalists by Tito in

1972. In consequence, the anticommunist nationalists (churches being the best organized among them) were gaining more influence. In other words, by purging party "liberals" and "nationally sensitive" communists, who were nonetheless secular nationalists, Tito unwittingly played into the hands of the clerical nationalists. During the last two decades of Yugoslavia's life, the two churches would successfully appropriate and virtually monopolize ethnic nationalist causes.

Tito's error

4

THE CATHOLIC CHURCH AND THE MAKING OF THE CROATIAN NATION, 1970–1984

As a consequence of the liberal course of the Yugoslav communist regime of the 1960s, the six-republic federation was swamped by an upsurge of ethnic nationalism in all the republics and autonomous provinces.[1] The carriers of this nationalism were not initially the conservative anticommunist forces such as, the churches and surviving World War II enemies of the Partisans but were "ethnonationally sensitive" communist leaders in the republics and autonomous provinces. They demanded more power and autonomy at the expense of the federation. Nonetheless, they unwittingly became allies of conservative nationalists who saw the process as a step toward their separatist ideal. Although secular forces dominated these movements, religious institutions were not dormant.

The most massive of the Yugoslav nationalist movements of the late sixties was the Croatian National Movement, also referred to by its supporters as Croatian Spring, or, in the old regime's jargon, the "Croatian Mass Movement" (1967–72). The Croatian national movement, triggered by a Serbo-Croatian linguistic dispute in 1967, expanded into spheres of culture, economy, education, foreign and military affairs, interethnic relations, constitutional politics, and so on. Croat communists and noncommunists came together, bound by the appealing nationalist agenda. Thus, the secretary of the League of Communists of Croatia, Miko Tripalo, said that "national and class interests were the same as nation and class had become identical."[2] The movement's leaders believed that Croatia without the rest of Yugoslavia (especially if released from the "Balkan burden" of Serbia, Kosovo, and Macedonia), would attain the prosperity of western European countries.[3] The movement reached its pinnacle in the spring of 1971. Croatia was on the verge of revolution. Street protests and strikes took place in several Croatian cities. In December 1971, the unchallenged supreme authority in Yugoslavia, Josip Broz Tito, summoned the Croat communist leaders who sided with the movement to his Karadjordjevo hunting lodge and threatened military intervention. Between 1972 and 1973 the regime jailed a large number the Croat National Movement's leaders and activists. Tito purged Croatia's League of Communists and established a rigid structure of power. The period from roughly 1973 to 1989 would come to be known as the "Croatian silence." During the same period, however, the Catholic Church in Croatia was agile and outspoken as both the carrier of the national idea and fighter for greater religious liberty.

The Catholic Church and the Croatian National Movement, 1970–1972

The Movement's ideas and initiatives found support and sympathy in the clerical ranks of the Croatian branch of the Catholic Church. Yet the episcopate did not directly support the movement. This does not mean that the Church ignored it, or adopted a "wait and see" policy, as one analyst argued.[4] As I will show, the Church hierarchy had a mobilizational agenda of its own. Nevertheless, the Movement's leaders hoped that the Church would more explicitly and directly support them. In a speech at the 1970 Catholic student convention at Rijeka, the student leader and Catholic layman Ivan Zvonimir Čičak urged the Church to

> get involved actively in political life. . . . [T]he Church, Catholic lay movement, and other forces must come together, united within one single movement operating under one single leadership, and in accordance with this leadership's policies. It is time for the forces other than the Communist Party to assume the leading role in this society and set in motion social and historical process. . . . Christianity is not merely prayer and conversation but also concrete action. We must become more active.[5]

Church leaders were not impressed by such calls. The archbishop of Split, Frane Franić, as he recalled in our 1989 interview, jokingly asked his colleague bishops on a meeting held late in 1970: "So are we going to put the Church under command of those Catholic students whose leaders have ambitions to replace the Pope, or perhaps we ought to let Marxists have command over the Church?"[6] On the other hand, the Capuchin theologian Tomislav Šagi-Bunić, who was one of the Movement's outspoken advocates, told me in our 1990 interview that the bishops had abandoned the Croatian people.[7] According to Šagi-Bunić, the archbishop of Zagreb, Franjo Kuharić, refused to see the prominent nationalist leaders Franjo Tudjman and Marko Veselica, who pleaded for the Church's support.[8] Some bishops even collaborated with the regime. Early in 1972, when the backlash against the Movement's leaders had already begun, Archbishop Franić assured representatives of the government of Croatia that the Vatican was keeping its commitment to the Church's noninterference in domestic political affairs in Yugoslavia. In several meetings with high state officials, Archbishop Franić said that Pope Paul VI had urged the episcopate not to participate in or assist the movement.[9] The Church, according to the archbishop, sought to avoid bloodshed because the situation in spring 1971 was explosive. The archbishop argued that the regime should have been grateful to the Church for mitigating conflicts and curbing extremism. Franić, who worried most about the regime's blockade of construction of the new St. Peter's cathedral in Split (during the antinationalist campaign the authorities reduced the cathedral's size and relocated it on less attractive location) protested the regime's attacks on clergy but stopped short of protesting the regime's repression of the movement's leaders.

Even though the bishops abstained from direct involvement in politics, religious symbols were ubiquitous and churches were crowded. The Croatian Catholic lay movement was witnessing a second golden age after the interwar period. Religious life was dynamic: spiritual panels, catechism for adults, worship services for students and intellectuals, and Sunday sermons dedicated to the current social issues attracted large audience, especially in the major Croatian cities such as Zagreb, Split, Rijeka, Osijek, Zadar, Dubrovnik, and elsewhere. The Institute for the Theological Culture of Laypeople at Rijeka, with the affiliated lay group Sinaxis, were centers of the movement's Catholic wing. In the capital city of Zagreb, people flocked to the city's churches to hear popular preachers.[10] In Split, the Friars Minor Conventual ran a "Spiritual Panel for Adults" that was frequented by prominent student leaders and intellectuals.

The theologian Šagi-Bunić was a popular preacher in Zagreb and a member of the cultural forum Matica hrvatska, the umbrella organization that operated as the movement's "party" and its headquarters. From February to August 1972, Šagi-Bunić wrote a series of essays in the periodical Glas koncila about democratization and the interaction between religion and the Yugoslav national question.[11] Šagi-Bunić argued that a Church-state rapprochement through dialogue, if it resulted in greater democratization, would be for the benefit of both institutions. But he warned that believers could not consider the regime, as it was, a legitimate government because, according to the program of the League of Communists, its members must be nonbelievers and only they are allowed to hold power.[12] Šagi also criticized the regime's religious policies. He correctly observed that the ruling elite unwittingly boosted clericalism, trying to make a power-sharing deal with the episcopate rather than granting full religious liberty to citizen believers.[13] However, Šagi also admitted that the Church should do more to reform itself in the spirit of Vatican II, in order to help the democratic transformation of Yugoslav society.

Šagi-Bunić also wrote a series of essays on nationalism. He inferred that the Tito regime tend to magnify the nationalist threat to society. Šagi pointed out that Vatican II, the papal encyclical Populorum progressio, and the Third

Synod of Bishops that took place in Rome in October 1971 made it clear that the Church was against "excessive nationalism" and hatred rooted in ethnicity, religion, or race.[14] Šagi-Bunić argued that the regime was over-reacting to "cultural nationalism," for example, ethnic patriotic songs, folk-lore, and an emphasis on ethnic history. He called for more freedom, which would provide a safety valve and eventually ease tensions in the multina-tional state. The regime was unreceptive toward Šagi Bunić's ideas. Only a few liberal Marxist intellectuals joined the debate.

According to an analysis released by the League of Communists of Cro-atia, the Catholic Church "sympathized with the movement's ideas, but only a few clergy and no religious leader joined the nationalists."[15] "The Church as a whole remained within the limits of legal religious activity," the doc-ument reads, "thanks to our good relations with the Vatican, and also be-cause the nationalist leaders had failed to appreciate the Church's potential and find a proper role for the Church in the movement."[16] Croatia's com-missioner for religious affairs, Zlatko Frid, thanked Archbishop Franić on the January 1972 meeting in Zagreb, saying that "although a few cases of na-tionalism and chauvinism have been observed in the Church, the nationalist ideas did not penetrate the clerical rank and file."[17]

Nonetheless, the Church carried out its national mission. To begin with, the Church reintroduced the cult of the Virgin Mary as the major religious and national symbol of Catholic Croatia. Further, as noted earlier, the ex-pansion and consolidation of the Croatian Catholic Church abroad, through the establishment of the Bishops' Conference's Council for Croatian Migrants in 1969, had improved the Church's financial status and exerted a far-reaching impact on the Croatian national homogenization under the aegis of the Church. In addition, the Church reinvigorated Croatian nationalism through several specific initiatives. On 10 February 1970, the archbishop of Zagreb, Franjo Kuharić, held the first public commemoration dedicated to the controversial church leader Alojzije Cardinal Stepinac. Within the next decade the commemoration at Stepinac's tomb in the Zagreb Cathedral would attract large audiences and evolve into an unofficial Croatian national holiday—Cardinal Stepinac's Day. The first native Croat saint of the Catholic Church, Nikola Tavelić, was canonized in September 1970.[18] Thousands of jubilant Croat pilgrims attended the proclamation of the new saint at Rome. In 1971, the Vatican made another concession to Croatian nationalism: de-spite bitter protests from the Yugoslav embassy, the Church renamed the former Illyrian Institute and Church of Saint Girolamo at Rome (linked with the escape of Croatian fascists) the Croatian Institute and Church of Saint Girolamo.

The revival of the Marian cult was especially important. On 15–22 Au-gust 1971 the Church organized the "Mariological and Marian Congress" in Zagreb and at the nearby shrine of Marija Bistrica. According to a Church monograph, it was "the first in a series of grand jubilees and celebrations blessed with church-historical and Marian elements, which came to us inseparable in mutual interaction."[19] The congress hosted 126 theologians, experts on Marian spirituality from 30 countries. The Archbishop of Zagreb, Franjo Kuharić, entitled his opening speech "The Tribulations of Croatia and the Virgin Mary." Kuharić pointed out that "small, oppressed nations worship the cult of Mary with an extraordinary piety."[20] The Franciscan Karlo Balić, a Mariologist from Rome, proposed that the Marian shrine of Marija Bistrica be consecrated as a "national" shrine of Croatia. Balić was actually reviving an official initiative made by the Archbishop of Zagreb Alojzije Stepinac. As early as 1939, Stepinac had begun preparations for the establishment of Marija Bistrica as the central Croat Catholic tabernacle. During the period of the Independent State of Croatia, Stepinac, in collaboration with the Pavelić government and financially assisted by the regime, organized works in Marija Bistrica conceived as a "national" shrine of the new Croatian state. In September 1971, the Bishops' Conference of Yugoslavia supported the initiative for a special status for Marija Bistrica presented by the archbishop of Zagreb. In the early seventies, emulating the Catholic Church in Poland, the Catholic Church in Croatia launched the mobilization of the Croats under the aegis of "the Virgin Mary, Queen of the Croats."[21] In 1971, Marija Bistrica became the Croatian equivalent to Czestochowa in Poland. Incidentally, the Croats, like the Poles, kept at Marija Bistrica a "Black" Madonna. The cult of "black" statues of the Virgin originated in the sixteenth century. It was believed that the Croat Black Madonna had saved the area from Turkish raids. The Croatian Black Madonna was referred to as the Queen of the Croats and the "advocata fidelissima Croatiae" (the most faithful advocate of Croatia). The cult of the Queen of the Croats emerged at the end of the eighteenth century, when someone engraved under the Madonna's icon at the Remete shrine, near Zagreb, the inscription *"Advocata Croatiae fidelissima mater"* (Advocate of Croatia, the most faithful mother). In the absence of native saints prior to 1970, the Virgin Mary Queen of the Croats had become the central cult of Croatian Catholicism as well as one of the most popular symbols of Croatian nationalism. Marian statues, shrines, and pilgrimages symbolically unify territories that Croatian nationalists considered historically Croatian. Icons of the Queen of the Croats, circulated across the multiconfessional Yugoslav labyrinth, symbolically embracing the ethnic nation.

The International Marian Congress concluded at the newly consecrated national shrine at Marija Bistrica on 22 August 1971. Over 150,000 pilgrims came to pay tribute to the Madonna Queen of the Croats. "Catholic Croatia has never seen anything like this before," reported the church press.[22] "The small but united Croatian people," said Archbishop Kuharić in a homily at Marija Bistrica, "came together from this country and from abroad; the Croats have come here to embrace each other and the whole of Croatia."[23] The crowd chanted the Croatian national anthem "Our Lovely Homeland" and the religious hymn "Virgin of Paradise, Queen of the Croats." Archbishop Kuharić concluded that "the Marian congress reasserted Croatian

Catholic identity and unity." In Kuharić's words, "the main purpose of Marian festivals and congresses is bringing the Croatian people together while quenching the people's thirst for the spiritual."[24]

The year 1971 became one of the milestones in recent Croatian history, not only because of the Croatian National Movement but also regarding the activities of the Catholic Church of Croatia. In August 1971, at the shrine of Trsat near the Adriatic port of Rijeka, 40,000 pilgrims celebrated the feast of the Assumption. It became customary for pilgrims to display the Croatian colors, wear ethnic attire, and sing patriotic songs and church hymns. Occasionally the police intervened, confiscated what was viewed as nationalist insignia, and fined the violators. In August, the archbishop of Zadar, Marjan Oblak, led a pilgrimage to the early medieval Croatian diocesan seat of Nin in Dalmatia's hinterland. On 1 August 1971, the Archbishop Franić convened a metropolitan Marian congress at the second largest Croatian Marian shrine of Sinj. The Sinj congress was announced under the slogan "Let Our People Not Lose Their Identity." Archbishop Franić presided over a "Prayer for the Croatian People."

In 1972, church-state relations worsened. After Tito's purge of the League of Communists in Croatia, the first arrests of Croatian nationalists occurred in December 1971 and continued through 1972. The Church was attacked by the state press, and some churchmen were persecuted. In January 1972, at the session of the Intermunicipal Conference of the League of Communists of Croatia for Dalmatia, the state prosecutor reported that "certain circles from the Catholic and Orthodox churches are resisting the new political course . . . in defiance of warnings, they continue to wave national flags without the socialist symbols [and] publicize anti-Party and antistate articles in the church press, and some even organize worship service for the former political leaders."[25] Even in the traditionally nonnationalist Croatian province of Istria the Church was publicly attacked, so that the parish priest from Rovinj complained in a letter to the Municipal Commission for Religious Affairs, published in *Glas koncila*, that "political leaders in public statements contend that the Church and the clergy have always been and will remain ugly nationalists, the worst of all."[26]

In response to state repression, the archbishop of Zagreb, Franjo Kuharić, delivered a stern message to the communists, while his counterpart from Split, Archbishop Franić, was again in the role of the appeaser.[27] By contrast, Archbishop Kuharić held a series of protest sermons in the Zagreb cathedral from January through March 1972. The homilies were entitled "Let us Not Capitulate before Evil" and "Our People Needs Its Church."[28] On the occasion of Lent in 1972, the archbishop Kuharić released an epistle in which he attacked the regime's restrictions of religious liberty. The letter also addressed the issue of equality of nations in the multiethnic country of Yugoslavia. "Believers will never put up with discrimination against anyone because of his faith," Archbishop Kuharić wrote, emphasizing that political authorities have no right to command what philosophy and view of the world citizens should espouse. It is a duty for us believers to love our Croatian people. We understand that good relations with other nationalities are important and necessary, but these relations among nationalities must be just and based on freedom for all, equality and rule of law that is equal for all.[29]

At the regular spring session of the Bishops' Conference of Yugoslavia, held in Zagreb on 18–21 April 1972, the bishops released a public statement expressing unity and support for Archbishop Kuharić and said that Kuharić's Lent message was written in the spirit of the Second Vatican Council and based on the evidence of numerous documented human rights violations in Croatia.[30]

Concurrently, the theologian Šagi-Bunić wrote in *Glas koncila* an essay on the role of the Catholic Church in the formation of the Croatian nation.

> The Church and the Croatian nation are inseparable, and nothing can sever that connection. Catholicism cannot be deleted from the people's collective memory or the Croatian national identity, either by theoretical persuasion and propaganda or by a revolutionary act. The Catholic Church in our country has done nothing bad or harmful in recent years, no moves or gestures that could have possibly hampered the development of the Croatian people or that have been at the expense of any other nationality in Yugoslavia.[31]

In June 1972, Šagi-Bunić published in *Glas koncila* his boldest piece on the Church and nationalism. "The Church is not to blame for the formation of the Croatian nation," he wrote, concluding that "the Croatian nation is the finished product in which Catholicism is one among several key components of Croatian national identity."[32]

The Croatian crisis continued. Although domestic unrest was short-lived, the regime worried about an intensification of activities by Croatian exile groups. Between 1968 and 1972, exile anti-Yugoslav organizations carried out a series of deadly terrorist attacks.[33] The Belgrade government asked the Vatican and moderate bishops to intervene and condemn the attacks. The Vatican urged clergy to ease tensions, but no Catholic Church leader publicly condemned terrorism. In July 1972, Archbishop Franić met with the Croatia government officials Frid and Petrinović and informed them that the pope had urged church leaders to unite forces in order to make the Church stronger while helping stabilization of Yugoslavia, according to the current foreign policy of the Holy See. According to records of Franić's meetings with Croatian officials, Franić, whom Croatian officials viewed as a moderate church leader, was explicitly asked by state officials to publicly condemn terrorist activities (some of them with fatal consequences) carried out at the time by Croat extremist groups abroad. State officials reminded the archbishop that the Vatican was obliged to condemn such attacks by the Protocol of 1966, Franić promised that he would put the issue on the Bishops' Conference's agenda and would himself condemn such violent activities. There is no evidence, however, that this church leader or the Bishops' Conference released any pronouncement in connection with the Croat terrorists who had been active between 1970 and 1972 (some were sentenced by criminal courts in Western countries), although they were obliged to do so by the Protocol of 1966 between the Holy See and the Belgrade government.

On 14–15 August 1972, the Catholic Church in Croatia celebrated the feast of the Assumption of Mary at the national shrine at Marija Bistrica. Archbishop Franić convened his congregation in the historic Solin "by the graves of the Croatian kings" on 8 September 1972. Over 30,000 people chanted the Croatian anthem and Marian songs. After the collapse of the Croatian (secular) nationalist movement, the Church became the only driving force of Croatian ethnic nationalism. Many secular nationalist leaders recognized the Church's leadership and became practicing Catholics.[35]

A Symbolic Revolution: The Great Novena

After the Croatian Church–state quarrel in the spring of 1972, the Vatican sought to ease tensions in Yugoslavia. The domestic episcopate cooperated. Archbishop Kuharić, who vehemently protested the regime's policies after the collapse of the Croat National Movement, kept a low profile, while Archbishop Franić and Slovene bishops labored to ameliorate relations with the state. The Church was preparing the ground for the commencement of the nine-year-long jubilee, or the Great Novena, Thirteen Centuries of Christianity in the Croat People. Instead of commencement it would be more accurate to say continuation, for the jubilee had begun in 1941 and had been interrupted by war.

In September 1974, the Croatian episcopate announced the resumption of the Great Novena.[36] The bishops' committee for organizing the Great Novena explained the purpose of the jubilee as follows:

> Facing the phenomena of secularization, urbanization, industrialization, and atheism, the Church in Croatia wanted in the first place to revive the historic-redemptional consciousness and responsibility for the Christian legacy, as well as to strengthen the harmony of the Church by means of a profound Eucharistic revival.[37]

The pope proclaimed the year 1975–76 the "International Year of Mary." On that occasion the Catholic episcopate in Yugoslavia released a pastoral letter, "Thirteen centuries of Christianity in the Croat people," and announced the beginning of the jubilee. The jubilee's logo, showing a replica of the Madonna's image from the tenth-century king Zvonimir's basilica at

Biskupija near Knin, was labeled "Our Lady of the Great Croatian Christian Covenant." It would be circulating over nine years through parishes across Croatia and Croatian enclaves in neighboring areas. The nine-year jubilee was conceived not only as a liturgical and pastoral animation but also as a course in national and Church history. The Church monthly for the young, *Little Council*, initiated in parishes and missions at home and abroad a quiz in Church history: "The Catechism Olympiad for Prince Višeslav's Trophy." The contest became traditional and was accompanied with several editions of the new history textbook "A Little Key for the History of the Church in the Croat People."

Celebrations of the International Year of Mary were associated with the Croatian "Year of Queen Helen," in honor of the oldest Marian shrine at Solin, near Split, founded by Queen Helen in 976. The thousandth anniversary of this first known Marian shrine in Croatia was marked by a three-day international Marian congress in Split and liturgical ceremonies on 8–12 September at nearby Solin. The final liturgical celebration was preceded by a vigil at Queen Helen's shrine. The purpose of the vigil was to teach the faithful "A Course in Croatian Catholic History at the Tombs of our Catholic Kings."[38] The final ceremony, entitled "Day of the Great Covenant," with a congregation of 60,000 in attendance, took place at Solin on 12 September 1976.[39] The concluding "Prayer of the Great Covenant" mentioned Marian shrines dispersed across Yugoslav lands from Istria to Bosnia and Kosovo.[40] The Church underscored religious history as the hallmark of nationhood.

The Church evaluated the opening of the Great Novena as a success, with special compliments to the host, Archbishop Franić.[41] The Croatian Church leader had studied the precedent in Poland, held consultations with the Polish prelates, and emulated the Polish jubilee of the "Great Novena of the Millennium, 1956–1965." In many respects, Franić's strategy recalled the work of Stefan Cardinal Wyszyński.[42] As a result, Croatia's commissioner for religious affairs, Ivan Lalić, in his toast at the 11 September reception for the participants, declared that all Church activities were strictly religious and therefore legal. However, a confidential document originated by the League of Communists of Dalmatia described the beginning of the Great Novena as "a nationalistic escalation and regrouping of the defeated nationalist forces around the Catholic Church."[43]

In 1977, the Church celebrated the eight-hundredth anniversary of the first papal visit to Slavic lands. The jubilee invoked a legend according to which Pope Alexander III, when he arrived at the Adriatic port of Zara (Zadar) was impressed as local Slavs chanted hymns in their native language. According to a Church document, the jubilee's goal was "to underscore the importance of the language for national self-determination."[44] Next year the Church marked the nine-hundredth anniversary of the basilica at Biskupija, built by King Zvonimir, who during his reign (1076–88) solidified Croatia's place in Western civilization. In preparation for the Zvonimir jubilee, the leading Church historians Josip Soldo, Bonaventura Duda, and Tomislav Šagi-Bunić wrote and lectured about the historic consequences of the King Zvonimir's consolidation of Roman Catholicism and rejection of Eastern Orthodoxy, thus cementing the character of Croatia as a Western nation. They referred to Serbian Church historians who describe Zvonimir as an enemy of the Orthodox faith.[45]

The final ceremony of the King Zvonimir jubilee took place on 14–17 September 1978 at the village of Biskupija, which harbors the relics of a basilica built by him and dedicated to Mary. The Zvonimir basilica is one of numerous important sacred landmarks posted along communal boundaries amid the Yugoslav ethnoreligious maze (the village of Biskupija, not very far from the regional centers of Knin and Drniš, is located in the area overwhelmingly populated by Orthodox Serbs). At the Zvonimir jubilee, a new practice was introduced: the icon of "Our Lady of the Great Croatian Christian Covenant" on display inside the church was decorated by the Croatian national flag. The flag differed from the official state flag of the Socialist Republic of Croatia (there was no red star in the middle). The Church was attacked by the official press. Still the disputed flag remained on display in all ensuing events of the Great Novena. The regime press also criticized the chanting of the Croatian national anthem as inappropriate practice for religious events.[46]

Over 30,000 pilgrims, clergy, and bishops, with the papal legate the cardinal Silvio Oddi, and state officials and representatives of the Serbian Orthodox Church were in attendance at the mass in Biskupija on 17 September 1978. The ceremony was dedicated to the consecration of the renovated replica of the historic church of King Zvonimir. In the evening, at the vigil in the magnificent sixteenth-century romanesque cathedral at the nearby diocesan center of Šibenik, Archbishop Franić spoke in his homily about the importance of sacred rebuilding, which, according to his words, epitomized the perpetual process of renewal and continuity of the Church and the nation.[47]

In 1979 the Catholic Church in Croatia commemorated another medieval ruler, Prince Branimir. The Year of Prince Branimir was a continuation of the previous jubilee dedicated to the crucial connection between the Croat medieval rulers and the popes.[48] On the occasion, Tomislav Šagi-Bunić wrote: "in the Year of Branimir, we commemorate the return of the Croatian Church and people into the Church of Rome, which also means appropriation of Latin culture and inclusion into the West."[49] In the light of the contesting Catholic and Orthodox interpretations of history, Prince Branimir (who ruled from 879 to 887), made the critical choice between Rome and Constantinople in favor of the former. Branimir had his rival, Duke Sedeslav (878–79), who favored alliance with Constantinople, executed. Serbian Church historiography views Sedeslav as a martyr of the Orthodox church and Branimir's ascension to power as a disaster that separated two Slavic peoples who both leaned toward the Orthodox church. The Serbian Church historian Bishop Milaš built his historiography on the assumption that Serb and Croats were ethnically the same people, predetermined to form a unified nation had the fatal religious split not occurred.[50] Milaš's most often quoted Croatian Catholic opponent is the Franciscan historian Dominik Mandić, who argued that the Serb and Croat have different ethnic origins and so many distinct characteristics that the ideal solution for each people is to have a nation-state of its own.[51] Updating the classical Milaš-Mandić debate and accommodating it to the ecumenical spirit of the Second Vatican Council, Tomislav Šagi-Bunić argued in a lecture delivered to the clergy of Istria in Pazin of 9 July 1979 that the churches of East and West (and their respective Serb and Croat branches) had been separated in the course of history because of the interaction of multiple "historical-cultural factors" and also because of a "lack of mutual understanding and love" rather than because of Branimir's feud with Sedeslav.[52]

As a part of the 1979 jubilee, the Church organized a "Croatian national pilgrimage" in honor of the first Slavic pope, John Paul II. The pope officiated at the mass for the Croat pilgrims at Saint Peter's Basilica on 30 April 1979. Speaking in Croatian, the Pope stressed the importance of the Great Novena. He praised "the love and loyalty of the Croats to the Holy See" and encouraged the pilgrims to be "faithful, fearless, and proud of the Christian name."[53] The "Year of Branimir" concluded on 2 September 1979 in Zadar and Nin. More than 150,000 people paid pilgrimage to the eighth-century Basilica of the Holy Cross at Nin, which is the oldest preserved church in Yugoslavia. Cardinal Franjo Šeper presided over the jubilee as a papal legate and celebrated the mass with cardinals and bishops from Italy, Austria, Poland, France, Hungary, and domestic bishops and clergy. The congregation loudly applauded when the announcer mentioned the names and tiles of the state officials and representatives of the Orthodox Church. Yet again, the national flag without the red star was displayed, and the crowd chanted the two Croatian anthems. According to a Church document, the Branimir jubilee "has shown to all, this time with thus far unseen massive turnout, that the Church in the Croat People is strong, alive, and visible, and that people are expecting from this Church to accomplish important things."[54]

In 1982, the Church expanded the jubilee in the neighboring Yugoslav republics. In Sarajevo on 1–4 July 1982 and later in other Bosnian diocesan centers the Church commemorated the one hundredth anniversary of the restoration of the regular ecclesiastical authority in Bosnia-Herzegovina. The Church paid tribute to the Austrian bishop of Croatian background, Josef Stadler (1843–1918), who had administered Bosnia-Herzegovina from the Austrian occupation of Bosnia in 1878 to the collapse of Habsburg rule. In September 1982, Croatian pilgrims set out to Istria to commemorate the one hundredth anniversary of the Istrian native bishop, Juraj Dobrila (1812–82), who defended the national rights of the Croats under Italian rule. On 1 October 1982, on the occasion of the centennial of the cathedral in the northern Croatian town of Djakovo, the Church honored the most notable bishop of Croatian origin, Josip Juraj Strossmayer (1815–1905), a reform-minded participant in the First Vatican Council, philanthropist, and church-builder, the founder of the Yugoslav Academy of Arts and Sciences, and the champion of ecumenical dialogue between the Catholic and Orthodox churches in Slavic lands. On 16 October 1983, the Great Novena commemorated the Catholic past of what is now Montenegro. Catholic pilgrims from Herzeg Novi, Montenegro, joined by other Croatian pilgrims and clergy, went to Rome to pay tribute to another saint of Croatian descent—the Franciscan Capuchin monk and popular confessor Leopold Bogan Mandić, a native of Herzeg Novi. Growing enthusiasm of the faithful Catholics after the canonizations of two native Croatian saints within twelve years propelled the Great Novena toward a triumphant climax.

From 1981 to 1984, the Church organized a series of massive pilgrimages and festivals in the form of diocesan Eucharistic congresses. According to a Croatian government analysis, the Church, through Eucharistic congresses, "sought to flex muscles, deliver a message to enemies, encourage the faithful, revitalize the faith, and mobilize believers in response to crisis and challenge."[55] The total number of active participants and organizers in local parish congresses, as estimated by the government source, was between 1,052,000 to 1,315,000. The number of pilgrims and participants at the last congressional festivals held at the level of the deanery and diocese varied from several thousand up to 20,000. According to the regime's sources, the Church employed between 690,000 to 920,000 activists in the preparation of the congresses. "The Church is obviously in a state of general mobilization, and we can expect a massive turnout, possibly in the hundreds thousand, at the final ceremony of the National Eucharistic Congress at Marija Bistrica," concluded a 1984 governmental analysis of church-state affairs.[56] Finally, the most massive diocesan Eucharistic congresses took place in Split. On 6 September 1981, Archbishop Franić convened 100,000 pilgrims at the final ceremony of the diocesan Eucharistic congress of the metropolitanate of Dalmatia at the shrine of Vepric near the one-time diocesan seat of Makarska. The papal legate Silvio Cardinal Oddi, joined by 11 bishops and 220 priests, presided over the Mass. According to a Church source, 17,600 pilgrims received Holy Communion on the day of the main event alone.[57]

As the main event of the Great Novena, the National Eucharistic Congress (NEK '84), was nearing, the regime in Yugoslavia became conscious of the growing power of Croatian Catholicism. The regime's press frequently featured articles on Church-state relations. Communist experts on religion and church politics were warning of the danger. In a series of articles, the semiofficial newspaper of the League of Communists, *Komunist*, argued that the activities of the Great Novena were

carefully designed to make a synthesis of the nationalist and religious agendas through the manipulation of symbols, themes, and dates from Church and national history, in order to penetrate popular consciousness with both of two key themes, religion and ethnic nationalism, fused and merged into a single whole. Through the Great Novena, the Catholic Church is closing the ranks of the Croatian nation, while emphasizing the leading, essentially political role of the hierarchy."[58] *Komunist* concluded: "The Great Novena simply means the clerical exploitation of ethnicity, folklore, history, and Croatian cultural heritage, coupled with the transformation of national history, into a myth. The Church's objective is to reinvigorate the reactionary consciousness, which, in this multinational country, may produce destructive outcomes."[59]

Seeking to appease the Orthodox Church and the regime, the National Eucharistic Congress included ecumenical activities in the jubilee's program. From January to September 1984 numerous interfaith meetings and ecumenical vigils took place in Croatia. "In the hope of overcoming our differences, Catholics always appeared as prime movers of all ecumenical activities," a Catholic Church document summarized the historic experience of Catholic-Orthodox relations.[60] Cardinal Kuharić invited Patriarch Germanus to attend the congress as a guest of honor. The Patriarch of the Orthodox Church also wrote to Cardinal Kuharić to inform him that the Serbian Church was preparing for a commemoration of a new chapel at Jasenovac on 2 September 1984, only a week before the NEK, and invited the cardinal to attend the Jasenovac commemoration. Kuharić excused himself but announced that a high Catholic delegation led by Bishop Djuro Kokša would be in attendance at Jasenovac. Then the patriarch refused to attend the NEK and nominated Metropolitan Jovan Pavlović as the representative of the Orthodox Church.

On 8–9 September 1984 several hundred thousand people turned out at the national shrine of Marija Bistirica. State television mentioned gave number as 180,000. The Church press wrote of 400,000 to half a million pilgrims in attendance at the final ceremony of the Great Novena. On 8 September, at the evening Mass in the Zagreb cathedral, the papal legate, the archbishop of Vienna, Franz Cardinal Koenig, opened the National Eucharistic Congress. Pope John Paul II addressed the jubilee through Radio Vatican. The papal message was broadcast live in and around the cathedral. The controversial Alojzije Cardinal Stepinac was mentioned several times in prayers and sermons. After the opening ceremony, the pilgrims attended the "Great Congressional Vigil," which proceeded simultaneously in Zagreb and Marija Bistrica. The vigil consisted of spiritual and folk music, prayer, and a history course taught in form of a drama, a chronicle of the "Thirteen Centuries of Christianity in the Croats." The vigil was labeled by the Church press the "Vigil of the Century." The purpose of the vigil was to present a survey of a new history of the Croatian Church and people from 641 to 1984.

The course in the new Croatian history authorized by the Catholic Church, designed as a dramatized chronicle, was written by the Catholic historian Josip Turčinović. The chronicle included narrative, poetry, prayer, music, and singing performed by students of theology, nuns, and pilgrims. The narrative began with a poetic account on the baptism of the Croats in the eighth century. It described the growth of the Church under the medieval ethnic rulers, balancing between Rome and Constantinople and exposed to the pressure of the powerful Franks and the Magyars. The controversial topics of Zvonimir and Branimir were also elaborated. The chronicle also mentioned relations with rival religions, in particular Serbian Orthodoxy and Islam. The historic role of the Serbian Orthodox Church was portrayed in dark colors. The foundation of the Serbian Church was described as a political trickery of Saint Sava, who had played off the pope against the church of Constantinople and finally sided with the latter in accordance with interests of the Nemanjić ruling house. The Great Migration of Serbs under Patriarch Arsenije III in 1691 was viewed as an invasion of Croatian territory. The chronicle emphasized that the Serbian Church leaders had launched a war for the reconversion of Uniate communities in northern and western Croatia. According to the chronicle, the so-called concordat crisis of 1937, when the Serbian Church led demonstrations in Belgrade against the concordat between the Belgrade government and the Holy See, was evidence of the Serbian Orthodox Church's support for Serbian hegemony in the multinational state. No mention was made of the genocidal massacres committed by the Croat fascist Ustašas (the Church considered these massacres to be lesser in scope than the terror against Croats carried out by the Serb nationalist guerilla Četniks and the communists). World War II is a gap in the chronicle. However, the new history rewritten through the Great Novena dwelled at length on the postwar communist persecution of the Church and the trial of Archbishop Stepinac. Stepinac and the clergy who were persecuted by communist regime were portrayed as saints and martyrs. The chronicle concluded by stating that Church-state relations had improved since 1966, when the Church acquired more freedom than elsewhere in communist countries, although "numerous contradictions in the ideologically monolithic one-party state that is also a multiethnic and multiconfessional country have not yet been resolved."[61]

On the eve of the National Eucharistic Congress Archbishop Franić delivered an important homily at the Great Congressional Vigil in the Zagreb cathedral. Among other things he emphasized that the Slavic pope John Paul II, in his message to the 1976 jubilee at Solin, had drawn parallels between the churches of Poland and Croatia. Franić referred to the current situation in Poland and found it analogous to the situation in Yugoslavia. He reminded the faithful that the pope had pointed out the following three similarities shared by the churches of Poland and Croatia. First, both churches played a paramount role in the defense of the eastern borders of Catholicism. Second, both churches worship the cult of the Blessed Virgin Mary with an extraordinary piety fused with patriotism. Third, both churches are especially devoted to the popes. Franić concluded that the two

Catholic Slavic peoples stand again in the first line of defense of the Catholic West against the Orthodox East and exclaimed: "God rendered to us Catholic Croats this land in which we have lived for a thousand and three hundred years, and we will not let anyone else rule over us in our own land." As the eruption of patriotic zeal swamped the packed cathedral, the archbishop urged the faithful not to succumb to euphoria.[62]

The Polish-Croat analogy was strongly emphasized by the Croatian episcopate in the Croatian Great Novena so as to suggest that in the 1980s both Catholic nations were again the bulwark of the West against the danger from the East—communism, incidentally emanating from Orthodox Russia and Serbia, respectively (concurrently, the Serbian Orthodox Church sought to upgrade relations with the patriarchate of Moscow and the Russian Church—see more later). Visitations by Polish Church dignitaries during the jubilee (especially in 1979 and 1984) were to show symbolically the restored "natural" and traditional "brotherhood and unity" between the two western Catholic Slavic nations, as opposed to the communist-Titoist "artificial" brotherhood and unity between Catholic Croats and Orthodox Serbs. At the historic meeting between a Croatian delegation representing the Great Novena organizers and participants with the Polish pope in the Vatican, on 30 April 1979, Karol Wojtyla said in his address, among other things, the following: "you also commemorate your ancestral homeland that you call White Croatia, which was located precisely in the area where I was born."[63] Thus the pope espoused the Great Novena's myth of the Croats' fourth-through sixth-century migration southward from the western slope of the Carpathian Mountains, where they allegedly lived side by side with the Poles, while no trace could be found of the Serbs.[64] The organizers of the Croat Great Novena sought to fortify the restored Croat-Polish brotherhood by inviting the pope to the NEK and emphasizing the role of the Croats as helpers to the Roman missionaries who had evangelized the Poles. On 13 February 1984, the archbishop of Zadar, Marjan Oblak, met with the Polish pope in a private audience in the Vatican. The purpose of Oblak's visit was to inform Wojtyla that the Croatian Church would like in the program of the Great Novena to stress the role of the Croats in the evangelization of Poland, according to Oblak, they welcomed the papal missionaries traveling to northern Slavic lands from Rome via the Croatian port of Zadar.[65] At the meeting with the Pope, Oblak cited some Polish as well as Croat historians as sources of the theory about the Croatian role in the evangelization of Poland. Oblak also emphasized that a cathedral in Zadar proudly housed the oldest icon of the holy queen Jadwiga, who made possible the evangelization of the Poles. The Croatian *Glas koncila* wrote that the pope was delighted with the initiative and encouraged the Croatian episcopate to underscore the historic ties between the two Slavic Catholic nations.[66]

Birth of the Catholic Nation

The final ceremony of the National Eucharistic Congress on Sunday, 9 September 1984, at Marija Bistrica was labeled by the Church press the "Grand Convention of the People of God." The night before the main event, tens of thousands of people took part in spectacular torch parades and vigils along the "Way of the Cross" at Marija Bistrica. On Sunday morning, a crowd of 400,000 packed the liturgical area in front of the Bistrica church and the surrounding hills. The ceremony commenced with a procession moving slowly from the church to the altar in the open for over two hours. The procession displayed religious and ethnic symbols, including Marian icons from 32 Marian shrines across Yugoslavia. The participants carried artifacts from museums and collections of Croatian medieval history. The march concluded with a procession of the Croatian Church's clerical resources, including thousands of monks and nuns followed by a "white wave" of 1,100 priests in liturgical attire. In front of the clerical column marched a young Uniate (Greco-Catholic) deacon carrying the Bible. Finally came the hierarchy: foreign and domestic superiors of monastic orders, bishops and high prelates, 5 cardinals, sixty archbishops, and representatives of state authorities, the Orthodox Church, the Islamic Community, and several Protestant denominations.

During the Mass, which the Church press labeled "Mass of the Century," more than 100,000 believers received Holy Communion from Cardinal Koenig, with several bishops and more than three hundred priests circulating in the crowd.[67] The chairman of the Bishops' Conference of Yugoslavia, Cardinal Kuharić, delivered a homily. After wrapping up the proceedings and events of the Great Novena, he brought up the case of Cardinal Stepinac as the crowd applauded. Kuharić then demanded the lifting of all restrictive provisions from laws on religious communities and an unambiguously favorable of the regime policy toward the churches.[68] At the conclusion of the "Grand Convention of the People of God" at the Croatian national shrine of Marija Bistrica, a choir of several hundred thousand people chanted "Virgin of Paradise Queen of the Croats" and "Our Lovely Homeland."

Scenes from the national shrine appeared on Sunday evening on state television prime-time news program. The British magazine *Economist* compared the Catholic Church in Croatia to the Church in Poland.[69] The Croatian edition of the League of Communists weekly *Komunist* lamented:

Religion is *en vogue* again. The Valley of Tears, as Marx has labeled Christianity, looks fresh, vital, and attractive to people, although we thought that it would wither away. Religion seems to be attractive for the young, too: How to explain this paradox? And we in Yugoslavia also believed that we have resolved the national question in this country once and for all, but it seems that it is not so. The Church is defending its people from something or someone, but from whom? From atheism, for example. In

Marija Bistrica Cardinal Kuharić said that atheists are bad people. He refers to nonbelief as evil. Further, the Church again commemorates Stepinac. Our Constitution guarantees freedom of religion, but nobody has a right to utilize religion for political purposes. Some churchmen think that the political use of religion is perfectly normal.[70]

The chairman of the Central Committee of Croatia's League of Communists, Mika Špiljak, accused the Church of manipulating ethnic identity and nationalist sentiments in order to restore clerical wealth and power in society.[71] The party daily, *Borba* (Belgrade), wrote that "some church dignitaries sought to exploit the National Eucharistic Congress inaugurate a clerical strategy that equates religion and nationality, glorifies Stepinac, and sanctions the Church's meddling in politics."[72]

Nonetheless, the Great Novena had succeeded, despite the pressure in the media and from the ruling circles, and in spite of the fact that from 1973 to 1985 (which roughly coincides with the Great Novena), 85 people were jailed on account of Croatian nationalism, including seven Catholic priests.[73] The Church could only profit from more Stepinacs. The Catholic Church, operating autonomously and independently from Croatian secular nationalists, accomplished mobilization and homogenization of the Croat masses. The Great Novena supported the Church as a political force and affirmed the episcopate as national leadership. The numbers of socially active Catholics grew from the 60,000 at Solin in 1976 to nearly 200,000 at Nin in 1979. Several hundred thousand people took part in the diocesan Eucharistic congresses of 1981–83. Nearly half a million came to Marija Bistrica in September 1984. The crowds of the Great Novena operated as a plebiscite for the new Croatia as designed by the Catholic Church. The Church supplied the newborn nation with the necessities such as a new history and new symbols and myths. The key component of the new nation was its new history, authorized by the Church. The new Croatia was reinvented as a "100 percent Western" nation though its interaction with the Byzantine ecclesiastical and political authority and tradition, and Orthodox Christianity was underrated and portrayed in overall negative colors (as a "hegemony," as opposed to the papal and Western imperial patronage, presented as civilizing mission and protection). Further, the Great Novena revived and "resolved" the classical controversy of church versus national historiography regarding the early medieval religious split caused the by policies of the Croat and Serb feudal lords and rulers. The Great Novena denounced the Serb Church historian Bishop Milaš, who had laid the foundations of Serbian ecclesiastical historiography (which coincides with the nationalist perspective in the secular Serbian historiography) on the assumption that Serbs and Croats were ethnically the same people, predetermined to form a unified Slavic (Orthodox) nation, had the popes not intervened and prevented these two fraternal Slavic peoples from becoming all Greek Orthodox. The Great Novena reasserted the main argument of the Croatian nationalist ideology that Serbs and Croats were "two ancient distinct peoples" each entitled to a nation-state of its own. Finally, concerning very recent controversies from church history, the dark spots from the history of the Croatian Church and nation during World War II were "forgotten," while the leading church figure of this period, Alojzije Cardinal Stepinac, was portrayed as a martyr, the victim of a conspiracy masterminded by the enemies of the Catholic Church, namely, the Serbs and communists.[74]

The jubilee "Thirteen Centuries of Christianity in the Croat People" was a well-organized political as well as religious mobilization of the people by the Church. Yet this mobilization was in its essence nationalistic and religious only in form. The spiritual impact was definitely weaker than the political. Fighting modernization, secularization, communism, the Yugoslav multinational state, and the rival faiths, the Church worshiped itself and consecrated new ethnic and ecclesiastical histories as part of the making of the new Croatian nation. The clerical leadership in the Croat national movement was established in the 1970s, paradoxically, with the communist regime's implicit help and owing to the communist suppression of the Croatian secular liberal opposition. By the mid-eighties, the Church would also challenge another secular rival: the pro-Yugoslav League of Communists of Croatia. After the triumph of the Great Novena, Croatian Catholicism became an increasingly influential social and political force. Yet the advancing "Church in the Croat People" had yet to confront its most powerful rivals: the Serbian Orthodox Church and Serbian nationalism. Incidentally, as I have shown in the preceding chapter and will show further, a similar Serbian ethnic nationalist revolution was unfolding and corresponded with the Croatian mobilization on an ethnoreligious basis. In this Serbian revolution the Serbian Orthodox Church emerged as one of the driving forces. In the second half of the 1980s, the history of Yugoslavia witnessed, not surprisingly, a "war of the churches."

5

THE BOSNIAN ULEMA AND
MUSLIM NATIONALISM

During almost the entire communist era until 1989, the Muslim religious organization—the Islamic Community in the *Socialist Federal Republic (SFR) of* Yugoslavia—had been managed by leaders recruited from World War II Partisan veterans dedicated to Titoist brotherhood and unity. This Muslim organization had been a factor of stability in religious and ethnic relations and the source of religious legitimation for the Yugoslav regime. Leaders of the Muslim organization were appointed with the regime's consent from the rank and file of the Bosnian ulema associated with the Ilmija clerical organization. The top Muslim leaders were all Partisan veterans of the Anti-fascist People's Liberation Struggle. Their policy was based on the belief that the Muslims scattered across Bosnia-Herzegovina, Serbia, Macedonia, Montenegro, and other Yugoslav regions should live in a united Yugoslav state with Bosnia and Herzegovina as its federated republic.

In the late sixties and early seventies, the patriotic leadership of the Islamic Community encountered a challenge from Muslim ethnic nationalism that came from above, namely from the League of Communists of Bosnia and Herzegovina, as well as from below, for example, in the religious nationalism advanced by the outlawed "Young Muslims" organization. Even though Yugoslav Muslims thought of themselves as a distinct entity, before 1968 they were not recognized as a nationality on a par with other Yugoslav constituent ethnic nations. The Muslim religious organization did not establish itself, like the Christian Churches, as a guardian of national identity. In contrast to Serbian and Croatian Christian clergy, Muslim clerics (*hodjas, imams*) and ulema did not systematically worship medieval native rulers, native saints, shrines, territory, and ethnic myths. According to the mythology advanced by the Christian churches, Bosnia and Herzegovina were Catholic or Orthodox but unquestionably Christian lands. Muslims did not have myths of their own—they were aliens in their native land. The weakness or total absence of religious nationalism as exemplified in a churchlike hierarchical organization dedicated to the worship of ethnic nationalism made Serbo-Croatian-speaking Muslims uneven partners in the religious-nationalist competition in Yugoslavia. For the same reason the communists had a relatively easier task in controlling the Muslim religious organization. A government analysis of church-state relations in the 1960s reported that the Muslim religious organization, the Islamic Religious Community, "was placed under direct supervision of the state, and even though in the early 1960s administrative control had been eased, this religious organization is still unable to operate without governmental financial support."[1] The loyalty of the ulema to the communist regime was unquestionable. One of the radical Bosnian Muslim nationalists who came to the fore in the late 1980s, Djemaludin Latić, argued that many Muslims ignored the reis-ul-ulema and other authorities and recognized as their genuine religious leaders recitators of the Holy Koran and Islamic theologians.[2] In reality, the so-called Young Muslims, radical Bosnian nationalists who emerged in World War II, and other Muslim extremists were isolated and virtually unknown, while the Reis-ul-ulema and other religious leaders managed to keep the Muslim organization going and rebuilt it and expanded its activities.

A Nationality with a Religious Name

In February 1968, the Central Committee of the League of Communists of Bosnia and Herzegovina declared that Bosnian Muslims, as well as other Yugoslav Muslims who thought of themselves as a distinct nationality, be granted the status of a full-fledged nationality recognized by the federal constitution. The new Yugoslav ethnic nation was given the religious label "Muslim" as a national name. The national label was capitalized, as opposed to the religious term. The Socialist Republic of Bosnia-Herzegovina was designated a national state of Serbs, Croats, and "Muslims by nationality." Muslims welcomed the new status. In the 1971 census 1,482,430 citizens of Yugoslavia declared themselves Muslims by nationality, in contrast to the census of 1961, when 842,247 persons were registered as "ethnic" Muslims. The number of "undecided" dropped from 275,883 in 1961 to 43,796 in 1971.[3] The new identity appealed not only to the Muslims of Bosnia-Herzegovina but also to Serbo-Croatian-speaking Muslims in Sandjak and Kosovo and Macedonian-speaking Muslims in the Socialist Republic of Macedonia. Similarly, Montenegrin Muslims had to choose whether to declare themselves as Montegrins or go under the new religious-ethnic name.[4] Some minor Muslim groups such as the Torbesh, Pomaks, Gorans, and Turkic Muslims also came under pressure to make the choice.

The "religious" name for the new nation triggered a polemic. The founder of the Yugoslav Sociology of Religion, Esad Ćimić, viewed the use of the religious label as a national name as inappropriate. The exiled Muslim leader Adil Zulfikarpašić proposed the term "Bosniak" as the solution. Muslim religious leaders pleaded for more time, the establishment of Muslim cultural institutions, and more religious liberty, thereby to empower the Muslims to solve the controversy by themselves.[5] The communists disagreed. In the words of the communist leader Nijaz Duraković, the label "Muslim" as a national name was "the only possible name, whether one likes it or not."[6]

Another consequence of the birth of the "religious" nation in Bosnia was the friction between Muslims, who stressed ethicity and modern secular national identity, and Muslims, who considered religion the key ingredient of the new national identity. The regime noticed growing pressures by local ethnic nationalists (Muslim and Albanian) on Muslim religious officials in Bosnia, as well as in Macedonia and Kosovo, to emphasize religious identity. In Sarajevo, members of the outlawed Young Muslims group (most of whom were jailed by the communists as collaborators with the foreign invaders during the war and/or as religious zealots and Bosnian nationalists) criticized the Islamic Community's head reis-ul-ulema and high clergy for collaborating with the antireligious regime and neglecting the religious component in Muslim national identity. The Young Muslim group was established in the 1930s as a radical wing of the moderate Jugoslav Muslim Organization (YMO). As opposed to the JMO, which advocated autonomy for Muslims as a religious group within the Yugoslav state, the Young Muslims perceived themselves as a full-fledged ethnic nation in which Islam constituted the main ingredient of national identity. The Young Muslim organization always involved some, but not very many, imams. Young Muslims were the outgrowth of the right-wing nationalism of the 1930s, and they fought for an independent homogenous Muslim nation. During World War II, Young Muslims constituted an independent faction in the Bosnian civil war and sided with various factions, except the Četniks.[7] The Islamic religious institutions and the Bosnian ulema had struggled for their own autonomy in religious matters ever since the Ottoman era and continued the quest under Austrian and Yugoslav rule. The Muslim religious organization and the Young Muslims (that is, their successors), however, did not come together and unite over the issue of the Muslim nation-state until the 1990s.

The upsurge of nationalism in all Yugoslav ethnic nations during the communist liberal reforms of the 1960s provided an impulse for the mobilization of various Muslim factions. Communists of Muslim background sought to forge a Muslim national identity and restructure Bosnia within the Yugoslav federation. At the same time, nationalist anticommunists, notably the Young Muslim group, led by the Sarajevo lawyer Alija Izetbegović (jailed by the communists in 1948), also became active. Concerning the Islamic Community (IZ), its leaders sought greater autonomy through cooperation with the regime and were supportive of the concept of Bosnia-Herzegovina as a federated republic within socialist Yugoslavia with the recognition of the Muslim nationality. To be sure, not all clergy were pro-Titoist as the IZ leaders were. For example, the young imam Hasan Ćengić, with a group of students of the medresa (Islamic seminary), at Sarajevo and with the participation of ex–Young Muslims Alija Izetbegović, Omer Behmen, and others, envisioned a new Muslim national identity in which religion would play key role and a Muslim that state would operate in accordance with *Sharia* (traditional Muslim law). Proregime Muslim religious leaders helped to isolate this group. According to a government document, "although the Islamic Community's leaders had successfully rebuffed nationalistic and extremist pressures, it is evident that some Muslim clerics tend to overrate the importance of the religious factor for Muslim national identity, arguing that religious and ethnic identity is all the same."[8]

The Izetbegović group outlined its ideology in a document, entitled "The Islamic Declaration—A Program for the Islamization of Muslims and Muslim Peoples," written in 1970.[9] In the document, Izetbegović envisioned that Muslims of the world would unite and launch a "religious as well as social revolution" but did not explicitly refer to the situation in Yugoslavia or Bosnia-Herzegovina. The transformation of a non-Islamic into an Islamic society, according to Izetbegović, would begin with a "moral reconstruction" and "inner purification" and evolve into "social and political revolution."[10] In spite of the omission of any direct reference to Yugoslavia and Bosnia-Herzegovina, the Declaration made it clear that once Muslims become a majority in one country (thanks to their relatively high population growth) they should demand a state of their own, organized according to Islamic laws and norms because, in Izetbegović's words, "Islam and non-Islamic systems are incompatible."[11] The Declaration designated Pakistan as a model country to be emulated by Muslim revolutionaries worldwide. The Pakistan parallel also revealed Izetbegović's vision of Yugoslavia's fate as analogous to that of India after 1948.

The Islamic Declaration was copied and circulated but did not reach a large audience. The communist secret police, SDB, in Sarajevo called up Alija Izetbegović several times and warned him not to continue political and religious agitation, but the Sarajevo radical was not prosecuted. The Islamic Community had a played critically important role in the peaceful containment of Izetbegović's "Islamic revolution." The chairman of the Socialist Alliance of Working People, Todo Kurtović, had asked the reis-ul-ulema and leaders of the Ilmija to explain to the clergy the danger of Alija Izetbegović's ideas. Muslim clergy in Bosnia and elsewhere throughout the country held meetings and were briefed about Izetbegović's activities. The IZ leaders often spoke publicly about values of brotherhood and unity and Muslims' vital interest in supporting united Yugoslavia.

In order to emphasize its role as a "national" (rather then merely religious) institution of the Muslim people, in November 1969 the Supreme Islamic Assembly changed the official title of the organization from "Islamic Religious Community" to "Islamic Community." The principal legislative body of the Islamic Community, the Supreme Islamic Assembly, convened on 5 November 1969 in Sarajevo and adopted a new constitution under the organizations' new title, "The Islamic Community in the Socialist Federal Republic of Yugoslavia." The Federal Commission for Religious Affairs noticed the change and described it as "a strange and unexpected move whose real purpose and motives need to be further examined."[12] The new Islamic Community defined itself not merely as religious but also as a national institution for all Muslims. From 1969 through 1970 the Islamic newspaper *Preporod* complained in a series of articles and editorials that Muslims were not allowed to establish national institutions of their own that would serve as an equivalent to national cultural institutions in Croatia and Serbia. Under the new name, the Islamic Community aspired to become a de facto Muslim national institution that would compensate for the lack of what were national academies of sciences and arts and cultural umbrella organizations (*maticas*) in Serbia and Croatia.

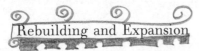

Rebuilding and Expansion

Relying on state support and foreign assistance from Islamic countries, the leaders of the Islamic Community in Yugoslavia managed to rebuild the organization and upgrade religious life. From 1950s to late 1980s, the Islamic Community had been the most patriotic among mainline Yugoslav religious organizations and was particularly instrumental in championing the official plan of brotherhood and unity for all Yugoslav ethnic nations and national minorities. Islamic religion and culture and the Muslim religious organization had benefited from the Muslim leaders' patriotic policy. Muslims earned the regime's confidence and in return were granted more religious liberty. Thus, for example, one of the first religious services shown on state television in the communist era was the 1975 Muslim funeral in honor of the mother of Prime Minister Djemal Bijedić (a popular native of Herzegovina and Partisan fighter against both Ustašas and Četniks). As the *Washington Post* Balkan correspondent Dusko Doder observed, "the mother of Djemal Bijedić, who served as Prime Minister in 1975, was given a religious funeral that year with top state and party leaders marching in the traditional Moslem funeral procession (the pictures of the funeral were shown on national television)."[13]

Between 1969 and 1980 more than 800 Muslim places of worship had been built, and the Community operated over 3,000 mosques in the early 1980s.[14] In the first half of the 1980s, the Islamic Community had 1,600 officials—imams; in the first half of the 1980s, the Islamic Community had 1,600 officials—imams, hafezs (recitators of the Koran), religious instructors, and other employees.[15] As noted earlier, the Muslim religious organization had the most favorable cleric-per-believer ratio among the three major religions in Yugoslavia: one imam for every 1,250 Muslims.[16] In 1977 the new Islamic Theological School was opened in Sarajevo, and a new medresa was to be opened in Skopje, Macedonia, in 1982. Between 1978 and 1988, 52 students graduated from the Sarajevo Islamic Theological School. In the academic year 1979–80, 366 students were enrolled in medresas in Sarajevo and Priština, with 62 students in the female section of the Sarajevo Gaze-Husrev-Bey seminary.[17] In the academic year 1987–88, there were 310 male students and 140 female students in the Sarajevo medresa alone.[18] Nevertheless, Ahmed Smajlović, one of a few high officials of the Islamic Community close to the fundamentalist Izetbegović (according to my conversations with the Community's officials in the 1980s, Smajlović was annoying for moderate officials and staff in the Community but the leaders did not know how to get rid of him) complained in the Arab press that Islam was suppressed in Yugoslavia. A U.S. expert on political Islam took Smajlović as a reliable source for the conclusion that "there was no great Islamic learning in Yugoslavia" and that the Tito regime oppressed Muslims.[19] To provide more evidence about the good standing of Yugoslav Islam after the 1960s, it is worth noting that the Sarajevo-based Islamic biweekly *Preporod* (Renewal) increased its circulation from 30,000 in the early 1980s to over 70,000 at the end of the decade.[20] Among other publications, the *Preporod* publishing house and the Sarajevo Oriental Institute published in the 1985 a luxury edition of the Holy Koran and a two-volume Arabic-Serbo-Croatian dictionary in 1987. Finally, in the late 1970s, the Islamic Community of Yugoslavia began developing its own foreign branch (in North America, western Europe, and Australia), with ten years' delay in comparison with the two Christian churches. Nevertheless, Yugoslav Islam in the country's last decade was by all means an expanding religious institution.

In contrast to the centralized and hierarchical Christian churches linked to their respective ethnic communities, the Islamic Community was a Pan-Yugoslav, multiethnic federation of autonomous Muslim institutions and associations. The constitution of the Islamic Community was congruent with the Yugoslav "self-management" system. Self-administered regional assemblies in Macedonia, Montenegro, Kosovo (for all Serbia), and Bosnia-Herzegovina (including Croatia and Slovenia) influenced the central authority at Sarajevo through representatives and delegations. Sarajevo religious authorities also granted broad autonomy to local muftis and Muslim assemblies in Kosovo, Macedonia, and Belgrade.[21] The reis-ul-ulema had special prerogatives as the religious authority and head of the clergy but could not veto decisions passed by the autonomous assemblies. Tuzla, Belgrade, Priština, and Skopje also enjoyed considerable autonomy. Some Sufi (or dervish) orders and monasteries (*tekijas*) recognized the Sarajevo authorities, while some others were independent. Sixty percent of all the Yugoslav tekijas were located in Kosovo and Macedonia. Mostly Albanians by nationality, the Sufis of Kosovo and western Macedonia parted ways with the reis-ul-ulema and his Sarajevo headquarters in 1974. Albanian Sufis founded an autonomous association of Sufi orders under Sheik Djemali Shehu Rufai, a Kosovar Albanian, headquartered at Prizren. Sheik Djemali, according to his words a one-time associate of the American Black Muslim leader Elijah Mohammed, also directly manages a four-thousand-member monastic community with tekijas in Yugoslavia, western Europe, the United States, (Washington, D.C., Cleveland, New York), and Canada. Sheik Djemali was an admirer of Josip Broz Tito, who, as the Sheik said in an interview with me, had done great things for the Albanian people in Kosovo.[22]

In the last decade of the six-republic federation, when the Christian churches spearheaded ethnic nationalist movements, the Islamic Community remained pro–Yugoslav. After the spring 1982 elections in the Socialist Alliance of Working People of Yugoslavia (SAWPY), 169 religious officials (mostly Muslim imams with a few Orthodox priests and several Bosnian Franciscans) were elected members of local boards of this communist-sponsored political organization.[23] According to a SAWPY report,

> the participation of clergy in the elections was very encouraging now that a resolute resistance to religious nationalism is badly needed . . . the elections have demonstrated that a large number of religious officials in Bosnia-Herzegovina support the legacy and achievements of the Popular Liberation War and Socialist Revolution and refuse to accept ideas advocated by some nationalist clerics who often occupy high positions in the religious institutions' hierarchies.[24]

Patriotic leaders of the Islamic Community were instrumental in backing the Titoist foreign policy of nonalignment. In 1982, as *Preporod* reported, the reis-ul-ulema Naim Hadžiabdić met with several foreign statesmen, such as the president of India and representatives of the Tunisian and Malaysian governments. Hadžiabdić discussed problems of the Community's activity and used the occasion to stress that Yugoslav Muslims enjoy full religious liberty. However, according to the same report, while visiting Algeria in March 1982, the Yugoslav reis was welcomed by a government representative who said to him that "Yugoslavia and Algeria would play an important role in the renaissance of Islam, and actively promote the faith worldwide."[25]

After the death of Tito in 1980, the leader's memory lived among patriotic Yugoslavs. In March 1982, the Islamic newspaper *Preporod* featured a travel report from the Muslim community of Bijelo Polje, Monetenegro, in which the reporter described a renovation of the local mosque, surrounded with a memorial to President Tito, who had died at the age of 88. The Islamic newspaper wrote: "In the mosque's garden in Bijelo Polje, 88 roses blossom. Their scent and beauty remind us of the noble image and great deeds of Comrade Tito, who built the foundations of brotherhood and unity, liberty, independence, and prosperity for our Socialist Yugoslavia."[26]

The spirit of the Titoist brotherhood and unity continued to live in the Islamic Community of Yugoslavia, even though at the time the nationalistic mobilizations of the Christian churches were in full swing. On 18 May 1985 at Sarajevo, the reis-ul-ulema Naim Hadziabdić spoke at the opening session of the Supreme Assembly of the Islamic Community:

> We have gathered today to discuss questions and problems of the Islamic Community. But let me first remind all of you, that we mark this year two great jubilees. The first is the 40th anniversary of the victory over fascism and liberation of our country. Along with Victory Day, we are commemorating the fifth anniversary of the death of our dear president Tito, who is not physically with us; nonetheless we remain loyal to him, and we shall proceed to march down the Tito's path of brotherhood and unity for the benefit of all of us, for our own happiness. . . . Only united as brothers will we be able to march forward and defend our freedom and self-management. Religious officials in our mosques will have special responsibility to preserve these ideals and achievements.[27]

The dynamic rebuilding of Muslim places of worship continued through the 1980s. In Bosnia-Herzegovina, Kosovo and Macedonia 80 new mosques were built, and several new mosques were to be built in Croatia and Slovenia.[28] An extravagant new mosque came under construction in 1981 in Zagreb. Although the Zagreb city authorities were angered as it became evident that the size of the new mosque had exceeded the approved blueprint, the regime eventually endorsed the ambitious project. The mosque was completed in the second half of 1987. The new structure occupied 10,000 square meters, instead of the 3,000 originally approved by the city authorities. The Zagreb mosque became the third largest mosque in Europe, almost as big as the new mosques in London and Rome. It was a modern mosque with an elegant minaret, a library, offices, conference rooms, classrooms, and a restaurant. The Bosnian architects Mirza Goleš and Djemal Ćelić designed a modernized version of the classical Islamic architecture in white marble. The minaret was 49 meters high with two *sheferets* (small balconies). The mosque could receive a thousand believers in prayer on the floor covered with carpets donated by the governments of Iran and Libya. According to speculations by the state press at the time of the mosque's opening, the total costs of the construction exceeded 6 million U.S. dollars.[29] The money was raised mostly in Libya (Libya's leader Quadafi donated half a million dollars), Iran, and Saudi Arabia. Two million U.S. dollars were put on hold by Yugoslav customs and later released. In September 1987, the mosque was solemnly opened with 30,000 visitors in attendance. Pilgrims arrived in 500 buses from all parts of Yugoslavia, and delegations came from 10 Islamic countries.

The local Zagreb Muslim community (*djemat*) and the new mosque were managed by two young imams educated in Arab countries, Ševko Omerbašić and Mustafa Cerić. Omerbašić said in an interview that the mosque's mission is "to make Islamic civilization closer to the people of Croatia and the whole of Yugoslavia, so as to facilitate better mutual understanding and togetherness."[30] A governmental document expressed concern over the foreign involvement in the Zagreb religious enterprise, particularly regarding alleged activities of diplomatic representatives of Iran and Iraq, whose "governments, by all accounts, are playing certain political games with our Muslims."[31] The same document was critical of the imam Mustafa Cerić, who spoke about Islamic revival in Yugoslavia on Iraqi television and maintained contacts with the chargé d'affaires of the Iranian embassy, who, drawing on his talks with Cerić, reported to his government that '100,000 Zagreb Muslims support the Islamic revolution in Iran.' "[32]

The symbolic expansion of Yugoslav Islam was observed with growing concern in the Serbian press. A Belgrade newspaper wrote in 1987 that the Zagreb grand mosque was "too big and lavish, far above the religious needs of the local Muslim community," designed by its builders to symbolize "rising Muslim self-awareness fostered by the fusion of religion and nationality in Islam."[33] The newspaper warned that "the proliferation of the new extravagant mosques can aggravate ethnic and religious relations and cause tensions and conflicts—although a high Muslim religious official had said that such mosques are built to defy communism, other religious institutions do not feel comfortable with that."[34] It is noteworthy that at the time when the Serbian press was publishing such texts on the rise of Islam, the Serbian Orthodox Church in Belgrade was rebuilding one of the largest Byzantine cathedrals in the world, while Belgrade city authorities were repeatedly denying construction permits for the new mosque.

Religious Nationalism in Bosnia-Herzegovina

After the Islamic revolution in Iran in 1979 and the death of Tito in 1980, Alija Izetbegović's faction made an attempt to revive its activities. In contrast to the 1970s, the secret police this time did not merely warn Izetbegović. In July and August 1983, Bosnian authorities brought Izetbegović and 11 others (a Muslim cleric was among them) before the court in the capital of Bosnia-Herzegovina. The members of the group were sentenced to a combined total of 90 years in jail. The Iranian press wrote that "the Yugoslav model of socialism proved incompatible with Islam and hostile to Muslims . . . the Belgrade regime can no longer maintain its high reputation among the Non-Aligned."[35] The regime asked the reis-ul-ulema to support the sentence, but except for several announcements regarding inaccurate information in the foreign press, no explicit official statement on the issue was released from the Islamic Community's Sarajevo headquarters.[36]

A few years later, the regime realized that the Sarajevo trial had been a mistake; it alienated from the Belgrade government many erstwhile allies in the nonaligned movement and Third World countries while prompting Muslim nationalism at home. By 1987, the imprisoned Muslim radicals had been released through amnesty and reduced sentences. The regime's efforts to employ the reis-ul-ulema and other patriotic imams in proregime propaganda activities further discredited the leaders of the Islamic Community. At the same time Izetbegović's popularity was growing. In the second half of the 1980s, particularly when aggressive Serbian nationalism began spread through the media and even ordinary people became worried, the influence of Alija Izetbegović's faction among Bosnian Muslim clergy had increased. According to a British Balkan correspondent at the time,

> [t]here is a religious movement in Yugoslavia routinely ignored by western observers of this country: the growth of Islam, particularly in Bosnia, the land converted to Islam in the 16th century by the Ottoman Turks. In recent years, several hundred new mosques have been built; some with substantial financial aid from Islamic countries. Last month, the *Borba*, a Belgrade daily newspaper close to the government, was complaining about numerous attempts of Islamic propaganda and religious agitation among Yugoslav Muslims. The newspaper asserted that some hundred Yugoslav students were currently enrolled into Islamic universities in the Arab and other Islamic countries. In 1983, a group of Yugoslav Muslims received long prison terms for alleged political and religious activity. The recent signs of an Islamic religious revival are evidently bothering Yugoslav authorities.[37]

In the late 1980s, the Titoist leadership of the Islamic Community began losing control over the increasingly anticommunist clergy, including many sympathizers with Izetbegović's Bosnian religious nationalism and imported fundamentalist ideas. In the winter of 1988 and through the spring and summer of 1989, the Bosnian and Herzegovinian ulema held a series of protest meetings in Sarajevo. Imams criticized the policies of the Islamic Community's leaders and demanded reforms in the Yugoslav Muslim religious organization. The protesters urged that the newly appointed reis-ul-ulema, Hasan Mujić (the regime's candidate), be removed from his post. They also asked for full autonomy for the Ilmiya clerical association; self-administration of the Islamic Community without the regime's interference; stricter application of Islamic norms regarding everyday life of Muslims; and improvement of imams' living and working conditions. After the meeting in Sarajevo held on 3 July 1989, a commission of imams led by the mufti of Mostar, Seid Smajkić, announced the early retirement of Hasan Mujić and opened a process for the revision of the Islamic Community's constitution.

In spite of several noisy meetings and fiery statements, the Islamic Community was able to normalize the situation and proceed with reform. However, the movement of imams in Sarajevo caused alarm in Serbia. In an interview with a Sarajevo University newspaper, the Serbian politician Vuk Drašković accused the imams of inciting a religious and national war in Bosnia-Herzegovina. "Those Islamic hawks and followers of Khomeini," said Drašković.

want to overthrow the legitimate head of the Yugoslav Muslim organization; they would force Muslim women to wear Muslim attire like they do in Iran; they demand separate kindergartens for Muslim children, and special nutrition according to religious norms for Muslim servicemen in the Yugoslav Army. . . . [I]f their demands are met, that would cause religious and national war . . . a catastrophe in Bosnia-Herzegovina.[38]

On 25 May 1989, the Committee for Religious Affairs of the Socialist Alliance of Working People of Serbia held a conference in which the Serbian politician Živomir Stanković asserted that "the Sarajevo movement of imams is dominated by Islamic extremists and is under the influence of the international Islamic factor."[39] At the same meeting, an Orthodox priest, a member of that forum, argued that the Islamic Community in Yugoslavia had turned radical fundamentalist and accused the imams of inciting ethnic and religious hatred.[40] As I will show, the media and some scholars in Serbia argued that religion (Islam) was the major catalyst of Albanian nationalism and Kosovo separatism, although according to government investigations and trials of clandestine nationalist organizations, the principal fomenter of anti-Yugoslav sentiments among ethnic Albanians of Kosovo was communist Albania under the Stalinist dictator Enver Hoxha. Islam was quite influential in Bosnia but not in Kosovo.

After the early retirement of Reis Mujić, the top position in the Islamic Community remained vacant, until the first democratic elections and a new constitution. Ferhat Šeta, a professor at Sarajevo Theological School and a moderate religious leader dedicated to the Titoist brotherhood and unity, served as acting reis. Šeta was soon replaced as acting reis by another prominent moderate religious leader, Jakub Selimoski, a Muslim from Macedonia. In February 1990, the Islamic Community submitted to the Federal Executive Council of Yugoslavia a proposal for further democratization of church-state relations in a "time of hope and encouragement."[41] In April 1990, the Supreme Assembly of the Islamic Community in Yugoslavia adopted a new constitution. It provided that "the Islamic Community operate on the Islamic principles and widely accepted norms and values of the contemporary world, in accordance with Islamic religious doctrine and under the constitutional and legal system of the Socialist Federal Republic of Yugoslavia."[42] The new supreme law proclaimed that the Islamic Community is independent from the state and its elected officials accountable to the electorate in local community assemblies. The Supreme Assembly was given more authority at the expense of the reis-ul-ulema. A new executive body, the *Rijasset*, shared authority with the reis and the assembly. The new constitution incorporated new Muslim communities under the religious authorities (meshihat) in the western republics of Croatia and Slovenia; brought all Sufi dervish orders (except those in Kosovo) under the jurisdiction of Sarajevo, and gave even broader autonomy to regional assemblies and their executive bodies (meshihat). The new labels *meshihat* and *rijasset* came from the Ottoman era, when the Bosnian ulema was part of the Meshihat in Istanbul. The two institutions had been abolished in the Serb-dominated interwar Yugoslav kingdom. In May 1990, imams restructured the Ilmiya clerical association as an autonomous professional association concerned with the imams' status and living and working conditions and also capable of influencing the Islamic Supreme Assembly. With the demise of communism in sight, the Islamic Community was able to democratize itself and became independent from the state.

In March 1991, the Islamic Community of Yugoslavia acquired its first democratically elected reis-ul-ulema, Jakub Selimoski. He was elected by a secret ballot among three candidates. Selimoski's opponents Senahid Bristrić, Mustafa Cerić, and Jusuf Ramić held advanced degrees from Islamic universities in Arab countries and were considered "Islamic hawks" close to Izetbegović. The moderate cleric from Macedonia was to secure an all-Yugoslav character for the Islamic Community and to testify to the organization's commitment to the country's unity. Selimoski functioned as a counterweight to the group around Izetbegović, which, in the meantime, had recruited a large number of sympathizers in the clerical rank and file. Having a Macedonian Muslim as reis-ul-ulema also worked as a check against growing ethnic nationalism among Muslims of Albanian background in western Macedonia and Kosovo.

In spite of the obvious victory of moderates in the Islamic Community, the Belgrade press portrayed Selimoski as a fundamentalist whose intentions were to establish an Islamic state in Muslim-populated regions of Sandjak, Kosovo, Macedonia, and Bosnia-Herzegovina.[43] In order to counter the Serb propaganda, the reis-elect rushed to announce the Community's new course. On the occasion of the 1991 holiday of Ramadan-Bajram, Jakub Selimoski presided over a televised religious ceremony in the new mosque at Zagreb. He said:

> On this occasion, I want to make it clear that the Islamic Community is for Yugoslavia. Muslims live in the territory of the whole of Yugoslavia from Triglav to Gevgelija and view this whole country as their own fatherland. The Islamic Community will not interfere in the debates about Yugoslavia's future political arrangement, but we will support the country's unity.[44]

However, the new Islamic Community sought to make itself more visible under the changing conditions in the country, which was then in the midst of dynamic ethnic and religious ferment as well as in the process of the transfer of power from the communists into the hands of ethnic nationalists. From 1989 to 1991, the new leadership of the Islamic Community launched a dynamic program of religious festivals. In consequence, Islam became as visible as the two rival Christian churches. In 1990, at the end of the holy month of Ramadan, state television in all Yugoslav republics except Serbia, Montenegro, and Macedonia broadcast live religious ceremonies from the Sarajevo Gazi-Husrev Bey mosque. In June 1990 the Islamic Community, emulating the earlier described Christian churches' practices, organized a landmark commemoration of the sixteenth-century conversions to Islam in Bosnia. Concurrently the IZ symbolically restored the "national" Muslim shrine at Ajvatovica in western Bosnia via massive pilgrimage under green banners of Islam. The pilgrimage had originated in 1463 and had continued as an established tradition until it was interrupted by a police action in 1947. Legend has it that Ottoman religious instructors came to the Prusac area in the 1460s to establish regular religious instruction and convert local members of the Bogumil "Bosnian Church" to Islam. On 16–17 June 1990, over 100,000 people made pilgrimage to Ajvatovica to commemorate the beginning of the conversion to Islam in Bosnia. At the mountain shrine where Muslim mystics meditate above the valley of the historic conversion, Jakub Selimoski (then acting reis-ul-ulema) said:

> With the help of the Almighty Merciful Allah, this is the time when we Muslims are restoring the right to express our religious identity in a dignified and humane way; this is the time when we restore our traditions and customs in liberty, though being aware of the responsibility and constraints the freedom we have acquired are imposing upon us. . . . Congregating here at Ajvatovica, as our ancestors before us did, we are paying tribute to literacy and education. . . . We are today also paying tribute to our history and our forefathers.[45]

The next year, the "little haj" at Ajvatovica brought together over 150,000 pilgrims and guests. In addition to the traditional march to the holy site in the mountains, the organizers included a cultural program and pilgrimage for women. Yugoslav television and press ran previously unseen images, such as green banners with Arabic inscriptions and columns of Muslim women in traditional attire.

The new momentum in Yugoslav Islam came in the late 1980s when the Serbian, Albanian, and Croatian ethnic nationalist movements swamped Yugoslavia. Bosnian Muslims also became increasingly preoccupied with articulating their national identity and defining the territory and boundaries of their nation. Muslim religious leaders renounced Serbian threats as well as the nationalistic appropriations of Bosnian Muslims by other ethnic groups and urged the establishment of Muslim national and cultural institutions in Bosnia and Herzegovina.[46] In 1990 the Islamic newspaper *Preporod* wrote presumably the first "nationalist" text since the death of Tito. This article on Muslim national identity in Bosnian literature describes a Muslim as *homo duplex*—"schizophrenic creature"—and quotes the novelist Mehmed "Meša" Selimović: "Bosnians belong to no one. Settled in the middle of a crossroad, we were always being given to someone as a dowry."[47]

The tactful reform inaugurated by the moderate leadership of the Islamic Community was facing a challenge not only from the Izetbegović fundamentalist group but also from growing anti-Muslim sentiment in Serbia, which made it possible for Izetbegović's faction to build an image of being the only defender of the endangered Muslim nation. As early as 1990, Izetbegović began secretly purchasing weapons and organizing a Muslim militia, the so-called Muslim Patriotic League.[48] The Islamic Community came under pressure to respond to the patriotic appeals for national defense and homogenization. Ironically, as soon as the Islamic Community, for decades the least autonomous among the Yugoslav denominations, had won independence from the communist regime, the new Community's status was challenged by the Izetbegović's movement, which aspired to evolve into a Muslim ethnoreligious party and national umbrella movement and absorb the religious organization.

In 1990, Izetbegović fulfilled his old dream of the foundation of an Islamic religious and national party in Bosnia. The founding convention of the Party of Democratic Action (SDA) as a "party of Muslim cultural-historic circle" took place in Sarajevo on 26 May 1990. The new party had to avoid an ethnic or religious label so as to comply with state laws that prohibited the establishment of ethnic or religious parties in multiethnic Bosnia-Herzegovina. Yet the new party was "evidently a Muslim party, which the party's founders openly declared," reported the Islamic newspaper *Preporod*.[49] Many members of the Islamic Community, including high officials and a number of imams, took part in the foundation of the Party of Democratic Action.

Alija Izetbegović was elected the new party's chairman amid ovations from 2,000 participants in the Sarajevo founding convention. Izetbegović chose to play a role of a "moderator" between the SDA radical nationalist-fundamentalist wing, led by Izetbegović's Young Muslim comrade Omer Behmen (who would become the first Bosnian ambassador to Iran), and the liberal secular Muslims, whose most prominent advocate was the exile "Bosniak" Adil Zulfikarpašić. In his inaugural speech as the new party's chairman, Izetbegović spoke about full religious freedom for all in Yugoslavia and denounced unfriendly sentiments toward any of the Yugoslav peoples.[50] The SDA founding convention released a declaration on religious liberty according to which religious pluralism and tolerance were viewed as a fundamental preconditions for success of the new democratic Bosnia and Herzegovina. As Adil Zulfikarpašić put it, "we were aware that playing games with religious sentiments of the other had always been the same as playing with fire—it was a matter of life and death in Bosnia."[51]

Although Izetbegović and Behmen spoke about "five hundred imams employed by SDA to organize the election campaign and win political support for the Muslim party,"[52] the authorities of the Islamic Community made an attempt to preserve the organization's newly acquired autonomy instead of merging with the SDA. At the Rijasset's session of 9 June, 1990, the Islamic

Community banned direct involvement in partisan politics for the Community's officials and clergy. Religious leaders and clergy terminated their party membership.[53] Reis Selimoski, the Rijasset general secretary, Haris Silajdžić, and members of the Supreme Assembly of the Islamic Community (most of them SDA founding members) declared noninvolvement in party politics. Until mid-1990, Yugoslav Islam was still relatively the least nationalistic and militant organized religion in Yugoslavia. "Islam as a religion and culture cannot be nationalistic," *Preporod* wrote in an editorial: "a truly devout Muslim cannot be a nationalist—Islam in Yugoslavia will be waiting until this nationalistic frenzy is over."[54]

Alija Izetbegović and the SDA pursued Bosnian nationalism with a strong religious dimension. One of first foreign policy moves by Izetbegović was an official visit to Quadafi's Islamic Republic of Libya. The Belgrade press wrote about Izetbegović's "fundamentalism and global geostrategic ambitions."[55] During the first multiparty elections in Bosnia and Herzegovina, Izetbegović continued to use Islam as the principal force of homogenization and mobilization of Bosnian Muslims. Between August and November 1990, the SDA needed Islam both as the vehicle of popular mobilization and the key component of the newly emerging Bosniak national identity (the possibility of statehood, though never explicitly mentioned, could be taken for granted). Besides, SDA voters were mostly of the rural population of Bosnia-Herzegovina, and Izetbegović could not organize the election campaign without assistance from the local Muslim clergy. Despite protests by the liberal Zulfikarpašić and Reis Selimoski, Zulfikarpašić testifies, hundreds of clerics remained associated with the SDA and took part in organizing rallies, voting, and, later, helping in the formation of the party's armed echelon—the so-called Muslim Patriotic League.[56] The fear of Serbia had played the decisive role in the rise of Alija Izetbegović and the SDA.

The first democratically elected reis-ul-ulema had become a problem for the SDA and Izetbegović, and imams loyal to him contemplated a coup in the Islamic Community. Selimoski's pro- Yugoslav course and attempts to preserve the Islamic Community's autonomy collided with Izetbegović's desire to put the religious organization in the service of his politics. Meanwhile, Izetbegović, Behmen, and other SDA hawks hoped to take advantage of the disintegration of the Titoist federation and, through negotiations with Serbs and Croats (or if necessary through war, carve out of Bosnia-Herzegovina (including possibly Sandjak) an Islamic state. As the threat from Serbia worsened, the reis from Macedonia became more and more alienated from the Bosnian ulema. Selimoski would be formally removed from his post in 1993. The SDA and the IZ in Bosnia-Herzegovina were closing their ranks. The Islamic Community of Bosnia-Herzegovina was in the process of becoming another Yugoslav "national church," dedicated, like the Christian churches of Serbia and Croatia, to the making of ethnic nations.

Figure 1. Saint Sava's Memorial Orthodox Church in Belgrade. Symbol of Serbia's national renaissance, one of the largest Byzantine churches in the world, under construction in 1991. PHOTO BY DUŠAN MITIĆ. PHOTO ARCHIVE *NEDJELJNA DALMACIJA*.

Figure 2. Rebuilding of places of worship under communism: the grand mosque in Zagreb, Croatia, opened in 1987. *FERAL TRIBUNE* PHOTO ARCHIVE. COURTESY OF ZORAN MANDIĆ.

Figure 3. Rebuilding of places of worship in postcommunism. The Catholic cathedral in Zagreb, Croatia, the site of the first commemoration of Cardinal Stepinac, under reconstruction in 1998. *FERAL TRIBUNE* PHOTO ARCHIVE. COURTESY OF ZORAN MANDIĆ.

Figure 4. (*left*) Archbishop Metropolitan of Zagreb Franjo Cardinal Kuharić (standing below). In the 1970s, Kuharić was the first church leader to publicly commemorate the anticommunist prelate Cardinal Alojzije Stepinac. FERAL TRIBUNE PHOTO ARCHIVE. COURTESY OF ZORAN MANDIĆ.

Figure 5. (*below*) The author interviews Bishop of Mostar Monsignor Pave Žanić in the diocesan office in Mostar, Herzegovina, in 1991. The themes include the Medjugorje miracle and pre-war crisis in former Yugoslavia. AUTHOR'S ARCHIVE.

Figure 6. A scene from Marija Bistrica near Zagreb, central Marian shrine in Croatia where the final ceremony of the jubilee "Thirteen Centuries of Christianity in the Croat People" took place in September 1984. Note that vendors offer religious paraphernalia and Croation national symbols. PHOTOGRAPH BY NIKSA ANTONINI. PHOTO ARCHIVE *NEDJELJNA DALMACIJA*. COURTESY OF DRAŽEN GUDIĆ.

Figure 7. Pope John Paul II is greeted by a crowd in Zagreb during the second papal visit to Croatia in October 1998. PHOTO ARCHIVE *NEDJELJNA DALMACIJA*. COURTESY OF DRAŽEN GUDIĆ.

Figure 8. Medjugorje, Bosnia and Herzegovina, where, allegedly, the Virgin Mary has been visiting several seers since June 1981 to deliver messages to the world. A scene from the Seventh World Youth Prayer Meeting held in June 1996. PHOTO ARCHIVE *NEDJELJNA DALMACIJA*. COURTESY OF DRAŽEN GUDIĆ.

Figure 9. Visitors in the 1980s gather at the memorial site near Jasenovac in northern Croatia. During World War II, Jasenovac was the largest concentration camp run by Croatian native fascists the Ustaše. The flower-shaped concrete monument was designed by the Belgrade architect Bogdan Bogdanović and installed at the site near the memorial museum dedicated to the victims of the concentration camp in the 1960s by the Tito regime. The monumental concrete flower at Jasenovac was one of the major memorials to Yugoslav World War II antifascist resistance and symbol of the communist-era multiethnic patriotic ideology of brotherhood and unity. PHOTO ARCHIVE *NEDJELJNA DALMACIJA*. COURTESY OF DRAŽEN GUDIĆ.

Figure 10. Jakub Selimoski, Muslim from Macedonia, was the first democratically elected and last supreme religious authority, *Reis ul ulema*, of the united Islamic Community in the Socialist Federal Republic of Yugoslavia. Selimoski supported Yugoslav unity and was removed from his post in 1992 by the militant Muslim nationalist faction led by Alija Izetbegović. PHOTO BY BOZIDAR VUKICEVIC. PHOTO ARCHIVE *NEDJELJNA DALMACIJA*. COURTESY OF DRAŽEN GUDIĆ.

Figure 11. During the Bosnian War of 1992–1995, Archbishop of Sarajevo Vinko Puljić became the youngest cardinal in the Catholic Church thanks to his support for a united Bosnia-Herzegovina and multi-ethnic cooperation. In the second half of the 1990s, Cardinal Puljić lost faith in the international community and feasibility of a Bosnian multi-ethnic nation-state and turned into a champion of Croatian separatism. PHOTO BY MARIO TODORIC. PHOTO ARCHIVE *NEDJELJNA DALMACIJA*. COURTESY OF DRAŽEN GUDIĆ.

Figure 12. Metropolitan of Zagreb-Ljubljana and all Italy Jovan (Pavlović) was the supreme authority of the Serbian Orthodox Church in Croatia and a member of the Holy Synod of the Serbian Orthodox Church for most of the pre-war and wartime period in Yugoslavia. In the summer of 1995, as the Croation Army re-conquered the Serbian enclave of Krajina, Metropolitan Jovan led an exodus of Serbian clergy and two hundred thousand Serbs from Croatia only to return and restore church life in 1998. PHOTO BY MILIVOJ KEBER. PHOTO ARCHIVE *NEDJELJNA DALMACIJA*. COURTESY OF DRAŽEN GUDIĆ.

6

UNITED WE STAND, DIVIDED WE FALL

The Civil Religion of Brotherhood and Unity

Nations are held together largely by force and by emotion.
Reinhold Niebuhr

The art of government is the organization of idolatry.
George Bernard Shaw

The president of the Socialist Federal Republic of Yugoslavia and chairman of the League of Communists of Yugoslavia, Marshall Josip Broz Tito, celebrated New Year's Day 1980 in the company of close aides at the Kardjordjevo hunting lodge on the Croatian-Serbian border. Three days later Tito was admitted to the hospital in the capital of Slovenia, Ljubljana, where he had to undergo a difficult surgery (leg amputation). Tito died on 4 May 1980. During the last four months of Tito's life, the Ljubljana Clinical Center received thousands of letters for him from his fellow Yugoslavs. According to a volume released right after Tito's death, state and party organs and firms dutifully wrote to the president, but the warmest letters came from ordinary people, particularly from members of ethnic minorities. "Most esteemed and dear President," reads a letter signed by "two retired women from Kosovo, the Turk Zehra and Albanian Ćeba Redžepagu," and goes on: "blessed are you who live in the hearts of the people of our country, because we are all worried about your health, and we wish, if it were possible, to make you immortal. But your deeds will live forever."[1] Other letters also mirror the vox populi, being written in a similar frank manner and emotional tone, for example: "Dear Comrade Tito: I and my 45-member-strong family wish you a quick recovery and long life," Rahim Hodža, Belanica village, county of Suva Reka, Kosovo.[2] "Our Dear Comrade Tito: Today on Friday, 25 January 1980, as we gathered for our weekly worship; you

89

are with us in our thoughts and prayers. We beg the Almighty Allah to give you the strength to conquer your illness as you used to overpower your enemies. Members of the Ustikotlina *džemat* (parish) of the Islamic Community, Bosnia and Herzegovina."[3] May God bless you and care for you for the benefit of all of us, our dear comrade Tito," from men and women villagers of Uzdolje, Knin, Croatia.[4] From Zvonimir Jović, priest-poet from Donji Stajevci, Serbia:

> Mister President: your illness has befallen you when you are needed more than ever to lead the struggle for a brighter socialist future, for better human relations in our socialist community unrivaled in the whole world, and for better relations among nations of the world. You, most esteemed Mr. President, were among the founders of the movement of nonaligned countries working together with the late Nehru of India, Nasser of Egypt and His Beatitude Archbishop Makarios president of Cyprus, who had done tremendous efforts for peace in the world and made possible that this Balkan powder keg never explodes again. All our people wish that you, Mr. President, get well soon. With kindest regards I salute you on behalf of the people of Gornje Plinje where I serve as a priest.[5]

"Dear Comrade Tito: I wish that you get well soon. I wish that you live long and endure so long as our bridge on the Drina," Meho Hurem, Višegrad, Bosnia.[6] "Today is Friday, day of worship and prayer in our tekija. By the dervish prayer, we implore God to give you quick and successful recovery from illness. All dervishes from Yugoslavia are today with us in a prayer for you. Get well soon and get back to your mission of peace. We all need you for a long, long time, our beloved comrade Tito. Always with you," Sanja ul Mesajih Nadži Sejn Džemali, Prizren, Kosovo.[7] "I want to know the date of birth of your doctor, dear comrade Tito, to bake him for his birthday a big beautiful cake," Adem Elezi, pastry-shop owner, Jadranovo, Croatia.[8] "Dear President: The Roma Society of Obrenovac, and all Roma people, wish you recovery from your illness soon and we hope you will lead us again. The Association of the Roma People, Obrenovac, Serbia."[9] "Tito, my son! I saw you this morning at 7:30 on TV. You were sitting on your hospital bed with your two son warriors. I am a 74-year-old woman, my legs are paralyzed and I've been tied to bed for 13 years now. I see you, and I am waving to you with tears in my eyes. You can't see me but I see you and I say: long live justice, how fortunate we have been for having you! Here I enclose the holy picture of your mother's namesake, Maria, Our Gospa, Mother of God, to help you during your grievous illness. I, a sick old woman, wish you a long and healthy life," Djove, Split, Croatia.[10] "We pray for your health and may God help you in your service for our people and our beautiful country, those are wishes of our community the Church of Evangelical Christians, Yours, Milka Panić," Valjevo, Serbia.[11] "Dear Comrade Tito: We, Slovaks, employees of 'Zvezda' supermarket no. 8 in Kisać, love you and respect you so much that we cannot describe."[12] "Dear Tito: we are proud to be Yugoslavs and have you as our leader." Nada Mitevska and the family, Skopje, Macedonia.[13] "Dear Tito, two young people in love wish you a quick recovery from illness," Svetlana and Bata, Belgrade.[14]

Yugoslavia's Swan Song, 1980–1984

On Sunday, 4 May 1980, in Split, the national league's soccer game between archrivals the Croatian *Hajduk* and the Serbian *Crvena Zvezda* was interrupted early in the second half. When loudspeakers announced the news of Tito's death, the players, referees, stadium crew, policemen, and 50,000 spectators burst into tears. The crowd chanted: "Comrade Tito, we pledge to you that we will never stray from your path." Only a year earlier, Tito had been there, at the opening of the Eighth Mediterranean Sport Games. Official commemoration and funeral ceremonies were held at Belgrade on 5–8 May 1980. Belgrade welcomed 209 delegations from 127 countries. The delegations included 38 heads of states, 10 premiers, 7 vice-presidents, 6 presidents of parliaments, 12 foreign ministers, 2 kings, and 5 princes.[15] A hundred and sixty reporters and 58 television networks from 42 countries provided the news coverage of the funeral ceremonies.[16] From 4–8 May 7,768 prominent citizens and state officials held vigils by Tito's bier in the antechamber of the Federal Assembly at Belgrade, and five hundred thousand people made pilgrimages to the capital city.[17]

Yugoslav newspapers published statements by and interviews with foreign leaders, politicians, diplomats, and delegates of liberation movements who portrayed Tito as one of the greatest statesmen of the twentieth century. Tito's nonaligned friends, such as the prime minister of India, Indira Gandhi, President Kenneth Kaunda of Zambia, and other Third World leaders were favored by the domestic media, as if to suggest that a country with so many friends had little to worry about. The regime launched a slogan: "And after Tito, there will be Tito!" A discourse of eternity and continuity was echoed in the media. Poet Velimir Milošević echoed the "mood of eternity" in the following verses:

> If Heaven exists, he flew up there to bring us stars
> If eternity exists, then he met with it, on his way to the sun.
> The people, down here, await the eternal wanderer who
> went to the future to see what is going to happen with his people.[18]

Tito's burial place and mausoleum, officially called the 25 May Memorial Complex, was labeled in the press the "eternal house of flowers." There, according to Tito's last wish, "people will come to rest and children will play."[19] Tito was laid to rest on 8 May (i.e., on V-E Day and the thirty-fifth anniversary of the end of World War II in Europe) in the "house of flowers." The white marble tomb bore no symbols but the name and dates of birth and death. A Yugoslav journalist at the scene wrote: "Tito is gone but his Yugoslavia remains. She is eternal."[20]

The ensuing years seemed to corroborate the optimistic prophecy. Yugoslav pride soared when in February 1984, the capital city of Bosnia-Herzegovina, Sarajevo, hosted the Fourteenth Winter Olympic Games, the first Olympics held in Eastern Europe. In the same year, Belgrade was recognized as a prospective candidate for the 1992 Summer Olympics (eventually be held in Barcelona, Spain). No other phenomenon better symbolized the pride, elan, and relative prosperity of Tito's Yugoslavia than internationally recognized Yugoslav sports. The Sarajevo Olympics came as an international recognition of Yugoslavia's success as a nation and an award for its sports development. The globally televised opening ceremony of the Olympiad on 8 February was spectacular. At the Sarajevo Koševo Stadium, thousands of performers took part in the artistic program. The Sarajevo Olympics hosted 49 countries with 2,500 athletes and officials, 7,283 reporters and media people, and 12,500 invited guests. The host country employed 30,000 people with the organization committee and the Games' services. All employees and retirees in the country donated 2.5 percent of their incomes for more than four years for the Games. In addition, 1.5 million people made special donations for the construction of Olympic facilities. Construction firms with experts and workers from all Yugoslav republics built 167 main facilities and 400 accessory building for the Games. The country, caught up in a galloping economic crisis (the number of unemployed persons neared a million in 1983), bore an enormous financial burden. "When Sarajevo was selected ahead of Sapporo or Gothenburg," a Western sport historian would later write, "even the host's organizing committee was surprised; nevertheless, 1984 saw the Winter Games held in the Balkans for the first time . . . after the Olympic torch had been carried through Yugoslavia by 1,600 relay runners, the Olympic flame was lit by the figure skater Sanda Dubravčić in Sarajevo's Olympic Stadium."[21]

According to some assessments, two billion people watched the television broadcast of the opening ceremony. The spectacle, designed by the Olympic Organization Committee under the chairmanship of the Bosnian politician Branko Mikulić, put on parade Yugoslavia's diversity, folklore, youth, energy, and optimism. The Olympic Organization Committee pointed out in a welcoming message to athletes and guests that the Fourteenth Winter Olympic Games had come to this city and this country to reassure the world that the Balkans, Yugoslavia, and Sarajevo were no longer what used to be viewed as a "powder keg" and zone of conflict.[22]

A monograph published that year in Sarajevo by the Olympic Organization Committee cited greetings, letters, and telegrams received from foreign viewers and visitors. Most of the letters came from the United States of America, which was warming up for the upcoming Summer Olympics in

Los Angeles and the ensuing Winter Olympics at Lake Placid, New York. In one letter, Jonnie Mundt from Dallas, Texas, exclaimed: "the wonderful people of Sarajevo worked together and showed a fascinating talent, creativity, honesty and self-sacrifice. . . . Your people gave to the world such a wonderful example of peaceful cooperation."[23] Laureen Ruffner, from Las Vegas, wrote as follows: "Nothing in the world is so badly needed as mutual understanding and cooperation among different peoples; your country is the best example in the world! Americans can learn a lot about the special spirit and compassion of the Yugoslav peoples. I was touched by the sincere togetherness and warmth of the Yugoslav people."[24]

"You have shown to the world that peace and cooperation among all peoples are possible," wrote Charles C. Dierks when he returned from the Balkans to his native Hemet, California, and added: "thank you for the most beautiful Olympic spectacle I have ever seen. Your wonderful children look so healthy; may the good Lord bless you all!" Jack and Agnes Mudry from Grand Junction, Colorado, dedicated to the host country of the Fourteenth Winter Olympic Games the following piece of poetry:

> Oh amazing Yugoslavia, country of many nationalities,
> United in a magnificent single whole,
> Full of beauty, customs, folklore and taste
> Your children are wonderful, your men are courageous
> Let the wonderful Yugoslavia live forever![25]

The Yugoslav press boasted that the Sarajevo Olympics was the world's reward to Yugoslavia as a factor of stability in international relations and honored its success in international sports. The host city of Sarajevo, with its domes, crosses, synagogues, and minarets, epitomized the Olympic ideal of peace and cooperation in the world. The host country took the opportunity to show the world a new kind of socialism different from the Soviet model. For example, the Olympic Organization Committee provided halls for prayer and worship in the Sarajevo Olympic village. The Committee chairman, Branko Mikulić, held meetings with religious officials to discuss how to improve spiritual services for guests and athletes. Even though Mikulić was a "liberal communist" in economic matters, he showed no compromise over the issue of a multiparty system in Yugoslavia. At the 7 February 1984 press conference, a Western journalist, having declared that Yugoslavia seemed more democratic than other communist countries, asked Mikulić why the League of Communists still hesitated to allow the multiparty system. The Yugoslav leader replied:

> If we allow [a] multiparty system in this country, all . . . the people would get would be several new ethnic and religious parties without any specific political or economic agenda and issues except hatred for one another and their leaders' cries for partitions and secessions. We would have another Lebanon in this country, and the League of Communists of Yugoslavia will never let it happen![26]

At the Sarajevo Olympic Games, even the otherwise mediocre Yugoslav ski team, propelled by national pride, managed to win an Olympic medal. Yugoslav pride also energized other more competitive Yugoslav sports. Before and after Tito, Yugoslav sports in international competition was the source of national pride and cohesion. The national team (*reprezentacija*) was an efficient instrument of official nationalism. The *reprezentacija* epitomized the patriotic idea of brotherhood and unity and brought the idea into action before a large popular audience. The victories of the multiethnic national team testified to the strength in unity among diverse groups in the multinational federation.[27] The communist founders of the second Yugoslav state appreciated sports as an effective political tool. As early as during the Partisan resistance in World War II, the movement's communist leaders had put sports in the service of the liberation struggle, nation-making, and communist revolution. Members of the soccer team "RŠK Split" from Split, Croatia, were among the first martyrs ("people's heroes") captured after a battle with the Italians and Ustašas and executed in the summer of 1941. In 1942, an "Olympiad" was held in Foča, in eastern Bosnia. In the summer of 1944, soccer and water polo teams representing the People's Liberation Army of Yugoslavia played international games against British and U.S. teams in Italy. In August 1944 in Rome, a British military newspaper praised the water polo skills shown by "Marshall Tito's Dolphins."[28] After 1945, The communist regime in Tito's Yugoslavia encouraged a rapid development of all sports. The national team, sponsored by the federation, had a special place in the Yugoslav system. As a Croatian basketball coach put it, the state forged a "cult of the national team" that mirrored the nation's pride and diversity.[29]

According to the records of the Yugoslav government sports association, in the year of Tito's death, the Yugoslav national team won 93 world or European trophies (gold, silver, or bronze medals, that is, winning one of three first places in official international competition) and 105 trophies in 1981. In 1982, 175 Yugoslav athletes from 54 Yugoslav cities and from all of the Yugoslav republics and autonomous provinces, competing as members of the national team in official international competition in 22 sport disciplines, won 70 trophies worldwide; in the same year Yugoslav athletes won seven gold medals in world championships with 11 first places in European contests: Yugoslavia was ranked, according to the total output in international competition, tenth in the world.[30] In the Olympic year 1984, the Yugoslav national team won a total of 88 international trophies, including 24 first places, and was ranked third in total number of medals won in world championships.[31]

Civil Religion in a Communist Country

After World War II, a new sizable South Slav nation-state was forged in southeastern Europe. The keystone of the new Yugoslav nationalism was the concept of "brotherhood and unity." The new nationalism was combined with the Tito cult, the myth of the Pan-Yugoslav antifascist struggle during World War II, the victory over Soviet hegemony, the Yugoslav model of socialism, and the country's nonaligned foreign policy. Yugoslav communists sought legitimacy as guardians of ethnic harmony to which the only alternative seemed to be a civil war and genocide. No nation-state is just a state (i.e., bureaucracy or state apparatus plus "people") and it cannot be made and maintained by force alone. Nations are held together largely by force and by emotion, wrote Reinhold Niebuhr.[32] Accordingly, nationalism means both the method of nation-construction and the human emotion that bind the individual with the collective in point. All successful nation-states developed vital and meaningful civil religions. Civil religion is an alloy of myths, quasi-religious symbols, cults, rituals, beliefs, and practices that secure the nation's legitimacy and convince the people that the system is "good." Typically, civil religions entail a myth-narrative about the national origin, usually through struggle and martyrdom; cults of "founding fathers," liberators and heroes; a sense of "exceptionalism," and success, victory, or redemption.[33] Monuments, patriotic rituals, commemorations, and the often-forgotten phenomenon of sports fuel civil religions as living a spiritual force.[34]

The Yugoslav civil religion of brotherhood and unity consisted of the following main components. First, the myths of the nation's origin during the World War II Partisan struggle (1941–45) and the rebirth of the nation after the anti-stalinist Cominform affair (or the Tito-Stalin split of 1948). Second, brotherhood and unity of all ethnic groups and minorities, that is, the "Yugoslav spirit," as one of core values. Third, the cult of Josip Broz Tito as the nation's founding father, war hero, and successful world statesman. The peculiar patriotic quasi-sporting ritual "Tito's Relay," or the "Youth Relay," could be viewed as part of the Tito cult. Fourth, the foreign policy of nonalignment and the Yugoslav model of socialism (self-management or *samoupravljanje*). Finally, an important role in the new patriotic system was given to Yugoslav sports particularly the national team of Yugoslavia (*reprezentacija Jugoslavije*). I will be briefly describe some of these components hereafter.

The Myth of the Nation's Origin: Yugoslav Victories over Hitler and Stalin

The Anti-Fascist People's Liberation Struggle, or the Yugoslav Partisan war, was a European World War II resistance movement. In contrast to the communist wings of other European resistance movements, which remained relatively small factions, the Communist Party of Yugoslavia was able to mobilize millions of people as combatants or supporters of the movement.

In Yugoslavia, wrote C. L. Sulzberger, "Tito's partisans had created history's most effective guerilla army."[35] This antifascist "popular front" became a base for nation-formation and the communist revolution. Yet, prior to 1945, the Partisan movement's appeal was not excessively Marxist and communist. As Tito's top commissar Djilas testifies, Partisan leaders promised to each of the major Yugoslav ethnic nations, and even to those previously unrecognized as nations, a state of its own.[36]

In the Moscow Declaration of 1955, the Soviet Union officially admitted that the Yugoslavs had defeated fascism largely through their own efforts. In a similar vein, some post–Cold War accounts acknowledged that the Yugoslav Partisan war was not a communist myth but one of the most massive and successful World War II resistance movements.[37] The Balkan forests and mountains provided a setting favorable of guerilla warfare, but this alone would not have sufficed for both the successful military resistance and the Pan-Yugoslav nationalist-later-turned-communist revolution. The Allies recognized the qualities of Tito's movement as early as 1943, and, after the Cold War, Western military literature as well as college history textbooks acknowledged Tito's resistance as one of the most successful local movements in World War II.[38]

The struggle of the Partisans was a pan-Yugoslav popular nationalist liberation movement. The anti-Fascist People's Liberation Struggle was successful militarily and politically. As military force it started with 40,000 in 1941, of these most were members of the Communist Party and Communist Youth. In the summer of 1944, the former guerilla Partisans had 39 divisions, a navy, and an air force, with a total of 350,000 combatants, and in May 1945 there were 800,000 troops organized in four armies and 52 divisions.[39] In the People's Liberation Struggle, 305,000 fighters lost their lives and 425,000 were wounded.[40] The Communist Party of Yugoslavia lost 50,000 members in combat. Three-fourths of the prewar cadres were killed, as were over half of those admitted to the Party during the war.[41] The communists led charges and were expected to sacrifice their lives. In a bizarre note from his memoirs, Tito's one-time close aide Milovan Djilas wrote that the communists believed that God was one their side—Djilas allegedly experienced a religious vision of Jesus Christ, whom Djilas considered a protocommunist.[42]

The movement's political success was exemplified in the building of a broad antifascist coalition, or "Popular Front." From 1942 to 1944, the country was covered with a web of "People's Liberation Committees," the organs of government of the emerging Yugoslav federation, founded at Jajce in central Bosnia on 29 November 1943. These committees included a number of noncommunists and relatively large numbers of women. In 1944 in Dalmatia alone, 965 women were active in military and civilian service with the People's Liberation Committees.[43] Finally, ethnic minorities (e.g., Jews, Slovaks, Czechs, Ukrainians, Poles, Italians, Magyars, Roma, Turks, Albanians, and others) were also represented in Partisan ranks. More than 2,000

Yugoslav Jews fought in Tito's Partisan Army.[44] At any rate, the success of the Partisan political and military movement would have not been possible without broad popular support (of course, the support from the Allies must not be neglected). Yet it took many civilians, towns, and villages to feed such a massive military force, assist the wounded, maintain channels of communication, and provide other forms of support. It was not only Tito and several thousand communists who won the war but the Yugoslav people.

After the communist consolidation of power and the launching of the revolution, the Partisan War became the founding myth and energizer of the new nationalism. The new myth legitimatized communist rule. The Yugoslav people en masse took part in the worship of the new nation. According to Dedijer, more than 40,000 pieces of folk poetry were inspired by the People's Liberation Struggle.[45] The new civil religion established its shrines and memorial sites commemorating battles and sites of martyrdom from World War II, such as Sutjeska and Neretva-Jablanica (sites large-scale battles between the Partisans and Germans and their domestic allies); Kozara, Igman, and Romanija; Jajce (the birthplace of the Republic); Drvar (Tito's base, attacked by German paratroopers in 1944); Užice (the first larger town captured by the Partisans in 1941); Šumarice (a hill in the Serbian town of Kragujevac where the Germans executed 7,000 civilians in retaliation for Partisan attacks), Jasenovac, and so forth. Statues of Tito and heroes of the Partisan war were ubiquitous. Almost every town and village had a memorial to the People's Liberation Struggle. An order of "national saints" of sorts was inaugurated under the name "people's heroes" (narodni heroji). Tito was awarded the Order of the "People's Hero" three times. As with saint-making and commemorations of martyrdom in religious organizations, school curricula contained detailed descriptions of the enemy's methods of torture and atrocities against the civilian population. Many towns were named after Partisan heroes. Major state holidays were the Day of the (founding of the) Republic (29 November 1943) and the Day of the (Partisan) Uprising (4 July 1941). While official historiography, patriotic monuments and rituals, film, literature, and television commemorated Partisan casualties and people's heroes' martyrdom, no mention was made in public of victims of Partisan revenge and communist revolution. The term "domestic traitors" in reference to all enemies of the system became part of the country's official discourse, justifying revenge and implying that there were no innocent victims among the defeated. Nevertheless, massive Partisan executions during the war and the postwar destruction of "class enemies" and "domestic traitors" remained engraved in popular memory. Domestic clergy and antiregime emigre groups filled this void by commemorating the victims of the Tito system. Some of these groups followed the established pattern of mythmaking by magnifying the number of victims and portraying themselves as infallible. Consequently, while justification of revenge became a tenet of the civil religion of brotherhood and unity, the opposition also fostered lust for revenge against the communists and other rival groups.

The 1948 the Tito-Stalin split came as a second trial for the new nation and became its new founding myth. Stalin's pressure involved an economic blockade, terrorism, military threats, and a schism within the Communist Party of Yugoslavia. Tito fought Yugoslav Stalinists with Stalin's methods by incarcerating thousands of pro-Soviet communists at Naked Island concentration camp in the Adriatic.[46] Tito survived and even received recognition in the form of the Khrushchev's humiliating visit to Belgrade, on which occasion the Soviet leader extolled the Yugoslav autonomous antifascist struggle and gave Tito the green light to build his own model of socialism. The myth of the People's Liberation Struggle was fused with the new myth of Tito's victory over Stalin and the Cominform. Both victories were ascribed to the power of Yugoslav brotherhood and unity, that is, Yugoslav nationalism. In an interview, the American historian Arthur M. Schlesinger, Jr., argued that Tito owed his triumph over Stalin to the fact that nationalism is a more powerful emotion than that of class consciousness and proletarian solidarity, to which Stalin had appealed.[47]

Jaroslav Krejči and Vitezslav Velimsky argued in a 1981 study on European nationalism that the "Yugoslav defiance of Soviet aspirations for incontestable leadership in the 'Socialist' bloc is her most unifying factor."[48] While Eastern European Slavs remained under the humiliating Soviet yoke, the Yugoslavs, as Drago Jančar wrote, "were more free and better off, only in comparison with the Poles, Czechs, Rumanians, Magyars, Bulgarians. Yugoslavs looked at them with a mixture of pride, contempt, and compassion.[49] In reality, life in Yugoslavia in the 1960s and 1970s was much better than the Slovene author Jančar was prepared to admit. A brief look at destinations of Yugoslavs' private foreign travel, spanning from Hawaii to Bali via New York with routine "weekend shopping trips" to northern Italy and Austria, shows that the Yugoslavs could match western Europeans while Easterners could not even fit the comparison.

Yugoslav "national communists" sought to discover a system that would be different from Stalinism and Leninism but still Marxist and socialist. Djilas believed that such an ideal system would be democratic socialism as it existed in Sweden and elsewhere in western Europe. Yet Tito's Slovene confidante Edvard Kardelj prevailed, developing a loose, "decentralized" federation and workers' self-management, inspired by nineteenth-century socialism, liberalism, and anarchism. At the same time, Tito's own focus remained unchanged: the resolution of the Yugoslav National Question in a strong and stable nation-state. Consequently Titoism became a remarkable nationalism, competing at the same time with "socialist nations" and with domestic ethnic nationalisms. Tito's nation was the first overtly nationalistic independent communist regime in Europe, or perhaps in the world (because at the time China still recognized Soviet primacy). As Emil Lengyel insightfully observed in his 1969 study *Nationalism—The Last Stage of Communism*, Yugoslavia, "a nation of many nations," was the place "where the Heresy Began."[50]

Self-Management and Nonalignment

In the 1950s, the Tito regime abandoned the communist "command economy." The party denounced economic statism (in the official jargon: *etatism*), and the economy was restructured, based on enterprises that were more or less autonomous from the state and party. These enterprises were managed by "workers' councils" and autonomous (often too independent and uncontrollable) executive directors. Many Yugoslav firms, but not all, of course, became profitable and intentionally successful. This "Yugoslav experiment," that is, businesses run as cooperatives in which employees shared profit and took part in the management, was not, again, the invention of Marxism-Leninism. After Western democratic socialists such as Robert Owen and Charles Fourier, this economic model was advocated by the liberal John Stuart Mill.[51]

Furthermore, after getting rid of the Soviets, Tito quickly moved from being a survivor to being a world statesman. Having been luckily expelled from the Soviet camp, Yugoslavia was among the founders of the world movement of nonaligned countries. In the 1950s, Tito built personal friendship with independent nationalist leaders such as Nasser of Egypt and India's premier, Jawarharlal Nehru. The "big three" of the Third World, soon joined by independent leaders of Africa and Asia (while most of the South American opposition still preferred the Soviets as role models), organized an efficient lobby in the United Nations General Assembly. The nonaligned movement, as Henry Kissinger called it, took advantage of the Cold War rivalry between the superpowers and learned how to play them off against one another.[52] Egypt's Anwar el-Sadat testified that Tito, for whom Third World leaders felt "gratitude and loyalty" (as a senior and most experienced leader who was willing to give counsel and support even in for him risky situations), was acknowledged as first among equals in the organization of nonaligned countries.[53]

For Yugoslavia, nonalignment was not only an efficient foreign policy but also had a strong reinforcement of the new national identity and a boost to Yugoslav pride. Nonalignment and "socialist self-management," along with the civil religion of brotherhood and unity, became pillars of the new nation. These three pillars facilitated one of the crucial components of every nationalism: the nation's sense of "exceptionalism." In contrast to both local ethnic myths and Soviet satellite states in Eastern Europe that could not restore national pride despite communist efforts to appropriate rich traditions, Yugoslav pride in the Tito era was real and was recognized by other nations.

The Myth of Brotherhood and Unity

The main tenet of the new patriotic ideology was the idea of "brotherhood and unity" (*bratstvo i jedinstvo*). This idea bound together Serbs, Croats, Slovenes, Muslims, Montenegrins, and Macedonians, recognized as ethnically distinct groups, and overcame their differences in language and dialect, religion, customs, mentality, and so forth. Tito's nation did not inaugurate a new supranational "Yugoslav" nationality (although an unofficial Yugoslav-by-nationality group did emerge in the 1970s—see hereafter). Tito's Communist Party of Yugoslavia was anti–Great Serbian and therefore against any unitarian and "melting pot" approach to the national question. The new national consciousness did not generate a new "national identity." The new "Yugoslavism" entailed the idea of the necessity as well as fruitfulness of "fraternal" relations among several distinct groups. In contrast to the Yugoslav kingdom's ideology of "popular unity" (*narodno jedinstvo*), which had aimed at fusing several distinct nations into a single Serbian-dominated supernation, Tito and the communists emphasized the diversity and distinctiveness of the nation's ethnic groups but taught the people, through patriotic education and rituals, that unity means freedom, pride, and prosperity as opposed to ethnic strife, which brings all groups back into poverty and humiliation. This kind of "national consciousness" (i.e., the ideology of brotherhood and unity) basically made people conscious that disunity and partition would be an insane, tragic blunder, among other things, because the country's core could not be partitioned without a genocide, as the World War II experience had taught the people.

According to testimony by the American diplomat Averell Harriman, Tito "firmly believed that the nation would remain united after him, because every constituent nation of Yugoslavia has its own identity and distinct national spirit, but there is also a "Yugoslav" spirit or soul emanating from brotherhood and unity."[54] In his 20 June 1978 address to the Eleventh Congress of the League of Communists of Yugoslavia, Tito expounded what constitutes the strength of Yugoslavia (*snaga Jugoslavije*). The first point was, in Tito's words, "the unity of Yugoslavia's nations and nationalities built on the consciousness that this unity, in this world as it is, is the precondition of not only our prosperity but of our very survival."[55]

Brotherhood and unity became the nation's civil religion. The idea of brotherhood and unity was conceived as a counterweight to ethnic nationalisms that tore the country apart, incited hatred, and caused bloody massacres while at the same time perpetuating people's misery and foreign hegemony. As brotherhood and unity was sanctioned by the state as the highest patriotic value, the communists declared that the complex Yugoslav National Question had been solved once and for all. "From an ethical viewpoint," Vladimir Dedijer wrote,

the brotherhood and unity idea gave a profoundly humane element to Tito's political program. In contrast to hatred (rooted in nationalist manipulations with ethnicity and religion), Tito urged love among all Yugoslav peoples. . . . We have eradicated hatred, turned it into dust and ashes, we have eliminated the chauvinism incited and spread among our peoples by various antipeople's elements who have exploited the sensitive nationality problem whenever it suited them.[56]

The most famous quotation from Tito's speeches on brotherhood and unity was the "apple of the eye" analogy. ("You must keep brotherhood and unity as the apple of your eye!") To keep something as an apple of the eye was a popular adage in use by all Slavic peoples. The metaphor entered the political discourse of the Left in the 1930s and probably came from Russia. Both this metaphor and the phrase "brotherhood and unity," which Tito made a keystone of Yugoslav patriotism, are ordinarily used by Orthodox priests in liturgy and daily discourse.[57]

Without popular patriotic commitment, that is, faith in brotherhood and unity and the "Yugoslav spirit," espoused by a large number of the people, the loose multiethnic Yugoslav federation of six republics might have not been possible. Tito's country was not kept together by force. The Western analyst Harold Lydall noted this, and argued in his monograph on Yugoslav socialism that "a major reason for communist success was the party's advocacy of 'brotherhood and unity.'" . . . The outcome has been that Yugoslavia is the most genuinely federalized country in the world (not excluding Switzerland).[58] By contrast, most Western observers espoused a "realist" perspective on Yugoslav unity as maintained by the Party and Tito through force and manipulation. Thus Sabrina Petra Ramet downplayed brotherhood and unity and concluded that the country was maintained as a balance-of-power system with a key role for Tito.[59]

The faith in brotherhood and unity even facilitated the development of a new nationality, the so-called Yugoslavs by nationality. Many people, for various reasons (the most common being interethnic marriages), refused to accept or did not feel comfortable with the traditional ethnic labels. After the 1960s, censuses allowed the option "Yugoslav by nationality." In 1981, in the aftermath of Tito's spectacular burial, the number of Yugoslavs by nationality reached an all-time record high of 1,216,463.[60] The largest number of these Yugoslavs was recorded by the census of 1991 in Bosnia-Herzegovina (5.5 percent of the population). According to a 1992 study, around 4.5 million persons were uncertain about their ethnic identities actually seeing themselves as Yugoslavs by nationality.[61]

The negative attitude of Yugoslavs by nationality toward the traditional Yugoslav mainstream religions was a response to the traditional conjunction between religious and ethnonational identities. According to several surveys of religiosity and nationality conducted in the late 1970s through the first half of the 1980s, the Yugoslavs by nationality despised both traditional identities, ethnic as well as religious, and opted for the Yugoslav label as a nationality, while declaring no religious affiliation.[62] A survey of religiosity in the Zagreb region completed in 1984 indicated that disapproval of traditional religiosity among Yugoslavs by nationality was striking: 55.2 percent declared no religious affiliation; 45.2 percent declared themselves atheists;

88.8 percent never attended church, and 86.2 percent never prayed.[63] However, Yugoslavs by nationality declared a relatively greater affinity for attendance at official patriotic rituals (e.g., state holidays, the Youth Relay) and more interest in participating in various social activities than groups that showed relatively high commitment to traditional religiosity and church attendance (e.g., Croats).[64] In other words, these "ethnic Yugoslavs" were believers in the Yugoslav civil religion.[65] According to a 1986 survey of the values and orientations of Yugoslav Youth, Yugoslavs by nationality demonstrated the lowest degree of ethnocentrism and national exclusiveness, in contrast to ethnic Albanians, who manifested the relatively highest degree of ethnocentrism and national exclusiveness of all Yugoslav ethnic groups, as well as a high degree of traditional religious affiliation.[66] The survey director, Srdjan Vrcan, said that Yugoslavs by nationality were "the most secularized section of contemporary Yugoslav youth" and concluded that "it seems that the refusal to identify oneself in traditional national terms and the refusal to identify oneself religiously go hand in hand and mutually reinforce each other. It could be even argued that both arise from the same historical experience."[67]

Finally, although brotherhood and unity was not the same as the nineteenth-century ideology of Slavic brotherhood, it could be, at least hypothetically, perceived as a current in Pan-Slavism as, for instance, Titoist nationalism was identified by Hans Kohn.[68] Titoist Yugoslavism indeed manifested Pan-Slavic characteristics. In 1944, on the occasion of a soccer match between Tito's army and British troops on the isle of Vis in the Adriatic, the new Yugoslavia adopted as the nation's anthem a modified version of one of hallmarks of the nineteenth-century Pan-Slavism, the Slovak song "Ej Slovane" (Hey, Slavs!). The original hymn was written in 1834 by Samuel Tomašik and performed for the first time at the 1848 Pan-Slavic Congress at Prague. The hymn appeared in many versions (for awhile reflecting the growing Slav-Teuton strife, i.e., Slavo-German rivalry) and became, as the historian of Pan-Slavism Hans Kohn wrote, "a demonstrative assertion of Slav national vitality and eternity."[69] The hymn invokes a "Slavic spirit" (*duch Slovanski*). After the first phase of Pan-Slavism (and Slavo-German tensions), World War II, as Kohn pointed out, "gave a new impulse to the stalling Pan-Slavism," and this time again the old anti-Germanism was awakened.[70] After 1945, modified versions of "Ej Slovane" became national anthems of Poland and Yugoslavia, two Slavic nations that then shared the same communist system (but, as I showed in chapter 4, the anticommunist Catholic opposition in Yugoslavia and Poland was constructing an alternative, Polish-Croatian "brotherhood and unity" based on common Catholic faith and anticommunist ideology). After Tito's successful struggle with Stalin, Hans Kohn concluded in 1953, Titoism represented a shift toward the Western variant of Pan-Slavism, as opposed to the old Russian messianism and post–World War II Eastern Pan-Slavism that was revived by Stalin and advanced in the communist bloc of Eastern Europe under the aegis of the Soviet Union.[71]

The alloy of Pan-Slavism and the mythology of the Partisan war with brotherhood and unity as the country's civil religion created an effective nationalist ideology without repeating the flaws of the interwar kingdom that had sought to devise some kind of a new supranationality. The civil religion of brotherhood and unity was an important source of legitimacy for the communist regime. The system and the idea were inextricably linked. It was taken for granted that any struggle against communist rule in Yugoslavia would involve the destruction of brotherhood and unity, with the risk of another ethnic war.

The Tito Cult

According to Milovan Djilas, the apotheosis of Tito began spontaneously at the Second Session of the Anti-Fascist Council of the People's Liberation of Yugoslavia (AVNOJ) on 29 November 1943.[72] Dedijer has written that most of the thousands of pieces of patriotic poetry glorified Tito.[73] In 1970, the historian Franjo Tudjman wrote about the Tito worship as follows: "Only the people capable of being great in times of suffering and magnificent in combat; only the people who are terrible when they hate, but noble when they love and trust . . . could create such wonderful verses of honor, loyalty and love for man whom they embraced as their leader and symbol of national and revolutionary ideals."[74] In Yugoslav patriotic mythology, Tito was portrayed as a creator and savior ("if were not for you comrade Tito, we would not exist"), as a peacemaker who "abolished the religious hatred and united all Yugoslavs" and as a "defender of truth" whose power derived from the love of the people.[75]

Accounts by Tito's contemporaries and colleagues described him in terms such as "a contrast to other contemporary dictators," "more humane," "willing to experiment," "never taking ideology very seriously," "nonascetic," and a "practical politician with a Byzantine mind."[76] According to Djilas, Tito was an agnostic rather than an atheist, with a "sense of committing sin. . . . [He] had qualms of consciousness . . . a need for meditation and reflection . . . a sentiment of the tragic in human existence . . . [and] a doubt about the basic premises of materialist philosophy."[77] Anwar el-Sadat wrote that Tito possessed "qualities of world leadership . . . strength, self-assurance and courage" as well as personal charm and capability to build longtime and true friendship.[78] One of the most politically relevant traits of Tito's psyche, at least according to Dedijer, was an obsessive and deepseated fear that Serbs, Croats, Muslims and others would be killing each other again, that is, that the World War II genocidal massacres would be repeated. Otherwise a courageous and stable personality, Tito remained paranoid about this. Another fear was of assassination. Stalin masterminded numerous attempts on Tito's life,[79] as did exiled Balkan ethnic nationalists.

Tito's lifestyle earned him envy from many, especially from Soviet leaders who referred to him as the "communist emperor."[80] Tito was also compared with Franco of Spain rather than with Soviet leaders.[81] Royal palaces, a personal chef and physicians' council, fashionable suits and uniforms, luxury Mercedes cars, the befriending of kings, emperors, and movie stars, and hunting, yachting, and vacationing on private isles were some hallmarks of Titoism. The main symbols of this lifestyle were Tito's "private" isle of Vanga, full of exotic plants and animals, and his flamboyant yacht *Galeb* (Seagull), on which he sailed to Africa, Asia, and in the Mediterranean and on which he organized conferences and held meetings with world leaders.[82] According to Sadat's testimony, Tito believed that the Soviet system was not socialism except in name and other ideological phrases—socialism, in Tito's words, meant above all good life for the people, so he secured a better life for the Yugoslav peoples and he himself did not hide his luxuries as communist leaders routinely did.[83] Yet after his death, he bequested this property to the state rather than to his family.

From 1945 to 1990, Tito's image was ubiquitous. Every republic and autonomous province named a city after Tito. Every city and town had a boulevard, plaza, avenue, or school named after the Yugoslav president-for-life. During the erosion of the League of Communists of Yugoslavia and the decay of communist ideology in the 1980s, the Tito cult was still vital. In 1987, the Yugoslav Federal Assembly passed a special law for the protection of Tito's image and the use of his name.[84] In 1988 the Belgrade weekly *NIN* opened a panel about the new symbolism of the post–Titoist Yugoslavia. According to a public opinion poll presented to the panel, the most effective symbolic cohesive force of Yugoslavia was still the Tito cult.[85]

A Patriotic Ritual: Tito's Relay

Tito's Relay (*Titova štafeta*), or the Youth Relay, was a ritual of the Yugoslav civil religion that was closely associated with both Tito's cult and brotherhood and unity, combined with the construction of the new nation's image as youthful, colorful, and sportive. In 1945, according to Party archives, "the Alliance of Communist Youth set out to organize a sports event aimed at reaching out to all the young in the country and thereby to consolidate brotherhood and unity."[86] The event was conceived as a race through the whole of Yugoslavia. The runners carried a baton in which political organizations and institutions enclosed messages for Tito's birthday. In 1957, Tito proposed that Tito's Relay be renamed the Youth Relay. His birthday (25 May) became Youth Day, and the festival celebrated the nation's immortality and eternal youth.

Nonetheless, the new concept of a youth festival never superseded the original tribute to the charismatic leader. Thirty-sixth Youth Relay commenced on 23 March 1980 at Novi Sad, the capital of the Socialist Autonomous Province of Vojvodina. Traveling through every provincial and municipal center, the Youth Relay stopped on 25 April at the Clinical Hospital Center at Ljubljana, Slovenia, where Tito was concluding the relay of his life. The carriers of Tito's baton were not allowed in the patient's room. They sent flowers to Tito with a letter expressing assurances of commitment to the ideals of brotherhood and unity. On this occasion, the chairman of the Federal Conference of Socialist Youth, the Macedonian Vasil Tupurkovski, wrote: "each of the thirty-six batons went along Tito's path, for all paths of Yugoslavia are Tito's . . . that path will never change, for we are Tito's."[87]

Tito's baton did not end up in Tito's hands. On 7 May, the relay's last runner, Zoran Ostojić, laid the baton on Tito's bier in the antechamber of the Federal Assembly. The Federal Conference of Socialist Youth announced: "having heard the news of the death of Comrade Tito, the Presidency of the Federal Conference of the League of Socialist Youth of Yugoslavia decided that the Youth Relays—the symbol of love and loyalty toward Comrade Tito and his achievements, the symbol of the brotherhood and unity of the nations and nationalities of Yugoslavia—should be terminated."[88] Youth Day continued until 1987, when the organization of Socialist Youth of Slovenia demanded a profound change in the whole concept and eventually refused to participate, thus bringing the tradition to an end.

The last runner of the Youth Relay who delivered the baton of brotherhood and unity into Tito's living hands was the ethnic Albanian Sanije Hiseni, a student at the University of Priština (Kosovo). She pronounced the last brotherhood and unity pledge in the Albanian language. A year before, in 1978, the Youth Relay had commenced at the Trepča lead mine near the town of Kosovska Mitrovica (then called Titova Mitrovica), with the ethnic Albanian miner Rahim Mehmeti as the first runner. In sum, Tito's Relay was not a "Marxist" invention. Similar practices such as marathon races across the whole country or car and bike racing, moving from town to town thereby creating a sense of belonging to the nation have become traditions in many western countries.[89]

The Myth of the Yugoslav
Synergy: Was There
a Secret Link?

"A nation cannot be forged or changed," wrote Robert Bellah, "by rational politics alone, without the appeal to the nation's soul."[90] The making of the second Yugoslavia involved modernization of a backward society and harmonization of ethnic relations. This project could not work without a powerful irrational stimuli. The Yugoslav diversity harmonized through the civil religion of brotherhood and unity is the case in point. The idea of brotherhood and unity, forged by the communists during World War II, legitimized a multinational state and the Communist Party's status in power, but, most important, a new nation was born. In his accusation of Tito in 1948 of an excessive nationalism, Stalin was basically right. Later came the Yugoslav revision of Marxism-Leninism, and the Soviet-Chinese charges of "dangerous revisionism" were, again, from their point of view, justified.

In contrast to East European Soviet satellites, Tito's regime generated a legitimate government. The spirit of brotherhood and unity will live after Tito and after the demise of his country for as long as the pain, nostalgia, and pride live in individuals and the works of art and scholarship they created about Tito's country, even in cases when Tito (as basically a dictator unwilling to make faster and more radical changes) is accused of having contributed to the country's tragic fate. The young urban Yugoslav generation, devoted to Titoist, as opposed to ethnic, nationalism were without ethnic and religious prejudices and were convinced that diversity both constituted the source of progress and enriched society (see chapter 11). A popular tune of the 1980s, "There is some secret link, a secret link for all of us," performed by the popular rock band from Sarajevo, Bijelo Dugme, became this generation's anthem.[91] The "secret link" meant the love among diverse ethnic and religious groups and patriotic sentiments for the beloved country. The land and society of remarkable diversity and of "brotherly" unity among diverse individuals and groups and their spirits, habits, and cultures, as the Sarajevo singer-songwriter Davorin Popović would put it in one of his songs, "radiated the eternal glow." In a similar vein, a nostalgic writer asked rhetorically in a 2001 article what the source was of the "ecstasy" in the generation that, especially between the 1960s and 1980s, created outstanding achievements in art and scholarship, music, film, sports, and so forth.[92]

Anticommunists and ethnic nationalists will have to manufacture ethnic and religious hatred and start another civil war, among other things, in order to prove that the civil religion of brotherhood and unity never really existed except as an empty ideological slogan and sham that was an instrument in the communist monopoly of power. Ethnocentrists were presumably the most frustrated when they saw that the spirit of brotherhood and unity "worked" and that the multiethnic nation ruled by the communists seemed viable.[93] Yet, for example, the Croatian Catholic school of sociology of religion perceived the Yugoslav civil religion of brotherhood and unity as essentially the same kind of "political religion" that was created in the Soviet Union and in Mao's China.[94]

Internal critics and pro-Yugoslavs, especially after Tito's death, called for a reform of the Yugoslav civil religion. In the 1980 study inspired by the scholarship of Bertrand Russell, Glenn Vernon, and Robert Bellah, the Croatian sociologist Nikola Dugandžija expressed the hope that the coming period of democratization in Yugoslavia would involve "demystification" of the excessive forms of state-sponsored secular religiosity, concurrently with curbing similar excesses, myths, and exaggerations on the part of ethnic nationalists.[95] Many disillusioned Yugoslav communists who found an "exit" in becoming radical ethnic nationalists in the late 1960s and thereafter viewed the Titoist brotherhood and unity as a diabolic trap in which their respective ethnic nations got caught. One of those, the Croatian nationalist historian Franjo Tudjman, discovered behind Titoism the continuity of the same great Serbian nationalism that had tormented the first Yugoslav state. For the Serbian nationalist author Dobrica Ćosić, who, in 1989, published a novel with the telling title "The Believer," both Marxism and Titoism were false religions that stole the souls of millions of Serbs while their ethnic enemies, such as Albanians, Muslims, Croats, and others, benefited at the expense of the Serb capability to fight heroically and believe faithfully. An artistic account presented by the Sarajevo-born film director Emir Kusturica in his motion picture *Underground* (the winner of the "Golden Palm" at the 1995 Cannes Film Festival) also explores the question of true and false faiths, reality, myth, and deception within the Yugoslav historical context from 1941 to 1993. There is an interesting thesis in this motion picture, perhaps best epitomized in Goran Bregović's music and lyrics: "Something is shining from the Heavens but nobody really knows what it is." The "shining light" of Tito's Yugoslavia moved the people momentarily, but eventually, the mass disillusionment came when the people unmasked the deception, when they learned the truth about the world "above," about their leaders' real lives and character, and so forth. As one of Kusturica's characters, a German psychiatrist, puts it, "communism was an underground force, a large cellar," but, he went on to explain, sometimes it seems that the whole world might have been built on the dichotomy epitomized in a large underground cellar and the section above (the Earth's surface and Heaven), and many choose or are forced to live in this under-world.

At any rate, while forms of ideology, myth, and religion vary, they also produce various historical outcomes, which still does not help to "solve" the general question of "true and false faiths." Concerning the civil religion of the Yugoslav communist period, in spite of its defects and ultimate tragic failure, a blueprint for a viable multiethnic nation of considerable potential was outlined, and the civil religion of brotherhood and unity was its important building block. The Yugoslav "antifascist nationalism" and the civil religion of brotherhood and unity could have outlived communism. Neither of the two was in conflict with democracy. The mixed "market socialist" economy based on workers' cooperatives could have adjusted to the capitalism of the 1980s and 1990s more easily than Soviet-style regimes. The Tito cult, as an antifascist and anti-Stalinist movement and unifier of diverse and often adverse ethnic groups, could have survived and even been cele-

hatred + Genocide (fears - pg 104)

brated in the new Europe and postcommunist world.[96] Third World countries, as Sadat testified in his memoirs, held Tito and nonalignment in high regard.[97] At the home front, the Tito memory could have been a vibrant check against the danger of ethnic nationalism. Internationally competitive Yugoslav sports, another product of the Tito era, could have remained an effective cohesive force of the nation and source of national pride, as is the case in many countries worldwide.[98] Concurrently, Yugoslav sports operated as a safety-valve for mitigating intergroup tensions.[99] Of course, pan-Yugoslav nationalism, born during the Tito era, alone could not help the country to completely succeed. Yugoslavia should have been earlier and fully democratized. Yet was that possible?

Big question

7

MARY-MAKING IN HERZEGOVINA

From Apparitions to Partitions

order of Lady of bishops

As noted earlier, during the Great Novena (1975–84) the Croat episcopate carried out ethnic mobilization and religious awakening of Catholic Croats under the symbolic guidance of the Virgin Mary, referred to as the "Queen of the Croats." However, in June 1981, a *when* rival Croatian Virgin Mary appeared, seemingly, without the church au- *where* thorities' knowledge and approval. On 24 June 1981, six children from the *to whom* village of Medjugorje in western Herzegovina reported that they had en- countered a Croatian-speaking Madonna. They received divine messages *origin.* that were announced and translated into foreign languages by the local Franciscans. Within a few weeks, columns of pilgrims from the country and abroad swamped the area and set in motion what would become the longest series of Marian apparitions in the history of the Catholic Church.[2] The apparitions of the Virgin Mary in Herzegovina unfolded into a massive devotional movement that resembled such sporadical occurrences else- where in the Catholic world.[3] Almost as a rule, the histories of each of these movements show concurrent church-state or interfaith conflict and crisis in society.[4]

Before the apparitions of 1981, the toponym Medjugorje had been little known even in Yugoslavia. The region of western Herzegovina was over- whelmingly populated by Catholic Croats, with some Muslims and only a few Orthodox Serbs (a sizeable Orthodox community was decimated by the *why* Ustašas in World War II). Natives of the area, however, were better known in western Europe. Many had spent years in the jails of Germany, Austria, France, Italy, and other countries, where, as the Croat author Ivan Raos tells in the novel *Prosjaci i sinovi* (In a free translation: "Beggars & Sons, Inc."), they practiced their trade as professional beggars, black marketeers, and petty thieves. The local Franciscans were a mirror image of their flock. The area was a stronghold of militant Catholics, whose anger mounted during the ecclesiastical tensions in the 1930s (see chapter 1). In 1934, the Catholic

beotawd'n to chusch + clergy

Croats of the Čitluk-Medjugorje parish erected, in honor of the 1900th anniversary of the death of Jesus, a thirty-foot-high concrete cross on the
Križevac hill, less than a mile from the site of the 1981 apparitions. During
World War II, Catholics from the area filled the ranks of the Croat fascist
Ustaša. Many Ustaša leaders received education at the Franciscan monastery
at Široki Brijeg, not very far from Medjugorje. In February 1945, Široki Brijeg
was the site of a bitter battle between joint Ustaša-German forces fortified
in the monastery and the communist-led Partisan brigades. After taking
heavy casualties, the Partisans captured the stronghold and executed 12
clerics they found there. After 1945, 70 priests, monks, and relatives of
Ustaša leaders from western Herzegovina were sentenced to death.[5] Among
the executed, 67 were Franciscan monks, the most faithful Ustaša allies. The
surviving members of the Herzegovinian Franciscan Province of the Assumption of Mary, as one of them proudly reported to me in an interview,
served a total of 500 years in prison in the following decades.[6] In the midst
of the persecution, several apparitions of the Virgin Mary, followed by pilgrimages and crowding at apparitions sites, were reported in 1945 and 1946.
According to William Christian Jr., who carried out research on Marian
apparitions in European history, four visions were said to have taken place
at mass graves in the Catholic republics of Slovenia and Croatia where the
communists had executed their wartime opponents.[7]

The 1981 apparitions of the Virgin Mary at Medjugorje could best be
understood within the broader context of the struggle between the Roman
Catholic Church and communism in the twentieth century, as well as with
the context of the anticommunist backlash in Yugoslavia after the death of
Tito in May 1980. In addition, the Medjugorje "miracle" occurred in the
midst of a deep social and economic crisis[8] and growing ethnic tensions in
the country.

The Medjugorje "miracle" had drawn a massive following but also encountered bitter opposition. The oppositions came from the bishop of Mostar,
the regime, and the Serbian Orthodox Church. The bishop of Mostar, Monsignor Pave Žanić, was convinced that members of the Franciscan Province
of the Assumption, who had disobeyed the episcopal authority for over a
hundred years, had engineered the miracle in order to forestall the bishop's
plan for a redistribution of parishes in favor of diocesan clergy. The bishop's
initial assumption was that the child visionaries were either mentally ill or
hypnotized by the Franciscans or both. After an investigation that included
medical testing, no abnormalities in any of the visionaries could be found.
The visionaries underwent several rounds of subsequent testing, which also
included investigations of numerous healings reported by pilgrims to Medjugorje.[9] Meanwhile, both the bishop and the friars from Medjugorje were
interrogated by the local police in Mostar and brought to the headquarters
of the secret police in Sarajevo. Bishop Žanić, eager to discredit the Franciscans and heal once and for all the old sore in the Church, was happy for

the opportunity to collaborate with the SDB against the friars. Žanić gave to secret police operatives in Sarajevo his findings based on the bishop's investigation as well as other useful information about the friars of Medjugorje, whom both the bishop and the communists held accountable for the engineering of the apparitions.[10] Bishop Žanić was furious when the Franciscans announced through one of the Madonna's messages, allegedly entrusted to the Franciscans by the visionaries, that the Mother of God viewed the Franciscans as the righteous party in the dispute with the bishop over the distribution of parishes. The bishop urged the communist police to put the friars under arrest, while at the same time demanding that the Vatican discipline them.

According to Bishop Pave Žanić, the principal suspects of the manipulation of the child visionaries were the Herzegovinian Franciscan friars Slavko Barbarić and Tomislav Vlašić, with two friars who had been expelled from the Church.[11] One of the excommunicated, Ivica Vego, who went furthest in opposing the bishop while also showing propensity for fishy business and licentious behavior, was first suspended and warned to stop bothering the children.[12] Later, Bishop Žanić published and circulated a booklet report on the case. It included his interviews with the seers and interrogations of Barbarić, Vlašić, and Vego. According to the bishop, friar Slavko Barbarić, chaplain in Blagaj, had become impressed with mysticism and Catholic charismatic movements while studying pastoral psychology in Italy. Barbarić earned a master's degree in child psychology and during his studies in Rome joined the Catholic charismatic movement *Comunione e liberazione*. In Medjugorje, Barbarić trained the children together with Friar Tomislav Vlašić, then chaplain in the nearby village of Vitina, and Vego. Even the archbishop of Split, Metropolitan Franić, who would become one of most ardent supporters of the Medjugorje cult among Croatian bishops, once told me that Friar Barbarić, as a top expert in charismatic religiosity, was "coaching" the child visionaries, thus preparing them for visions and miracles. Yet in contrast to his colleague Žanić, Franić would argue that the children's experience was authentic and inspired by true faith that would result in a devotional movement of paramount importance for the Church. In Franić's view, Barbarić's work with the children was not a manipulation motivated by immoral or nonreligious goals, quite the contrary, the friar did an excellent job at what he was supposed to do.

In 1982, three Franciscans in west Herzegovina were jailed for "hostile propaganda," a criminal offense from the Federal Penal Code. One of the friars, Jozo Zovko, served in the time of the apparitions as a parish administrator in Medjugorje, while the other two issued a religious newspaper in which the regime found seditious and anti-Yugoslav content. Zovko was accused of making hostile and malicious allusions to the Yugoslav political system, which he portrayed as a prison system and a "40-year-long slavery" in which the people were exposed to "false teachings."[13] According to the indictment, Zovko made the speeches during his 11 July 1981 sermon at the Saint James Church and two weeks later on the occasion of Bishop Žanić's visit to Medjugorje. In the bishop's presence, Zovko sermonized about the "false teachings" of some Church authorities. The false teachings allegation, according to the state prosecutor, were interpreted as an attack on the League of Communists of Yugoslavia, Marxism, and self-management socialism. Bishop Žanić argued with Zovko after the mass and warned him that the Church teachings about Marian apparitions were to be respected.[14] The friar Zovko, who would later (especially on television and interviews for the press in the United States and other Western countries) contend that he himself had seen the Virgin Mary at Medjugorje, argued that the apparitions at Medjugorje occurred as a spontaneous spiritual experience of exceptionally gifted believers, mystics, and, as he put it, "lovers of prayer" (ljubitelji molitve).[15] Of course, there is no reason to doubt the visionaries' special talents and devotion. They grew up in a sectarian community permeated by devout Catholicism, excessive ethnicism, and memories of World War II Croatian martyrdom (the children did not know about Serb mass graves). The seers of Medjugorje were not merely someone's puppets. Christian, the scholar of Marian apparitions, observed visionaries' autonomy in other cases comparable to that of Medjugorje.[16]

Friar Zovko was portrayed by Western media as a martyr and hero of democratic opposition to communism. Yet the bishop of Mostar did not change his opinion. In an address to a group of young pilgrims at Medjugorje on 25 July 1987, Žanić said that in 1982 he had appointed a special commission of 15 theologians, psychologists, and psychiatrists to study the case and after three years of investigation, 2 members accepted the apparitions as genuine, 1 member abstained, and 11 declared that "there was nothing supernatural in the Medjugorje apparitions."[17] Two more commissions were appointed by the Bishops' Conference of Yugoslavia and by the Holy See. The bishop of Mostar remained intransigent: "The Madonna has never said anything at Medjugorje . . . all that is merely a mass delusion, euphoria, and spectacle for tourists."[18]

In the meantime, the Herzegovinian hamlet became world famous. In 1985 some 25,000 believers with 80 foreign and native priests gathered to mark the third anniversary of the miracle.[19] In 1988, according to rough estimates, almost 10 million people from all over the world made pilgrimage to Medjugorje. Most of the foreign visitors came from Italy, the United States, Canada, Australia, Spain, Austria, Germany, and France, as well as Asia, Africa, and Latin America.[20] The Italian Christian Democratic Party, caught up in a crisis caused by the worst corruption scandal since its foundation, urged party leaders, officials, members, and supporters to go to Medjugorje for inner purification and spiritual renewal. Flaminio Piccoli, Gulio Andreotti, and many other Christian Democrat ex-officials traveled privately to Medjugorje a number of times. Italian newspapers calculated that Italian tourist enterprises alone had harvested a total of 10 billion dollars since the pilgrimages began, which then equaled half of the total Yugoslav foreign debt.[21] In the United States, the Franciscan center in Steubenville, Ohio, took charge of propaganda and the coordination of the swiftly growing Medjugorje devotional movement. "Medjugorje centers" were established in Ohio, Louisiana, Massachusetts, Texas, Iowa, and elsewhere throughout the United States. *U.S. Support.*

The Yugoslav regime in 1987 changed its policy toward Medjugorje, and in 1988, systematic registration and taxation of pilgrims was introduced. Domestic travel agencies took over the religious tourism business, and a new chain of hotels was completed in a rush during 1988.[22] A U.S. magazine estimated in the early 1990s that "no fewer than 11 million people" had made pilgrimage to Medjugorje.[23] Meanwhile thousands of articles, books, videos, several documentaries, and a feature film on the Gospa of Medjugorje were released in Yugoslavia and abroad.[24] Testimonies about miraculous healings puzzled international councils of doctors. The visionaries and their Franciscan spiritual advisors toured foreign countries to be interviewed by journalists and experts, Church and security officials, doctors, the pious, and the curious. All the visionaries continued to report occasional encounters with the Virgin Mary. Four out of the six original seers claimed that the Gospa was appearing to them occasionally. Through Marija Pavlović, the divine messages to the world come routinely on the twenty-fifth of every month. The Croatian episcopate, after successfully completing the Great Novena, tacitly supported the Madonna of Medjugorje. The Vatican released a recommendation for "private" pilgrimages to Medjugorje, while keeping busy theological commissions investigating the case.[25] Meanwhile, Medjugorje acquired information center, hotels and golf courses. New businesses grew and residents increased their otherwise good living standard.

Beyond Mysticism: The Politics of Marian Apparitions

The cult of the Virgin Mary has been widely used for a long time as symbol of national identity and vehicle of nationalistic movements. The "Black Madonna" of Czestochowa is the national symbol of Poland. The statue harbored at the Jasna Gora shrine was a driving force of numerous nationalistic movements in the history of Poland, among them the struggle between the Church of Poland and communism, which has become a celebrated Cold War Myth. The Virgin of Guadalupe is revered as a patron saint of Mexico and as symbol of identity for Mexicans in Mexico and Mexicans in the United States. Likewise, the Virgin of Montserrat, located in a monastery near Barcelona, inspired the Catalan people's sense of national identity and fueled the long struggle for autonomy of Catalonia under various regimes. "In many ways Montserrat is to Catalonia what the Jasna Gora monastery is to Poland," wrote Hank Johnston, and went on to explain that "Montserrat has a long Catalan nationalist tradition. And is home of Catalonia's patron saint—a black image of the Virgin Mary (the 'Virgin of Montserrat'). . . . In 1947 the monastery was the scene of the first mass demonstration of Catalanist sentiment after the Civil War. Religious Catalanism was important in the development of Catalan nationalism."[26] Consequently the Virgin Mary could be correctly designated the founding mother of many nation-states and a weapon for stateless nations in their quest for statehood.

In the historical perspective of the twentieth century as a century of ideological wars, the Medjugorje "miracle" fueled both Croat nationalism and anticommunist struggle. It was initiated shortly after Tito's death in the region that was a fortress of the pro-Axis domestic ethnic nationalists and anticommunist fighters during World War II. At Medjugorje, the Virgin appeared on the sixty-fourth anniversary of the Marian apparitions at Fatima, Portugal. The Fatima "miracle" of 1917 and subsequent "Fatima movement" in the Iberian peninsula and in the Church worldwide were aimed at opposing the spread of communism; they coincided with the Bolshevik revolution and rise of communism worldwide. At Fatima, in June 1917, the Virgin, as the Church would teach decades later—not immediately, of course, because church leaders as well as religious "visionaries" are ordinary people who do not really and exactly know what is happening around them in the world and in history—delivered some sort of an "early warning" to the world about the oncoming menace spreading from Russia and continued to "predict" what would follow as the consequence of the Russian October. According to the 1917 Fatima "secret messages"—revealed not by the visionaries but by Pope Pius XII (who allegedly had the knowledge of the visionaries' confessions to the priests in charge), incidentally, between 1942 and 1943, that is, before it became clear that the Soviet Union would defeat Nazi Germany—Russia "will convert" eventually, after a long struggle and suffering; this "conversion" will occur during "the "last Madonna's apparitions on Earth," to be followed by a long-lasting "reign of peace" and renaissance of religion worldwide.[27] The Fatima myth would develop into one of most efficient forms of popular anticommunist mobilization in the twentieth century created and carried out by the Roman Catholic Church. Explaining the historical significance of Fatima apparitions on the occasion of the millennial jubilee of Christianity in 2000, one of highest ranked Vatican officials, Cardinal Angelo Sodano, said: "The vision of Fatima concerns above all the war waged by atheist systems against the Church and Christians, and it describes the immense suffering endured by the witnesses to the faith in the last century of the second millennium."[28]

How was the myth made? The "miracle" and visionaries, as already noted, occurred initially as a local affair, a religious event in an obscure Portugese hamlet in June 1917. In the 1930s, one of the visionaries from Fatima, Lucia Dos Santos, became a Catholic nun. The Church would subsequently "reveal" some "secrets" allegedly told by the Madonna to Lucia, which Lucia confessed to the Church authorities and no one else. Thus between 1917 and the 1940s, a great twentieth-century myth was born. Of course, Fatima was not without precedents, and Church experts in myth-making were not without experience. In the modern era, the Church utilized ever-popular Marian apparitions as weapons in the struggle against secu-larization, liberalism, liberal nationalism, freemasonry, socialism, and com-munism and against hostile regimes and rival religions. Seven apparitions in the modern era were officially "approved" by the Vatican. The first great wave of Marian apparitions in modern Europe occurred in the aftermath of the church-state struggle triggered by the French Revolution. The Commune of Paris in 1871, during which the anticlerical Communards executed the archbishop of Paris, prompted a vehement Church response through mas-sive pilgrimages to Lourdes, Rue du Bac, and Pontmain; consecrations of the Virgin's statues and shrines, and Marian festivals and commemorations. Apparitions were reported during the unification of Italy and Germany in the 1870s, during the Carlist Wars of the 1840s and the liberal-conservative struggles in the 1890s in Spain, and in the wake of the foundation of the Spanish Republic in 1931.

The Fatima myth and the symbol known as "Our Lady of Fatima" became the battering ram of the Catholic Church's anticommunist crusade in the twentieth century. In 1917, the "Militia of the Immaculate Conception" was founded, and in 1921 the "Legion of Mary" enhanced the ranks of Catholic Action. The Church responded to the persecution of religion in the Soviet Union and to the struggle between the Church and the Republicans during the Spanish Civil War, by revealing a first package of Fatima Prophecies.[29] In 1925–41, the Fatima visionary Lucia Dos Santos wrote memoirs and revealed those "secrets." Sister Lucia lived throughout the whole century, so that she could "reveal" Madonna's "secrets" in the 1960s, in the 1980s, and again, at the age of 93, on the threshold of the new millennium.

The Fatima myth has a special role in the history of the Cold War. Wil-liam Christian Jr. found that between 1947 and 1954, 112 visions and ap-paritions were reported, which is on average four times as many visions per year in this period as in the rest of the years from 1930 to 1975.[30] Moreover, during the critical period of the Cold War, between 1948 and 1958, over 126 Marian Congresses were held in various countries and the year of 1954 was proclaimed the Marian Year by the anticommunist Pope Pius XII.[31] According to estimates given by the leading Marian theologian Rene Lau-rentin, by the late 1950s nearly thousand new books on Mary were being published every year, and this includes only scholarly works, let alone thousands of devotional books and pamphlets.[32] In this period a new prac-tice was introduced—the feasts of the consecration to the Immaculate Heart. It was carried out through "voyage-missions" of the Madonna's statue or image from parish to parish in towns and villages.[33] In Spain, the dictator Franco received and welcomed the traveling image of Our Lady at the Prado Palace in Madrid. In Italy, the Church and Christian Democratic Party (DC), came together in attendance of Marian "voyage missions" during electoral campaigns.[34] The anticommunist use of Mary was conspicuous in Chile in 1973. As the Marxist Salvador Allende and his socialists were heading toward an electoral victory (they won, only to be shortly toppled in a bloody military coup led by Augusto Pinochet), the Church, the rightist groups, and the Virgin Mary's statue stepped in. The symbol of the "Our Lady of Fatima" arrived in Brazil. According to a report released by the local Catholic lay movement the Brazilian Society for the Defense of Tradition, Family and Property (TFP), Brazil welcomed the "Pilgrim Statue of Our Lady of Fatima which had miraculously shed tears in New Orleans, U.S.A.," and it toured the country until "the fiasco of the Marxist 'experiment' in Chile."[35] The voyages of the "miraculous statue" continued throughout South America in 1974, organized by the so-called Blue Army of Our Lady of Fatima in Brazil. Finally, in Poland, in the course of the Catholic Church jubilee, the Great Novena of the Millennium, in 1957–66, the replica of the Black Madonna Queen of Poland was touring the country to mobilize anticommunist forces. The Second Vatican Council (1962–65) made an attempt to curb the uncontrolled use of Mary, urging the bishops to carefully scrutinize each case of mystical experiences. Yet the apparitions continued. During the historic council, millions flocked to San Damiano (in Piacenza, Italy) and Garabandal (in northern Spain), where new Marian apparitions had been reported.[36]

To be sure, the Marian apparitions at Medjugorje did not suit quite well the official version of the Fatima myth. As noted earlier, the final triumphant Madonna's apparitions were to occur in Russia at the moment of the collapse of communism. The Medjugorje miracle, viewed from the vantage point of the Fatima "prophecies," came both prematurely and in the wrong place. The official Church tolerated but never recognized Medjugorje. Pope John Paul II consecrated Russia to the Immaculate Heart of Mary on 13 May 1982. Apparitions of the Virgin Mary were reported at Hrushiv, in western Ukraine, in 1987, on the occasion of the seventieth anniversary of the Fatima miracle. Thus in 1987, for the second time since 1954, the Madonna visited Ukrainian Uniate communities, while in Kiev, the Russian Orthodox Church (with government support) celebrated the grand jubilee of the Millennium of Orthodoxy in Russia. Russia might have "converted" from atheistic communism, but Orthodox faith was growing stronger.

The apparitions in the Ukraine were overshadowed by the Balkan spectacle at Medjugorje. While only a few thousand people turned out at Hrushiv, millions from all around the globe had flocked to Medjugorje. The Fatima scenario was disrupted.[37] Incidentally, in 1987 the Madonna of Medjugorje announced through the Croatian visionaries that Medjugorje apparitions would be the last Marian apparitions on Earth.

The Apparitions in Herzegovina
and the Yugoslav Crisis
of the 1980s

The Catholic Church never in history fully controlled the mountainous Bosnia-Herzegovina. In the fourteenth century, Franciscans were sent to Bosnia to wipe out the so-called Bogumil heresy. In the fifteenth and sixteenth centuries, Catholicism had to retreat from advancing Islam. A few Catholic communities survived around Franciscan monasteries at Olovo, Fojnica, Kreševo, Kraljeva Sutjeska, and elsewhere, while Orthodox Serb enclaves also held out around the monasteries of Mileševo and Žitomislić and others. Bosnian Franciscan monasteries, wrote Ivo Andrić, "throughout the centuries of Turkish rule . . . constituted a kind of storage battery of popular energy, and monks enjoyed the people' sympathy and respect far more than did the diocesan clergy."[38] In 1573, the pope appointed Fra Anton Matković the first bishop of Bosnia from Franciscan ranks. After the Austrian occupation of Bosnia-Herzegovina in 1878, the official Church sought to solidify episcopal authority and restore regular ecclesiastical organization. "With Bosnia's occupation by the Austro-Hungarian monarchy in 1878," wrote Ivo Andrić, "and the establishment of normal social and ecclesiastical conditions, the historic mission of the Bosnian Franciscans came to an end."[39] The Austrian archbishop of Sarajevo, Josef Stadler (1843–1918), installed after the Austrian occupation, attempted to reduce Franciscan influence by bringing the Jesuits to Bosnia-Herzegovina. Stadler also initiated redistribution of parishes in favor of secular clergy. The Franciscans resisted. Yet they were themselves divided over the Austro-Hungarian policies in Bosnia and emerging native nationalistic movements. The once-unified Bosnian Franciscan province, so-called Silver Bosnia, split into two parts. In 1846, a group of monks seceded from the Kreševo monastic community to establish the monastery of Široki Brijeg in western Herzegovina. In 1892, the new monastery became the main center of the new Herzegovinian Franciscan province (the Franciscan Province of the Assumption of Mary in Herzegovina). Although secular clergy and bishops labored on the redistribution of parishes, at the beginning of the 1940s, the Franciscans in Bosnia-Herzegovina (both provinces) were still unchallenged: they held 63 of the total of 79 parishes, 29 monasteries, five seminaries, a few hospitals, various business establishments, and a considerable number of landholdings.[40] Under communism, many of the Franciscans of the Silver Bosnia province sympathized with the Yugoslav civil religion of brotherhood and unity. By contrast, west Herzegovinian friars who during the war had sided with the Ustaša labored against Yugoslavism and communism and dreamed about the restoration of the Croat state. In the 1970s, the west Herzegovinian Franciscan province recovered, thanks to financial help from Herzegovinian guest workers in

West Germany and other west European countries. In the 1980s, the Herzegovinian Franciscan province had 80 monks who served 40 parishes.[41]

Yet, as early as the mid-1970s, some of the Franciscan parishes in western Herzegovina, notwithstanding a bitter opposition, had been taken over by the bishop of Mostar and secular clergy. In order to counter the official Church's campaign, the friars of Herzegovina established an association of priests and laypeople, called Peace and Goodness. The association developed into a local movement for church autonomy that opposed diocesan policies in Herzegovina and provided popular support for the Franciscans' self-rule. The Vatican strongly backed the local bishop. According to 1975 papal decree entitled *Romanis pontificibus*, the Franciscans were ordered to abandon most of the parishes to the bishop and withdraw into monasteries. In the years that preceded the apparitions at Medjugorje, the bishop made an effort to execute the papal decree. The friars sought support at home and abroad.[42] Church leaders acted cautiously, trying to avoid conflict with a stubborn opponent.[43]

In the 1980s, Catholic–Orthodox relations had worsened. In the context of the conflict of the churches, the Medjugorje movement added much fuel to the fire of the growing enmity. The Serbs and their Orthodox Church looked at the apparitions angrily. For them there was no doubt about the character of the "miracle" of Medjugorje: it could be only a relapse to Ustašism. The Ustašas left a bloody legacy and bitter memories among Orthodox Serbs in Herzegovina. During the Ustaša terror of 1941–42, the Ustašas ethnically cleansed half of the Serb population of Herzegovina. The area is full of mass graves. Natural pits (*jamas*), trenches, ravines, and underground cracks in the Herzegovinian limestone karst were burial sites of Ustaša victims but also harbored relics of the Croats—victims of the communists' and the Serbian nationalist militant Četniks' revenge. According to a map of mass graves and execution sites based on research by a Serbian author, there are 17 jamas and mass graves in the zone around Medjugorje, which includes the Mostar, Čapljina, and Gabela regions.[44] Four mass graves, Šurmanci, Prebilovci, Vidonje, and Bivolje Brdo lie within several miles of Medjugorje. In August 1941 the bishop of Mostar, the Franciscan Alojzije Mišić, wrote to the archbishop of Zagreb, Alojzije Stepinac: "those Ustaša brought six wagons full of mothers, girls and children under eight, to the station of Šurmanci, where the victims were taken out of the wagons, brought into the hills and thrown alive, mothers and children, into deep ravines."[45] The Franciscan assistance to the criminal Ustaša provided an opportunity for the bishop to discredit the disobedient friars.

In the 1980s, the bishop of Mostar and the Franciscans of Herzegovina were at odds, as always. However, as the possible breakup of Yugoslavia became possibility, especially when Slobodan Milošević came to power in Serbia, many Croat church leaders saw the Marian movement in Herzegovina as an instrument of national homogenization of the Croats from Croatia and Bosnia-Herzegovina. For example, the archbishop of Split, Frane

Franić, encouraged the new Marian cult and urged the faithful in his diocese to make pilgrimage to Medjugorje. As the pilgrims flocked to Medjugorje, the statue of Our Lady "Queen of Peace" of Fatima set out for "voyage missions" through parishes in Dalmatia. Monsignor Alojzije Bavčević, then the rector of Catholic seminary in Split, in the fall of 1983 brought several statues of the Queen of Peace from Italy to Southern Croatia and distributed them to rural parishes in the hinterland of Dalmatia. The Madonnas were packed into polished wooden altarlike boxes, with the Fatima's messages on the "conversion of Russia" typed on a sheet of paper attached to the box. In the Marian shrine of Sinj and surrounding villages, apparitions of the Madonna were reported during the "voyage missions." A 16-year-old girl from the village of Gala announced that she had seen the Virgin Mary. The familiar scenario of Medjugorje and other apparition sites was repeated. Thousands of pilgrims flocked to the apparition site, and many buses carrying pilgrims to Medjugorje turned from the Split-Mostar highway to take a look at the site of the newest miracle. The police surrounded the site, searched houses, arrested the visionary and the local clergy, and repeatedly dismantled wooden crosses erected on the apparition site, until the faithful built in a six-foot high concrete cross which the police finally let stand there.

The girl visionary from Gala was sentenced to two weeks in prison for "disseminating false news" and "alarming the public."[46] Police carried out an investigation that resulted in the indictment if three Catholic priests of the Split-Makarska diocese. Alojzije Bavčević, the rector of Catholic seminary in Split, who purchased the Madonnas in Italy and imported them to Yugoslavia, with two parish priests from the Sinj area who organized the "voyage missions," were charged with violating the federal criminal code by allegedly "insulting a foreign country" (Russia). The indictment alleged that

in the period from October 1983 to April 1984, the suspects conceived, planned, and carried out a ceremonial tour of the statue of the so-called "Our Lady of Fatima"—an icon revered by the church-going people as sacred and capable of performing miracles—throughout the parishes and villages of Trilj, Košute, and other places. . . . The statues were purchased and imported from Italy by the indicted Bavčević, who retyped and attached to the box with the Madonna's statue a text titled "Mary's Words from Fatima to the World," in which a foreign country, the USSR, is ridiculed and insulted. . . . Bavčević handed out the incriminated statues to the indicted Milan Vrdoljak and Vjenceslav Kujundžić, who exposed them in parish churches and organized their circulation among believer's families and homes.[47]

The indictment never reached the court. In order to mollify the increasingly frustrated authorities, the archbishop of Split, Frane Franić, decided to discontinue the Madonna's voyage missions and revised the text of the Fatima message so that the word "Russia" was replaced by "the world."[48]

Some members of the Bishops' Conference of Yugoslavia, including the chief architect of the Great Novena jubilee, Metropolitan Franić, began to argue that the Medjugorje apparitions merited support as a promising instrument of mobilization for the anticommunist struggle as well as energizer of the Croatian national struggle. The Vatican seemed to have arrived at the same conclusion. According to a statement in a U.S. magazine, Castellano Cervera, a specialist in Mariology who visited Medjugorje and held consultations in the Vatican, said: "it seems clear to me that one can go to Medjugorje, just as one goes to any sanctuary, to deepen one's Christian life."[49] Finally, the Bishops' Conference of Yugoslavia held its regular session in Zadar on 9–11 April 1991 and released a communiqué on Medjugorje, which proclaimed: *non constat de supernaturalitate!* The bishops said that the Church would be nonetheless following the course of events and would provide special pastoral services and any other necessary assistance to the numerous pilgrims at Medjugorje[50] Further, the Church recognized Medjugorje "as a holy place, as a shrine" and presumed that the people who come to Medjugorje do so in order to "venerate the Mother of God in a manner also in agreement with the teaching and belief of the Church so that the Church has nothing against it."[51] The American Catholic priest Richard J. Beyer wrote in his book on Medjugorje that "from all accounts, and looking at the new (postcommunist) world around us, Medjugorje has ushered in a new age of peace."[52] According to Beyer, in July 1989 the visionaries reported that the Blessed Virgin Mary had said the following: "Love your Serbian Orthodox and Muslim brothers, and even the atheists who persecute you."[53]

In the meantime, the Medjugorje movement was closely watched by the increasingly frustrated Serbian Orthodox Church. As early as the mid-1980s, the Orthodox Church press pointed out that the Catholic Bogoroditsa had appeared amid the unmarked mass graves in which the Croatian Fascists had dumped hundreds of thousands of Serbs who refused conversion to Catholicism and even those who had been converted.[54] The Serbian scholar Milan Bulajić called the Medjugorje apparitions an introduction to another genocide against Serbs, again unfolding under the auspices of the Catholic Church like the genocide of World War II.[55] Bulajić contended that the jailed Franciscan friar Jozo Zovko had allegedly taught the children of Medjugorje the Fascist salute.[56] The Holy Bishops' Sabor of the Serbian Orthodox Church released from its session held in Belgrade on 26 June 1989 a letter on Catholic-Orthodox relations in which Serb Orthodox bishops wrote about the concentration camp of Jasenovac and "countless pits and mass graves such as that near Medjugorje."[57] In October 1990, the Serbian Church began a year-long commemoration dedicated to the Serbian victims of World War II.[58] The commemorations began at Jasenovac and moved to Bosnia-Herzegovina. In Bosnia-Herzegovina, commemorations and requiems are held in Glamoč, Šipovo, Gacko, Ljubinje, and several sites near Mostar, Čapljina, and Čitluk, all in the vicinity of Medjugorje. In the village of Prebilovci, near Čapljina, and not very far from Čitluk and Medjugorje, the Serbian Orthodox Church built a chapel memorial in June 1991. The chapel, dedicated to "New Serbian Martyrs" with a memorial cemetery, was to harbor the remains of some eight hundred Ustaša victims from Prebilovci, excavated from the Šurmanci mass grave.[59]

The central commemoration in western Herzegovina was held on 2–3 February 1991 at the Žitomislić monastery in the Mostar area and in the village of Prebilovci near Čapljina, 10 miles from Medjugorje. For the occasion, the Serbian Orthodox Church organized excavations of the remains of the massacred from the pits and ravines at Šurmanci 2 miles from Medjugorje and Bivolje Brdo near Čapljina and 6 miles from Medjugorje. Standing in front of the skulls and bones of some 1,500 victims, to be reburied under the memorial chapel at the Prebilovci cemetery, preachers recalled August 1941, when "Catholic Croats massacred all Serb villagers, allegedly 54 families, and leveled to the ground Prebilovci and other Orthodox villages in the area, then sung the jubilant slogan: Serbs have perished. . . . Their (Orthodox Church) candles will never flame again!"[60]

After the funeral liturgy at Žitomislić, on Sunday, 3 February 1991, the patriarch spoke before a crowd of 20,000, which included Radovan Karadžić, the nationalist leader of Bosnian Serbs. The patriarch of Serbia, Paul I, invoked the names of eight Serbian Orthodox clerics who had been tortured and murdered along with several thousand Orthodox peasants. The patriarch stressed that the murderers and torturers were Roman Catholic Croats and that the victims lost their lives "in concentration camps, ravines and pits, only because they were 'guilty' of having been born in the religion and nationality different from that of their executioners."[61] Concluding the sermon, the patriarch urged the faithful to remember and commemorate, but not to retaliate, particularly not against unarmed opponents.[62] In a similar vein, Bishop Metropolitan Vladislav recalled "the time of madness in the summer of 1941, when Roman Catholic Croats massacred the monks from Žitomislić monastery and the Orthodox population from surrounding villages."[63] At the end of the convention, the nationalist leader Radovan Karadžić called the Serbs to gather around the Church and the Orthodox faith.[64]

Marian apparitions in Herzegovina reignited Catholic-Orthodox tensions (the case of the Ukraine was mentioned earlier). The Serbian Orthodox Church viewed the spectacle around the mass graves of Medjugorje as a slap in the face of the Serbian Church and people. Nonetheless, the Vatican found the movement in Herzegovina serviceable to the Church. The bishop of Mostar, Pave Žanić, remained isolated. In Žanić's words, many religious apparitions in history eventually proved hallucinations or frauds, and some visionaries subsequently denied their experiences and confessed mistakes.[65] The pope sent Žanić into retirement in 1992. After the electoral victory in 1990, the nationalist regime in Croatia exploited the global popularity of the Medjugorje cult. In 1995, a Croatian-American joint production generated the feature film Gospa (Madonna), directed by the native western Herzegovinian and Croatian regime's official propagandist, Jakov Sedlar. The movie, starring Martin Sheen as Father Jozo Zovko, Michael York as Zovko's lawyer Milan Vuković, Morgan Fairchild as Sister Fafijana Zovko, and Frank Finlay as the Bishop Žanić, was shown with modest success in the United States, western Europe, and elsewhere. In the movie, the Croats are portrayed as pious and peaceful Catholics eager to join the Western democratic world but prevented from that and oppressed by Orthodox Serbs and communists. Herzegovinian Franciscans were featured as good shepherds admired by their flocks so that the local bishop (a negative character in the movie) envies them. The Madonna, and the whole of Medjugorje, were, paradoxically, presented as forces of peace and freedom. In the meantime, the Madonna of Medjugorje had clearly affected Catholic-Orthodox relations negatively and disrupted stability in the vulnerable multiethnic Bosnia-Herzegovina. The Medjugorje apparitions of the 1980s were not a "peace and prayer movement," as the Western media stubbornly reiterate, but a prelude to partition, war, and genocide in Bosnia-Herzegovina.

8

FLAMES AND SHRINES

The Serbian Church and Serbian Nationalist
Movement in the 1980s

As noted in chapter 3, during the liberal phase of Yugoslav communism, that is, in the 1960s and 1970s, the Serbian Orthodox Church, as the League of Communists of Serbia had observed in the analysis quoted earlier, had emerged as the lone domestic carrier of Serbian ethnic nationalism. As a matter of fact, secular nationalists operating within the establishment were all purged (e.g. Dobrica Ćosić, Marko Nikezić, and Latinka Perović in Serbia and political leaders in Croatia mentioned earlier) so that the churches at home and exiled anti-Yugoslav groups remained the only opposition to the regime. The Serbian Church's role would be reasserted and strengthened in the 1980s, thanks to the worsening crisis in Kosovo. The third massive Albanian demonstrations in two decades broke out in Kosovo in 1981. This time the Albanians demanded a status of a federal republic for their province. The demonstrations of 1981, like earlier ones, were violent and accompanied with acts of terrorism. Thus, according to an observer, 680 fires attributed to arson broke out in Kosovo between 1980 and 1981.[1] The landmark Serbian sacred center in Kosovo, the patriarchate at Peć, was set on fire in the night on 15 March 1981. The fire destroyed the large 2,000-square-meter residential section along with valuable furniture, rare liturgical books, and some artifacts from the monastery's treasury. As the *Pravoslavlje* reported, the most precious valuables, rare manuscripts, and icons from the treasury had been rescued from the blaze by nuns and monks with the help of two local Albanian construction laborers employed by the monastery.[2] Patriarch Germanus were received by Vidoje Žarković, then the highest official of the Yugoslav Federation. Žarković promised an investigation, but the cause of the fire was never determined.[3] The government of Serbia promptly allocated financial aid for the renewal of the shrine at Peć, and on 16 October 1983, the section damaged by the 1981 fire was solemnly reopened, with 10,000 pilgrims in attendance.

The Holy Assembly of Bishops held several sessions in Kosovo, while church leaders frequently visited the troubled zone. After the incident at the old patriarchal seat, the media and public opinion in Belgrade and Serbia began to show increasingly interest in the crisis in the southern province. On Good Friday in 1982 a group of Serb Orthodox clerics led by the Archimandrite Atanasije Jevtić, then professor at Belgrade School of Orthodox Theology, released a document entitled "Appeal for the Protection of the Serbian Population and Their Sacred Monuments in Kosovo" (also known as the Appeal of 21 Serbian Priests). The appeal, an open letter, contained 21 signatures of prominent Orthodox clergymen and was addressed to the Presidency of the Socialist Federal Republic of Yugoslavia, the Presidency of the Socialist Republic of Serbia, the People's Assembly of Serbia, and the Holy Bishops' Sabor of the Serbian Orthodox Church. The *Pravoslavlje* published the text of the appeal in full on 15 May 1982, and some Belgrade newspapers reprinted shorter versions. "The Kosovo issue," says the appeal,

> is the issue of the spiritual, cultural, and historical identity of the Serbian people. . . . [L]ike the Jewish people who return to their Jerusalem in order to survive, the Serbian people are fighting once again the very same battle of Kosovo that our ancestors began to fight in 1389 at the Kosovo field. . . . And when it seemed that the battle has been won once and for all, Kosovo is being taken away from us and we are no longer what we are! . . . Without an exaggeration, it could be said that a planned *genocide* has been carried out against the Serbian people in Kosovo. The Albanian quest for an ethnically homogenous Albanian Kosovo free of Serbs is the evidence of genocide.[4]

The priests' letter also revived the analogy between the shrines of Kosovo and Palestine made by the author Jovan Dučićs in "Letter from Palestine" published in the 1930s.[5] In 1985, the Serb author Vuk Drašković published an open letter addressed to the writers of Israel, in which he refers to the Serbs as "the thirteenth lost and the most ill-fated tribe of Israel," calls Israeli writers brothers, and recites the Jeremiad applied to the current Kosovo situation: "If I forget thee, O Jerusalem, let my right hand be afflicted."[6] The leading author Dobrica Ćosić drew parallels between the tragic historical destinies of the Serbs and the Jews, according to him, both martyr-nations and innocent victims of genocide.[7] In the words of Ćosić, the Serb is "the new Jew at the end of the twentieth century."[8] The professor of the Belgrade Theological School, Archpriest Žarko Gavrilović, wrote in his 1986 collection of essays that "the Serbian people and their Orthodox Church, are the greatest martyrs of humankind . . . no other people in the world, except the Jews, have suffered so much for their faith and nation, as the Serbs have suffered."[9]

On its 20 May 1982 session, the Holy Bishop's Sabor made public a chronicle of Albanian anti-Serbian activities in Kosovo since 1968. The bishops underscored that the document contained only a small part of the material gathered by the Church.[10] The chronicle also recorded official urges, interventions, and appeals released by church leaders, beginning with the patriarch's letter to President Tito of May 1969. Meanwhile, the *Pravoslavlje* ran regular column about what was termed Albanian terror in Kosovo. According to the *Pravoslavlje*'s perspective on the Kosovo crisis, the roots of anti-Serbianism lie preeminently in religious hatred.[11] Between 1982 and 1986, the Church filed 12 petitions on alleged Albanian attacks on local Serbs and church property, addressed to authorities in Kosovo, Serbia, and in the Federation.[12] Archimandrite Atanasije Jevtić toured the country from Kosovo to Croatia, reporting from this trip in the church press he argued that Serbs were persecuted by Muslims and Catholics.[13] In a 1985 interview, Jevtić warned that the spiritual power of the Kosovo myth might cause a Serbian nationalist volcano unless the government suppressed Albanian nationalism.[14] Jevtić was echoed by his colleague, the theologian Dimitrije Bogdanović, who wrote in 1986 that "in spite of some anti-Albanian Serbian governmental policies. . . . Albanian irredentism has always been real force in the province. The exodus of Serbs and Montenegrins from Kosovo is the consequence of a genocide against one nationality!"[15]

As early as the mid-1980s, the Belgrade press began reporting daily from the restive province. It was the Belgrade press, the Archimandrite Atanasije had acknowledged, that "made the decisive shift in favor of the struggle for the Serbian truth about Kosovo."[16] The leading Belgrade political weekly *NIN* applauded the Church-induced "struggle against oblivion" in an article that concluded: "For how can the Serbian nation exist at all, separated from its spirituality in the spiritual centers of the Peć Patriarchate, Dečani, Gračanica, and other shrines of Kosovo and Metohija?"[17] In 1986 the Serbian Academy of Sciences and Arts (SASA) released a document cited as "Memorandum SASA." The document blamed Titoist policies, communist ideology, and non-Serbian ethnic nationalisms for the tribulations of Serbs and proposed a radical restructuring of the Yugoslav federation as a solution for the Serbian question.[18] Church leaders quoted the Memorandum in sermons and interviews. Members of the Academy and authors of the Memorandum made pilgrimages to Kosovo and Jasenovac.

Religion and the Serb Nationalist Mobilization

Shrines were the powerful symbolic energizer of the Serbian nationalist movement of the 1980s. In addition to drawing public attention to the attacked shrines of Kosovo, in 1985 the Serbian Orthodox Church began to continue the 1935–41 construction of memorial church of Saint Sava, located atop the Vračar hill, where, as legend has it, the Turks burned the relics of Saint Sava in 1594. From 1935 to 1941, Saint Sava's memorial temple rose to 45 feet, with 515 concrete pillars and 48 marble columns engraved with insignia of the Serbian kings and princes. Between 1960 and 1984, Patriarch Germanus, as he said in an interview, filed 88 petitions for the construction permit.[19] A chronicle of the new church's construction noted that the rebuilding, allegedly, had become possible only after the death of Tito.[20] According to the patriarch's words at the 12 May 1985 consecration ceremony at the construction site, the new church would be the material evidence of how the Serbs, guided by Saint Sava's spirit, survived trials and catastrophes from Kosovo to Jasenovac.[21]

The Holy Synod nominated Branko Pešić of the Belgrade University Department of Architecture chief designer of the new cathedral. Pešić's project envisioned a neo-Byzantine church, allegedly one of largest in the world. It would be 65 meters from the floor to the top of the main dome, with 9 more meters for the cross atop the central cupola. The church would have two galleries, with the upper gallery 40 meters high. The church would be capable of receiving 11,000 to 15,000 people. In 1985, the costs of construction were estimated at 15 million US dollars. In the course of construction, the costs rose above all previous calculations.[22] According to predictions, the new Belgrade Orthodox cathedral would be about the same size as Hagia Sophia of Constantinople, with even more ambitious program of mosaics frescoes, and other forms of arts inspired by the Serbian medieval sacred painting.[23] According to the chief designer Branko Pešić, the construction of the new cathedral at Belgrade was "certainly the world's greatest enterprise in church construction in this century."[24] The church would have 50 bells and 18 gilded crosses atop the temple's domes. The cross at the central cupola weighs four ton and is 40 feet high. The audience of 15,000 people is more than any other Orthodox church in the world can receive.[25] When the cupola was placed upon the church walls, the new church became the highest landmark dominating the capital city of Yugoslavia. In 1989, the *Pravoslavlje* editorial staff ran on the paper's front page a photograph of the rising giant towering above the Yugoslav Federal Parliament.[26]

After opening ceremonies and the consecration in 1985, construction work at the Vračar hill resumed on 14 April 1986. The great enterprise mobilized the Serbs at home and abroad, and donations poured into the patriarchate from the faithful, churches, governments and other sources. Among the first who made donations were the ecumenical patriarch Dimitrios I of Constantinople, the premier of Greece, Andreas Papandreou, and the Catholic archbishop of Ljubljana, in Slovenia, Alojz Šuštar. Excursions, schools, and visitors from Yugoslavia and foreign countries came to Belgrade to see the rise of one of the largest Byzantine cathedrals in the world. In May 1989, the 40-foot-high golden cross was installed atop the main cathedral's cupola. On 25 May 1989, the first liturgy was held inside the unfinished church, with 100,000 people in attendance inside the temple and around it. On the occasion, the holy relics of the holy prince Lazar of Kosovo were transferred to the temple and exposed for the worship of the faithful. When the new temple acquired a cupola, a nationalist poet wrote on the

Pravoslavlje's front page: "[with] hope of the nearing harvest tenaciously shining, Saint Sava is rising atop the Vračar hill, and all wretched Serbia rises with him."[27]

During the 1970s and 1980s, 30 new churches were built in Serbia proper; the ancient monastery of Gradac in Serbia was renovated with government assistance; in the capital city of Belgrade alone, in addition to 32 existing churches, the Serbian church began rebuilding three new large churches; began new buildings for theological school and seminary; built eight parish houses; renovated three churches and one chapel; and finally, increased pressure for permits for new churches in the suburbs of several new cities (but city authorities denied a permit for the construction of a new mosque). In Croatia, a parish church-memorial was to be completed at historic Jasenovac and another one in the coastal city of Split (see more on this later); the new monastery of the Holy Three Hierarchs was built at Krka Seminary near Knin (Croatia); new churches were built in the Bosnian towns of Tuzla and Drvar and in Nikšić in Montenegro; the fourteenth-century monasteries of Morača and Piva in Montenegro were under renovation and conservation; and the Raška-Prizren diocese obtained permits for new churches in Priština and Djakovica and elsewhere in Kosovo.[28]

In 1987 Slobodan Milošević came to power in Serbia. In the same landmark year the Holy Synod of the Serbian Orthodox Church issued an encyclopedic, richly illustrated atlas of the sacred Kosovo heritage entitled "Debts to God in Kosovo: Monuments and Symbols of the Serbian People. "It presented in text and pictures all the ancient shrines of Kosovo, or, as they were officially called, "debts to God and symbols and monuments of the Serbian people." "This monograph, in 880 pages," wrote the volume's editor, the archimandrite Atanasije Jevtić, "contains the visible and verifiable historical, cultural, spiritual, and artistic artifacts and documents about achievements of Kosovo in Serbian, Balkan, and European culture and civilization."[29] In April 1987 the Belgrade press published sensational findings according to which historic Orthodox churches and monasteries in Kosovo, including the famous fourteenth-century Dečani monastery, had been registered as mosques by the local Albanian administration.[30] In May 1987, the Holy Bishops' Sabor changed its regular meeting place and held its annual session at the old patriarchate of Peć. Two more bishops' assemblies took place at the Kosovo cities of Peć and Prizren. In October 1987, Patriarch Germanus, with the ecumenical patriarch Dimitrios I from Istanbul, visited the shrines of Kosovo. In 1987, the nationalist poet Matija Bečković published his elegy "The Kosovo Field," charging the Albanians with "stealing Serbia's memory and history."[31]

From 1987 to 1990, the new leader of Serbia, Slobodan Milošević, pacified the restless Kosovo. The Church took advantage of this to rebuild its resources in the province. On 29 November 1990 the Church solemnly opened excavations and restoration of the Holy Archangels monastery near Prizren. On 16 May 1991 church dignitaries and cheering crowds of local

Serbs attended a ground-breaking ceremony at the Holy Savior Cathedral in the Kosovo capital of Priština. The new Holy Savior Cathedral, like the Saint Sava Memorial Temple at Belgrade, was viewed, as its designer said, as "conflict-mitigating architecture."[32]

The Church simultaneously carried out a dynamic program of pilgrimages, jubilees, and church-national festivals in preparation for the 600th anniversary of the battle of Kosovo in 1989. In 1983, the Church marked the sixty-fifth anniversary of the Entente's forces breakthrough at the Salonica front, emphasizing the memory of World War I, underrated in communist Yugoslavia. In September 1986, the Church marked the 800th anniversary of the monastery at Studenica. More than 150,000 pilgrims paid tribute to the "mother of all Serbian churches," the Holy Bogoroditsa church at Studenica in southern Serbia, where the Church's founder, Saint Sava, served as the first head of the monastic community.[33] After a two-hour liturgy, the patriarch in a brief address emphasized that Studenica "had preserved the Serbian soul— the soul which lives on and today is again providing guidance for its children."[34] Reporting from the Studenica pilgrimage, the Balkan correspondent for the German daily newspaper *Die Welt* wrote that "what was happening in the monastery of Studenica these days was a unification of the Church and the people similar to that in Poland when the Pope recently visited his homeland."[35] In 1987, the Church joined the state in commemorating the 200th anniversary of the birth of the language reformer Vuk Karadžić (1787–1864). In 1988 and 1989, as an overture to the 600th anniversary of the Kosovo battle, the Church carried across Serbia and Bosnia the relics of the saintly prince Lazar. In 1989 the Church brought together 100,000 pilgrims on the occasion of the opening of the newly built Orthodox monastery at Knežija on Mount Romanija in Bosnia-Herzegovina. In 1990, Church and state came together to commemorate the 300th anniversary of the First Great Migration of Serbs under Patriarch Arsenius III.

The most massive in the sequel of jubilees was the 600th anniversary of the Kosovo battle. The June 1989 celebration was preceded by a year-long tour of the holy relics of the martyr of that battle, Prince Lazar, throughout Serbia, Montenegro, and Bosnia-Herzegovina. The jubilee's conclusion took place on 28 June, St. Vitus' Day, when, according to Belgrade press, a million Serbs gathered at the historic battlefield of Gazimestan. Slobodan Milošević delivered a speech to the crowd in which he used a phrase often quoted later, announcing new battles for Serbia, including armed ones.

In the 1980s, the Serbian Orthodox faith and Church were obviously coming back in public life. As early as 1982, the German daily *Die Welt* reported from Belgrade that

historical consciousness, national consciousness, and religion have penetrated politics in Serbia. The Kosovo myth is in the consciousness of every Serb. Kosovo has had a great impact on the Serbs, perhaps even greater than the epic of the Nibelungens or the legend of Emperor Friedreich Barbarossa have on the Germans. The Kosovo theme is ubiquitous in Serbia today.[36]

Religious and historical themes inspired singers and songwriters of urban rock music.[37] In 1987 NIN reported that on Christmas Eve (6 January) it was nearly impossible for the reporter to approach the patriarchate's church as crowds spilled all over the surrounding streets.[38] A sociological survey carried out in Belgrade in the mid-1980s showed that 21 percent of those included in the survey (about half of them were nonbelievers) thought that the Serbian Orthodox Church was the most trustworthy national institution.[39] In 1984, Belgrade press and television recorded an example of ethnic awakening through the shrines of Kosovo when a group of Partisan war veterans paid pilgrimage to the shrines under the guidance of the village priest. A scandal broke out afterward when the pilgrims, members of the League of Communists, were disciplined. After media uproar, they were readmitted.[40] In the ensuing years, pilgrimages from Serbia to Kosovo became frequent and included worship services and group baptisms near ancient monasteries.[41] The Church also revived the traditional Saint Sava's Day—27 January. The traditional Saint Sava Day ball, the first since the 1945 communist takeover, took place on 27 January 1989 in the Hotel Yugoslavia. More than eight hundred guests turned out at the ball. The Belgrade daily *Politika* reported: "the traditional *svetosavski* ball shines with its old glamour. With the Srbijanka folk dance, the ball was opened by the ball hostess, Mrs. Nada Golubović and the archmaster architect Professor Branko Pešić, builder of Saint Sava's Memorial Temple. . . . [G]enerous donations were made for the construction of the Saint Sava's Temple."[42]

Slobodan Milošević's personal attitude toward Serbian Church and religion remained ambiguous. Although the new national hero played the central role in the secular part of the 1989 Kosovo jubilee, Milošević did not attend the holy liturgy at the Gračanica church. He continued to avoid church services, even though at the same time elsewhere in Europe political leaders, especially former communists, flocked to churches and mosques. Nevertheless, the powerful tradition influenced the new Serbian leader. In 1991 Milošević's minister for religious affairs, Dragan Dragojlović, implied that Milošević had experienced some sort of moving spiritual experience or even a conversion. It occurred during the highest Serbian state delegation's 1991 visit to the thirteenth-century Hilandar monastery at the holy mountain of Athos in Greece. According to Dragojlović's article in a Belgrade weekly,[43] the Greek hosts took their Serb guests by helicopter to Hilandar. The ex-communist Milošević and his entourage came to the spiritual oasis founded by Stephen-Simon and Sava of the Nemanjić dynasty at a critical moment, disillusioned with Marxism, communism, and Tito's Yugoslavia, "which the Serbs embraced with faith and devotion as a long-desired common permanent home, in contrast to other Yugoslav nationalities, for whom Yugoslavia seemed to be only a provisional solution and transitional model toward formation of their ethnic states."[44] Milošević, Dragojlović, and other former believers in the communist utopia and Tito's idea of brotherhood and unity of the Yugoslav peoples had been in Dragojlović's words, "for a long time prisoners of a false ideology."[45] It is worth noting that Dragojlović, the communist-era commissioner for religious affairs, would become an outspoken convert to Serbian Orthodoxy and ethnonationalist ideologue of the 1990s.[46]

The historic pilgrimage to the holy mountain empowered the disenchanted Milošević and his ex-communist comrades with new spiritual and ideological impulses and, perhaps even more important, armed them with new myths and symbols without which they could not maintain the momentum of their movement. The Belgrade delegation arrived at Hilandar as the local monastic community, financially supported by the Belgrade government, was undertaking renovations of the monastery's church and residential section. The monks thanked Milošević and warmly received the guests. Milošević and Dragojlović looked with awe at the legendary monastery's grape tree. The tree, legend has it, was planted eight centuries ago over the tomb of the founder of the Serbian kingdom, Stephen Nemanja, who became Simon the monk. The Saint Simon grape tree is believed to heal infertility. As Dragojlović explained, the pilgrimage to Hilandar helped him and Milošević to overcome their sense of loss, emptiness and disenchantment. At Hilandar, wrote Dragojlović, "standing under the Saint Simon's grape tree, leaders of new Serbia came to believe, that even if the sacred tree planted by the Serb king some day stops bearing fruits, Serbia, Greece, and the Orthodox faith will survive and continue to live forever."[47]

Milošević's 1991 pilgrimage to the holy mountain accelerated Milošević's conversion to Serbian myths. Milošević's minister for religious affairs, Dragojlović, presented himself through his poetry as a religiously and ethnically awakening Orthodox Serb and argued that Serbia and the Serbian state should honor the Serbian Orthodox Church and protect it as a state religion against expanding Islam and papacy.[48] Milošević himself was torn between his close associates, such as Dragojlović, who became faithful Orthodox and as such represented his Socialist Party's "right" faction, and a whole array of "leftists," or national-socialists, represented, notably, by his spouse, Mira Marković.

Several "national programs" that appeared in Serbia in the late 1980s outlined the new role for the Church and religion in society. In June 1989 a group of Orthodox clerics and laymen released a document entitled "A Proposal of Serbian Church-National Program" (PSCNP).[49] The Serbian Orthodox Church, the PSCNP argued, must be recognized according to its traditional historic role as a leading national institution; Church property confiscated by the communists must be recovered; the Church should return in public life, "for there cannot be a strong state without a strong Church."[50]

The PSNCP did not call for a breakup of Yugoslavia. Instead it demanded "mutual respect among groups that worship God in different ways" and legal guarantees for the religious, cultural, and national rights of the Serbs who live outside Serbia. Yet the document urged caution concerning the euphoric quest unfolding in the western Catholic Yugoslav republics aimed at joining the (western) European Union. "We do not want to be servile junior partners of western Europe and blind emulators of alien models; we want a truly Christian Europe, with a genuine and creative theodemocracy instead of a formal, arid, Western democracy," the document concluded.[51]

Another Serbian church-national program, somewhat broader in scope and presented as a scholarly article, was elaborated by a professor at Belgrade's Orthodox Theological School, Archpriest Mitar Miljanović, in the Christmas 1991 issue of the *Voice of the Church*.[52] Writing about "[t]he Serbian Orthodox Church's patriotic agenda under contemporary conditions," Miljanović points out that "the Serbian Orthodox Church is not only a religious organization, but also a leading national institution committed to the cause of national unity—national leadership is the Church's historical mission as a national church and national institution."[53] According to this Orthodox theologian, the nationalist or patriotic agenda of the Serbian Orthodox Church contains the following eight themes, ranked in order of importance: (1) the national history of the Serbs; (2) Kosovo; (3) World War II and in particular the memory of the concentration camp of Jasenovac and Ustaša genocide of Serbs; (4) the memory of World War I; (5) the issues of Serbian national culture; (6) the Serbian Orthodox Church, its social status, and historical role; (7) the lifestyle, customs, and value system of the Serbian people; (8) the cult of and the status of churches dedicated to Saint Sava, the saintly founder of the Serbian Orthodox Church.

According to this document, the Church set out to be a guide for the Serbian people in the time of the great transformation in Europe. The Church, Miljanović explains, "has always held that its mission is to lead the Serbian people and evaluate their history and culture."[54] Miljanović points out that a coherent national-church program is needed. He gives his support to the PSCNP, proposing that Church leaders issue an imprimatur for the program. He concludes that the Serbian Orthodox Church will be carrying on its traditional "mission of national church and national institution, regardless of which particular political, social, and economic system will come out of the current social change."[55]

According to sociological surveys of religiosity, the currents of the 1980s were ambiguous. In the 1980s in Yugoslavia, the Serbian Orthodox Church had the most unfavorable distribution of priests per number of believers: one Orthodox priest provided services for 5,714 Orthodox believers, whereas the Catholic Church had one priest for every 2,239 Catholics; the Islamic Community had one imam to assist 1,250 Muslims.[56] Despite the relative advantage of ethnic Serbs as the major Yugoslav nationality, the Catholic Church was the largest Yugoslav religious institution. In 1986, for example, the Serbian Church had 27 bishops, 3,084 priests, monks, and nuns, 4 seminaries, and one theological school. At the same time, the Catholic Church in Yugoslavia had 36 bishops, 5,500 priests, monks, and nuns, 7 theological schools, and 22 seminaries, let alone the Church abroad, the Catholic publishing houses, and the Church press that dwarfed the Orthodox church resources.[57]

In 1984, the newspaper of the Alliance of Socialist Youth of Serbia, *Omladinske novine* (Youth Paper), revealed the results of its study entitled "Social Activism of the Young." According to this project, 77 percent of the polled in the age group 12 to 18 declared themselves atheists. The percentage increased to 81 percent in the older age groups (18 to 27).[58] A University of Zagreb study showed a slight decline of religious affiliation during the decade 1975–84.[59] According to this research, the relative number of non-religious is ordinarily high among Orthodox Serbs, including Serbs living outside Serbia. Whereas 70 percent of the interviewees of Orthodox background said that they did not believe in God, only 30 percent of Catholics and 40 percent of Muslims made such a declaration.[60] The number of self-declared atheists was highest among Yugoslavs by nationality (45 percent), followed by the Serbs (42 percent), while only 12 percent of the interviewees of Croatian background said they were nonreligious. Another survey, entitled "Status, Consciousness, and Behavior of the Young Generation in SFR Yugoslavia" polled a sample of 6,500 respondents and revealed an overall decline of religiosity during the period between 1953 and 1985–86. Thus, among the Orthodox the decrease was 35.5 percent to 28.9 percent; the decrease was for the Catholics 25.2 percent to 21.9 percent and for the Muslims 15.6 percent to 13.4 percent.[61] The sociologist of religion Srdjan Vrcan noted that church leaders, clergy, and lay movements had become overall more active and visible in the public sphere, while at the same time nothing had changed concerning general trends of secularization.[62] In other words, people did not seek God more or less than before, while ethnic nationalism was growing and mainstream religious organizations were seeking to influence sociopolitical changes at the moment when the end of communism could have been envisioned. The "conversion" of Slobodan Milošević is highly instructive because it exemplifies the character of "religious revival" in Serbia in the 1980s. Milošević remained indifferent toward God and despised the clergy, but he was moved by the Serb anger over the Albanian uprising in Kosovo. This emotional charge was enhanced with the frustration over the status of Serbia in the Yugoslav federation and the appeal of Serbian tradition, history, and ethnicity.

9

THE SECOND STRIFE

*Religion as the Catalyst of the Crisis in
the 1980s and 1990s*

Only that which never stops hurting stays in the memory.
Friedrich Nietzsche

After Tito's death, ethnic nationalism was simmering in all parts of the country, from Slovenia in the northwest to Kosovo in southeast. The secular politics of the regime's establishment involved factional quarrels, and the activities of secular intellectual elites have been analyzed at length in domestic and foreign literature. The religious scene, where important things occurred, has remained obscure. Yet visible religious symbols and movements were no less telling harbingers of what was to happen in the 1990s.

The Clerical Offensive and the
Regime's Last Stand, 1979–1987

In the 1980s, the regime's experts for religious affairs sensed that the dynamic religious institutions' mobilization called for new policies and responses. In 1984, Radovan Samardžić defined official policy as follows: "struggle against abuses of religion, religious activity, and church service for political purposes . . . must be conducted through a free debate, education, instruction, and persuasion, rather than by state repression."[1] This mirrors a continuity of the new religious politics inaugurated in the 1960s, when church-state relations had relatively improved and religious liberties had expanded. After 1966, the secret police abolished departments for "hostile activities" of the clergy founded as early as 1944. Yet, after Tito's crackdown of ethnic nationalism in the republic and autonomous provinces in the early 1970s, clandestine police control of religious organizations had resumed. Nevertheless, the secret police maintained no reliable and efficient network of agents in the clerical rank and file. According to secretly recorded minutes from sessions of the Bishops' Conference of Yugoslavia that I read in the Croatian republic's office for relations with religious communities at Zagreb, one source agent (presumably a bishop) appears under the same code name from the mid-1970s to late the 1980s, and there was no other significant agent in the Church. The dominant source of information for the police was electronic espionage, that is, eavesdropping using electronic devices. In 1990, a Slovene journalist who was allowed access to police archives in Slovenia found that the SDS relied chiefly on electronic espionage, that is, "bugging," wiretapping, and control of phone and postal communications.[2] This contradicts the Croatian journalist Chris Cviić's argument that the Church was "heavily penetrated" by the communist secret police.[3] As would be revealed in 1999, electronic spying on church leaders continued after the fall of communism and Tito's Yugoslavia in all successor states, including Slovenia.[4]

Since the 1960s, state commissions for religious affairs (renamed after 1974 as commissions for relations with religious communities) were instructed to develop cordial relations with clergy and religious leaders and help them to overcome unnecessary difficulties such as rebuilding of new facilities and places of worship and other problems in church-state relations. These commissions' status and influence in the system was modest. Commissions were defined as advisory committees, and no law was made their establishment obligatory. In the 1980s in Croatia, for example, only a few commissions operated continuously as small offices in several of the largest cities. The situation of other republics was similar—in fact, in Croatia, because of the relative strength of the Catholic Church, these commissions were taken more seriously.[5] According to a 1988 survey conducted by Croatia's "religious commission" chief secretary, Vitomir Unković, in addition to the republic's central commission, headquartered in Zagreb, which maintained a permanent office staffed with six employees, there were two active commissions, in Split and Rijeka. Although 80 municipalities formally established commissions for relations with religious communities, these bodies rarely or never met and had no permanent offices.[6] After 1974, the Federal Commission for Relations with Religious Communities was affiliated with the Federal Executive Council. It had a chairperson appointed by the federal premier and would meet once or at best twice annually for informal consultations among chairs of the similar commissions from the republics and autonomous provinces. For experts interested in the forms of the struggle between church and state under communism, it would be worthwhile to compare the role of "commissions for religious affairs" in the former Yugoslavia and the Soviet Union.[7]

In consequence, clergy hostile to Tito's system saw their chance in the

1980s and met little regime resistance. According to a 1980 confidential police report, during the illness and death of Josip Broz Tito, many clerics, particularly Serb Orthodox and Catholic, were jubilant, as well as impatient to see the collapse of Tito's country.[8] Many used the pulpit to call for regime change. At the same time, the Central Committee of the League of Communists of Yugoslavia praised the Vatican for its support of the "genuine principles of nonaligned policy" and stressed that the Holy See and Yugoslavia shared the same views on most of the main issues in international relations, although "some domestic clericalists tend to abuse religious freedom for nationalist propaganda and incitement of ethnic hatred."[9]

In the mid-1980s, the Central Committee of the League of Communists of Croatia worried over the growing power of the Catholic Church as carrier of what was apparently an ethnonationalistic mass mobilization. Catholic lay youth organizations revived their activity in big cities and university centers. In 1985, on the occasion of "International Year of the Young," Catholic youth movements organized numerous marches and pilgrimages, and some were banned by authorities because of nationalistic excesses.[10] On 10 June 1985, the Central Committee of the Croatian League of Communists released a new program on religion that only inaugurated a more liberal rhetoric and did not bring about any profound change in the regime's views on religion.[11] Two years later, the Eighth Session of the Central Committee of the League of Communists of Croatia, held on 23–24 April 1987, declared the Catholic Church "the most dangerous fountainhead of nationalism" and indicated that Church-state tensions were rising anew.[12]

Party and state authorities in the vulnerable multiethnic Bosnia-Herzegovina were even more concerned. At a 1983 meeting with the city communist organization in Mostar, Herzegovina, the chairman of the Bosnian presidency, Branko Mikulić, said that "nationalists and clericalists from all the three ethnic nations and their respective organized religions have recently raised their voices against the brotherhood and unity of Yugoslavia and equality of its nations."[13] These nationalists in Bosnia-Herzegovina, according to Mikulić, labored to establish ethnically pure villages and city quarters, while the clergy divided people in order to gain more power and privileged status for themselves.[14] In the similar vein, an influential pro-regime columnist called for stern state action against ethnic nationalism championed by clergy:

If we let the clergy continue their apology for clerical fascists like Stepinac and processions and marches across Yugoslavia, we must fear the repetition of the horrors of the Second World War. The clergy pulled out swords in the name of the people, who never entrusted them with such religion! . . . We communists began to believe that the crimes of the Second World War would never be repeated, especially not in Europe at the end of the 20th century. But I am afraid that we have been wrong. Now we have a right to demand of our state courts that they halt nationalism and fascism. Clerical robes do not provide immunity from persecution: law must be equal for all.[15]

The regime combined sporadic repression with talks and conferences about reforms. In the 1980s, most political prisoners were ethnic Albanians who took part in the Kosovo secessionist movement.[16] Among the political prisoners listed in the 1985 Amnesty International annual report, a number of persons persecuted as "prisoners of conscience" included seven clerics.[17] In addition, several dozen clerics, most of them Catholic, had been sentenced or fined for minor offenses. It is worth noting that military courts persecuted Jehovah's Witnesses and Nazarenes for refusing to bear arms while in military service. According to official Yugoslav sources, as reported in December 1986, "over the past 15 years . . . 152 Yugoslav citizens have been convicted for refusing to carry weapons for religious reasons during military service."[18]

The repression of radical nationalist clergy was balanced with appeasement of religious leaders. Party officials and commissions for religious affairs made every effort to speed up administrative procedure for the construction of religious facilities.[19] Concurrently, the so-called New Year greetings between religious leaders and state officials were held with a significant media attention.

A Promise of Peaceful Transition: Moderate Religious Policies and the Regime's Belated Democratization, 1988–1990

The Croatian episcopate's policy toward the regime in the 1980s was ambivalent. An account read at the National Eucharistic Congress and published in the jubilee's monograph by the Bishop's Conference of Yugoslavia in 1988 acknowledged that the Church enjoyed relatively more favorable conditions in Yugoslavia in comparison with other communist countries. According to the document,

> in contrast to other socialist countries, here the state does not interfere in the Church's internal affairs: the bishops are nominated without governmental influence; they administer diocesan affairs autonomously; the state imposes no restrictions on the number of candidates for the clerical profession. . . . The Church autonomously trains priests, and no state commissars are placed at the church's offices. In addition, Yugoslavia was the only socialist country that has maintained direct diplomatic relations with the Holy See, except for the period between 1953 and 1970.[20]

Church leaders applied different methods and echoed mutually contesting views. While Archbishop Kuharić stepped up annual commemorations and the beatification campaign for Cardinal Stepinac, thereby irritating both the regime and the Serbian Church, the archbishop of Split-Makarska, Frane Franić, urged appeasement and dialogue. In his Christmas epistle of 1985, Franić asked believers "to love the concrete plural society in which we live, to identify ourselves with that society."[21] Franić also expressed a positive attitude toward the World War II Partisan struggle and urged the faithful to work together with "our brethren the Orthodox and the Muslims" for stability, the common good, and greater progress for "our multiethnic country."[22]

In 1983 and 1984, the federal government was negotiating with the Holy See a papal visit to Yugoslavia. The Croatian bishops officially invited the pope to the National Eucharistic Congress in September 1984. The Belgrade government was obliged to receive the pope, who had several times been invited by Yugoslav leaders to visit their country. The Vatican secretary of state, Cardinal Silvestrini, attended the Tito funeral in 1980, and a Yugoslav invitation to visit Yugoslavia was extended to the pope in 1981 during a meeting between the chairman of the federal presidency, Cvijetin Mijatović, and the pope in Rome. On this occasion the Vatican declared support for the federal-multiethnic, socialist, and nonaligned Yugoslavia.[23] A Croatian government document released in May 1981 recommended that the federal government allow the papal visit because, the document reads, "the papal visit, if properly managed, can produce far-reaching positive political consequences in our country."[24] Pope John Paul II made several appeals for interreligious cooperation and democratic transition in Yugoslavia. The Croatian program of Vatican Radio quoted on 18 March 1983 a papal address to Yugoslav bishops *ad limina apostolorum*. Wojtyla urged Catholic-Orthodox cooperation through an interchurch council for dialogue, extended special papal greetings to Yugoslav Muslims, and told the bishops that he held them responsible for maintaining interfaith harmony in the multiethnic country.[25] According to the Italian state news agency *ANSA*, the pope gave instructions in November 1983 to Michele Checchini, then a papal nuncio to Yugoslavia, to launch formal negotiations with the Belgrade government about the papal visit.[26] The nuncio Checchini, along with Cardinal Archbishop Franz Koenig of Vienna, held talks with federal government officials in Belgrade in January and February 1984. These meetings failed to reach agreement on the interfaith program of the papal visit. According to my interview with Radovan Samardžić, who was then the general secretary of the federal commission for relations with religious communities, the Serbian Orthodox Church indicated that the pope should visit Jasenovac and meet there, as well as in Belgrade, with the patriarch of Serbia. The Croatian episcopate had a number of objections to such an agenda, while demanding that interfaith prayers should commemorate all victims of war. The Serbian Church insisted that the pope mention specifically that most of those murdered at Jasenovac were ethnic Serbs. In consequence, the papal visit was called off. The two parties found a diplomatic formula for the controversy over the papal visit: the pope would come as soon as "circumstances permit" and both parties agree that the visit would not aggravate ethnic and interconfessional relations in Yugoslavia.[27]

Ethnically homogenous Catholic Slovenia, whose local Church did not seek a beatification of the World War II anticommunist and pro-German bishop Rožman and whose political leaders did not worry about ethnic minorities, rushed to inaugurate religious liberty without restrictions as early as 1987. From 1989 to 1990, in all Yugoslav republics except in Serbia, worship services were broadcast on Television, religious dignitaries read their messages to the faithful, and state officials delivered greetings to citizen believers. Even the Yugoslav military announced in November 1990 that "regulation of religious rights for military personnel is under review."[28] The federal government, under the premier Ante Marković, announced democratization of religious affairs in the context of the constitutional reform initiated in 1987. The Catholic episcopate released two documents concerning the constitutional reform. The bishops promised loyalty to the Yugoslav state provided that it honor religious values and recognize religious institutions as respected and benevolent social institutions.[29] In 1988, the Holy Synod of the Serbian Orthodox Church also submitted a set of proposals for the ongoing constitutional reform to federal authorities. The Serbian Church demanded that Christmas and Saint Sava's Day become state holidays.

Finally, the first private interfaith associations were formed in 1989. In October 1989, the Belgrade press published a document, entitled "An Interconfessional Petition," submitted to the federal government by a human rights group that brought together prominent clerics from various denominations. This interfaith group was led by a Serb Orthodox prelate Ljubodrag Petrović, with assistance from Belgrade Jesuits, some Muslim clerics, and leaders of local Jewish community.[30] The document called for greater religious liberty, advancement of religious culture, and the formation of interfaith advocacy groups.[31]

Ethnoreligious Realignment and the Multiparty Elections

As the first multiparty elections were announced in all Yugoslav federal republics, the question of religious liberty and religious affairs in general became a highly important issue in the preelection campaign. All pretenders vied to gain support from religious institutions. Aware of the Church's strength in Croatia, party leaders decided to start negotiations about power-sharing with the Catholic episcopate. Croatian communist reformers pinned their hopes on the diplomatic skills of Zdenko Svete, a Partisan veteran and former ambassador to the Holy See, who was nominated head of the state delegation for top-level secret church-state negotiations that began in February 1989 in Zagreb.[32] The Bishops' Conference of Yugoslavia nominated Bishop Ćiril Kos of Djakovo as the head of the Church delegation, assisted by the bishop of Šibenik, Antun Tamarut, the auxiliary bishop of Zagreb, Djuro Kokša, and the general secretary of the BKJ, Vjekoslav Milovan. The talks were held in the Croatian government's luxury residence, known as Villa Weiss (in Prekrižje).

According to my interviews with members of the state negotiation team, Svete's authority was rather limited.[33] His job was to buy time and make sure that the Church did not overtly side with ethnic nationalists. The Church, however, was in a hurry. At the first meeting Church representatives demanded unconditionally the lifting of all restrictive laws and policies in the domain of religious affairs. The bishops did not yet pose the issue of the restitution of Church property. The other party was stalling. The Croatian reformers could not simply meet all the Church's demands as the Slovenes had because, among other reasons, the Croatian government also had the task of conducting similar negotiations with the Serbian Orthodox Church. Svete tried to assure the bishops that the Church's possible support of the nationalists would carry a grave risk of interethnic strife. Svete made it clear to the bishops that both the Croatian League of Communists and the Croatian government were determined to resist Slobodan Milošević's great Serbian politics. The bishops applauded this. Svete also announced the beginning of separate talks between the federation and the Holy See about the revision of the "Protocol" of 1966. The chief secretary for relations with religious communities, Radovan Samardžić, told me that the leading reformer in the federation, Prime Minister Ante Marković (a Croatian business leader), urged new regulation in church-state relations emulating the West European model (e.g., Sweden, the Netherlands, Belgium).[34] Marković even put pressure on one of the most rigid institutions of the old regime—the Yugoslav People's Army—to begin revising military rules that banned active military personnel from attending worship service in uniform and reading religious publications inside garrisons.[35] However, neither Prime Minister Ante Marković and his "Alliance of Reform Forces" (backed by Western governments) nor any other nonnationalist or prounity party or movement won endorsement from religious authorities. In January 1990, the Bishops' Conference of Yugoslavia evaluated the course of the church-state talks in Croatia and ordered the delegation to obtain some written concessions to the key Church demands or to withdraw from the talks. The talks were interrupted by the first multiparty elections in April 1990.

In the meantime, the Croatian government faced growing ethnic nationalism and militancy from the apparently conflict-prone Serbian Orthodox Church. As early as the first half of the 1980s, a Croatian government document emphasized that "while interest in religion and the quality of spiritual life in the Orthodox Church has been for a long time now declining at an alarming rate, the Serbian clergy is intensifying nationalist propaganda in order to mobilize people on the platform of ethnic nationalism."[36] The document also pointed out that some clerics tend to magnify minor disputes over land, property, or trivial conflicts between the locals and the authorities in Serb-populated areas, in order to charge discrimination against the Serbian minority and unequal status for the Serbian Orthodox Church in predominantly Catholic Croatia. Furthermore, the source blames zealots among monks and bishops and the church press, especially the biweekly *Pravoslavlje*, for pressing the issue of World War II Ustaša crimes in order to aggravate interchurch and interethnic relations.[37]

In 1989 the Serbian Orthodox Church released a statement by the Holy Bishops' Sabor in which the bishops demanded from the authorities in Croatia and Bosnia-Herzegovina financial reparations for the loss of human resources and material damage the Serbian Church had suffered at the hands of the Ustašas.[38] The Croatian press noted that the Serbian Church had been for decades the major recipient of governmental subsidies and financial aid.[39] Nevertheless, the Croatian government tried to appease the Orthodox bishops, giving a lavish financial assistance for the celebration of the 600th anniversary of the Battle of Kosovo. The Croatian portion of the jubilee was held in northern Dalmatia at the village of Kosovo near Knin. During preparations for the jubilee, the Zagreb government donated 10 billion dinars (approximately 100,000 dollars) for rebuilding the Orthodox seminary at the Krka monastery in the Knin district. The government fully funded the construction of a 4.5-kilometer-long section of road giving access to the same monastery (the costs were equivalent to 1 million U.S. dollars). The government of Croatia also financially assisted the main ceremony of the jubilee of the Kosovo Battle in the village of Kosovo near Knin. Despite the regime's concessions to the Church, a massive nationalist demonstration erupted at the main event of the jubilee.[40] Perpetuating the pressure, Orthodox bishops and clergy (except a few Partisan veterans and members of priestly associations) boycotted the New Year church-state meeting in Zagreb in January 1990.

Between 4 October 1989 and 17 March 1990, the national Catholic bishops' conference released several statements, epistles, and instructions to the clergy and faithful about how to vote and prepare believers for the elections. These statements were tactful and diplomatic. Meanwhile, in Croatia, most of the clergy welcomed the 1989 foundation of the ethnic nationalistic party Croatian Democratic Community (HDZ) under the nationalist historian Franjo Tudjman. Tudjman had earlier distinguished himself by denying a Serbian "new historiography" of the World War II (more on this later), although he inclined toward minimizing NDH crimes against Serbs and Jews. Hence Tudjman was at the same time a good and bad choice. Good because he had been a Partisan, not Ustaša, during World War II but bad in that he was a red flag for the raging bull of Serbian nationalism because he used historical scholarship to debunk Serb myths, not in the name of the old Titoist brotherhood and unity but in order to exculpate the NDH and prepare ground for another independent Croatian state. In spite of his communist past, Tudjman was sufficiently nationalistic and ethnocentric to earn the Catholic Church's sympathies. A strong and rigid man and a former general,

Tudjman made the bishops feel less afraid of the Serbian menace. The leading Catholic weekly *Glas koncila* favored Tudjman. Many ordinary clerics agitated for the HDZ and some became party officials. The Franciscan Tomislav Duka, the Bosnian prelate Anto Baković, and the theologians Adalbert Rebić and Juraj Kolarić became members of the Tudjman party. The friar Duka told me in an interview that Pope John Paul II, Michael Gorbachev, and Franjo Tudjman were prophets sent by Jesus Christ to finish off communism and bring eternal happiness to humankind.[41] Baković became president of the "Croatian Population Movement," promising generous rewards for families with more than two children and threatening higher taxes for bachelors and unmarried women under 40. Both the Church and the HDZ promised to the people a national renaissance epitomized in high population growth and prosperity through quick privatization of the socialist economy, quick admission into the European Union, generous investments by rich countries that were friendly to Croatia, notably Germany and Austria, and the return to the homeland of wealthy Croatians from Western countries.

Tudjman conducted fundraising campaigns among exile Croat communities with the assistance of the Croatian Catholic missions. Catholic priests, such as the Franciscans Ljubo Krasić from Canada, Tomislav Duka from Germany, and other Croat clerics from Croatian parishes and missions in the diaspora raised millions in hard currency for Tudjman's electoral campaign.[42] Father Ljubo Krasić, a Herzegovinian Franciscan who served as parish administrator in Sudbury, Ontario (Canada), with his fellow Herzegovinians Gojko Šušak and Ante Beljo from Ottawa and others from the so-called Norwal group, with which Tudjman had collaborated during his American tours between 1987 and 1990, supplied Tudjman with dollars as well as very reliable cadres.[43] Šušak would become Tudjman's defense minister, and Beljo took over as the HDZ propaganda chief. According to a later testimony by General Martin Špegelj, who was Croatia's defense minister in 1990–91 (and was succeeded by Šušak after Špegelj resigned in protest of Tudjman-Milošević secret contacts), the Tudjman regime recruited police, military, and political officials from among a number of ordinary criminals, wanted by Interpol, who took refuge in Croatia as patriots returning to defend the country.[44] The same could be observed in Serbia, where, for example, the internationally wanted criminals Željko Ražnatović Arkan and the mysterious "Captain Dragan" from Australia returned to led paramilitary units "defending" Serbs in Croatia and Bosnia. Tudjman's top aide, Gojko Šušak, was designated by Western observers one of persons directly responsible for the outbreak of the Serbo-Croat war in 1991—it was he who launched armed attacks on Serb villages and ordered the assassination of Croats and Serbs who labored for peace.[45] Tudjman would later refer to the war of 1991 as a "war forced upon us" but in reality the HDZ wanted sovereignty and statehood for Croatia at any price and by all means, including war.

In the spring 1990 elections in Croatia, Tudjman's HDZ won a relative plurality of 43 percent and beat former communists, who gained 34 percent. The Church's support might have been a decisive factor for the election's outcome. The clerical support also had strong impact on the elections in Bosnia and Herzegovina. According to the moderate Bosnian politician Ivo Komšić, the Bosnian branch of the HDZ was organized and prepared for the 1990 elections through the parish system of the Catholic Church in Bosnia and Herzegovina.[46] Bosnian Catholic bishops and most of the Bosnian-Herzegovinian clergy, contends Komšić, made possible the electoral victory of the HDZ, even though it was obvious that this party's goal was the dismemberment of the republic. All in all, ethnic nationalistic parties, namely, the Serbian Democratic Party (SDS) in Croatia and Bosnia-Herzegovina, the HDZ in Croatia and Bosnia-Herzegovina and the Muslim Party of Democratic Action (SDA) in Bosnia-Herzegovina, backed by the largest religious institutions, won the elections by narrow margins of votes.[47]

At the same time in Bosnia-Herzegovina, the Serbian Orthodox Church provided overt support for the extreme Serb nationalist Radovan Karadžić, while Bosnian Muslim clergy backed the Muslim SDA party. The Muslim leader Izetbegović needed Islam both as the vehicle of popular mobilization and the key component of the newly emerging Bosniak national identity. Besides, the weak Muslim SDA could not organize the election campaign without the local Muslim clergy. Although leaders of the Islamic Community had declared their neutrality in party politics, in reality, imams and other officials of the Islamic Community unequivocally supported the SDA in the first multiparty election in Bosnia-Herzegovina held in November 1990. In the words of an SDA activist from Mostar, Herzegovina, "without the help from our imams and villages, Alija [Izetbegović] would have not become the new president of Bosnia and Herzegovina."[48] According to my interviews with Muslim religious officials and SDA leaders in 1989 and 1990, the ulema took part in the foundation of the SDA and carried out most of the logistics for the election campaign.[49] Among 40 founding members of the SDA, eight were former "Young Muslims" and some two dozen included prominent imams from the Sarajevo theological school and the Zagreb mosque, the mufti of Mostar, and officials of the Community's Sarajevo headquarters. Despite the decision on clerical noninvolvement in politics by the Islamic Community and protests by the liberal Zulfikarpašić and the Reis Selimoski, hundreds of clerics remained associated with the party, backed its fundamentalist wing, and, according to Zulfikarpašić, took part in organizing the party's military wing, the so-called Muslim Patriotic League.[50] Islamic religious symbolism dominated the new party's mass gatherings. The moderate Muslim Zulfikarpašić argued that the display of symbols imported from Arab countries was "unseen in Bosnia, alien to its culture, and harmful for the idea of tolerance."[51] Izetbegović, according to Zulfikarpašić, was pretending to be a mediator between the liberals and zealots, though in reality he backed the latter. The zealots also recruited prominent former communists, who rushed to demonstrate their new religious conversion.[52] Thus, the most massive SDA convention under the green banners of Islam and Arab inscriptions from the Koran took place in the western Bosnian town of Velika Kladuša, with the sponsorship of the former communist official and local business magnate Fikret Abdić, as a part of his bid for the office of Bosnia's presidium.

Up to the outbreak of the Bosnian war in 1992, the leaders of the Islamic Community remained nonetheless less nationalistic and militant than the Christian Churches. The Reis Selimoski took part in a joint prayer for peace with Pope John Paul II and organized several ecumenical meetings and peace vigils. Yet, after it became clear that Slovenia and Croatia were fighting for secession while Milošević launched a war for Greater Serbia, in October 1991 the Rijasset in Sarajevo released a document in support of an independent and sovereign Bosnia-Herzegovina. Muslim leaders established collaboration with the Islamic Conference and urged this organization to watch closely the crisis in Bosnia-Herzegovina and be prepared even for international recognition of Bosnia as a sovereign state in case Milošević and Tudjman attempted to dismember it.

In contrast to the cases of Croatia and Bosnia, where clerical support had a palpable impact on the elections' outcome, in Serbia and Montenegro, Slobodan Milošević retained power without the Serbian Orthodox Church's help and even in spite of some criticism from the clerical rank and file. At the time of the elections, the Church was without a patriarch. Germanus was on his deathbed, and the new patriarch had not been elected yet. Many clerics in the Serbian Church believed that Milošević was the long-awaited liberator and unifier of all Serbian lands. Although Patriarch Germanus did not explicitly mention Milošević's name, even this cautious Church leader said (in the 1987 interview quoted earlier) that Serbia and the Serbian Orthodox church were waiting for a national leader capable of defending Serbian interests and if necessary, accomplishing partition of the country.[53] Some prelates, especially those aspiring to replace the ailing Germanus at the patriarchal throne, lauded Milošević in interviews with the secular press. Metropolitan Amfilohije said in his 1990 interview with the Belgrade weekly *NIN* that "Milošević and other leading politicians in Serbia should be commended for understanding the vital interests of the Serb people at this moment. . . . If they continue as they have started, the results will be very impressive."[54] According to Bishop Amfilohije's interview with the foreign press, "between 1987 and 1989, as it was so clear during the jubilee of the Kosovo Battle, Serbia has demonstrated a national unity, unseen probably since 1914."[55] Another outspoken Milošević supporter was the acting patriarch, Metropolitan Jovan of Zagreb. Nevertheless, many Church leaders remained suspicious of Milošević because of his communist past and nonattendance of Church services and jubilees, let alone the issue of Church property, which he ignored.

The confused Serb episcopate held the elections for the new patriarch on 6 December 1990, one week before the multiparty elections in Serbia. Milošević tried to secure control over the Church through his favorites for the patriarchal seat, the incumbent patriarch's deputy, Metropolitan Jovan of Zagreb and the metropolitan of Montenegro, Amfilohije Radović. Yet both proteges of the Serbian strongman suffered a fiasco, not even having been elected to a short list of three candidates. The new patriarch-elect was the bishop of Raška-Prizren (Kosovo), Pavle (Gojko Stojčević), born in 1914. At the same session the bishops' assembly released a preelectoral message to the Serbian people. The message was vehemently anticommunist, with the following relatively easily identifiable anti-Milošević note: "we are convinced that the Serbian people will be capable of recognizing and electing candidates sincerely faithful to God and to the nation, in contrast to those who make big promises behind which they hide their quest for power and selfish interests."[56] The Church, through the preelectoral message, also announced its own expectations for "full freedom of the Church's mission . . . and return of the Church as spiritual mother of the Serbian people in schools, hospitals, the mass media and public life . . . in the new democratic society."[57] Two weeks before the election day in Serbia, the patriarchate's weekly, *Pravoslavlje*, lashed out at Milošević and his communists, renamed "socialists." In the strongest words possible, *Pravoslavlje* called on the people of Serbia to renounce "the new wave of dishonor, dishonesty, brainwashing and media-terror," "neo-Bolshevism," and "neo-Titoism" and vote against "the arrogant, self-appointed Hazyain Milošević."[58] However, following Milošević's 65 percent electoral triumph, on 24 December 1990, the patriarch-elect paid a visit to the president-elect on the patriarch's request. Milošević, who earlier had avoided encounters with the clergy, this time allowed the meeting be televised and praised by the media as evidence of national unity around the new democratically elected leader. Nevertheless, the Church was still upset by the fact that Milošević did not improve the social and financial status of the clergy or recognize the Church as a specific national institution.[59] In spite of the Church's desire for collaboration, President Milošević did not attend the enthronement of patriarch-elect Paul I in the Saborna church, and his government did not grant a day off for Christmas, as the western republics had done two years earlier. Not even Saint Sava's Day was restored as a school feast. The patriarch and the *Provoslavlje* protested not only the Christmas issue but also the "arrogant manipulations with the Church and the patriarch, for the Serbian president's self-promotion and other propaganda purposes, in Milošević's daily *Politika* and state-run TV."[60]

The Serbian Church, however, strongly backed Serb nationalist parties and their leaders in Croatia and Bosnia-Herzegovina. In Croatia, as I have shown, the Serbian Church turned militant and anti-Croatian even before Tudjman's electoral triumph. Since 1987, the Church press had alleged numerous cases of anti-Serbian discrimination by the new regime.[61] After the regime change in Spring 1990, the Serbian Church overtly designated Tudjman a new Pavelić. On 13 September 1990, a group of Orthodox priests released a message in which they accused the Croatian authorities of "daily cases of terror and intimidation, insults, loss of jobs, demolition of homes, assaults and even proven cases of murder and rape . . . the major targets of the violence being Orthodox priests, their families, and especially children."[62] The clergy "hold the state responsible for the violence."[63] In January 1991, president-elect Franjo Tudjman officially invited all bishops and other dignitaries of the Serbian Orthodox Church in Croatia to the traditional church-state meetings inherited from the communist era. None of 14 invited Orthodox dignitaries appeared in the Croatian state assembly. A written notice addressed to the president-elect said that the representatives of the Orthodox Church would stay away to protest against assaults on Serbian clergy, people, and church property in Croatia.[64]

The War of the Churches

In the late 1980s and early 1990s, Catholic–Orthodox relations, observed at the level of Croat and Serb religious elites, seemed strikingly analogous to the Concordat crisis of the 1930s and the prewar mobilization of the churches from 1937 to 1941. This time, points of conflict included an even larger number of concrete issues, plus a propaganda war over the causes of the current crisis and controversies from the history of World War II. The Kosovo crisis and the Macedonian ecclesiastical schism widened the rift between the Serbian Orthodox Church and the other two major Yugoslav religious institutions. Both the Islamic Community and the Catholic Church came under the Serbian barrage. Orthodox clergy, Belgrade media, and Serb scholars argued that Islamic fundamentalism was the driving force of Albanian separatism.[65] "Islamic fundamentalism has played a great role in the Kosovo drama and tragedy for the Serbian people and the Church," wrote the archimandrite Atanasije Jevtić in his Kosovo chronicle.[66] In 1987 Patriarch Germanus said in an interview that the influence of Islam on the situation in the part of Yugoslavia where Albanians live was "enormous" and blamed Muslim leaders for "doing nothing to keep Albanian separatism under control."[67] In reality, proregime officials of the Islamic Community, urged by the state, labored for years to mitigate tensions in Kosovo. Besides, the influence of Muslim clergy was rather limited. Albanian nationalism was ethnic and tribal, not religious. Albanian riots in 1968, 1971, and 1981 were led by pro-Tirana Marxist students and intellectuals. The mufti of Kosovo told me in an interview that the religious culture of the Kosovo population was poor and the attendance of worship services and religious instruction worryingly low.[68] The Kosovo crisis also affected Catholic–Orthodox relations negatively. The Croatian church press, Radio Vatican, and some Catholic churchmen expressed support for the 1981 Kosovo movement and backed the Albanian quest for greater autonomy in Kosovo. In 1982 Vatican Radio broadcast a series of programs in the Albanian and Croatian languages supportive of the Albanian struggle against the Serbs. One of the Jesuit editors in the Croatian language program lost his position after a diplomatic note filed by Belgrade to the Vatican. In 1982, Archimandrite Atanasije Jevtić accused the Croatian secular and church press of encouraging the secession of Kosovo while covering up the truth about the Croat genocide of Serbs during World War II.[69] A foreign analyst of Balkan affairs wrote about the Catholic–Orthodox rift over Kosovo as a "detonator of the Serbo-Croat conflict threatening to explode."[70]

The Vatican angered the Serbian Church by maintaining ties with the schismatic Macedonian Orthodox Church. The Macedonian Orthodox Church established annual May commemorations at St. Cyril's tomb in Rome. The pope received Macedonian clergy in a private audience. The papal sympathy for the Macedonians also derived from the tradition of the 1859 ecclesiastical union of Kukuš. The once-expanding Macedonian Kukuš Uniate church was suppressed through a joint Serbo-Bulgarian-Greek effort and abolished after the Balkan wars. However, several parishes survived and a Uniate bishop was installed in Skopje. Yugoslav diplomacy was thankful to the pope for supporting the Macedonians. On 18 June 1982, on the occasion of the consecration of the newly built Catholic cathedral in the Macedonian capital of Skopje, representatives of the Holy See were in attendance with Yugoslav regime officials and the Macedonian clergy. On 22 May 1985, the pope received a delegation of the Macedonian Church accompanied by Yugoslav regime officials. In September 1985, the Macedonian Orthodox Church delegation, despite bitter protests by the Serbian Orthodox Church, took part in the main ceremony of the Year of Saint Methodius at Djakovo, Croatia. In October 1987, a high-ranking delegation of the Catholic Church visited Skopje to participate in the Macedonian Church's jubilee of the twentieth anniversary of the proclamation of autocephaly. The embittered patriarch of Serbia, Germanus, complained (in the 1987 interview cited earlier): "No other Orthodox Church has accepted the forceful separation of one part of the Serbian Orthodox Church from the rest of it. On another side, they (Macedonians) are recognized by the Vatican! Doesn't this one detail alone really tell you enough?!"[71] It is also noteworthy that the Vatican and Catholic press further infuriated the Serbian Orthodox Church by supporting the movement for an autocephalous Orthodox Church in Montenegro. The Montenegrin ecclesiastical movement argued that the oldest church in Montenegro (in the historic Dioklea-Duklja and Zeta provinces) was the Catholic archdiocese of Bar. The same argument emphasizes that the autonomous national Orthodox Church in the Kingdom of Montenegro was abolished and incorporated into the Serbian Orthodox Church in 1920.[72]

The Churches and the World War II Controversy

After Tito's death, the official history of World War II that had constituted the keystone of the civil religion of brotherhood and unity and the six-republic federation's patriotic myths was questioned by authors, historians, and journalists—nationalists as well as liberal communists.[73] One of keystones of Titoist historiography of World War II, according to which the Croat Ustaša NDH was an aberration in the history of the Croat people and was imposed by fascist Nazi invaders, was challenged in the mid-1980s by intellectual, cultural, and religious circles in Belgrade. A "new Serbian history" was then in the process of being written, concurrent with the unfolding ethnic nationalist mobilization of Serbs aimed at restructuring the Tito federation. This "new history" was influenced by the following fours factors and sources: (1) Serbian ethnic nationalist ideology; (2) nationalism emanating from the Orthodox Church and church historiography; (3) Serb émigré myths and propaganda; and (4) Holocaust and genocide studies (according to which the Serbs identified themselves with the Jews and the crimes against Serbs were perceived as equivalent to the Holocaust). The influence of the fourth factor I have already noted and will further elaborate hereafter, although a proper understanding would presumably require from readers familiarity with Holocaust historiography since the 1960s.[74]

The "new" Serbian historians argued that the NDH was above all a very efficient instrument of genocide against Serbs, conceived in Croatia several centuries before the genocide took place. The NDH genocide, argued Serb historian Vasilije Dj. Krestić, among many others, targeted the Serb people for annihilation, while the idea of genocide is, allegedly, several centuries old, one of the key peculiarities in the history of the Croats, and even a remarkable idiom of Croatian culture, religion, and national character.[75] The new Serbian historiography, to which both Church and secular historians contributed, emphasized the role of religion as the key catalyst of Serbo-Croat hatred, designating the Roman Catholic Church as the chief carrier of hatred and inspirer of the idea of genocide against the Serb people.[76] After inaugurating this new history, the Serbian nationalist movement moved on to argue that, allegedly, another independent state of Croatia was in the process of reemergence in what was then the Socialist Republic of Croatia (then still ruled together by Croat and Serb communists devoted to Tito's ideology of multiethnic "brotherhood and unity"). Serbs in Croatia and Bosnia-Herzegovina were cautioned to be prepared for a possible repetition of the genocide of 1941.

Croatian historians, nationalists and moderates alike, rebuked the genocide thesis.[77] The nationalist historian Franjo Tudjman was one of the most outspoken defenders of the Croats against the Serb "genocide thesis," but his proclivity to minimize Ustaša crimes and explain them as an overreaction against the long Great Serbian pressure on Croats in Croatia and Bosnia, especially during the interwar monarchy, fueled the anger from Belgrade so that new genocide charges mounted.[78] Tudjman also used his scholarly skills to write an apology for the Catholic Church and Archbishop Stepinac, designated as accomplices in Ustaša crimes.[79] Monsignor Pave Žanić, who was the bishop of Mostar in the 1980s, told me in an interview that all Croat bishops admired both Tudjman's scholarship and courage.[80]

The churches, of course, began rewriting history and challenging each other earlier through grand jubilees and commemorations of various anniversaries from ethnic past. Regarding the Stepinac controversy, in 1979, the Archbishop of Zagreb, Franjo Kuharić, inaugurated annual mementoes for Cardinal Stepinac, publicly calling for a "new" truth about the allegedly falsely accused cardinal. In 1981, the Zagreb archdiocese submitted Stepinac's candidacy for martyrdom to the Vatican's Congregation for the Causes of Saints. The Curia initiated procedure de virtutibus, which includes study of the candidate's life and demeanor, in order to determine whether, as the proposal argued, the candidate lived strictly according to Christian norms, thereby setting an example for others. In 1984, the Stepinac case was elevated to the stage de martyrio, focusing on the candidate's struggle against communism and his years in jail. In the meantime, the Catholic Church was completing the nine-year entitled Great Novena "Thirteen Centuries of Christianity in the Croat People." In September 1984, at the final ceremony of the jubilee, Cardinal Kuharić spoke about the Stepinac case. Yet only a week before the National Eucharistic Congress of the Church in the Croat People, the Church of Serbia staged its "countercommemoration" at Jasenovac.

Forgive but Not Forget: Liturgy in the Concentration Camp

Four years after Tito's death, Serbian Orthodox Church leaders dared to undertake what Bishop Nikolaj Velimrović had urged as early as the 1950s: a liturgical commemoration of Jasenovac as a site of martyrdom of the Serb people second in importance to Kosovo. During Tito's life such an act would have been impossible, for two basic reasons. First, Titoism emphasized antifascist Partisans, not ethnic Serbs, as the principal victims of the Jasenovac concentration camp. As noted in chapter 6, Jasenovac became a shrine of the civil religion of brotherhood and unity and a memorial to the Partisan struggle in which all ethnic groups and minorities took part and suffered. At the site where the Ustaša death camp once stood, state authorities established a museum and memorial park with a 140-foot-tall concrete flower-shaped memorial monument.[81] Second, Titoism would have not allowed separate ethnically based commemorations and uses of Jasenovac to imply that "the Serb people" were a victim of a genocide carried out by "the Croat people" as the Serb nationalistic message established in the late 1980s did.

The Serbian Orthodox Church viewed Jasenovac as a latter-day Kosovo, that is, a sacred site of martyrdom and "eternal memory" that would rejuvenate the nation. A new Serbia was emerging, with its secular capital and the patriarchal seat in Belgrade and two spiritual centers in Kosovo and

Jasenovac, plus the web of monasteries and shrines in the region. The connection between the old myth of Kosovo and the new Jasenovac myth was carefully knitted by church leaders. Yet Jasenovac needed "desecularization." In 1988, the church journal *Glas crkve* revealed that Bishop Velimirović had bequeathed funds for the construction of what he envisioned as a "Temple of Atonement" to be built at Jasenovac, "in honor of the victims and as symbol of forgiveness to the executioners for the crimes they committed."[82]

An Orthodox chapel at Jasenovac was rebuilt between 1973 and 1984 with financial aid from the Croatian government and donations from Serbs abroad. After the Tito's 1971 crackdown on the Croat nationalist movement, the new Croatian republic's authorities felt a sense of guilt and sought to appease Croatian Serbs in a number of ways, including providing the permit and money for the chapel. The original parish church at Jasenovac had been destroyed and burned to the ground by the Ustašas in August 1941. In 1983, a replica of the prewar parish church was completed and the new temple was scheduled to be consecrated in the same week that the Roman Catholic Church in Croatia was to hold the final ceremony of the Great Novena—the National Eucharistic Congress.

On 2 September 1984, the Serbian Church convened 20,000 faithful at Jasenovac for the consecration of the new St. John the Baptist parish church. The purpose of the event, according to the Orthodox theologian Mitar Miljanović, was the consecration and inauguration of Jasenovac as "the memorial site of the most horrible suffering of the Serbian people next to Kosovo. Jasenovac is not only a symbol of genocide of the Serbian people—Jasenovac is the specific location in which genocide was committed preeminently against the Serbian people."[83] In the words of the Serb-Orthodox metropolitan of Zagreb-Ljubljana, Jovan Pavlović, the commemoration was the Serbian Orthodox church's response to "attempts to obliterate the traces of Jasenovac, to reduce the total immense number of victims, to deny the crime and forget it! We cannot, and will not, ever forget the sufferings of the innocent children in Jasenovac. . . . A too easy forgetfulness of evil means that it could be repeated."[84] In his homily, the patriarch of Serbia, Germanus, drew parallels between Jasenovac and Jerusalem (Golgotha) and between Jasenovac and the Nazi concentration camps of Auschwitz, Mauthausen, and Dachau. The patriarch stressed that those who had committed the crimes at Jasenovac were Christians who killed and tortured other Christians, all in a belief that thereby they were doing a patriotic service to their nation. The head of the Orthodox Church concluded: "Brothers, we have to forgive, because such is the Gospel's commandment—but we cannot forget. Let the great-grandsons of our great-grandsons know that this enormous concrete flower on the field of Jasenovac is the witness of madness, which must never take place again."[85]

After the 1984 commemoration at Jasenovac, the memorial site became the destination of Serb pilgrimages. In search of inspiration, the members of the Serbian Academy of Sciences and arts, then working on the "Memorandum of the Serbian Academy of Sciences and Arts," made pilgrimage to Jasenovac twice, in 1985 and again in 1989. In the meantime, the Serbian Church continued annual commemorations at Jasenovac (the most massive would be the liturgies held in 1990 and 1991). In August 1990 the Holy Synod published a massive monograph dedicated to Jasenovac. This book argued that the Vatican and Croatian Catholic clergy were liable for the Ustaša genocide against Serbs.[86] Metropolitan Jovan of Zagreb established a local feast in honor of the 1984 consecration of the Jasenovac memorial church. The new local Orthodox bishop, Lukijan Pantelić, was installed in 1985. He inaugurated the Day of the Jasenovac Martyrs, to be commemorated annually on Saint John's Day, 7 July.

The Serbian Church's 1984 liturgy at the World War II concentration camp memorial site rebutted the history symbolically presented by the Croat Catholic Great Novena entitled "Thirteen Centuries of Christianity in the Croat People" and was an assault by the Serbian Church on the civil religion of brotherhood and unity. Many Serb, Croat, Montenegrin, Muslim, Slovene, and other Partisan communists were killed in Jasenovac because they were communists and Partisan. The Serbian Church wanted this to be forgotten. The "new" Jasenovac became a "death camp," a "Yugoslav Auschwitz" for extermination of the Serb people. Serb historians and church leaders borrowed concepts and ideas from Holocaust historiography and applied it to World War II in Yugoslavia. Serbs became equivalent to the Jews and Croats to the Nazi Germans. In the ensuing years, Serb prelates commemorated "genocide against the Serb people" in other memorial sites from World War II where Partisans fought major battles against Germans and Ustašas as well as Serb nationalist Četniks. The Kozara mountain in western Bosnia, Romanija in eastern Bosnia, Užice and Kragujevac in Serbia, Petrova Gora in Croatia, St. Prokhor Pčinjski in Macedonia, and other places of Partisan heroism were converted into memorials to the martyrdom of the Serb people. In 1990, the last federal prime minister, Ante Marković convened some 100,000 supporters at the Kozara mountain in western Bosnia. There, in 1942, Germans and Ustašas (with indirect support from the Serb Četniks, who blocked Partisan reinforcements) surrounded a few Partisan brigades and hundreds of thousands of people, mostly Serbs, and after a massacre of the Partisans sent whole villages and families into concentration camps. Yet, while Ante Marković spoke about reform and brotherhood and unity, thousands in attendance waved Serbia's flags and displayed portraits of the Serb communist-turned-nationalist Slobodan Milošević along with icons of Saint Sava and King Dušan.

A Battle of Myths: The Yugoslav
Auschwitz versus
the Martyr Cardinal

Estimates of the number of people killed at Jasenovac varied from 28,000 to 40,000, as Croat "minimalists" (notably Franjo Tudjman) alleged, to

700,000 Serbs murdered in Jasenovac alone, with over a million in NDH concentration camps, as Serb nationalists alleged.[87] Moderate analysts, such as Vladimir Žerjavić, estimate the total war losses of the population of prewar Yugoslavia at 1,027,000, out of which 50,000 were killed at the Jasenovac camp.[88] The Milošević regime and Serb historians found it extremely important to win over eminent Yugoslav Jewish organizations and individuals for the idea of the joint Serbo-Jewish martyrdom. In order to accomplish this, Serbia had to falsify history by obscuring the fact that the Serb quislings Milan Nedić and Dimitrije Ljotić had cleansed Serbia of her sizeable Jewish population by deportations of Jews to East European concentration camps or killing them in Serbia.[89]

Nevertheless, some Yugoslav Jews collaborated with the new Serbian historiography. The eminent legal scholar Andrija Gams backed Milošević.[90] Another Belgrade professor of Jewish background, Enriko Josif, was asked by the Holy Synod of the Serbian Church to promote the new church monograph about Jasenovac at Belgrade's Kolarac's University in October 1990. In his address, Josif drew parallels between Jasenovac and Auschwitz, between Jasenovac and Stalin's concentration camps, and between the Holocaust and the Ustaša massacre of Serbs, Jews, and Gypsies in the Independent State of Croatia.[91]

The Serbian Orthodox Church accepted as accurate the figure of 700,000 Serb victims killed in Jasenovac alone.[92] Echoing Bishop Nikolaj Velimirović, Archimandrite Jevtić accused Croat Catholic clergy and the Vatican of inciting a genocide against the Serbian people. In Jevtić's words, "countless murders of Serbs had begun in the sacristy and parish offices of the Roman Catholic Church in the Independent State of Croatia."[93] The Serb legal scholar Smilja Avramov wrote in several books that the Vatican's influence on the wartime Zagreb regime was strong enough to halt what she viewed as a genocide.[94] According to Avramov,

the crime of genocide in the Independent State of Croatia was carried out according to a fixed plan, with the active assistance of the Zagreb Archbishopric. . . . In Croatia, for instance, the Catholic church was the high priest and theoretician of the cult of exterminating the Serbs, Jews, and Gypsies, but this was not the case with the Catholic Church in Slovakia, Poland, etc., as regards to the Jews or any other enemies. . . . There was a similar situation in Denmark and the Netherlands. In contrast, various Croatian Catholic priests and even nuns were directly involved in massacring the Serbs, albeit many Catholic priests attached to the Italian forces of occupation helped organize the escape.[95]

The Serb anti-Catholic campaign also included the issue of the so-called "Croatian Orthodox Church" established by the Ustašas in 1942 and the massive conversions of Serbs to Catholicism under Ustaša rule.[96]

In response to these charges, the Catholic Church of Croatia vociferously continued the apology of Cardinal Stepinac. Catholic historians underscored Stepinac's resistance to communism but argued that the prelate had also rescued Jews and other persons persecuted by NDH regime and was not on good terms with the Ustaša fuhrer Pavelić.[97] It is noteworthy that exiled Ustašas also joined the dispute defending the Catholic Church.[98]

At the 1979 commemoration of Stepinac's death, Cardinal Kuharić said that "even the history of the church is subject to analyses, scientific messages and assessments" and invited a scientific inquiry into the wartime role of Cardinal Stepinac, provided the research is "honest, fair and objective, devoid of any hatred or biased approaches. . . . We are never afraid of the judgment of history, because we are not afraid of the truth. There exist documents; there exist works; there exist statements."[99] The Church opened secret archives and announced that Stepinac had saved the lives of a number of Serbs, Jews, and Partisans.[100] The editor-in-chief of the *Glas koncila*, Živko Kustić, wrote a weekly column and editorial in which he defended Stepinac and rebuked other Serbian charges, such as exaggerations of the number of victims of Jasenovac and the role of the Catholic Church in the forcible conversions of Serbs to Catholicism (Kustić argued that these conversions were few and that through them the Church allegedly saved lives of Serbs condemned to death by the Ustašas). In defense of Stepinac, Kustić published a monograph, *Stepinac*, written for a wide popular audience.[101] The Serbian church newspaper *Pravoslavlje* called the book "another apotheosis of Cardinal Stepinac, as part of the neo-Ustaša revival in Croatia."[102] Kustić's book," *Pravoslavlje* writes, "encourages and incites young Croats to fight the Serbs because the moment has come to establish another NDH."[103]

The apology of Cardinal Stepinac angered the Serbian Church. Patriarch Germanus said in an interview: "Had it not been for the Serbian holocaust in the Independent State of Croatia, I believe that Stepinac would never have become a saint."[104] Serb clerics advocated that Bishop Nikolaj Velimirović and Archimandrite Justin Popović be made saints of the Serbian Church.

Disputes over Holy Places

Envisioning the possible breakup of the Yugoslav federation, the Serbian Orthodox Church press frequently wrote about the origins of ancient churches and monasteries in ethnically mixed areas. Church leaders held liturgies near long-forgotten ruins where no religious activity had occurred for decades or, in some cases, centuries. For example, in May 1990, Catholic and Orthodox press argued over the historic origins of an ancient church of the Ascension, also called the Holy Savior, located in Croatia's predominantly Serb-populated Krajina region, where Serb militants had already agitated for an armed Serb uprising and secession from Croatia. Secular and church archeologists, historians, and art historians came up with various hypotheses about the origins of the church, but according to the most credible research and literature, the original church was built in the Western style of sacred architecture by a medieval Catholic ruler. In May 1990 (in the midst the first multiparty elections in Croatia), both Orthodox and Catholic churches announced that worship services would be held at the contested church. At the eleventh hour, the local Franciscan leader in Split decided not to aggravate the crisis and canceled the pilgrimage. On 24 May 1990, the Serb Orthodox Bishop Nikolaj Mrdja officiated before a crowd of two hundred Serbs led by the militant nationalists Jovan Rašković, Vojislav Šešelj, and Željko Ražnatović Arkan. "Even if there was an older church underground, as some people argue these days" the bishop said in his sermon at the Holy Savior, "that underground church must also be Orthodox, because all Christian churches in Dalmatia at the time when that church was built, that is in the ninth or tenth century, were Byzantine churches under the jurisdiction of the patriarch in Constantinople, which means that they are Orthodox, and by succession, should belong to the Serbian Orthodox Church."[105] Similar disputes drew considerable attention from the media. For example, in the coastal city of Split the Serbian Orthodox Church quarreled for years with city authorities over an unfinished Orthodox memorial temple and eventually refused to rebuild the church once the permit was obtained, thus keeping the crisis simmering. In 1986 the Croatian secret police notified the Central Committee of the League of Communists of Croatia that the leaders of the Serbian Church, allied with Serb nationalists in Serbia and Croatia, sought to provoke incidents between local Serbs and authorities of the Republic of Croatia in order to mobilize the Serbs in Croatia for a massive armed uprising.[106]

This police warning proved correct. On 17 August 1990, church bells rang throughout Serb-populated zones in Croatia calling Serbs to arms. A secessionist "Krajina" province was established, backed by Belgrade. In the summer of 1991, Serb insurgents destroyed hundreds of Catholic churches in the areas under their control. Many armed clashes and massacres occurred in the vicinity of previously disputed holy places and historic sites. The Serbs massacred Catholic villagers at Škabrnja, within a province where several ancient churches were disputed. Another large massacre occurred near the parish church at Kusonje in western Slavonia. The village of Kusonje is known as a Partisan base in World War II where the Ustašas locked up Serb men in the parish Orthodox church and set the church ablaze. In 1989, a local Orthodox priest from Kusonje launched a public polemic over the renovation of local church and thus mobilized the villagers, drawing them into a conflict with the Croatian government. And it was near Kusonje, on 8 September 1991, that Serb militants ambushed and killed a Croatian police unit. The Serbian Church also commemorated historic seats of Orthodox dioceses at Dalj in Slavonia and Ston near Dubrovnik in Dalmatia. The town of Dalj is also the site of a Serb martyrdom of World War II, where the Ustašas forced local Serbs (who had earlier converted to Cathol-

,icism) to demolish the Orthodox parish church on Orthodox Christmas Day in 1942. In 1991 Serb militants carried out massacres and expulsions of Croats from the Dalj area. Not far from there, in the town of Vukovar on the Danube, a major battle of the Serbo-Croat 1991 war would take place. Needless to say, the villages around the mixed Serbo-Croatian town of Vukovar were during World War II predominately Serb populated and supportive of the communist-led Partisan movement and therefore were "cleansed" by the Ustašas, who massacred a large number of Serbs, converted others to Catholicism, and destroyed all Orthodox churches in the area.[107] Also in 1991, anticipating the Yugoslav army invasion, the Serbian Church held a commemoration at the strategically important Prevlaka peninsula on the border between Montenegro and Croatia in order to reassert church history–based Serbian clams on the territory. The metropolitan of Montenegro, Amfilohije, held a religious ceremony at Prevlaka on 17 February 1991 commemorating the historic church of the Holy Archangel.[108]

Serbian prelates concurrently fought similar symbolic wars in Macedonia and Montenegro.[109] At its emergency session in December 1990, the assembly of bishops of the Serbian Orthodox Church demanded immediate eviction of the Macedonian national museum from the Saint Prokhor Pčinjski monastery.[110] On Saint Elijah's Day in 1991, several incidents occurred in and around the monastery. Two groups of demonstrators—the radical Serbian nationalists led by Vojislav Šešelj and Macedonian nationalists confronted each other without casualties. The Serbian Church continued legal and propaganda battles with the Macedonian Church and authorities in Skopje.[111] In Montenegro, in February 1990, Serbian bishops and clergy and pro-Serbian Montengrins made a pilgrimage to the site of Ivanova korita, near the top of the mountain of Lovćen, in order to consecrate the remains of the destroyed Njegos chapel. Meanwhile, Montenegrin proindependence political parties advanced the case for an autocephalous national Orthodox church of Montenegro. Metropolitan Amfilohije attacked what he labeled the "Montenegrin sect" and accused Tito and the communists of inventing the Montenegrin nation in order to weaken Serbia.[112]

The Collapse of the Interfaith Dialogue

In 1989, the Balkan correspondent for the British daily newspaper the *Independent* wrote that "attacks on the pope from the Serbian Orthodox Church and the Belgrade media are as popular as in Protestant Belfast."[113] Even the earlier proregime Association of Orthodox clergy turned nationalistic.[114] The influential theologian Bishop Irenej (Bulović) said in an interview in May 1990 that the pope, if he still wanted to visit Yugoslavia, must come to Jasenovac together with the Catholic episcopate, to perform "an act of repentance, not merely a verbal condemnation of the crimes, and to promise that such a crime will never happen again."[115]

After ignoring several Catholic Church leaders' official and unofficial calls for ecumenical meetings released between 1982 and 1986, the Holy Assembly of Serb Orthodox bishops sent in June 1989 to the Catholic bishops' conference a letter entitled "Preconditions for Ecumenical Dialogue." This letter was, according to a statement by the moderate Slovene archbishop France Perko in an interview with an Austrian daily newspaper, "only another unpleasant move within the Orthodox church's ongoing anti-Catholic campaign full of accusations and ultimate demands."[116] The Serb bishops' epistle expressed a strong resentment both over the past and present. On the World War II controversy, the letter charged a genocide-denial, and regarding the current crisis in Yugoslavia, Serb bishops accused the Catholic Church of backing enemies of the Serbian people. "It is an astounding and horrible fact that (during the Second World War) the Roman Catholic Church hierarchy, led by the late Archbishop Stepinac (who was also the military vicar of Pavelić's army), could agree to collaborate with the Ustaša regime," the Serb Church leader wrote, and went on to say: "The Catholic Church also actively collaborated in rebaptism [forcible conversion of Serbs to Catholicism] that took place amid widespread violence and Serbs' fear of a biological extinction."[117] On the current crisis, the letter argued that there is "a tendency toward minimizing the crimes and not telling the truth about the tragic fate of the Serbian Church and people clearly visible in the Catholic weekly *Glas koncila* and the public statements of Catholic prelates, including Cardinal Kuharić. . . . The Serbian Church does not demand penance for someone else's crimes—we only want your restraint from further insults."[118] In the letter, the Serb bishops also complained about the language policies in Croatia, the Vatican's support for the secessionist Macedonian Orthodox Church, the Catholic Church's support of Albanian separatism in Kosovo, and alleged antiecumenical statements and writings by Monsignor Kolarić, the secretary for ecumenism of the bishops conference.[119] In the letter concluding paragraph, Serb Church leaders implied that some kind of an eleventh-hour rapprochement might be possible. Although they did not specify concrete demands, Serb prelates had probably hoped that the worried Croatian Church leaders, frightened by the aggressive Milošević and looming ethnic war, would release a public apology to the Serbian Church and modify their views on Kosovo, Macedonia, and other issues of the Yugoslav crisis.

The Catholic bishops' conference of Yugoslavia convened at Zagreb on 12 November 1990 to compose an official response to the Serb bishops' letter. The Catholic reply was published in all major newspapers. On behalf of the bishops' conference, Cardinal Kuharić accused the Serbian Church of paying lip service to "certain politics" (i.e., the politics of Serbia's nationalist leader Slobodan Milošević) rather than being concerned about discouraging tendencies in the ecumenical dialogue.[120] Kuharić also delineated the new interpretation of recent church history, according to which the Archbishop Stepinac was an independent church leader who publicly protested against Ustaša crimes and specifically against crimes committed in the Jasenovac concentration camp. As evidence Kuharić quoted Stepinac's wartime homilies delivered in the Zagreb Cathedral and Stepinac's letters to the Croat fuhrer Pavelić.

From an emergency session held early in December 1990, the Holy Assembly of Serb bishops released a statement on ecumenical relations with the Roman Catholic Church in which the bishops:

> having received the Catholic Church's reply to our letter, this Sabor with deep regret declares that the intolerant attitude on the part of some Catholic clerics and Catholic intelligentsia in Yugoslavia toward the Orthodox faith and the Serbian Orthodox Church, has brought ecumenical relations in our country almost into an impasse. Nevertheless, this Sabor remains open for a fraternal dialogue and will do anything it can to improve the climate of interchurch relations.[121]

The post–Vatican II ecumenical movement came to an end in 1990. The traditional interfaculty ecumenical symposia, held every two years since 1974, was terminated in 1990 because of the Croatians' absence in protest of Milošević's coups in the autonomous provinces and threats to the republics. The "Ecumenical Octave for Christian Unity," held in January 1990 in Osijek in northern Croatia, was one of the last interfaith vigils before the outbreak of the Serbo-Croat war in 1991. On 25 January 1991 the participants met at an interfaith worship service, and on that occasion the Serb Orthodox bishop of Srijem, Vasilije Kačavenda, pointed out that "Croats, Serbs, and others, despite the different religions and nationalities in which they were born, want to show that common worship could be the way for mitigating the tensions and difficulties of the moment."[122]

Untimely Commemorations

From June 1990 to August 1991, the Serbian Orthodox Church carried out a series of commemorations in honor of "the beginning of the Second World War and the suffering of the Serbian Church and Serbian people in that war."[123] Those commemorations came as a continuation of the September 1984 consecration of the Saint John the Baptist memorial church at Jasenovac. These religious events coincided with Slobodan Milošević's so-called antibureaucratic revolution, that is, the Serb nationalistic mobilization carried out through street protests and an aggressive media campaign.[124] Concurrently the Serbian Church's commemorations bred popular sentiments of pride and self-pity as well as a lust for revenge.[125]

In June 1990, the Holy Synod published the second landmark monograph since the 1987 "Debts to God in Kosovo," this time dedicated to Jasenovac. The volume was entitled *Ve čan pomen: Jasenovac: mjesto natopljeno krvlju nevinih 1941/1985/1991—Eternal Memory—Jasenovac—the Place Soaked in the Blood of Innocents, With Summaries in English.*[126] In the monograph, one of the editors, the Metropolitan Jovan Pavlović, concludes the introduction with a quotation from a public statement released early in 1990 by Enriko Josif, a Yugoslav intellectual of Jewish background and a member of the central committee of the Federation of Jewish Communities of Yugoslavia. The statement reads as follows:

> One of the horrible spiritual crimes is the fact that what happened to the Serbs was hushed up in the whole world. This is a postwar continuation of the horrible crime. . . . The worst service to the West, and particularly to the Roman Catholic Church of the Croats, was to hush up the religious and biological crime of genocide committed against the Serbian people during World War II. In the name of Christ and Christian love, the head of the Roman Catholic church should have raised his voice and condemned the eternal sin of Cain. This should be done as soon as possible.[127]

In June 1990, the Holy Synod issued a church calendar dedicated to the fiftieth anniversary of the beginning of World War II in the Balkans, with special emphasis on the Serbian Orthodox Church's casualties during the war in the Independent State of Croatia.[128] The calendar ran on its cover page the previously banned text by Bishop Velimirović, "The Most Horrible Inquisition," written in exile in the 1950s. In this article Nikolaj accused the Catholic Church of inciting numerous crimes, among which Ustaša genocide is perhaps the most horrible.[129] In the Easter 1991 issue of the patriarchate's newspaper *Pravoslavlje*, Patriarch Pavle repeated Germanus' words: "We have to forgive, but we cannot forget," and cited the figure of 700,000 Serbs killed at Jasenovac. The calendar opened year-long commemorations at Jasenovac and other sites of Ustaša massacres and mass graves in Croatia and in Bosnia-Herzegovina. Those commemorations involved excavations and reburial of the Serb victims massacred by the Ustašas during World War II. The church organized reburial and funerals and erected a number of monuments, memorials, and chapels to mark Serbian mass graves.

While the Serbian Church's activities drew broad popular support, a few Serb voices of criticism are worth noting. A group of Serb intellectuals from France wrote in an open letter to Serbian Church leaders that "calling for revenge against the living descendants of those who committed the crimes—cannot be justified. The World War II Ustaša terrorists were a minority among the Croatian people!"[130] In the similar vein, the author Svetislav Basara wrote in May 1991 in the Belgrade weekly *NIN*:

> Maniacs are screaming all around: "Survival of our nation is at stake!" Nonsense! There cannot be endangered nations and races. Only the indi-

vidual can be endangered. They refer to Christian values and tradition. They say "our people" are threatened by some other people! That is sheer hypocrisy! Christianity is basically a-national! To identify religion with nationality is not only nonsensical, but also blasphemous! We all have sinned, we've been punished as we deserved. All the people around us are equally helpless and imperiled. Look around you, your neighbor needs help—please, take your neighbor seriously.[131]

Incompatible Worlds: Serbs Call for Partition

In the year of Milošević's ascent to power, Serbian Church leaders and church press openly proposed the idea of the partition of Yugoslavia between the two largest ethnic nations, Serbs and Croats. In a 1987 interview (published in 1990), the Patriarch Germanus had said that Serbia awaits a leader with "the strength and intelligence to select the right portion of land for the Serbs."[132] The Orthodox Church newspaper *Pravoslavlje* called for partition on 1 October 1987. In an article entitled "A Commentary on a Speech," written by the patriarchate official Svetozar Dušanić, this church newspaper proposed the partition of Yugoslavia into an "Eastern Orthodox-Byzantine sphere of influence" and "western Roman Catholic sphere of influence," because "the two incompatible worlds sharply differ from one another in religion, culture, historical development, ethics, psychology and mentality, and therefore previous conflicts that culminated with massacres in the Second World War could be repeated."[133] The article ridiculed the western republics of Croatia and Slovenia for their rush to join the European Community, calling on the Serbs to form a commonwealth of Orthodox countries.[134] The text concluded by prophetically calling for partition to be accomplished as soon as possible, otherwise, "suicidal and self-destructive wars over borders will break out in the disintegrating Yugoslavia . . . [and] Western Europe will be watching it indifferently."[135]

Orthodox Church leaders voiced the partition idea in sermons and public statements. In an interview for the Serbian-language Kosovo newspaper *Jedinstvo* in June 1990, the metropolitan of Montenegro, Amfilohije, said that "there cannot be a reconciliation over the graves of innocents, there will be no reconciliation until the Croatian people renounce the evil. . . . Today we Serbs are all determined to build a country of our own, and at the same time we must respect the centuries-old desires of our brethren Roman Catholic Croats and Slovenes to establish their national states."[136] In a similar vein, in September 1990, the church-national assembly at Gračanica (Kosovo) urged the defense of the "sovereignty and integrity of Serbian territories and [the] resistance to disintegration of the Serbian ethnic nation."[137] The assembly released a message to the public in which it offered two options for Yugoslavia's future: first, a common state based on "the organic cultural-historical unity" of the Slavic founders of the country, that is, Serbs, Croats, and Slovenes as constituent nations while the new nationalities, republics, and provinces created in communist Yugoslavia, such as Macedonians, Montenegrins, Muslims and Albanians as the privileged minority; second, the country's partition into communities of Orthodox, Islamic, and Catholic faith.[138]

The Serbian Orthodox Church also intensified its foreign policy activism to obtain the support abroad needed for the restructuring of Yugoslavia. Serbo-Russian friendship was the capstone of this new Church foreign policy agenda. After four summit meetings in the 1970s, the Russian patriarch Pimen again came to Yugoslavia in November 1984, when he visited Kosovo and received a spectacular welcome by a crowd of local Serbs at the historic Gračanica church.[139] Germanus pointed out in the 1987 interview that he and Russian Patriarch Pimen shared same views about the need for a mutual defense of Orthodox peoples against the West and other threats such as Islam and communism.[140]

As the old Uniate issue reappeared with the collapse of communism, Orthodox churches gathered on a conference in Moscow and urged that the Uniate problem be renegotiated between the Orthodox churches and the Vatican.[141] Responding to the appeal of Alexei II, patriarch of Moscow and all Russia, for "fraternal assistance" to all Orthodox churches on the occasion of the occupation of the Cathedral of Saint George in Lviv by Ukrainian Uniates,[142] the Serbian Orthodox Church lobbied through the Geneva-based Conference of European Churches for a pan-Orthodox solidarity in support of the Russian Orthodox Church.[143]

On 10–13 December 1990, the Ecumenical Patriarchate of Constantinople organized an international symposium of Orthodox churches to discuss conflicts between local Orthodox churches and Uniate communities in the Ukraine, Czechoslovakia, Romania, and Poland. At this conference, the Serbian Orthodox Church delegation urged that "an ecumenical dialogue with the Roman Catholics under current circumstances is not possible and must be halted until an agreement is reached through negotiations with the Vatican regarding the Uniate problem."[144] The Serbian Church delegation also took part at the First All-Church Sabor of Orthodox Youth, held in Moscow on 25–28 January 1991. In March 1991, Serbian Church representatives again voiced radical views at the pan-Orthodox symposium, called "Roman Catholicism and the Orthodox World," held at the historic monastery of Pachaev, near Kiev, in the Ukraine. The objective of this international meeting was a show of solidarity among Orthodox nations with support for the endangered Orthodox peoples such as the pro-Moscow Orthodox of Ukraine, the Orthodox Serbs in Yugoslavia, and Orthodox minorities elsewhere in excommunist countries. The conference released messages to the pope, the patriarchates of Moscow and Constantinople, and to Mikhail Gorbachev. In the message to the pope, the participants said: "Your Holiness, the Orthodox peoples will not be intimidated by the alliance between you and the powerful international forces. Amen."[145] Mikhail Gorbachev was invited to defend the rights of Orthodox countries and Orthodox peoples, in accordance with to the tradition of Russian Orthodox tsars.[146] The conference's resolution said that the anti-Orthodox policies and Uniate crusades instigated by the Vatican generated tragic conflicts, such as the current church strife in western Ukraine and "in another Slavic land of Croatia, where the Catholics slaughtered 700,000 Orthodox Serbs."[147] The document said that "once again in history, Roman Catholicism has become a weapon in the hands of anti-Christian dark forces."[148]

Continuing the dynamic pan-Orthodox campaign, a high delegation of the Serbian Church visited Moscow in May 1991. On that occasion Alexei II gave his apostolic blessing to the newly founded "Society of Russo-Serbian Friendship" and received a joint delegation of the Serbian Orthodox Church and the Belgrade government. The *Pravoslavlje* reported on the meeting under the headline "Now It Is Time for All Orthodox Peoples to Join Forces."[149] Further, on 13 December 1991, during the escalation of the Serbo-Croatian war in Croatia, the patriarch of Serbia, Pavle, released a circular letter to all Orthodox churches seeking the protection of Croatian Serbs from "the Croatian neo-fascist regime—the successor of the Ustašas who massacred 700,000 Orthodox Serbs in World War II."[150]

The Serbian Church delegation attended the Orthodox ecclesiastical summit conference convened in Istanbul on 12–15 March 1992. At the conference, 14 Orthodox churches discussed current ecclesiastical and world affairs. In a public statement released by the participants in this historic convention, Orthodox church leaders wrote:

> [A]fter the collapse of the godless communist system that severely persecuted Orthodox Churches, we expected fraternal support or at least understanding for grave difficulties that had befallen us. . . . [I]nstead, Orthodox countries have been targeted by Roman Catholic missionaries and advocates of Uniatism. These came together with Protestant fundamentalists . . . and sects.[151]

The conference issued an appeal for a more respectful and influential role of Orthodox countries in the process of European unification and postcommunist transitions. The Orthodox church summit conference called for peace in the current conflicts in Yugoslavia and in the Middle East but did not include the Serbian Church's proposal to condemn the "Croatian aggression against the Serbian people."[152] After the Istanbul conference, the Serbian Church maintained the same course in foreign policy, though not always overtly, continuously anti-West and seeking closer ties with the churches of Russia and Greece and advancing the idea of the Orthodox commonwealth.[153]

In the meantime on the home front, the Serbian Orthodox Church sought contacts with the Catholic Church in order to negotiate the partition of

Bosnia-Herzegovina and a readjustment of borders between Serbia and Croatia in the north. Two such meetings took place in 1991. The first was held in Srijemski Karlovci on 8 May 1991. The day before, Patriarch Pavle had been at Jasenovac for a commemoration. At Srijemski Karlovci, the two churches released an appeal for a peaceful and political solution of the conflict in Croatia. The second meeting took place at Slavonski Brod on the Sava River on 24 August 1991. That meeting also resulted in a similar, abstract peace appeal but without specific references to the causes of conflict, the warring parties, or feasible solutions. The meetings of church leaders coincided with negotiations conducted by the two secular nationalistic leaders Franjo Tudjman of Croatia and Slobodan Milošević of Serbia. The 8 May church summit meeting, incidentally, came as a follow-up to the Milošević and Tudjman meeting at Karadjordjevo on 25 March, where the two leaders tried to negotiate a peaceful breakup of Yugoslavia that would include the partition of Bosnia-Herzegovina between Serbia and Croatia and the exchange of territories and population.[154] It is noteworthy that both church summit meetings were initiated by the Catholic bishops of Croatia, who desperately tried to stop the escalation of war. According to Croatian prelate Vinko Puljić's statement on a panel in the United States, during the 1991 meetings between church leaders, the Serbian Church seized the opportunity to put the border issue on the table and the bishops discussed changes of borders in conjunction with the breakup of the communist federation and the formation of its successor states.[155]

An Eye for an Eye, a Tooth for a Tooth: The Serb Call for Revenge

The Serb historian Milan Bulajić argued that the main cause of the 1991 Serbo-Croat war was the anger and fear of the Serbs and the Serbian Orthodox Church facing the resurgence of Croatian neo-Ustašism.[156] Bulajić also found anti-Serbian attitudes on the part of the Croatian episcopate in the bishops' epistle to the bishops of the world released on 1 February 1991 in the aftermath of the first Serbian armed attacks on Croatian police and the first Croatian casualties. According to the Catholic episcopate's views expressed in this letter (quoted by Bulajić), the main source of the crisis in the country was "the resistance to democratic changes by Serbia," coupled with "the aggressive quest for Serbian domination, and the military solution of the crisis advocated by the leading Serbian politicians, army officers and unfortunately certain leading figures in the Serbian Orthodox Church."[157] The Croatian bishops' letter accused the Serbian Orthodox Church of ruining the ecumenical dialogue and joining Serbian nationalist historians in attacking the Catholic Church for alleged genocide against Serbs during World War II.[158] These accusations are, according to the bishops, false, because the genocide never happened, except for what the bishops described as occasional minor punitive actions by the Croatian state authorities provoked by the communists and Serb nationalist Četniks who sought to destroy the new Croatian state.

In reality, several years prior to Tudjman's electoral victory, notably since the Jasenovac liturgy of September 1984, Serb nationalists in Croatia had mobilized local Serbs against their neighbors, preparing the ground for the secession and the partition of Yugoslavia. Tudjman's demonstration of Croatian pride, fury, and nationalistic symbols only added fuel to the already rampant fire of Serbian nationalism. As early as July 1990, the policemen of Serbian nationality from the predominantly populated Knin district refused to wear new uniforms, allegedly resembling those of the Ustaša police, thus precipitating the secession of Krajina from Croatia.[159] Speaking before a crowd of 50,000 Serbs gathered around the church of Saint Lazar of Kosovo at the village of Kosovo in southern Croatia on Saint Vitus' Day 1990, Jovan Rašković, the president of the Serbian Democratic Party, said:

> The Serbs were dormant for nearly 50 years. We forgot our name, our faith, our roots. Now, the time for awakening has come. What the Serbs must do first, is to pay tribute to our Serbian Orthodox Church. . . . Our Orthodox Church is our mother. . . . She was a weeping and lonely mother deserted by her children. We must return to its altar, because the Serbian Church is our mother. The Serbian nation was born at the holy altar of our Serbian Orthodox Church in the year of 1219 as the first European political nation.[160]

In a similar vein, the nationalist leader of the Bosnian Serbs, Radovan Karadžić, spoke in a 1990 interview for a Sarajevo newspaper. "The Serbian Orthodox Church is not merely a religious organization," said Karadžić, "it is a cultural institution and part of national leadership; the Church is highly important for all Serbs, and it is irrelevant whether one believes in God or not."[161]

On 13 September 1990, the Orthodox episcopate from Croatia released a statement in which they described the status of local Serbs as a "life under occupation."[162] In March 1991, the patriarchate's newspaper ran a report from Slavonia written by Bishop Lukijan entitled "Anti-Serbian March of the Ustaša State." In the article the bishop described armed attacks by Croatian police on the city of Pakrac, assaults on Serbs, and desecration of Orthodox churches.[163] In April 1991, Bishop Lukijan made his "eye for an eye" statement, often quoted later, calling on the Serbs to retaliate for past crimes and prevent the new Ustaša assault on the Serbian people.[164]

On 15 January 1992, Germany and the Vatican, followed by other western European countries, granted diplomatic recognition to the republics of Slovenia and Croatia, which earlier had declared independence from Belgrade. This provoked an outburst of anger in Serbia. The Belgrade Foreign Ministry filed a protest note to the papal nuncio, saying that the Vatican would be held responsible for the imminent war in Bosnia. The Serbian historian Milan Bulajić argued that the 1992 diplomatic recognition of Croatia and Slovenia by the Vatican was more evidence of the long historical continuity of the Vatican's anti-Serbian and anti-Yugoslavian policies.[165]

At the time of the 1992 recognition, the Serbian Orthodox Church had finally settled the poignant North American schism. Church leaders were in the midst of preparations for celebration. Ironically, they viewed the war in Croatia as a part of the historic process of reunification of the Serbs. On 16–17 January 1992 the Holy Bishops' Assembly of the Serbian Orthodox Church held an emergency session in the patriarchate and issued a document entitled "Appeal of the Sabor of the Serbian Orthodox Church to the Serbian People and to the International Public." In addition, the Serb bishops dispatched a letter to Pope John Paul II in which they said they "protest[ed] the premature diplomatic recognition of Croatia and Slovenia as independent countries without taking into account the legitimate national and political rights and equality for the Serbian people" and expressed "a deep sorrow" for the pope's "one-sided and un-Christian attitude toward the ethnic, civil, and historic rights and Christian dignity of the Serbian people."[166] The Serb episcopate disapproved of Slobodan Milošević's 1992 agreement to allow a United Nations peacekeeping mission in Croatia. Church leaders wrote that the Church's "trust in the political leadership of Serbia and Yugoslavia and in the command of the Yugoslav Army has been seriously undermined" because "nobody was authorized by the Serbian people to make political deals on behalf of all Serbs, without the people's consent and without the blessing of the Serbian people's spiritual Mother, the Serbian Orthodox Church."[167]

The Vatican's recognition of Croatia and Slovenia was an unexpected move. From 1966 to 1989, the Vatican diplomatically supported unity of the six-republic federation. After the 1990 elections, the Holy See was prepared to support the transformation of Yugoslavia into a confederation, leaving the borders intact while the successor states of Yugoslavia would peacefully negotiate future arrangements. Thus, in November 1990, the bishops' conference of Yugoslavia outlined a new statute that provided for, instead of one unified bishops' conference, three autonomous bishops' conferences linked with a high-ranking church official as a liaison officer without prerogatives in decision-making. This "confederate" model of church organization provided that the Catholic Churches of Croatia and Bosnia-Herzegovina would work together with the so-called central division of the new bishops' conference.[168]

In the spring of 1991, as the Serbo-Croatian war was escalated, the Catholic Church abandoned the confederation idea and began to support Tudjman's visions of an independent Croatia.[169] On 25 May 1991, Pope John Paul II received Tudjman in a private audience, on which occasion Tudjman appealed for international recognition. The Holy See finally granted it. The pope accepted the explanation of the Yugoslav crisis given by the Croatian episcopate and Croat clergy in the Curia.

In addition, the Vatican's decision was determined by the fact that the pope never trusted the Miloševic regime and eventually lost patience in expecting any moderation from the Serbian Orthodox Church. It is worth noting that as early as 31 May 1991, Pope John Paul II released a "Letter to European Bishops on the Changes in Central and Eastern Europe" in which the Vatican made an attempt to invoke the Council's ecumenical friendship toward Orthodox churches. Furthermore, during the same period, the Holy See successfully worked together with the patriarchate of Moscow on the mitigation of the serious conflict between Catholicism and Orthodoxy in western Ukraine.[170] According to a high official of the Moscow patriarchate, Moscow and the Vatican also made an attempt to mitigate tensions in Yugoslavia, but the success from the Ukraine could not be repeated.[171] Consequently, the pope entrusted management of the Balkan crisis to the Rome-based ecumenical and conflict resolution body called the Community of Saint Egidio. This body worked to arrange papal meetings with Serbian Church leaders and papal visits to Serbia, Kosovo, Montenegro, and Macedonia, especially during the papal visits to Croatia, Slovenia, and Bosnia in 1994 and 1997. According to Belgrade sources, the Holy Synod of the Serbian Orthodox Church rejected these initiatives for various reasons.[172]

10

RELIGION AS HALLMARK OF NATIONHOOD

Popovi pa topovi.
"First came priests, then guns."
Headline in the Montenegrin weekly *Monitor*, alluding
to the genesis of the Yugoslav conflict of the 1990s

From 1991 to 1995, for a second time in six decades, the Yugoslav peoples were drawn into a bloody fratricidal war fought in Croatia and Bosnia-Herzegovina. Wars would continue in 1998 between Serbs and Albanians in Kosovo and between Albanians and Macedonians in 2001 in Macedonia. While other eastern and central European nations, liberated from Soviet hegemony, were starting a new happier era, the golden age for the Yugoslav peoples came to an end. The 1991–95 war came as a result of ethnic nationalistic revolutions aimed at destroying the multiethnic federation founded by the communists and establishing independent ethnically homogenous states in its stead. In 1995 at an international conference in Paris, the Croatian sociologist Stipe Šuvar presented the following data about casualties and war damage: at least 150,000 people had died, and the relatively largest number of the killed were Bosnian Muslims, followed by ethnic Serbs and Croats; 250,000 were injured; two and a half million people were expelled from their homes; at least half a million mostly highly educated people moved out of the territory of the former Yugoslavia to western countries; the number of Serbs in Bosnia and Herzegovina had been brought down from the prewar 1.3 million to 700,000, and Croats from 750,000 to 400,000; the number of employed in the whole territory of former Yugoslavia has been reduced from 6.7 million in the late 1980s to 3 million in the mid-1990s, of which 900,000 belonged to armies and police forces engaged in some forms of combat.[1] According to the following data about the war

165

in Bosnia-Herzegovina presented in December 2001 by the Belgrade-based journal *Republika* (no. 274–275), in this war alone, from 1992 to 1995, 236,500 persons lost their lives: 164,000 Bosnian Muslims (126,000 civilians and 38,000 members of the Bosnian Armed forces), 31,000 Croats (17,000 civilians and 14,000 members of various Croatian military forces engaged in the Bosnian war), some 27,500 Serbs (6,500 civilians and 21,000 soldiers), and 14,000 members of other nationalities (9,000 civilians and 5,000 in uniform). Also during this war, the number of wounded and injured was estimated at 225,000. As noted earlier, the war damage included thousands of intentionally destroyed places of worship. Thus, 1,024 mosques and other Muslim religious sites—almost all Muslim historic and cultural landmarks located in the areas occupied by Serbs and Croats—were destroyed. In addition, 182 Catholic churches were destroyed, mostly by Serbs, while Muslims and Croats are responsible for the destruction of 28 Serb Orthodox churches and monasteries.

International observers singled out massive war crimes, such as confining people to concentration camps, massive executions without trial, mass expulsion of civilian population and creation of ethnically homogenous territories, mass rapes of women, and 1,600 children under the age of 15 killed by snipers and artillery shells during the siege of Sarajevo alone. The United Nations established a new international institution, the International Criminal Tribunal for the Former Yugoslavia (ICTY), in the Hague. The tribunal indicted hundreds of individuals who took part in genocidal massacres and war crimes. Drawing on the Balkan case, comparative genocide studies inaugurated the concept of "ethnic cleansing" as a form of genocide.[2]

The Balkan wars of the 1990s were fought among several united ethnic nationalistic fronts each seeking statehood and nationhood and each contesting borders, myths, and identities of rival groups. This time there was no "pan-Yugoslav front" and no communists with their antinationalistic program and multiethnic armies. Almost all of the members of the League of Communists of Serbia turned into radical Serb ethnic nationalists, most of whom become members of Milošević's "Socialist Party of Serbia" (a national-socialist or neofascist party that, in contrast to the similar Croatian HDZ, has not directly allied with the national church). A large number of members of the League of Communists of Croatia also transferred loyalty to ethnic nationalist parties, mostly to Tudjman's HDZ.[3]

The three largest religious organizations, as impartial foreign and domestic analysts have agreed, were among the principal engineers of the crisis and conflict.[4] Western analysts noticed religious insignia on the battlefield, prayers before the combat and during battles, religious salutes, clergy in uniforms and under arms; elite combat units labeled "the Muslim Army" or "Orthodox Army" accompanied by clergy; massive destruction of places of worship; forms of torture such as carving religious insignia into human flesh; and so on. Foreign "holy warriors" came to engage in a global "civilization clash" on the Bosnian battlefield.[5] The Serbian Orthodox Church is held the most directly responsible for the advocacy of ethnic cleansing, but radical faction tendencies were found in Croatian Catholicism and in the Islamic Community as well.

The Serbs did not deny that they struck first in Kosovo, in Croatia, and in Bosnia-Herzegovina, but, as a Serb nationalist leader explained in an interview, "in contrast to 1941, this time we were prepared to defend ourselves from genocide . . . had Serbs not armed themselves and attacked first, they would have been eradicated."[6] A group of Serbian Orthodox Church leaders and Serb intellectuals defined the war as a spontaneous civil war in which the Serbs, by striking first, were only trying to avoid the genocide that happened to them in 1941.[7] A "Museum of Victims of Genocide" was opened in Belgrade in 1992. The museum sought contacts with Jewish organizations and Holocaust museums in Israel and other countries, presenting the Serbs as the principal victims of both ethnic wars that had befallen Yugoslavia within six decades.[8] The museum and the Milošević regime organized international conferences on the genocide against the Serb people.[9] Milošević managed to obtain support from the Federation of Jewish Communities of Yugoslavia.[10] Only a few Serbs of Jewish descent (notably the author Filip David) spoke out against the Milošević regime and Serbian nationalism. A political scientist from Belgrade, Dragan Simić, echoing the "Serbo-Jewish analogy," said:

> I think that we Serbs must unite in the desire to preserve Kosovo forever. We must be like the Jews. The Jews and Israel should be our role models and we must emulate their perseverance and their long-term plan. For two thousand years, the Jews have greeted one another with "I'll see you next year in Jerusalem!" And they eventually returned to Jerusalem and made it the capital of the Jewish state. Why can't we Serbs introduce in our everyday communication the slogan "I'll see you next year in Peć, Prizren, Priština, and Knin"?[11]

However, the Belgrade psychiatrist and prominent Orthodox Church layman, Vladeta Jerotić emphasized the impact of the memory of World War II and the Serb lust for revenge. He wrote:

> We were unprepared to present the facts about what happened in 1941 before Europe (and Europe was not very enthusiastic to listen about the dark and bloody Balkan past). In consequence, we set out to publish intensely about the crimes against the Serbian people, to reveal the facts about those crimes. This search for truth was accompanied with angry, bitter, resentful comments. Thus we incited bitterness, anger, and hatred among the Serbs against Croats and Muslims. The current war had been manufactured over several years through these specific efforts.[12]

Yet not only the Serbs, but also the Croats and Bosnian Muslims espoused the martyr-nation concept. A scholarly symposium held under the aegis of the Catholic Church in Croatia designated Serbs and Serbian clergy as instigators of the war and termed it a genocide against the Croat people.[13] The Croatian daily *Slobodna Dalmacija*, citing an article from the Austrian press that, drawing from Daniel Goldhagen's study about ordinary Germans as Hitler's accomplices in the execution of the Holocaust, referred to the Serbs as "Slobodan Milošević's willing executioners."[14] The new Croatian historiography portrayed Serbia as warlike nation whose leaders forged a secret plan to commit genocide against the neighboring peoples as early as the 1840s.[15] In 1990 the Tudjman regime founded the "Croatian Holocaust Information Center." New historical studies appeared in Croatia arguing that the Serbs started the genocide against the Croat people in May 1945 (the "Bleiburg Massacre") under Communism continued it through the secret police (UDBA), and tried to conclude with the 1991–95 war incited from Belgrade.[16]

Religion and Nationalism in the Successor States

In all successor states of the former Yugoslavia except perhaps in Slovenia, religion became the hallmark of nationhood. To be sure, new languages were introduced in lieu of Serbo-Croatian and sanctioned by constitutions (the Croatian, Bosnian, and Serbian languages were inaugurated between 1990–92 and a new Montenegrin language emerged in linguistic and political debates in the second half of the 1990s). Yet a primacy of religious identities could be observed. In addition, religious organizations became co-rulers with the new regimes in all the successor states except Milošević's Yugoslavia.

Islam and Muslim Nationalism in Bosnia-Herzegovina

Slavic Muslims and their Islamic Community were primary targets of genocide carried out against them by the Serbs while also being endangered by, post-1990, the increasingly unfriendly Croats. The prewar turmoil, war, and genocide, however, facilitated a historically unprecedented politicization and "nationalization" of Islam. The Muslim nationalist party SDA utilized Islam as the principal instrument for the making of the Muslim nation. Alija Izetbegović became convinced that nothing else but the creation of an Islamic state (his secret agenda in the Islamic Declaration of 1970) could secure survival for Europe's only native Muslim community. Muslim countries rushed to help their coreligionists in Europe. During the 1992–95 war in Bosnia-Herzegovina, the heartland of the ex–communist federation became another Mecca. As Samuel P. Huntington observed in his *Clash of Civiliza-*

tions (1993), the plight of the "blue-eyed Muslims" of the Balkans mobilized the whole Muslim world in an effort to provide military, economic, and political assistance to their coreligionists. According to a Croatian newspaper, in 1995 more than 190 various Islamic organizations (including branches of the militant Hamas, Islamic Jihad, and Taliban) operated in Bosnia and Herzegovina.[17] In spite of an extremely difficult situation on the battlefields, Alija Izetbegović and his Party of Democratic Action exploited such favorable international circumstances to launch an Islamic revolution aimed at creating an Islamic republic in Bosnia-Herzegovina. The one-time pro-Yugoslav Islamic Community became one of the principal mobilizational resources and the equivalent of the "national churches" in Serbia, Croatia, the Serb Republic, Montenegro, and Macedonia. On 28 April 1993 in besieged Sarajevo, Bosnian Muslim clergy, urged by Alija Izetbegović, held a "congress of renewal." Mustafa Cerić, the former imam of the Zagreb mosque, was elected the head of the new organization adopting, the title *naibu-reis*. Cerić later became reis-ul-ulema of Bosnia-Herzegovina. The ousted pro-Yugoslav reis, Jakub Selimoski, blamed Izetbegović, the SDA, and the aspiring Reis Cerić for turning the Serbian aggression on Bosnia into a civil war and also accused Izetbegović of being partly responsible for the outbreak of the 1993 war between Bosniaks and Croats.[18]

In contrast to accounts according to which religious fundamentalism, was a driving force of Muslim militancy, a French analyst noticed that Izetbegović and his group were in fact ethnic nationalists (similar to Serbs and Croats).[19] Religion boomed, but so did a "new" history, without which a nation cannot exist. School textbooks glorified the Ottoman era. The Bosniaks have become a martyr-nation, victim of a genocide perpetrated against Muslims by the two neighboring Christian nations. Emulating the Serbian Church's prewar activities, the Islamic Community carried out massive commemorations and reburials of victims of the 1992–95 war. The new regime encouraged homogenization of Muslims and separation from the neighboring groups. In counties with a Muslim majority, as well as in the offices of the Muslim-dominated Federation, everyone was required to use the traditional Muslim salute, "Selaam aleikum." The reis-ul-ulema, Mustafa Cerić, argued that interfaith marriages were blasphemous acts.[20] During the Christmas holidays of 1998, Reis Cerić complained about what he saw as excessively Christian content on state television.[21] The Bosniak nationalist poet Djemaludin Latić, speaking in the capacity of official ideologue of Izetbegović's Party of Democratic Action, was widely quoted in the press as saying that "a Muslim from Malaysia is closer to him than a Catholic or Orthodox Slav from Sarajevo."[22] The imam-preacher Nezim Halilović, who was the commander of a Muslim combat brigade during the 1992–95 war, earned postwar fame with his zealous sermons in the Sarajevo "King Fahd" Mosque. Halilović urged faithful Muslims to reject the "alien and hostile influence of the West" and demonstrate solidarity with the holy struggle of Muslim brethren in Chechnya and elsewhere.[23]

New mosques mushroomed in areas under Muslim control. The massive rebuilding was funded by Islamic countries. According to a Sarajevo journal, Saudi Arabia financed the rebuilding of 72 mosques and other religious facilities; Kuwait donated money for a hundred new mosques and religious facilities; Indonesia paid for the construction of the currently largest mosque in Bosnia; Malaysia helped the renovation of 40 mosques; and so forth.[24] According to the same source, in the Sarajevo county of Novi Grad alone, three new mosques were under construction in 1997, with 27 other religious facilities to be built soon; in the town of Bugojno, a new Islamic center will cost 15 million US dollars; one of the newly built mosques, as local believers had proposed, was to have a 250-foot-high minaret, thus aspiring to become one of largest mosques in the world and, as a Muslim leader pointed out, higher than the Saint Sava Serb-Orthodox Cathedral at Belgrade.[25] In September 2000, a Croatian daily announced that a new Islamic center with the second largest mosque in Europe was opened in Sarajevo by an official from Saudi Arabia and that that country alone had financed, since 1995, 157 new Islamic centers, mosques, and other buildings of the Islamic Community in Bosnia-Herzegovina.[26] The archbishop of Sarajevo, Vinko Cardinal Puljić, calling Europe's attention to what he called the "Islamization" of Bosnia-Herzegovina, presented similar data (49 new mosques in Sarajevo and 156 elsewhere in Bosnia-Herzegovina) in his October 2000 interview with the Italian Catholic weekly *Famiglia Christiana*, but the Bosnian Muslim press replied that the cardinal was exaggerating about the new mosques while himself launching construction of a new cathedral in Sarajevo.[27]

New mosques sponsored by Arab states were designed as "Islamic centers" with schools, cultural centers, and restaurants. A number of segregated schools for men and women (boys/girls) were opened, and various Muslim cultural and political organizations affiliated with Islamic centers were founded in Sarajevo, Zenica, Tuzla, and other Muslim-dominated cities and towns. The so-called Active Islamic Youth (*Aktivna islamska omladina*), inspired by militant Arab revolutionary Islam, became the most conspicuous among these organizations. This organization's leaders carried out bitter polemics with liberal Sarajevo press and secular youth press such as *Dani*, but a large number of young Muslims joined this organization and adopted its ideology and program.

The Bosniak-Muslim liberal politician Muhamed Filipović admitted in an interview that the incumbent chairman of the Bosnian presidency, Alija Izetbegović, backed by the SDA party and the ulema, was driving Bosnia-Herzegovina toward partition and the foundation of a small, homogenous Islamic state.[28] To be sure, many moderate and nonnationalist Muslims in Sarajevo, Tuzla, and other large cities did not support the movement for an Islamic state in Bosnia and Herzegovina. Not even the alliance between the SDA and the Islamic Community held for very long. Tension between the clerical and secular Muslim elites arose as religious leaders demanded restitution of IZ property confiscated by the state under communism. According to these demands, the Islamic Community should be given the property it owned under Ottoman rule and prior to the 1878 Austrian occupation of Bosnia-Herzegovina. Roughly, this would include over one-fourth of all arable land plus buildings, estates, and other forms of property.

In 1999 and 2000 when the ailing Izetbegović retired from politics, the attempted Islamic revolution in Bosnia and Herzegovina lost momentum. The influential Muslim leader Haris Silajdžić opted for a European-oriented secular and moderate "Party for Bosnia and Herzegovina." The party viewed future government in Bosnia-Herzegovina as a coalition of moderate secular Muslims, former communists, and other supporters of Bosnia's independence and secular democracy. A large number of urban Muslims espoused the Silajdžić's Europeanism and even saw Bosnia-Herzegovina as a "region" of Europe rather than the strong nation-state that SDA wanted to establish. The elections of November 2000 mirrored the following situation: Silajdžić's coalition did not dominate but still changed the erstwhile stalemate, in which three mutually hateful ethnic parties maneuvered waiting for the opportunity to dismember the country. Silajdžić also saved the face of Islam and distinguished his faith from that of the discredited nationalistic Christian neighbors. Although Islamic radicalism and Muslim nationalism have not been completely defeated, a large portion of the Bosnian Muslim population have chosen democracy, secularism, and new Europe, in spite of the lack of help they experienced during the war.

The Madonna of Medjugorje and Croatian Nationalism in Bosnia-Herzegovina and Croatia

In the second decade of its life, the longest sequence of Marian apparitions in religious history, the Medjugorje "miracle," had followed the same pattern of "fall," erosion, and disenchantment that manifested in other concurrent religious and quasi-religious phenomena such as nationalism, ethnoclericalism, and communism. While local and international pilgrims continued their blind worship of what they viewed as the "Queen of Peace" of Medjugorje during the Bosnian War, Croatian nationalists in Herzegovina, assisted by the Tudjman regime in Zagreb, founded a secessionist-minded Croatian state-regime under the name "The Croatian Community of Herceg-Bosna." The Republic of Croatia provided regular financing of the administration of the Croatian enclave in western Herzegovina.[29] The capital city, Mostar, became known as "the city of the bridges"—with remnants of its ancient Ottoman bridge over the Neretva river destroyed by artillery shells of the Croat Army in 1993—cleansed of Muslims and Serbs, as were many other towns and villages in the area. Medjugorje became a "sacred capital" of this new Balkan state. The local Franciscans strengthened ties with the separatist authorities of the Herceg-Bosna and with the Tudjman regime, thereby insulating themselves even further from the authority of the local bishop. According to a Croatian opposition weekly, the Franciscans from Medjugorje and the nearby Široki Brijeg monastery amassed wealth through the ownership of the Bank of Herzegovina and other forms of Mafia-style businesses that boomed in the broader region during the 1990s.[30] In the midst of the bloody war, the Herzegovina Franciscans, assisted by Croatia's defense minister, Gojko Šušak, built in Croatia's capital, Zagreb, a new mammoth church and pastoral center worth 12 million German marks.[31] A Sarajevo antinationalist newspaper described Medjugorje simply as a center of massive fraud and crime.[32] Reporters for the Split daily *Slobodna Dalmacija* investigated organized prostitution in Croatia, in which, according to the newspaper's findings, almost all pimps and prostitutes came from western Herzegovina.[33] At the same time, according to a "who rules in Croatia" analysis in the opposition weekly *Feral Tribune*, thousands of natives of western Herzegovina moved to neighboring Croatia and became members of the new ruling elite: cabinet members, leaders in military and security apparatus, business and media tycoons.[34] The four probably most infamous figures in postcommunist Croatian politics, the defense minister Gojko Šušak, the business tycoon Miroslav Kutle, President Tudjman's senior adviser and HDZ vice-president Ivić Pašalić, and the film director Jakov Sedlar, who directed the movie on the Medjugorje miracle, *Gospa* (1995), and the neo-Nazi film *Četverored* (1999), were all natives of west Herzegovina linked with the Franciscans. An Italian political analyst of Balkan affairs designated Medjugorje a fulcrum of the new Croat nationalism and wrote that the Medjugorje cult was under the control of the neo-Ustašas.[35]

The official Church struggled to tame the Balkan friars while trying not to harm Medjugorje's religious, political, and financial benefits. As early as 1994, Cardinal Kuharić attacked the politics of the west Herzegovinian HDZ party concerning the Bosnian War. Vatican inspectors were constantly busy dealing with the issue of the administration of parishes and mediating between the bishop and the friars. In February 1999, the bishop of Mostar, Ratko Perić, backed by the Vatican and with the personal involvement of the superior general of the Order of the Friars Minor, made one among numerous attempts to implement the papal decree *Romanis pontificibus*, which commands the monks to withdraw to monasteries and leave the disputed parishes to secular clergy.

The political, military, and "Mafia" background of local affairs, however, did not harm the Madonna's cult. According to a *Newsweek* article published in January 2000, the seer of 1981, Ivan Dragičević, who lives in Boston with his wife, Laureen Murphy (a former Miss Massachusetts), attracted thousands of American Catholics to his daily encounters with Mary.[36] On the occasion of the nineteenth anniversary of the Medjugorje miracle, Dragičević said to the press that the Madonna of Medjugorje appeared in 1981 in Bosnia-Herzegovina to warn the people of the imminent war and that the contemporary world is experiencing a "spiritual revolution."[37] The Medjugorje cult burgeoned in many countries, being the most popular in the United States, in spite of several well-documented critical books published there.[38] Pilgrims were coming to the land of genocide from Italy, Poland, Korea, France, the United States, Canada, the Baltic states, Ireland, Slovakia, Hungary, Romania, Albania, and elsewhere.

In June 2001, the celebration of the twentieth anniversary of the first apparitions brought together at Medjugorje more than 200,000 pilgrims. This event may be also designated the first straightforward clerical manifesto on the political, ethnonationalistic background of the Medjugorje apparitions. At the mass, held near the apparition site on 24 June 2001, the local Franciscan provincial Tomislav Pervan said that without the miracle at Medjugorje there would not have been the Croatian independent state existing today, and that it was the Madonna of Medjugorje who put Croatia on the map of world nation-states.[39]

Religion and Nationalism in Other Successor States

Close ties between church and state were established in the so-called Serb Republic (RS), a territory "cleansed" of Muslims and Croats during the war. The constitution of the Serb Republic granted to the Serbian Orthodox Church a "special status." Orthodox Christianity became the de facto state religion ("de facto" means a real religious monopoly as in other successor states, but without being put in writing lest the western providers of financial aid object to it due to their liberalism). The RS government and foreign-aid givers funded renovation of more than 100 Serb churches damaged in the 1992–95 war. Serbian churches in Sarajevo and Mostar were rebuilt thanks to financial assistance from Greece and Germany. Meanwhile, Muslims and Croats in the Serb Republic were stopped from rebuilding their shrines by Serb police and angry crowds incited by clergy (in some enclaves, Croats applied similar tactics against Serbs and Muslims). According to an insider in RS ruling circles, "amidst the reign of crime and robbery, everyone celebrates the *slava* [traditional Serbian feast of baptism or family patron-saint] and pays lip service to the Orthodox Church,"[40] According to a U.S. human rights organization, the RS continued to be governed by internationally wanted war crimes suspects.[41] No Serb cleric or bishop ever condemned any Serb criminal, not even those tried and sentenced at the Hague War Crimes Tribunal for the Former Yugoslavia. The internationally wanted war crimes suspect and former president of the Bosnian-Serb Republic, Radovan Karadžić, was seen in the company of Church leaders. In 1996 and 1997, the patriarch of Serbia, Pavle, was among several dozen nationalistic intellectuals who signed declarations demanding that Karadžić and another war crimes suspect, General Ratko Mladić, be pardoned by the International War Crimes Tribunal in the Hague.[42] The Greece-based Hilandar monastery offered Karadžić monastic life as protection from the prosecution. Serbian Church leaders such as Metropolitan Amfilohije, praised Karadžić's defiance of the Dayton Peace Accord. The Orthodox Churches of Serbia, Greece, and Russia honored Karadžić with high church decorations for the defense of the Orthodox faith. According to a British newspaper; Karadžić was made a candidate for sainthood in the Serbian Orthodox Church.[43] Serb prelates, including the patriarch, also frequently met with the paramilitary leader and Belgrade mafia boss Željko Ražnatović Arkan. Arkan made generous donations to the Church, especially for the rebuilding of churches in Kosovo and Metohija. Arkan is also remembered for his wartime statements that the patriarch of Serbia was his supreme commander.

In the province of Kosovo, between 1989 and 1998, the Serbian Church, taking advantage of Milošević's police rule, was rebuilding churches and renovating ancient monasteries. New cathedrals came under construction in Priština and Djakovica, while monasteries and ancient shrines were being renovated. The Church, however, remained in a less favorable situation in Serbia proper. The Church could not recover property confiscated by the communists. Milošević annoyed Church leaders by retaining many symbols and memorials of the communist era and ignoring Church events. Many churchmen, according to a Belgrade analysis of Church affairs, became disappointed with the Serbian nationalist revolution, while zealots increasingly spoke out against Milošević.[44]

In the Former Yugoslav Republic of Macedonia, the Macedonian Orthodox Church became the main pillar of the tiny, barely viable nation. The national church, with shrines it controlled, and the new cathedral at Skopje helped resolved the difficult question: "Who are the Macedonians" (Greeks, Slavs or Albanians)? by providing a simple answer: the Macedonians (by nationality) are members of the Macedonian Orthodox Church. In the meantime, the Serbian patriarchate continued its struggle against the Macedonian clergy and Macedonian state. Several Serb bishops and prelates were evicted from the border zone by the Macedonian police upon violation of the Macedonian law that prohibited Serb clergy from wearing clerical attire in the republic's territory. The Belgrade patriarchate continued to complain that the Skopje government had denied the Serb clergy access to the shrines and tombs of Serbian kings and military cemeteries from the Balkan War of 1912 and the Salonica Front of 1918.[45] In October 1998, the Orthodox Church of Greece unsuccessfully attempted to mediate between Skopje and Belgrade. In 1998 the Macedonian Orthodox Church contributed to the electoral victory of the radical Slavic Macedonian nationalistic party VMRO-DPMNE. The new premier, ethnic nationalist Ljupčo Georgijevski, promised to the national Church of Macedonia status of a state religion and promptly allocated to the Church lands in the Ohrid region. Finally, in 2001, as Albanians took up arms and, emulating their cousins in Kosovo, rebelled against the Skopje government, the Macedonian Orthodox Church got a chance to demonstrate militant patriotism similar to that of the Serbian

Church. As the fighting went on, the head of the Macedonian Orthodox Church, Metropolitan Stefan, called for a holy war against the Albanian "terrorists who are stealing our territory."[46]

In Montenegro, two parallel rival ecclesiastical structures coexisted. The Serb metropolitan, Amfilohije, controlled the metropolitanate of Montenegro-Primorje, with 160 clerics, nuns, and monks who served more than 90 percent of all parishes and monasteries in the country. The schismatic self-declared Montenegrin Autocephalous Church (MAC), under the unrecognized Metropolitan bishop Miras Dedaić, established a headquarters at the old national capital of Cetinje. There adherents of the Serbian Church and the Church of Montenegro challenged each other on occasions of church festivals and holidays in a ritual and symbolic fashion. Occasionally the rivals used traditional means such as fist-fighting and pistol-shooting—thus far, only in the air. In the late 1990s, several plebiscites were held in parishes, and the schismatic church thus acquired 26 temples. Step by step, reminding one of the case of Macedonia, the schismatic Church of Montenegro was institutionalized. According to an advocate of Montenegrin ecclesiastical independence and statehood, "the autocephalous Montenegrin Orthodox Church will unify all Montenegrins around our native Montenegrin cults and saints in a single Montenegrin national state, instead of inciting hatred, turning us against our neighbors, and sending us to Heavenly Serbia."[47] In an attack on the schismatic church of Montenegro, Metropolitan Amfilohije chided the Montenegrins for adopting what he called "tribal identity."[48] Urged by Belgrade, the assembly of Orthodox churches held in Sofia, Bulgaria, from 30 September to 1 October 1998, released a special pronouncement by which the schismatic clergy of Montenegro was denied priesthood. After the 1998 elections, the new president of Montenegro, Milo Djukanović, inaugurated a proindependence course and supported the quest for autocephaly of the Montenegrin Church as a symbol of distinct Montenegrin national identity and statehood. The Holy Assembly of the Serbian Orthodox Church repeatedly condemned "the apostate Miras Dedaić and his schismatic godless group backed by the separatist forces in Montenegro."[49] In December 2000 in Cetinje and around other shrines a new round of quarrels exploded between a sizable "army" of followers of the Metropolitan Amfilohije and Montenegrin separatists and culminated on Orthodox Christmas, 7 January 2001. In his sermons and interviews, Metropolitan Amfilohije repeatedly spoke about civil war as he had in 1990–91.

The Politics of Saint-Making

After the bloody 1991–95 wars in Croatia and Bosnia-Herzegovina, the rival churches of Serbia and Croatia continued the course in interfaith relations begun in the 1960s. This course could be briefly described as intransigence with a sporadic display of ecclesiastical diplomacy (see more on this later).

While the postcommunist Croatian nationalist regime established Catholicism as the de facto state religion and the Stepinac cult as the key patriotic symbol, the Serbian church and Serb nationalists established cults of the martyrdom of Serbs in the World War II and published books that portrayed Cardinal Stepinac as an instigation of genocide. In 1995, the Zagreb archdiocese issued a collection of allegedly authentic Stepinac wartime sermons (earlier kept in secret Church archives) as evidence of the prelate's humanitarian work and criticism of the Ustaša regime for its excessive cruelty.[50] In 1997 the renovated Cardinal Stepinac shrine was opened in the Zagreb cathedral. In addition, the Croatian government and the Church had a nine-foot-high bronze statue of what became the nation's new founding father erected in Stepinac's native village of Krašić. Local authorities began building monuments to Stepinac in every village. In the meantime, the Vatican concluded the beatification cause and announced that the head of the Roman Church would come to Croatia in October 1998 for the beatification of Alojzije Stepinac, the servant of God.

As the beatification in Croatia approached, foreign Jewish organizations (and some individual Croats of Jewish descent) vehemently protested the beautification of Alojzije Cardinal Stepinac. Early in 1998, the Simon Wiesenthal Center asked the Zagreb government for a delay of the Stepinac beatification. A Croatian human rights organization close to the regime replied angrily by saying that "the Jews cannot appropriate the exclusive right to pass historical judgments and to bear the aura of the only martyr-nation, because many other nations, such as notably, the Croatian nation, have suffered, too."[51] The Catholic Church announced that Cardinal Stepinac, "according to solidly based data . . . saved several hundred Jews during the Second World War: either by direct intervention, or by secret prescripts to the clergymen, including mixed marriages, conversion to Catholicism, as did some Righteous in other European countries."[52] One the basis of documents in possession of the Catholic Church, the Zagreb regime and the Church twice requested from Yad Vashem—The Holocaust Martyr's and heroes' Remembrance Authority at Jerusalem—that Cardinal Alojzije Stepinac be honored as one of the "Righteous among the Nations," but Yad Vashem declined. The Vatican did try, however, to pursue something that could be described as a politics of "balancing the saints." While the Stepinac beatification was scheduled for 2 October 1998 during the second papal visit to Croatia, similar event, aimed at appeasing the Jews, would occur in the Vatican on 11 October—the papal canonization of Edith Stein, a Carmelite nun of Jewish descent who perished in Auschwitz.

On 3 October 1998, the most massive congregation since the 1984 National Eucharistic Congress welcomed the pope at the national shrine of Marija Bistrica. On this occasion Pope John Paul II consecrated Alojzije Stepinac a blessed martyr of the Roman Catholic Church. According to the papal message from Marija Bistrica, the Croat church leader Cardinal

Stepinac became a martyr "to the atrocities of the communist system" and "humanist who opposed the three twentieth-century evils of Nazism, fascism, and communism."[53] Thus, construction of the Stepinac myth was completed. It started in the 1950s during the critical moment in the Cold War when anticommunists in the Church and Western countries used the jailed Croatian prelate to energize the global anticommunist struggle. Under the Tudjman regime, the beatified churchman became some kind of a "cofounding father" of the new Croatia. In the words of the Archbishop of Zagreb, Josip Bozanić, "Cardinal Stepinac has become a compass that makes possible proper orientation for the Croatian people."[54] As the "nation's" myth, the new Stepinac myth highlights a link between the past and present of Croatia, sustaining the thesis about the Church as the nation's original founder and guide through history. On the Balkan interethnic and multiconfessional front, the Stepinac myth operated as a check against Serbian nationalism while also whitewashing the Church's World War II past. It rebuffs the Serb genocide charges and redeems the Croats from the sense of guilt that Serbian nationalists attempted to impose in order to curb Croatian nationalism. For the Holy See, the Stepinac myth was expected to help the cause of the ongoing beatification procedure of the wartime pope Pius XII, who has been continuously attacked, especially by Jewish circles, for his alleged silence about the Holocaust. Incidentally, in the same year the Vatican issued a kind of a public apology to the Jews, entitled "We Remember: A Reflection on the Shoah."[55] Finally, the 1998 beatification of Cardinal Stepinac was also part of the Catholic Church's construction of a new mythical history of the twentieth century during which the Church, as its leaders asked the faithful to believe, purportedly opposed all the three "evils" of fascism, Nazism, and communism.

intention of Vatican

While the "Shoah" document and the Edith Stein canonization might have somewhat appeased the Jews, the Stepinac beatification certainly did not meet with approval from domestic and foreign Jewish circles, let alone the response of the embittered Serbian Orthodox Church, which coincided with the beatification. In anticipation of the beatification and papal visit, the Serbian Orthodox Church responded: in May 1998 the Holy Assembly of Bishops of the Serbian Orthodox Church canonized eight new Serbian saints. Although many clerics and faithful in the Serbian Church expected that the answer to Stepinac's beatification would be canonization of the anti-Catholic and anticommunist bishop Nikolaj Velimirović, whose relics were solemnly transferred to Serbia from the United States in 1991, church leaders chose a more telling response. In the regular spring session of the Belgrade patriarchate, the Holy Assembly of Bishops had announced the forthcoming canonization of these eight new saintly martyrs. Seven of the new saints had been executed between 1941 and 1945 by the Ustašas and one by the communists. The following church leaders, priests, and believers were to become "new martyrs" and members of the Assembly of Saints of the

Orthodox Church: the metropolitan of Zagreb, Dositej Vasić, who was imprisoned and beaten to death by Croat Ustašas (allegedly, as the *Pravoslavlje* writes and as was included in the official saintly biography, Catholic nuns took part in the torture); the metropolitan archbishop of Sarajevo, Petar Zimonjić, killed by the Ustašas at Jasenovac; the bishop of Banja Luka, Platon Jovanović, executed by the Ustašas near Banja Luka and thrown into a river; the bishop of Karlovac, Sava, killed by the Ustašas; the archpriest Branko Dobrosavljević, tortured and executed by the Ustašas; the archpriest Djordje Bogić, tortured and killed by the Ustašas; and the Serb peasant Vukašin, a parishioner from Klepci, Herzegovina, who, according to survivors' testimonies, died under torture while calmly telling his executioners: "Just keep on doing your business, son"; and the metropolitan of Montenegro, Joanikije Lipovac, executed by the communists in 1945 after his failed attempt to escape across the Austrian border to the West.[56] All except Joanikije Lipovac were victims of the Croat fascist Ustašas, while the metropolitan of Montenegro (Joanikije) was executed by the communists.[57]

The announcement of the canonization of the new Serbian saints in May 1998 was an immediate response to the Stepinac canonization. An official and liturgical canonization ensued two years latter. In the meantime the list of the new martyrs was expanded with the new name of Rafail, who during the World War II was the abbott at the Šišatovac monastery near the Serbo-Croatian border. The ninth martyr was also a victim of the Ustašas and died under torture in the prison camp of Slavonska Požega. The solemn canonization of the new Serbian saints took place during the central commemoration of the two thousand years of Christianity, on 21 May 2000, at the memorial Saint Sava's church in Belgrade. The new Serb saints were to consolidate one of the founding myths of the new Serbia—the Jasenovac myth. As the "second Serbian Golgotha," the Jasenovac myth combined the myth of the nation's origin, that is, the Kosovo myth, with the myth of the nation's rebirth in the 1990s. It consecrated the link between past and present and between heavenly and earthly Serbia. Finally, it boosts the Church's historic role as a leading national institution. The two new myths, the Stepinac myth and the Jasenovac myth, according to their clerical architects, were designed to become building blocks in the making of two new European nations: postcommunist Serbia and Croatia. The Serbo-Croat hostility of the 1930s and 1980s was thus reinforced, and the historic strife between Catholicism and Orthodoxy in southeastern Europe was continued in the twenty-first century. Things have settled in their proper place, as the Serbian patriarch had announced in his 1987 interview. The Partisan struggle during World War II and the communist era of Serbo-Croatian brotherhood and unity was meant to be some kind of a temporary disorder. The harmony was engineered by "godless" forces, so that the godly clerical forces had to correct it by manufacturing hatred and securing its endurance—in which they seem to have succeeded.

Religious Organizations and the
International Peace Process

During the Balkan wars, leaders of the mainstream Yugoslav religious organizations maintained hostile relations and deepened the hatred but issued a number of appeals for peace. With increasing international involvement in the Balkan conflict, domestic clergy encountered a new challenge: foreign missionaries as peacemakers, also known as "religious statecraft."[58] Willy-nilly, the archrivals had themselves to turn to peacemaking diplomacy.

After the outbreak of the Yugoslav war of 1991, numerous relief programs and conflict mitigation activities were initiated and carried out by foreign and domestic religious groups and individuals. Though it would be difficult to give credit to whole institutions for humanitarian and peace-building activities, because religious institutions and religious authorities carried out, to say the least, an ambiguous strategy that involved simultaneous backing of the nationalistic factions while playing the role of peace mediators before the international observers, a number of individual clerics and religious leaders have done an invaluable service for peace. The evangelical scholar from Osijek, Croatia, Peter Kuzmić, convened in spring 1991 at Osijek a "Peace and Justice" conference aimed at raising awareness in the West about the imminent war threat in the Balkans; during the war, Kuzmić conducted relief work through centers based in Boston, Massachusetts, and in Osijek. In 1994, the Evangelical Theological Seminary in Osijek inaugurated a course in "Christian Peace-Making" and held in September 1998 the Second International Conference for Theological Education in the Post-Communist World. In Bosnia and Herzegovina, Bosnian Franciscans of the province called "Silver Bosnia," as opposed to their brethren in western Herzegovina, excelled in the peace effort in the 1990s. The Bosnian Franciscan leaders Petar Andjelović and Luka Markešić, with the friars Ivo Marković, Marko Oršolić, and others, fought on the humanitarian front while also agitating for a united Bosnia-Herzegovina. Provincial Andjelović took part in one of the first interreligious peace vigils held in besieged Sarajevo on 4 October 1993 and has continued to partake in peace efforts since. Fra Ivo Marković directed the conciliation project "Face to Face" sponsored by U.S. ecumenical foundations and American Presbyterian mediators. The project involved regular interreligious meetings, conversations among clergy of all Bosnian religious communities, and mutual visitations on the occasion of religious holidays. During the Easter holidays of 1998, Fra Ivo set up the first interfaith Catholic-Orthodox children's chorus in the church of Saint Anthony in Sarajevo. In Croatia, the bishop of Šibenik, Srećko Badurina, the bishop of Djakovo, Marin Srakić, and a priest from Trnava, Luka Vincetić, labored to maintain dialogue with the Serbian Orthodox Church and ease tensions. In addition, Bishop Badurina was the chief initiator of the

"Epistle on the Occasion of the Fiftieth Anniversary of the Ending of the Second World War in Europe," released by the Conference of Croatian bishops on 1 May 1995, in which the Croat bishops for the first time in history mentioned the persecution of the Serbian Orthodox Church by the Croat wartime state and called for reconciliation. Bishop Badurina was also an outspoken critic of crimes against Serb civilians committed by the Croatian military during the Croat victories against the breakaway Serb republic of Krajina in 1995. Furthermore, the chief imam of Croatia and Slovenia, Ševko Omerbašić, promoted Christian-Muslim understanding and organized relief work during the Bosnian war. The bishop of Banja, Luka Franjo Komarica, fought under extremely difficult conditions for survival of the local Catholic community (while also helping Muslims persecuted by Serbs) through a patient dialogue with Serb authorities and cooperation with the international community. In the Serbian Orthodox Church, the bishop of Srijem, Vasilije, took part in several ecumenical meetings and prayers for peace before, during, and after the war. In addition, a few individual Serb churchmen who took part in the peace process were veterans of the Partisan war and leaders of the Titoist clerical association, such as the archpriest Jovan Nikolić from Zagreb and Krstan Bjelajac from Sarajevo.

Foreign relief organizations, conflict resolution specialists, and ecumenical groups and other governmental and nongovernmental organizations involved in the otherwise booming political business of conflict resolution (accompanied with peace research and conflict analysis as advancing branches in international relations studies) provided mediation, financial aid, relief, and humanitarian and peace-building programs and organized numerous interfaith round tables and conferences.[59] According to one account, the religious peace-building operation in the Balkans expanded into the most massive such operation in the history of humanitarian work and peacemaking.[60] As I will show later, the impressive quantity but low quality of this "religious statecraft" (i.e., little if any real effect in eliminating the causes of the conflict) is one of its most remarkable characteristics.

The new "religious statecraft" and religious humanitarian work carried out by foreigners posed challenges for mainstream domestic denominations and required their response. Patriotic clergy and the church press, as well as secular nationalistic regimes, attacked foreign religious peace advocates (predominantly Protestants), asking for state protection against the "invasion of sects." The first Balkan Evangelical conference, held in September 1996 in Belgrade, complained about police harassment and a propaganda war against Western peace and relief workers in Serbia, Croatia, and Bosnia alike.[61] Prominent prelates in Serbia and Croatia and Bosnian imams released studies on "sects" and guidebooks on how to deal with them. According to the Serbian Church's "anti-sectarian" pamphlet, "religious sects of various names and 'doctrines' all lead toward destruction of integrity of the individual, while undermining homogeneity of the nation and stability of the state, making them prone to self-destruction and the abandonment of the centuries-old spiritual, cultural, and civilizational heritage and identity."[62] In 1997, 280 monks and 40 priests of the Serbian Orthodox Church released an "Appeal against Ecumenism." The appeal was published in all major church and secular newspapers and read on state television. This appeal argued that interfaith ecumenical dialogue was a weapon of Western missionaries' proselytism and quoted the famous statement of Archimandrite Justin, from his 1974 antiecumenical study.

Gradually, most religious leaders came to collaborate with Western supervisors of the peace process. The archbishop of Sarajevo, Vinko Cardinal Puljić, the reis-ul-ulema Mustafa Cerić, the bishop of Kosovo, Artemije, and Western-educated monks from the Kosovo Visoki Dečani Abbey, and some others, understood the importance of lobbying, public relations, fund raising, and so forth. Even some earlier outspoken militants espoused the rhetoric of peace and human rights. For example, the Serb Orthodox bishop of Slavonia, Lukijan Pantelić, who in 1991 made the "eye for an eye, tooth, for tooth" statement, in June 1996 met with the Catholic bishop of Djakovo, Marin Srakić, at an interfaith peace meeting arranged by the Conference of Catholic Bishops of the United States and said: "We were drawn into a horrible war from which both churches emerged as losers. Someone used us and played games with us. We all need help now."[63] In a similar vein, at an interfaith conference that took place on 16 March 1998 in Tuzla, the participants released a joint statement according to which "we feel remorse and regret the evil committed in this war by some members of our respective communities, although the perpetrators of the crimes did not act on behalf of the churches. . . . We pray for mutual forgiveness."[64]

The Catholic Church had undertaken relatively more conciliatory activities of all major religious institutions in the successor states. Pope John Paul II, during his 1997 visit to Sarajevo, appealed: "Forgive and beg for forgiveness." The Catholic Church also attempted, without much success, to restart the interfaith dialogue that began in 1965 and was interrupted in 1990. As noted earlier, in 1995 the Croatian Catholic episcopate released a statement on the occasion of the fiftieth anniversary of V-E (Victory in Europe, i.e., the Allies' triumph over the Axis) Day. In this epistle the episcopate said that "the wartime regime in the Independent State of Croatia established an ideology of racial and ethnic discrimination [and] committed crimes which cannot be justified as self-defense," and that "many suffered during the war, [and] particularly gravely affected was the Serbian Orthodox Church."[65] The Catholic Church in Croatia also assisted in the restoration of the religious life of Orthodox Serbs and the return of the Serb clergy in the Krajina region (abandoned by people and clergy in the aftermath of the Croatian "Storm" military offensive in the summer of 1995).

The archbishop of Sarajevo, Vinko Cardinal Puljić, became a media favorite, portrayed as a leading peacemaker. Thus Puljić was one of the founders of the American-funded "Interfaith Council of Bosnia-Herzegovina" established at Sarajevo in June 1997. The prelate toured the world and raised significant funds for various conflict resolution and peace-building programs while also using this activity to advance the Croat Catholic perspective on the Balkan conflict and discredit enemies of the Church and Croatian nationalism. Cardinal Puljić insisted that religion and religious organizations had nothing to do with the making of the Yugoslav conflict. The archbishop portrayed the religious institutions as victims of communist oppression as well as manipulation by secular politicians (many of whom were ex-communists). In Puljić's words, religious organizations could not aggravate the crisis because before the war "[c]hurches had influence on a relatively small number of people who regularly attended worship services, church press had a small circulation, and churches had no access to radio and television."[66] Puljić's appointee as coordinator to the U.S.-funded Interfaith Council, Niko Ikić, said in an interview with Voice of America that the Interfaith Council had to focus on foreign relations in order to explain to the Western governments that the war in Bosnia was ignited by "atheists and others who manipulated and deceived the religious institutions and dragged them into conflict."[67] On one occasion Cardinal Puljić argued that only practicing believers and others who enjoyed Church leaders' confidence could take part in the peace process and receive financial aid.[68] Cardinal Puljić, his vicar Mato Zovkić, and Church leaders in Bosnia and Croatia found common ground with the reis-ul-ulema Mustafa Cerić and the Serb Orthodox archbishop of Bosnia, Nikolaj Mrdja, in attacking unanimously several notable domestic clerics who were peace advocates as alleged "Marxists, communists, and Titoists" demanding that the international community exclude them from the peace process.[69] Such discredited clerics were, among others, the Bosnian Franciscan Marko Oršolić and the Serb-Orthodox priest from Croatia, Jovan Nikolić. Yet Oršolić and Nikolić (who had been Partisan resistance fighter in World War II) were by no means Marxists or communists, although both were sympathetic to the united Yugoslav state and the brotherhood-and-unity idea of Tito. Like many other pro–brotherhood and unity clerics, the two contributed to the ecumenical dialogue of the 1960s and 1970s. During the wars of the 1990s, the two clerics excelled in the antiwar campaign, relief work, and peace-building (Father Nikolić was a member of the Helsinki Committee in Croatia). In short, it is obvious that Cardinal Puljić and the top religious leaders of all denominations sought a total control over the religious dimension of the peace effort in order to protect various "higher interests" other than mere assistance to victims of war and genocide.

In April 1998, Puljić jumped into a public polemic with the UN High Commissioner for Bosnia, Carlos Westendorp. In a statement to the U.S. press, Westendorp drew analogies between the role of the Church in the Spanish Civil War and in the recent Bosnian war. Westendorp argued that the churches took sides and bore a large degree of responsibility for the conflict and its consequences. He concluded that peace would come provided that the churches took the blame and withdrew from political and public life while ethnic nationalist parties were abolished. Cardinal Puljić attacked Westendorp in a Croatian newspaper accusing him of underrating the legacies of communism and atheism and the influence of secular politicians, especially ex-communists.[70] The Bosnian-Croat author Ivan Lovrenović pointed out that at a round table held in Sarajevo in September 1999 and televised in prime time by the state television, all the religious leaders and members of the Western-funded Interfaith Council of Bosnia and Herzegovina reiterated the charges against secular forces while denying any clerical liability and saw no connection between religion, ethnic nationalism, and genocide in Yugoslav lands. The most outspoken in advancing such ideas was the representative of the Serbian Orthodox Church.[71]

In the meantime, the Serbian Church was also active on the peace-making and humanitarian front. During his first visit to Croatia after the war, in the spring of 1999, the patriarch of Serbia, Pavle, spoke about forgiveness and urged local Serbs to be loyal to the new Croatian regime.[72] Patriarch Pavle also made several moves to improve relations with the Islamic Community. In June 1999, Patriarch Pavle invited and cordially welcomed a Muslim delegation to the Mileševo, monastery, the most sacred Serbian shrine in Bosnia. According to the Muslim newspaper *Ljiljan*, the Serb political leader Biljana Plavšić "kissed the hand of the mufti of Sandjak," while the patriarch and the Serbian Church, according to the newspaper, "signaled that some kind of change might be in process in the Serbian Church."[73]

While improving its image via this new "interfaith cooperation," staged for the eyes of Western peace-builders, the Serbian Church also improved its image by attacking Slobodan Milošević, who in the meantime had evolved into an archenemy of the international community. A Church assembly at Belgrade on 9–11 June 1998 denied the right to "any individual or the incumbent regime in Serbia which conducts of an unnational and nondemocratic politics, to negotiate and sign treaties and contracts about the fate of Kosovo and Metohija."[74] In May 1998, Patriarch Pavle received Harriet Hentges, the vice-president of the United States Institute of Peace. Thereupon Bishop Artemije visited Washington several times and spoke against Milošević.[75]

Numerous projects aimed at promoting reconciliation either collapsed or produced ambiguous results. While religion posed as a general differences-sharpening but not unsurmountable obstacle, history proved "unmanageable." Religious institutions failed to conduct a tolerant dialogue about their common past and find like views on any important issue. Here is one example. In 1995 foreign mediators tried to convince religious leaders in the successor states to abandon the myths and take a realistic look at the past in order to discover a minimum they could agree about. The principal mediator in this project, entitled "South Slavic Religious History," was the Austrian bishops' conference. Religious leaders and scholars from all major religious institutions from ex-Yugoslavia were invited to Vienna to discuss

controversies from church history. The Austrian church institution "Pro Or-
iente" established and funded a "Commission for South Slavic Church History" whose members were Croat Catholic, Serb-Orthodox, and Bosnian
Muslim religious leaders and scholars. Cardinal Franz Koenig, the retired
archbishop of Vienna, said at the commission's first session that a new
church history of South Slavs must be written *sine ira et studio* (without
anger and prejudice) if the Yugoslav peoples and the new Europe wanted to
have a future.[76] Yet, after the first meeting, the project was ignored by the
leaders of the two major churches. As was pointed out by a U.S. conflict
resolution agency, "the necessity of establishing the historical truth" will
remain one of the principal tasks in the peace process in southeastern Europe.[77]

Although "religious statecraft," as an instrument of the management of
worldwide conflicts, received much encouragement and recognition, and in
spite of considerable Western investments in the religious dimension of the
Balkan peace process, the religious peace-making in the former Yugoslavia
seemed anything but successful. In some cases it only helped religious leaders who were candidates for prosecution by the Hague Tribunal as war
crimes suspects to avoid it and become "peace-makers," speaking as guests
of honor in the United States and other countries where religion is part of
established conservative politics. Many Western nongovernmental organizations (NGOs) continued their support of the discredited Balkan religious
leaders, some of whom have been designated in the liberal press as war
crimes suspects and candidates for the Hague Tribunal. For example, in
January 2001, the Washington-based International Crisis Group released a
report on the role of religion in the Kosovo conflict. The report extends the
Western support for the ineffective albeit expensive "religious peacemaking"
similar to the Interfaith Council in Bosnia and Herzegovina and says

> contrary to common belief, religion has not been a direct cause of conflict
> in Kosovo and may offer a way to reconciling some of the bitter social
> and political divisions between Albanians and Serbs. Religious leaders of
> all faiths in Kosovo—Orthodox, Muslim and Catholic—are prepared to
> enter an interfaith dialogue, but more support from the United Nations
> Mission is needed to give these talks appropriate standing. This report
> argues that UNMIK should establish and fund a permanent Kosovo Inter-
> faith Council, provide adequate financing for the repair and protection of
> all religious monuments, and ensure that education in Kosovo remains
> secular.[78]

Those who are well informed about the history of interfaith relations and
religious aspects of the Yugoslav conflict remained unimpressed with the
new "religious statecraft." One of the prominent ecumenical advocates in
the former Yugoslavia and a Vatican-appointed mediator between Croat
Catholic and Serb-Orthodox hierarchies, the Catholic archbishop of Bel-

grade, France Perko, voiced disappointment with the peace process. In his 1999 Christmas message he called for forgiveness and reconciliation among all ethnic communities in the Balkans. Yet he also told a Belgrade weekly in a Christmas interview that at present there is "no sincere wish for reconciliation on any of the sides."[79] Perko echoed the same concern, skepticism, and fear he expressed in a 1990 interview with me.[80] At the Religious Peace Conference that took place on 27–28 November 1999 at Amman, Jordan, under the aegis of the New York–based World Conference on Religion and Peace, representatives of religious organizations from ten Balkan countries released another abstract appeal for peace but, according to a BBC report, "refused to accept direct responsibility for the decade of conflict in the Balkans, saying that religion and religious institutions had been manipulated by nationalist politicians."[81]

Balkan religious leaders used interfaith institutions for pursuing their common interests, such as the restitution of church property and public pressure on all anticlerical forces. On 5 July 2000 in Sarajevo, Serb Orthodox bishops met with Croat Catholic church leaders to set up a joint committee for the celebration of two-thousandth anniversary of the birth of Jesus. After the meeting, which was advertised as ecumenical, the bishops said in a press release that they again demand from the authorities the restitution of church property confiscated by the communists 50 years ago and used the opportunity to strongly reject the charges that religious organizations bore any responsibility for wars and war crimes in former Yugoslavia and its successor states.[82] In November 2000, "religious statecraft" was again used as a battering ram of clericalism. The Interfaith Council of Bosnia and Herzegovina refused to approve a proposal made by international secular peace-building initiatives that ecumenical courses in religious culture be introduced in all Bosnia's public schools. Instead they insisted that catechism under control of religious authorities be taught in segregated classes. In a commentary, the Sarajevo author Ivan Lovrenović concluded that "[t]he 1992–1995 Bosnian war may have not been a religious war. But the next one will be for sure."[83]

11

THE TWILIGHT OF BALKAN IDOLS

In this part of the world a man has no chance to be born and
buried in the same country.

Macedonian rock performer Vlatko Stefanovski

After the Eastern European revolutions of 1989, Eastern Europe
ceased to exist as a geopolitical unit and cultural concept and
was replaced by "Central Europe" and "the Balkans". The successor states
of the one-time open and proud Yugoslavia became "the Balkans," mired
again in ethnic bloodshed. From the 1950s through the 1980s, Yugoslavia
was, in spite of its official "Third World" (nonaligned) course, de facto part
of the West. After the collapse of communism, Yugoslavia's successor states,
except Slovenia, were despised by the West and, in the case of Serbia and
Croatia, came into conflict with the West, while Bosnia-Herzegovina, Kosovo,
and Macedonia became Western protectorates. The Yugoslav peoples became
again what nineteenth-century western European statesmen termed "bits
and refuse" of nations.[1] Local ethnic nationalist revolutions ended in failure.
New regimes that emerged during the wars of the 1900s were labeled
"Mafia-states" by an Italian analyst of world affairs.[2] Each post-Yugoslav
"successor state" went down its own path of degradation. And only the
growing influence of myth and religion helped some people to believe that
the new was better than the old.

The Catholic Church and Croatia's
Return to the West

At least twice in the modern era, the Croatian branch of the Catholic
Church got the opportunity to decisively influence political transformations

and contribute to the resolution of the crucial Croatian statehood-nationhood issue. During World War II Church leaders came to believe that the Independent State of Croatia (NDH) should have the Church's legitimation. The only currently available alternatives were another Serb-dominated Yugoslavia similar to the interwar kingdom or—in the eyes of the Church, even worse—a new Yugoslav state ruled by the communists. From the clerical point of view, it was reasonable to believe that a Croat national state, while it might not be a paradise on earth, still could not be worse than another kingdom under a Serb dynasty or a communist republic. Yet somehow the NDH *was* even worse. Nevertheless, the clerical assistance in the Ustaša government and the domestic Church leaders' legitimation of the state helped the NDH to function as a state and survive for four years. After 1945, the NDH legacy seriously damaged both the image and national interest of the Croatian people. Nonetheless, the Church was never prepared to learn from history and recognize clerical policies toward the NDH as a mistake. Instead, like most religious organizations, Croat church leaders sought to substitute myth for history. After the collapse of communism the Catholic Church in Croatia again became a kingmaker of sorts. As described in chapter 10, both reform-minded communists and their ethnic nationalistic opponents wooed the Church in the hope that clerical support would decide the elections. This time the Church had relatively easier task than during World War II because there was no communist alternative to compel the Church to side with the nationalists. Nevertheless, the Church helped the coming-to-power of the nationalistic historian Franjo Tudjman and his Croatian Democratic Community (HDZ). This time the legitimation was not even ambiguous, as it had been during the World War II. After the domestic church helped Tudjman's electoral campaign, on 14 January 1992 the Vatican led several Western countries to recognize Croatia as an independent state. Yet again, as in the case of the NDH, the Tudjman regime proved another failure in the Croatian quest for statehood, nationhood, and a good reputation in the community of nations. Paradoxically, both zealous worshipers of the nation—ethnic nationalists and the Church—thus have eventually earned their stripes in national history within the same camp as empires, foreign invaders, and others responsible for the Croatian curse of missing or bad nationhood. And the Church, instead of confession and repentance, will again try to suppress this historical fact with new myths.

A new grand myth arose in Croatia as soon as the nationalists defeated the coalition led by the reformed communists in the spring of 1990. Tudjman's 1990 election victory was advertised by the winners as the fulfillment of the nationalist myth of "Croatia's return to the West" after some kind of a Babylonian captivity in the multiethnic federation dominated by atheistic communists and Orthodox Serbs. In numerous interviews Tudjman talked about his country's return in the sphere of Western civilization. In his address on the occasion of the promulgation of Croatia's new Constitution on 22 December 1990, the new president mentioned the terms "Europe" and

"European" as many times as the terms "Croatia" and "Croatian" and insisted on Croatia's image as a Western country.[3] The new secular myth was adjusted to the central church myth of "Thirteen Centuries of Christianity in the Croat People" (see chapter 4). Tudjman insisted on the continuity between the ancient Western Christian Croatian principalities and the three modern Croat states (Tudjman included the communist-era Croatian republic). The key national institution—a national council or assembly known long ago under the common Slavic term *sabor* (assembly, diet) adopted the World War II title *Hrvtaski Državni Sabor* (the Croatian State *Sabor*). The new currency was called the *kuna*, a currency coined by Croatian medieval rulers and again put in use during the World II in the NDH. Symbols were changing in the new Croatia. Memorials were erected in honor of and streets named after World War II Ustaša leaders. Old Ustašas, as well as Croatian nationalists who were associated with emigre terrorist groups during the cold War, returned to Croatia. Many of them assumed high posts in the government and prominence in political life. Their principal targets became ethnic Serbs, former members of the League of Communists who had not joined HDZ, and symbols of alien cultures and of the communist era.

Neo-Ustašas dynamited thousands of memorials to the World War II antifascist struggle.[4] The Partisan memorial at the Zagreb Mirogoj cemetery was dynamited. An explosive was found near Josip Broz Tito's bronze statue in his birthplace of Kumrovec. In the midst of a right-wing rally, a HDZ official urinated publicly on the local Partisan memorial at Veljun in Istria; and so forth. Concurrently, HDZ activists in some cities were "cleansing" politically or religiously incorrect books from schools and city public libraries. Primary targets were books written in the Cyrillic alphabet (after 1990 no longer taught in Croatian elementary schools) and books written by left-wing authors, Serbs, or pro-Yugoslavs, such as Ivan Cankar, Ivo Andrić, August Cesarec, and Branko Ćopić, and even foreign authors guilty of socialism, atheism, and homosexuality, such as Jack London, Mark Twain, and Oscar Wilde.[5] Public discourse in postcommunist Croatia was permeated with ethnic slurs targeting Serbs, Muslims, Jews, Russians, Greeks, Africans, and countries that criticized the Zagreb regime. President Tudjman himself opened the barrage ("I've been blessed by the fact that my wife is neither a Serb nor Jewish"). The leader was echoed by returning old Ustaša emigres and leaders of right-wing parties who insulted Serbs, Jews, leftists, and other in speeches, articles, and interviews. Militant neo-Ustaša groups attacked opposition leaders, disrupted opposition rallies, and physically attacked union leaders and antifascists who commemorated the World War II Partisan resistance.

The Tudjman regime inaugurated a new history that minimized Ustaša crimes. An international commission established to supervise the new Croatian school history courses in high schools found that new textbooks minimized World War II Ustaša crimes (barely mentioning the Jasenovac camp) while magnifying the number of victims of communist repression and crimes committed against Croats by the World War II Serb guerilla Četniks.[6] A "new" world history was also taught in a similar fashion. Thus, in 1999 on the sixtieth anniversary of the ending of the Spanish Civil War, a pro-regime daily newspaper obscured the causes of the conflict and blamed Spanish communists and the Soviet Union for persecution of the faith, causing civil war, and attempting communist revolution in Spain.[7] President Tudjman himself encouraged the writing of a new national historiography that portrayed the Ustašas as patriots and blamed Serbs and communists for provoking allegedly sporadic and not excessively cruel Ustaša reprisals.[8] The government established a "Commission for Verification of the Exact Number of Victims of the Second World War and Postwar Era." Twenty-four of the commission's members were politicians chiefly from the ruling party, with forty historians and experts of whom most were close to the regime. This commission submitted to the Croatian Sabor a report that minimized the number of Ustaša victims and blamed the communists for most of the atrocities. The commission estimated the total number killed during and after the war at 161,415, of which 4,797 persons were executed in jails and concentration camps. In Jasenovac only 2,238 were supposed to have lost their lives, and the total number of Jews executed by the NDH regime was 203. The communist-led antifascist Partisans and the communists regime of the postwar Yugoslavia were accountable for 37,800 executions, as opposed to the Ustašas, who allegedly killed 15,705 persons.[9] Domestic opposition and Western media designated the report as scandalous neofascist propaganda based on false data.[10]

Thus this neo-Ustaša revival was not merely symbolic. One more example is in order to highlight a legal dimension of this revival. On 14 February, 1992, the Croatian Sabor declared null and void all verdicts passed by state courts of the federated Republic of Croatia and the Federal Republic of Yugoslavia between 1945 and 1990 against "innocent victims of communism and Croatian patriots." All persons sentenced as nationalists, including war criminals and terrorists, were considered "innocent victims of communism." Croatian Catholic prelates present at this session of the Sabor jubilantly applauded because the declaration applied to the Stepinac case and other clergy sentenced by Yugoslav criminal courts during the revolutionary period of 1945–1953 and thereafter. Yet the declaration made no distinction between a few clerics who might have been innocent and those who wore Ustaša uniforms, belonged to Ustaša and NDH organizations, and took part in wartime massacres of civilians, not to mention Ustašas sentenced for war crimes and wanted also by international police forces, criminal courts in foreign countries, and Jewish organizations investigating the Holocaust.

The status of the Catholic Church as de facto state religion was another similarity between Tudjman's Croatia and the NDH. On 30 November 1998, only two days before the second papal visit to Croatia and the beatification of Cardinal Stepinac, the Sabor ratified a package of "treaties," a de facto concordat between Zagreb and the Vatican. The agreement, which quickly became Croatia's law, granted permanent financial assistance to the Church from the state budget. Parishes were entitled to financial aid, and the clergy obtained pensions from the state pension fund (officials of other faiths were not granted this privilege). The law set terms and deadlines for a swift restitution of Church property confiscated under communism (no other religious institution or private individual or firm received such guarantees). It also established a military vicariate, with 18 priests and a bishop military vicar (the auxiliary bishop of Zagreb, Juraj Jezerinec) placed on the Defense Ministry's payroll. Needless to say, no other faith was allowed to delegate its cleric to the armed forces, not even without pay. The law also introduced Catholic catechism in all schools and even in preschool and daycare centers. Candidates for positions in state bureaucracy had to provide letters of recommendation from parish priests and bishops as well as warrants about holy communion, confirmation, and children's participation in religious training. According to a U.S. State Department report on religious freedom in Croatia, Catholicism was de facto a state religion in Croatia, while discrimination against other faiths was also practiced.[11]

Tudjman's close aide Jure Radić (earlier a prominent Catholic layman and counsel to top Church leaders) became vice-premier and minister for religious affairs. Radić said in an interview that all state laws should be based on the Holy Gospel and announced the abolition of "the communist abortion law that violates the Gospel."[12] According to the Evangelical pastor Peter Kuzmič, all decisions concerning religious affairs and Church-state relations were made through secret channels between President Tudjman and the Bishops' Conference.[13] Kuzmič revealed in an interview that, in the midst of a public debate about the teaching of an ecumenical religious culture in public schools, Tudjman and the bishops' conference of the Catholic Church, ignoring the debate as well as protests by religious minorities, reached a secret agreement about teaching only Catholic doctrine in schools.[14] The Church launched a national Catholic radio station ("Radio Marija") and obtained considerable air time on state-run television. Constructions of Catholic religious facilities were booming. According to a Croatian weekly, the Catholic Church had become the largest construction investor in postcommunist Croatia—in 1999, in Zagreb and Split alone, the Church had under construction new churches and other church facilities worth 104 million German marks.[15] The gothic Zagreb cathedral was thoroughly renewed and a new shrine to Cardinal Stepinac was built behind the main altar. Croatia became a "Catholic nation." According to a Croatian sociologist, the number of people who declared themselves practicing Catholics rose from 64.8 percent in 1988 to more than 90 percent by the late 1990s.[16]

At the fourth general party Convention held in February 1998 in Zagreb, the ruling Croatian Democratic Community (HDZ) officially presented itself as a "Christian-Democratic party" and HDZ adopted the social teachings of the Roman Catholic Church as official party doctrine. President Tudjman's speeches regularly included Biblical quotes and analogies. The president regularly attended Sunday masses at the Zagreb Cathedral; he also took private lessons in Catholic theology. Inspired by his new theological knowledge, Tudjman inaugurated in daily political jargon the concept of the *pretvorba* (literary meaning; "transformation"; also used by the Church as a liturgical term for the Eucharistic transubstantiation) to refer to the process of post-communist privatization. "The Croatian president," wrote columnist Slaven Letica, "exploited the holy notion of the Eucharist to legitimize the quick and ruthless grabbing of national wealth by the ruling elite."[17]

Tudjman's domestic and foreign policies alienated Croatia from the West and postponed her mythical "return." The new Croatian state was not only authoritarian but so excessively nationalistic that Croatia became a stumbling block in the Balkan peace process. Members of the regular Croatian army committed atrocities during the wars in Croatia and Bosnia-Herzegovina. Dozens of Croat military and some political leaders were indicted by the International War Crimes Tribunal for the Former Yugoslavia in the Hague. A HDZ branch loyal to Tudjman was set up in the Herzegovina town of Mostar. Herzegovina's HDZ was responsible for the outbreak of the Croat-Muslim war in 1993. During the Bosnian war of 1992–1995, the Zagreb government sent Croat divisions to protect Croatian interests, that is, to prepare ground for partition of the former Yugoslavia's heartland. To maintain the Croatian enclave in Herzegovina, Zagreb employed 22,000 state officials, military, and police and provided pensions for war veterans and other funds needed to prepare the ground for the possible annexation of this predominantly Croatian-populated province that had been cleansed of its Serbs during World War II by the Ustašas.[18]

Tudjman's construction of the new Croatian nation also included a new wealthy elite and key state and social institutions. The new Croat postcommunist aristocracy would consist of some "two hundred families" (Tudjman's words) selected by Tudjman and the HDZ and enriched through the privatization programs plus a few already wealthy Croats returning from foreign countries to their homeland and investing in its economy. Other pillars of society were the military, the intelligence services headed by Tudjman's son Miroslav, and the Catholic Church. As the state-run news agency HINA has revealed, in the second half of the 1990s, Croatia had put on the Defense Ministry's payroll the largest number of generals of any country in the world in proportion to the number of inhabitants and ordinary soldiers.[19] Croatia's intelligence and state security apparatus included the following: the domestic security and public surveillance service (UNS) and the service for the protection of the Constitution (SZUP), both protecting prominent political leaders and fighting various enemies in the country (e.g., ethnic minority organizations, foreign-based and domestic human rights associations, various independent voluntary associations, individual social critics, socialists, communists, liberals, and religious sects, organized crime and criminal gangs, etc.); counterintelligence services (SIS, HIS) focusing on foreign intelligence activities in Croatia; the Ministry of Foreign Affairs' Seventh Department, and the Ministry of Defense's Fifth Department.

Last but certainly not least important, the decade of HDZ rule destroyed the Croatian economy and impoverished the population. Once the most advanced economically of all Yugoslav republics, Croatia came to resemble the most backward parts of the Balkans. According to the economist Vladimir Gligorov, during the 1960s and 1970s, Croatia's businesses became internationally competitive and the republic demonstrated a potential to develop into the most prosperous East European region—yet during the 1990s Croatia became a backward and autarkic economy and one of the poorest countries in Europe.[20] According to a recent analysis, in 2001 Croatia had 180,000 unemployed persons, more than in 1990, and the total number of persons without a job reached one-fifth of the total population. At the same time, the country's foreign debt tripled the 1990 amount to reach 9 billion U.S. dollars in 2001 ($2,600 per capita).[21] An expert listed the following major causes for this economic disaster: first, the autarkic national economy, influenced by nationalistic politics; second, the ruling HDZ party's privatization program and criminal appropriations of socialist-era property and wealth; third, war.[22]

According to an independent U.S. research agency, in the 10 years of HDZ rule, 8 billion dollars appropriated through privatization and abuses of the state budget was taken out of Croatia and deposited in private accounts in foreign banks, and an additional 7 billion dollars of profit was acquired by top HDZ officials and their partners from these transactions. [23] What was once the wealthiest of the six republics in socialist Yugoslavia became an eroding society in which the number of users of illegal drugs rose from 4,000 in 1990 to 13,000 in 2000.[24] According to an opposition weekly, women of the prosperous Istria province, who in the 1960s and 1970s frequently travel to Trieste and Venice to buy fancy clothes, have become a major source of recruitment for the most difficult physical labor in neighboring Italy.[25] Antun Bogetić, the bishop of Istria, lamented in a 1992 interview that "thousands young people had left Istria" and "many of Istria's Croats had declared themselves Italians by nationality only to get a job in neighboring Italy."[26] The Bishop's Conference of Bosnia and Herzegovina met on 9–10 November 1999 in Sarajevo to discuss a massive exodus of young Croat Catholics to western Europe and overseas.[27] A survey of young people in Bosnia and Herzegovina conducted by two international organizations in 1999 has shown that 62 percent want to leave this country (from 1996 to 1998, some 42,000 persons under 40 years of age went abroad went with no intention to return).[28]

Regimes like Tudjman's are relatively short-lived and terminate either with dictators' deaths, corruption scandals, coups, or a combination of these factors. Corruption scandals and abuses of privatization policies shook the country as early as 1993. It became public after Tudjman's death in December 1999 that the regime's as well as the Church's officials were involved in money laundering, profiteering, speculations in real estate, and financial scandals.[29] Tudjman's daughter was allegedly involved in criminal appropriations of national wealth.[30] Leaders of the HDZ from North America accused Franjo Tudjman and Gojko Šušak of stealing millions of dollars donated by the Croatian diaspora for the defense of Croatia against Milošević's aggression. The transfer of the money from America into Tudjman's and Šušak's possession was carried out through the Catholic Church, which often served as a channel for similar operations.[31] Tudjman's son Miroslav was accused by a newspaper of stealing a number of secret files from the police archives and the ex-president's residence.[32]

Small wonder that anti-Tudjman voices also came from the Catholic Church and other religious circles. I noted earlier that Cardinal Kuharić criticized Tudjman's Bosnia policy and the Croatian army's cruelty to Serb civilians during the war in Croatia. Kuharić's successor, Archbishop Josip Bozanić, attacked privatization laws and was momentarily celebrated as a hero by the desperate opposition media. The Christian ecumenically oriented theologian Peter Kuzmić, who had earlier figured as a friend of the Catholic Church, wrote about the Church's "uncritical equation of Catholicism, national identity, and patriotism" and pointed out that some religious leaders, prominent prelates, and Church media often overtly threatened non-Catholics, secularists and liberals, or atheists who criticized the Church, calling on the state to prosecute them and mobilizing public opinion against anyone who dared to criticize the Church.[33] The theologian Bono Z. Šagi wrote about "post communist neocommunism," in which the Church supports another ideological monopoly and does not apply the same moral standards to those in power and the people.[34] The eminent priests Stjepan Kožul and Josip Ćorić attacked in their sermons and articles the regime's corruption and Church leaders' inaction. Eminent Catholic laymen such as Ivo Banac, Krsto Cviic, Boris Maruna, and others also publicly criticized the Church for contributing to the failure of democratization in Croatia and the country's international isolation. The Catholic priest-sociologist Ivan Grubišić said in an interview that "the Church today, as well as earlier in history, was tempted by the offer of high social status, wealth, and power . . . [and] the Church could not resist the temptation."[35] Grubišić also condemned in interviews the Church's manipulations of national history, in process, in his view, since the Great Novena of 1975–84, and Tudjman's confidence in hardline Croat nationalists returning from exile in 1990 to assume, without merit and qualifications, high posts in the government.[36] As a matter of fact, antiregime criticism from clerical and lay Catholic circles in Croatia, if observed in comparison with that of the Serbian Orthodox Church, was quite remarkable. Yet it is cold comfort for Croatian Catholicism to be somewhat less bad than Serbian Orthodoxy.

Church leaders have been consistent in their support of Tudjman and HDZ. The only "controversy" of sorts among Church leaders concerning the Church's support for the Tudjman regime occurred in 1996. In anticipation of the 1996–97 local, regional, and presidential elections, Church leaders debated the corruption issue and the Church's relations with the HDZ at the regular autumn session of the national Bishops' Conference in Djakovo on 3–5 October 1996. The conference's chairman, Franjo Cardinal Kuharić (who exceeded 75 years of age and was to retire in 1994) insisted on the Church's independence from the ruling party and government and urged the Church press and clergy to publicly criticize the regime's corruption, class tensions, impoverishment and unemployment, growing crime, and police ineffectiveness. He also insisted that Croatia back the legal authorities and sovereignty of Bosnia-Herzegovina. According to the well-informed Zagreb weekly *Globus*, a personal existed animosity between Tudjman and Kuharić.[37] While most bishops vacillated, the retired metropolitan of Split-Makarska, Archbishop Frane Franić, rose as the most outspoken opponent of Kuharić Franić campaigned in the media, calling on the Church to forge the same kind of relations with the HDZ as the Church in Western Europe had done with Christian democratic parties during the Cold War. In Croatia, Franić argued, communism was not completely defeated and might be back under the guise of social-democratic and liberal parties. Eventually, the year 1997 brought a great victory for Tudjman's and Franić's views and policies. The pope sent Kuharić into retirement, and the HDZ emerged triumphant in the elections. Tudjman was re-elected, the Church-state symbiosis was fortified from the parish to the national level, and the Church reasserted itself as the regime's trusted ally. Only briefly did Kuharić's successor, Bozanić, warm the hearts of the opposition by his criticism of corruption and privatization; he did not propose any change in the established system and was on better personal terms with Tudjman than his predecessor. Tudjman thus won the battle on the domestic front but seemed to be losing abroad.

All things considered, in spite of a few liberal voices, since the 1980s, clerical zealots and extremist ethnic nationalists seem to have exerted a strong influence in the Catholic churches of Croatia and Bosnia-Herzegovina. It was the quarrel of the churches in the 1980s and the impact of the 1991–95 was that turned most of the clergy in parishes and monasteries into zealots. Regarding church leadership, the situation in Croatian church remained ambivalent—or at least more complex than in the Serbian Orthodox Church, which was staffed by extremist nationalistic bishops and monks with only a few moderates among theologians and parish priests. Recently the Vatican has been striving, as always to "balance" its policies concerning new bishops' appointments. Thus, after 1989, the Holy See tried, first of all, to rejuvenate the Croatian episcopal elite and boost bishops' intellectual and educational background. Most of newly appointed bishops during the 1990s in Croatia and Bosnia-Herzegovina were highly educated prelates between the ages of 45 and 55. In addition, new church leaders were selected according to the following three criteria: episcopal candidates were sought among, first, those who had excelled in anticommunism before 1989; second, those who had distinguished themselves as ecumenical theorists and practitioners, and third, those who possessed expertise in rival faiths such as Serbian Orthodoxy and Islam. Thus, the two largest archdioceses in Croatia, Zagreb, and Split-Makarska, acquired bishops selected according to the first two criteria. While Kuharić's successor Josip Bozanić was a cautious churchman unsympathetic toward any form of radicalism and extremism, even anticommunism and anti-Yugoslavism, two candidates for the seat of the archbishop-metropolitan of Split-Makarska were selected among notable anticommunists. Thus, Petar Šolić, who served as auxiliary bishop of Split until he was killed in a 1993 traffic accident, had had troubles with communist authorities in the mid-1980s for organizing provocative marches of Catholic youth. The incumbent archbishop of Split, Marin Barišić, was attacked by the old regime's press and pursued by the police in the early 1980s for his alleged nationalistic agitation among students of the University of Split. The Vatican also appreciated prelates' being knowledgeable about rival faiths and ecumenical affairs, which resulted in the appointments of Ratko Perić at Mostar (Herzegovina) and Mile Bogović in Lika. interestingly, the "expert on communism" Marin Barišić, together with the expert on Serbian Orthodoxy, Mile Bogović, and the military vicar Juraj Jezerinac, had emerged by the end of the decade as among the leading ethnonationalistic "hawks" in the Croatian episcopate. Regarding Croatian Church leaders in neighboring Bosnia and Herzegovina, the hopeless situation in this ruined country, especially the disappointment with the Dayton Accords and rapid erosion of the ethnic Croat population, has transformed the archbishop of Sarajevo, Vinko Cardinal Puljić, from an intelligent moderate churchman similar to Archbishop Bozanić into an ethnonationalistic hawk like Barišić, Bogović, and Jezerinac. It is also noteworthy that the communist-era "media warrior," the ex-editor of *Glas Koncila*, Živko Kustić (a Greek-Catholic or Uniate priest), has remained during the past two decades the most outspoken of all Croat clerical "hawks."

The West to which Tudjman's country was supposed to belong could not embrace such a regime. Croatia was popular in Germany only briefly, during the Serbian aggression on Croatia and Bosnia in 1991 and 1992, and was never popular in the United States, France, or Britain. By 1995, public opinion in all western democracies, including Germany, despised Tudjman's country, viewing him and Milošević as two of a kind. Tudjman's foreign ministry found it nearly impossible to arrange official state visits for the Croatian president. Few if any world statesmen came to Croatia during Tudjman's reign expect to apply pressure and demand concessions regarding the Balkan peace process. Tudjman's Bosnia policy, dictatorial manners, faltering democracy, corruption, and reminiscences of World War II Ustašism angered many in the West even among the most conservative circles. Influential Jewish organizations in the United States, Israel, and elsewhere agitated against the Zagreb regime.[38] This pressure resulted in the trial of one Ustaša war criminal and the dismissal from diplomatic service of another ex-Ustaša leader.[39] Tudjman sought to appease Jewish groups in the United States and

Israel by revising his historical studies on World War II while Croatia also issued official apologies regarding the persecution of Jews in the Independent State of Croatia.[40] Nevertheless, the pressure from Jewish organizations continued and reached an apex in 1998 in numerous attempts to block the papal beatification of Cardinal Stepinac.

In the 1990s, numerous reports critical of Croatia's government were released in the West.[41] Croatia's infamy mounted in December 1999 as the international community accused the Zagreb regime and its extended arm in Herzegovina of sabotaging the peace process in Bosnia-Herzegovina by spying on the peacekeepers and undermining interethnic cooperation.[42] A U.S. congressman called Croatia one of gravest disappointments among the former communist countries in the transition to democracy.[43] On the occasion of Tudjman's death, world leaders chose to boycott the 13 December 1999 burial in Zagreb.[44] Thus, during the decade of Tudjman's rule, the Catholic Church was the only foreign friend of his regime. Small wonder that Tudjman's last foreign policy move was his October 1999 visit to the Vatican.

After the January 2000 electoral triumph of the coalition of Croatian social democrats and liberals, Croatia seemed to have finally begun its real "return" to the West. Twelve heads of state and 60 foreign delegations attended the inauguration of Croatia's new president, Stipe Mesić, on 18 February 2000. The U.S. secretary of state, Madeleine Albright, traveled twice within three weeks to Zagreb, to congratulate, support, and encourage the change in Croatian politics. Yet the new government inherited a ruined country.

The 2000 elections in which Tudjman's regime was defeated caused much worry in the Church. According to the priest-sociologist Ivan Grubišić, Archbishop Bozanić had to tour Church communities to calm down clergy and convince them that the winning coalition of social democrats and liberals was not the same as the old communists and that 1945 would not be repeated.[45] A Croatian daily published a protest letter written to Archbishop Bozanić by a group of lower clergy in which the new government was called "atheistic and evil," the archbishop was said to be a communist sympathizer, and the new premier Ivica Račan was accused of atheism, polygamy, and drug abuse.[46] Račan, however, was a former communist bureaucrat happy to be in power again and seemingly determined to retain the status quo. On Statehood Day, 30 May 2000, the new Premier Račan (who had been chairman of the Central Committee of the League of Communists of Croatia in the 1980s) dutifully attended the Mass for the Homeland. Over the mass, Archbishop Bozanić sermonized about what he saw as 10 years of freedom and democracy. The archbishop also spoke about the legacy of communist totalitarianism and Croatia's martyrdom in the recent Balkan wars. Premier Račan promised in a statement to the press that he would regularly attend Church services. Račan did not indicate that he intended to question the Tudjman cult and the Church's privileged status in society.

The feared rightist backlash began in the fall of 2000. After the government had arrested several Croat war crimes suspects (wanted by the Hague-based United Nations International Tribunal for War Crimes in the Former Yugoslavia), some of whom were also involved in organized crime after the war, a right-wing group that called itself the Emergency Headquarters for the Defense of the Dignity of the War for the Fatherland launched street protests and a media campaign against the government. In the midst of the crisis, extremists assassinated the war veteran Milan Levar, who had testified against Croat war crimes suspects in The Hague. A group of 12 military leaders published an open letter criticizing the government and calling for the defense of the honor of the "War for the Fatherland." The defeated nationalist HDZ party released a declaration "to the Croat people in the homeland and worldwide" calling for resistance against "the communist regime of an anti-Croatian spirit that draws the homeland into a civil war."[47]

President Mesić said in an interview that a coup d'etat was attempted in Croatia during late 2000 and early 2001 by the formerly ruling HDZ party, rightist groups, and several military leaders.[48] During the crisis, the Archbishop Bozanić appealed for calm and required the noninvolvement of the Church, but many clergy overtly supported the attempted coup. The archbishop of Split-Makarska, Marin Barišić, sent a letter of support to the war crimes suspect General Norac, who refused to surrender to the Hague Tribunal. The Catholic weekly *Glas knocila* accused the international community of bias and hate against the Croat people.[49] The Croatian province of the Dominican Order released an open letter to the republic's president in which monks and nuns called on him to resign.[50] In a similar vein, the military vicar, Bishop Juraj Jezerinac, held fiery sermons at gatherings of police and military servicemen expressing doubts in the new government's patriotism. On 21 September the national bishops' conference, meeting at Poreč, Istria, released a statement in which they accused the government of disrespect toward both the highest ideal of statehood and nationhood and the "brave defenders of the independent Croat state thanks to whom the aggressor was prevented from committing crimes against the people and destroying the Croat state."[51] Right-wing marches and street protests continued through February and March 2001. At these meetings President Mesić and Premier Račan were labeled "gypsies," "traitors," and "red bandits," while mobs called for the lynching of the two democratically elected leaders. The upheaval was accompanied by terrorism; Voice of America Croatian Service reported on two terrorist attacks in March 2001 in Zagreb. In the first, a World War II memorial to fallen antifascist Partisans was demolished by a military explosive; in the second, a bomb exploded in front of the city hall.[52]

In neighboring Bosnia and Herzegovina, the secessionist enclave called the "Croatian Community of Herceg-Bosna" and its local HDZ boycotted the federal authorities and incited riots in Mostar and other western Herzegovina towns. The Catholic Church, led by the archbishop of Sarajevo, Vinko Puljić, and Herzegovina Franciscan monks, backed local HDZ leaders' call for a plebiscite on the independence of the Croat people. On 22 March in New York, the UN Security Council issued a warning statement according to which the HDZ of Bosnia-Herzegovina was planning to establish a so-called Croatian self-administration in western Herzegovina that would constitute a violation of the Dayton Peace Agreement.[53] In short, the situation in Croatia in the fall of 2000 and early 2001 invoked a historic analogy with Spain in the summer of 1936, or at least was nearing that. The return of the nationalists to power in Croatia seemed to be only a matter of time. For that matter, the church's support seemed crucial and would presumably be granted to the nationalist. Church leaders, in spite of their rhetoric, presumably agreed that the pre-2000 regime was overall more favorable for the Church. Small wonder that in the summer of 2001, the Croatian bishops' conference announced a "dramatic" decrease in the numbers of Croat Catholics who received holy baptisms and confirmations, accompanied by a significantly decreased number of marriages in the Church during 2000.[54] The church's public campaign against the government was not the only form of the new clerical politics. Concurrently, the church lobbied through prominent laymen who occupied influential posts in important institutions to keep HDZ members in positions of power and influence while also forging right-wing coalitions in local administration in towns and provinces. Thus, Croatian academic circles were shocked when in September 2001 a mediocre theologian Tomislav Ivaničić (recently appointed, by conservative church leaders, dean of Catholic Theological School in Zagreb) defeated in the elections in the University Senate several Croatian scientists of world fame and became new rector of the largest Croatian public institution of higher education, the renowned University of Zagreb. Similar political trickery engineered by clergy and Catholic laymen through lobbying and secret deals took place in the coastal cities of Šibenik, Zadar, and Dubrovnik, where local HDZ branches regained control over the local administration, although HDZ did not win the necessary votes in the 2000 elections. The well-informed Zagreb weekly *Nacional* wrote as follows: "Such a vehement antigovernment activity as the Church has carried out since the 2000 elections in Croatia, the clergy had never undertaken against the communists in Tito's Yugoslavia."[55] The same source revealed that President Mesić launched in August 2001 a vigorous diplomatic campaign against clerical interference in politics in general and clerical support of right-wing groups in particular. Mesić complained in a letter to Pope John Paul II and urged the European Union to intervene. The intervention occurred in October in form of diplomatic pressure on the Vatican, carried out by ambassadors of several leading western European countries and backed by the United States. The Vatican urged clerical restraint from politics, but the pope and the moderate Zagreb archbishop Bozanić have encountered a stern opposition in the broad front of radical nationalistic clergy led by militant rightist prelates, namely, the archbishop of Split-Makarska, Marin Barišić, the bishop of Lika province, Mile Bogović, and the chief military vicar, Juraj Jezerinac.[56]

President Mesić also angered the HDZ and the Church by publicly condemning the "new Croatian history" written during the Tudjman regime, criticizing its policies of minimizing Ustaša crimes and taking pride in the World War II Croatian antifascist legacy. Mesić traveled to Israel and publicly apologized there for Ustaša crimes against Croatian Jews. (Croatian state TV, in which nationalists still maintained strong influence, did not show this news among top stories of the day.) In Israel, the Croatian president praised the partisans, often mentioning Josip Broz Tito and other Croatian communist leaders. The Jewish community of Zagreb thanked President Mesić for his support of the publication of an objective historical study about the Ustaša genocidal assault on Zagreb Jews during World War II.[57] It is worth mentioning that no Croatian Catholic church dignitary attended the 6 November 2001 promotion of the new book, *Holocaust in Zagreb*, by two eminent Croatian-Jewish authors, Ivo Goldstein and Slavko Goldstein, who were also known as outspoken critics of the Tudjman regime. It is difficult to say whether the Church was more irritated by the fact that prominent Zagreb Jews such as the Goldsteins and the historian Mirjana Gross were outspoken Tudjman critics or by the fact that all had been members of the League of Communists of Yugoslavia during the Tito era.

In spite of Western support for the government, the leaders of the Catholic Church in Croatia did not discourage the antigovernment offensive launched by the far right after the 2000 elections. On 9 November 2001 the national conference of bishops released the strongest antigovernment indictment hitherto, entitled "Croatian Bishops' Message about the Current Social Situation in Croatia." The ultranationalist Croatian clergy's gift for political maneuvering was combined with a bitter, deep-seated hatred against all Croats who were not faithful ethnic nationalists "appointed" to govern the state by the Catholic bishops. Taking advantage of the harsh consequences of the new Račan government's liberal economic transitional policies (i.e., "shock therapy," as successfully tested earlier in Poland, Hungary, and the Czech Republic), imposed on this government by the European Union and the West, the bishops' message targets the government's social policies. The prelates attacked the low pensions for the retired, the dramatic rise of unemployment, the alleged lack of state support for families with many children, the alleged mistreatment of the veterans of the 1991–95 "War for the Fatherland," the Račan administration's alleged liability for corruption, and the exodus of thousands of young Croats to foreign countries—although all of these problems had arisen and gained momentum under Tudjman. The bishops' message cynically uses leftist rhetoric and socialist arguments to attack a left-center government hated by the bishops as such (because some of its members are former communists who did not earlier join Tudjman and HDZ and moderate nationalists who disliked HDZ).

The bishops lashed out at the government's orthodox liberal capitalism and alleged insensitivity to social welfare. In reality, as a Croatian weekly pointed out, the real motives for "the Church's overt and all-out war against government" is the Croatian Catholic clergy's ultranationalism, conservatism, nostalgia for Tudjman, and desire to bring HDZ back to power.[58]

The case of the Croatian Church's war against the Račan government provides an opportunity for analysts to illuminate one of the controversial themes in the history of Roman Catholicism in the twentieth century—the controversy over the church's alleged "silence" about massive crimes such as the Holocaust and other atrocities committed by right-wing nationalists, racists, and anticommunists often backed by the Church. The charge of "silence" seems rather too strong and not quite true. As a matter of fact, the church rarely remained completely silent about any massive crimes. In Yugoslav history I have found only one example when the Roman Catholic church remained completely silent. That was in the wake of Croatian extremist nationalist groups' terrorist attacks, including the assassinations of Yugoslav diplomats, gurilla raids, and the hijacking of civilian aircraft in the post-1945 years and notably in the 1960s and 1970s. Croatian church leaders refused to condemn these criminal acts, although the Church became obliged to do so under the Protocol between Yugoslavia and the Holy See of 1966. On all other occasions the Church did speak out and condemn atrocities, especially strongly and unambiguously in case of communist crimes. Yet church leaders carefully chose the form and method by which the Church responded to these moral issues. Basically, two methods have been utilized. First is the less official and less strong method of private channels—that is, private talks and correspondence between Church and political leaders—Church press' editorials, or Church leaders' statements from the pulpit during worship services. Second is the much more effective and stronger form of public reactions such as epistles and messages issued by national conferences of bishops from church leaders' regular or extraordinary conventions. Here are a few examples from the recent history of the Catholic Church in Croatia. In the 1930s, the national conference of Catholic bishops of Yugoslavia released strong messages and letters against the Serbian-dominated government's management of the so-called Concordat crisis. During World War II, individual church leaders occasionally criticized some policies of the government (e.g., as did the Archbishop of Zagreb, Alojzije Stepinac, in private letters to NDH leaders and a few homilies at the Zagreb cathedral), but the national conference of bishops never released an official document containing any antigovernment criticism regarding persecution of Jews, Serbs, Gypsies, and antifascist Croats. In 1945, the national conference of Catholic bishops released a strongly worded pastoral letter condemning the communist regime's persecution of clergy and confiscation of church property. The Church never used any form of public reaction to protest the often deadly terrorist attacks against Yugoslavia carried out between 1945 and the 1970s by extremist Croatian exile groups. During the

1991–95 war the Church used the strongest form of national bishops' conferences messages to the world and the faithful to condemn Serbian crimes. Concurrently, the Church utilized private channels and individual Church leaders' statements (but not official bishops' conference messages to the world) to condemn Croatian crimes against Serbs civilians in Croatia and Bosnia and the Croatian military involvement in the Bosnian war. In the 1990s, the Archbishop Bozanić voiced a mild antiregime criticism of corruption during Tudjman's tenure, but the bishops' conference never released any epistle or similar official statement against the HDZ regime. Finally, the church utilized all available methods (private clerical criticism, the church press, and national bishops' conference letters to the public) against the left-center government that replaced the HDZ in power in 2000. Thus in the final analysis, the Catholic Church in Croatia condemned much more strongly and unambiguously the democratically elected left-center government in post-communist Croatia than it had the crimes of the pro-Axis NDH regime and Cold War–era Croatian nationalists' terrorist attacks. Accordingly, in Yugoslav history, the conference of Catholic bishops would officially and most strongly attack only governments they considered illegitimate, such as the Serbian-dominated government of the interwar kingdom, the communist government of the former Yugoslavia, and the post-2000 left-center government in Croatia. This rationale and practice are even more strikingly clear in the history of the Serbian Orthodox Church. Of course, it is not a new discovery that political parties backed by religious organizations enjoy the extraordinary privilege in the possibility that even most brutal mass murderers among their members can become saints, or at least the churches can help their crimes to be forgotten.

In the long run, the successful "return" of Croatia to the West, which, in spite of the national church's resistance, began with the elections of 2000, was crowned by two events in November 2000. First, the Sabor, amid protests from HDZ delegates, passed the resolution of Croatia's intention to join the European Union. The resolution affirmed Croatia's willingness to collaborate with European institutions, including the International War Crimes Tribunal. Then, on November 2001 10 in Washington, D.C., an official state meeting took place between the US president, George W. Bush, and the Croatian president, Stipe Mesić. On this occasion the American president (whose administration was in place at the time that diplomatic pressure was put on the Vatican to curb clerical nationalists in Croatia) emphasized the Western character of Croatia and announced its forthcoming admission to the NATO alliance. Thus, contrary to scenarios that would have sustained the myth of "The Thirteen Centuries of Christianity in the Croat People," it was not the Catholic Church that brought Croatia back in the orbit of Western civilization but a regime led by former communists that the Church had resisted in an attempted coup.

To conclude, the history of Church-state relations in postcommunist Croatia had several milestones: 1990, 1992, 1997, 1998, and 2000. In 1990, the Church helped the HDZ to win elections. In 1992 the Vatican was first to grant international recognition to Croatia. In 1997, the Church again assisted the new electoral victory and consolidation of power of the HDZ. In the same year Croatia and the Holy See agreed on treaties by which Catholicism became the de facto state religion in Croatia. In 1998, Pope John Paul II came to Croatia for the beatification of Cardinal Stepinac and the symbolic legitimation of the system in which the new saintly candidate became the most revered patriotic icon. Finally, after the democratic elections of 2000, the Church took part in a right-wing coup attempt aimed at bringing the radical ethnonationalistic HDZ back to power. Accordingly, trends in Croatian Catholicism since the end of the communist era have followed the pattern of Balkan politics and resembled much more the Serbian Orthodox Church than, for example, the Catholic Church in neighboring Slovenia. In Slovenia, domestic Catholicism assisted the postcommunist democratic transition, restrained from ethnic nationalistic politics, and did its part in the story about the most (and the only) successful new democracy among successor states to the former Yugoslavia. Yet, as noted earlier, it is fair to say that the happy, ethnically homogenous Catholic Slovenia never shared the same problems, fears, and concerns as Bosnia and Herzegovina, Croatia, and Serbia.

Jerusalem Lost: The Serbian Church, the West, and the Failure of the Serbian Revolution

Since 1990, Serbs and Serbia have been at war not only with all non-Serbs in Yugoslavia but also with the West. On 24 April 1990, the local bishop from Kosovo and future patriarch Pavle visited Washington. He argued before the Senate Foreign Relations Committee that the principal sources of the problem in Kosovo were Islamic fundamentalism, Albanian nationalism, and the legacy of Tito's communism.[59] The delegation complained that international observers avoided visiting ancient shrines such as the patriarchate of Peć, Dečani, or Gračanica. Those shrines, Pavle said in Washington, "are the most valuable pieces of evidence to prove the Serbian, Christian, European and civilizational character of the culture they represent."[60]

In August 1990 US Senator Robert Dole arrived in Kosovo on a factfinding mission. According to a report dispatched by the archimandrite Atanasije Jevtić from Priština to the Holy Synod and written as an article in the Belgrade daily *Politika express*, "all attempts of Kosovo Serbs to provide any explanation to American senators were in vain—Bob Dole came as a prosecutor of the Serbian people and an advocate of their Albanian enemies."[61] Jevtić, as he himself claimed, invited the guests to visit the shrines of Kosovo and Serb villages, but they refused. Thus, he explained in his article, the foreigners showed disrespect toward Serbian culture, religion, and the truth about Kosovo.[62]

During the wars in Croatia and Bosnia, the conflict between Serbia and Western democracies worsened. The international community blamed the Belgrade regime for massive human rights abuses in Kosovo. In 1996, Albanian émigré groups, Albanians from Albania, and some natives of Kosovo launched a guerilla war against Serbian rule in Kosovo. In 1998, a Serbo-Albanian war broke out. The Albanians overtly came up with the idea of an independent Albanian state in the Albanian-populated areas of the former Yugoslavia. Emulating the practice of the Serbian Orthodox Church, a monograph was published in Albania according to which numerous historic monuments located in Kosovo sustain Albanian territorial claims and rights to statehood.[63]

Slobodan Milošević's regime refused to endorse the international plan for Kosovo, and on 24 March 1999, NATO resumed massive air raids on Serbia. While Western democracies supported the bombing, Russia emerged as Serbia's principal ally. The Russian Orthodox Church provided symbolic and spiritual help for its Balkan coreligionists. On 31 March 1999, the holy icon of the miraculous Madonna of Kazan arrived in Belgrade and was presented before the faithful in several Belgrade churches. On 20 April 1999, the patriarch of Moscow and all Russia, Alexei II, who had visited Serbia, Bosnia, and Kosovo during the Bosnian war, again came to the Yugoslav capital. After the holy liturgy in the memorial temple of Saint Sava, the head of the Russian Orthodox Church addressed the crowd of 15,000 in the church and nearly 100,000 around it. "We are witnessing lawlessness and we cry for justice," said the head of the largest Orthodox Church in the world, and continued:

Several mighty and wealthy countries arrogantly ascribed to themselves the role of a supreme arbiter who determines what is good and what is evil. They violated the sovereign will of those people who only want to live in a way that differs from the life of the mighty. NATO's bombs and rockets striking at this country do not defend anyone. NATO military actions have another objective: to impose a new world order based on their dictate and their power. But injustice and hypocrisy will not prevail. . . . God is on your side my dear Serbian brothers. . . . But I beg you to make peace in the holy Serbian land of Kosovo and let all peaceful people return to their homes. Thus no one will be able to blame you and thereby justify his own sin.[64]

As bombs continued to fall on Belgrade, anti-Western sentiment exploded both in Serbia and Russia. In Russia, violent demonstrations took place in several cities. An Italian observer of global affairs noted that the NATO intervention triggered a vehement anti-Westernism in which the Orthodox churches of Serbia and Russia appeared as founders of a new "anti-Western Axis."[65] The Serbian Church press portrayed the Americans as barbarians who, having no respect for history and tradition, damaged several dozen ancient sacred monuments.[66] The *Pravoslavlje* wrote that "America, which views itself as a new Rome, is seeking to destroy Serbian Jerusalem as the Romans despoiled the Jerusalem Temple."[67] A June editorial entitled "Moral Crisis of the West Causes Political Crises in the World" declared that "America, which had some blessed moments in the past, is now under the rule of Satan. The dollar became God. Lies are presented as truth. The system of ethical values has been destroyed. Christianity is buried alive."[68] The newsletter of the Serbian Orthodox North American Diocese called the United States the "Anti-Christ's army," engaged in the creation of a "diabolic new world order" aimed at total destruction of the Christian faith, the Church, and ethnic communities.[69] An editorial in the *Pravoslavlje* said that "the Serbs have encountered a de-Christianized America as a force of evil no better than the evil forces of Nazism and Bolshevism."[70] The Belgrade monthly journal *Duga* ran an article arguing that the United States of America set out to turn the world into its own mirror image by undermining homogenous nations and forcibly intermixing the world population. According to the *Duga*, the principal hindrances to this US plan have been Serbia and Germany—the two homogenous European nations "with the most vibrant and enduring national identities and nationalist sentiments."[71] America's plan, the article concludes, involves a gradual destruction of those two world champions in nationalism by establishing new Islamic states in Europe such as Bosnia and Albania, as well as encouraging the growth and consolidation of Muslim communities in Germany, France, and other western European countries, along with simultaneous support for Muslim states along the borders of Russia. Finally, in May 1999, the Yugoslav federal parliament voted in favor of Yugoslavia's adherence to the Union of Russia–Belarus, but Moscow remained reserved.

A few weeks before Saint Vitus' Day in 1999, Serbian military and police withdrew from Kosovo. Columns of Serb refugees followed the troops, and the new great migration of Serbs was recorded in church chronicles. By the summer of 2000, less than a hundred thousand Serbs were left in the province. Yet the Church and the shrines remained. Serb church leaders put all the blame on Milošević. The disillusioned zealot bishop Atansije Jevtić requested a retirement from the Holy Synod (allegedly due to poor health). The Bishop of Kosovo, Artemije, and the patriarch began tactfully collaborating with the West. In June 1999, on the occasion of the 610th anniversary of the Kosovo battle, Patriarch Pavle called Slobodan Milošević, before Western television cameras, the source of evil. Western-educated Serbian monks advanced the Serbian cause via the internet. The Kosovo bishop Artemije, representing Patriarch Pavle, joined the pro-Western Serbian party the "Alliance for Change" founded by the American businessman Milan

Panić. Artemije spoke against Milošević on several panels in the United States.[72] On another occasion Artemije said that Milošević "carved out the cross on which the Serbs and Serbia were crucified."[73]

failure

Three decades after launching the movement for the recovery of Serbian Kosovo, the Serbian Church found itself in an even worse position than under Tito. There was no longer a Yugoslav state in which all ethnic Serbs lived together under the same state and church authority. Kosovo was occupied by foreign troops and governed by local Albanians. A handful of Serbs were left to live in "Old Serbia." Macedonia was a sovereign state, and Serb priests were not welcome there. The Serbian state in Bosnia and Herzegovina remained the only model of a state arranged according to clerical wishes. The one-time sizable Serb community in Croatia was cut in half and had lost the status and influence it had once enjoyed in this republic. Finally, Montenegro seemed to be preparing to leave the Yugoslav federation.

As always amid crises, the Church kept faith in the capacity of the Kosovo shrines and the myth to heal wounds and to give new impetus for the nation's rebirth. Analogous to the historic patriarchate of Peć in the sixteenth century, Serbia remained visible in the province solely through the Church. International authorities accepted the bishop of Kosovo, Artemije, as a political representative of Kosovo Serbs.[74] In Serbia, the Church contributed to the fall of Milošević, who had failed to create a greater Serbia and abandoned the sacred battle for Kosovo. In other words, the Serbian Orthodox Church did condemn the war criminal Milošević but not because he was a bad man. Actually, the Church blamed him for not having been even worse.

The new Serbian leader, Vojislav Koštunica, came to power in October 2000, and in 2001 the British-born crown prince Alexander Karadjordjević returned to live permanently in his father's royal palace in Belgrade. Koštunica, unlike his predecessor, paid respect to the Church and occasionally attended liturgies. Church press and prelates, in frequent meetings with authorities, lobbied for state salaries and pensions for clergy, laws against abortion, military chaplains, Orthodox catechism in public schools, and the expulsion of the Latin alphabet from state administration, schools, and public use in general. In September 2001 the new Belgrade regime introduced the Orthodox catechism in public schools. Keston News Service reported in September 2001 that Christian Protestant denominations in Serbia called for dialogue with the government and the Orthodox Church about Serbia's new law on religious communities, which these denominations found discriminatory, yet both government and the official SOC ignored such calls.[75] The Belgrade opposition journal *Republika* observed that a "new" nationalism was coming into shape and that the Serbian Orthodox Church was working on a regrouping the nationalistic bloc and jumpstarting a new nationalistic revolution, fueled by the living Kosovo myth.[76]

Some analysts of Balkan affairs rushed to announce that Yugoslavia's fall was "inevitable."[77] Thus, General Brent Scowcroft, a high U.S. official in charge of the Balkans during the Cold War, said in a December 1999 interview that "the entire Yugoslav experiment may have been a mistake committed in good faith by President Wilson and other statesmen at Paris 1919" and that the United States "could never properly understand those distant peoples and mentalities."[78] In a similar vein, the U.S. representative to the United Nations and the chief negotiator at the Dayton Peace Conference, Richard Holbrooke, revived the theory of Woodrow Wilson's well-meaning Balkan mistake that resulted in US support of an "artificial country."[79] Such historical assessments are neither surprising nor new. "Every enterprise that does not succeed is a mistake," said one of the prominent participants in the 1919 Paris conference, Eleutherios Venizelos, the premier of Greece. In a similar vein, the historian E. H. Carr pointed out in his study entitled *The Twenty Years Crisis, 1919–1939*, that men are generally prepared to accept the judgment of history by praising success and condemning failure.

However, as Reinhold Niebuhr has pointed out, nations are held together largely by force and by emotion. In the midst of the crisis of the 1980s, millions loved the united Yugoslavia and thought it would survive. When Slovene and Croatian delegates were walking out from the session of the last, fourteenth congress of the League of Communists of Yugoslavia in January 1990, they did not shout hateful ethnic slogans but shed tears. From the 1950s, a new pan-Yugoslav elite had been taking shape in Yugoslavia's towns and cities. Yet this generation was fragile and needed more time and better circumstances to salvage their country. This generation was well educated, multicultural, and worldly in outlook and by all means capable of securing a peaceful transition toward democracy and restructuring the country's pattern of development. When the federation began to crumble in the 1980s, the country was defended by emotions alone and by the fragile lost generation alone. Yugoslav civil religion, sports urban youth culture, pop and rock music and humor and satire unsuccessfully tried to save the country from the looming disaster. The Tito funeral, the last Tito's Relay, the Sarajevo Olympics, and the trophies and victories of the Yugoslav national team in international sport arenas propelled the last wave of Yugoslav patriotism. The remarkable youth press, Yugoslav film, and satire, such as the Sarajevo-based Television show *Top lista nadrealista* ("The Surrealists' Chart"), served the cause of democratization and, while still developing a critical view on communism, tried to water down nationalistic passions by ridiculing nationalists and nationalistic myths. In a similar vein, integrative currents in youth culture proliferated during the whole decade until the catastrophe of 1991–92 when the war began. Pop, rock, and folk singers and bands voiced pro unity more often than ethnic nationalist sentiments.[80] Artists defended the country that inspired them. In a 1991 interview with me, a leading Yugoslav rock performer, Branimir Štulić, identified himself as a "Balkanian."[81] In 1992 in Sarajevo, snipers fired on a column of 7,000 people marching peacefully and chanting about brotherhood and unity. A 22-year-old Sarajevo University student was shot to death. One of the peace marchers told a Western observer: "We were here because we thought there was still time to change people's minds, to save Sarajevo . . . as a place where Muslims, Serbs, and Croats could live together as they had for five hundred years. . . . The idea was to . . . show that the city still belonged to the people—all the people."[82] At the time posters of Tito still hung in many homes from Sarajevo to Kosovo.[83] One of the most effective cohesive forces of Yugoslav unity, sports, also continued to celebrate Yugoslavia after its collapse. Yet urban youth with its education, rock-and-roll, film, and sports could not counter the forces of destruction and the wars of the 1990s. The six-republic federation was destroyed. An all-Yugoslav plebiscite to decide the fate of the federation never took place.

Although the name was appropriated by the Milošević regime, during the 1990s, vestiges of the former Yugoslavia began to disappear. A million-strong group known not long ago as "Yugoslavs by nationality" has vanished. As early as 1992, American reporters from Balkan battlefields noticed the revival of the primordial ethnic identities at the expense of the Yugoslav identity.[84] Some of the "Yugoslavs by nationality" were forced to change nationality and others became disillusioned and undetermined about who they are, while many discovered the traditional religious and ethnic identities and became neophytes.[85] The ethnic nationalist leaders Milošević and Tudjman tried to emulate Tito's lifestyle and used Tito's memory for foreign policy purposes.[86] The two postcommunist dictators appropriated for themselves and their families property of Tito that he had bequeathed to the Yugoslav People's Army, museums, and other federal institutions. Tito's wife, children, and relatives had to fight legal battles for their shares.[87] The pride of the old regime, Yugoslav sports was appropriated and put in the service of new nation-building projects. In Croatia, the new patriotic sports journalism glorified athletes who supported the Croatian "War for the Fatherland."[88] In 1998, Tudjman's first lieutenant, the Defense minister Gojko Šušak, received 11 patriotic athletes and awarded each a handgun.[89] Croatia was caught up in another nationalist euphoria in 1998 when the Croatian national soccer team took the third place in the World Soccer Cup in France. In Serbia, the Milošević regime took pride in several international triumphs by the Serbo-Montenegrin national basketball team, although in the meantime sports began crumbling under the management of postcommunist Mafia bosses, such as the war crimes suspect Željiko Ražnatović Arkan.[90] From 1992 to 1999 international ratings of Yugoslav sports dropped overall. There was no longer an internationally competitive Yugoslav national team. To be sure, individual athletes, outgrowths of the once-successful school of Yugoslav sports continued to win most prestigious international trophies, for example, the Croatian tennis star Goran Ivanišević, who won the Wimbledon tournament in 2001, Yugoslav basketball players in the American NBA and European leagues, numerous soccer players and coaches working for foreign employers, and so forth.[91]

While nationalist regimes labored at prolonging nationalist euphoria, more and more people experienced nostalgia. A public opinion survey conducted in 1997 by Croatian state Television showed that 70 percent of the respondents perceived Tito as a great statesman, and in a sociological survey conducted in Croatia in April 1998, respondents viewed Tito as a more skillful and a reputable leader than the incumbent President Tudjman.[92] A new social sentiment, termed by the press *Yugonostalgia*, spread among the young and old generations of once much more free, proud, and prosperous Yugoslavs.[93] In the second half of the 1990s, nostalgic overtones reverberated in literature, music, film, media, sports arenas, and concert halls and spread around the world via the internet. The 1996 Croatian feature film *Maršal* (The Marshall) tells of a Medjugorje-styled "religious apparition" of the communist icon Marshall Josip Broz Tito witnessed by a group of Partisan veterans.[94] "Of course, I used to believe in all that patriotic stuff. I lived in the country of world champions in many sports," said the singer-songwriter Djordje Balašević in an interview.[95] The head coach of the Italian basketball national team, Bogdan Tanjević, who used to coach the former Yugoslavia's national team, proposed in a 1999 interview a basketball league among the successor states of former Yugoslavia, as part of the Balkan Peace Process. His idea was financially supported by the international community, and as a result the so-called Adriatic League, with several basketball teams from Croatia, Slovenia, Bosnia-Herzegovina, and Montenegro was begun in 2001 as an effort toward peacemaking and reconciliation through sports. Yugonostalgia sites mushroomed in cyberspace. One website presented a new country called "Cyber Yugoslavia." It was a "virtual nation," without a territory, existing only in cyberspace and bringing together all those who had left the country to live abroad or who had left but shared nostalgic sentiments for the old times of brotherhood, unity, and dignity.[96]

Presumably the most valuable outgrowth of Yugoslav socialism, Yugoslavia's human capital, saw no future in the successor states. According to a survey, among the youth in former European communist countries, only young Serbs and Croats preferred going overseas with no intention to return.[97] A proregime Croatian newspaper reported in 1999 that 130,000 young people left Croatia between 1991 and 1998 and were replaced by some 150,000 Catholic refugees, as well as members of the "new elite" from Bosnia and Herzegovina.[98] Yet the relentlessly anti-Tudjman *Feral Tribune* weekly from Split has revealed that more than 250,000 mostly young and educated Croatians left their homeland during the last decade of the twentieth century.[99] If close to the truth, this sounds devastating for a country of four million people. According to another report on demographic trends in successor states, the young would rather go to foreign countries than return to ethnically mixed areas, even in the case of such fertile and one-time prosperous regions such as Eastern Slavonia.[100]

Demography and migration replaced Marxism as the new key menace for the churches. A dramatic exodus of the young from the successor states of the former Yugoslavia was presumably the hardest blow to the new Balkan nationalism and its carriers. Antun Bogetić, bishop of Croatia's province of Istria on the Croat-Italian border, lamented in a 1992 interview that "thousands of young people left Istria," and that "many of Istria's Croats declared themselves Italians by nationality only to get a job in neighboring Italy."[101] The bishops' conference of Bosnia and Herzegovina met on 9–10 November 1999 in Sarajevo to discuss what Bishop Pero Sudar described as a massive exodus of young Croat Catholics to western Europe and overseas.[102] A survey of young people in Bosnia and Herzegovina conducted by two international organizations in 1999 showed that 62 percent want to leave this country (from 1996 to 1998, some 42,000 persons under 40 years of age went abroad with no intention to return).[103] According to the same survey, the worldview and values of young people in Bosnia-Herzegovina have profoundly changed in comparison to the youth that demonstrated in 1992 for peace and brotherhood and unity in the streets of Sarajevo. Now 71 percent of the polled young Bosnians say that religious instruction in schools should be mandatory and 62 percent say that they would never marry a person of a different nationality.[104] In an opinion poll conducted in Serbia's northern province of Vojvodina, out of 2,500 persons polled, 1,946 responded they would chose to live permanently in the West.[105] Another blow for the nationalists and the Churches was that the number of children and young people was shrinking overall. Thus, since 1990, Croatia has recorded a negative population growth.[106] An almost identical situation came about in Serbia, another hopelessly diminishing Slavic ethnic nation. The Milošević era forced many Serbs into exile. A British defense ministry policy analysis described the Balkan exodus as follows:

> The task of creating democracy and civil society . . . will be immense and will probably take generations. In their tens of thousands, educated, decent young people, the future of any nation, have emigrated to escape a corrupt, criminal, repressive regime that has destroyed such social harmony as existed, the economy and the reputation of their former country. They have left a society that has become pauperized, criminalized, brutalized, cynical and/or apathetic and helpless.[107]

IMP

Legacies of bygone states, systems, and regimes typically entail good and bad things, and history needs to record both. The most successful products of the socialist era in Yugoslavia were the country's human capital and the idea of multiethnic brotherhood and unity, out of which grew a "culture of immunity" to ethnic and religious differences. Had the "lost generation" born between 1950 and 1980 stayed at home in the multiethnic, democra-tized, "fraternized and unified" country, the former Yugoslavia might have accomplished a successful democratic transition relatively faster and maybe much earlier than did the former Soviet satellite states of Eastern Europe. Chances existed in the 1950s, in the 1960s and 1970s, and even in the 1980s. In the words of Goran Radman, currently the director of the Micro-soft Corporation in Croatia,

> speaking of information technology, in the early 1990s we in Yugoslavia had better infrastructure than, say, Italy and Austria (not to mention the former Soviet satellites in Eastern Europe). At that time in Croatia almost all large companies had information centers, trained computer experts, as well as necessary technology and equipment. That was our springboard for a successful transition. Today we lag behind countries such as Romania and Bulgaria.[108]

In a similar vein, one of the newly elected post-Tudjman Croatian leaders, Josip Kregar, described postcommunist regimes as "governments of bad stu-dents."[109] International organizations dealing with rebuilding the Balkans also realized this and, according to a 2001 initiative will encourage and finance the return of the lost human capital home.[110] In the meantime, many members of the lost Yugoslav generation dispersed around the world have so far distinguished themselves in science, scholarship, sports, arts, entertainment, and business, remaining a living proof of a country's talent and promise.

12

CONCLUSIONS

As high as mind stands above nature, so high does the state stand above physical life. Man must therefore venerate the state as a secular deity.... The march of God in the world, that is what the State is.

G. W. F. Hegel

The state is the coldest monster of all. It lies coldly; and this is the coldest lie that slithers out of its mouth: "I, the state, am the people."... The state lies in the language of good and evil. ...I offer you this sign as the sign that marks the state: confusion of the language of good and evil.

Friedrich Nietzsche

A ruler... should seem to be exceptionally merciful, trustworthy, upright, humane and devout. And it is most necessary of all to seem devout.

Niccolo Machiavelli

Saints should always be judged guilty until they are proved innocent.

George Orwell

False gods do not always result in bad state-building. On the contrary, at least according to Niccolo Machiavelli, whose fascinating knowledge of politics cannot be denied in spite of his unforgivable straightforwardness in presenting it, some kind of popular cult and worship, combined with a ruler capable of deftly pretending to be devout, are *conditio sine qua non* of every efficient government. The problem of "legitimation by religion," however, grows complicated in multiethnic and multiconfessional countries. If in such a country, each of several ethnic and religious communities worships its own false gods (and gods never come alone but accompanied with mutually contesting myths), unity at the "national" level is very hard to achieve. This problem was one of numerous factors of instability in Yugoslav states, most of which happened to be multiethnic and multiconfessional. The balance sheet of the eight decades of state-building in the Yugoslav section of southeastern Europe reveals the following. In an area about the size of Italy, there existed 12 different states, of which four collapsed and the survival of five seems uncertain. During eight decades, these states and peoples witnessed two cycles of wars and civil wars, two rounds of revolutions, and two cycles of genocide. In contrast to this political fragility and transitoriness stand "eternal" faiths and ethnic communities. It seems indeed difficult to design a regime, economic system, and state-building model capable of "taming" or pleasing them all at once.

To be born in a setting such as Yugoslavia is called bad luck. "In this part of the world," as the epigraph to chapter 11, from Macedonian rock performer Vlatko Stefanovski, notes, "a man has no chance to be born and buried in the same country." God's role in history is difficult to scrutinize, but it seems that religious organizations share with secular forces not only the worship of false gods but also the responsibility for the notorious instability and failure of Balkan state-building. It is not so tragic that religious leaders perceive themselves as highly competent, although only a few may be, because that is not something peculiar to religious but to all leaders; yet it is tragic that religious organizations came to believe that they had discovered an ideal model of state and society. This ideal system should be achieved via partition of "artificial" states and found in "natural" and "eternal" homogenous ethnoreligious communities.

At any rate, events of great historical significance have occurred in the twentieth century within the Balkan landscape adorned by Byzantine domes, Gothic spires, and minarets, the part of the world where western and eastern Christianity and Islam cut through several large ethnic groups and numerous minorities, trespassing and obfuscating boundaries and testing models of nation-state formation, modernization and development, while coping for eight decades with regime changes, social movements, wars, revolutions, and civil wars. The making and unmaking of Yugoslav states as a case study, in general, and its religious dimension, in particular, offers scholars a kind of "laboratory" in which important findings and conclusions can be made. Here are some of those conclusions.

Multinational States and
Legitimacy by Religion

At least since Thomas Hobbes's *Leviathan* (1651), in which this political thinker expressed concern over the "sectarian threat," religion has been a hindrance to successful modern state-building. In multiethnic and multiconfessional states, religious organizations have found it hard both to accommodate to pluralist-minded secular regimes and maintain interfaith cooperation. With one notable exception—the United States of America—all multiconfessional states have experienced crises of religious legitimacy, and none has accomplished a noteworthy breakthrough in interfaith cooperation. This is not to say that the United States will be permanently immune and safe from some kind of a Yugoslav-type crisis. In a number of cases, religion has played a part in serious conflicts and civil wars (e.g., India and Pakistan, Lebanon, Palestine, Yugoslavia, Ethiopia, Sri Lanka, Indonesia, Northern Ireland, and so forth). While the quintessential religious ideal is harmony, the historical reality is conflict. Religious scholars are well aware of what Scott R. Appleby termed "the ambivalence of the sacred."[1] In a similar vein, Peter Berger has admitted that "religion much more often fosters war, both between and within nations, rather than peace although occasionally, religious institutions do try to resist warlike policies or to mediate between conflicting parties."[2]

Multiconfessional and multiethnic Yugoslav states have suffered from the lack of religious legitimation from the onset of Yugoslavism. Many regime types were tested and none pleased all of the country's faiths at the same time. Was this so because Yugoslav states never discovered an ideal regime type for such a complex setting? What would be the ideal form of political organization in this part of the Balkans? During the World War I debate on the final phase of the so-called "Eastern Question" and nation-formation in the Balkans, one of the Western scholars cognizant of all relevant factors and then most popular nation-building models, the British diplomatic historian J. A. R. Marriott, published in 1918 a proposal for the new political order in southeastern Europe. Marriott argued as follows:

> It will always be difficult to maintain in the Balkans a single centralized state. . . . Unification is prohibited alike by geography and by ethnography. Even federalism presupposes the existence of unifying forces which have not as yet manifested themselves in this region. Things being as they are, a *Staatenbund* would therefore be preferable to a *Bundesstaat*: Switzerland is a model more appropriate to the Balkans than Germany. . . . Even this measure of union is unattainable without a thorough territorial readjustment. No confederation, however loose in structure, could be expected to endure for six months, unless a fairly satisfactory settlement of outstanding difficulties can be previously effected. And that settlement must come from within. The Treaties of London and Bucharest (May and August

1913) are a sufficient warning against the futility of European intervention in Balkan affairs.[3]

The Yugoslav state existed in various forms, but Marriott's proposal was never tested or fully applied. The Yugoslav peoples and their leaders experienced and experimented with various types of regimes, except what Marriott termed a Staatenbund, or "Swiss model." Something that could be considered close to this ideal model was attempted in the 1974 constitution of the Socialist Federal Republic of Yugoslavia. However, not even this model earned legitimation from all of the country's major faiths at the same time. Had someone other than the communists sponsored the "ideal" model of a "Balkan Switzerland," accompanied by a liberal-democratic civil religion of multiethnic and interfaith brotherhood and unity, would the major Yugoslav faiths have legitimized such a system? Probably not. After all, the interwar kingdom was notoriously anticommunist but it never consolidated church-state relations and never witnessed any encouraging interfaith cooperation. For religious organizations that vied with regimes and each other for centuries within multinational empires and lamented in their liturgies about ancient ethnic kingdoms, no multinational state could become an ideal model of statehood and nationhood. For the Serbian Orthodox Church, the ideal form of statehood would always be ethnically homogenous Serbia under a Serbian king and patriarch. Likewise, the Croatian Catholic clergy have always idealized and idolized an ethnically compact Croat nation-state with Catholicism as the de facto state religion. Finally, it would be gullible to say that most of the Bosnian Muslim ulema and other adherents of Islam, in spite of their long-practiced accommodation with various multinational Yugoslav states, have not always idealized an Islamic state in Bosnia. This is not even a Balkan peculiarity or a novelty. Theocracies, state religions, religious or ideological states are hardly anything new in history. As established faiths grow stronger and expand, they seek what sociologist David Martin termed a "religious monopoly." This monopoly is best maintained in a theocracy or authoritarian regime in which the official church and government legitimized by religion rule together. In societies where religious and ethnic identity and nationality are congruent and there exists a religious institution perceived as a "progenitor and guardian of the nation," religious monopoly (i.e., authoritarianism) is more likely to establish and maintain itself as a "natural" political order. This phenomenon in its specific Balkan variant has been designated in this study as ethnoclericalism.

Ethnoclericalism

The concept of ethnoclericalism is the Balkan case's contribution to the recent scholarship dealing with religious fundamentalism, "religious nationalism," and various challenges to the secular state and western liberal thought about religion. Key components of ethnoclericalism are the idea of ethnically based nationhood and a "national church" with its clergy entitled to national leadership but never accountable for political blunders as are secular leaders. This "new" ethnoclericalism can be seen as a reinvention under new circumstances of the ancient function of "religious traditions and distinctive priesthoods," which, as Anthony D. Smith pointed out, have been critical for the preservation and maintaining of ethnic identity and ethnic nations ever since ancient times. [4] As noted earlier, the major religious institutions of Yugoslavia are "ethnic churches." The Serbian Church which the Catholic "Church in the Croat People" came to strikingly resemble) remarkably exemplifies what A. D. Smith, using the case of the Armenian church, termed the *ethnic church*, which provides "a tangible expression of identity, a framework for community and a latent political goal of the restoration of the ethnic state."[5]

Excessive ethnic nationalism is relatively most enduring and vibrant in the Orthodox Church. Michael Radu has termed it "the burden of Eastern Orthodoxy."[6] By contrast, the most outspoken theologians critical of excessive ethnic nationalism and nationalism in general carried out via religion have been Protestant Christian theologians, with a few Catholic colleagues.[7] With regard to Islam, many Western experts on Islam have pointed out this religion's difficulties with Western secular nationalism, so that Islam has remained the repository of what is called "fundamentalism."[8]

"Ethnic churches" are designed as instruments for the survival of ethnic communities. Small wonder they have always abhorred liberal ideas—they decay when no outside threat exists. Due to their "survivor nature" they cannot be liberal within either. They are authoritarian-minded and centralized organizations capable of organizing resistance against an outside threat and maintaining stability inside the community. The upper section of clerical hierarchies exercise a hegemony in ecclesiastical affairs (at the expense of lower clergy and lay members). Ethnoclericalism is thus both an ecclesiastical concept and political ideology. It champions a strong homogenous church in a strong homogenous state, with both institutions working together as guardians of the ethnic community. Ethnic churches depend on the nation-state as much as the nation depends on them. Needless to say, ethnoclericalism as an ideology holds that the ethnic community would perish without its own church and state. Thanks to its church and state, the ethnic community becomes a nation.

"National churches" become hallmarks of nationhood. A nation cannot exist as such without an independent national religious institution whose independence and status are protected by the strong state, whose governing elite has common ethnicity and faith. The phenomenon of ethnoclericalism makes it possible, for example, to answer the hard question "Who are the Macedonians?" that has been bothering many politicians and scholars for quite awhile. The Macedonians are, very simply, "members of the Macedonian Orthodox Church." Likewise, who are the Montenegrins and how do they differ from their Serb cousins? The Montenegrins are members of the national autocephalous church of Montenegro. Montenegro will become a full-fledged nation not when it is admitted to the United Nations, or when the great powers say so, but when the Orthodox Church of Montenegro is granted autocephaly by other Orthodox churches. Ethnoclericalism has also generated the most autonomous national branches of Roman Catholicism, such as the Church of Croatia, the Church of Ireland, the Church of Poland, and so on. Finally, thanks to the vital Balkan ethnoclericalism, Bosnian Islam resembles more the Balkan churches than mainstream Islam in the Arab world. While only some Bosnian Muslim clergy find Islamic fundamentalism and Arab revolutionary Islam attractive, all of the Bosnian ulema would be happiest in a Muslim republic under a Muslim government and with an independent national religious organization staffed by native clergy all of whom are ethnic Bosniaks or Muslims from Bosnia and Herzegovina.

Ethnoclericalism dominates Balkan faiths and determines church-state relations. In the case of Serbia, for example, the Serbian Orthodox Church has made clear what kind of government it will sincerely legitimize: a government composed of ethnic Serbs practicing the faith and securing for the national church the status of a state religion while developing an educational curriculum aimed at fostering national ideology, patriotic historiography, and ethnic customs. In Croatia, the Catholic hierarchy wants to "appoint" governments and dismiss them if the bishops dislike them. In Macedonia, the church demands a status in accordance with its function as the creator of the nation and the factor that makes its existence possible.

Ethnoclericalist religious institutions are both antiliberal in general and antisecular in particular, that is, they are opponents of the principle of separation between church and state. It was noted earlier that members of the government are expected to be practicing believers and government policies are expected to uphold one specific church and faith rather than "religious culture" or faith in general. The concept of religious liberty and equality of all faiths in the country is alien and "unnational." The clerical profession is not open for all. All clergy, as well as the chief saints and cults, must belong to the ethnic group under consideration. For example, Serb national saints carry more weight than other Christian saints, who are called "foreigners," and in the "Church in the Croat People" only Jesus Christ himself rivals in importance the native Croats saints and blessed martyrs. Finally, ethnoclericalism is much the same as right-wing political ideology. "Christians must side with the political right, and right-wing ideology is an imperative for each genuine Christian who strives in the afterlife toward sitting to Jesus' right side," the Croatian Catholic weekly *Glas koncila* expounded in July 2001.[9] While being antiliberal and antisecular, ethnic churches could serve the purpose of the Cold War anticommunist struggle. Yet the same religious institutions that earlier earned fame in the West as anticommunist forces have, according to scholarly research, so far failed to adequately assist democratic transition in the former communist countries of eastern Europe.[10]

Ethnoclericalism is not confined to, although it appears especially strong in, multiethnic and multiconfessional societies in which ethnic and religious identities coincide. Introduced in the Yugoslav conflict by the Serbian Orthodox Church, the extremist Serbian kind of ethnoclericalism affected Croatian Catholicism and Bosnian Islam and eventually was espoused by their leaders. It is noteworthy that, although the Catholic Church in Croatia and Bosnia-Herzegovina manifested clericalist tendencies in the second half of the nineteenth century, the "ethnicization" of the clergy and the saints is of recent origin. This "ethnicization" of Croatian Catholicism has accelerated since the 1960s thanks to the Vatican's emphasis on ethnicity and pastoral work in ethnic communities worldwide. The encyclical *Populorum progressio* and the papal *motu proprio* on ethnic communities and "people on the move," both released in the second half of the 1960s, urged clergy to foster ethnic identities, to "awaken" diaspora communities and link them with their matrix nations, and, last but not least, to utilize ethnic nationalism as a weapon against communism. As a result, among other things, of the Serbian church's influence combined with the Vatican's emphasis on ethnicity, the new "ethnoclerical" concept of the so-called Church in the Croat People, as a church in form and nationalistic party in substance, came to life in the 1970s to became the powerful patron of the new Croatian nation after the collapse of communism. In this "Church in the Croat People," universal Catholicism can find a result of its experiments with the uses of nationalism and ethnicity against secularization (communism was merely a part of the general problem of secularization and modernity that have bothered the Church for the last two hundred years). Hypernationalistic "national Catholic" churches such as the "Church in the Croat People" (and a number of others) have departed from the original purpose of Roman Catholicism or "Christendom." They have come to resemble the Orthodox churches of the East. Paradoxically, the "Church in the Croat People" and the Serbian Orthodox Church could be described as "Balkan twins," invoking the old nursery rhyme about Tweedledee and Tweedledum. Such cases of enmity between two of a kind have often generated the bitterest and worst conflicts in history.

Finally, ethnoclericalism is not merely about domestic politics. It entails a foreign policy agenda, too. The consolidated "national churches" and clerical elites, in symbiosis with the state, influence their countries' foreign policies by seeking to build Huntingtonian "cultural" and "civilizational" alliances" (e.g., Orthodox Serbia's "natural allies" would be Russia and Greece, and Muslim Bosnia would get closer to Turkey and the Arab countries). They also urge the formation of defensive alliances against "alien cultures" and hostile civilizations, thus getting ready for the inevitable; in their eyes, "clash of civilizations." In the former Yugoslavia, as I have shown in preceding chapters, the formation of such alliances had begun nearly a decade before the outbreak of the domestic conflict.

The Myth of Religious Revival

While sociologists of religion publish studies, hold conferences, and argue, still uncertain, over whether secularization is "real" or not and, if yes, how much it has really weakened religion during the modern era, religious organizations have taken the frightening impact of secularization as a giver. Since the onset of modernity, people of faith have been waiting for some kind of a large-scale "global" religious revival. Atheistic communism was presumably the strongest secularizing factor ever in history, and its demise seemed the right time for the long-awaited global revival. Even otherwise quite skeptical scholars came to believe that a large-scale religious awakening was in process. Samuel P. Huntington built his much-debated "Clash of Civilizations" thesis on such an assumption.[11] Of course, Huntington and other secular scholars and analysts of political affairs are primarily interested in statistics and the potential for political mobilization of persons who share certain religious convictions, values, and practices—not in the quality and purity of moral and spiritual life. By contrast, some sociologists of religion, and perhaps most notably religious scholars and theologians, have always been more concerned with the question of "genuineness" and the ethical dimensions of religious experience than with statistics about church-mosque-synagogue attendance and the display of religious symbols in street marches. Peter L. Berger has written that "upsurges of religion" in the modern era, are, in most cases, political movements "that use religion as a convenient legitimation for political agendas based on non-religious interests" as opposed to "movements genuinely inspired by religion."[12] To be sure, Berger has also noted that every religious "upsurge," including the recent dynamics of religion worldwide, is accompanied with an increasing religious commitment, that is, that the numbers of religious people grow.[13] However, the content and character of such religiosity should be (and invariably is) congruent with each concrete movement's ideas, aims, values, and concrete experience. For example, religious and ethnic revolutions and movements in the Balkans during the period under consideration could generate only more hatred and fear and faith in state power although no religion officially professes hatred, fear, and idolatrous worship. That is to say, believers and converts whose "spiritual experience" made them "aware" of divine support for their group and of rival groups' "evil character" and turned them into worshipers of ethno-religious nation-states, are almost invariably intolerant, authoritarian-minded, and conflict-prone. Even though as an outcome of such movements numbers of "religious" people may have been growing, both these "converts" and their religious leaders seem strikingly analogous to adherents of secular ideologies if not basically the same regardless of symbols and rituals they use. Speaking with relatively highest certainty about the Balkans but cautiously implying about the dominant religion worldwide (which in my view is patriotism and nationalism), I would argue that a genuine faith is only an unambiguously apolitical and *antipolitical* faith. That is, it is not only anti-nationalistic but also explicitly anti-statist religiosity, such as for example, the faith of Jehovah Witnesses and similar sects and the faith of mystical and sufi orders.

According to the sociological concept of religious revival, it is characterized by the growth of new cults and sects that both challenge established religious institutions and respond to secularization trends in society.[14] Accordingly, genuine religious revival typically comes "from below." Yet what was happening in the former communist countries was the opposite: religious elites and established institutions mobilized the people against atheistic regimes and, once they were brought down, turned against liberal parties and policies, religious and ethnic minorities, and each other. As presented in the preceding chapters, during the most of the period under consideration in the Yugoslav states, religious beliefs and practices in mainstream faiths have been in decline and no growth of new cults and sects has been observed. Sociological surveys of religion conducted in the 1980s by both Yugoslav neo-Marxists and Catholic schools of sociology of religion, as well as an independent study carried out in Serbia, found that the secularization accelerated by the post-1945 abrupt modernization of previously backward rural society had not been reversed.[15] As noted earlier, under communism, the numbers of believers were in decline although religious organizations grew and expanded from the 1960s. Findings from international surveys of religiosity, conducted during and shortly after the fall of communism, did not reveal any striking difference.[16] Yugoslav religious minorities (e.g., various Christian denominations of Protestant origin, Islamic sufi-dervish orders, and other cults and sects) manifested less political religiosity but did not reverse secularization trends.[17] Finally, activities of Western missionaries and nontraditional cults bloomed in postcommunist eastern Europe and the former USSR during the 1990s. Yet, according to Sabrina Ramet's research, these activities did not bring about a profound change in religious life and could not challenge the consolidation of traditional faiths that fostered nationalism and frustrated liberalization in postcommunist societies.[18]

To be sure, ethnic nationalistic revolutions in the former Yugoslavia's successor states did, at least temporarily, give momentum to a new "patriotic" religiosity. The Catholic priest-sociologist of religion Ivan Grubišić wrote that, according to new surveys of religiosity conducted at the end of the 1990s, more than 90 percent of the population in Croatia were self-declared practicing Catholics, in contrast to 64 percent in the 1980s.[19] This cleric scholar, however, was frustrated with the quality of this new spirituality. He remarked once that during the 10 years of postcommunism, the most prosperous and influential people in Croatia became "tycoons, crooks, war profiteers, professional politicians, union leaders, religious leaders, drug dealers and those in the prostitution business."[20] In another commentary, which he voiced in a 2001 interview in the wake of the bishops' attack on the left-center government in Croatia, he repeated that no matter what church leaders do, even if it is struggle with regimes and governments, evidently nothing can halt secularization because the influence and quality of faith relentlessly erodes, fewer people worship regularly, and fewer young people are interested in the clerical profession.[21]

In a similar vein, a Croatian lay theologian described the apparently growing new religiosity as the consequence of the establishment of Catholicism as a virtual state religion; that is, as he sarcastically wrote, clerics and believers see "Jesus Christ as an archbishop, Mary as his secretary, and St. Peter as Jesus' chief of staff."[22] Another survey echoed the thesis that European Catholicism owes much of its recent strength to anticommunism and nationalism. According to a 2000 survey designed by Sergej Flere, religious convictions have relatively the strongest impact on political attitudes in Poland, Croatia, and Slovakia—all predominantly Catholic nations in which the Church led the struggle against communism while championing nationalism. Poland and Croatia also lead the group of six surveyed countries in the number of respondents who consider inappropriate the Church's too-strong impact on government's policies. By contrast, a relatively weak influence of religion is found in Germany (eastern section), Slovenia, and the Czech Republic.[23] It is worth noting that the only successful new democracy among the successor states of former Yugoslavia, the Republic of Slovenia, has followed the western European trend of dazzling secularization and religious indifference rather than the pattern of the Balkan "religious revival" of the 1980s and 1990s. According to a 2000 survey, only 19% of the surveyed Slovenes said they were church members and 60% declared that they did not practice religion (AIM dossier "Religion in the Balkans," available at http://www.aimpress January 2001).

A patriotic religion similar to that in Croatia and Bosnia-Herzegovina was growing in Serbia, too. An international symposium (funded by Western initiatives for democratization and conflict resolution in the Balkans) held in Belgrade in 1998, praised the Serbian Orthodox Church as part of an emerging "civil society" in Serbia and concluded that Serbian society was experiencing a "desecularization."[24] The Serbian sociologist of religion Dragoljub Djordjević, who in the early 1980's wrote that Serbs ignore the Serbian Church, discovered a profound change in the 1990s. He entitled his 1994 study: "The Return of the Sacred."[25] In a similar vein, on the occasion of Orthodox Easter in 2000, a Belgrade weekly revealed that 84 percent of the surveyed citizens of Serbia contended that they believed in the existence of God, 74 percent said they firmly believed in the resurrection of Christ, and 62 percent would attend Easter liturgies.[26] Yet a few voices of dissent, denying these findings as a genuine spiritual awakening, could be heard in Serbia, too. In a 1997 interview, a Serb-Orthodox archpriest-scholar argued that Serbia's awakening was, above all, an upsurge of ethnic nationalism, while the quality of Orthodox spirituality and religious culture remained poor.[27] The renowned Serb Orthodox laymen Vladeta Jerotić and Mirko Djordjević criticized Serbian nationalistic extremism carried out through the Church and Orthodox faith.[28] Similarly, the Belgrade author Filip David and the opposition circles around the bimonthly *Republika*, among others, called the national church a carrier of nationalism that would outlive Milošević.[29]

Accordingly, in spite of dynamic religious organizations' activities in some periods, no genuine religious revival ever occurred in any of the Yugoslav states. The only possible genuine revival in Yugoslavia would have been a rise of the influence of minority faiths. This did not occur, and mainstream faiths even attempted to check the influx of foreign missionaries while harassing domestic minorities. I introduced the Yugoslav minority faiths ("minor religious communities" or sects) in the religious portrait of Yugoslav states in chapter I, where I said that they were not linked with any particular ideology, ethnic group, or state. As noted, these minor faiths are multiethnic, and while their members have not been the agents of the Yugoslav conflict, they have contributed to the interfaith dialogue and religious peacemaking. Minor Protestant Christian communities were the only religious organizations in Yugoslavia that did not take part in the Yugoslav ethnic conflict. Minor religious organizations and individual religious figures, operating autonomously, successfully contributed to interfaith dialogue, religious peacemaking, and relief work—all this with no strings attached (in contrast to the large religious organizations, which always compete with one another and pursue political and economic interests). In addition to the quixotic Bosnian Franciscans Marko Oršolić and Ivo Marković, and several other autonomous religious figures mentioned in chapter 10, the champions of religious peacemaking and interfaith dialogue in the successor states of the former Yugoslavia have been members of minority groups, such as Jakob Finci of the Sarajevo Jewish community and the Pentecostal Christian scholar from northern Croatia, Peter Kuzmić. It is in order to note in this conclusion (as I did in chapter I) the benign role of minority faiths in the former Yugoslavia and its successor states. This "different kind of faith" has survived amid all the Balkan idols. This example, like many similar cases, provokes the assumption that genuine religion may be possible only in sects, cults, and individuals, most likely hermits and heretics. A genuine religious revival exemplified in the rise of new cults and sects could be observed in recent decades, for example, in South America, Asia, and Africa, but not in countries where "godless" communism had collapsed. There, traditional faiths sought to fill the space vacated by communist parties. This process had to do not with spiritual and moral recovery of society but with religious organizations' struggle for ideological monopoly and the spoils of postcommunism—power and privatization of former socialist property. New theocracies, state religions, and religious states have succeeded in recent decades more often than liberal democracies. There are a large number of semitheocracies, state religions, and religious states in our world today—notably in the Muslim world but also elsewhere. During the same period, many new liberal democracies experienced the clerical challenge and remained threatened by antisecular forces.

Phenomena similar to the mobilization of mainstream faiths in former Yugoslavia could be observed elsewhere. The most massive and effective religious movements in several recent decades were not quests for the spiritual but quintessential "anti"-movements. Anticommunism and anti-Westernism have been two dominant vehicles in recent religious movements. Anticommunism was predominant in the West. During the Cold War, taking advantage of communist antireligious policies, anticommunists fought their opponents by encouraging religious dissent in communist countries.[30] Likewise, according to an analyst of American anticommunism, between 1950 and 1960, that is, during the height of the Cold War, the percentage of the American population with a church affiliation jumped from 55 to 69 percent, "an increase unprecedented in the twentieth century."[31] Concurrently, anti-Westernism fueled Islamic and Eastern Orthodox "revivals," while Judaism gained importance thanks to Arab-Israeli strife. "Mass movements can rise and spread without a belief in a God, but never without belief in a devil," said philosopher-longshoreman Eric Hoffer.[32]

Concerning specifically the dynamic religious activity during the crisis and collapse of communism in Europe, which was enthusiastically described in the West as another "great awakening" and "spiritual renaissance," perhaps the most valuable views are expressed by Czeslaw Milos and Mirko Djordjević. Commenting on the role of the Catholic Church in postcommunist Poland, Milos has noted that the Church was seeking for itself the status and authority that earlier belonged to the Communist Party and that the people began to fear priests and bishops and look at religion with disgust because of "sins of triumphalism" and the tendency toward establishing state religions.[33] Even more explicit was Djordjević writing about the Serbian Orthodox Church's responsibility for the Yugoslav wars. Djordjević argues that, contrary to hopes that religion in former communist countries, while recovering from persecution and rebuilding its appeal on this martyrdom, would revitalize itself, no genuine spiritual renewal took place. What has taken place instead of a popular "return to God," Djordjević asserts, was religious organizations' struggle for property and status as state religions during the period of transition. This was accompanied with a rising clerical influence in politics and in some cases such as Yugoslavia, clerical contribution to nationalistic extremism and war.[34]

In sum, the "return of God" predicted in the late 1980s and early 1990s did not take place. From the globally televised scenes of the burning Bosnian government towers in Sarajevo in 1992 to the smoke, fire, and death at the World Trade Center in New York in September 2001, the world seems to have experienced some kind of apocalypse rather than a religious renaissance. And it must be noted that religion was a factor instrumental in bringing about both those catastrophic events. In last two decades, established religions have temporarily increased their influence in society, especially in ex-communist countries, only to recede when the anticommunist euphoria was over. In spite of pivotal changes in the world since the 1980s, there have been no heretical voices within religious institutions nor even cautious church reforms resembling the Second Vatican Council. To be sure, religious organizations have contributed to advocacy of human rights, charitable work, conflict resolution, education, discussion of environmental issues, and other praiseworthy activities. Yet these relatively modest achievements have been overshadowed by two chief functions and "missions" of religion in our time—as the source of mobilization and justification of extremist ethnic and religious nationalism or fundamentalism, and the source of support and legitimation of conservative politics. ⟩ MYTH.

The terrorist attacks on the United States on September 11, 2001, posed new challenges to tradiational faiths. As U.S. military forces sought the terrorists, among whom were many clerics and practicing religious believers who justified terror and violence by faith, the hero of the anticommunist struggle, Pope John Paul II, convened an interfaith meeting of world religious leaders. On January 24, at Asisi, the pope and leaders of dozens of faiths, including Muslims, Jews, Christians, Buddhists, and others, made an attempt to address the issue of responsibility for the rising violence inspired by religious extremism. "Clearly, a principal motive for the pope's convening the gathering was the claim by the Islamic fundamentalists who carried out the attacks on the United States that they had acted in God's name," reported the *New York Times*.[35] On the occasion, as many times before, religious leaders prayed for peace. Yet they did not designate religion as a source of any specific problem or assume any responsibility.

To conclude, after the short-lived mood of triumph during the collapse of "godless" communism in Europe, the past decade witnessed upsurges of religious extremism and conflicts related to religion in many parts of the world. This process accompanied the wars in the Balkans and the worsening of the crisis in Palestine and culminated in the Islamic radicals' attack on the United States on September 11. Despite all, religion remains an influential factor in our world. And while religious organizations claim their rights to influence almost every dimension of life and society, not just spiritual life, charitable work and culture, religious leaders hardly ever admit the responsibility of religion for any bad things. The standard explanation is that bad things associated with religion are "aberrations" and "misuses" of an inherently good and immutable religious faith. However, these aberrations and misuses have been quite frequent since the dawn of civilization to the present.

A Godly Idea in A Godless Regime: Religion and Yugoslav Communism

Like religion, communism and state socialism could also be described as essentially good but "aberrant" or "utopian" ideas abused and exploited by evil individuals. Somehow, only communism and no other ideology (e.g., Nazism, racism, imperialism, colonialism) earned the label "godless." Two key findings underlie Western literature on religion under communism. The first is that Marxist regimes were hostile toward traditional religions, seeking to eradicate them. The second is that methods for attaining a religion-free society combined sporadic state-sponsored terror with various "religious surrogates" such as secular cults, nationalism, sports, science, and dogmatic applications of Marxist ideology as an "absolute truth." Many excellent analyses of religion under communism have been written, but somehow no convincing and complete work has addressed the question of why no communists anywhere in the world completely eradicated religion (it is still little known that only communist Albania came close to the "final solution" of the religious question). Concerning Yugoslav communism, no evidence exists that the Tito regime, from its Partisan years to its collapse, ever intended to eradicate religion. After the 1945–53 bloody anticlerical terror, driven more by post–civil war passions than revolutionary zeal, the regime was prepared to grant religious liberty and even many privileges to religious organizations that were instrumental in championing the official patriotism of brotherhood and unity, designated in this study a civil religion.

To be sure, the Yugoslav civil religion of brotherhood and unity did share many features with phenomena such as the cult of Chairman Mao or the making of the new Soviet man or what George L. Mosse termed the "new politics" of secular worship and "nationalization of the masses" in the Third Reich.[36] Yet the rationale of Titoism was not the consolidation and conservation of state-party systems as in China and USSR but reform that eventually weakened the state and the party. This "Yugo-experiment" eventually brought the system to a point when it was safeguarded by "emotion" alone, that is, by the few people who valued brotherhood and unity squeezed between diehard ethnic nationalists and communists turned into ethnic nationalists. Nor was the rationale for rituals and symbols utilized in the Titoist "nationalization of the masses" the same as that in the Third Reich. That is to say, had Hitler at Nazi rallies called for brotherhood and unity between Germans and Jews in order to make Germany stronger in its diversity, would the Holocaust have come out of it? The Yugoslav civil religion of brotherhood and unity was a public worship compatible with the Western liberal idea of religious toleration. Further, in contrast to Soviet and Chinese-styled secular worship, Titoist brotherhood and unity was neither a religious surrogate nor channel for imposing Marxism on society, because it sought not to exclude but to embrace and activate religious organizations on an ecumenical agenda and did not refer to Marxism. To be sure, Titoism did dwarf religion in order to maintain ethnic harmony and prevent the ethnonationalistic groups from unification with religious organizations. In the end, however, forces of conflict have prevailed. For that matter, Yugoslavia seems analogous for example to India, although Tito and Mahatma Gandhi had different religious views and pursued different religious policies. In contrast to the atheist Tito and his restrictive or antireligious policies, Gandhi was an outspoken believer who honored faith and labored to create an "ecumenical multireligion" in his country. Yet both leaders ended up defeated by hatred and bigotry. Had Tito allowed full religious liberty in the 1950s, he might likely have met Gandhi's fate.

Accordingly, brotherhood and unity was designated a civil religion. Even the phrase itself ("brotherhood and unity") was borrowed from traditional religions, specifically from the Orthodox church. Alexei Khomjakov, Leo Tolstoy, and Vladimir Soloviev, among many others, spoke and wrote about it. Tito, who routinely struggled with words and ideas, borrowed the phrases "brotherhood and unity" (*sobornost, koinonia*) and "keeping Orthodox faith as the apple of the eye" (which he would change into "keep brotherhood and unity as the apple of your eye") from the discourse of the Comintern during his Moscow years (as E. H. Carr noticed, Comintern leaders used the "apple of the eye" metaphor stolen from Orthodox priests).[37] At any rate, the brotherhood and unity idea entailed both spiritual and ethical dimensions. The Second Vatican Council viewed socialists and communists as potential Christians who live in error. Milovan Djilas might have had this in mind when he argued that there was a difference between communists and Nazi-fascists (i.e., extreme nationalists and racists) because, in Djilas's interpretation, the communists, in their quest for "humanity," equality, and justice, were always inclined toward heresy and, when confronted with the truth about the failures of their venture, sought repentance—as opposed to nationalistic and racist extremists, who never generated massive heresies and renegades in their ranks; never repented (even when confronted with the shocking evidence on genocide trials); and continued to the bitter end to worship themselves and hate others.[38]

As a political concept, the civil religion of brotherhood and unity imposed on the chief enemies of united multiethnic Yugoslavia, that is, the ethnic nationalists, the following Hobson's choice: either undermine the regime using the most effective weapon, which is ethnic hatred, and thus risk another genocide after having been responsible for the first one; or form a benevolent opposition by embracing the ideal of brotherhood and unity and try to prove that not only the communists but also noncommunists and even anticommunists are capable of bringing together in peace peoples of diverse faiths and cultures. As I have shown, the clerical search for interfaith dialogue as a path toward an united, religiously inspired alternative to communism did not succeed. On the other hand, Tito's regime succeeded in discrediting its opponents while, for most of the communist era, avoiding excessive use of force. Thus when the Yugoslav communist system was strongest, its religious policies were softest.

In a nutshell, Tito's national communism prevented its enemies from taking a "godly idea" from the hands of "the godless." The chief "instrument" left to ethnic nationalists was genocide, and they would do it twice. Of course, Titoism is by all means a part of the dark legacy of communism.

However, as one of the competing nationalisms seeking to resolve the notorious Yugoslav National Question, the Titoist multiethnic federation appeared *relatively* good, or "less bad," when compared with Serbian, Croatian, Muslim, Albanian, and other ethnic nationalisms and their ideologies, concrete regimes, and crimes against humanity. In other words, what makes Titoism seem relatively good is above all the fact that its rivals were proven so obviously bad. If observed in a broader context, Titoism again seems relatively good because of its historically discredited enemies such as Nazism and fascism, Stalinism, the wretched regimes in the Soviet satellite states of eastern Europe, and the Balkan ethnic nationalisms. It was a strike of luck for Titoism to have had such an ugly "other." While looking at the Yugoslav ethnic nationalisms and other rivals of Tito in the hindsight of the post-Yugoslav era, and thinking of the fact that two cycles of genocide preceded and succeeded the communist era as a time of relative peace and prosperity, I could not help perceiving the communists as much nicer than they really were. Unfortunately, to this day, nothing better than Titoism has been seen in this part of the world.

Finally, after the Yugoslav wars of the 1990s and so obtrusive failures of its successor states, Josip Broz Tito has been acknowledged in the West as an important twentieth-century statesman, unifier of the "impossible country" of Yugoslavia. College history textbooks, chronicles of the Holocaust, and new documentary videos have highlighted his remarkable role in the anti-Nazi resistance. After the terrorist attacks on the United States in September 2001, the West seem to be prepared for giving Tito even more credit than earlier. After September 11, many in the United States may have realized that Tito, with Nasser of Egypt, Nehru of India, and other modernizers of the Third World, were they more successful and better assisted by the West in the 1950s through the 1970s, could have helped avert the religious and ethnic extremism and terrorism that the world has witnessed in recent years.

The Myth of the Three Evils of the Twentieth Century and Other New Myths

The most crucial single characteristic of the religion under consideration is worship of history. History as the principal object of worship entails myths that facilitate coming to terms with various historical controversies coupled with the worship of the nation (or ethno-religious community). I would single out three sets of new myths that most critically affected the period under consideration and are likely to exert significant influence on future events in successor states to the former Yugoslavia. These myths could be named as follows:

1. The Deep Roots Myth
2. The Jerusalem Myth
3. The Myth of the Three Evils of the Twentieth Century

These myths challenged the patriotic mythologies of the Yugoslav nation while building mythical foundations for the rebirth of the ethnic nations. They also challenged each other as rival ethnic nationalistic myths. Furthermore, they contributed to the construction of broader "civilizational" myths. To begin with, the Deep Roots Myth is about group pride and identity based on the belief in tradition and continuity. As already noted, both Serb and Croat nationalistic leaders claimed that their respective nation was "the first political nation in Europe." The Deep Roots Myth is a myth of national origin. It narrates the two largest Yugoslav churches' and ethnic groups' origins, their quest for independent statehood, and their struggle with foreign invaders, with each other, and with the Yugoslav multinational state, especially with the young communist federation that they sought to defeat by the power of their long traditions. The myth draws its power from the two ethnic nations' cultural longevity and various forms of autonomy and statehood. The recent states are perceived as an extension of medieval ethnic principalities that with the help of native clergy maintained the continuity of nationhood. The Croatian version of the myth worshiped the conversion of the Croat ethnic chieftains ("kings") to Christianity and the development of statehood between the seventh and twelfth centuries, after which the nation continued through various forms of cultural activity and political autonomy. The myth portrays Croatia as a western European nation much older than Serbia and allegedly culturally superior both to Serbia and the twentieth-century product called Yugoslavia. The Serbian version of the myth emphasizes the relatively greater territory and power of the Serbian medieval state and the achievements of the modern Serbian state between 1804 and 1918, during which period no independent Croatia existed. In both versions of the Deep Roots Myth, the churches worship themselves, glorifying clergy as wise leaders, heroes, and patriots and presenting religion as a hallmark of nationhood. Appropriating for themselves the role of progenitors of ethnic nations and guardians of their identity during a long history of survival, struggle, and redemption, the two churches each vied to claim grater cultural, political, and military achievements than the other, while both tried to dwarf the young Yugoslav state—especially its communist federal version, founded in 1945. While it proved effective against the communists in the 1980s, the Deep Roots Myth deepened mutual animosity and rivalry between the allegedly older and more cultured "Western" nation of Croatia and the younger but purportedly "stronger, more courageous, glorious, and martyred" Serbian nation. The two myths were commemorated and reinvented through the church activities undertaken between 1939 and

1998 described earlier. The old myths were recently reinvented to incorporate reinterpretations of the past and constructions of histories of the Yugoslav state, World War II, the Cold War, and the recent Balkan wars suitable to the mythmakers and new relations of power in the successor states. The two versions of the Deep Roots Myth today constitute the bases for two official national patriotic historiographies in Croatia and Serbia.

In sum, architects of the Deep Roots Myth have labored to create a "visible" link between ancient ethnic communities and nation-states founded after the collapse of communism and disintegration of the former Yugoslavia. Their favorite word is "tradition," which they perceive as something immutable in ever-changing history, created centuries ago yet somehow coming to us intact and unaltered. As they make people conscious of these allegedly immutable things that resisted the power of historical change and invite the people to "wake up" and "return" to their "genuine" identities, their chief aim is to profoundly alter the current situation in the society, culture, economy, government, identity, and mentality of the people. In other words, ethnic nationalists say that nothing has changed since the Middle Ages in order to change everything today.

Second, the Serbian Orthodox Church, assisted by Serb nationalist intellectuals, has constructed the Jerusalem Myth. The myth draws from the established Kosovo myth while also borrowing from the immensely influential post-1945 histories, narratives, and uses of the Holocaust, the state of Israel, and the Jews. The Serbian Church consecrated two national "sacred centers"—sites of Serbian glory and martyrdom located in Kosovo (the Kosovo battlefield and medieval shrines) and in northern Croatia (Jasenovac). The myth was symbolically inaugurated between 1984 and 1989 by commemorations at Jasenovac and Gazimestan and consolidated between 1998 and 2000 by the canonization of eight Serbian martyrs or "new saints," victims of the Jasenovac concentration camp who thus joined the army of Serbian saints who reside in the mythical Heavenly Serbia. The myth prepared the ground for Serbian ethnic cleansing in Croatia, Bosnia-Herzegovina, and Kosovo. It generated the lust for revenge and justified crimes committed by Serbs during the Balkan wars of the 1990s. The lasting function of the Jerusalem Myth will be to boost national pride and cohesion, strengthen the status of the Serbian Orthodox Church as partner in the national leadership, and secure Jewish sympathies for the Serbs. In addition, the myth's future functions include undoing the Serbian territorial losses in Kosovo and in Croatia, maintaining a perpetual stigma against Croats, Albanians, and Muslims, and creating a symbolic rallying point for another national awakening and possible Serbian reconquest of the lost territories.

The Balkan version of the Jerusalem Myth is an archetypal myth. It evolved from archetypal civilizational myths such as the Myth of Lost Jerusalem and the Myth of Lost Paradise and the "Eternal Return," phrases familiar to students of myth and identified by Mircea Eliade as progenitors of myths that occupy a pivotal place in all religions.[39] The Jerusalem Myth is not merely about Kosovo (and its Jasenovac extension). Every group involved in the Balkan conflict (analogies can be found in many other troubled zones worldwide) has worshiped some variant of the Jerusalem Myth. The ruins of the former Yugoslavia are full of tombs and monuments of all sorts and all ages, sites of martyrdom, wailing walls and sacred centers both above and under ground, to which the damned groups want to return but cannot. What the Jerusalem Myth really narrates is a story about a land of ceaseless resentment inhabited by eternal losers.

The third and presumably the most important among the new myths I have termed "The Myth of the Three Evils of the Twentieth Century." As described earlier, in October 1998, Pope John Paul II beatified the Croatian cardinal Alojzije Stepinac, who was persecuted by the communists in the former Yugoslavia. According to the papal words at the beatification ceremony, the brave and autonomous church leader consistently opposed, with an even strength and determination, "the three evils of the twentieth century: Nazism, fascism, and communism." This papal interpretation of twentieth-century history drew much criticism worldwide. Protest was especially vocal among local Balkan Orthodox Serbs and Jewish organizations in Israel, the United States, and Europe. They had earlier campaigned against the beatification because this Croatian church leader was associated with the pro-Axis Croatian World War II regime responsible for the deaths of hundreds thousands of Jews, Serbs, Gypsies, and Croatian antifascists. To be sure, Cardinal Stepinac did indeed bravely confront the communists and was imprisoned by them in 1946 after convening the national conference of bishops and issuing a strong letter protesting the brutality of the communist revolution. Yet during Second World War II Stepinac never convened the national bishops' conference in order to condemn Croatian fascists' crimes, although he, for various reasons, did privately criticize the Croatian regime's excessive brutality. Nor did Cardinal Stepinac ever discipline any of the numerous priests and prominent Catholic lay leaders who served as the discredited regime's officials, some of whom actively participated in drawing up the regime's racist laws, which led to the massive persecution of the hated ethnic groups and political opponents. Finally, the controversial cardinal (who had access to the public and was, as a victim of communism, interviewed by Western journalists) never made any public statement of regret or apology regarding the crimes for which the Croatian World War II regime was found responsible, on the basis of strong evidence gathered after 1945. Thus, contrary to the 1998 speech in which the head of the Catholic Church justified Stepinac's beatification, this saintly candidate did not treat evenly all the "three evils" of the twentieth century. It is rather clear that he was, first of all, a diehard Croatian nationalist, prepared to sanctify the ideal of Croatian statehood even under the worst kind of government—even if that statehood was achieved at the expense of massive crimes. Second, there is no doubt that Stepinac viewed communism as the gravest evil. He was prepared to tolerate Nazism and fascism as efficient instruments of anticommunism. Because of his anticommunism he did not even protest the Italian fascist occupation of the predominantly Croatian-populated provinces of Dalmatia and Istria. So why does the Church portray him now as an opponent of not just communism, but also fascism and Nazism?

The Stepinac case is not an isolated historical episode or another of those notorious "Balkan affairs." It is important to place it in the broader context of twentieth-century history as it has been reinterpreted after the end of the Cold War. In this context, the Stepinac case is associated with the following two myth-making projects. The first I see as the writing and promoting, via religion among other things, of a new history of the twentieth century, concerning the ideological conflict between Nazism, fascism, communism, and democracy that I have termed the "Myth of the Three Evils of the Twentieth Century." The second, and a component of this myth, is the controversy over Pope Pius XII and his much-debated silence about the Holocaust. The Vatican inaugurated this "new history" (later to be articulated as the Myth of the Three Evils of the Twentieth Century) in 1989 on the occasion of the German invasion of Poland and the fiftieth anniversary of the beginning of World War II. In his encyclical, Pope John Paul II utilized the concept of "totalitarianism," invented by secular scholars between the 1930s and 1950s.[40] The pope designated the Church an "antitotalitarian" force and a consistent opponent of all societies and regimes that could be identified as totalitarian.[41] The Church perceived itself as one of the earliest "warning systems," identifying "totalitarianism" as early as 1846 and opposing it since. This is based on the papal encyclicals *Qui pluribus* (1846) *Mit brennender Sorge*, and *Divini redemptoris* (1937), which condemned, among other things (such as, for example, the tolerant interfaith dialogue championed by some Christian Protestant groups from western Europe and the United States, not to mention other encyclicals that attacked liberalism, movements for women's rights, and so forth), atheistic communism, racism, and extremist nationalism. The myth of an autonomous church consistently opposing all forms of evil amid the horror, chaos, and confusion of the long twentieth-century ideological war provided a hope that the epoch under consideration was not so terrible (as it actually was). Secular scholars who argued that communism might have been the single greatest evil of the terrible century often praised the Roman Catholic Church as the leading anticommunist force and perhaps the only remaining moral and intellectual "compass" in our world.[42] Concurrently, a related secular debate has continued between historians who perceive communism as being as terrible as fascism, or the same as fascism,[43] and historians who make a sharp distinction between the innately evil and by far most destructive ideology and politics of Nazism-fascism, and the inherently good but abused and mismanaged communist utopia that still managed to achieve some good things before its eventual failure.[44] At any rate, recent world historiography, as a new epoch's historical perspective on the bygone age, has coincided with and exerted mutual influence on religious organizations' mythmaking concerning the same period. This phenomenon is a reminder and an enlarged picture of the ethnic nationalistic and revisionist-anticommunist "new histories" that were accompanied by church mythmaking and saint-making during the decades of the disintegration and transformation of Yugoslavia. Accordingly, speaking again about Catholicism, one of the chief objectives of the Myth of the Three Evils of the Twentieth Century is to bring the Church on the side of the post–Cold War winners, that is, the Western democracies, in the conclusion of the twentieth-century ideological conflict between Nazism, fascism, communism, and democracy. That is to say, if the Church were, for example, not only acknowledged as a champion of anticommunism but also perceived as a supporter of right-wing authoritarianism, including Nazism and fascism, it could not become one of the post-1989 winners and architects of the new world order. The myth presumably aims to achieve even more than merely consolidating post-1989 gains of the Catholic church and established faiths in general by reasserting moral and intellectual supremacy of religious over secular thought.

Furthermore, the Myth of the Three Evils of the Twentieth Century is, like many myths that originated in religious organizations during that terrible century, an anticommunist myth. It aims at hurting communism even posthumously. The myth portrays the anticommunist struggle as a holy war of sorts and rebuffs the criticism of excesses in anticommunism, its ambiguous character and aims.[45] More specifically, the Myth of the Three Evils of the Twentieth Century aims to preclude the "vampire" of communism from rising again in the form of a "revisionist" history of the twentieth century— a history that may attempt to rethink communism without the pressure of the Cold War and acknowledge it as, not an inherent evil but a good idea with sporadic "aberrations" and "misuses," and the major contributor in the struggle against Nazism and fascism. However, religious organizations have shown no such remarkable effort in order to prevent revivals of Nazism, racism, fascism, and right-wing tyrannies now routinely fused with religious monopolies. Not to mention that religious organizations that do not merely tolerate capitalism but explicitly declare this system as "good" must be held responsible for this moral blunder. It is fair to say that the Roman Catholic Church is not among those.

In close connection with this myth's functions as just presented, it also aims at softening and watering down the strong impact of Holocaust historiography and genocide studies. This scholarship studies many dimensions of modern genocidal crimes and convincingly argues for making religious organizations responsible, either as having been "tolerant" of evil or, in some cases, operating as instigators of genocide and accomplices in crimes.[46] By the same token, another major implication of the Stepinac beatification concerns the controversy about the role of the Vatican and Pope Pius XII during World War II. I believe that the Vatican conceives of Stepinac's case as a stepping-stone toward the beatification of Pope Pius XII and that both future saints will operate as building blocks in the construction of the Myth of the Three Evils of the Twentieth Century. Pius XII has been the target of a controversy much wider and better known than Stepinac's case, concerning Christianity as a source of anti-Semitism and Christian churches' responsibility for the Holocaust.[47] It seems likely that the formula from the Stepinac case (resistance against all the three "evils," not just against communism) will be applied to the case of Pius as well. Recent papal beatifications and canonizations have indicated that the Myth of the Three Evils of the Twentieth Century is gradually taking shape and that the anticipated beatification of Pius should be its capstone. In addition to Stepinac, several other recent beatifications and canonizations sustain the Myth of the Three Evils of the Twentieth Century in general and the Pius XII cause in particular. Thus, for example, after the beatification in Croatia on 2 October 1998, on 11 October in Rome (as the Stepinac beatification was still drawing protests from Jewish organizations worldwide), Pope John Paul II canonized the Carmelite nun Teresa Benedicta, born as Edith Stein into a Jewish family from Wroclaw, Poland, who perished in Auschwitz in 1942. While the pope hoped that this tribute to a victim of Auschwitz would appease the Jews, many Jewish associations found Stein's canonization offensive. Furthermore, on 11 March 2001, the pope beatified 233 clergy and prominent lay leaders killed during the 1936–39 Spanish Civil War. All of those new blessed martyrs died at the hands of the leftists defenders of the Spanish Republic battling Francisco Franco's right-wing movement, backed by the hierarchy of the Catholic Church in Spain and by churches abroad. The vast majority of Franco's victims, including many priests, have not, of course, been beatified, among other reasons because the pro-Franco clergy assisted with the post–Civil War massive persecution of the regime's opponents so that many Spanish Catholics were de facto victimized by the Church. Concluding the series, in June 2001, Pope John Paul II went to western Ukraine to canonize Ukrainian Uniates—victims of Soviet communism.

The new Myth of the Three Evils of the Twentieth Century, not only from the vantage point of the Church and conservative right-wing politics but also from the point of view of all the disappointed in humanity after the terrible twentieth century, may sound like a good idea. Yet it seems hard to sustain the myth with a usable past because of the striking imbalance between the church's concrete attitude toward the right and left. The Church's favoring of the former and upholding it in numerous ways, as opposed to a few declarations critical of the latter, has been quite obvious. It should be also noted that leftist church members, Marxist fellow travelers, and true Catholic antifascists cannot qualify for sainthood and cannot be used as corrections to the imbalance. To be sure, the Church had earlier canonized and beatified a large number of Polish clergy killed by the Germans during World War II. These martyred Poles were designated antifascists although most of them did not actively fight against Germans or take part in the resistance. At any rate, while the Church cannot afford to canonize and recognize as martyrs any of its rather numerous clergy and members who sided with the forces of the Left against Nazism and fascism, the grand Myth of the Three Evils of the Twentieth Century will be sustained by inventing a more "balanced" approach, even in cases where it did not exist (e.g., the remarkable right-wing figures Pope Pius XII and Cardinal Stepinac, both tolerant of Nazi-fascism and rigid nationalism).

Finally, from a historian's perspective, one of the presumably weakest components of the Myth of the Three Evils of the Twentieth Century will be convincing historical interpretation of one of the milestone events in the history of the Roman Catholic Church: the Second Vatican Council, 1962–65. As noted in chapter 2, this church council is still considered one of the boldest church reforms in the long process of the church's accommodation to the modern world. Yet what were the aims of the council perceived in the light of the mythical past according to the Myth of the Three Evils of the Twentieth Century? Did the Church make an attempt to come to terms, to collaborate with then seemingly powerful and growing forces of global socialism and communism? If this is not so, if the Council inaugurated a subtle trickery aimed at deceiving and weakening the enemy, as some recent reinterpretations of the council have argued (see chapter 2), what about the council's ecumenical agenda—was that a trickery, too? Were, for that matter, Serbian Orthodox zealots right? How could rival faiths trust Catholic leaders who began to engage in a dialogue, that is, collaborate with the communists? Did John XXIII and Paul VI, in fact, carry out similar policies with regard to communism as Pius XII did regarding fascism and Nazism? In other words, has the Church always been ready to collaborate with whatever form of evil predominates in order to preserve its own privileged status in society? How could the Church proclaim via the council its, if not overt accommodation with, than at least toleration of a system that had been all along inherently evil, as Pope John Paul II has recently discovered? Neither "Gaudium et spes" ("The Church in the Contemporary World") nor any other council's document indicated that church leaders had been aware that communism was evil. Pope John Paul II declared communism evil in retrospect. Yet if this becomes an official Church stance, it will require a new council to revise Vatican II.

In conclusion, a myth-in-the making termed here the Myth of the Three Evils of the Twentieth Century has already become one of the dominant perspectives on twentieth-century history. Many secular historians have already accepted it. The Catholic Church (and many other religious organizations, too) will turn this myth into an object of mass worship and as such it will become true history. Yet many will oppose it. Contrary to the myth-makers' desire to foster consensus and cement order, myth cannot indefinitely maintain order. After all, the collapse of the one-time powerful and enduring communist mythology within only a few years in the late 1980s is one very instructive lesson from history. Where are now the myths of the international workers' movement and proletarian revolution? Where are now the myths of the Yugoslav brotherhood and unity? Also, as in the case of the warring Balkan ethnic myths, the contradiction between myth and reality almost invariably results in conflict. Typically, myth solidifies certain social order by obscuring its contradictions, which then continue to work under the surface only to erupt like a volcano, disrupting the order momentarily consolidated by myth. Likewise, myth strengthens and unites "communities of fear." It can help the survival of a group and even propel its rise. Yet this success simultaneously brings about hostile responses in rival groups whose myths are challenged. It is true that without myth there is no dignity and identity, but sooner or later myth turns against its creators.

The Balkan Nightmare Continues

I shall now conclude this journey where it began—in the Balkan land of Byzantine domes, gothic spires, and Islamic minarets. These have been razed, damaged, and newly built and renovated, and they still stand side by side, defying all attempts to profoundly change the legacy of the Balkan past. Today, however, there exists a changed broad context known as "the new Europe." Instead of rushing to identify it as another new or rejuvenated old myth, it must be acknowledged that in contrast to nineteenth-century western and central European statesmen, princes, and emperors, who looked with much contempt on the Balkans and their peoples, the leaders of the European Union (EU) look on Europe's southeastern corner with mixed feelings of concern, contempt, and compassion. Today European leaders seem prepared for and capable of healing the Balkan malady.

Prominent intellectuals of Yugoslav descent, such as, for example, the authors Ivo Andrić and Miroslav Krleža, died before the invention of the new Europe. These two Slavic intellectuals, among many others, despised western Europe and were notorious pessimists regarding the prospects for stability and civilization in Europe's southeastern corner. Among others, they believed that the Yugoslav peoples are damned. According the famous metaphors from Andrić's and Krleža's stories and novels, moments of peace and light in the history of the Yugoslav peoples are short-lived, as opposed to long-lasting violence and darkness. Short moments of peace and light are always brought to an end as someone "turns the lights off," thus giving a signal for a mass slaughter in this "Balkan Inn." Hatred, frustration, and anger emanating from ignorance, superstition, prejudice, and misrule are never fully cured—they only change forms, from lethargy to vehement outburst. The local establishment is everywhere composed of "fools" and "newly enriched bastards," while the wise are for most of the time silent and ignored. Needless to say, both literary giants were outspoken anticlericalists. For Andrić, the clergy of all major faiths in Bosnia are carriers of the fateful everlasting hatred, and for Krleža, bishops and archimandrites march down the streets in front of a "schizophrenic mob" while ruling elites "worship the golden calf." According to their views of the history of the Yugoslav peoples, short periods of normalcy are interrupted by long dark moments "when fools speak out, the wise shut up and bastards get rich," as Andrić has written. Andrić died in 1975 and Krleža a few years later. If they were alive today they would probably have little to revise in their conclusions expect perhaps to add a few more bitter notes. Would these two, who also blamed Europe for much of the Balkan misfortune, have changed their views on Europe, hoping for her healing role in the Balkans?

At this writing, neither the EU project has been completed nor the Balkan problem solved. There exist again "two Europes." Symbols and landmarks of the wealthy, stable, religiously indifferent, and seemingly happy one are Brussels, Maastricht, the rebuilt whitewashed city of Berlin, and rejuvenated east-central European urban centers such as Warsaw, Prague, and Budapest. By contrast, symbols of the new "Other Europe" are zones of conflict such as Bosnia-Herzegovina, Kosovo, Macedonia, Northern Ireland, Cyprus, and the Basque country. At any rate, while Europe is "reinventing" itself, the Balkan nightmare continues. From the 10-day war in Slovenia in the spring of 1991, followed by the long wars in Croatia, Bosnia-Herzegovina, and Kosovo, to the most recent Macedonian-Albanian strife of 2001, the dismembered country, at this writing, commemorates one of its history's darkest decades.

During 2000–2001, the infamous ethnic nationalistic leaders Slobodan Milošević, Franjo Tudjman, and Alija Izetbegović, designated by Western media and politicians the principal architects of the Yugoslav tragedy, have all been removed from positions of power. At this writing Slobodan Milošević is being prosecuted for war crimes before the Hague International War Crimes Tribunal for the Former Yugoslavia. Yet neither Milošević nor other two ethnic leaders were the sole agents of the conflict, and their departure cannot alter the situation profoundly. And while Milošević, along with many Serb, Croat, and Muslim military and police officers and other executive officials of the Balkan conflict, face prosecution, other agents of the conflict will not. Nationalistic historians, novelists, and intellectuals, and religious leaders who mobilized people in pursuit of criminal projects will get away with it. Accordingly, the Hague trial is analogous to the Nuremberg trials in that all the culprits are not there.

In the meantime, the heirs and ideologies of Milošević, Tudjman, and Izetbegović, as well as parties they founded, together with the religious institutions that helped their rise to power, have continued to exert considerable influence in politics and public life in the successor states and even in international affairs. New wars are probable while local incidents recur. Most recently, an all-out war broke out between the government of the Republic of Macedonia and an Albanian guerilla force. Incidents continue in Kosovo, in the Preševo region bordering Serbia and Kosovo, and throughout Bosnia and Herzegovina. The fates of Bosnia-Herzegovina, Macedonia, and Montenegro as viable nation-states are uncertain. Six years after the Dayton

Peace Accords, the international community has begun to realize that Bosnia and Herzegovina cannot survive until the two secession-oriented enclaves ruled by ethnic parties, gangs, and nationalistic clergy, namely, the "Serb Republic" and the "Croatian Community of Herzeg-Bosna," are abolished. The UN High Commissioner for Bosnia and Herzegovina virtually outlawed the Croatian enclave early in 2001. Later that year pressure was mounting from NGOs toward doing away with the bankrupt and criminal "Serb Republic."[48] In spite of all existing problems and destruction and loss in the past, Bosnia and Herzegovina, with remarkable diversity and resources, has the greatest potential of all the successor states of the former Yugoslavia. Some day this former Ottoman province may indeed become a Switzerland of the Balkans. Among numerous obstacles toward this goal, Bosnian and Herzegovinan clergy are still this country's curse. The Serbian Orthodox Church is a Trojan horse stubbornly hoping for the secession of the "Serb lands" and unification with Serbia. Catholic hierarchy will insist on a concordat between Sarajevo and the Vatican, but the Serbian Church will veto it. Many Catholic clergy, let alone the notorious Herzegovina Franciscans, will be laboring for the secession of "Croatian lands" and unification with Croatia. The nationalist-fundamentalist faction within the Islamic Community will be hoping and laboring for an Islamic state even at the expense of some territorial concessions. Presumably the only point of agreement among the members of the "Interfaith Council" of Bosnia and Herzegovina (which involves top leaders of the major local faiths and is funded largely by the United States) was to reject the liberal secular initiative for teaching a course in an ecumenically oriented religious culture in public schools. Instead, religious leaders pursue further divisions in the multiethnic society, insisting on traditional religious instruction carried out by clergy among students divided into estranged religious enclaves. The only patriotic clergy committed to the country's unity based on multiethnic and interfaith cooperation are the Franciscans of the "Silver Bosnia" province.

Bosnia is not the only successor state threatened by secession. Such outcomes are probable in Serbia and Croatia, too. Serbia today invokes the analogy of her old enemy, the Ottoman Empire, once known as the "sick man of Europe." Montenegro is heading toward secession from the still-living monster called the "Federal Republic of Yugoslavia." Kosovo Albanians have worked toward the same goal for quite awhile. The popularity of the regional autonomous movement is growing in Serbia's northern province of Vojvodina, although the autonomy or secession of the province seem unlikely. Serbia has changed little since Milošević's fall. According to a public opinion survey conducted by an independent (i.e., financed by the West) Belgrade agency early in 2001, the greatest heroes of the Serbian people are (in order of degree of popularity) Radovan Karadžić, General Ratko Mladić, Željko Ražnatović Arkan, and Slobodan Milošević—the "gang of four" most wanted by the International War Crimes Tribunal in the Hague.[49] At the level of official politics, the Koštunica government encourages "special ties" with the Serb Republic of Bosnia and advocates Dobrica Ćosić's "solution" for Kosovo via partition of the province into a Serbian section (with most of the medieval shrines included) and an Albanian section (free of Serbs and free to join Albania).[50]

In Croatia, the strong ethnic nationalistic forces envision the country's future as a conservative, centralized, Catholic nation-state, possibly enlarged by the acquisition of a Western section of Bosnia-Herzegovina. The Catholic Church and right-wing parties have labored to overthrow the democratically elected left-center government. Since the 2000 elections the powerful national church has flexed its muscles, seeking to reassert itself as a kingmaker in Croatian politics. The Croatian church hierarchy wants its "own" party in power, regardless of the outcomes of the democratic process and that party's actual performance in the economy and the building of a democratic polity. In the meantime, in the northwestern Croatian region of Istria, the strong regional party of Istrian Democratic Sabor (IDS) is cautiously preparing a ground for the country's federalization and, if necessary, the secession of Istria and its inclusion in the European regional association and eventually in the EU.

Wars of myths and symbols with mutually provocative commemorations have continued in all successor states. After the 1991–95 wars in Croatia and Bosnia-Herzegovina that left thousands of places of worship in ruins, religious organizations strove to rebuild their resources but found it difficult to break the barriers erected by war and cross new boundaries of the successor states and "ethnically cleansed" areas. Since 1995, the Catholic Church in Bosnia has made a number of unsuccessful attempts to restore regular worship and rebuild churches in Serb-held territories. Likewise, returning Muslim pilgrims were unwelcome both in Serb and Croat territories. In the town of Stolac, "cleansed" of Muslims by Croat militants, the local Croats several times blocked the Islamic Community's attempt to rebuild the city mosque. The Serbs were even more militant. On 11 July 2000 and again on the same day in 2001, the Islamic Community of Bosnia, with thousands of Muslim pilgrims, protected by international peacekeepers from angry Serb mobs, commemorated the massacre of several thousand Muslim prisoners of war by Serbs at the town of Srebrenica. Attempts to held commemorations and rebuild mosques caused incidents, as in Srebrenica and Banja Luka in May 2001, when a Muslim pilgrim was killed. After the Banja Luka incident, the reis-ul-ulema Mustafa Cerić reiterated in several public speeches that life in the same state with the Serbs (whom he designated racists, fascists, and people sick with hatred) would not be feasible.[51]

Shrines, monuments, and sites of history and memory continue to be potential flashpoints. Memorials to victims of genocide (committed by all and denied by all) have been held every now and then. The Serbian Orthodox Church has lamented over the lost "Serbian Jerusalem." Serb church leaders call for pilgrimages to Kosovo, as well as to Jasenovac and elsewhere in Croatia, and to historic sites in Macedonia, Bosnia-Herzegovina, and Montenegro. The Serbian Orthodox Church may sooner or later demand from the Croatian government the construction of the old project of the "Temple of the Atonement" at Jasenovac. The Serbian Church is likely to request from the Macedonian government in Skopje the rebuilding of memorials at World War I battlefields in Macedonia, not to mention the renovation and better care of Macedonian monasteries built by the Serbian medieval kings. Of the Albanian authorities in Kosovo, the Serbian Church will be asking permission to rebuild the Djakovica cathedral and other destroyed churches and monasteries, along with numerous projects concerning the renovation and maintenance of the Serbian sacred heritage in Kosovo. If Kosovo is granted statehood, the Serb myth will be only reinvigorated. The major slogan of Serbian right-wing politics will be "We shall return." And as long as the shrines built by medieval Serb kings stand, this return, in the form of apparently peaceful, devout pilgrims or armed soldiers in tanks, must not be ruled out. If the shrines are destroyed, the Serbs will return to rebuild them. Kosovo will remain "Serbian Jerusalem." The news that a moderate Albanian party has won the November 2001 Kosovo elections should not be considered very good news, because all Albanian parties demand the full-fledged statehood and independence of Kosovo, thus playing into the hands of Serb nationalists. There is no politics or economy that can insulate Kosovo Albanians from the power of the Kosovo myth and cast a shadow over the Christian shrines of "Serbian Jerusalem." The Albanians may have statehood, but the Serbs have the shrines and the Albanians don't. Albanian statehood in Kosovo is about politics and the economy. "Serbian Jerusalem" is about what Mircea Eliade, drawing from Nietzsche, termed the Myth of the Eternal Return. In a nutshell, Kosovo will remain the fountainhead of Serbian nationalism. There will be always someone in Belgrade calling on the Serbs to do something similar to Israel's 1967 reconquest of Jerusalem. These "eternal returns," symbolic or material, are likely to continue in Kosovo and elsewhere in the region. The may surface as cultural movements, with commemorations, pilgrimages, lamentations, nostalgia, and traditional motives in literature, film, music, art, and religion but no dramatic political implications. They also may evolve into political movements and even revolutions. It is difficult to say which scenario is more likely to occur. If secularization and globalization keep on advancing concurrently with European integration and a successful transition to democracy in postcommunist countries, the "culture only" scenario seems more likely. If new socioeconomic crises hit the area and the power of myth and religion is recalled by local nationalistic elements, new battles are not to be ruled out.

Crises, of course, are not only possible—they are the reality. The economic situation has been critical for more than two decades now. Ethnic political parties in Bosnia-Herzegovina, Kosovo, Macedonia, Croatia, Serbia, and Montenegro are often linked with international organized crime. It is not uncommon for members of governments, party leaders, and even premiers of local regimes to be investigated by international and domestic police or indicted for criminal activities and corruption by independent press, but prosecutions and resignations have rarely occurred, police investigators, justice ministers and judges, and independent journalists give up more often. According to a 2001 analysis by an international nongovernmental organization, "both the fighting in Macedonia and the move by the Croatian Democratic Community in Bosnia highlight the strong link between nationalist forces and criminal activity."[52]

International faith-based conflict management, reconciliation efforts, religious relief, and interfaith understanding have made noticeable progress, but, as noted in chapter 10, have generated ambiguous outcomes. It would be fair to acknowledge, however, that "religious statecraft" has become an established and welcome "missing dimension" of international diplomacy. After all, international diplomacy has always lacked a moral dimension, so any kind of moral support should be welcome. At the same time, religious organizations, like any group or individual, merit an opportunity to redeem religion for the centuries-old grim record of conflict and mass crime rooted in religion or aggravated by religion, and often incited by religious organizations. Regarding the concrete post-1991 religious peacebuilding effort in what used to be Yugoslavia, according to a 2001 analysis released by United States Institute of Peace, numerous religious relief missions, programs for promoting interfaith dialogue, and concrete peace and development programs funded by American and other western NGOs, private groups, individuals, and governments have been implemented in Bosnia and Herzegovina, Kosovo, Macedonia, Croatia, Serbia, and Montenegro.[53] It must be noted that U.S. Christian denominations have been, as always, the most active: Quakers, Mennonites, Methodists, Baptists, and others have established themselves as a relevant global factor in conflict management and peace-building.[54] These American religious peace-builders merit gratitude for their good will and effort, although their Balkan operation was based on the mistaken assumption that local mainstream faiths need help as victims of Marxist atheism instead of as people pushed into the excessive worship of ethnic nations by, among others, religious institutions. Thus, in the words of William Vendley, of the World Conference for Religion and Peace, "some conflicts derive from too little religion rather than too much, from spirituality that has been enfeebled by such forces as communist rule in Yugoslavia."[55] By now these benevolent foreigners may have realized (although they do not say it in public and on conferences) that the local established faiths and their hierarchies pose the major problem in peace-building, as opposed to the many helpful and cooperative individual clergy and believers who are otherwise attacked by ethnic nationalists as the old regime's "fellow travelers." Bosnian Franciscans such as Marko Oršolić and Ivo Marković, who have contributed remarkably to the international peace process in Bosnia-Herzegovina, have been targets of attacks from their own church leaders, such as Cardinal Vinko Puljić and others, not to mention the Muslim reis Mustafa Cerić and his militant clerics and the nationalist Serb clerics of the

Serb Republic. According to the Bosnian author Ivan Lovrenović, Cerić accused Oršolić of founding a "private multireligion" in cooperation with the West by which he helps "Serbs, Muslims, and children of the communists."[56] I also recall that during my 1997 tenure at United States Institute of Peace some Catholic Church leaders from Croatia and Bosnia who visited Washington denounced to their American hosts the peace-making Friar Oršolić as "Marxist." If only there had been more Marxists like him.

Speaking further of the religious contribution to peace-building, it must be acknowledged that the Catholic Church also has contributed a great deal, especially American Catholic organizations and the Vatican-based Community of St. Egidio.[57] Unfortunately, contribution from the Orthodox Church, otherwise critical for the Balkans, remains unsatisfactory. Some representatives from the Orthodox Church took part in an international "Truth and Reconciliation Conference" in May 2001 in Belgrade, but no self-criticisms have been heard so far from the hierarchy. Consequently, while foreign religious mediators with cooperative domestic lower clergy struggle for Balkan peace, the leaders of the Serbian Orthodox Church, the Catholic Church in Croatia and Bosnia-Herzegovina, and most of the Muslim ulema in Bosnia and Herzegovina remain hostile to each other and linked with ethnic nationalistic parties all pursuing the ideal of sectlike states. As I showed in chapter 11, the Catholic Church in Croatia launched a full-fledged war against a liberal government in order to bring back the ethnonationalistic HDZ to power. The same church continued lobbying on behalf of Croatian military and paramilitary leaders wanted by the Hague war crimes tribunal. For that matter, the Croatian Catholic hierarchy does not differ from that of the Serbian Orthodox Church, whose leaders never supported the international prosecution of Radovan Karadžić, Ratko Mladić, and other Serb war crimes suspects. In a 2001 regional report, the Institute for War and Peace Reporting quoted Serbian Orthodox scholar Mirko Djordjević as saying, "Our Church has been inconsistent in this matter, blinded by nationalist feelings. Thus it takes the view that we all sinned equally, but the Serbian side suffered more." According to the same report, another inside critic has been discovered in the Serbian Church, by the name of Mirko Tomović, who said as follows: "I'd like to see Patriarch Pavle (the head of the Orthodox Church), accompanied by a crowd of Serb people and oxen, candles in hand, travel 200 kilometer to Srebrenica on foot, in an effort to beg for forgiveness for everything the Serbian people did to others in this war. That is what Christ would have done, it is a Christian thing to do. Then let others consider what was done to us."[58]

Accordingly, it seems that the theory about good lower clergy and "citizens of faith" but problematic leaders and hierarchies of mainstream religious organizations that originated in the liberal phase of the communist era was not a mere product of the old regime's failure to exploit religious leaders as champions of brotherhood and unity. Ever since the 1930s, the most difficult problems in interfaith relations as well as church-state relations within mainstream faiths have come "from above." However, this theory is still an oversimplification. Although I generally hesitate to seek excuses for leaders, focusing rather on their responsibilities, it must be noted that hard historical circumstances that affected the Balkan peoples in general have often transformed moderate religious leaders into zealots. The political outlook of Cardinal Alojzije Stepinac was decisively shaped by two historical events: the concordat crisis of the 1930s and the communist revolution in 1945. Likewise, the moderate Serb Orthodox patriarch Germanus Djorić turned into a zealot and ethnic nationalist extremist at the age of eighty-seven under the pressures of several combined factors, such as the "triple schism" within the church, the relative progress of Catholicism and Islam, the worsening of the Kosovo crisis, the rise of Milošević, the nationalistic responses from the Catholic Church in Croatia, the European anticommunist euphoria of 1989, and so forth. I would also argue that the Islamic Community has always been relatively less nationalistic and militant. The Serb anti-Muslim campaign of the 1980s and, most of all, war and genocide in Bosnia-Herzegovina have produced numerous Islamic hawks in the IZ and made Arab revolutionary Islam popular in Bosnia-Herzegovina. Thus, for example, the currently ultrahawkish reis-ul-ulema Mustafa Cerić appeared to me, when I interviewed him on the occasion of the Gulf War, to be an ambitious Arab-educated Muslim cleric, and I described him as a moderate. Yet, fueled by the horrors of the Bosnian war and Milošević's assault on Albanians in Kosovo, militancy swamped Muslim communities not only in Bosnia but also in Kosovo and Macedonia. Now Islamic hawks could be found even among the two most moderate Muslim religious communities I found in the Balkans, the Slavic Muslims of Macedonia and the sufi (dervish) orders in Kosovo. I think that I can conclude the same about the recently increasingly nationalistic archbishop of Sarajevo, Vinko Cardinal Puljić. Although I spoke with him only briefly, I followed his career and came to the conclusion that he is one of the young, highly competent members of the Vatican's "cadres for the twentieth first century." Puljić was originally a moderate church leader and turned into a militant after his disappointment with the international community, combined with his frustration over the decline of the Croat population in Bosnia-Herzegovina and his conviction that neither the local Serb nor Muslim communities will communities will ever sincerely cooperate. Nonetheless, although religious leaders operating in such a rough setting as the Balkans might have had more or less compelling reasons for feeling what Mircea Eliade has termed the perennial religious communities' "fear of extinction," which often turned them into zealots, it is strange and discouraging how quickly and easily religious leaders succumb to this fear and lose faith and patience. Besides, one can never be sure when the religious leaders' "fear of extinction" is real and when they intentionally magnify it in order to mobilize the faithful against the "other," to revitalize faith, boost the cohesion of the religio-national community, and consolidate privileged social status of the clergy.

All things considered, it seems that, generally speaking, religious leaders still pose a relatively less difficult problem than the nature of the religious faiths, corrupted by ethnic nationalism, ethnoclericalism, antisecularism, fundamentalism, and similar "isms," combined with these faiths' notorious inability to coexist in multinational states or to accomplish any significant breakthrough through interfaith dialogue on a either regional or global scale. Serbian Orthodoxy, Croatian Catholicism, Bosnian Islam, and Macedonian Orthodoxy may not even be considered faiths but ideologies and nationalistic (i.e., political) organizations. As such, they may not qualify for tax relief and international aid normally granted to religious institutions and should not be viewed as a part of civil society but as components of the state. Likewise, attacks on them would definitely not constitute "religious persecution" but civic duty and a struggle for civil liberties. Small wonder that many NGOs and democratic forces view these national churches as the chief obstacles to a more efficient transition to democracy. However, I have found that religious leaders' responsibility concerns above all their ability to make proper assessment of whether rival faiths and ethnic groups, new ideologies, and other challenges constitute a "clear and present danger." In other words, religious leaders are in charge of the survival of their communities, but one will never know when a challenge is real and dangerous and when leaders are magnifying and dramatizing it so as to mobilize the faithful and revitalize faith, whose chief enemies are indifference, monotony, and decay.

An optimistic note is, of course, in order in the concluding paragraph. Because we all must believe in something, let us pick up from the garden of currently most appealing idols the one known as the new Europe, and let us believe that that is what distinguishes the Balkan case from those of the hopeless Palestine, Lebanon, Kashmir, Somalia, and so on. Europe must be the key to the problem under consideration, because the peculiarity of Balkan history has remained unchanged—that is, that the Balkan peoples shed blood propelled by the desire to master their own destiny, only to realize after each bloody cycle of local wars that the masters of their destiny are outsiders. Finally, one really must be an arch-pessimist to say that the Europe of the Congress of Berlin and that of the Maastricht Treaty are completely the same.

The new Europe seems to be looking more self-confident than it was during the Renaissance and the age of discoveries. Europe is bent on "absorbing," overcoming, and healing many formidable problems, from the Holocaust to the legacies of communism and the Cold War, from Cyprus to Catalonia, the Basque country, and Northern Ireland. The Balkans stand halfway between Cyprus and Catalonia and cannot be skipped over. After all, the EU, UN, and private groups or governments from many countries have done much so far to help stabilization, recovery, and democratization in the Balkans. The European Union, led by Germany as the major donor, has provided a great deal of assistance for the region. Massive material and human resources have been employed in service of peace, stability and democratic transition of the new Balkan states. Relieved by the departure of the three ethnic extremist leaders, the EU officials in charge of the troubled Southeast have called for more financial and other effort.[59] Moreover, in 1999, the European Union founded an ambitious and expensive long-term program known as the Stability Pact for South Eastern Europe.[60] This pact, although it has hitherto made ambiguous progress, is based on the correct assumption that the Yugoslav peoples depend on each other and must work together in the region, emulating what Europe is doing at the continental level; that is, the peoples of southeastern Europe should solve their problems by themselves, and Europe will help.[61] To all intents and purposes, this kind of international community differs from the foreign supervisors of southeastern Europe in earlier epochs. The EU and the world seem to be willing to help and have already helped a great deal. In order to make use of the opportunity, however, the Yugoslav peoples have been again invited by the EU to work together. Yet this time they are not being expected to accomplish such an ambitious goal as brotherhood and unity. The rational postmodern EU and the West do not go that far. The Yugoslav peoples are invited to a rational collaboration based on mutual respect, tolerance, and observance of the laws, norms, and standards under which Western democracies operate. This presumably will not result in brotherhood, yet some degree of unity, without the risk of another fratricidal war may be accomplished. The East, willy-nilly, emulates the West, and the Balkans have no choice but to follow Europe. After ages of war, the new Europe—more religiously indifferent and less ideologically passionate than ever—seems to be making progress in attaining unity with little concern about any kind of brotherhood.

just respect, you don't have to preach BROTHER-HOOD etc.

NOTES

Preface

1. Samuel P. Huntington, *Religion and the Third Wave: Democratization in the Late Twentieth Century* (Norman: University of Oklahoma Press, 1991).

2. See, for example, George Weigel, *The Final Revolution: The Resistance Church and the Collapse of Communism* (New York: Oxford University Press, 1992) and Jonathan Luxmoore and Jolanta Babiuch, *The Vatican and the Red Flag: The Struggle for the Soul of Eastern Europe* (London: Chapman, 1999).

3. According to Richard J. Beyer, *Medjugorje Day by Day* (Notre Dame, IN: Ave Maria Press, 1993).

4. Eric J. Hobsbawm, *The Age of Extremes: A History of the World, 1914–1991* (New York: Vintage Books, 1994).

5. "Cross vs. Crescent: The Battle Lines Are Being Redrawn in Bosnia along Old Religious Scars: The Roots Go Back to the Great Schism and the Ottoman Turks," *New York Times*, 17 September 1992.

6. See Mark Danner, series of essays, *New York Review of Books*, November 1997–April 1998; Sarah A. Kent, "Writing the Yugoslav Wars: English-Language Books on Bosnia (1992–1996) and the Challenges of Analyzing Contemporary History," *American Historical Review* 102 (October 1997); Quintin Hoare and Noel Malcolm, eds., *Books on Bosnia: A Critical Bibliography of Works Relating to Bosnia-Herzegovina Published Since 1990 in Western European Languages* (London: Bosnian Institute, 1999); John B. Allcock, Marko Milivojevic, and John J. Horton, eds., *Roots of Modern Conflict: Conflict in the Former Yugoslavia—An Encyclopedia* (Santa Barbara, CA: ABC-CLIO Books, 1998); and Rusko Matulic, *Bibliography of Sources on the Region of Former Yugoslavia* (Boulder, CO: East European Monographs, 1999).

7. Including Rebecca West, *Black Lamb and Grey Falcon: The Record of a Journey through Yugoslavia in 1937* (London: Macmillan, 1941). I used the 1995 reprint *Black Lamb and Grey Falcon: A Journey through Yugoslavia* (New York: Penguin Books, 1969; rpt. 1995).

8. Robert Kaplan, *Balkan Ghosts: A Journey through History* (New York: Random House, 1994); *Eastward to Tartary: Travels in the Balkans, the Middle East and the Caucasus* (New York: Random House, 2000).

9. See "The Middle East and the Balkans" *Foreign Affairs*, 80, 1 (January–February 2001).

10. Sabrina P. Ramet, *Balkan Babel: Politics, Culture, and Religion in Yugoslavia* (Boulder, CO: Westview Press, 1992, 1996, 1999, and 2002); Paul Mojzes, *Yugoslavian Inferno: Ethnoreligious Warfare in the Balkans* (New York: Continuum, 1994); Paul Mojzes, ed., *Religion and the War in Bosnia* (Atlanta, GA: Scholar Press, 1998).

11. Samuel P. Huntington, *The Clash of Civilizations and the Remaking of World Order* (New York: Simon and Schuster, 1996), pp. 95–101; Peter L. Berger, "Secularism in Retreat," *National Interest* (winter 1996–97), pp. 3–12; "Symposium: The Impact of Religion on Global Affairs," *SAIS Review* (summer–fall 1998). "Faith and Statecraft—A Special Issue on Religion in World Affairs," *Orbis* 42, 2 (spring 1998); Peter L. Berger, ed., *The Desecularization of the World: Resurgent Religion and World Politics* (Washington, DC: Ethics and Public Policy Center, 1999); and Gilles Kepel, *The Revenge of God: The Resurgence of Islam, Christianity and Judaism in the Modern World*, trans. Alan Braley (University Park: Penn State University Press, 1994).

12. See for example, Hobsbawm, *The Age of Extremes*, p. 566; John Lukacs, *The End of the Twentieth Century and the End of the Modern Age* (New York: Ticknor and Fields, 1993), pp. 225–231; and Sabrina P. Ramet, *Nihil Obstat: Religion, Politics, and Social Change in East-Central Europe and Russia* (Durham, NC: Duke University Press, 1998).

13. See for example, Mark Juergensmeyer, *The New Cold War? Religious Nationalism Confronts the Secular State* (Berkeley: University of California Press, 1993), and *Terror in the Mind of God: The Global Rise of Religious Violence* (Berkeley: University of California Press, 2000). Peter Van Der Veer, *Religious Nationalism: Hindus and Muslims in India* (Berkeley: University of California Press, 1994); Peter Van Der Veer and Hartmut Lehmann, eds., *Nation and Religion: Perspectives on Europe and Asia* (Princeton, NJ: Princeton University Press, 1999), and John L. Esposito and Michael Watson, *Religion and Global Order* (Cardiff: University of Wales Press, 2000).

14. See, for example, Zdenko Roter, *Katoliška cerkev in država v Jugoslaviji 1945–1973* (The Catholic Church and the state in Yugoslavia 1945–1973) (Ljubljana: Cankarjeva Založba, 1976); Ivan Mužić, *Katolička crkva u Kraljevini Jugoslaviji: Politički i pravni aspekti konkordata izmedju Svete Stolice i Kraljevine Jugoslavije* (The Catholic Church in the Kingdom of Yugoslavia: Political and legal aspects of the Concordat between the Holy See and the Kingdom of Yugoslavia) (Split: Crkva u svijetu, 1978); Esad Ćimić, *Metodologijski doseg istraživanja unutar sociologije religije u Hrvatskoj* (The methodological breakthrough in the research in the sociology of religion in Croatia) (Zagreb: IDIS, 1991); Ivan Grubišić et al., *Religija i Sloboda: Prilog socioreligijskoj karti Hrvatske* (Split: Institut za primjenjena društvena istraživanja, 1993); Stella Alexander, *Church and State in Yugoslavia since 1945* (London: Cambridge University Press, 1979); and *The Triple Myth: A Life of Archbishop Alojzije Stepinac* (Boulder, CO: East European Monographs, 1987); Paul Mojzes, *Religious Liberty in Eastern Europe and USSR—Before and After the Great Transformation* (Boulder, CO: East European Monographs, 1992); Pedro Ramet, *Cross and Commisar: The Politics of Religion in Eastern Europe and the USSR* (Bloomington; Indiana University Press, 1987).

15. See Ivo Banac, "The Dissolution of Yugoslav Historiography," in *Beyond Yugoslavia: Politics, Economics and Culture in a Shattered Community*, ed. Sabrina P. Ramet and Ljubisa S. Adamovich (Boulder, CO: Westview Press, 1995), p. 40.

16. Ivo Banac, *The National Question in Yugoslavia: Origins, History, Politics* (Ithaca, NY: Cornell University Press, 1984): Milorad Ekmečić, *Stvaranje Jugoslavije 1790–1918* (The creation of Yugoslavia 1790–1918), 2 vols. (Belgrade: Prosveta, 1989).

17. Banac, *National Question*, p. 410.

18. Ibid. See also Jure Krišto, *Prešućena povijest: Katolička crkva u hrvatskoj politici 1850–1918* (An untold history: The Catholic Church in Croatian Politics 1850–1918) (Zagreb: Hrvatska Sveučilišna naklada, 1994).

19. Ekmečić, *Stvaranje Jugoslavije 1790–1918*.

20. Ibid. In a series of essays published during the prewar crisis, Ekmečić drew analogies between Yugoslavia, Lebanon, and Northern Ireland. Milorad Ekmečić, "Jugoslavenski krst, križ, i polumesec," series of 13 articles and interviews, *Borba*, February–March 1990.

21. See Ljubo Boban, *Kontroverze iz povijesti Jugoslavije* (Controversies from the history of Yugoslavia), vols. 1–3 (Zagreb: Školska knjiga, 1987; 1989; 1990); Banac, "Dissolution of Yugoslav Historiography."

22. See Robert N. Bellah, introduction to *Varieties of Civil Religion*, by Robert N. Bellah and Phillip E. Hammond (San Francisco: Harper and Row, 1980), pp. i–xv. See also Sabrina P. Ramet, "Sacred Values and the Tapestry of Power: An Introduction," in *Render unto Caesar: The Religious Sphere in World Politics*, Sabrina P. ed. Ramet and Donald W. Treadgold, pp. 6–9; Van Der Veer and Lehmann, *Nation and Religion*; Roland Robertson, *The Sociological Interpretation of Religion* (Oxford: Blackwell, 1970), esp. pp. 38–39.

23. Paul Mojzes, *Yugoslavian Inferno: Ethnoreligious Warfare in the Balkans* (New York: Continuum, 1994) and Paul Mojzes, ed., *Religion and the War in Bosnia* (Atlanta, GA: Scholar Press, 1998); Miroslav Volf, *Exclusion and Embrace: A Theological Exploration of Identity, Otherness and Reconciliation* (Nashville: Abingdon Press, 1996); Mirko Djordjević, *Znaci vremena* (Belgrade: Janus, 1998) and "Ratni out Srpske crkve" in *Republika*, Belgrade, no. 273, 16–30 November 2001; and Michael A. Sells, *The Bridge Betrayed: Religion and Genocide in Bosnia* (Berkeley: University of California Press, 1996).

24. Reinhold Niebuhr, *The Nature and Destiny of Man*, vol. 1 *Humane Nature* (Louisville: Kentucky: Westminster John Knox Press, 1996), p. 210; Robert N. Bellah, *The Broken Covenant: American Civil Religion in Time of Trial*, 2d ed. (Chicago: University of Chicago Press, 1992), p. 162.

25. Misha Glenny, *The Balkans, 1804–1999: Nationalism, War and the Great Powers* (London: Granta Books, 1999).

1. Religion, Ethnicity, and Nationhood

1. Dečani monastery website: http//www.decani.com/destruction.html, 21 May 2000. According to Serbian church sources, between 13 June and 20 October 1999, 74 Christian churches, monasteries, and cemeteries had been destroyed by Albanian Muslim militants. See *Raspeto Kosovo: Uništene i oskrnavljene Srpske pravoslavne crkve na Kosovo i Metohiji, Jun-Avgust 1999* (Crucified Kosovo: Destroyed and desecrated Serbian Orthodox churches in Kosovo and Metohija, June–August 1999) (Prizren: Raška-Prizren Diocese, 1999).

2. See Andrew Herscher and Andras Riedlmayer, *Architectural Heritage in Kosovo: A Post-War Report* (London: Bosnia Report, September 2000); "Libraries and Archives in Kosovo: A Postwar Report," http//www.bosnia.org.uk/bosrep/

decfeboo/libraries.htm, "Museums in Kosovo: A First Postwar Assessment," http: //www.bosnia.org.uk/bosrep/marjuneoo/museums.htm.

3. In 1996, the Croatian bishops' conference announced that Serbs had destroyed 571 churches in Croatia. In 1998, Bosnian bishops reported about 269 destroyed Catholic churches in Bosnia. See Ilija Živković, ed., *Ranjena Crkva u Hrvatskoj—uništavanje sakralnih objekata u Hrvatskoj 1991–1995* (Wounded Church in Croatia—Destruction of places of worship in Croatia 1991–1995) (Zagreb: Hrvatski Informativni centar, 1996); Ilija Živković, ed., *Raspeta Crkva u Bosni i Hercegovini—uništavanje Katoličkih sakralnih objekata u Bosni i Hercegovini 1991– 1996* (The crucified Church in Bosnia and Herzegovina—Destruction of Catholic sacred buildings in Bosnia and Herzegovina 1991–1996 (Zagreb: Hrvatski Informativni centar, 1998).

4. According to the Rijasset (supreme administrative body) of the Islamic Community, out of 1,112 mosques that existed before the war in Bosnia-Herzegovina, the Serbs destroyed 534 mosques, three Muslim monasteries, and several hundred other religious facilities. In the 1993–94 Croat-Muslim war, Croat militants destroyed 80 mosques, 43 masdjids, one Muslim monastery, and 70 other religious facilities. "Djamija po glavi stanovnika," *Dan*, no. 61, October 1997.

5. Slobodan Mileusnić, ed., *Duhovni genocid: pregled porušenih, oštećenih i obesvećenih crkava, manastira i drugih crkvenih objekata u ratu 1991–1993* (Spiritual genocide: A survey of destroyed, damaged, and desecrated churches, monasteries, and other church buildings during the war 1991–1993) (Belgrade: Muzej Srpske pravoslavne crkve with Privredne vesti Europublic, 1994). Three more volumes of Mileusnićs "Spiritual Genocide" were published in 1996, 1998, and 2000. See also data in *Duga*, no 1733, 26 February 2000.

6. The Croatian church historian Josip Turćinović argued that Bosnia-Herzegovina was evidently a Christian, preeminently Catholic country before the sixteenth-century Ottoman conquest. Yet numerous Christian churches were destroyed by the Muslim invaders. Turćinović noted that in the northern Bosnian Banja Luka area, "where once there were more than 120 churches and 15 Franciscan and many Dominican and Templar monasteries, Catholics were reduced to an evident minority group." Josip Turćinović, *Katolićka crkva u južnoslavenskim zemljama* (The Catholic Church in South Slav lands) (Zagreb: Kršćanska sadašnjost, 1973) pp.35–38.

7. Dusko Doder, *The Yugoslavs* (New York: Random House, 1978), pp. 18–19.

8. John A. Armstrong, *Nations before Nationalism* (Chapel Hill: University of North Carolina Press, 1982), pp. 5–6.

9. Peter Van Der Veer, *Religious Nationalism: Hindus and Muslims in India* (Berkeley: University of California Press, 1994), p. 214.

10. George L. Mosse, *The Nationalization of the Masses: Political Symbolism and Mass Movements in Germany from the Napoleonic Wars through the Third Reich* (Ithaca, NY: Cornell University Press, 1975). See also, on the interaction between religion and the nationalist politics, Sabrina Petra Ramet and Donald W. Treadgold, eds., *Render unto Caesar: Religion in World Politics* (Washington, D.C.: Catholic University of America Press, 1995).

11. Civil religion is defined by Bellah as an institutionalized pattern of symbols and practices that evokes people's commitment and legitimizes the political authority. Robert N. Bellah, "Civil Religion in America," *Daedalus* 96 (1967), pp. 1–21.

12. See Chrystel Lane, *The Rites of Rulers: Ritual in Industrial Society—The*

Soviet Case (Cambridge, UK: Cambridge University Press, 1981); James Thrower, *God's Commissar: Marxism-Leninism as the Civil Religion of Soviet Society* (Lewiston, NY: Mellen Press, 1992).

13. Mircea Eliade, *Images and Symbols: Studies in Religious Symbolism*, transl. Philip Mairet (New York: Sheed and Ward, 1961), p. 56.

14. Bronislaw Malinowski, *Magic, Science and Religion, and Other Essays* (Westport, CT: Greenwood Press, 1984).

15. Eric J. Hobsbawm, *Nations and Nationalism since 1780*, p. 12.

16. According to the 1882 lecture by Ernest Renan, "What Is a Nation?" in *Becoming National: A Reader*, ed. Geoff Eley and Ronald Grigor Suny (New York: Oxford University Press, 1996). See also Benedict Anderson, *Imagined Communities: Reflections on the Origin and Spread of Nationalism* (London: Verso, 1983), pp. 198–201.

17. Quoted in Stephen Metcalf, ed, *Hammer of the Gods: Selected Writings by Friedrich Nietzsche* (London: Creation Books, 1996), pp. 211–214.

18. *Austrian History Yearbook* 3 (Minneapolis: Center for Austrian Studies, 1967), p. 217.

19. According to the census of 1921, in the first Yugoslav common state (1918–1941) the total population of Yugoslavia was 46.6 percent Orthodox; 39.4 percent Roman Catholics; 11.1 percent Muslims; 1.8 percent Protestants; 0.5 percent Jews; 0.3 percent Greek Catholics, and so forth. In 1953, there were 41.7 percent Serbs; 5.2 percent Macedonians and 2.7 percent Montenegrins (the Orthodox by religion made up 41.5 percent of the total population); 23.4 percent Croats and 8.7 percent Slovenes (31.8 percent Catholics by religion); and 5.8 percent Muslim by religion or "Muslim by cultural background" who declined to specify ethnic background, presumed to be Serb or Croat. Srdjan Vrcan, "Religion, Nation and Class in Contemporary Yugoslavia," in *The Influence of the Frankfurt School on Contemporary Theology—Critical Theory and the Future of Religion*, ed. James A. Reimer (Lewiston, NY: Mellen Press, 1992), p. 92.

20. Ibid., p. 92.

21. "Strahinja Maletić: XX vek u tridesetak slika" (Strahinja Maletić: The twentieth century in thirty fragments and images), *NIN*, no. 2570, 30 March 2000.

22. Michael Radu, "The Burden of Eastern Orthodoxy," *Orbis* 42, 2 (spring 1998), p. 283.

23. Ibid., p. 285.

24. Michael B. Petrovich, *A History of Modern Serbia: 1804–1918* (New York: Harcourt Brace Jovanovich, 1976), p. 10.

25. The Monasteries of Sopoćani and Studenica in southwestern Serbia are the only Serbian monasteries on the UNESCO World Heritage List (no monument in Kosovo is on this list).

26. According to church sources, two thousand more or less preserved temples and other religious facilities, harboring the relics of native Serbian saints and rulers, with some twenty thousand holy icons, frescoes, and mosaics, are scattered across Kosovo, Macedonia, and southern Serbia. Over a thousand shrines are located in Kosovo alone. *Pravoslavlje*, 15 January 1991; Atanasije Jevtić, *Stradanja Srba na Kosovu i Metohiji od 1941 do 1990* (Tribulations of Serbs in Kosovo and Metohija from 1941 to 1990) (Priština: Jedinstvo, 1990), p. 449.

27. Charles Jelavich, "Some Aspects of Serbian Religious Development in the Eighteenth Century," *Church History* 23 (1954), pp. 144–152.

28. J. Gardner Wilkinson, *Dalmatia and Montenegro*, vol. 1 (London: John Murray, 1848), pp. 530–531.

29. Ibid., p. 472.

30. See among numerous works on the meaning of Kosovo, Vojin Matić, *Psihoanaliza mitske prošlosti* (A psychoanalysis of the mythical past) (Belgrade: Prosveta, 1976); Wayne S. Vucinich and Thomas A. Emmert, eds., *Kosovo: Legacy of a Medieval Battle*, Minnesota Mediterranean and East European Monographs, vol. 1 (Minneapolis: University of Minnesota, 1991); Warren Zimmermann, *Origins of a Catastrophe: Yugoslavia and Its Destroyers. America's Last Ambassador Tells What Happened and Why* (New York: Times Books, 1996); and Warren Zimmermann, "The Demons of Kosovo," *National Interest*, 52 (spring 1998).

31. See Vuchinich and Emmert, *Kosovo: Legacy of a Medieval Battle*.

32. According to official Yugoslav census data, in 1921, 65.8 percent of Kosovo's population were Albanian and 26 percent were Serbian. The first postwar census in 1948 shows that the percentage of Albanians grew and that of the Serbs decreased: Serbs were 23.6 percent and in 1981, only 13.2 percent Serbs lived in Kosovo. According to the last census in 1991, there were 81.6 percent Albanians and 9.9 percent Serbs. *Nacionalni sastav stanovništva SFRJ* (Population structure in SFRY by nationality) (Belgrade: Savremena administracija, 1991).

33. See Thomas A. Emmert, "Kosovo: Development and Impact of a National Ethic," in Ivo Banac, John G. Ackerman, and Roman Szporluk, eds., *Nation and Ideology: Essays in Honor of Wayne S. Vucinich* (New York: Eastern European Monographs, 1981), p. 80.

34. Hobsbawm, *Nations and Nationalism since 1780*, pp. 75–76.

35. Radoslav M. Grujić, *Pravoslavna srpska crkva* (The Orthodox Serb Church) (Kragujevac: Svetlost-Kalenić, 1989), pp. 93–94.

36. Ekmečić, *Stvaranje Jugoslavije 1790–1918*, vol. 1, p. 41.

37. Slobodan Mileusnić, *Sveti Srbi* (Saintly Serbs) (Kragujevac: Kalenić, 1989), p. 9.

38. See Ekmečić, preface to *Stvaranje Jugoslavije 1790–1918*, vol. I.

39. Ranković, Bigović, and Milovanović, *Vladika Nikolaj*, p. 224.

40. Ibid., p. 217.

41. The data come from *Relazioni religiose*, 29 March 1986; Radovan Samardžić, *Religious Communities in Yugoslavia* (Belgrade: Jugoslavenski Pregled, 1981), p. 38; *Intervju*, 29 March 1991.

42. See for example, Karlo Jurišić, "Ranije pokrštenje Hrvata i problem nedostatka arheoloških spomenika" (The earlier evangelization of the Croats and the problem of the lack of preserved archeological monuments), in *Počeci hrvatskog kršćanskog i društvenog života od VII do kraja IX stoljeća; Radovi drugog medjunarodnog simpozija o hrvatskoj crkvenoj i društvenoj povijesti* (Origins of Croatian Christian and social life from the Twelfth to the end of the Nineteenth Century: Works of the Second International Symposium on Croat Church and Social History) (Split: Nadbiskupija Splitsko-Makarska, 1990). See also Nenad Gatin et al., *Starohrvatska sakralna arhitektura* (Ancient Croatian sacred architecture) (Zagreb: Nakladni zavod Matice Hrvatske; Kršćanska sadašnjost, 1982).

43. See Karlo Jurišić, *Fra Lujo Marun, osnivač starohrvatske arheologije: 1857–1939* (Franciscan Lujo Marun, the founder of Croatian Archeology: 1857–1939) (Split: Zbornik Kačič, 1979).

44. See, among many sources on this, the Roman Catholic Church of Poland website: http//www.ipipan.waw.

45. See Mileusnić, *Sveti Srbi*, p. 8.

46. According to Samardžić, *Religious Communities in Yugoslavia*, p. 37; *Adresar Katoličke crkve u SFRJ* (Directory of the Catholic Church in SFRY) (Zagreb: Kršćanska sadašnjost, 1986); and *Katolička Crkva i Hrvati izvan domovine* (The Catholic Church and Croats out of the homeland), a monograph published by the Council of the Bishops' Conference for Croatian Migrants (Zagreb: Kršćanska sadašnjost, 1980), p. 55.

47. Ferdo Hauptman, *Borba Muslimana Bosne i Hercegovine za vjersku i vakufsko-mearifsku autonomiju* (The struggle of Muslims of Bosnia and Herzegovina for autonomy in legal and economic matters), vol. 3 (Sarajevo: Arhiv SR BiH, 1967).

48. According to Samardžić, *Religious Communities in Yugoslavia*, p. 39.

49. Ibid., p. 38.

50. According to the data from the Federal commission for relations with religious communities published in abbreviated form in Samardžić, *Religious Communities in Yugoslavia*.

51. Nikola Dugandžija, *Božija djeca—Religioznost u malim vjerskim zajednicama (uz zagrebačko istraživanje)* (God's children—Religiosity in the minor religious communities, on the occasion of the Zagreb Research Project) (Zagreb: Republička konferencija Saveza socijalističke omladine Hrvatske and Institut za društvena istraživanja Sveučilišta u Zagrebu, 1990). The survey included the following established religious organizations registered in Croatia: the Baptist Church; the Church of Jesus Christ of Latter-Day Saints; the Evangelical Church; the Croatian Catholic Church; the Jewish Community in Zagreb; the Christian Adventist Church; the Church of Christ; the Christ Church of Bethany; the Christ Church of Brethren; the Christ Spiritual Church; the Christ Spiritual Church of the Baptized; the Pentecostal Church of Christ; the Christian Reform Church, the Christian Community of Jehovah's Witnesses in the SFRY; the Reform Movement of Seventh-Day Adventists; and the Free Catholic Church.

52. Dugandžija, *Božja djeca*, pp. 50–51.

53. Ibid., pp. 104–105.

54. Komisija Saveznog Izvršnog vijeća (SIV) za odnose s vjerskim zajednicama (Commission of the Federal Executive Council for Relations with Religious Communities), "Odnosi s vjerskim zajednicama—Izveštaj o radu komisije" (Relations with religious communities—Annual report on the Commission's activity), Belgrade, 4 December 1982.

55. "Yugoslav religious relations," wrote Ivo Banac in his study on the origins of nationalism in Yugoslavia, "never occasioned religious wars on the scale of those fought in Western Europe after the Reformation." *The National Question in Yugoslavia*, p. 410.

56. ENM (Bishop Nikodim Milaš), *Pravoslavna Dalmacija* (Novi Sad: Knjižarnica A. Pajevića, 1901; reissued in Belgrade, 1989).

57. See Srećko M. Džaja, *Konfessionalitat und Nationalitat: Bosniens und der Herzegowina. Voremanzipatorische Phase 1463–1804* (Munich: Oldenbourg, (1984).

58. Drago Roksandić, "Religious Tolerance and Division in the Krajina: The Croatian Serbs of the Habsburg Military Border," in *Christianity and Islam in Southeastern Europe, occasional paper* no. 47 (Washington, DC: Woodrow Wilson Center for East European Studies, January 1997), p. 75. See also Sugar, "Nationalism and Religion in the Balkans since the Nineteenth Century."

2. The First Strife

1. Mužić, *Katolička crkva u Kraljevini Jugoslaviji*, pp. 218–221.

2. Nikolaj Velimirović, "Konkordatska borba 1937 godine" (The Concordat struggle in 1937), in *Vladika Nikolaj: izabrana dela. Knjiga XII*, ed. Ljubomir Ranković, Radovan Bigović, and Mitar Milovanović (Valjevo: Glas Crkve, 1997), p. 310.

3. Ibid., p. 342.

4. On 8 November 1929, the Yugoslav state assembly passed the "Law on the Serbian Orthodox Church." According to this law, the state provided salaries for the clergy and financial assistance to the church but also interfered in church affairs by influencing the election of the patriarch.

5. The Serbian Church perceived the new state as "the restoration of the state of the Serbian people.... Serb warriors defeated the enemy, liberated the country, united all our ethnic brothers, and created a state more spacious than Dušan's empire. The magnificent dreams of generations have come true.... By the political liberation and unification of the Serbian people, conditions for liberation and unification of all Serbian Churches and Church provinces have been thereby created." *Glasnik Srpske pravoslavne crkve*, no. 10, October 1970, p. 299.

6. According to a secular Catholic historian, "the foundation of the Kingdom of Serbs, Croats and Slovenes, the Catholic episcopate welcomed not only as a political necessity, but also as an opportunity for Roman Catholic penetration to the East." Mužić, *Katolička crkva u Kraljevini Jugoslaviji*, p. 202.

7. Also in the capital city, the grandiose church of Saint Mark was built in the 1930s. It was designed as an enlarged replica of the famous historic Gračanica church at the historic Kosovo battlefield. In the Kosovo province, the Serbian Orthodox Church was building new churches, renovating ancient ones and sponsoring archaeological excavations at historic sites. A new cathedral was built at Djakovica, six miles from the Albanian border. It had a mausoleum dedicated to four hundred heroes who died for Serbia in the Balkan wars of 1912–13 and in World War I. New Orthodox churches also appeared in the homogeneous Catholic Slovenia and predominantly Catholic Croatian coastline. The Slovene cities of Ljublijana, Maribor, and Celje acquired Orthodox byzantine temples. In Croatia, new Serbian churches were built at Sušak near Rijeka (Fiume), in Split, at Ston near Dubrovnik, and on the naval base of Vis.

8. A Catholic priest complained in a pamphlet on church affairs in the interwar kingdom that interfaith marriages "at the expense of the Catholic Church were deftly arranged and encouraged. Orthodox army officers were bound by a confidential circular to celebrate matrimony with a Catholic girl solely according to the Orthodox rite. Up to 1940 there were more than 30,000 of these mixed marriages." Guberina, "The Catholic Formation of Croatia," in Carlo Falconi, *The Silence of Pius XII*, trans. Bernard Wall (Boston: Little, Brown, 1970), p. 267.

9. In 1921 the census registered in the total population of Yugoslavia as 46.6 percent Orthodox and 39.4 percent Roman Catholics. In 1931, the census registered 48.7 percent Orthodox and 37.4 percent Catholics. Vrcan, "Religion, Nation and Class in Contemporary Yugoslavia," p. 92.

10. A church commission requested 3,997,472,632.50 dinars. In January 1940, the government agreed to pay 1,142,262,283.11 dinars. Risto Grbić, "O crkvenim finansijama" (On the Church's finances), in *Srpska Crkva na istorijskoj prekretnici* (Belgrade: Pravoslavlje, 1969), p. 7; see also Mužić, *Katoličk q crkva*, p. 31.

11. See Milo Mišović, *Srpska crkva i konkordatska kriza* (The Serbian Church and the Concordat crisis) (Belgrade: Sloboda, 1983), p. 170.

12. Ivo Guberina, "The Catholic Formation of Croatia," p. 269.

13. Ibid., p. 204.

14. Jevtić, *Sveti Sava i Kosovski zavet*, pp. 346–347.

15. Ranković et al., *Vladika Nikolaj*, p. 42.

16. Quoted in Emmert, "Kosovo—Development and Impact of a National Ethic," p. 80.

17. Eucharistic congresses were a form of mass mobilization of the faithful introduced in nineteenth-century France. The Catholic Church in the Yugoslav kingdom held Eucharistic congresses in 1923, 1930, and in 1935.

18. See James J. Sadkovich, *Italian Support for Croatian Separatism, 1927–1937* (New York: Garland, 1987).

19. Eric J. Hobsbawm, *Nations and Nationalism since 1780: Programme, Myth, Reality* (Cambridge, UK: Cambridge University Press, 1990), pp. 146–147.

20. On Četnik massacres of Muslims in Bosnia, see Vladimir Dedijer and Antun Miletić, *Genocid nad Muslimanima 1941–1945: zbornik dokumenata i svedočenja* (Sarajevo: Svijetlost, 1990). For an account on Četniks in Croatia and their crimes against the Catholic population, see Mile Vidović, *Povijest Crkve u Hrvata* (Split: Crkva u svijetu, 1995), pp. 403–411, and Fikreta Jelić-Butić, *Četnici u Hrvatskoj, 1941–1945* (Zagreb: Globus, 1986). See also generally on the Četniks "The Collaboration of D. Mihailovič's Chetniks with the Enemy Forces of Occupation: 1941–1944," in *Tajna i javna saradnja četnika i okupatora. English*, ed. Jovan Marjanović and Mihailo Stanišić (Belgrade: Arhivski pregled, 1976).

21. A Croatian independent analyst listed 22 such camps and noted that there were more. Vladimir Žerjavić, *Population Losses in Yugoslavia, 1941–1945* (Zagreb: Dom and Svijet, 1997), pp. 233–234.

22. See Ladislaus Hory, *Der Kroatische Ustascha-Staat, 1941–1945* (Stuttgart: Deutsche Verlags-Anstalt, 1964); Peter Broucek, ed., *Ein General in Zwielicht: Die Erinnerungen von Edmund Glaise von Horstenau* (Cologne: Bohlau, 1992).

23. Misha Glenny, *The Balkans: Nationalism, War and the Great Powers, 1804–1999* (London: Granta Books, 1999), pp. 494–506.

24. A list of names of Catholic clergy associated with the Ustašas, with accounts of these clerics' wartime activity based on communist authorities' post-1945 investigations, is given by Viktor Novak, in his *Magnum crimen—Pola vijeka klerikalizma u Hrvatskoj* (Belgrade: Nova Knjiga, 1986; 1st ed. 1946). Another different list of Catholic clergy, including those who supported the communist-led Partisan movement, can be found in Ćiril Petešić, *Katoličko svećenstvo u NOB-u 1941–1945* (The Catholic clergy in the People's Liberation Struggle 1941–1945) (Zagreb: Vjesnikova Press agencija, 1982). For information about Muslim clerics supportive of the Partisans, see *Spomenica Ilmije* (Sarajevo: Udruženje Islamskih vjerskih službenika, 1971). *Almanah—Srbi i pravoslavlje u Dalmaciji i Dubrovniku* (Zagreb: Savez udruženja srpskog pravoslavnog pravoslavnog sveštenstva u SR Hrvatskoj, 1971) provides an incomplete list of Serb Orthodox clergy who sided with the Partisans. Finally, information about Orthodox clergy in Macedonia during World War II can be found in Slavko Dimevski, *Istorija na Makedonskata pravoslavna crkva* (Skopje: Makedonska knjiga, 1989).

25. Veljko Djurić, "Pravoslavna crkva u tzv. Nezavisnoj Državi Hrvatskoj" (The Orthodox Church in the so-called Independent State of Croatia), in *Crkva 1991–Kalendar Srpske pravoslavne patrijaršije za prostu 1991 godinu: 1941–1991 Nezaceljene rane na telu Srpske crkve* (The Church 1991—A calendar of the Serbian

Orthodox patriarchate for the year 1991: 1941–1991, unhealed wounds in the body and flesh of the Serbian Church) (Belgrade: Sveti Arhijerejski Sinod, July 1990), p. 84.

26. According to estimates by a Croat secular historian, the conversions affected around 240,000 Orthodox Serbs. Jelić-Butić, *Ustaše i Nezavisna Država Hrvatska*, p. 175.

27. Edmond Paris, *Genocide in Satellite Croatia, 1941–1945: A Record of Racial and Religious Persecutions and Massacres*, trans. from the French by Lois Perkins (Chicago: American Institute for Balkan Affairs, 1961), p. 289–290.

28. Žerjavić, *Population Losses in Yugoslavia, 1941–1945*, p. 98.

29. "Fascist movements," wrote Hobsbawm, "had trouble in appealing to the genuinely traditional elements in rural society (unless reinforced, as in Croatia, by organizations like the Roman Catholic Church)." Eric Hobsbawm, *The Age of Extremes: a History of the World, 1914–1991*. (New York: Vintage Books, 1994), p. 122. See also Sugar, *Native Fascism in the Successor States 1918–1945*.

30. Krunoslav S. Draganović, ed., *Croazia sacra* (Rome: Officium libri catholici, 1943).

31. Fikreta Jelić-Butić, *Ustaše i Nezavisna Dr žava Hrvatska* (Zagreb: Liber, 1977), pp. 218–219.

32. As pointed out by the Croat Catholic journalist Chris Cviić, who quoted Ivan Jakovljević's book *Konclogor na Savi* (The concentration camp on the Sava River). *Nacional*, no. 234, 11 May 2000.

33. Milo Bošković, *Antijugoslavenska fašistička emigracija* (Anti-Yugoslav fascist émigré organizations) (Belgrade: Sloboda, 1980), p. 280.

34. Mark Aarons and John Loftus, *Unholy Trinity: How the Vatican's Nazi Networks Betrayed Western Intelligence to the Soviets* (New York: St. Martin's Press, 1991).

35. See, Dušan Čalić and Ljubo Boban, eds., *Narodnooslobodilačka borba i socijalistička revolucija u Hrvatskoj 1944 godine* (Zagreb: JAZU, 1976), and Ćiril Petešić, Katoličko Svećenstvo u NOB-u, 1941–1945 (Zagreb: VPA, 1981).

36. See the preamble to the Constitution of the Republic of Croatia, "Izorišne osnove," in *Ustav Republike Hrvatske*, 9th ed. (Zagreb: Informator, 1995), pp. 7–9.

37. Ibid., p. 8.

38. See the data in Ramet, *Cross and Commisar*, p. 30. The Catholic Church published testimonies on communist attacks on clergy with biographies of priests executed without trial in Šimun Jurišić, *Zaboravljeni sve ćenici: Životopisi 1882–1941* (Forgotten priests: Biographies 1882–1941) (Split: Zbirka Niko Duboković, 1995).

39. See Milovan Djilas, *Rise and Fall* (San Diego: Harcourt Brace Jovanovich, 1985).

40. Stephane Courtois et al., *The Black Book of Communism: Crimes, Terror, Repression*, trans. Jonathan Murphy and Mark Kramer (Cambridge: Harvard University Press, 1999), pp. 424–425.

41. *Yugoslavia: History, Peoples and Administration*, vols. 1–3 of *Geographical Handbook, Series B.R. 493A* (London: British Admiralty Naval Intelligence Division, October 1944), p. 229.

42. See Bošković, *Antijugoslavenska fašistička emigracija*, pp. 64–71, 350–353.

43. Ibid.

44. According to John R. Schindler, "Overturning Tito: Yugoslav Exiles and Western Intelligence, 1945-1950," presentation at the thirty-third National Con-

vention of the American Association for the Advancement of Slavic Studies, 18 November 2001, Crystal City, Virginia.

45. According to a 1973 scholarly analysis, between 1962 and 1971, 50 violent acts classified by the state prosecutor of Sweden as terrorism were perpetrated against Yugoslavia in western Europe. See Vladimir Vodinelić, *10 verzija više jedna jednako istina: zapisi o bonskom i stokhlomskom procesu ustaškim teroristima* (Split: Marksistički centar, 1973). According to the Yugoslav Federal Secretariat of Internal Affairs, between 1962 and 1976 exiled groups assassinated four Yugoslav diplomats, wounded two, and attempted 16 various terrorist attacks on Yugoslav diplomatic representatives. In 1968, Ustaša terrorists planted a bomb in a Belgrade movie theater; in the same year, Četniks carried out several bombings on Yugoslav targets in Belgium and the Ustaša bombed the Yugoslav Club in Paris; in 1969 a bomb was planted at the Belgrade railway station; in 1972 the Croat terrorists highjacked a Swedish airliner and a year later bombed an Austrian train; in 1974, explosive device mailed by Ustašas from Germany exploded in the Zagreb Postal office; in 1976, Croat terrorists highjacked a TWA airliner and bombed the New York airport, and so forth. Many anti-Yugoslav exile militants were sentenced by foreign courts, particularly in West Germany, where the government cracked down on far-right groups, with which Yugoslav exiles were linked. From 1975 to 1978, exile militants attempted 80 terrorist attacks, most of which were prevented by the Yugoslav secret police. See Bošković, *Antijugoslavenska fašistička emigracija*, pp. 212–217.

46. Dušan Janković, "Pakleni plan 'Feniks,'" series of articles, *NIN*, July 1975.

47. On emigré politics in general, and in particular on exile groups' links with organized crime, see a journalistic perspective by Marko Lopušina, *Ubij bližnjeg svog* (Kill thy neighbor), vols 1–3: *Jugoslavenska tajna policija od 1945 do 1997* (The Yugoslav secret police, 1945–1997); *Akcije dr žavne bezbednosti protiv špijuna od 1946 do 1997* (Activities of the state security against spies, 1946–1997); *Istorija Jugoslavenskog podzemlja* (A history of the Yugoslav underworld) (Belgrade: Narodna knjiga—Alfa, 1996–1998).

48. Sreten Kovačević, *Hronologija antijugoslavenskog terorizma 1960–1980* (A chronology of anti-Yugoslav terrorism, 1960–1980) (Belgrade: ISRO Privredno finansijski vodič, 1981).

49. See Aarons and Loftus, *Unholy Trinity*. See also Michael J. Phayer, "Pope Pius XI, the Holocaust, and the Cold War," *Holocaust and Genocide Studies* 12, 2 (fall 1998), pp. 233–256.

50. Most radical among these priests were former Ustašas, namely, Vilim Cecelja, Vjekoslav Lasić, Rafael Medić, Josip Kasić, Dragutin Kamber-Kelava, Josip Bujanović, and Mladen and Ante Čuvalo. Četnik priests, Stojiljko and Živko Kajević, Nikola Kavaja, and Radiša Stević took part in Serb nationalist propaganda activities, while the Kajevićs and Kavaja also participated in terrorist attacks and were sentenced by the foreign court. See Bošković, *Antijugoslavenska fašistička emigracia*, pp. 279–281. See also Joža Vlahović, "Tajni rat protiv Jugoslavije" (Secret war against Yugoslavia), series of articles, *Politika*, May–June 1969; and Boro Komljenović, "Sudjenje pripadnicima četnicke i saradnicima ustaške emigracije," *Politika*, 5 April 1972.

51. See Aarons and Loftus, *Unholy Trinity*, pp. 88–119.

52. See Hansjakob Stehle, *Eastern Politics of the Vatican, 1917–1979*, trans. Sandra Smith (Athens: Ohio University Press, 1981).

53. "Memorandum on Crimes of Genocide Committed against the Serbian People by the Government of the 'Independent State of Croatia' during World War Ii, Addressed to the fifth General Assembly of the United Nations, 1950," by Adam Pribičević, Hon. President of the Democratic Party of Yugoslavia, Dr. Vladimir Belajčić, former Justice of the Supreme Court of Yugoslavia, and Dr. Branko Milijuš, former Minister of Yugoslavia. Quoted in Edmond Paris, *Genocide in Satellite Croatia, 1941–1945*, p. 291. See also *The Crime of Genocide—A Plea for Ratification of the Genocide Pact* (Chicago: Serbian National Defense Council of America, 1951).

54. *Martyrdom of the Serbs: Persecutions of the Serbian Orthodox Church and Massacre of the Serbian People* (Chicago, Serbian Eastern Orthodox Diocese for the United States of American and Canada, 1943), pp. 21, 65, 171–72. See Herve Lauriere, *Less assassenes au nom de Dieu* (Lausanne, Switzerland: L'Age d'Homm, 1993). Avro Manhattan published in 1967 his *Threat to Europe*, reissued as *The Vatican's Holocaust: The Sensational Account of the Most Horrifying Religious Massacre of the twentieth Century* (Springfield, MO: Ozark Books, 1986).

55. "Opomena Srbima rodoljubima" (An exhortation to Serb patriots), in Ranković et al., *Vladika Nikolaj*, p. 210.

56. Vinko Nikolić, *Bleiburška tragedija hrvatskog naroda. Na temelju španjolskog izdanja "La tragedia de Bleiburg" (1963) priredio Vinko Nikolić*, (The Bleiburg tragedy of the Croat People. According to the Spanish edition "La Tragedia de Bleiburg" [1963] prepared by Vinko Nikolic), 3rd ed. (Zagreb: Knjižnica hrvatske revije, 1993); Ivo Omrčanin, *Le Martyrologe Croate, 1940–1951: Pretres et religieux assasines en haine de la foi* (Martyrdom of the Croats, 1940–1951: Priests and religious murderers hateful of the faith) (Paris: Nouvelles editions Latines, 1962); *Dramatis Personae and Finis of the Independent State of Croatia in American and British Documents* (Bryn Mawr, PA: Dorrance, 1983); *Holocaust of Croatians* (Washington, DC: Samizdat, 1986); *Croatia rediviva* (Washington, DC: Ivor Press, 1995). See also Beljo, *YU-Genocide: Bleiburg, death marches, UDBA (Yugoslav secret police)*.

57. Žerjavić, *Population Losses*, pp. 99, 177.

58. Djordje Ličina, *Dvadeseti čovjek* (The twentieth man) (Zagreb: Centar za informacije i publicitet, 1985); and *Roverova braća* (Brothers of the Ustaša Srećko Rover) (Zagreb: Centar za informacije i publicitet, 1987).

59. Dragutin Kamber-Kelava, *Kardinal Stepinac* (Detroit, MI: 1953).

60. *Alojzije Stepinac, hrvatski kardinal* (Alojzije Stepinac, Croatian cardinal), written in the Vatican by the Benedictine Aleksa Benigar (Rome: ZIRAL, 1974), can be considered a classic in the massive ensuing literature on Stepinac. The book was banned from circulation in communist Yugoslavia. The first collection of Stepinac's wartime sermons that was aimed at testifying that the cardinal protested Ustaša crimes was published in 1967 in Spain. See Eugen B. Kostelić, ed., *Stepinac govori: život i rad te zbirka govora, propovijedi, pisama i okružnica velikog hrvatskog rodoljuba i mučenika Dra Alojzija Stepinca* (Valencia, Spain: 1967).

61. See a detailed account on Christian-Marxist dialogue in Yugoslavia in comparison with other communist countries, in Paul Mojzes, *Christian-Marxist Dialogue in Eastern Europe* (Minneapolis: Augsburg, 1981).

62. *Svesci* (Communio) (Zagreb: Kršćanska sadašnjost, September 1968).

63. Špiro Marasović. "Samoupravljanje i religija," *Crkva u svijetu* 15, 3 (1980).

64. Pope John Paul II, *Centesimus annus*, encyclical letter (Rome: Vatican, 1991), pp. 9–10.

65. A portion of this section is taken with the publisher's permission from

my article "Interfaith Dialogue versus Recent Hatred: Serbian Orthodoxy and Croatian Catholicism from the Second Vatican Council to the Yugoslav War, 1965–1992," *Religion, State and Society* 29, (March 2001), pp. 39–66.

66. *Nedjeljna Dalmacija*, 26 November 1989. Franić recorded the historic prayer in his chronicle of diocesan affairs as follows: "Ecumenical prayer in the Cathedral was held on the occasion of the *Octave of Prayer for Christian Unity* together with the archpriest Marko Plavša as representative of the Orthodox bishop of Dalmatia, and with Mr Stojanac Marko on behalf of Orthodox church community in Split. The archpriest Plavša read in the crowded cathedral Ephesians 4: 1–7 and 13–21 and when finished, gave the bishop a fraternal hug. The congregation was moved, many had tears in their eyes. The archbishop addressed the Orthodox with special words, greeting them as beloved Christian brethren." *Vjesnik biskupije splitske i makarske*, no. 1 (1966).

67. Juraj Kolarić, *Pravoslavni* (The Orthodox) (Zagreb: Veritas, 1985), p. 187.

68. A lengthy article about this movement and interfaith relations during the communist era was published by this author in 2001. See Vjekoslav Perica, "Interfaith Dialogue versus Recent Hatred: Serbian Orthodoxy and Croatian Catholicism from the Second Vatican Council to the Yugoslav War, 1965–1992 *Religion, State and Society* 29, 1 (March 2001), pp. 39–66.

69. Petar Ćebić, *Ekumenizam i vjerska tolerancija u Jugoslaviji* (Ecumenism and religious tolerance in Yugoslavia) (Belgrade: NIRO Mladost, 1988), pp. 170, 182.

70. Quoted in English translation from Serbo-Croatian in Bulajić, *The Role of the Vatican in the Breakup of the Yugoslav State*, p. 183.

71. According to a Serbian church historian, the Serbian Patriarchate received from the World Council of Church generous financial support: "the tremendous help . . . had kept pouring in from Geneva . . . in 1958: $18,558,933; in 1959: $9,128,749; in 1960: $9,339,189; in 1961: $5,960,042." Paul Pavlovich, *The History of the Serbian Orthodox Church* (Toronto: Serbian Heritage Books, 1989), p. 4.

72. In 1974 in Greece, Popović published a study on ecumenism in which he condemned both factions of the global ecumenical movement, that is, the so-called Geneva ecumenism, dominated by American Evangelicals, and Roman ecumenism, launched by the Second Vatican Council. Popović designated the Orthodox Church as the only true and credible spiritual force capable of accomplishing the ideal of Christian unity. Justin Popović, *Pravoslavna crkva i ekumenizam* (The Orthodox Church and ecumenism) (Salonika: Hilandar, 1974), p. 190.

73. Dimitrije Bogdanović, "Dijalog kakav nam ne treba" (A dialogue we do not need), *Vesnik*, no. 525–526, 1971. Quoted in Ćebić, *Ekumenizam i vjerska tolerancija u Jugoslaviji*, p. 168.

74. Quoted in Ćebić, *Ekumenizam i vjerska tolerancija u Jugoslaviji*, p. 133.

75. Bogdanović, "Dijalog kakav nam ne treba," p. 168.

76. Savezna komisija za vjerska pitanja (Federal Commission for Religious Affairs), "Informacija broj 26, Povjerljivo—O nekim aspektima stanja i djelovanja verskih zajednica u Jugoslaviji" (Information no. 26, confidential—On some aspects of the situation and activity of the religious communities in Yugoslavia) Belgrade, December 1969, p. 12.

77. In the first sentence of the brief paragraph on religion (in which religion was described as a product of backwardness), it was written that religion should not be fought against by administrative repression—however, the program explicitly said that party members must be atheistic Marxists. For an

English translation of the Party program, see *Yugoslavia's Way: Programme of the League of Communists of Yugoslavia*, trans. S. Pribichevich (New York: 1958).

78. The rapprochement came in 1966 as an agreement under the abbreviated title "Protocol." See Vjekoslav Cvrlje, *Vatikan u suvremenom svijetu* (Zagreb: Školska knjiga, 1980).

79. Krsto Leković, *Svijet*, 13 June to 19 September 1986; Siniša Ivanović, *Špijun u mantiji* (A spy in clerical attire) (Belgrade: Nova knjiga, 1987). Aarons and Loftus in *Unholy Trinity* also speculate that Draganović worked for the UDBA.

80. Komisija za odnose s vjerskim zajednicama Izvršnog vijeća Sabora Socijalističke Republike Hrvatske (Commission for Relations with Religious Communities of the Executive Council of the Assembly of the Socialist Republic of Croatia), "Informativni bilten broj 5/1969" (Informative bulletin no.5/1969), with report on the conference held in Zagreb on 11 November 1969, "Naša politika prema najnovijim kretanjim u vjerskim zajednicama u Hrvatskoj" (Our policy toward the newest currents in religious communities in the SR Croatia), 30 December 1969, Zagreb.

81. Ibid., p. 30.

82. Savezna Komisija za vjerska pitanja, "Informacija broj 26, Povjerljivo— O nekim aspektima stanja i djelovanja verskih zajednica u Jugoslaviji" (Belgrade, December 1969), p. 31.

83. Komisija Saveznog Izvršnog vijeća za odnose s vjerskim zajednicama (Commission of the Federal Executive Council for Relations with Religious Communities), "Izveštaj o radu komisije u 1973 godini" (Annual report on the Commission's activity in 1973) (Belgrade, April 1974).

84. Komisija za odnose s vjerskim zajednicama Izvršnog vijeća Sabora Socijalističke Republike Hrvatske (Commission for Relations with Religious Communities of the Executive Council of the Assembly of the Socialist Republic of Croatia, "Odnosi s vjerskim zajednicama u SR Hrvatskoj" (Relations with religious communities in the Socialist Republic of Croatia—Annual report) (Zagreb, March 1981); and "Informacija o problemima vezanim za izgradnju vjerskih objekata u SRH" (Information about problems regarding construction of places for worship) (Zagreb, 26 February 1982).

85. Savezna Komisija za vjerska pitanja, "Informacija broj 26," p. 31.

86. Ibid., pp. 31–32.

87. Ibid., In my translation.

88. Ibid.

89. Manojlo Bročić, "The Position and Activities of the Religious Communities in Yugoslavia with Special Attention to the Serbian Orthodox Church," in *Religion and Atheism in the U.S.S.R. and Eastern Europe*, ed. Bohdan R. Bociurkiw, John W. Strong, and Jean K. Laux (Toronto: University of Toronto Press, 1975), p. 362.

90. Komisija za odnose s vjerskim zajednicama Izvršnog vijeća Sabora Socijalističke Republike Hrvatske, "Informativni bilten broj 5/1969."

91. Ibid.

92. *Glasnik Srpske pravoslavne crkve* 7, July 1971, p. 150; *Glasnik Srpske pravoslavne crkve* 6, June 1973, p. 128.

93. Two issues were withdrawn from circulation upon court orders in 1972 and 1973.

94. A Catholic researcher pointed out that "almost all empirical studies in sociology of religion have indicated a relatively high degree of correlation be-

tween the phenomena such as industrialization, urbanization and the like, and a crisis of people's religious behavior." Stipe Tadić, "Clerical professions in Croatia from 1945 to 1990," in Grubišić et al., *Religija i Sloboda*, p. 207.

95. Vrcan, "Religion, Nation and Class in Contemporary Yugoslavia," p. 94. Only the number of Moslems increased, from 12.3 percent to 13.4 percent.

96. Cited in Bročić, "The Position and Activities of the Religious Communities in Yugoslavia," p. 356.

97. Milomir Glišić, *Odnos mladih prema religiji* (The attitude of young people toward religious—A supplement to empirical research of religious attitudes and behavior of high school seniors in Serbia) (Gornji Milanovac: Dečije novine, 1982).

98. Pedro Ramet, ed., *Catholicism and Politics in Communist Societies* (Durham, NC: Duke University Press, 1990), pp. 200–203.

99. Bročić, "The Position and Activities of the Religious Communities in Yugoslavia," p. 362.

100. See John Anderson, *Religion, State and Politics in the Soviet Union and Successor States* (Cambridge, UK: Cambridge University Press, 1994), p. 55.

101. Bročić, "The Position and Activities of the Religious Communities in Yugoslavia, pp. 362–363.

102. Ibid.

103. *Srpska pravoslavna crkva 1219–1969. Spomenica o 750-godišnjici autkofalnosti* (The Serbian Orthodox Church 1219–1969. Special issue on the occasion of the 750th anniversary of the Church's autocephaly (Belgrade: Sveti Arhijerejski Sinod, 1969).

104. Ibid.

105. Slobodan Reljić, "German Djorić: Crveni patrijarh ili Gandi sa Balkana" (Germanus Djorić: Red patriarch or Gandhi from the Balkans?), *NIN*, 7 September 1990, p. 47.

106. Ibid.

107. Pedro Ramet, ed., *Eastern Christianity and Politics in the Twentieth Century* (Durham, NC: Duke University Press, 1988), p. 241.

108. From "Official Section" of the three volumes of *Glasnik srpske pravoslavne crkve*, 1966.

109. *Pravoslavlje*, 1 June 1984.

110. Komisija za odnose s vjerskim zajednicama Izvršnog vijeć Sabora Socijalističke Republike Hrvatske, "Informacija o problemima vezanim za izgradnju vjerskih objekata u SRH" and "Odnosi s vjerskim zajednicama u SR Hrvatskoj."

111. *NIN*, 7 September 1990, p. 47.

112. The rest went to the Evangelical Church, the Baptist church, the Pentecostal Church, and two minor religious groups. Most of the monies given the Orthodox Church were paid to the association of the Orthodox clergy for the pensions of its retired members and for church museums and repair of several church facilities. A modest sum was also listed, allocated by local municipal authorities in Dalmatia to a church museum administered by the Franciscans. According to the governmental report: Komisija za odnose s vjerskim zajednicama Izvršnog vijeća Sabora Socijalističke Republike Hrvatske, "Odnosi s vjerskim zajednicama u SR Hrvatskoj."

113. Komisija Saveznog Izvršnog vijeća (SIV) za odnose s vjerskim zajednicama (Federal Executive Council's Commission for Relations with Religious Communities, Office of the Commission), "Izeštaj o radu komisije" (Annual report on the Commission's activities) (Belgrade, April 1980).

114. According to *Katolička Crkva i Hrvati izvan domovine*, p. 13. Most of these worked in West Germany.

115. According to the 1971 census, 330,000 migrant workers were from Croatia and 137,351 from Bosnia-Herzegovina, mostly from Croatian-populated areas. Idid., 116. Vatican documents, *Motu Proprio—Pastoralis Migratorum Cura* and *Instructio de Pastoralis Migratorum Cura*, released on 20 August 1969, urge spiritual care of migrant workers, refugees, and people without a homeland.

116. Vatican documents, *Motu Proprio—Pastoralis Migratorum Cura* and *Instructio de Pastoralis Migratorum Cura*, released on 20 August 1969, urge spiritual care of migrant workers, refugees, and people without a homeland.

117. The Croatian Church abroad was distributed most densely throughout western Europe, with 110 missions, pastoral centers, and offices and some 140 priests, about 100 social workers, and another 100 pastoral assistants (57 laypeople and 43 nuns). Ignacije Vugdelija, "Političko-ekonomska migracija Hrvata i religijsko-moralna problematika te briga Crkve," in Grubišić et al., *Religija i Sloboda*, p. 271.

118. From Stanković's interview with me, *Nedjeljna Dalmacija*, 1 July 1990, p. 19.

119. Ignacije Vugdelija, "Političko-ekonomska migracija Hrvata i religijsko-moralna problematika te briga Crkve," in Grubišić et al., *Religija i Sloboda*, pp. 276–282.

120. I picked up these terms on my journalistic tours and talks with village priests in Dalmatia's hinterland.

121. Doder, *The Yugoslavs*, p. 83.

122. Ibid.

123. Komisija za odnose s vjerskim zajednicama Izvršnog vijeća Sabora Socijalističke Republike Hrvatske (Commission for Relations with Religious Communities of the Executive Council of the Assembly of the Socialist Republic of Croatia), "Zabilješka o razgovoru predsjednika komisije Dr. Frida i Nadbiskupa Dr. FRane Franića održanog 21 Aprila 1972 u prostorijama komisije" (Memo on meeting between the Commission's Chairman, Dr. Frid, and the archbishop of Split, Dr. Frane Franić, held on 21 April 1972 in the Commission's Office), confidential, 08-41/2-1972) (Zagreb, 25 April 1972).

124. Interview with me. *Nedjeljna Damacija*, 1 July 1990. According to information I obtained through the Ministry of Foreign Affairs of the Republic of Croatia in May 1991, in the late 1980s, the total number of Yugoslav diplomatic staff and consular officials working abroad was 1,110, of whom 78 were ethnic Croats. *Informacija.o zastupljenosti kadrova iz republike Hrvatske u SSIP-u i DKP* (An information on diplomatic and consular cadres from the Republic of Croatia in the Federal Ministry of Foreign Affairs) (Zagreb: Ministry of Foreign Affairs of the Republic of Croatia, 1990).

125. Grbić, "O crkvenim finansijama," p. 6.

126. According to the Church's official statistics for 1969, the Catholic Church ran 19 seminaries with 2,109 students, and 11 theological schools (including two universities) with 1,256 students at home and 70 students studying theology abroad. Bročić, "The Position and Activities of the Religious Communities in Yugoslavia," p. 363.

127. For example, "parish catechism" was practiced in the Croatian diòcese of Split in 40 locations in the academic year 1947–48—by 1983, 60 percent of all elementary school children and 19.7 percent of high school students regularly attended the parish catechism. Ivan Grubišić, "Župski vjeronauk (kataheza) i

marksistička indoktrinacija u odgojno-obrazovnom sustavu u Hrvatskoj" (Parish catechism and Marxist indoctrination in the educational system in Croatia), in Grubišić et al., *Religija i Sloboda*, pp. 195–197.

128. Roter, *Katoliška cerkev in država v Jugoslaviji 1945–1973*, pp. 273–276.

3. The Other Serbia

1. See more about the wave of nationalism in the republics and autonomous provinces in Sabrina P. Ramet, *Nationalism and Federalism in Yugoslavia: 1962–1991*, 2nd ed. (Bloomington: Indiana University Press, 1992).

2. Most of the doctorates were in the Albanian language, the humanities, history, and the social sciences. *Slobodna Dalmacija*, 7 June 1999.

3. Vrcan, "Religion, Nation and Class in Contemporary Yugoslavia," p. 91.

4. Slijepčević, *Istorija Srpske Pravoslavne Crkve*, p. 271.

5. Ibid., pp. 271–272.

6. Savezna komisija za vjerska pitanja, "Informacija broj 26," p. 12.

7. Ibid. See also Wayne S. Vuchinich, ed., *Contemporary Yugoslavia—Twenty Years of Socialist Experiment* (Berkeley: University of California Press, 1969), pp. 260–261.

8. According to Bishop Pavle's correspondence with Vitomir Petković, chairman of the Commission for Religious Affairs of Serbia. Courtesy of Radovan Samardjić, general secretary of the government commission for religious affairs. See also Atanasije Jevtić, *Od Kosova do Jadovna* (Belgrade: Sfairos, 1984).

9. A brief note on the letter was published in *Glasnik Srpske pravoslavne crkve* in 1969. The full text of the letter (here my translation from Serbo-Croatian) was published for the first time after Tito's death by the Holy Synod in May 1982 and was quoted from the Italian news bulletin *Relazioni religiose in Religion, Politics, Society*, 9 December 1982.

10. "I have received your letter in which you inform me that the Serbian Orthodox Church and its believers have been hurt by unlawful activities. I am sorry to hear that and I regret that the activities, described in your letter, which violate Constitution of the SFRY have been committed. As President of the SFRY I will do all that is necessary to halt the incidents and illegal activities and to secure the freedom and integrity of all citizens as well as security for their property. Your letter will be forwarded along with my opinion on the need to undertake resolute measures that will guarantee legality to the Executive Council of Socialist Republic of Serbia. President of the SFRY Josip Broz Tito." Quoted from *Religion, Politics, Society*, 9 December 1982.

11. Quoted in *NIN*, 21 September 1990, p. 64, my translation. It is noteworthy that *Pravoslavlje* used the official title "comrade."

12. For a summary of this, see Jevtić, *Stradanja Srba na Kosovu i Metohiji od 1941 do 1990*; and by the same author, *Od Kosova do Jadovna*. In the second book, the same charges were extended to Croatia.

13. This was the explanation given by Archimandrite Atanasije Jevtić to American observers in the Balkans. See Jevtić, *Stradanja Srba na Kosovu i Meohiji od 1941 do 1990*.

14. Pešić's research on rapes in Kosovo "indicates that as of 1987, there was not a single "interethnic" rape (i.e., a Serbian woman raped by an Albanian), although such cases were constantly mentioned in the press. Under enormous public pressure regarding the rape of "Serbian women," new criminal proceedings were introduced if the rape involved individuals of "different nationalities."

In addition, "the rate of such sexual assaults in Kosovo was the lowest compared to other Yugoslav republics, and the greatest number of rapes in Kosovo occurred within the same ethnic groups." Vesna Pešić, *Serbian Nationalism and the Origins of the Yugoslav Crisis*, Peaceworks Series (Washington, DC: United States Institute of Peace, 1996); Vesna Pešić, "O krivičnom delu silovanja: Uporedna analiza sa SFRJ, užu Srbiju, Kosovo i Vojvodinu," in *Kosovski čvor; drešiti ili seći?* (Belgrade: Chronos, 1990), p. 47.

15. Ramet, *Nationalism and Federalism in Yugoslavia*, pp. 198–201. See also Milan Vučković, *Stanovništvo Kosova u razdoblju of 1918 do 1991 godine sa osvrtom na prethodni istorijski period* (Los Angeles: Loyola Marymount University, 1998).

16. Vučković.

17. In 1920, Belgrade obtained from the Ecumenical patriarchate in Istanbul jurisdiction over part of the area where Serbian ruler Stephen Dušan made himself emperor in 1346. The three Macedonian dioceses were under the patriarchate of Serbia, and a unilateral act could not reverse the status of the Macedonian dioceses.

18. Dimevski, *Istorija na Makedonskata pravoslavna crkva*, p. 988.

19. As implied by the patriarchate's financial adviser Risto Grbić in his pamphlet-report "O crkvenim finansijama," pp. 6–7.

20. Savezna komisija za vjerska pitanja, "Informacija broj 26."

21. In an interview, Patriarch Germanus said about the Macedonian *raskol*: "The arbitrary, that is forceful separation of one of its parts from the Serbian Orthodox Church, as a living organism, causes terrible pains to our church, it is our unhealed wound. The communists want to divide and rule. Only, the days are going to come when everything will find its proper place. So it will also be with the southern part of Yugoslavia. . . . Illusions come to an end, but truth is eternal." Svetislav Spasojević, *The Communists and I: The Serbian Patriarch German and the Communists*, trans. Todor Mika and Stevan Scott (Grayslake, IL: Free Serbian Orthodox Diocese of the United States of America and Canada, 1991), pp. 98–99.

22. The Macedonian (proindependence) historian Ilija Velev listed and described a total of 887 medieval churches and monasteries in Macedonia and designated which of them were built by Serbian kings, though often on the foundations of Greek and sometimes Bulgarian churches. Ilija Velev, *Pregled na srednovekovni crkvi i manastiri vo Makedonija* (Skopje: Naša knjiga, 1990).

23. Saint Prokhor is situated in the border zone between the federated republic of Serbia and Macedonia. It was founded by the Byzantine emperor Romanus IV Diogenes in the eleventh century and renovated by the Serbian king Milutin early in the fourteenth century; several times damaged and rebuilt under Ottoman rule, it was renovated during the Serbian kingdom at the end of the nineteenth century.

24. Dimevski, *Istorija na makedonskata pravoslavna crkva*, p. 1024.

25. The most outspoken critic of the domestic Church was the Bishop Nikolaj Velmirović. In a similar vein, the jailed theologian Justin Popović wrote in a 1960 *samizdat*, or secretly circulated pamphlet: "Not collaboration, but coexistence. . . . Our communists impose collaboration instead of coexistence upon the Church. In the meantime, those same communists are championing the foreign policy of 'peaceful coexistence' among various ideologies, regimes, and systems." Justin Popović (Otac Justin), *Istina o Srpskoj pravoslavnoj crkvi u komunističkoj Jugoslaviji* (Father Justin: The truth about the Serbian Orthodox Church in communist Yugoslavia), (Belgrade: Ćelije Monastery, 1990), p. 29.

26. "Strahinja Maletić: XX vek u tridesetak slika," *NIN*, no. 2572, 15 April 2000.

27. Slijepčević, *Istorija Srpske Pravoslavne Crkve*, p. 419.

28. According to annual reports on the status of religious communities and church-state relations in the Socialist Republic of Croatia in 1979–85, obtained through the Commission for Relations with Religious Communities of the Executive Council of Municipal Assembly of Split, Croatia.

29. *Almanah—Srbi i pravoslavlje u Dalmaciji i Dubrovniku*, p. 300.

30. Wilkinson, *Dalmatia and Montenegro*, 1: 425.

31. In 1845 the original chapel was consecrated, and Njegoš was laid to rest there in 1855. In 1916, the Njegoš memorial chapel was demolished by Austrian troops. The ruler's relics were transferred to the Cetinje monastery. In 1925, a replica of the chapel was rebuilt at the same location by the Royal Yugoslav Army and solemnly opened by King Alexander I Karadjordjević.

32. "Njegoš and Lovćen (4)", *NIN*, 4 February 1990.

33. See Komisija za vjerska pitanja Izvršnog vijeća Sabora Socijalističke Republike Hrvatske, "Informativni bilten broj 5/1969."

34. Radna grupa Sekretarijata Centralnog komiteta Saveza komunista Srbije (Working group of the Secretariat of the Central Committee of the League of Communist of Serbia), *Aktivnost SKS u borbi protiv nacionalizma i šovinizma u SR Srbiji: Aktivnost Srpske pravoslavne crkve na platformi srpskog nacionalizma* (Activity of the League of Communists of Serbia in the struggle against nationalism and chauvinism in the Socialist Republic of Serbia; Activities of the Serbian Orthodox Church on the platform of Serbian nationalism) (Belgrade: IC Komunist, 1972), pp. 200–201.

35. The 1960 survey examined the largest (4,000) sample of respondents—students of the University of Belgrade selected from across Yugoslavia. In terms of ethnic distribution, 33 percent of the Croatian students, 23 percent of Catholic Slovenes, and 23 percent of Muslims declared themselves to be religious. Among those who are traditionally Orthodox, the highest percentage of students who declared themselves to be religious were Macedonians (19 percent) while 16 percent were of Serbian background. Bročić, "The Position and Activities of the Religious Communities in Yugoslavia with Special Attention to the Serbian Orthodox Church," in *Religion and Atheism in the U.S.S.R.*, edited by Bohdan R. Bociurkiw, John W. Strong, and Jean K. Laux (Toronto: University of Toronto Press, 1975), pp. 364–365.

36. Bogdan Denitch, "Religion and Social Change in Yugoslavia," Bociurkiw, Strong, and Laux, in *Religion and Atheism in the U.S.S.R. and Eastern Europe*, pp. 378–379.

37. See Pedro Ramet, ed., *Catholicism and Politics in Communist Societies* (Durham, NC: Duke University Press, 1990), pp. 200–203.

38. Vrcan, "Religion, Nation and Class in Contemporary Yugoslavia," p. 95.

39. Ibid.

40. See Bročić, "The Position and Activities of the Religious Communities in Yugoslavia," p. 366.

41. Milan Kašanin, *Glasnik Srpske pravoslavne crkve*, no.10, October 1969 p. 298 (my translation).

42. Pavlovich, *The History of the Serbian Orthodox Church*, p. 116.

43. *Glasnik Srpske pravoslavne crkve*, no.10, October 1969, p. 281.

44. Ibid., p. 287.

45. Welcoming Patriarch Germanus at the 1975 Gomirje feast, Ivan Lalić,

chairman of Croatia's Commission for Relations with Religious Communities, said that the 375th anniversary of Gomirje says enough about a century-old brotherhood between Serbs and Croats in Croatia who live side by side in this area and elsewhere in Yugoslavia, "all the time preserving fraternal love, concord, and peace despite many attempts to separate the two fraternal nations." *Glasnik Srpske pravoslavne crkve*, 10 October 1975, p. 183.

46. Ibid., p. 209.

47. *Glasnik Srpske pravoslavne crkve*, 11 November 1972, p. 282.

48. Ibid., p. 275.

49. Savezna komisija za vjerska pitanja (Federal Commission for Religious Affairs), "Izveštaj o poseti patrijarha Ruske pravoslavne crkve Jugoslaviji" (Report on the visit of the patriarch of the Russian Orthodox Church to Yugoslavia) (Belgrade, 2 November 1972).

50. Ibid., p. 293.

51. *Glasnik Srpske pravoslavne crkve*, 11 November 1974, p. 237.

52. Ibid.

53. Spasojević, *The Communists and I: The Serbian Patriarch German and the Communists*, p. 81.

54. Radna grupa Sekretarijata Centralnog komiteta Saveza komunista Srbije, "Aktivnost SKS u borbi protiv nacionalizma i šovinizma u SR Srbiji," pp. 199–203. (my translation).

4. The Catholic Church and the Making of the Croatian Nation, 1970–1984

1. This chapter is a revised version of an article published under the same title in *East European Politics and Societies* (Fall 2000), pp. 532–564. Reprinted from *East European Politics and Societies* 14, 3, by permission of the University of California Press. ©2000 by The American Council of Learned Societies.

2. Quoted in Dennison Rusinow, *The Yugoslav Experiment 1948–1974* (Berkeley: University of California Press, 1977), p. 296.

3. See more about the movement in Ramet, *Nationalism and Federalism in Yugoslavia: 1962–1991*; Ante Čuvalo, *The Croation National Movement, 1966–1972* (Boulder, CO: East European Monographs, 1990) and Rusinow, *The Yugoslav Experiment.*

4. See Čuvalo, *The Croation National Movement*, pp. 155–157.

5. According to a report of the League of Communists of Croatia, Committee of Rijeka, 25 February 1971, cited in Ćiril Petešić, *Što se dogadja u Katoličkoj crkvi u Hrvatskoj?* (Zagreb: Stvarnost, 1972), pp. 54–55.

6. Interview with me in Split, Croatia, November 1989.

7. As asserted by Šagi-Bunić in a 1990 interview with me. The interview appeared in *Nedjeljna Dalmacija* on 24 June 1990.

8. Ibid.

9. Franić had talks with the newly appointed premier of Croatia, Ivo Perišin, on 22 January 1972 and with the chairman of Croatia's Commission for Religious Affairs, Zlatko Frid, on 20 January 1972. Franić also discussed the Croatian crisis several times with the mayor of Split, Jakša Miličić. This is according to the following documents: Komisija za odnose s vjerskim zajednicama Izvršnog vijeća Sabora Socijalističke Republike Hrvatske (Commission for Relations with Religious Communities of the Executive Council of the Assembly of the Socialist Republic of Croatia), "Zabilješka o razgovoru predsjednika komisije Dr. Zlatka

Frida i Nadbiskupa Dr. Frane Franića održanog 20 sije čnja 1972 u prostorijama komisije" (Memo on meeting between the chairman of the Commission, Dr. Zlatko Frid, and the archbishop of Split, Dr. Frane Franić, held on 20 January 1972 in the Commission's Office), confidential, no. 15 (Zagreb, 1972); "Zabilješka o razgovoru Dr. Ive Perišina i Nadbiskupa Dr. Frane Franića" (Memo on meeting between Dr. Ivo Perišin and Archbishop Dr. Frane Franić), confidential, 08-41/ 1-1972 (Zagreb, 23 January 1972); "Zabilješka o razgovoru predsjednika komisije Dr. Frida i Nadbiskupa Dr. Frane Franića održanog 21 April 1972 prostorijama komisije."

10. The most popular churches in Zagreb were the Franciscan church on Kaptol Hill; the cathedral; the Jesuit church on Palmotćeva Street; the Dominican chapel of Wounded Jesus on Ilica Street; and, among suburban churches, the Church of Blessed Mark of Križevci on Selska Road and the Capuchin Church of Saint Michael at Dubrava district.

11. Tomislav Šagi-Bunić, Glas koncila 4–16,19,20, February–August 1972.

12. Glas koncila, 6 August 1972.

13. Glas koncila, 20 February 1972.

14. Glas koncila, 2 April 1972.

15. Komisija za odnose s vjerskim zajednicama Izvršnog vijeća Skupštine Zajednice općina Split (Commission for Relations with Religious Communities of the Executive Council of the Association of Municipalities of Split), "Katolička crkva i masovni pokret hrvatskog nacionalizma," 1971–1975 (The Catholic Church and the Croatian nationalist mass movement, 1971–1975), confidential (Split, October 1975).

16. Ibid.

17. Komisija za odnose s vjerskim zajednicama Izvršnog vijeća Sabora Socijalističke Republike Hrvastke, "Zabilješka o razgovoru predsjednika komisije Dr. Zlatka Frida i Nadbiskupa Dr. Frane Franića održanog 20 sijećnja 1972 u prostorijama komisije."

18. The Dominican preacher Tihomir Zovko sermonized in a 1971 at Rijeka: "The Croats have finally got a saint of their own blood, at the time when the canonization of saints has become an outdated ecclesiastical practice; our turn came when all large nations not only satisfied their thirst for national saints but when they even got tired of it; thus, we Croats have kept the Catholic faith as well as the Croatian national consciousness alive for thirteen centuries without a single saint of Croatian background." Quoted in Petešić, Što se dogadja u Katoličkoj crkvi u Hrvatskoj? pp. 58–59 (my translation).

19. Eduard Peričić and Antun Škorčević, eds., Trinaest stoljeća kršćanstva u Hrvata, monografija Nacionalnog Euharistijskog kongresa—NEK 84 (Thirteen centuries of Christianity in the Croat People, A monograph of the National Eucharistic Congress—NEK 84), (Zagreb: BKJ, 1988), p. 23.

20. Glas koncila, 22 August 1971.

21. Mary of Czestochowa was proclaimed Queen of Poland by King Jan Kazimierz (1659), as the defense of Czestochowa (Jasna Gora) Monastery (1656) played a major role in stopping the Swedish flood across Poland and Europe in the seventeenth century. This title was confirmed in 1962 by Pope John XXIII.

22. Glas koncila, 22 August 1971.

23. Ibid.

24. Glas koncila, 5 September 1971.

25. Slobodna Dalmacija, 31 January 1972.

26. Glas koncila, 5 March 1972.

27. In his 1972 Easter message, "Nadati se protiv svake nade" (Hope against Hope), Franić urged dialogue and forgiveness : "We believe in a renaissance of familial, patriotic, and international love," he wrote, "although we live in hard times, we remain full of optimism." Frane Franić, *Nadati se protiv svake nade: Uskršnja poslanica Dr Frane Franiča Nadbiskupa Splitsko-Makarskog* (Split: Nadbiskupski ordinarijat, April 1972), p. 11.

28. *Glas koncila*, 6 February 1972.

29. *Glas koncila*, 19 March 1972 (my translation).

30. Ibid.

31. Ibid.

32. *Glas koncila*, 25 June 1972.

33. In April 1971 militant Croatian exiles assassinated the Yugoslav ambassador to Sweden, Vladimir Rolović. In January 1972 a Croatian terrorist group hijacked and downed a Swedish airliner; Croat exile groups were also behind the bombing of the Vienna-Belgrade train in 1970 and masterminded the raid of the 19-member armed guerilla group in Bosnia in July 1972; and so on (see chapter 2).

34. Komisija za odnose s vjerskim zajednicama Izvršnog vijeća Sabora Socijalistićke Republike Hrvatske, "Zabilješka o razgovoru predsjednika komisije Dr. Zlatka Frida i Dr. Ive Petrinovića, člana Centralnog komiteta Saveza komunista Hrvatske s Nadbiskupskog Dr. Franom Franičem održanog 17 July 1972 u prostorijama Nadbiskupskog ordinarijata u Splitu." (Memo on Conversation between the chairman, Zlatko Frid, and Dr. Ivo Petrinović, member of the Central Committee of the League of Communists, with Dr. Frane Franić, the archbishop of Split-Makarska, held in the Archdiocesan Office in Split of 17 July 1972), confidential, Pov. 08-41/1-72 (Zagreb, 1 August 1972).

35. For example, the prominent Croatian nationalist Stipe Mesić said in an interview that one of the Croat nationalist leaders, Marko Veselica, turned into a "religious fanatic" after the disaster of 1971 and came close to the Catholic Church, although he had earlier been an atheist. *Slobodna Dalmacija*, 31 January 2000.

36. According to Croatian Church historians, in the year 641 Croatian rulers established ties with Pope John IV. The pope dispatched Abbot Martin to the Slavic-populated lands of Dalmatia and Istria to redeem Christian slaves and bring to Rome the relics of local Christian martyrs. Peričić and Škvorčević, *Trinaest stoljeća kršćanstva u Hrvata*, pp. 19–20.

37. Ibid., p. 300.

38. Šimundža, eds., *Godina velikoga zavjeta* (Year of the Great Covenant) (Split: Crkva u svijetu, 1977).

39. On the occasion of the twentieth anniversary of the beginning of the jubilee "Thirteen Centuries of Christianity in the Croat People," the church press asserted that 120,000 people gathered at the Mass in Solin on 12 September 1976. *Glas koncila*, no. 23, 9 June 1996.

40. The prayer led by the Archbishop Kuharić mentioned the following shrines: "Our Lady of the Isle" (southern Croatia); "Our Lady of Bistrica" (the national shrine in northern Croatia near Zagreb); "the Gospa of Sinj" (southern Croatia–Dalmatian hinterland), "the Gospa of Trsat" (northern Adriatic littoral); "the Madonna of Olovo" (Bosnia); "the Gospa of Siroki Brijeg" (western Herzegovina); "the Madonna of Letnica" (Kosovo-Serbia); "the Madonna of Aljmas" (eastern Slavonia); "the Madonna of Vocin (Vojvodina); "the Gospa of Krasno" (northwestern Croatia).

41. Šimundža, *Godina velikoga zavjeta*. According to the Croatian prelate Živko Kustić, Archbishop Francić was the chief architect of the Great Novena. *Vjesnik*, 24 January 1997.

42. According to a study on the Great Novena in Poland, Cardinal Wyszynski "created a new religious nationalism that was detached from partisan politics, a nationalism that made the very existence of the nation dependent on the Church and her royal/divine Protectress, the Virgin Mary, Queen of Poland"; Maryjane Osa, "Creating Solidarity: The Religious Foundations of the Polish Social Movement," *East European Politics and Societies* 11, 2 (spring 1997), p. 353.

43. Komisija za odnose s vjerskim zajednicama Izvršnog vijeća Skupštine Zajednice općina Split (Commission for Relations with Religious Communities of the Executive Council of the Association of Municipalties of Split; Together with the Intermunicipal Conference of the Socialist Alliance of Working People for Dalmatia), "Dan velikog hrvatskog krsnog zavjeta i druge crkvene manifestacije u Splitu i Solinu u rujnu 1976—analiza" (Day of the Great Covenant and other Church manifestations in Split and Solin in September 1976—An analysis), confidential (Split, 2 December 1976).

44. Peričić and Škvorčević, *Trinaest stoljeća kršćanstva u Hrvata*, p. 44.

45. The Serb Orthodox bishop-historian Nikodim Milaš wrote about Zvonimir as traitor who, after maintaining ties with Constantinople, converted to Roman Catholicism for personal benefit. ENM (Bishop Nikodim Milaš), *Pravoslavana Dalmacija*.

46. The hymn "Croatian Homeland," popularly known as "Our Lovely Homeland," originated in the 1830s. In communist Yugoslavia it was first outlawed and then reintroduced as an unofficial national anthem during the Croatian Spring of 1971. After 1974, "Our Lovely Homeland" was authorized for official use, provided that it was performed after the official hymn of the Yugoslav Federation, "Hey Slavs."

47. "Today we are witnessing another renewal. We see that the people have prevailed because the people, not those who have arms and wealth, will be victorious, because the people are armed with much stronger morale. Neither practical nor dialectical materialism can overpower contemporary Christianity. Inspired by our history, we are building a living Church that lives inside and outside church buildings and will continue to live. If someone denies us a permit for construction of a church, the Church will nevertheless continue to live. We will never renounce our religious freedom!" Peričić and Škvorčević, *Trinaest stoljeća kršćanstva u Hrvata*, p. 248.

48. The Church commemorated the 1,100th anniversary of five letters exchanged in 879 between the Croatian native chief Branimir (879–92), and Pope John VIII. In this historic correspondence, Branimir obtained from the pope the nomination of the monk Theodosius, who was of Croatian ancestry, as bishop at the diocesan seat of Nin (or the ancient Nona).

49. Tomislav Šagi-Bunić, "Smisao proslavljanja Branimirove godine 1979" (The meaning of the Branimir Jubilee 1979), in *Katolička crkva i hrvatski narod* (Zagreb: Kršćanska sadašnjost, 1983), p. 93.

50. ENM, *Pravoslavna Dalmacija*.

51. Dominik Mandić, *Hrvati i Srbi—dva stara različita naroda* (Croats and Serbs—Two ancient distinct peoples) (Zagreb: Nakladni zavod Matice Hrvatske, 1990).

52. Šagi-Bunić, in *Katolička crkva i hrvatski narod*, p. 97.

53. *Branimirova godina—Od Rima do Nina* (The Year of Branimir—From Rome

to Nin), a photo-monograph (Zadar: Odbor za proslavu Branimirove godine, 1980), pp. 64–65.

54. Šagi-Bunić, in *Katolička crkva i hrvatski narod*, pp. 36–37.

55. Eucharistic congresses were inaugurated in the nineteenth century in France. In Yugoslav lands, Eucharistic congresses were held in 1902–4 at Rijeka and Dubrovnik and again in 1923, 1930, and 1941 in Zagreb and Marija Bistrica. The Catholic Church in Slovenia held its Eucharistic congress in Ljublijana in 1935. Komisija za odnose s vjerskim zajednicama Izvršnog vijeća Sabora Soci-jalističke Republike Hrvatske (Commission for Relations with Religious Commu-nities of the Executive Council of the Assembly of the Socialist Republic of Cro-atia), "Euharistijski kongresi 1981–1984—analiza" (Eucharistic congresses 1981–1984—An analysis) (Zagreb, 1984).

56. Ibid.

57. Peričić and Škvorčević, *Trinaest stoljeća kršćanstva u Hrvata*, p. 64.

58. *Komunist* (Croatian edition), 23 December 1983, p. 18.

59. Ibid.

60. Peričić and Škvorčević, *Trinaest stoljeća kršćanstva u Hrvata*, p. 94.

61. Ibid., pp. 139–161.

62. Ibid.

63. Ibid., p. 34 (my translation).

64. "Learned men believe that ancient Croats came to Europe from present-day Persia . . . and crossing the Caucasus and the Ukraine, arrived to what is today Poland . . . there near the city of Krakov, they founded a mighty, well-organized state known as Great or White Croatia." Krunoslav Draganović and Josip Buturac, *Poviest crkve u Hrvatskoj* (Zagreb: Hrvatsko književo društvo svetog Jeronima, 1944), p. 5 (my translation).

65. *Glas koncila*, 8 March 1984. See *Religion, Politics, Society*, 27 March 1984.

66. Ibid.

67. Peričić are Škvorčević, *Trinaest stoljeća kršćanstva u Hrvata*, p. 203.

68. The cardinal said: "The Church demands freedom without restrictions. It means that each believer can participate in religious activities and church life. In this society, freedom of religion has not yet been fully accomplished. Full freedom of religion includes the freedom of religious instruction for our children and the young, free construction of adequate religious facilities wherever the faithful live, the right of the sick and those at the deathbed to receive holy sacraments while in state hospitals, the right of the imprisoned to receive spir-itual assistance, [and] the right of military servicemen to receive religious peri-odicals, attend worship services, and receive sacraments. All these rights and liberties protect the dignity of the individual and cultivate the whole society." Ibid., pp. 225–226.

69. *Economist*, 15–21 September 1984. In Serbo-Croat translation, according to *Religion, Politics, Society*, 27 September 1984.

70. *Komunist* (Croatian edition), 14 September 1984.

71. Speaking on the commemoration of an anniversary from the Partisan war, Špiljak said that "the Church appropriates for itself rights it does not should not have—to represent and lead the Croatian people. If we look into the past, the Church had a good number of opportunities to side with the people, but it did not—instead it always sided with the powerful and wealthy, often in the service of foreign powers . . . and now, when the Croatian people and other Yugo-slav peoples, by their own effort, have succeeded in building a sovereign, self-managed socialist country, the Catholic hierarchy is trying to impose itself as

the only real defender of people's interest and national identity. Well, enough is enough." *Vjesnik*, 17 September 1984.

72. *Borba*, 12 September 1984.

73. *Religion in Communist Lands* 15, 3 (winter 1987), pp. 65–81.

74. On the occasion of the twentieth anniversary of the beginning of the Great Novena, *Glas koncila* underlined in an editorial the importance of the jubilee's historical agenda: "That was the Church's service to the people, aimed at safeguarding its historical identity. Generations in 'Yugo-communist' schools could not learn the truth about their nation's past. Studying church and national history through the jubilee "Thirteen Centuries of Christianity in the Croat People," the people reinvigorated their faith and restored national pride." *Glas koncila*, no. 23, 6 June 1996.

5. The Bosnian Ulema and Muslim Nationalism

1. Savezna komisija za vjerska pitanja, "Informacija broj 26, Povjerljivo—O nekim aspektima stanja i djelovanja verskih zajednica u Jugoslaviji," pp. 16–17.

2. *Intervju*, 1 March 1991.

3. *Statistički godišnjak Jugoslavije* (Belgrade: Savezni zavod za statistiku, 1979).

4. According to the census of 1981, in addition to 1,630,033 Muslims in Bosnia-Herzegovina, 151,674 Muslims by nationality lived in Serbia proper (mostly in Sandjak), with 39,513 in Macedonia, 78,080 in Montenegro, and 58,562 in Kosovo. Most of some 35,000 Muslim migrants in the western republics of Croatia and Slovenia were ethnic Muslims, too. *Statistički godišnjak Jugoslavije* (Belgrade: Savezni zavod za statistiku, May 1982).

5. From my interview with the mufti Ševko Omerbašić, *Nedjeljna Dalmacija*, 20 May 1990.

6. Nijaz Duraković, "Muslimani od vjerskog do nacionalnog" (Muslims from the religious toward the national), in *Religija i društvo* (Religion and society), ed. Štefica Bahtijarević and Branko Bošnjak (Zagreb: Centar za idejno-teorijski rad Gradskog komiteta SKH, 1987), p. 122.

7. See Irfan Sijerčić, "The Activites of the 'Young Moslems' at the End of the War, 1944–1945," *Bosanski pogledi* 2, 10, ed. Adil Zulfikarpašić (Zurich, May 1961); reprinted in *South Slav Journal* 8, 1–2 (1985), pp. 65–71.

8. Savezna komisija za vjerska pitanja, "Informacija broj 26, Povjerljivo—O nekim aspektima stanja i djelovanja verskih zajednica u Jugoslaviji," p. 17.

9. Alija Izetbegović, *The Islamic Declaration: a Programme for the Islamization of the Muslim peoples* (Sarajevo: published by the author, 1990), p. 1.

10. Ibid., p. 41.

11. Ibid., p. 23.

12. Komisija Saveznog Izvršnog vijeća (SIV) za odnose s vjerskim zajednicama, "Odnosi s vjerskim zajednicama—Izveštaj o radu komisije" (Relations with Religious Communities—Annual report on the Commission's activity) (Belgrade, 4 December 1982).

13. Doder, *The Yugoslavs*, p. 112.

14. Samardžić, *Religious Communities in Yugoslavia*, p. 39.

15. Ibid.

16. By comparison, the Catholic Church had 1 priest per 2,239 Catholics, whereas the Serbian Orthodox Church had 1 priest per 5,714 believers. *AKSA*, 31 August 1984.

17. Samardžić, *Religious Communities*, p. 39.

18. *Slobodna Dalmacija*, 22 May 1988.

19. Ahmad Smajlović, "Muslims in Yugoslavia," *Journal of Muslim Minority Affairs* 1, (1979), quoted in Fouad Ajami, "Under Western Eyes: The Fate of Bosnia," *Survival* 41, 2 (summer 1999), p. 37.

20. According to the League of Communists' Organ Medjuopćinska konferencija Saveza komunista za Dalmaciju, Marksistički centar (Intermunicipal Conference of the League of Communists of Croatia of the Association of Municipalities of Dalmatia, Marxist Center), "Pregled pisanja vjerske štampe" (A survey of the church press) (Split, June 1988).

21. Only after the constitutional reform in 1990 (see hereafter) did Kosovo Albanians, in the words of the supreme Islamic official in Kosovo, mufti Jetiš Bajrami, become satisfied with the degree of autonomy granted them by Sarajevo. Interview with me held in Prizren, 4 August 1990.

22. Sheik Djemali Shehu granted an interview to me in Prizren on 5 August 1990. *Nedjeljna Dalmacija*, 12 August 1990.

23. Seventy-four imams became members of municipal and district SAWPY committees. *Religion, Politics, Society*, 27 May 1982.

24. Ibid.

25. Ibid.

26. *Preporod*, 15 March 1982; see TANJUG bulletin, *Religion, Politics, Society*, 11 April 1982, p. III/36.

27. *Preporod*, 1 June 1985. See *Religion, Politics, Society*, 20 June 1985, p. III/45.

28. Komisija za odnose s vjerskim zajednicama Izvršnog vijeća Skupštine općine Split (Commission for Relations with Religious Communities of the Executive Council of the Municipality of Split), "Izgradnja objekata za potrebe vjerskih zajednica, 1983–1987—informacija" (Information on construction of religious facilities and places of worship, 1983–1987) (Split, 14 April 1987).

29. *NIN*, 18 January 1987; *NIN*, 13 September 1987; "Muslims: Religion and Politics," in *Nedjeljni Vjesnik*, 14 April 1991.

30. Quoted from Omerbašić's interview with me held in Zagreb on 14 May 1990. *Nedjeljna Dalmacija*, 20 May 1990.

31. Komisija za odnose s vjerskim zajednicama Izvršnog vijeća Sabora Socijalističke Republike Hrvatske, "*Odnosi s vjerskim zajednicama u SR Hrvatskoj.*"

32. Ibid.

33. *NIN*, 13 September 1987.

34. Ibid.

35. *Religion, Politics, Society*, 18 October 1984.

36. In an editorial, the Islamic newspaper *Preporod* wrote that the Islamic Community regretted "the misfortune incident" and wanted to correct some allegations in the foreign Islamic press, such as that not Yugoslav communists but the Serbian Cetniks committed massacres against Muslims in World War II, and that Muslims enjoy in socialist Yugoslavia relatively more freedom than their coreligionists in other communist countries. *Religion, Politics, Society*, 18 October 1984.

37. *Economist*, 15–21 September 1984. See *Religion, Politics, Society*, 27 September 1984.

38. *Valter*, 7 April 1989.

39. *Politika express*, 26 May 1989.

40. Ibid.

41. *Preporod*, 15 February 1990.

42. "The Constitution of the Islamic Community," *Preporod*, 15 April 1990.

43. A Belgrade weekly wrote: "Jakub Selimoski is the winner of the elections—the man under whose leadership all cards have been disclosed, which indicates that our Muslims are moving toward an Islamic state." *Svet*, 3 April 1991.

44. "Muslimani za Yugoslaviju" (Muslims for Yugoslavia), *Slobodna Dalmacija*, 23 June 1991.

45. *Preporod*, 1 July 1990.

46. From my interview with Mufti Omerbašić. *Nedjeljna Dalmacija*, 20 May 1990.

47. *Preporod*, 1 June 1990.

48. Milovan Djilas and Nadežda Gće, *Bošnjak Adil Zulfikarpašić*, 3rd ed. (Zurich: Bošnjački institut, 1995), p. 134.

49. *Preporod*, 1 June 1990.

50. Ibid.

51. Djilas and Gaće, *Bošnjak Adil Zulfikarpašić*, p. 134.

52. Ibid.

53. In an interview with me, Mufti Omerbašić said that he himself and many other imams participated in the organizing of the SDA but decided to comply with the decision on political neutrality of the Islamic Community. Yet, according to Omerbašić's words, many clerics virtually remained party activists without a membership card. *Nedjeljna Dalmacija*, 20 May 1990.

54. *Nedjeljna Dalmacija*, 15 October 1989.

55. *Nedjeljna Dalmacija*, 21 April 1991.

56. Djilas and Gaće, *Bošnjak Adil Zulfikarpašić*, p. 134.

6. United We Stand, Divided We Fall

1. *Titu: poruke, želje zaveti, 4 Januar—4 Maj 1980* (To Tito: Messages, wishes, vows, 4 January–4 May 1980) (Belgrade: Borba, 1981), p. 38.

2. Ibid., 58.

3. Ibid., 139.

4. Ibid., 91.

5. Ibid., p. 91.

6. Ibid., p. 100

7. Ibid., p. 139.

8. Ibid., p. 127.

9. Ibid., p. 191.

10. Ibid., p. 173.

11. Ibid., p. 179.

12. Ibid., p. 150.

13. Ibid., p. 119.

14. Ibid., p. 115.

15. *Bilo je časno živjeti s Titom* (It was an honor to be a contemporary of Tito) (Zagreb: Vjesnik, 1980), p. 226.

16. *NIN*, 11 May 1980.

17. Ibid.

18. Velimir Milošević, in *Pjesme o Titu*, ed. Husein Tahmiščić (Zagreb: Spektar, 1983), p. 141.

19. *NIN*, 11 May 1980.

20. *Bilo je časno živjeti s Titom*, p. 239.

21. *Chronicle of the Olympics* (New York: DK, 1996), pp. 159–161.

22. Ibid., p. 10.

23. *Hvala Sarajevo: poruke zahvalnosti gradu i zemlji domaćinu XIV zimskih olimpijskih igara* (Thanks Sarajevo: Messages of gratitude to the host city and host country of the XIV Winter Olympic Games) (Sarajevo: Organizacioni komiter XIV zimskih Olimpijskih Igara, July 1984), pp. 149–166.

24. Ibid., p. 151.

25. Ibid., p. 159.

26. After this statement, a Western newspaper wrote that the chairman Mikulić was "a hard-line communist whose primary concern was to preserve the communist ideological and political monopoly." *Religion, Politics, Society*, 12 February 1984.

27. For example, among 206 Yugoslav athletes who won gold, silver, or bronze medals in international contests in 1980, 81 were from Serbia (2 from Kosovo and 24 from Vojvodina), 58 from Croatia, 27 from Slovenia, 23 from Bosnia-Herzegovina, 9 from Macedonia, and 8 from Montenegro. In 1984, 220 athletes won prestigious international trophies; 77 of these athletes came from Serbia (3 from Kosovo and 22 from Vojvodina), 69 from Croatia, 39 from Slovenia, 18 from Bosnia and Herzegovina, 11 from Montenegro, and 6 from Macedonia. *Almanah jugoslavenskog sporta* (Belgrade: Savez za fizičku kulturu Jugoslavije, 1984), p. 10.

28. Tonči Petrić "Provijest sporta u Splitu" (History of sports in the city of Split), *Slobodna Dalmacija*, 15 May 200.

29. See more on Yugoslav sports as a nation-unifying force in Vjekoslav Perica, "United They Stood, Divided They Fell: Nationalism and the Yugoslav School of Yugoslav Basketball, 1968–2000," *Nationalities Papers* 29, (June 2001), pp. 267–291.

30. *Almanah jugoslavenskog sporta* (Belgrade: Savez za fizičku kulturu Jugoslavije, 1982), p. 5.

31. Ibid., pp. 2–4.

32. Reinhold Niebuhr, *The Nature and Destiny of Man*, vol. 1 (Louisville, KY: John Knox Press, 1996), p. 210.

33. See Bellah, *The Broken Covenant: American Civil Religion in Time of Trial*, 2nd ed. (Chicago: University of Chicago Press, 1992); see also Bellah and Hammond, *Varieties of Civil Religion*.

34. See Bellah and Hammond, *Varieties of Civil Religion*; Eric Hobsbawm and Terence Ranger, *The Invention of Tradition* (Cambridge, UK: Cambridge University Press, 1983); and Hobsbawm, *Nations and Nationalism since 1780: Programme, Myth, Reality*. On the role of sport and patriotic rituals see also the Wilbur Zelinsky, preface to *Nation into State. The Shifting Symbolic Foundations of American Nationalism* (Chapel Hill: University of North Carolina Press 1988).

35. C. L. Sulzberger, *World War II* (Boston: Houghton Mifflin, 1969), p. 225.

36. Milovan Djilas, *Wartime*, trans. Michael B. Petrovich (New York: Harcourt Brace Jovanovich, 1977).

37. See Hobsbawm, *The Age of Extremes: A History of the World, 1914–1991* (New York: Vintage Books, 1994), pp. 166–167, 206. See also John Keegan, *The Battle for History: Re-Fighting World War II* (New York: Vintage Books, 1995).

38. See "The 1998 US Army Handbook: Yugoslavia, History Briefings," in *NATO Yugoslavian Internet War: Resources*, available at http//www.users.bigpond .com (24 May 1999). See also Dennis Sherman and Joyce Salisbury, *The West in*

the World: A Mid-Length Narrative History, vol. 2, *From 1600* (Boston: McGraw-Hill, 2001) pp. 782–783.

39. Dušan Čalić and Ljubo Boban, eds., *Narodnooslobodilačka borba i socijalistička revolucija u Hrvatskoj 1994 godine* (The People's Liberation Struggle and the socialist revolution in Croatia in 1994) (Zagreb: JAZU, 1976), p. 133.

40. Pero Morača, *Narodnooslobodilačka borba Jugoslavije, 1941–1945* (The People's Liberation Struggle 1941–1945) (Belgrade: Radnička štampa, 1980), p. 192.

41. Vladimir Dedijer, *Novi prilozi za biografiju Josipa Broza Tita* (New supplements for biography of Josip Broz Tito), vol. 2 (Rijeka: Liburnija, 1981), chapter 12.

42. In his wartime memoirs, Djilas describes the following religious experience, which occurred to him in a life-threatening situation in the midst of the battle of Sutjeska in June 1943: "As I fell fast asleep . . . suddenly in my mind Christ appeared; the one from the frescoes and icons, with a silk beard and a look of pity. . . . I began to speak to him: If you came into the world and suffered for goodness and truth, you must see that our cause is just and noble. We are, in fact, carrying on what you began. And you have not forgotten us, nor can you abandon us. You live and endure in us. As I was saying this, I knew that I was not ceasing to be a communist . . . it never even crossed my mind that this was a miracle or that miracles occur, though the apparition inspired calm and courage." *Wartime*, p. 285.

43. Čalić and Boban, *Narodnooslobodilačka borba i socijalistićka revolucija u Hrvatskoj 1944 godine*, p. 254.

44. Some Western sources allege that 2,000–4,000 Jewish fighters joined Tito's army and hundreds died in combat. See *The Holocaust Chronicle* (Lincolnwood, IL: Publications International, 2000), pp. 231, 492.

45. Dedijer *Novi prilozi*, vol. 2, p. 929.

46. The largest opposition group within the party were the traditionally pro-Russian ethnic Serbs and Monetengrins. See Ivo Banac, *With Stalin against Tito-Cominformists Split in Yugoslav Communism* (Ithaca, NY: Cornell University Press, 1988).

47. Momčilo Stefanović, *Svet i Tito* (Zagreb: Globus, 1988), p. 351.

48. Jaroslav Krejči and Vitezslav Velimsky, *Ethnic and Political Nations in Europe* (London: Croom Helm, 1981), p. 145.

49. Drago Jančar, "Uspomene na Jugoslaviju (2)," (Remembrance of Yugoslavia, no. 2), *Slobodna Dalmacija*, 17 July 1991.

50. Emil Lengyel, *Nationalism—The Last Stage of Communism* (New York: Funk and Wagnalls, 1969), pp. 93–136. See also Walker Connor, *The National Question in Marxist-Leninst Theory and Strategy* (Princeton, NJ: Princeton University Press, 1984).

51. See Brian Readhead, ed., *Political Thought from Plato to NATO* (Chicago: Dorsey Press, 1988), p. 156.

52. Henry Kissinger, *Diplomacy* (New York: Simon and Schuster, 1994), p. 564.

53. Anwar el-Sadat, *Those I Have Known* (New York: Continuum, 1984), p. 96.

54. *NIN*, no. 1532, 11 May 1980.

55. *Bilo je časno živjeti s Titom*, p. 260.

56. Dedijer, *Novi prilozi*, p. 585.

57. See Andrew Donskov and John Woodsworth, eds., "Lev Tolstoy and the Concept of Brotherhood," *Slavic Review* 57, 3 (fall 1998), p. 686.

58. Lydall, *Yugoslav Socialism: Theory and Practice*, pp. 281–282.

59. Ramet, *Nationalism and Federalism in Yugoslavia: 1962–1991.*

60. Ibid.

61. "When Marriage Is Sleeping with Enemy," *Newsweek*, 5 October 1992. *Newsweek* cited a survey conducted in the late 1980s by the University of Belgrade.

62. See Nikola Dugandžija, "Religija i nacija u zagrebačkoj regiji" (Religion and nation in the Zagreb region), in *Religija i društvo*, ed. Štefica Bahtijarevic and Branko Bošnjak (Zagreb: Centar za idejno-teorijski rad Gradskog komiteta Saveza komunista Hrvatske, 1987), p. 100. See also Vrcan, "Religion, Nation and Class in Contemporary Yugoslavia," pp. 97–98.

63. Dugandžija, "Religija i nacija," pp. 99–100.

64. Ibid., p. 101.

65. Ibid., pp. 98–101.

66. For example, the number of respondents who considered nationality as very important in choosing one's friends and spouse was 61 percent in ethnic Albanians and 7.6 percent in Yugoslavs by nationality. Vrcan, "Religion, Nation and Class in Contemporary Yugoslavia," p. 98.

67. Ibid., p. 97.

68. Hans Kohn, *Pan-Slavism: Its History and Ideology* (Notre Dame, IN: University of Notre Dame Press, 1953).

69. Ibid., p. 71.

70. As Hans Kohn noted, "World War II brought an unexpected revival in an unprecedented breadth and intensity of the Pan-Slavic idea that seemed dead in the 1930s." Ibid., p. 251.

71. Ibid., p. 252. See more on Russian Pan-Slavism in Michael Boro Petrovich, *The Emergence of Russian Panslavism, 1856–1870* (Westport, CT.: Greenwood Press, 1985).

72. Djilas describes the atmosphere in terms such as "rapture," "intoxicating ecstasy," and "tumultuous rhythmic outbursts." *Wartime*, pp. 359–361.

73. Dedijer, *Novi prilozi*, 2:929.

74. See "Tako je pisao Tudjman (5)" (Thus wrote Tudjman, no. 5), *Feral Tribune*, 25 August 1997.

75. *Pjesme o Titu*, pp. 28, 81.

76. Doder, *The Yugoslavs*, p. 117.

77. Milovan Djilas, *Druženje s Titom* (Harrow, UK: Aleksa Djilas, 1980), pp. 118–119.

78. El-Sadat, *Those I Have Known*, pp. 90, 93, and 96.

79. Ibid., p. 89.

80. Ibid., p. 93.

81. One of the probably most interesting though little-known comparisons between Titoism and other contemporary dictatorships can be found in Enrique Triana Carrasquilla, *Franco-Tito: Espańńa-Yugoslavia, paralelo extraordinario* (Bogota: Fuerzas Militares, 1990).

82. In 1999, the government of Montenegro sold the *Seagull* to American businessman John Paul Papanicolau.

83. El-Sadat, *Those I Have Known*, p. 94.

84. *Zbirka propisa o upotrebi imena i lika i o čuvanju dela Josipa Broza Tita, o grbu, zastavi i himni SFRJ, o praznicima i odlikovanjima SFRJ, o nagradama i o proglašavanju opštenarodne žalosti u SFRJ* (Belgrade: Novinsko-izdavačka ustanova Službeni list SFRJ, 1987).

85. *NIN*, 14 August 1988.

86. *Titova štafeta—Štafeta mladosti*, 5th ed. (Belgrade: Muzej 25th Maj, 1981), p. 36.

87. Ibid., pp. 34, 47.

88. Ibid., p. 35.

89. Sporting institutions like the cyclists' Tour de France and the Giro d' Italia "were the concrete demonstration of the links which bound all inhabitants of the national state together, irrespective of local and regional differences." Eric Hobsbawm, "Mass-Producing Traditions: Europe, 1870–1914" in Eric Hobsbawm and Terence Ranger, *The Invention of Tradition* (Cambridge: Cambridge University Press, 1983), p. 301.

90. Bellah, *The Broken Covenant*, p. 162.

91. The rock anthem "Ima neka tajna veza" (There is some secret link) was performed by the Sarajevo rock band Bijelo Dugme. See more on the Yugo-rock scene of the 1980s in Sabrina P. Ramet, ed., *Rocking the State: Rock Music and Politics in Eastern Europe and Russia* (Boulder, CO: Westview Press, 1994).

92. *Feral Tribune*, no. 823, 23 June 2001

93. In a 1987 interview, the head of the Serbian Orthodox Church, Patriarch Germanus, argued that "brotherhood and unity cannot be accomplished by ignoring traditional religions and churches" and declared that ordinary people's patriotism "was not in harmony with this 'religion,' because the communists viewed themselves as the only true patriots." See Spasojevic, *The Communists and I*, pp. 85, 129.

94. Jakov Jukic, "Teorije ideologizacije i sekularizacije" (Theories of ideologization and secularization), in *Religija i sloboda-Prilog socioreligijskoj karti Hrvatske*, ed. Ivan Grubišić et al. (Split: Institut za primjenjena društvena istraživanja-Centar Split, 1993), p. 36.

95. Nikola Dugandžija, *Svjetovna religija* (Belgrade: Mladost, 1980), pp. 323–327.

96. Recently published world history and Western civilization textbooks for US college students portary Tito in a more or less positive light and recognize him as globally important statesman during World War II and the Cold War. See, for example, Sherman and Salisbury, pp. 782–783 and 803–840; R. R. Palmer and Joel Colton, *A History of the Modern World*, 8th ed., (New York: McGraw-Hill, 1995), p. 911; Philip J. Adler, *World Civilizations*, vol. 2, *Since 1500*, 2nd ed. (Belmont, CA: Wadsworth, 2000), p. 708, and Jerry H. Bentley and Herbert F. Ziegler; *Traditions and Encounters: A Global Perspective on the Past*, vol. 2, *From 1500 to the Present* (Boston: McGraw-Hill, 2000), p. 1013.

97. Sadat, *Those I Have Known*, pp. 90–96.

98. "Between the wars . . . international sport became, as George Orwell soon recognized, an expression of national struggle, and sportsmen representing nation or state, primary expression of their imagined communities." Hobsbawm, *Nations and Nationalism since 1780*, p. 143.

99. Hobsbawm, *Nations and Nationalism since 1870*, p. 142. For an analysis of nationalistic excesses in sports arenas and the use of religious symbols by ethnic nationalist fans, see Srdjan Vrcan, *Sport i nasilje danas u nas i druge studije iz sociologije sporta* (Sport and violence here today and other studies in the sociology of sports), (Zagreb: Naprijed 1990). See also Doder, *The Yugoslavs*, pp. 36–38.

7. Mary-making in Herzegovina

1. On 24 June 1981, at Medjugorje, two teenage girls reported to their parents and the Franciscans that they had an encounter with someone who looked like the Virgin Mary, Mother of God, or, in the local dialect, the Gospa. The girls, Ivanka Ivanković and Mirjana Dragičević, returned to the site the next day with their friends Vicka Ivanković and Marija Pavlovic and two boys, Ivan Dragičević and Jakov Čolo. The visions continued at the hill of Podbrdo above Medjugorje, but when large groups of pilgrims flocked to the barren Dinaric karst to pray for hours in the Mediterranean summer heat, the show moved, allegedly on the recommendation of the Gospa herself, to the interior of the spacious parish church of Saint James at Medjugorje. Two more children, Jelena Vasilj and Mirjana Vasilj, also reported communication with the Gospa on a daily basis.

2. From 1981 to 1997, over 22 million people made pilgrimage to Medjugorje. See Richard J. Beyer, *Medjugorje Day by Day* (Notre Dame, IN: Ave Maria Press, 1993).

3. See William A. Christian, Jr., *Visionaries: The Spanish Republic and the Reign of Christ* (Berkeley: University of California Press, 1996); Daniel H. Levine, ed., *Religion and Political Conflict in Latin America* (Chapel Hill:University of North Carolina Press, 1986). See also Jakov Jukić, *Religija u modernom industrijskom drušvu* (Religion in modern industrial society) (Split: Crkva u svijetu, 1973), p. 327.

4. See David Blackbourn, *Marpingen: Apparitions of the Virgin Mary in Bismarckian Germany* (Oxford: Clarendon Press, 1993).

5. According to information given to me by the monks from the Franciscan cloister in Duvno-Tomislavgrad, Bosnia-Herzegovian, in an interview with the monks and the monastery's superior Gabro Mioč in April 1991. An article about this was published in the special issue "Herzegovina," supplement to the weekly *Nedjeljna Dalmacija*, May 1991.

6. From my interview with Mioč in April 1991.

7. William A. Christian, Jr., "Religious Apparitions and the Cold War in Southern Europe," in *Religion, Power and Protest in Local Communities*, ed. Eric Wolf (Berlin: Mouton, 1984), p. 253.

8. According to Pedro Ramet, "in 1981, when the apparitions were first reported, the growth rate of industrial production slowed to 4 percent (from 5 percent in the 1970s), agricultural growth slid to 1.25 percent, domestic consumer demand declined by 3.5 percent, [and] unemployment rose 3 percent . . . over 1980 (there were 808,000 unemployed that year). . . . [I]nflation also began to accelerate sharply in 1981 . . . fixed investment as a share of the Gross Domestic Product declined steadily from 1979 to 1983 . . . [and] the mood in Yugoslavia [in] 1981–1983 was generally despondent, where economic matters were concerned." "The Miracle at Medjugorje—A Functional Perspective," *South Slav Journal 8* (1985), p. 17.

9. Henri Joyeux et al., *Etudes médicales et scientifiques sur les apparitions de Medjugorje* (Paris: OEIL, 1985).

10. Žanić implied (but did not explicitly say) this in an interview with me at the bishops' office in Mostar on 4 February 1991 and again on 15 June 1991. Vjekoslav Perica, "Deset godina kasnije: Novo čudo u Medjugorju" (Ten years later: New miracle at Medjugorje), *Nedjeljna Dalmacija*, 30 June 1991.

11. As said by Žanić in two interviews me conducted in July 1990 in Split and in February 1991 in Mostar.

12. Vego later married a nun from a nearby female monastic community and continued to live in Medjugorje—the couple made a living working as guides for foreign pilgrims and keeping a small shop with Medjugorje paraphernalia.

13. See Milan Vuković, *Cl.133 KZ SFRJ nad Medjugorjem—Sudski progon fra Joze Zovka* (Article 133 of SFR Yugoslavia's Criminal Code over Medjugorje—The trial of Father Jozo Zovko) (Zagreb: Helios, 1990).

14. From my interview with Monsignor Žanić in Mostar, February 1991.

15. Beyer, *Medjugorje Day by Day*. Zovko repeated this on 3 January 1997 in an interview on the US religious television channel EWTN.

16. Christian *Visionaries: the Spanish Republic and the Reign of Christ*.

17. *Religion in Communist Lands* 16, 1 (spring 1988), p. 87.

18. "The Mystery of Mary," *Life*, December 1996, p. 54.

19. Ramet, "The Miracle at Medjugorje: A Functional Perspective," p. 12.

20. The Medjugorje cult became widely popular in the United States. See for example, Dale Brown, *Journey of a Coach: The Testimony of Head Basketball Coach of the LSU Tigers about the Apparitions of the Blessed Mother of God in Medjugorje, Yugoslavia* (New Orleans: MIR Group, 1989).

21. *Religion in Communist Lands* 16, 1 (spring 1988), p. 87.

22. Ibid.

23. "The Mystery of Mary," p. 54.

24. This film was funded by the new Croatian regime and directed by the Croatian proregime filmmaker Jakov Sedlar, with an American crew.

25. Pope John Paul II "has watched the unfolding events with great interest and has privately affirmed the spiritual fruits of Medjugorje. 'Let the people go to Medjugorje if they pray, fast, do penance, confess, and convert,' the Pontiff said in 1986." Beyer, *Medjugorje Day by Day*, p.

26. Hank Johnston, *Tales of Nationalism: Catalonia, 1939–1979* (New Brunswick: Rutgers University Press, 1991), pp. 55–56.

27. See Robert A. Graham, *The Vatican and Communism during World War II* (San Francisco: Ignatius Press, 1996) pp. 93–94.

28. "Address of Cardinal Angelo Sodano Regarding the 'Third Part' of the Secret of Fatima at the Conclusion of the Solemn Mass of John Paul II," Fatima, 13 May 2000, quoted from the official website of the Holy See: http//www.vatican.va.

29. William Christian, "Religious Apparitions and the Cold War in Southern Europe," Eric Wolf, ed., *Religion, Power and Protest in Local Communities* (Berlin: Mouton, 1984), p. 243.

30. Ibid., p. 241.

31. Michael P. Carroll, *The Cult of the Virgin Mary: Psychological Origins* (Princeton, NJ: Princeton University Press, 1986), pp. 219–220.

32. Christian, "Religious Apparitions and the Cold War in Southern Europe," p. 220.

33. Ibid., pp. 246–249.

34. Jeffrey Pratt, "Christian-Democrat Ideology in the Cold War Period," in Wolf, *Religion, Power and Protest*.

35. *Tradition, Family, Property: Half a Century of Epic Anticommunism*, translated from the Portuguese by John Russel Spann in collaboration with Jose Aloisio A. Schelini (New York: Foundation for a Christian Civilization, 1981), pp. 439–440.

36. New apparitions triggered massive devotional movements in the ensuing decades. In the 1980s the Madonna allegedly appeared during the crisis in Nic-

aragua to support the Contras and chastise the communist Sandinistas. Then came the apparitions at Medjugorje and in western Ukraine. In the late 1980s and 1990s, new Marian apparitions were reported in Argentina, Syria, Spain, Rwanda, Egypt, and Italy.

37. The Procession with the statue of Our Lady of Fatima commemorating the Fatima apparition and symbolically demonstrating its fulfilment would take place in Moscow in June 1992.

38. Ivo Andrić, *The Development of Spiritual Life in Bosnia under the Influence of Turkish Rule*, ed. and trans. Zelimir Juričić and Hohn F. Loud (Durham, NC: Duke University Press, 1990), p. 65.

39. Ibid., p. 44.

40. Mart Bax, "The Madonna of Medjugorje: Religious Rivalry and the Formation of a Devotional Movement in Yugoslavia," *Anthropological Quarterly* 63, 2 (April 1990), p. 64.

41. In the 1980s, owing to the popularity of the Medjugorje miracle, the west Herzegovinian Franciscans brought 140 monks into the area who served the pilgrims and worked in 43 parishes and 4 monasteries, according to *Adresar Katoličke crkve u SFRJ*.

42. One of the founders of liberation theology, the Franciscan Leonardo Boff (who was disciplined by the Vatican), visited Bosnia-Herzegovina during the recent war. Boff said in an interview that he was "impressed and fascinated with the Franciscans of Bosnia-Herzegovina who remained faithful to their people even at the expense of martyrdom." Croatian Catholic news agency *IKA*, 27 September 1996.

43. In the words of the archbishop of Sarajevo, Vinko Cardinal Puljić, the friars of Herzegovina are a "stern, pigheaded, and weird kind of folks," according to my notes of the cardinal-archbishop's lecture delivered at the United States Institute of Peace in Washington, DC, 19 February 1997.

44. Strahinja Kurdulija, *Atlas of the Ustasha Genocide of the Serbs 1941–1945* (Belgrade: Europublic, 1994).

45. See Richard West, *Tito and the Rise and Fall of Yugoslavia* (New York: Caroll L. Graf, 1995), p. 385. See also Marco Aurelio Rivelli, *L'arcivescovo del genocidio: monsignor Stepinac, il Vaticano e la dittatura ustascia in Croazia, 1941–1944* (Milan: Kaos, 1999).

46. The girl's lawyer argued that the news was not false. He asked the judge to provide convincing evidence that the Virgin Mary does not exist and that the girl did not see what she was claiming she had really seen. In the local press, the whole affair was used to ridicule both the Church and the authorities.

47. From (in my translation) the original indictment filed in the Office of the Commission for Relation with Religious Communities of the Association of Municipalities of Dalmatia, Split, Croatia.

48. According to correspondence between Archbishop Metropolitan Franić and the municipal commission for relations with religious communities in Split.

49. "The Mystery of Mary," p. 54.

50. *Glas koncila*, 12 April 1991.

51. *Glas koncila*, 15 August 1993.

52. Ibid., p. 11.

53. Beyer, *Medjugorje Day by Day*,

54. The former Yugoslav state news agency TANJUG carried the information, as well as foreign news agencies. For example, the *Frankfurter Algemeine Zeitung* mentioned the massacres around Medjugorje in a lengthy December 1981 article

that was largely sympathetic to the Church; in October 1981, a daily newspaper in Melbourne, Australia, also noted this bizarre fact; also in October 1981, a Japanese daily in English, the *Mainichi Daily News*, wrote that the Virgin Mary appeared at the site where the Croatian Nazis Catholic Ustašas had massacred 2,500 Yugoslavs of Orthodox faith during World War II. All according to *Religion, Politics, Society* (October–December 1981).

55. Milan Bulajić, *Ustaški zločini genocida i sudjenje Andriji Artukoviću 1986* (The Ustaša crimes of genocide and the trial of Andrija Artuković 1986), vols. 1–4 (Belgrade: Rad, 1988, 1990).

56. Bulajić asserted in an interview that Zovko's guilt for teaching the children how to salute in the Fascist manner was proved before the court in the 1981 trial. *NIN*, Belgrade, 17 June 1988.

57. *Pravoslavlje*, 15 November 1990.

58. *Crkva 1991: 1941–1991 Nezaceljene rane na telu Srpske Crkve* (1941–1991 Unhealed wounds on the body of the Serbian Church), Church calendar (Belgrade: Holy Bishop's Synod, 1990).

59. In June 1992, following the Serbian attack on Bosnia-Herzegovina, the chapel was, according to Serbian Church allegations, dynamited by Croats. Patriarch Pavle sent a protest letter to the United Nations. According to Marko Karamatić, ed., *Znanstveni skup "Rat u Bosni i Hercegovini: uzroci, posljedice, perspektive"* (Scholarly conference "War in Bosnia-Herzegovina: Causes, consequences, perspectives") (Samobor, Croatia: Franciscan Theological School in Sarajevo, 1993), p. 209.

60. *Pravoslavlje*, 15 February 1991.

61. Ibid.

62. Ibid.

63. Ibid.

64. Ibid.

65. *Nedjeljna Dalmacija*, 30 June 1991.

8. Flames and Shrines

1. Ramet, *Nationalism and Federalism in Yugoslavia: 1962–1991*, p. 197.

2. *Pravoslavlje*, 1 April 1981.

3. In a 1987 interview, Patriarch Germanus indicated that the Albanians had set the patriarchate on fire and inferred that this was not revealed by the federal authorities because of concerns about security and the desire to maintain calm ethnic relations. Spasojević, *The Communists and I*, p. 90.

4. From Jevtić, *Stradanja Srba na Kosovu i Metohiji od 1941 do 1990*, pp. 401–402.

5. The Serbian Church reprinted the article in 1991. The text reads as follows: "Serbian kings earned a special place in European history by building the largest number of sacred Christian places of worship: two thousand churches and monasteries, still preserved or in ruins, stand today in ancient Kosovo and Macedonia on this Serbian soil so devoted to Christ! These sacred sites harbor twenty thousand frescoes and icons. Is there any other place in the East or in the West where something like this can be found?" *Pravoslavlje*, 15 January 1991.

6. From Marko Živković, "Stories Serbs Tell Themselves: Discourse on Identity and Destiny in Serbia since the Mid-1980s," *Problems of Post-Communism* 44, 4 (July–August 1997), pp. 22–29.

7. "Ćosić, following Camus, who undoubtedly had in mind the famous re-

mark of Hegel, that history can be explained as a sphere of exclusively tragic events, came to believe that nations and people can do little to change the nature and consequences of historical events." Branislav Milošević, "Ćosićeve mijene i ciljevi" (Ćosić's changes and objectives), *Danas*, September–October 1989.

8. In a 1993 interview with a foreign correspondent, Ćosić said: "The Serb is the new Jew, the Jew at the end of the twentieth century." Christina Posa, "Engineering Hatred: The Roots of Contemporary Serbian Nationalism," *Balkanistica* 11 (1998), pp. 69–77.

9. Žarko Gavrilović, *Na braniku vere i nacije* (In Defense of the faith and the nation) (Belgrade: IZ Patriaršije, 1986). Quoted from Gavrilović's presentation of the book according to *Borba*, 30 October 1986.

10. *Glasnik Srpske pravoslavne crkve*, no. 7, July 1982.

11. *"Kronika exodusa Srba s Kosova i Metohije"* (A chronicle of the Serb exodus from Kosovo and Metohija), *Pravoslavlje*, 1 October 1982.

12. Atanasije Jevtić et al., eds., *Zadužbine Kosova: spomenici i znamenja srpskog naroda* (Debts to God in Kosovo: Monuments and symbols of the Serbian people) (Belgrade: Eparhija Raško-Prizrenska i Bogoslovski fakultet, 1987), pp. 831–842.

13. Atanasije Jevtić, "Od Kosova do Jadovna," *Pravoslavlje*, 15 November 1983. The first edition of Jevtić's book appeared in 1984 with a more than dozen subsequent editions and supplements. Atanasije Jevtić, *Od Kosova do Jadovna* (Belgrade: Sfairos, 1984).

14. "We in the Serbian Church know the mystery and believe in the liberating power of Kosovo. We believe in the capability of all cults of the Serbian martyrdom to bring about resurrection of the Serbian people. But there is no resurrection without death, as (the famous poets) Njegš and Šantić have said. The Serbs have been martyred again. Expelled Serbs, while leaving Kosovo, are telling the Albanians: We will be back! That is not vengefulness, that is our faith. Kosovo is ours and will be ours again. I already see promising changes in Serbia." *Religion, Politics, Society*, 10 October 1985, p. III/43.

15. Dimitrije Bogdanović, "Istina prije svega" (Truth above all), quoted in Jevtić et al., *Zadužbine Kosova*, pp. 844–845.

16. Jevtić et al., afterword to *Zadužbine Kosova*.

17. *NIN*, 6 March 1988, p. 29.

18. "Memorandum SANU—Memorandum of the Serbian Academy of Science and Arts," in *Eastern European Nationalism in the Twentieth Century*, ed. Peter F. Sugar (Washington, DC: American University Press, 1995), pp. 332–346.

19. Spasojević, *The Communists and I*, p. 24.

20. In 1995, with the temple still unfinished, the Holy Synod had to release an appeal for "only 10 million dollars more" and accused the international community of imposing sanction on Serbia because of the Bosnian war, thus crippling the sacred rebuilding. Branko Pešić, *Godine Hrama Svetog Save* (Belgrade: M. komunikacije, 1995), p. 9.

21. Ibid.

22. Ibid.

23. *Politika*, 11 June 1988.

24. Pešić, *Godine Hrama Svetog Save*, p. 60.

25. Ibid.

26. *Pravoslavlje*, 1 November 1989.

27. *Pravoslavlje*, 1 March 1990.

28. *Pravoslavlje*, 1 June 1984; *Politika*, 11 March 1988; *Oslobodjenje*, 2 March 1988.

29. Jevtić, *Stradanja Srba*, p. 450.

30. The daily *Politika* wrote: "It is shocking and unthinkable that someone dared to register as an Islamic place of worship, even by mistake, one of the holiest landmarks of Serbdom and Orthodoxy, as well as the invaluable monument of world cultural heritage, [a place] such as the monastery of Visoki Dečani, which celebrates this year the 650th anniversary of its foundation . . . [I]t seems that someone is playing games with the Serbian cultural heritage." "I Dečani pokršteni" (Even Dečani have been converted), *Politika*, 25 April 1987.

31. A part of the poem follows (my translation):

> They are stealing my memory,
> They want to shorten my history,
> They are taking away my centuries,
> Converting my churches into mosques
> Transcribing my alphabet.
> They are hammering my cemeteries and tombs,
> They want to uproot me,
> They want to crush my cradle.
> But where I can move my Dečani?
> And how I can dislocate the patriarchate of Peć?
> *Pravoslavlje*, 1 March 1990

32. *Pravoslavlje*, 1 March 1990. The very same vision of new sacred buildings mushrooming in late communism as symbols with a "conflict-mitigating" function was expressed to me by the chief architect of the Saint Sava cathedral at Belgrade, Branko Pešić, in an interview on 26 April 1991 in Belgrade.

33. The cathedral of the Mother of God of Charity at the Studenica monastery near Ušće in southwestern Serbia was built by the founder of the Nemanjić dynasty, Stephen Nemanja (1169–96). The white polished marble structure fuses the Byzantine and Romanesque styles into what is known as the Raška type of sacral architecture.

34. *Glasnik Srpske pravoslavne crkve*, 6 June 1986, p. 133.

35. "Yugoslav communists, who seemed to put up with the self-assertive and dissenting Croatian Catholicism, now have also to turn more attention to the Serbian Orthodox Church, which they until recently routinely underestimated." *Religion, Politics, Society*, 28 May 1986. The article originally appeared in *Die Velt*, 25 May 1986.

36. Karl Gustav Stroem, "We Believe in the Spiritual Power of Tzar Lazar and the Martyrs of Kosovo," *Religion, Politics, Society*, 15 July 1982. The article was originally published in the German daily newspaper *Die Velt*, 7 July 1982.

37. The Belgrade rock band YU-Grupa hit the charts with "Kosovski Božuri," a tune about red flowers (božuri) blossoming on the Kosovo battlefield. Legend has it that the flowers are watered by the blood of the Serb warriors who died there in 1389. Another popular tune of the 1980s was "Jefimija," performed by Lutajuća Srca, about the fourteenth-century Serb-Orthodox nunpoet. In 1982 the Belgrade vocal-instrumental assemble Idoli released a record entitled *Apology and Last Days*, with a cover picture of Cyrillic letters and religious symbols that the band's songwriter, Vlada Divljan, had discovered in the library of the Serbian patriarchate (the title was borrowed from the Serb author Borislav Pekić's historic novel on the beginning of World War II). The Idoli enriched their music with chanting from the Orthodox church liturgy while evoking the Kosovo myth

and Slavophile sentiments about Russia. One of the most influential Serbian rock bands, Ekaterina Velika, dedicated to Kosovo one of their hit songs, "Zemlja" (Land), whose lyrics call on Serbs not to leave their land. Many other performers wrote songs inspired by religion and myth.

38. "Eppur si muove," *NIN*, 18 January 1987.

39. *Religija i društvo* (Religion and society) (Zagreb: Centar za idejno teorijski rad Gradskog komiteta Saveza komunista, 1987), p. 120.

40. *Pravoslavlje*, 15 January 1984; *Vjesnik Sedam Dana*, 3 March 1984; TV Belgrade, evening news, 26 February 1984.

41. The chronicle of the Visoki Dečani abbey on the Serbian-Albanian border recorded that "in September of 1992 over 2,000 people were christened in the Bistrica River. That was probably the first time—since the mass conversion of Slavs to Christianity in the 7th century—that so many people accepted the Christian Orthodox faith of their forefathers." See Monastery Visoki Dečani, at http//www.decani.yunet.com.

42. "U Beogradu održan prvi posleratni svetosavski ball" (First postwar Saint Sava's Ball held in Belgrade), *Politika*, 29 January 1989.

43. *NIN*, 26 April 1991.

44. Ibid.

45. Ibid.

46. In the 1990s, Dragojlović published spiritual treatises and nationalistic pamphlets. See Dragan Dragojlović, *Nebeska Srbija* (Belgrade: Srpska književna zadruga, 1990) *Dozivanje Boga* (Belgrade: Prosveta, 1995).

47. *NIN*, 26 April 1991.

48. See Dragojlović's article in Gordana Živković, ed., *Čovek i crkva u vrtlogu krize: šta nam nudi pravoslavlje danas?* (Man and the Church in the vortex of crisis: What Can the Orthodox faith offer us today?) (Niš: Gradina, 1993). See also his poetry and essays, *Nebeska Srbija* (Heavenly Serbia) (Belgrade: Srpska književna zadruga, 1990); *Dozivanje Boga* (Calling God) (Belgrade: Prosveta, 1995).

49. "Predlog srpskog crkveno-nacionalnog programa" (A proposal of the Serbian Church-National program), *Glas crkve*, no. 3, 28 June, 1989.

50. Ibid.

51. Ibid.

52. Mitar Miljanović, "Srpska pravoslavna crkva i nacionalno pitanje" (The Serbian Orthodox Church and the national question), *Glas Crkve*, no. 1, January 1991, pp. 61–69.

53. Ibid., pp. 67–71.

54. Ibid., p. 70.

55. Ibid., p. 71.

56. *AKSA*, 31 August 1984.

57. According to *Religion, Politics, Society*, March 1986, and *Adresar katoličke crkve u SFRJ*.

58. *Omladinske novine*, 15 April 1984; also *Religion, Politics, Society*, 19 April 1984.

59. Štefica Bahtijarević, ed., *Religijska situacija na području zagrebačke regije* (The Religious situation in the Zagreb region) (Zagreb: Institute za društvena istraživanja Sveučilišta u Zagrebu, 1985). The statement by one of the researchers Liudevit Plačko is quoted from *Religion, Politics, Society*, 30 May 1985, p. III/43.

60. Ibid.

61. Vrcan, "Religion, Nation and Class in Contemporary Yugoslavia," p. 94.

62. Srdjan Vrcan, "Mladi i religija danas" (The young and religion today), in *Religija i društvo*, pp. 46–60.

9. *The Second Strife*

1. Radovan Samardžić, "Religija i društvo, crkva i dr žava u SFRJ" (Religion and society—Church and state in the SFRJ), in *Religija i društvo* (Religion and society), ed. Štefica Bahtijarević and Branko Bošnjak (Zagreb: Center za idejno teorijski rad Gradskog komiteta SKH, 1987), p. 199.

2. The Slovene TV journalist Ljerka Bizilj was the first in Yugoslavia who, in 1990, after having examined police archives at Ljubljana, wrote about spying on the clergy by the communist political police. Ljerka Bizilji, *Cerkev v policijskih arhivih* (The Church in police archives) (Ljubljana: Cankarjeva založba, 1990).

3. Chris Cviic, "Throne and Altar in Croatia," *Tablet*, 19 July 1997.

4. The media in Slovenia revealed in 1999 that workers found several microphones planted in the offices of Maribor Bishop Franc Kramberger and one of his aides. Vatican Radio reported on this on 10 April 2000. The listening devices were discovered in September 1999, just before the visit by Pope John Paul II. The Slovenian leadership, says Radio Vatican, includes many former communists and others who fear that the Roman Catholic Church wants to regain the wealth and political power it enjoyed before 1945. Radio Free Europe/Radio Liberty, *Newsline, Southeastern Europe*, 11 March 2000.

5. Komisija za odnose s vjerskim zajednicama Izvršnog vijeća Sabora Socijalističke Republike Hrvatske, "Uputstvo za organizaciju i rad komisija za odnose s vjerskim zajednicama u općinama, gradovima, i zajednicama općina" (Instructions for organization and work of Commissions for Relations with Religious Communities in municipalities, cities and associations of municipalities), confidential (Zagreb, 24 April 1986).

6. Komisija za odnose s vjerskim zajednicama Izvršnog vijeća Sabora Socijalističke Republike Hrvatske, "Pregled stanja i rada komisija za odnose s vjerskim zajednicama u SR Hrvatskoj" (A survey of the status and activity of commissions for Relations with Religious Communities in the SR Croatia), prepared by the chief secretary Vitomir Unković with the Commission's staff in cooperation with municipal commissions (Zagreb, April 1988).

7. See John Anderson, *Religion, State and Politics in the Soviet Union and Successor States* (Cambridge, UK: Cambridge University Press, 1994).

8. Republički sekretarijat za unutrašnje poslove SR Hrvatske—Služba Državne Sigurnosti (The Republic Secretariat of Internal Affairs of the Socialist Republic of Croatia—Service of State Security), "Informacija o komentarima i ponašanju klera za vrijeme bolesti i pogreba Predsjednika Tita" (An information on comments and behavior of the clergy during the illness and funeral of President Tito), top secret, obtained through the Commission for Relations with Religious Communities of the Executive Council of the Association of Municipalities of Dalmatia (Zagreb, June 1980). According to this document, some clerics blamed God for keeping Tito alive so long.

9. *Vjesnik*, Zagreb, 21 April 1983.

10. In 1985, Monsignor Petar Šolić, a professor of theology from Split and spiritual advisor for the Catholic Youth Movement, was threatened with a jail sentence by the police for organizing a march on the diocesan shrine of Sinj. In an interview with me, Šolić said he saw nothing illegal in singing religious songs

and walking in public with religious insignia but still refrained from further massive marches. Instead he split his activists into smaller groups.

11. Centralni komitet Saveza komunista Hrvatske (Central Committee of the League of Communists of Croatia), "Program idejno-političke akcije Saveza komunista Hrvatske u ostvarivanju programskih načela u odnosu prema religiji, provodjenju ustavnih opredjeljenja o slobodi vjeroispovijesti i borbi protiv sektaštva, klerikalizma i kleronacionalizma" (A program of ideological-political action of the League of Communists of Croatia aimed at achieving application of the programmatic principles concerning religion, constitutional norms on religious liberty, and the struggle against sectarianism, clericalism and cleronationalism) (Zagreb, 10 June 1985); and Komisija za statutarna pitanja (Commission for Questions of the Statute), "Neka stutarna pitanja odnosa komunista prema religiji i vjerskim obredima" (Some questions of the statute regarding attitudes of communists toward religion and religious practices) (Zagreb, 10 June 1985).

12. *Vijesnik*, 25 April 1987.

13. *Vijesnik*, 22 January 1983.

14. Ibid.

15. Jug Grizelj, column in the *Slobodna Dalmacija*, 27 April 1985.

16. According to an incomplete list of political prisoners in Yugoslavia released by an international human rights group, in the period from March 1973 to October 1985, 527 persons were jailed for various forms of antiregime political activity, though some other sources estimated that 2,208 people had been charged with political offenses between 1980 and 1983 alone. Most of those sentenced were ethnic Albanian separatists arrested in the aftermath of the 1981 Albanian rebellion in the province of Kosovo. *Religion in Communist Lands* 15, 3 (winter 1987), p. 64.

17. Ibid., p. 65.

18. Most of these conscientious objectors were Jehovah's Witnesses, Nazarenes, and Seventh-Day Adventists. See *Religion in Communist Lands* 15, 3, p. 333.

19. In my personal experience, pressure on local administration to grant all demands for sacred construction, with an increase of state funding for the preservation of sacred heritage, and establishing friendly communications with clergy was the principal task of the commissions for relations with religious communities in the 1980s.

20. Peričić and Škvorčević, *Trinaest stoljeća kršćanstva u Hrvata*, p. 22.

21. See Franić, *Bit ćete mi svijedoci*, pp. 271–275.

22. On 22 January 1986 in the Split city hall, the Archbishop Franić said: "As we see that democratic processes in our society are making progress, we all realize that a chance is given to us by God, to create a better and more humane society in this Balkan region—a more humane and more civilized society than we have ever had here before in history. In this newly emerging society, in the foreseeable future, I believe, every individual, of any religious or ethnic background, will be given an equal opportunity, and free access to economic, cultural, and social goods as well as public offices and services, depending on each individual's own abilities, willingness to work and professional knowledge, humane characteristics, and patriotic love toward the concrete [i.e., socialist-communist] society. In such a free and just society, there will be no need for exploiting religion for political purposes, and no reason for the consecration of politics. I believe as a Christian that this society in which we all live is not created by the devil but by God, and God takes care of it. A tolerant dialogue among all of us is needed to achieve a consensus about what is freedom, what is truth, what is justice,

what does it mean to be good, what is love, what is peace, what is the social role of the Church. . . . A broad democratic consensus in this country is what we need to accomplish." The text of the speech was given to me by Archbishop Franić. It was later published in the official bulletin of the Archdiocese of Split-Makarska in January 1985, as *"The Archbishop's Address at the New Year meeting with State Authorities."*

23. Komisija za odnose s vjerskim zajednicama Izvršnog vijeća Sabora Soci-jalističke Republike Hrvatske, "Odnosi s vjerskim zajednicama u SR Hrvatskoj" (Zagreb, March 1981).

24. Ibid.

25. Radio Vatican, Croatian Service, *Evening News*, 18 March 1983. See *Religion, Politics, Society*, 24 March 1983.

26. *ANSA*, daily report, 25 November 1983. See *Religion, Politics, Society*, 8 December 1983.

27. TANJUG bulletin, *Religion, Politics, Society*, 11 May 1984. According to my 1989 interview with the Yugoslav ambassador to the Holy See, Zdenko Svete, the talks were private and informal and included a number of issues, including the Jasenovac issue. In Svete's words, John Paul II did not oppose the idea of prayer at Jasenovac. Yet Cardinal Kuharić and the bishops' conference of Yugoslavia argued that a consensus with the Orthodox Church should be reached in advance of the papal visit. That was not possible, because the Serbian Orthodox Church did not respond to the bishops' conference's 1982 and 1983 letters proposing new forms of ecumenical dialogue.

28. According to an interview I carried out in 1990 with some top-ranking officers of the Yugoslav navy, *Nedjeljna Dalmacija*, 11 November 1990.

29. "Prilog BKJ rasparavi o aktualnim promjenama Ustava SFRJ u svijetlu kršćanske etike" (A supplement of the BKJ to the debate on the current amendments to the Constitution of the SFRY in the light of Christian ethics), *AKSA* 42 (909), 10 October 1987.

30. The group included the Archpriest Ljubodrag Petrović, head of the Saint Alexander Temple in Belgrade, the Jesuit priest Vladimir Horvat, the mufti of Belgrade, Hamdija Jusufspahić, and the rabbi Alexandar Šibul, all from Belgrade. The petition was addressed to the federal and republican authorities as well as to religious authorities. I interviewed Archpriest Petrović and Monsignor Horvat.

31. In a conversation with me on 23 December 1990, at the Belgrade Saint Alexander Nevski temple, Archpriest Ljubodrag Petrović said that the group wanted to stress both the right of the clergy to act autonomously as citizens, as well as the participants' desire to form interfaith committees such as existed in the West.

32. The state delegation also included Svete's deputy, Pero Pletikosa; the commission's chief secretary, Vitomir Unković, and the chairman of municipal commission for relations with religious communities in Split, Marin Kuzmić.

33. I did not find a written record of the meeting in the Zagreb commission office. Chairman Svete reported about the talks verbally to a small group of top leaders that included the party general secretary, Drago Dimitrović, the executive secretary, Celestin Sardelić, and Croatia's premier, Antun Milović. I discussed the talks with Vitomir Unković and Marin Kuzmić, as well as with Bishop Tamarut and Archbishop Franić.

34. Vjekoslav Perica, "Prayer for Marković," *Nedjeljna Dalmacija*, 21 January 1990.

35. *Nedjeljna Dalmacija*, 11 November 1990. The article is based on my inter-

views with Radovan Samardžić and Rear Admiral Jovan Popović, then one of commanding officers of the military-naval district in Split, Croatia.

36. Komisija za odnose s vjerskim zajednicama Izvršnog vijeća Sabora Socijalističke Republike Hrvatske, "Odnosi s vjerskim zajednicama u SR Hrvatskoj."

37. The document reads: "Systematic and persistent efforts aimed to launch a public debate on the Ustaša crimes committed in World War II against Serbs and the persecution of the Serbian Orthodox Church in the territory of the so-called Independent State of Croatia, whereas the entire Croatian people is equated with the Ustašas, so that Orthodox zealots often speak about the "Croatian crimes" against Serbs without specifying that some militant Ustašas committed the crimes while thousands of Croats together with Serbs fought the invaders and their domestic servants." Komisija za odnose s vjerskim zajednicama Izvršnog viječa Sabora Socijalističke Republike Hrvatske, "Odnosi s vjerskim zajednicama u SR Hrvatskoj."

38. The office of the Serbian patriarchate in Belgrade claimed damages in Yugoslav currency from the federal government estimated at 2,432,618,334 Yugoslav dinars after the war and later asked for 878,019,175 dinars more. The office's legal representative said that damages were given to the Serbian Orthodox Church by the state. *Stav*, September 1990. In June 1989 the Holy Synod of the Serbian Orthodox Church addressed separate requests for damages to the government of the Socialist Republic of Croatia and the Socialist Republic of Bosnia-Herzegovina regarding World War II crimes against the Serbian Orthodox Church in the wartime Croatian state. See *Pravoslavlje*, 1 July 1989, and *Nedjeljna Dalmacija*, 17 September 1989.

39. The Serbian Orthodox Church in Croatia, newly built 64 churches, two monasteries, 15 parish homes, and nine chapels, 25 churches, four chapels, 16 parish homes, and two church museums were renovated. The construction was achieved with state financial assistance. *Nedjeljna Dalmacija*, 17 September 1989.

40. Vjekoslav Perica, "Strategija Kaosa: Kako je Srpska pravoslavna crkva pripremala teren za oružane ustanke Srba u Hrvatskoj" (A strategy of chaos: How the Serbian Orthodox Church prepared the ground for armed Serb uprisings in Croatia), *Nedjeljna Dalmacija*, 10, 17, and 24 March 1991.

41. *Nedjeljna Dalmacija*, 2 December 1990, p. 7.

42. In 1990 Duka became deputy minister for labor and social welfare. In an interview with me, this Franciscan friar said that a large amount of the money he raised for Tudjman in Germany would be allocated (according to a deal between Tudjman and Duka) to social welfare programs and aid to the unemployed affected by the economic transition from socialism to capitalism. By 1995, Duka left the HDZ and became Tudjman's critic. My interview with Duka appeared in *Nedjeljna Dalmacija*, 2 December 1990, p. 7.

43. According to Josip Manolić, at one time a close aide to Tudjman, the Yugoslav secret police kept track of all Tudjman's activities abroad. *Nedjeljna Dalmacija*, 30 December 1999.

44. Voice of America, Croatian Service, 28 April 2000.

45. See *Yugoslavia—Death of a Nation*, TV series, parts 1–4 (Discovery Channel, BBC, and ORF, 1995).

46. "Hrvatska okupacijska zona u BiH," interview with Ivo Komšić, president of the Croatian Popular Council, *Feral Tribune*, 12 July 1999, pp. 38–39.

47. In Croatia, Tudjman's Croatian Democratic Community won a relative plurality of 43 percent and beat the former communists, who gained 34 percent. The nationalistic Serbian Democratic Party, backed by the Church, won in the

municipalities throughout the Krajina region in which the armed uprising began in August 1990. In Bosnia, the Muslim Party of Democratic Action won 34 percent and the nationalistic Serbian Democratic Party 30 percent, while the multiethnic Reform Alliance led by the federal premier Ante Marković gained 10 percent of the vote, less than the Croat nationalists, who won 18 percent.

48. *Nedjeljna Dalmacija*, monthly supplement *Herzegovina*, March 1991.

49. The head of the Islamic Community of Croatia, Ševko Omerbašić, told me in May 1990 that several Muslim religious leaders, including Omerbašić and Mustafa Cerić from Zagreb, Senahid Bristrić form Sarajevo, and the mufti Seid Smajkić from Mostar, among others, took part in the foundation of the SDA in 1989. According to my talks with local Muslim leaders in Mostar in February 1991, Muslim clergy carried out the election campaign in Muslim villages and small towns (secular leaders were prominent in the big cities), including organization of rallies, speeches at the rallies, meetings with voters, and so forth. Ibid.

50. Djilas and Graće, *Bošnjak Adil Zulfikarpašić*.

51. Ibid., p. 149.

52. Ibid., p. 131.

53. Spasojević, *The Communists and I*, pp. 104–105.

54. *Naša Borba*, 8 April 1998.

55. The bishop's statement to the BBC evening radio news, 4 August 1989. *Religion, Politics, Society*, 17 August 1989.

56. "Poruka Svetog arhijerejskog sabora Srpske pravslavne crkve srpskom narodu povodom prvih višestranačkih izbora u Sriji i Crnoj Gori" (Message of the Holy Bishops' Sabor of the Serbian Orthodox Church to the Serbian people on the occasion of the first multiparty elections in Serbia and Montenegro), *Pravoslavlje*, 15 December 1990.

57. Ibid.

58. Atanasije Jevtić, front page editorials, *Pravoslavlje*, 1 November 1990, 1 December 1990.

59. On 18 April 1991 the People's Assembly of Serbia passed a law on restitution of the confiscated property (buildings, endowments, construction lots) to the Serbian Orthodox Church, but Milošević did not sign the law, despite the patriarchate's vigorous protests, addressed to the Popular Assembly and published in the Church press. *Pravoslavlje*, 15 May 1991.

60. *Pravoslavlje*, 15 January 1991.

61. In one such article the Serbian Church contended that the Croatian police tolerated murder and expulsions of Serbs in the Krajina region. *Pravoslavlje*, 15 April 1988.

62. *Pravoslavlje*, 1 October 1990.

63. Ibid.

64. *Nedjeljna Dalmacija*, 20 January 1991.

65. See Miroljub Jevtić, *Šiptari i Islam* (Prnjavor: Grafomotajica, 1995).

66. Jevtić, *Stradanja Srba na Kosovu i Metohiji od 1941 do 1990*, p. 442.

67. Spasojević, *The Communists and I*, p. 119.

68. The mufti of Kosovo, Jetiš Bajrami, said in an interview with me that the Islamic Community could not be held accountable for Albanian separatism because regular mosque attendance is low and the percentage of children enrolled in religious instruction is unsatisfactory. Interview in Prizren, August 1990. *Nedjeljna Dalmacija*, 5 August 1990.

69. *Pravoslavlje*, 15 June 1982; *Danas*, 22 June 1982.

70. *Religion, Politics, Society,* 15 July 1982. The article by Karl Gustav Stroem was originally published in the German daily newspaper *Die Welt,* 7 July 1982.

71. Spasojević, *The Communists and I,* p. 99.

72. See Turčinović, *Katolička Crkva u južnoslavenskim zemljama,* and Zarija Bešić et al., ed., *Istorija Crne Gore* (History of Montenegro), vols. 1–3 (Titograd: Redakcija za istoriju Crne Gore, 1967).

73. See a critical review of the debate in Ivo Banac, "The Dissolution of Yugoslav Historiography," in *Beyond Yugoslavia: Politics, Economics and Culture in a Shattered Community* ed. Sabrina P. Ramet and Ljubisa S. Adamovich (Boulder, CO: Westview Press, 1995), pp. 39–65.

74. See for example, Charles S. Maier, *The Unmasterable Past: History, Holocaust, and German National Identity* (Cambridge: Harvard University Press, 1988), and Norman G. Finkelstein, *The Holocaust Industry: Reflections on the Exploitation of the Jewish Suffering* (London: Verso, 2000).

75. See Vasilije Dj. Krestić, "O genezi genocida nad Srbima u NDH" Književne novine, 15 September 1986, and his expanded version of this article in English, *Through Genocide to a Greater Croatia,* trans. Boško Milosavljevie (Belgrade: BIGZ, 1998).

76. See, for example, ENM (Bishop Nikodim Milaš), *Pravoslavna Dalmacija* (Novi Sad: Knjižarnica A. Pajevića, 1901; reissued in Belgrade, 1989); Ljubomir Ranković, Radovan Bigović, and Mitar Milovanović, eds., *Vladika Nikolaj: Izabrana dela. Knjiga XII* (Valjevo: Glas Crkve, 1997); Atanasije Jevtie, *Velikomučenicki Jasenovac, ustaška tvornica smrti: dokumenti i svedo čenja* (Valjevo: Glas crkve; Belgrade: Sfairos, 1990); Veljko D. Djurić, *Prekrštavanje Srba u Nezavisnoj Državi Hrvatskoj: prilozi za istoriju verskog genocida.* (Belgrade: Alfa, 1991); Milan Bulajić, *Misija Vatikana u Nezavisnoj Državi Hrvatskoj: "Politika Stepinac" razbijanja jugoslavenske dr žave i pokatoličavanja pravoslavnih Srba po cijenu genocida: stvaranje "Civitas Dei" i "Antemurale Christianitatis,"* 2 vols. (Belgrade: Politika, 1992); Smilja Avramov, *Genocide in Yugoslavia* (Belgrade: BIGZ, 1995).

77. The moderate Ljubo Boban wrote a three-volume polemical study of the controversy. See Ljubo Boban, *Kontroverze iz povijesti Jugoslavije* (Controversies from the history of Yugoslavia), vols. 1–3. (Zagreb: Školska knjiga, 1987, 1989, 1990).

78. Franjo Tudjman, *Bespuća povijesne zbiljnosti: rasprava o povijesti filozofije zlosilja,* 2nd ed. (Zagreb: Matica hrvatska, 1989), and *Horrors of war: Historical reality and philosophy,* trans. Katarina Mijatović (New York: Evans, 1996).

79. See *Horrors of War,* pp. 125–126, 292–302, 309–312, 322–323.

80. Vjekoslav Perica, "*Deset godina kasnije: Novo čudo u Medjugorju*" (Ten years later: New miracle at Medjugorje), *Nedjeljna Dalmacija,* 30 June 1991. The interview took place at the Diocesan office in Mostar, 25 June 1991.

81. The construction of the Memorial Zone at Jasenovac began in 1964. The monument was designed by Bogan Boganović. The renovation of the memorial park was completed in the mid-1970s.

82. *Glas crkve,* no. 3, 1988. See the church calendar *Crkva 1991,* p. 59.

83. Miljanović, "Srpska pravoslavna crkva i nacionalno pitanje," p. 66.

84. Ibid.

85. Ibid.

86. Milan Bulajić, "Post-war Documents about the Responsibility of the Vatican and the Kaptol for the Jasenovac Crimes," in *Večan pomen: Jasenovac: mjesto natopljeno krvlju nevinih 1941/1985/1991—Eternal Memory—Jasenovac, the Place*

Soaked in the Blood of Innocents, with Summaries in English—On the 50th Anniversary of Martyred Jesenovac and of the 7th Anniversary of the Consecration of the new Church of the Nativity of St. John the Baptist—Memorial Church Jasenovac (Belgrade: Holy Synod of the Serbian Orthodox Church, 1990), pp. 359–363).

87. The Croat historian Franjo Tudjman estimates the number of all victims killed in Jasenovac (including many Croats) at 40,000 to 60,000. See Franjo Tudjman, *Horrors of War: Historical Reality and Philosophy*, trans. Katarina Mijatović (New York: Evans, 1996), pp. 15, 242–243. In Radomir Bulatović, *Koncentracioni logor Jasenovac, s posebnim osvrtom na Donju Gradinu* (Sarajevo: Svjetlost, 1990), the figure of Jasenovac victims rose to over one million—precisely 1,110,929.

88. Vladimir Žerjavić, *Population Losses in Yugoslavia 1941–1945* (Zagreb: Dom i svijet, 1997), pp. 97, 188.

89. See Walter Manoschek, *Serbien ist Judefrei: militarische Besatzungpolitik und Judenvernichtung in Serbien 1941/42.* (Munich: Oldenbourg, 1993).

90. Andrija Gams, *The Truth about "Serbian Anti-Semitism."* (Belgrade: Ministry of Information of the Republic of Serbia, 1994).

91. Josif, as quoted by the church newspaper *Pravoslavlje*, said: "As I was reading, horrified, about the horrors from the testimonies of survivors in this book of righteousness. Neither in the testimony of the misfortune prisoners of the Gulag Archipelago written by the confessional pen of Solzhenitsyn, nor in the testimonies from Kolyma recorded by the embittered pen of Shalamov, such inhumanities have been recorded . . . Jasenovac! That was the gravest, most horrible place of destruction of the Serbian people . . . The insane legal order passed to make possible the extermination of one-third of the Serbian people in the Independent State of Croatia (which had been far exceeded) was passed in the name of religion and based on the murderous slogan: "Kill the anti-Christ in the name of Christ" [and] was a bloody stain on twentieth-century Roman Catholicism, a stain that cannot be removed. Sin of all sins. An archsin with no repentance. Third Crucifix of Jesus. . . . Once again, stunned and thrilled, I am saying now: Jasenovac is the holiest shrine for every Serb, Jasenovac is a unifier of the Serbian popular soul, Jasenovac is the new spiritual capital of Heavenly Serbia! In the halls of endless Heavens, the Serbian people have been chosen to spearhead the advent in New Jerusalem among the nations to whom salvation will be granted." Enriko Josif, "Jasenovac prestolnica Nebeske Srbije" (Jasenovac—the capital city of Heavenly Serbia), *Pravoslavlje*, 15 November 1990.

92. See *Večan pomen: Jasenovac: mjesto natopljeno krvlju nevinih 1941/1985/ 1991.* See also the church calendar *Crkva 1991* and Atanasije Jevtić, *Velikomučenički Jasenovac, ustaška tvornica smrti: dokumenti i svedo čenja* (the great martyr Jasenovac, the Ustaša death factory: Documents and testimonies) (Belgrade: Sfairos, 1990).

93. According to a review of *Večan pomen: Jasenovac: mjesto natopljeno krvlju nevinih 1941/1985/1991, Pravoslavlje,* 1 October 1990

94. Shilja Avramov, *Genocide in Yugoslavia,* (Belgrade: Bigz, 1995), p. 34.

95. Ibid.

96. Sima Simić, *Prekrštavanje Srba za vrijeme drugog svetskog rata* (The forcible religious conversions of Serbs during the Second World War) (Belgrade: Kultura, 1990; original published in 1959); Veljko D. Djurić, *Prekrštavanje Srba u Nezavisnoj Državi Hrvatskoj: prilozi za istoriju verskog genocida* (The forcible religious conversions of Serbs in the Independent State of Croatia: Supplements for a history of

the religious genocide) (Belgrade: Alfa, 1991); Veljko D. Djurić, *Ustaše i pravos-lavlje: Hrvatska Pravoslavna crkva* (The Ustašas and orthodoxy: The Croatian Or-thodox Church) (Novi Beograd: Beletra, 1989).

97. See Ivan Mužić, *Pavelić i Stepinac* (Split: Logos, 1990).

98. One the conversions issue, see Ivo Omrčanin, *Forced Conversions of Cro-atians to the Serbian Faith in History*, paper presented to the Third World Congress for Soviet and East European Studies, 30 October–4 November 1985 (Washing-ton, DC: Samizdat, 1985).

99. Bulajić, *The Role of the Vatican in the Breakup of the Yugoslav State*, p. 10.

100. Croatian internet propaganda, for example, emphasized the saving of the Jews. See "Cardinal Alojzije Stepinac and Saving the Jews in Croatia during the WW2," available from the Website "Cardinal Stepinac and the Jews," at http://www.hr.darko/etf.jews; the web pages of the Croatian World Congress—*Hrvat-ski svjetski kongres*, at http://www.crowc.org; and Croatian Holocaust Informa-tion Center, Croatian Information Center.

101. Živko Kustić, *Stepinac* (Zagreb: Studio Promotion, 1991).

102. "Poziv u rat" (A war cry), *Pravoslavlje*, 1 July 1991.

103. *Pravoslavlje*, 1 July 1991.

104. The patriarch said: "We do not think that in the Catholic Church's desire to canonize Aloysius Stepinac there is anything so extraordinary that it should surprise us. . . . Aloysius Stepinac, as the Kaptol (i.e. Croatian Church) and the Vatican assert, has great merits for the Croatian people and their home-land. He is their spiritual leader . . . If . . . (the Croatian people think that Stepinac is responsible for concentration camps and the re-baptisms they will not accept him as a saint), if they do accept him as a saint, again it is good. Both extremes have their message. Only it is not good if the other nations, whose bones have been left in the places of execution and the pits, fail to comprehend those mes-sages in time, and fail to draw the logical conclusions." Quoted in Spasojević, *The Communists and I*, p. 127.

105. According to my personal notes taken while attending the ceremony.

106. Republički sekretarijat za unutrašnje poslove—Služba državne sigur-nosti, "Procjena stanja sigurnosti na području SR Hrvatske" (Assessment of the situation concerning state security in the Socialist Republic of Croatia), top se-cret, obtained through the office of the Commission for Relations with Religious Communities of the Association of Municipalities of Dalmatia, Split (Zagreb, 5 December 1986).

107. *Crkva 1991*, church calendar, pp. 76–77.

108. The Serbian Orthodox Church argued that the territory had been de facto under the jurisdiction of the Serbian Church since the foundation of the Orthodox diocese at Ston in the thirteenth century by Saint Sava. According to *Pravoslavlje*, the monumental cathedral of the Holy Archangel was built on the Prevlaka peninsula but destroyed by Venice in the mid–fifteenth century. *Pravos-lavlje*, 15 March 1991.

109. Ljiljana Stošić, "Srpski crkveni spomenici u Makedoniji 1282–1690," Ve-lika Sabja 219 (1990).

110. According to the session's press release, "this assembly, motivated by the continuing appropriation of the Saint Prokhor Pčinjski monastery by some peo-ple who never had rights on this church property; coupled with the Stalinist-Broz (Titoist) content in the Memorial Museum of the ASNOM and the disturbing monastic life, reaffirmed the earlier Sabor's decision that the Museum must be evicted from the monastery." *Pravoslavlje*, 15 December 1990.

111. In 1994 the Skopje government passed a law prohibiting Serbian clergy from entering the territory of the Republic of Macedonia (or the Former Yugoslav Republic of Macedonia [FYORM]) in clerical attire. The Belgrade Patriarchate announced pilgrimages and commemorations around Serbian monasteries and First Balkan war battlefields across the FYORM.

112. *Pravoslavlje*, 15 November 1990.

113. "Church—Symbol of the Serbs," *Independent*, 22 June 1989.

114. The official bulletin of the clerical association criticized the Croatian Marxist sociologist Srdjan Vrcan for his public statement that "an aggressive and sometimes disgusting anti-Catholicism is emanating from the Serbian Orthodox church press and Belgrade media." *Vesnik Udruženja pravoslavnog sveštenstva*, June–July 1988.

115. From Bulović's interview with *Politika express*; see *Glas koncila*, 20 May 1990.

116. *Die presse*, Vienna, 23 October 1989.

117. *Pravoslavlje*, 15 November 1990.

118. Ibid.

119. Monsignor Juraj Kolarić served for years as the secretary of the ecumenical committee of the bishops' conference. He was criticized by the Serbian Church for writing an "anti-ecumenical book." However, Kolarić's 1985 study, *Pravoslavni The Orthodox*, was, in the words of its author, "probably the most cordial book about the Orthodox Church ever written by a Catholic scholar.... [D]id they expect me to write a love letter...? Let us just take a look at the Serbian theologian Justin Popović's 1974 study that denounces every form of ecumenism." From Monsignor Kolarić's interview with me in Zagreb, February 1991. See also *Nedjeljna Dalmacija*, 3–10 March 1991.

120. *Pravoslavlje*, 15 December 1990.

121. Ibid.

122. *Pravoslavlje*, 15 February 1991.

123. *Crkva 1991*.

124. See more on this mobilization in Slavoljub Djukić, *Izmedju slave i anateme: politička biografija Slobodana Miloševića* (Belgrade: Filip Višnjić, 1994); and Laura Silber and Allan Little, *Yugoslavia—Death of a Nation* (New York: Penguin Books, 1997).

125. See Sabrina P. Ramet, "The Serbian Church and the Serbian Nation," in Ramet and Adamovich, *Beyond Yugoslavia*, pp. 101–122.

126. *Večan pomen: Jasenovac: mjesto natopljeno krvlju nevinih 1941/1985/1991*, pp. 349–350.

127. Ibid., p. 351.

128. The calendar's cover page featured a fresco-style illustration with the biblical Cain and Abel and the quotation: "What have you done? The voice of your brother's blood is crying to me from the ground" (Genesis 4:10).

129. The text reads: "In European history, the three cycles of the Catholic Church's persecution of its enemies took a combined 243,000 lives. Yet in the Yugoslav inquisition, 700,000 people lost their lives! The Inquisition against the Serbs in Yugoslavia, 1941–1945, was not only the most fatal according to the number of victims but also, according to various studies published in the West that examined the forms of tortures of Serbs, the cruelest of all inquisitions ... Bloody massacres of Serbs in the Croat Nazi state and conversions of Orthodox Serbs to Catholicism at gunpoint were carried out by 'murderers in the name of God.' " *Crkva 1991*, pp. 34–35.

130. *NIN*, 8 December 1991. The appeal was previously published by *Le Monde* of Paris and subscribed to by Pavle Rak, Milovan Danojić, Olivier Cleman, Nicola Losky, Tatjana Goricheva, and Elizabeth Behr-Siegel.

131. Svetislav Basara, "Pokora" (Penitence), *NIN*, 31 May 1991.

132. Spasojević, *The Communists and I*, pp. 104–105.

133. "Osvrt and jedan govor" (Comment on a speech), *Pravoslavlje*, 1 October 1987.

134. Ibid.

135. Ibid.

136. *Vijesnik*, 7 September 1990.

137. Ibid.

138. Ibid.

139. *Glas crkve*, no. 11, 1984.

140. Spasojević, *The Communists and I*, p. 86.

141. *Pravoslavlje*, 15 June 1990.

142. *Pravoslavlje*, 1 October 1990.

143. *Pravoslavlje*, 15 November 1990.

144. *Pravoslavlje*, 1 February 1991.

145. Ibid.

146. "If you take a look at Russian history, you will see that every time when Roman Catholicism, in one way or another, encroached on Russian soil, tragic consequences followed. We hope that the tradition and spiritual values of your ancestors will make you act in support of your Orthodox brethren." *Borba*, 13 March 1991.

147. Ibid.

148. Ibid.

149. *Pravoslavlje*, 15 July 1991.

150. *Pravoslavlje*, 15 December 1991.

151. Ratko Perič, *Ekumenske nade i tjeskobe* (Mostar: Crkva na Kamenv i Bishupki Ordinarjat, 1993), p. 329.

152. Ibid.

153. In June 1998, the Serbian Church sent a sizeable delegation to "Slavic Congress" at Prague. The congress, officially ignored by its host country (not even the Czech Orthodox Church participated), was dominated by Russian communists and nationalists.

154. Tudjman's former close aides and later critics revealed the Tudjman-Milošević partition plans in their interviews and memoirs published in Croatia. See Stipe Mesić, *Kako je srušena Jugoslavija* (Zagreb: Mislavpress, 1994); Hrvoje Šarinić, *Svi moji tajni pregovori sa Slobodanom Miloševićem: izmedju rata i diplomacije, 1993–1995* (Zagreb: Globus international, 1999).

155. In a public lecture delivered on 19 February 1997 at the United States Institute of Peace in Washington D.C., the cardinal archbishop of Sarajevo, Vinko Puljić, said, in response to my question whether the bishops of the two churches had ever discussed the partition issue, that the Croatian and Serbian episcopate did not talk about partition but about borders among the republics in the former Yugoslavia.

156. Ibid., p. 12.

157. Originally published in the Catholic weekly *Glas koncila* and reprinted by the Croatian daily newspapers, the bishops' letter is quoted here from Bulajić, *The Role of the Vatican in the Breakup of the Yugoslav State*, p. 173, in Bulajic's translation.

158. Ibid.

159. In an open letter to the Federal Ministry of Internal Affairs, the Knin police demanded exemption from Croatia's jurisdiction. *Politika*, 5 July 1990.

160. *Nedjeljna Dalmacija*, 8 July 1990.

161. Interview with Radovan Karadžić in the weekly newspaper *Nedjelja*, 2 September 1990.

162. *Pravoslavlje*, 15 September 1990.

163. *Pravoslavlje*, 15 March 1991.

164. "This conflict is a warning and reminder of the Croatian crimes of 1941 when Ustašas attacked and massacred the unarmed Serbian people. But this time, we Serbs will not repeat the mistake of '41. We shall remain Christians, but for now, let us disregard the Gospel of Christ and turn to the Old Testament, which reads: *An eye for an eye, a tooth for a tooth!* After justice has been done, we will return to the New Testament, which says: *To him who strikes you on the cheek, offer the other also.*" *Vijesnik*, 6 March 1991 (my translation).

165. Bulajić, *The Role of the Vatican in the Breakup of the Yugoslav State*, pp. 9–12.

166. *Politika*, 19 January 1992.

167. "Apel Sabora Srpske pravoslavne crkve Srpskom narodu i medjunarodnoj javnosti" (Appeal of the Bishops' Assembly of the Serbian Orthodox Church to the Serbian people and to the international public), *Politika*, 19 January 1992.

168. According to my interview with the general secretary of the bishops' conference of Yugoslavia, Monsignor Vjekoslav Milovan, conducted on 14 November 1990 in Zagreb, the new bishops' conference would be divided into three sections. The "western section" would include the national bishops' conference of Slovenia; the bishops of Croatia and Bosnia-Herzegovina would work together with the "central section"; and the "eastern" division would incorporate the Catholic diaspora in the parts of Yugoslavia with an Orthodox majority. "Catholic Confederation," *Nedjeljna Dalmacija*, 18 November 1990.

169. The *Glas koncila* wrote in an editorial four days before the plebiscite on sovereignty in Croatia: "We can say, with a clear conscience, that Yugoslavia, every one up to now and also the present one, was a negative experience for the Croats and Catholics." *Glas koncila*, 15 May 1991.

170. On 13–17 January 1990 in Moscow, delegations of the Vatican, led by cardinals Willebrands and Cassidy, and the patriarchate of Moscow, represented by the patriarchate's minister for foreign affairs, the metropolitan of Smolensk, Cyril, discussed the Ukrainian religious crisis. The two churches agreed to work together. As a result, the situation in western Ukraine had calmed down by the end of the year. *Glas koncila*, 21 January 1990. See also Vsevolod Chaplin, "The Church and Politics in Contemporary Russia," in The Politics of Religion in Russia and the New States of Eurasia, ed. Michael Bordeaux (Armonk, NY: Sharpe, 1995).

171. Chaplin, "The Church and Politics in Contemporary Russia."

172. *NIN*, No. 2577, 18 May 2000, pp. 58–59.

10. Religion as Hallmark of Nationhood

1. According to Independent Radio B92, Belgrade, 11 June 1995.

2. See Norman N. Naimark, "Ethnic Cleansing in Twentieth Century Europe," *Donald W. Treadgold Papers* 19, October 1998.

3. Speaking in March 1992 on Youth TV Zagreb, the sociologist Stipe Šuvar,

former chairman of the League of Communists of Croatia and Yugoslavia, said that 50 percent of the members of the then ruling Croatian Democratic Community (Tudjman's HDZ) were former communists, as well as 90 percent of the members of the liberal nationalist Croatian People's Party (HND), whereas 50,000 former members of the League of Communists of Croatia had joined the extreme nationalistic Serbian Democratic Party (SDS). According to Šuvar, from 1945 to 1990 over 650,000 people were registered as members of the Communist Party/League of Communists of Croatia. In 1992, according to this sociologist and ex-official, the surviving organization of reformed communists (social democrats) of Croatia had between 20,000 and 40,000 members who supported Croatia as a sovereign state and condemned the excesses of Titoism.

4. See Ramet, *Balkan Babel*, M. A. Sells, *The Bridge Betrayed: Religion and Genocide in Bosnia* (Berkeley: University of California Press, 1996); Paul Mojzes, ed., *Religion and the War in Bosnia* (Atlanta, GA: Scholar Press, 1998); Rudolph Grulich and Thomas Bremer, "Die Religionsgemeinschaften im ehemaligen Jugoslawien," in Dunja Melčić, ed., *Der Jugoslawien-Krieg: Handbuch zu Vorgeschichte, Verlauf und Konsequenzen* (Wiesbaden: Westdeutscher Verlag, 1999).

5. See M. M. Gorymov, *Russkie doborvoltsy v Bosnii, 1992–1995 gg.* (Moskva: Vestnik, 1997); Hashim Hussein, *Malaysian Tigers in Bosnia* (Kuala Lumpur: Berita, 1996). See also Huntington, *The Clash of Civilizations*; Ramet, *Balkan Babel*, 2nd ed., p. 3; Mojzes, *Religion and the War in Bosnia*; Michael A. Sells, *The Bridge Betrayed: Religion and Genocide in Bosnia*, (Berkeley: University of California Press, 1996).

6. Jović Momir, "Da se Srbi nisu oduprli bili bi zbrisani" (Had the Serbs not resisted, they would have been annihilated), *Jedinstvo* No. 39–40 (Priština, 1995).

7. *Jagnje božije i zvijer iz bezdana: filosofija rata, zbirka eseja* (The lamb of God and the beast from the abyss: A philosophy of war; A collection of essays) (Cetinje: Svetigora, 1996).

8. See *Muzej žrtava genocide* (Museum of victims of genocide), available from http://beograd.com/jasenovac; see also *Serbs and Jews*, ROM the Serbian Unity Congress's Website available from http://srpska-mreza.com/library/facts/Jews.

9. The most influential was the conference entitled "Jasenovac: A System of Croat Ustaša Death Camps," held in 1997 in New York.

10. See for example, Danon Cadik (the chief rabbi of Yugoslavia) et al., *An Open Letter to the American Jewish Committee*, available from http://www.srpska-mreza.com/library/facts/cadik. A pro-Milošević pamphlet was released by, among others, the Yugoslav legal scholar of Jewish descent, Andrija Gams: *The Truth about "Serbian Anti-Semitism"* (Belgrade: Ministry of Information of the Republic of Serbia, 1994).

11. *Duga*, no. 1738, 6 May 2000.

12. Vladeta Jerotić, *Vera i nacija* (Faith and nation), 2nd ed. (Belgrade: Tersit, 1995), p. 52.

13. Karamatić, *Znanstveni skup "Rat u Bosni i Hercegovini: uzroci, posljedice, perspektive,"* pp. 83–93.

14. "Srbi su dragovoljni izvršitelji planova Slobodana Miloševia" (The Serbs are Slobodan Milošević's willing executioners), *Slobodna Dalmacija*, 2 June 1999. The article cites Daniel J. Goldhagen, *Hitler's Willing Executioners: Ordinary Germans and the Holocaust* (New York: Knopf, 1996).

15. See, for example, *Southeastern Europe 1918–1995: Proceedings of the International Symposium, Zadar, Croatia, September 1995* (Zagreb: Hrvatski informativni centar; Hrvatska Matica iseljenika, 1996).

16. See Ante Beljo, *YU-Genocide: Bleiburg, Death Marches, UDBA (Yugoslav secret police)* (Toronto: Northern Tribune, 1995); Jozo Marević, ed., *U Bleiburgu iskra: zbornik radova o Bleiburgu i križnom putu: znanstveni, progodničarski i autobiografski prilozi s 1. medjunarodnog znanstvenog simpozija u Bleiburgu 15 i 16 svibnja 1993* (Zagreb: Vidokrug, 1993);

17. *Slobodna Dalmacija*, 2 November 2000.

18. "Izetbegović nas je upropastio!" (Izetbegović has ruined us!), interview with Jakub Effendi Selimoski, *Danas*, 2 July 1993.

19. Xavier Bougarel, "Bosniaks under the Control of Panislamists (1)", *Dani*, Sarajevo, 18 June 1999 (translated into Bosnian by Zijad Imamović).

20. *Feral Tribune*, 17 March 1997.

21. *Oslobodjenje*, 14 March 1999.

22. *Feral Tribune*, 10 November 1997.

23. See Ivan Lovrenović, column in *Feral Tribune*, no. 772, 1 July 2000.

24. *Dani*, no. 61, October 1997.

25. Ibid.

26. *Slobodna Dalmacija*, 27 September 2000.

27. *Feral Tribune*, no. 796, 16 December 2000.

28. *Feral Tribune*, 10 November 1997, p. 4.

29. *Feral Tribune*, no. 739, 16 November 1999.

30. *Nacional*, no. 203, 6 October 1999, p. 41. The Spit daily *Slobodna Dalmacija* reported later that Tudjman and Šušak deposited several billion German marks in a bank in Austria. The money was allocated for the two nationalist leaders' private needs as well as for the funding of the "Herzegovinian state." *Slobodna Dalmacija*, 31 January 2000.

31. *Tjednik*, no. 3, 22 March 1997.

32. "The Madonna of Barefoot Pilgrims and Deft Traders," *Hrvatski obzor*, no. 175, August 1998.

33. *Slobodna Dalmacija*, 8 February 2000.

34. *Feral Tribune*, no. 739, 16 November 1999.

35. Luca Rastello, "La Vergine Strategica: Medjugorje come fulcro del nazionalismo Croato," LIMES, no. 1/2000, June 2000.

36. "Visions of the Virgin: Thousands of Believers Throng to Hear the Mother of Jesus Speak through a Man Who Lives in Boston," *Newsweek*, 17 January 2000.

37. *Slobodna Dalmacija*, 26 June 2000.

38. See, for example, contesting views on Medjugorje in Wayne Weible, *The Final Harvest: Medjugorje at the End of the Century* (Brewster, MA: Paraclete Press, 1999), as opposed to Michael E. Jones, *The Medjugorje Deception: Queen of Peace, Ethnic Cleansing, Ruined Lives* (South Bend, IN: Fidelity Press, 1998).

39. See *Večernji list*, special issue, "Twenty Years of the Apparitions," 25 June 2001 (courtesy of Sabrina Patra Ramet). Pervan is quoted according to *Feral Tribune*, no. 824, 30 June 2001, pp. 7–8.

40. Nedjo Šipovac in *NIN*, no. 2547, 21 October 1999. Based on Šipovac's book *Rat 1992–1996. Preispitivanja* (The War, 1992–1996. A reconsideration) (Belgrade: published by the author, 1998).

41. A report by the International Crisis Committee (ICC) said that five years after the end of the Bosnian war, some 75 people linked to war crimes were in elected office or positions of authority in the Serb Republic. The list includes mayors, police officers, and members of the Bosnian Serb parliament. The ICC says UN documents and witness testimony implicate many of those officials in

"war crimes, like mass murder, ethnic cleansing, and mass rape" or in the running of prison camps. Radio Free Europe/Radio Liberty, *Newsline, Southeastern Europe*, 3 November 2000.

42. See *Naša Borba*, 18 October 1997.

43. "Karadžić Gets Saintly Status," *Independent*, London, 27 August 1993.

44. "Od Kosova do Kosova" (From Kosovo to Kosovo), series of essays, *Naša Borba*, Belgrade, 8–10 April 1998.

45. *Pravoslavlje*, 1 September 1998.

46. Radio Free Europe/Radio Liberty, Southeastern Europe 12 June 2001.

47. Stevo Vučinić, general secretary of the committee for the renewal of autocephaly of the Montenegrin Orthodox Church, in a speech on the occasion of the 1993 proclamation of the independent Montenegrin Church at Cetinje, *Monitor*, 5 November 1993.

48. *Pravoslavlje*, 15 November 1998.

49. *Pravoslavlje*, 1 June 2000.

50. Batelja and Tomić, *Propovijedi, govori i poruke zagrebačkog nadbiskupa kardinala Alojzija Stepinca 1941–1946*.

51. From a press release of the Croatian Victimological Society, in response to the Wiesenthal Center's appeal to the Vatican to call off the beatification of Croatian Cardinal Alojzije Stepinac in October 1998. Quoted from Croatian state television (*Dnevnik Hrvatske televizije*), 29 September 1998.

52. Josip Krišto, "Katolička crkva i Židovi u NDH" (The Catholic Church and the Jews in the NDH), in *Antisemitizam—Holokaust—Antifašizam* (Zagreb: Židovska općina, 1996).

53. "Pope Beautifies Croat Prelate, Fanning Ire among Serbs," *New York Times*, 4 October 1998.

54. Ibid.

55. On 16 March 1998, the Vatican released a 14-page document entitled "We Remember: A Reflection on the *Shoah*," prepared by the Holy See Commission for Relations with the Jews upon personal papal request. Presenting the document, Cardinal Edward Cassidy said that it is "more than an apology . . . an act of repentance . . . since as members of the Church we are linked to the sins as well as to the merits of her children." Cited from "Conferenza stampa di presentazione del documento della commissione della Santa Sede per i rapporti religiosi con L'Ebraismo: 'No ricordiamo: una roflessione sulla Shoah,' " *Holy See News Service*, 16 March 1998.

56. *Pravoslavlje*, 1 July 1998.

57. *Crkva 1991*, p. 110.

58. See R. Scott Appleby, "Religion and Global Affairs: Religious 'Militants for Peace,' " in "Symposium: The Impact of Religion on Global Affairs," *SAIS Review* (Summer–fall 1998), pp. 38–44; see also Douglas Johnston and Cynthia Sampson, eds., *Religion: the Missing Dimension of Statecraft* (New York: Oxford University Press, 1994.

59. To name only a few among the organizations involved: Moral Armament, the World Council on Religion and Peace (WCRP), Mercy Corps International, World Vision, the Appeal of Conscience Foundation, the Community of St. Egidio; the International Scientific Conference of Minorities for the Europe of Tomorrow (ISCOMET), the Foundation for Peace and Understanding, the Center for Strategic and International Studies, the Summer School for Interconfessional Dialogue and Understanding (SIDU), the United States Institute of Peace (USIP),

and many other governmental, nongovernmental, religious, and nondenominational organizations.

60. See Steven M. Riskin, ed., "Three Dimensions of Peacebuilding in Bosnia: Findings from USIP-Sponsored Research and Field Projects," *Peaceworks 32* (Washington, DC: United States Institute of Peace, December 1999). See also Vjekoslav Perica, *Deadline Doomsday? Yugoslav Religious Organizations in Conflict, 1981–1997* (Washington, DC: United States Institute of Peace Grant Program, 1998), with a summary in *Contributions to the Study of Peacemaking 6*, ed. Anne-Marie Smith (Washington D.C.: United States Institute of Peace, December 1999), p. 36.

61. Mennonite Central Committee News Service, 25 October 1996.

62. *Pravoslavlje*, 15 October 1998, reviewed the new patriarchate's semiofficial handbook on sects: Zoran D. Luković, *Verske sekte: priručnik za samoobranu* (Religious sects: A handbook for self-defense) (Belgrade: Pravoslavna misionarska škola, 1998).

63. As reported by the Croatian Catholic news agency IKA, 8 June 1997.

64. *Slobodna Dalmacija*, 20 March 1998.

65. *Glas koncila*, 7 May 1995.

66. Radio Free Europe/Radio Liberty, South Slavic Service, *Interviews*, 23 January 2000, available from the Radio Free Europe web site at http://www.rferl.org/bd/ss/index-eng.

67. Voice of America, Croatian Service, 3 November 1999.

68. According to my notes on a public lecture delivered by Cardinal Puljic on 19 February 1997 at the United States Institute of Peace in Washington, D.C.

69. This was revealed to me by David Little, senior scholar for Religion, Ethics, and Human Rights at the United States Institute of Peace, after Little's first trip to Bosnia in 1997.

70. Among other things, the cardinal said the following: "Religious leaders tried, but could not halt the outbreak of the war—clergy cannot perform miracles in peace-making, if politicians want war. . . . [T]he war and most of war atrocities were the work of nonbelievers and former communists turned nationalists. . . . [E]very criticism of religion and religious institutions is directed by the hidden communist hand. . . . [T]here will be no lasting and just peace without the decisive role of religious leaders—the international community must help further the religious peace in the Balkans." *Večernji list*, 30 April 1998, my translation. Reprinted in *Croatian Information Center—Review of the Croatian Press*, 30 April 1998.

71. Ivan Lovrenović, "Naličje religijskog suživota u Bosni i Hercegovini: Traganje za Jeruzalemom" (The other side of the religious cooperation in Bosnia and Herzegovina: In search of Jerusalem), *Feral Tribune*, no. 732, September 1999.

72. Pavle said: "In this war, grave evils have befallen the Croatian people, but the Serbs have suffered, too. Many Serbs took part in committing this evil. Yet I wish to emphasize that while the individual can be liable for crimes, a whole nation cannot. There are also victims on both sides. All secrets will be made public sooner or later. Time and history will put together the mosaic of good and evil and place every historical actor in his right place. That is why I ask you, the faithful, to be patient, love your neighbors and your country and be prepared to forgive." *Pravoslavlje*, 1 April 1999 (my free translation).

73. Quoted in *Oslobodjenje*, 30 July 1999.

74. "Deklaracija svesrpskog crkveno narodnog sabora, Beograd, 9–11 June 1998," *Naša Borba*, 14 June 1998.

75. See "Remarks by the Bishop Artemije," in *Current Issues* (Washington, DC: United States Institute of Peace, 15 September 1998). See also *Pravoslavna eparhija raskoprizrenska* (Orthodox Diocese Raška Prizren) at http://decani.yunet .com.

76. According to a report from Eisenstadt (Austria) released by the Croatian Catholic news agency IKA, 27 November 1995.

77. Steven M. Riskin, ed. "Three Dimensions of Peacebuilding in Bosnia: Findings from the U.S. Institute of Peace Sponsored Research and Field Projects," *Peaceworks 32* (Washington, DC: United States Institute of Peace, December 1999, p. 41.

78. International Crisis Group Crisis Web, "Latest Reports," at http://www. crisisweb.org

79. Radio Free Europe/Radio Liberty, *South Slavic Service*, 28 December 1999.

80. *Nedjeljna Dalmacija*, 26 December 1990.

81. Quoted from *BBC News: Europe*, 29 November 1999; available from http: //news.bbc.co.uk/hi.english/world/europe. In a similar vein, the Croatian sociologist Srdjan Vrcan accused religious leaders of issuing "abstract" pronouncements and conventional calls for peace without a real desire to contribute to it. See Srdjan Vrcan, "Religion and Churches and the Post-Yugoslav War," in *Religion and Nationalism*, ed. John Coleman and Tomka Mikols (London: SCM Press, 1995).

82. *Pravoslavlje*, nos. 801–802, 1–15 August 2000.

83. *Feral Tribune*, no. 794, 2 December 2000.

11. The Twilight of Balkan Idols

1. See Ivo Banac's preface to *The National Question in Yugoslavia*.

2. *"Gli Stati-Mafia: Criminalità e potere a cavallo dell' Adriatico—I pericoli per L' Italia."* LIMES—Quaderno Speciale, May 2000. States designated as "criminal" are the Yugoslavia (Serbia-Montenegro), Tudjman's Croatia, and Albania, including the Albanian nationalist organizations in Kosovo.

3. *Ustav Republike Hrvatske*, 9th ed., (Zagreb: Informator, 1995), pp. 3–4.

4. According to a foreign observer, "it has been estimated that, during the years the HDZ has been in power, 3,000 monuments of the national liberation movement have been demolished in Croatia—500 in Dalmatia alone." Jill A. Irvine, "Ultranationalist Ideology and State-Building in Croatia, 1990–1996," *Problems of Post-Communism* 44, 4 (July–August 1997), p. 35.

5. See Victor Ivančić's column in *Feral Tribune*, No. 840, October 20, 2001.

6. *Jutarnji list*, 9 May 1998.

7. *Slobodna Dalmacija*, 9–10 July 1999.

8. See for example, Mirko Valentić, ed., *Spomenica povodom 50-te obljetnice Bleiburga i križnog puta 1945–1995* (A recollection on the occasion of the fiftieth anniversary of Bleiburg and the way of the cross 1945–1955) (Zagreb: Quo vadis, 1995).

9. See Žerjavić, *Opsesije i megalomanije oko Jasenovca i Blajburga*.

10. *Voice of America, Croatian Service*, 22 October 1999.

11. According to the *Annual Report on International Religious Freedom for 1999* (Washington, DC: U.S. Department of State, Bureau for Democracy, Human Rights, and Labor, 9 September 1999), in the section on Croatia, "while there is

no official state religion, the dividing line between the Roman Catholic Church and the State often was blurred, and the ruling party throughout the period covered by this report attempted to identify itself closely with the Catholic Church." From *Voice of America, Croatian Service*, 10 September 1999.

12. *Feral Tribune*, no. 685, 2 November 1998.

13. *Feral Tribune*, no. 781, 2 September 2000.

14. Ibid.

15. *Globus*, no. 458, 17 September 1999, pp. 58–61.

16. Interview with Srdjan Vrcan in *Feral Tribune*, no. 814, 21 April 2001.

17. According to Christian theology, transubstantiation is the mode by which Christ's presence in the Eucharist is brought about through the conversion of the whole substance of the bread into the body of Christ and of the whole substance of the wine into the blood. "After the inauguration of the term *pretvorba* by Tudjman in 1990," writes Letica, "the notion of the *pretvorba* has become the generic term for all operations aimed at transferring socialist state property into private hands, thereby abusing the religious sentiments of the people. . . . [T]he greatest mystery of Christianity would come to designate the 'miracle' performed by the Croatian nouveau riches by the conversion of nothing into substantial personal wealth." *Globus*, no. 418, 11 December 1998 (my free translation).

18. *Feral Tribune*, no. 753, 19 February 2000.

19. According to Radio Free Europe/Radio Liberty, *Newsline*, 26 March 2001.

20. *Slobodna Dalmacija*, 2 June 2001.

21. *Nacional*, No. 309, 18 October 2001.

22. Ibid.

23. *Globus*, 8 June 2000; Voice of America, Croatian Service, 17 July 2000.

24. *Voice of America, Croatian Service*, 20 June 2000.

25. *Feral Tribune*, no. 779, 19 August 2000.

26. *Slobodna Dalmacija*, 27 November 1992,

27. Voice of America, Croatian Service, 10 November 1999.

28. *Feral Tribune*, no. 789, 28 October 2000.

29. Among many texts about the Church's shady business see, for example, a articles in the otherwise pro-HDZ daily *Slobodna Dalmacija*, 6, 28, and 30 January 2000. According to the 6 January article, the prominent HDZ supporter priest Anto Baković, had benefited from unlawful privatization, through which he became the owner of a firm that under his management quickly went bankrupt.

30. In November 2000, the District Court in Zagreb opened an investigation into Tudjman's daughter Nevenka, who was charged with corruption. Radio Free Europe/Radio Liberty, *Newsline*, Southeastern Europe, 3 November 2000.

31. *Slobodna Dalmacija*, 2 February 2000.

32. *Feral Tribune*, no. 800, 13 January 2001.

33. *Feral Tribune*, no. 7811, 2 September 2000.

34. Bono Z. Šagi, "Kriza morala" (The moral crisis), *Kana—Christian Family Review*, June 1997; and *"Neokomumizam i postkomunizam"* (Neocommunism and postcommunism), *Kana*, September 1997.

35. *Vijenac*, no. 106, 29 January 1998.

36. *Feral Tribune*, nos. 821, 822, June 2001.

37. Davor Butković, Slaven Letica, and their collaborators contributed with a valuable analysis of Church-state relations in *Globus*, 11 October 1996, pp. 9–10.

38. Tudjman earned a bad name in the West as early as the 1980s (especially in Jewish circles) as a historian who called the Holocaust a myth analogous to Great Serbian myths and cast doubt on the number of Holocaust victims. Robert D. Kaplan, "Croatianism: The Latest Balkan Ugliness," *New Republic*, 25 November 1991.

39. In 1997 the Simon Wiesental Center in Vienna designated as war crimes suspects these Argentine citizens of Croatian background: Dinko Šakić, former commander of the Jasenovac camp, and Šakić's wife, Nada, who ran a prison for women. The Šakićs were extradited to Croatia for a trial. Nada Šakić was released. Dinko Šakić was given a 20-year jail sentence for war crimes and crimes against humanity but was not tried for genocide.

40. In 1996 Tudjman's book containing his revised views on the Holocaust was published in English as *Horrors of War: Historical Reality and Philosophy*, trans. Katarina Mijatović (New York: M. Evans, 1996.). During the first top-level official visit of a Croatian state delegation to Israel, on 12 May 1998, Granić paid a visit to the Yad Vashem Holocaust memorial center in Jerusalem, where he laid a wreath on behalf of the Croatian government and released a statement to "express and testify to the deepest regret and condemnation of the persecution and suffering and the tragedy of the Jews on Croatian territory . . . during World War II and the Nazi occupation." Associated Press, 12 May 1998.

41. In the 1998 annual report of the US nongovernmental organization Freedom House, Croatia was classified as a "partly free country" with a downward trend in democratization (83 countries including the ex-Yugoslav republic of Slovenia were classified as "free," and the Serbo-Montenegrin Federation was classified as "unfree"); Voice of America, Croatian Service, 30 December 1998. In October 1999, the European Union decided to deliver two official diplomatic protest notes critical of the electoral law and organizations of the forthcoming parliamentary elections in Croatia and of its noncooperation with the Hague Tribunal. Voice of America, Croatian Service, 23 October 1999. Also in October 1999, Transparency International (TI) a on-governmental organization for struggle against corruption, released an annual report according to which Croatia's regime is one of the most corrupt in the world (Croatia was ranked at 74th place and Milošević's Yugoslavia 90th among 99 countries included in the report). Voice of America, Croatian Service, 26 October 1999. Human Rights Watch released in December 1999 an annual report on Croatia, according to which "serious restrictions of human rights and political liberties are the legacy of Franjo Tudjman and his regime." Voice of America, Croatian Service, 21 December 1999.

42. *BBC World*, 18 December 1999; *Washington Post*, 17 December 1999.

43. On 21 October 1999, Christopher Smith, member of the US House of Representatives and chair of the Congressional Committee for Security and Cooperation in Europe, issued a report entitled "When Will Croatia Become a Democratic Country?" The Smith report said that 10 years after the demise of communism, Croatia had failed to become a democratic country because of an authoritarian and corrupt regime in Zagreb. Voice of America, Croatian Service, 22 October 1999.

44. Such comments were released, for example, by the German television *Deutsche Velle* and Voice of America, Croatian Service, on 13 December 1999.

45. *Slobodna Dalmacija*, 30 January 2000.

46. *Slobodna Dalmacija*, 3 March 2000.

47. Voice of America, Croatian Service, 30 September 2000.

48. *Feral Tribune*, no. 817, 12 May 2001.

49. *Glas koncila*, no 37, 10 September 2000.

50. *Slobodna Dalmacija*, 21 September 2000.

51. *Slobodna Dalmacija*, 23 September 2000.

52. Voice of America, Croatian Service, 17 March 2001.
Radio Free Europe/Radio Liberty,

53. *Newsline*, 23 March 2001.

54. *Glas koncila*, no. 27, 8 July 2001.

55. *Nacional*, no. 306, 27 September 2001.

56. *"EU zatraŽila od Vatikana da zaustavi kaptolske desničare"* (The European Union asked Vatican to halt right-wing catholic clergy), *Nacional*, no. 308, 11 October 2001, internet edition available at www.nacional.hr/htm.

57. See Ivo Goldstein and Slavko Goldstein, *Holokaust u Zagrebu* (Zagreb: Novi Liber, 2001).

58. "Otvoreni rat Crkve i vlade" (All-out war between church and state), *Nacional*, no.313, 15 November 2001.

59. Jevtić, *Stradanja Srba na Kosovu i Metohiji od 1941 do 1990*, pp. 444–451.

60. Ibid., pp. 450–451 (my translation).

61. *Politika express*, 6 September 1990; Jevtić, *Stradanja Srba*, pp. 452–459.

62. The note reads as follows: "Honorable Gentlemen Senators and Congressmen of the United States of America: I declare that I with my people and our church are not communists and we cannot be aggressors in our own ancestral land. On the contrary, we are here victims of the Albanian bolshevik and fascist aggression and expansion of Islamic fundamentalism. Unfortunately, as I can see, you encourage the terror and aggression against us. Therefore, I have nothing else to speak with you. Things are all too clear and painful." Jevtić, *Stradanja Srba*, p. 458.

63. Valter Shtylla, *Monumente kulture ne Kosove* (Albanian cultural monuments in Kosovo) (Tirana:Butimet Toena, 1998).

64. *Pravoslavlje*, 1–15 May 1999.

65. Francesco Maria Cannata, "Mosca-Belgrado: L'Asse Ecclesiastico Antioccidentale," LIMES, no. 1/2000, June 2000.

66. *The Serbian Orthodox Church: The Bombardment of the Serb Holy Places*, at the Serbian Orthodox Church's Website, at http://www.spc.org.yu/Svetinje, 11 October 1999.

67. *Pravoslavlje*, 1 June 1999.

68. Ibid.

69. "The Anti Christ Has Arrived," *Istočnik*, no. 43 (Toronto: Serbian Orthodox Diocese of Canada, 1998)

70. *Pravoslavlje*, 15 June 1999; available at the Serbian Orthodox Church's website, at http://www.spc.org.yu/Pravoslavlje/774/kuca.

71. *Duga*, no. 1723, 9 October 1999.

72. The bishop of Raška-Prizren, Artemije, spoke at two 1998 U.S. Institute of Peace briefings on the prospects for democracy in Serbia and for resolving the conflict in Kosovo. At a 15 September meeting, the Serbian Orthodox Church and the Serb Resistance Movement of Kosovo presented a proposal for resolving the conflict in Kosovo that they posted on the Movement's website: http://www.kosovo.com. On 15 October, Bishop Artemije was joined on a panel by Alliance for Change members Dragoslav Avramović, former governor of the National Bank of Yugoslavia, and Milan Panić, former prime minister of Yugoslavia. The Serb representatives proclaimed that "the ethnic approach to forming a state

has brought us only disintegration in the Balkans . . . this has to end. All nationalities (within a state) must possess and enjoy full human rights." Bishop Artemije called for free elections in Kosovo and cautioned that "the international community should insist on freeing the media. Then the people will be able to choose which leader is better for their future. The international community also has to pressure both Albanians and Serbs in Kosovo to stop fighting, not just the Serbs," the bishop said. *Peace Watch* 5, 1 (Washington DC: U.S. Institute of Peace, 1998).

73. Bishop Artemije, Address at the presentation of the book *Crucified Kosovo: Destroyed and Desecated Serbian Orthodox Churches in Kosovo and Metohija, June–August, 1999*, in Belgrade, 16 September 1999. Available at the Serbian Orthodox Church Website, at http://www.Serbian-Church.net/Dogadjaji/Kosovo/raspeto_1.html.

74. During US president Clinton's November 1999 visit to Kosovo, he met with Bishop Artemije and promised the Serbian Church assistance in the rebuilding of the Serbian sacred heritage. *B92, Daily News*, 23 November 1999.

75. Keston News Service, 24–28 September 2001, at www.keston.org.ew

76. "Radjanje novog nacionalizma" (Birth of a new nationalism), *Republika*, nos. 230–231, 1–29 February 2000.

77. See, for example, Dennison Rusinow, ed., *Yugoslavia: A Fractured Federalism* (Washington, DC: Wilson Center Press, 1988); Sabrina P. Ramet, *Nationalism and Federalism in Yugoslavia: 1962–1991*, 2nd ed. (Bloomington: Indiana University Press, 1992); Susan L. Woodward, *Balkan Tragedy: Chaos and Dissolution after the Cold War* (Washington, DC: Brookings Institution, 1995); Sabrina Petra Ramet and Ljubisa S. Adamovich, eds., *Beyond Yugoslavia:Politics, Economics and Culture in a Shattered Community* (Boulder, CO: Westview Press, 1995) John R. Lampe, *Yugoslavia as History: Twice There was a Country* (London: Cambridge University Press 1996).

78. Voice of America, Croatian Service, 3 December 1999.

79. Voice of America, Croatian Service, 28 October 1999.

80. Sabrina Ramet and other Western observers of Yugoslavia have emphasized the relevance of rock culture in late communism. See *also* Kim Simpson, "The Dissolution of Yugoslav Rock," available from the University of Texas website at http://www.utexas.edu/ftb/pvb/eems. (June 1999).

81. *Nedjeljna Dalmacija*, 22 September 1991.

82. Quote in Nathaniel Harris, *The War in Former Yugoslavia* (Austin, TX: Steck-Vaughn, 1998), p. 4.

83. "As I entered the office of the Rufai dervish Sheik Djemali Shehu in Prizren, I was struck by the sight of a huge photograph on the wall behind the Sheik's desk. No, it wasn't Ayatollah Khomeni, it was Marshall Tito in his white uniform of the commander of the Yugoslav navy overlooking the blue Adriatic from the bridge of the presidential yacht *Galeb*." Vjekoslav Perica, "Derviški život dervišima," *Nedjeljna Dalmacija*, 5 August 1990.

84. "When Marriage Is Sleeping with Enemy," *Newsweek*, 5 October 1992.

85. The British observer of Eastern Europe Timothy G. Ash wrote about such a conversion of a young Belgrade man with a Serb father and a Croat mother, who "found that he was really a Serb . . . [and] discovered the glorious history of medieval Serbia—and the Serbian Orthodox Church." Timothy G. Ash, "Serbia's Great March," *New York Review of Books* 44, 7 (24 April 1997), p. 25.

86. In 1998, according to Slaven Letica's column in the weekly *Globus*, Tudjman boasted before diplomatic representatives of Israel, on the occasion of the

establishment of diplomatic relations between Zagreb and Jerusalem, that the two top leaders of the Yugoslav Partisans, Tito and Ivan Ribar, were ethnic Croats.

87. Tudjman privatized the Brioni archipelago in the northern Adriatic and Milošević, according to a Belgrade monthly, and confiscated Tito's valuable foreign decorations, medals, and pieces of art from the 25 May Museum. *Duga*, no. 1729, 1 January 2000.

88. Bože Šimleša, *Sportske bitke za Hrvatsku* (Sports battles for Croatia) (Zagreb: Meditor, 1995).

89. According to the Croatian state Television news of 27 January 1998, Defense Minister Šušak thanked the athletes for advancing Croatia's reputation worldwide and awarded handguns to the boxer Damir Škaro, the karate fighter Branko Cikatić, the tennis superstar Goran Ivanišević, soccer players Stjepan Deverić and Ivan Mustapić, the water poloists Dubravko Šimenc and Perica Bukić, and basketball figures Andro Knego, Veljko Mršić, and Boško Božć.

90. "Sport kao refleksija društvenih odnosa" (Sports as a mirror of social relations), *Republika*, no. 233, March 2000.

91. In 1999, more than 120 basketball players from Croatia alone had played in foreign countries. This number exceeded the number of active players in the domestic A1 league. During the 1998–99 season, the largest number of Croatians played in Slovenia (24), followed by Switzerland (16), the United States (11), Hungary (9), Turkey (9), Germany (9), Poland (7), Austria (6), and so forth. Source: Website of the International Basketball Federation http://www.eurobasket.comshcro.

92. Slaven Letica, "Tito i Tudjman," *Globus*, no. 386, June 1998.

93. The Croatian sociologist Županov described Yugonostalgia as a "social sentiment" rather than a movement. *Nacional*, 8 February 1996, p. 51.

94. Directed by Vinko Brešan, screenplay by Vinko Brešan and Ivo Brešan (Croatia, 1999).

95. *Feral Tribune*, 8 September 1997, p. 34.

96. "Cyber Yugoslavia" (CY) was officially established and posted on the World Wide Web on 9 September 1999. At that moment the new nation had five thousand "citizens" and a constitution. The CY "government" was issuing mock passports and appointing cabinet members. The CY founding manifesto reads as follows: "This is Cyber Yugoslavia. Home of Cyber Yugoslavs. We lost our country in 1991 and became citizens of Atlantis. Starting September, 1999 this will be our home. We don't have a physical land, but we do have nationality, and we are giving CY citizenship and CY passports. Because this is Atlantis, we are allowing double and triple citizenship. If you feel Yugoslav, you are welcome to apply for CY citizenship, regardless of your current nationality and citizenship, and you will be accepted. Please read our Constitution for the details. If you are just curious, you are welcome to visit us as tourists. This land will grow as our citizens wish. Neither faster, nor slower. Neither more, nor less. So, this site will always be under construction. For a solid country to grow, even a virtual one, it takes some time. When we have five million citizens, we plan to apply to the UN for member status. When this happens, we will ask 20 square meters of land anywhere on Earth to be our country. On this land, we'll keep our server." See http://www.juga.com.

97. In January 1999, the International Organization for Migrations revealed the results of its survey of migrations from former communist countries of eastern Europe. According to the survey, people from ex-communist countries, in

contrast to the communist era, did not want to leave their countries to settle in the West. Only a majority of those included in the survey who were from Croatia and Serbia declared that they wanted to leave their countries and go overseas (the United States, Canada, and Australia appeared to be the most desirable destinations) with no intention to return to their countries, which according to the respondents, had no other future but ethnic strife and economic backwardness. Reported by Voice of America, Croatian Service, 11 January 1998.

98. *Večernji list*, 1 March 1999, p. 3.

99. *Feral Tribune*, No. 797 23 December 2000.

100. Voice of America, Croatian Service, 14 November 1999.

101. *Slobodna Dalmacija*, 27 November 1992,

102. Voice of America, Croatian Service, 10 November 1999.

103. *Feral Tribune*, no. 789, 28 October 2000.

104. Ibid.

105. *Feral Tribune*, 19 July 1999.

106. Ibid.

107. *Reaction to Events in Kosovo*, p. 10.

108. Interview with Goran Radman, *Feral Tribune*, no. 770, 27 May 2000.

109. Interview with Josip Kregar, *Feral Tribune*, no. 771, 24 June 2000.

110. In February 2001, the Institute for Strengthening Democracy, based in Konjic, Bosnia-Herzegovina, and the University of Bergen in Norway launched a project entitled "The Balkans Students Return Home." They invited all students from Bosnia and other Balkan countries studying in the West to make contact and return to their countries of origin, from which they had escaped in the 1990s.

12. Conclusions

1. Scott R. Appleby, *The Ambivalence of the Sacred: Religion, Violence, and Reconciliation* (Lanham, MD: Rowman and Littlefield, 2000).

2. *National Interest* (Summer 1997).

3. J. A. R. Marriott, *The Eastern Question: An Historical Study in European Diplomacy* (Oxford: Clarendon Press, 1918), pp. 37–38.

4. *The Ethnic Origins of Nations* (Oxford: Blackwell, 1986), p. 119.

5. Ibid., p. 116

6. See Michael Radu, "The Burden of Eastern Orthodoxy," in "Religion in World Affairs," *Orbis* 42, 2 (Spring 1998), p. 283.

7. The first lengthy and explicit condemnation of nationalistic extremism, racism, and the secular worship of the nation-state was given in the encyclical *Mit brennender Sorge* (March 1937) by Pius XI and reiterated in several other Church documents, including most recently John Paul II's encyclical *Tertio Millennio Adveniente* (1994), which specifically refers to "exaggerated nationalism" in the Balkans. The antinationalistic Protestant Christian theologians most often quoted are Paul Tillich, Erich Voegelin, and Reinhold Niebuhr. See Paul Tillich, *The Encounter of Religions and Quasi-Religions*, ed. Terence Thomas (Lewiston, NY: Edwin Mellen Press, 1990); Erich Voegelin, *Political Religions*, translated by T. J. Di Napoli and E. S. Easterly II (Lewiston, NY: Edwin Mellen Press, 1986), and Reinhold Niebuhr, *The Nature and Destiny of Man*, vol. 1, *Humane Nature* (Louisville, KY: Westminster John Knox Press, 1996).

8. See, for example, the chapter on Islam in John Coleman and Miklos Tomka, eds., *Religion and Nationalism* (Maryknoll, NY: Orbis Books, 1995).

9. *Glas koncila*, no. 27, 8 July 2001, p. 2.

10. See Ramet, *Nihil Obstat*, and Vladimir Tismaneanu, "Nationalism, Populism, and Other Threats to Liberal Democracy in Post-Communist Europe," *Donald W. Treadgold Papers*, no. 20. (January 1999).

11. See Huntington, *The Clash of Civilizations and the Remaking of World Order*, pp. 95–101, 209–218, 254–265.

12. Berger, "Secularism in Retreat," *National Interest* (winter 1996–97), pp. 3–12.

13. Ibid., p. 6.

14. Sociologists of religion define revival as a "process countervailing to secularization and born out of secularization as protest groups, such as sects and cults, form to restore vigorous otherworldliness to a conventional faith." See Rodney Stark and Williams S. Bainbridge, *The Future of Religion: Secularization, Revival and Cult Formation* (Berkeley: University of California Press, 1985), p. 2.

15. See *Religija i društvo*, pp. 52–53; Grubišić et al., *Religija i Sloboda*, pp. 203, 220. For the situation in Serbia in the 1980s, see Dragoljub Djordjević, *Beg od Crkve* (Escape from the Church) (Niš: Gradina, 1984).

16. According to the 1990–93 World Values Surveys, church attendance in postcommunist Catholic Croatia was 22 percent, compared, for example, with 22 percent in Slovenia and 47 percent in postcommunist Catholic Slovakia, while in Orthodox Serbia, the percentage of the adult population that attends church at least once a week was 7 percent, compared with 2 percent in Russia and 10 percent in Bulgaria. Ronald Inglehart, Miguel Basanez, and Alejandro Moreno, *Human Values and Beliefs: A Cross Cultural Source Book* (Ann Arbor: University of Michigan Press, 1998).

17. See Nikola Dugandžija, *Boja djeca—Religioznost u malim vjerskim zajednicama (uz zagrebačko istraživanje)* God's children—Religiosity in the minor religious communities—on the occasion of the Zagreb Research Project) (Zagreb: Republička konferencija Saveza socijalističke omladine Hrvatske and Institut za društvena istraživanja Sveučilišta u Zagrebu, 1990).

18. See more about this in Sabrina Petra Ramet, *Nihil Obstat: Religion, Politics, and Social Change in East-Central Europe and Russia* (Durham, NC: Duke University Press, 1998) chap. 13.

19. *Slobodna Dalmacija*, 28 May 2000.

20. Ibid.

21. *Feral Tribune*, no. 845, November 2001. From the *Feral Tribune* website: www.feral.hr.

22. Quoted in *Feral Tribune*, no. 778, 12 August 2000.

23. Sergej Flere, "The Impact of Religiosity upon Political Stands: Survey Findings from Seven Central European Countries," *East European Quarterly*, 35, 2 (summer 2001), pp. 183–199.

24. See Slobodan Reljić, "Crkva, država, civilno društvo" (Church, state, and civil society), *NIN*, no. 2476, 11 June 1998.

25. Dragoljub Djordjević, *Povratak svetog* (Return of the sacred) (Niš: Gradina, 1994).

26. Slobodan Reljić, "Obnovljena religija" (Rejuvenated religion), *NIN*, no. 2574, 27 April 2000.

27. Interview with Radomir Milošević, priest from Smederevo, *Naša Borba*, Belgrade, 27 April 1997.

28. Vladeta Jerotić, *Vera i nacija*, 2nd ed. (Belgrade: Tersit, 1995); Mirko Djordjević, *Znaci vremena* (Belgrade: Janus, 1998).

29. Interview with Filip David, *Feral Tribune*, no. 767, 27 May 2000. "Radjanje novog nacionalizma," Republika, no. 230–231, 1–29 February 2000.

30. See for example, Leo Ribuffo, "Religion and American Foreign Policy," *National Interest* (summer 1998), pp. 36–51.

31. M. J. Heale, *American Anticommunism: Combating the Enemy Within, 1830–1970* (Baltimore: Johns Hopkins University Press, 1990), p. 170.

32. Quoted from Martin E. Marty with Jonathan Moore, *Politics, Religion, and the Common Good* (San Francisco: Jossey-Bass, 2000).

33. Czeslaw Milosz, "Panstwo wyznaniowe" in *Metafizyczna pauza*, (Krakow: Znak, 1995). Cited from "Prevod: Verska država," *Republika*, no. 273, 16–30 November 2001.

34. Mirko Djordjević, "Ratni put Srpske crkve" *Republika*, no. 273, 16–30 November 2001.

35. "Pope Denounces Violence in Religion's Name," *New York Times*, January 25, 2002.

36. George L. Mosse, *The Nationalization of the Masses: Political Symbolism and Mass Movements in Germany from the Napoleonic Wars through the Third Reich* (Ithaca, NY: Cornell University Press, 1975).

37. See E. H. Carr, *Twilight of the Comintern, 1930–1935* (London: Macmillan, 1982).

38. See Milovan Djilas and Nadežda Gaće, *Bošnjak Adil Zulfikarpašić*, 3rd ed. (Zurich: Bošnjacki Institut, 1995).

39. See for example, Mircea Eliade, *The Myth of the Eternal Return, Or, Cosmos and History*, trans. Willard R. Trask (Princeton: Princeton University Press, 1971); *The Sacred and the Profane: The Nature of Religion*, trans. Willard Trask (New York: Harcourt Brace Jovanovic, 1959); and *Images and Symbols: Studies in Religious Symbolism*, trans. Philip Mairet (New York: Sheed and Ward, 1961).

40. In August 1989 the Holy See released an apostolic letter that included a section on "Totalitarianism and Religion," or, in the original: "Totalitarismo e religione: Infatti, in ultima analisi, il paganesimo nazista e il dogma marxista hanno in comune il fatto di essere delle ideologie totalitarie, con una tendenza a divenire delle religioni sostitutive."

41. Quoted from the *Lettera Apostolica in Occasione Del Cinquantesimo Anniversario Dell'inizio Della II Guerra Mondiale*, Vatican City, 27 August 1989, available at the official website of the Holy See, http://www.vatican.va.

42. See, for example, Stephane Courtois et al., *The Black Book of Communism: Crimes, Terror, Repression*, trans. by Jonathan Murphy and Mark Kramer (Cambridge: Harvard University Press, 1999).

43. See James Gregor, *Phoenix: Fascism in Our Time* (New Brunswick, NJ: Transaction 1999) and *The Faces of Janus: Marxism and Fascism in the Twentieth Century* (New Haven: Yale University Press, 2000); François Furet and Ernst Nolte, *Fascism and Communism*, trans. Katherine Golsan (Lincoln: University of Nebraska Press, 2001).

44. See for example, Eric J. Hobsbawm, *The Age of Extremes: A History of the World, 1914–1991* (New York: Pantheon, 1994), and *On the Edge of the New Century* (New York: New Press, 2000). For a critique of Hobsbawm's views, see for example Neil McInnes, "The Long Goodbye: And Eric's Consoling Lies," *The National Interest*, 64 (Summer 2001), pp. 105–114.

45. For a critique of anticommunism, see, for example, John Lukacs, "The Poverty of Anticommunism," *The National Interest*, 55 (Spring 1999), pp. 75–83.

46. Omer Bartov and Phyllis Mack, eds., *In God's Name: Genocide and Religion in the Twentieth Century* (New York: Berghahn Books, 2001).

47. See for example, *The Holocaust Chronicle* (Lincolnwood, IL.: Publications International, 2000); David I. Kertzer, *The Popes against the Jews: The Vatican's Role in the Rise of Modern Anti-Semitism* (New York: Knopf, 2001); John Cornwell, *Hitler's Pope: The Secret History of Pius XII* (New York: Penguin Books, 2000).

48. See "The Wages of Sin: Confronting Bosnia's Republika Srpska," International Crisis Group, Sarajevo/Brussels, 8 October 2001, available at www.crisisweb.org/projects/showreport.

49. *Feral Tribune*, no. 819, 26 May 2001.

50. The Serbian deputy premier, Nebojša Ćović, said on 18 May 2001 in Belgrade that Kosovo should be divided into ethnic Albanian and Serbian entities, AP reported. Ćović told a panel of scholars and diplomats that the province could be split into a "Serb entity with most of the Serb historical and cultural monuments . . . and an ethnic Albanian entity where the majority of the population would be Kosovo Albanians." He declined to give details of any division but said that "the proposal means that both sides would have to give up their maximalistic demands." Radio Free Europe/Radio Liberty, *Newsline*, Southeastern Europe, 21 May 2001.

51. As reported by the moderate Bosnian Croat author Ivan Lovrenović, *Feral Tribune*, no. 820, 2 June 2001.

52. Florian Bieber, "Croat Self-Government in Bosnia—A Challenge for Dayton?" ECMI brief no. 5, May 2001. Available for viewing and download at: http://www.ecmi.de/publications/working_papers_reports.htm.

53. USIP Special Report: "Faith-based NGOs and International Peacebuilding," prepared by David Smock, Washington, DC, 22 October 2001. Available at the USIP website, www.usip.org/pubs.specialreports/.

54. Some of the participants in recent Balkan peacemaking efforts are the following: American Friends Service Committee; American Jewish Joint Distribution Committee; American Jewish World Service; American Muslim Council; Baptist Peace Fellowship of North America; Catholic Relief Services; Christian Peacemaker's Team; Cooperative Baptist Fellowship; Fellowship of Reconciliation; Foundation for Interreligious Diplomacy; Friends Committee for National Legislation; Global Peace Services; Institute for Global Engagement; Institute for Human Rights and Responsibility; International Center for Religion and Diplomacy; Joan Kroc Institute for Peace and Justice; Lutheran World Relief; Mennonite Central Committee; Mercy Corps International; Moral Rearmament; National Council of the Churches of Christ in the USA; Plowshares Institute; Tanenbaum Center for Interreligious Understanding; United Methodist Committee on Relief; United Methodist Women's Division; United Religions Initiative; World Conference on Religion and Peace; World Vision. Ibid.

55. Ibid., p. 2.

56. *Feral Tribune*, no. 846, 3 December 2001.

57. See the USIP special report "Catholic Contributions to International Peace" (Washington, DC: United States Institute of Peace, April 2001).

58. The Institute for War and Peace Reporting, *Tribunal Update*, no. 245, November 2001, p.

59. Early in 2001, the high EU official Carl Bildt wrote: "recent political transitions in Belgrade and Zagreb have created a historic chance to make lasting peace in the Balkans. Torn by ethnic strife for a century and a half, the region

must now choose between disintegration into ever-smaller ethnic states and integration into the European Union. The EU must actively facilitate the latter, or the Balkans could suffer another round of bloody war." Carl Bildt, "A Second Chance in the Balkans," *Foreign Affairs* 80, 1 (January–February 2001), p. 148. See also the European Commission, Directorate General—External Relations: *The European Union and Southeastern Europe: Building a Brighter Future*, (Brussels, September 2000), available at http://europa.eu.int/comm/external_relations/see-/various/publication.htm.

60. See the annual report on the Stability Pact Quick Start Package, 14 May 2001, at http://www.stabilitypact.org.

61. Johannes Varwick, "The Kosovo Crisis and the European Union: The Stability Pact and Its Consequences for EU Enlargement," in Kurt R. Spillmann and Joachim Krause, eds., *Kosovo: Lessons Learned for International Cooperative Security* (Bern: Peter Lang, 2000).

SELECTED BIBLIOGRAPHY

Documents in Croatian, Serbian, or Serbo-Croatian

Savez komunista (The League of Communists)
 Centralni komitet Saveza komunista Hrvatske (Central Committee of the
 League of Communists of Croatia), Zagreb
  Komisija za statutarna pitanja (Commission for Questions of the Statute),
   "Neka stutarna pitanja odnosa komunista prema religiji i vjerskim obredima" (Some questions pertaining to the statute regarding attitudes
   of communists toward religion and religious practices). 10 June 1985.
  "Program idejno-političke akcije Saveza komunista Hrvatske u ostvarivanju
   programskih načela u odnosu prema religiji, provodjenju ustavnih
   opredjeljenja o slobodi vjeroispovijesti i borbi protiv sektaštva, klerikalizma i kleronacionalizma" (A program of ideological-political action of
   the League of Communists of Croatia aimed at achieving application
   of the programmatic principles concerning religion, constitutional
   norms on religious liberty, and the struggle against sectarianism, clericalism, and cleronationalism). 10 June 1985.
 Medjuopćinska konferencija Saveza komunista za Dalmaciju (Intermunicipal
 Conference of the League of Communists of Croatia of the Association of
 Municipalities of Dalmatia), Split
  Marksistički centar (Marxist Center, "Pregled pisanja vjerske štampe" (A
   survey of the church press). May 1986; November 1986; March 1987;
   June 1988.
  Marksistički centar (Marxist Center), "Komunisti i religija. Program idejno-
   političkog ososobljavanja SKH, 1988" (Communists and religion. A pro-
   gram of ideological-political education of the League of Communists
   of Croatia, June 1988).
 Općinski komitet Saveza komunista (Municipal Committee of the League of
 Communist of Croatia) and Gradski komitet Saveza komunista (City
 Committee of the League of Communists), Split.

"Crkvene manifestacije i hodočašća mladih katolika" (Church Manifestations and Pilgrimages of Young Catholics), an information dispatch to the Central Committee. 16 August 1986.
Centralni komitet Saveza komunista Srbije (Central Committee of the League of Communists of Serbia), Belgrade.
Radna grupa Sekretarijata Centralnog komiteta Saveza komunista Srbije (Working Group of the Secretariat of Central Committee of the League of Communist of Serbia), "Aktivnost SKS u borbi protiv nacionalizma i sovinizma u SR Srbiji: Aktivnost Srpske pravoslavne crkve na platformi srpskog nacionalizma" (Activity of the League of Communists of Serbia in the struggle against nationalism and chauvinism in the Socialist Republic of Serbia—Activities of the Serbian Orthodox Church on the platform of Serbian nationalism). Belgrade: IC Komunist, 1972.

Socijalistički savez radnog naroda (The Socialist Alliance of Working People), Croatia
Medjuopćinska konferencija Saveza komunista i Socijalističkog saveza radnog naroda (Joint Conference of the Intermunicipal Conference of the League of Communists and of the Socialist Alliance of Working People of Croatia)
"Tendencije u djelovanju vjerskih zajednica u Dalmacij—analiza" (Tendencies in the activity of religious organizations in Dalmatia—An analysis). Split, January 1984.
Sekcija za društvena pitanja religije Općinske konferencije Socijalističkog saveza radnog naroda (Section for Social Issues concerning Religion of the Municipal Conference of Socialist Alliance of Working People)
Various documents, reports, memos, correspondence. Split, 1976–1990.

Komisije za vjerska pitanja (Commissions for Religious Affairs, 1953–19740) and Komisije za odnose s vjerskim zajednicama (Commissions for Relations with Religious Communities, 1974–1990)
Savezna komisija za vjerska pitanja (Federal Commission for Religious Affairs), Federal Executive Council, Belgrade
"Verske zajednice i medjunarodna situacija—informacija" (Religious communities and the international situation—An information). 2 August 1967.
"Pitanje javnog izvinjenja za ratne zločine kao problem u odnosina Srpsko-pravoslavne i Rimokatoličke crkve u Jugoslaviji—informacija, povjerljivo (Memo on the issue of apology for war crimes as a problem in Catholic-Orthodox relations—An information, confidential). Prepared by Petar Šegvić, counselor in the Commission for Religious Affairs. 2 December 1967.
"Informacija broj 26, Povjerljivo—O nekim aspektima stanja i djelovanja verskih zajednica u Jugoslaviji" (Information no. 26, confidential—On some aspects of the situation and activity of the religious communities in Yugoslavia). December 1969.
"Izveštaj o poseti patrijarha Ruske pravoslavne crkve Jugoslaviji" (Report on the visit of the patriarch of the Russian Orthodox Church to Yugoslavia). 2 November 1972.

Komisija Saveznog Izvršnog vijeća (SIV) za odnose s vjerskim zajednicama (Commission of the Federal Executive Council for Relations with Religious Communities), Belgrade

"Izveštaj o radu komisije u 1973 godini" (Annual report on the Commission's activity in 1973). Belgrade, April 1974.

"Odnosi s verskim zajednicama u Jugoslaviji, godišnji izveštaj" (Relations with Religious Communities in Yugoslavia, Annual Report). Belgrade, December 1979.

"Izveštaj o radu komisije" (Annual report on the Commission's activities). Belgrade, April 1980.

"Odnosi s vjerskim zajednicama—Izveštaj o radu komisije" (Relations with Religious Communities—Annual report on the Commission's activity). Belgrade, 4 December 1982.

"Izveštaj o radu komisije" (Annual report on the Commission's activities). Belgrade, April 1984.

Komisija za odnose s verskim zajednicama Izvršnog vijeća Skupštine Socijalističke Republike Srbije (Commission for Relations with Religious Communities of the Executive Council of the Assembly of the Socialist Republic of Serbia), Belgrade

"Informacija o osnovnim karakteristikama pisanja verske štampe u 1983 godini" (Information on basic characteristics of writings in the religious press in 1983). February 1983.

Komisija za odnose s vjerskim zajednicama Izvršnog vijeća Sabora Socijalističke Republike Hrvatske (Commission for Relations with Religious Communities of the Executive Council of the Assembly of the Socialist Republic of Croatia), Zagreb

"Informativni bilten broj 5/1969" (Informative bulletin no.5/1969), with report on the conference held in Zagreb on 11 November 1969—"Naša politika prema najnovijim kretanjim u vjerskim zajednicama u Hrvatskoj" (Our Policy toward the newest currents in religious communities in the SR Croatia). 30 December 1969.

"Zabilješka o razgovoru Dr. Ive Perišina i Nadbiskupa Dr. Frane Franića" (Memo on meeting between Dr. Ivo Perišin and Archbishop Dr. Frane Franić). Confidential, 08-41/1-1972, 23 January 1972.

"Zabilješka o razgovoru predsjednika komisije Dr. Frida i Nadbiskupa Dr. Frane Franića održanog 20 siječnja 1972 u prostorijama komisije" (Memo on meeting between the chairman of the Commission, Dr. Zlatko Frid, and the archbishop of Split, Dr. Frane Franić, held on 20 January 1972 in the Commission's Office). Confidential, no. 15, 1972.

"Zabilješka o razgovoru predsjednika komisije Dr. Frida i Nadbiskupa Dr. Frane Franića održanog 21 April 1972 u prostorijama komisije" (Memo on meeting between the Commission's chairman, Dr. Frid, and the archbishop of Split, Dr. Frane Franic, held on 21 April 1972 in the Commission's Office"). Confidential, 08-41/2-1972, 25 April 1972.

"Zabilješka o razgovoru predsjednika komisije Dr. Zlatka Frida i Dr. Ive Petrinovića, člana Centralnog komiteta Saveza komunista Hrvatske s Nadbiskupom Dr. Franom Franićem održanog 17 July 1972 u prostorijama Nadbiskupskog ordinarijata u Splitu." (Memo on conversation between the Chairman, Zlatko Frid, and Dr. Ivo Petrinović, member of the Central Committee of the League of Communists, with Dr. Frane Franić, the archbishop of Split-Makarska, held in the Archdiocesan Office in Split on 17 July 1972), confidential, Pov. 08-41/1-72. Zagreb, 1 August 1972.

"Izvještaj o radu komisije" (Annual report on the Commission's activities). February 1973.

"Izvještaj o radu komisije" (Annual report on the Commission's activities). February 1979.

"Odnosi s vjerskim zajednicama u SR Hrvatskoj" (Relations with religious communities in the Socialist Republic of Croatia—Annual report). March 1981.

"Informacija o problemima vezanim za izgradnju vjerskih objekata u SHR" (Information about problems regarding construction of places for worship). 26 February 1982.

"Euharistijski kongresi 1981–1984—analiza" ("Eucharistic Congress 1981–1984—An Analysis). 1984.

"Uputstvo za organizaciju i rad komisija za odnose s vjerskim zajednicama u općinama, gradovima, i zajednicama općina" (Instructions for organization and work of commissions for relations with religious communities in municipalities, cities, and associations of municipalities"). Confidential, 24 April 1986.

"Pregled stanja i rada komisija za odnose s vjerskim zajednicama u SR Hrvatskoj" (A Survey of the status and activity of commissions for relations with religious communities in the SR Croatia). Prepared by the chief secretary Vitomir Unković and the commission's staff in co-operation with municipal commissions. April 1988.

Komisija za odnose s vjerskim zajednicama Izvršnog vije ća Skupštine Zajednice općina Split (Commission for Relations with Religious Communities of the Executive Council of the Association of Municipalities of Split), 1974–1986; after 1986 renamed Komisija za odnose s vjerskim zajednicama Izvšnog vijeća Skupštine Zajednice Općina Dalmacije (Commission for Relations with Religious Communities of the Executive Council of the Association of Municipalities of Dalmatia), Split

"Katolička crkva i masovni pokret hrvatskog nacionalizma" (The Catholic Church and the Croatian nationalist mass movement, 1971–1975). Confidential, October 1975.

"Dan velikog hrvatskog krsnog zavjeta i druge crkvene manifestacije u Splitu i Solinu u rujnu 1976—Analiza" (Day of the Great Covenant and other Church manifestations in Split and Solin in September 1976—An Analysis). Together with the Intermunicipal Conference of the Socialist Alliance of Working People for Dalmatia. Confidential, 2 December 1976.

Various documents: memos and correspondence with religious institutions and the state administration.

Komisija za odnose s vjerskim zajednicama Izvršnog vijeća Skupstine općine Split (Commission for Relations with Religious Communities of the Executive Council of the Municipality of Split), 1965–1987; after 1987 renamed Komisija za odnose s vjerskim zajednicama Izvršnog vijeća Skupštine Gradske Zajednice Općina Split (Commission for Relations with Religious Communities of the Executive Council of the City Association of Municipalities of Split), Split

"Izveštaji o radu komisije, 1965–1989 (Annual reports on the Commission's activities, 1965–1989). Incomplete.

"Izgradnja objekata za potrebe vjerskih zajednica, 1983–1987—Informacija" (Information on the construction of religious facilities and places of worship, 1983–1987). 14 April 1987.

Various documents: memos and correspondence with religious institutions and the state administration.

Komisija za odnose s vjerskim zajednicama Izvršnog vijeća Skupstine općine Split, Split (after the multiparty elections of 1990)

"Odnosi s vjerskim zajednicama" (Relations with religious communities). In "Izvješće o radu Izvršnog vije ća Skupštine općine Split za razdoblje lipanj-prosinac 1990 godine s posebnim osvrtom na racionalizaciju općinske uprave (Annual report for the period of June–December 1990 with a special supplement on the restructuring of the municipal administration). January 1991.

Police Reports and Intelligence Sources: Republički sekretarijat za unutrašnje poslove SR Hrvatske—Služba Državne Sigurnosti (The Republic Secretariat for Internal Affairs of the Socialist Republic of Croatia—Service of State Security)

Informacija o komentarima i ponašanju klera za vrijeme bolesti i pogreba Predsjednika Tita (An information on comments and behavior of the clergy during the illness and funeral of President Tito). Top secret. Obtained through the Commission for Relations with Religious Communities of the Executive Council of the Association of Municipalities of Dalmatia. Zagreb, June 1980.

Sjednice Biskupske konferencije Jugoslavije u 1982 godini (Sessions of the Episcopal Conference of Yugoslavia in 1982). Classified. Courtesy of Vito Unković. Zagreb, February 1983.

Informacija o pojavama kleronacionalizma kroz krivični i prekršajni postupak (An information on clerical nationalism treated through criminal proceedings). Obtained through the Commission for Relations with Religious Communities of the Association of Municipalities of Dalmatia. Split, 20 April 1985.

Procjena stanja sigurnosti na području SR Hrvatske (Assessment of the situation concerning state security in the Socialist Republic of Croatia). Top secret. Obtained through the office of the Commission for Relations with Religious Communities of the Association of Municipalities of Dalmatia, Split. Zagreb, 5 December 1986.

Miscellaneous

Informacija o zastupljneosti kadrova iz republike Hrvatske u SSIP-u i DKP (An information on diplomatic and consular cadres from the Republic of Croatia in the Federal Ministry of Foreign Affairs). Zagreb, Ministry of Foreign Affairs of the Republic of Croatia, 1990.

Selected Interviews

Badurina, Srećko. Catholic bishop of Šibenik, Croatia. Unpublished as a separate interview but quoted in the column "Religion and Politics." *Nedjeljna Dalmacija*, 1990.

Bajrami, Jetiš. Muslim mufti of Kosovo. A short interview within a two-part story on Kosovo. *Nedjeljna Dalmacija*, 5 August 1990.

Cerić, Mustafa. At the time of the interview Muslim imam in Zagreb, now reis-ul-ulema of the Islamic Community of Bosnia-Herzegovina. Cerić's opinion on the Gulf War. *Nedjeljna Dalmacija*, 1991.

Duka, Tomislav. Franciscan priest and one of the founders of the Croatian Democratic Community (HDZ). Interview-portrait of a priest-politician. *Nedjeljna Dalmacija*, 2 December 1990.

Franić, Frane. Catholic archbishop and metropolitan of Split-Makarska, Croatia. Several interviews. One published in *Nedjeljna Dalmacija*, 1989.

Gugić, Ivo. Catholic auxiliary bishop of Split-Makarska and bishop of Kotor. Several interviews in 1987 and 1990. Unpublished.

Jurić, Ante. Catholic archbishop of Split-Makarska. Interview quoted in the column "Religion and Politics." *Nedjeljna Dalmacija*,

Kolarić, Juraj. Professor of Zagreb Catholic Theological School and former secretary of the Episcopal Conference's Council for Ecumenism. *Nedjeljna Dalmacija*, 1990.

Marasović, Špiro. Catholic theologian. *Nedjeljna Dalmacija*, 1990.

Milovan, Vjekoslav. Monseigneur and director of the National Office for Croatian Migrants of the Episcopal Conference of Croatia. *Nedjeljna Dalmacija*, 1990.

Omerbašić, Sevko. Chief imam and chairman of the Meshihat of the Islamic Community in Croatia and Slovenia. Several interviews. One published in *Nedjeljna Dalmacija*, 1990.

Perko, France. Catholic archbishop of Belgrade. *Nedjeljna Dalmacija*, 1990.

Pešić, Branko. Chief architect of Saint Sava's Memorial Temple in Belgrade and director of the Construction Office of the Serbian Orthodox Church. Several interviews. Quoted in the column "Religion and politics." *Nedjeljna Dalmacija*,

Petrović, Ljubodrag V. Serb-Orthodox archpriest, administrator of the St. Alexander Nevski temple in Belgrade. Quoted in the column "Religion and Politics." *Nedjeljna Dalmacija*, 1990.

Šagi-Bunić, Tomislav. Member of Croatian Academy of Arts and Sciences, dean and professor at Zagreb Theological School. Several interviews. One published in *Nedjeljna Dalmacija*, 24 June 1990.

Samardžić, Radovan. At time of the interview, chief secretary of the Commission for Relations with Religious Communities of the Federal Executive Council of SFRY. Several interviews. Quoted in *Nedjeljna Dalmacija*,

Šegvić, Petar. Former counselor at the office of the Federal Commission for Religious Affairs affiliated with the Federal Executive Council of SFR Yugoslavia (and the commission's general secretary 1963–1972). Several interviews, 1986–88. Unpublished.

Šešum, Vojislav. At the time of interview, Orthodox archpriest in Split. Several interviews. Quoted in the column "Religion and politics." *Nedjeljna Dalmacija*,

Šeta, Ferhat. Professor of Islamic Theological Faculty in Sarajevo, former chairman of the Supreme Eldership of the Islamic Community of Bosnia-Herzegovina. Quoted in *Nedjeljna Dalmacija*, 1991.

Shehu, Djemali. Sheik and religious leader of the ZIDRA (Association of Muslim Dervish Orders of Yugoslavia), Prizren, Kosovo. Quoted in two-part report from Kosovo. *Nedjeljna Dalmacija*, 5 August 1990.

Silajdžić, Haris. Former prime minister of Bosnia Herzegovina, at the time of the interview secretary general of the Islamic Community of Bosnia-Herzegovina. Quoted in *Nedjeljna Dalmacija*, 1991.

Smajkić, Seid. Mufti of Mostar. Several interviews. One published in *Nedjeljna Dalmacija*, supplement—*Herzegovina*, 1991.

Šolic, Petar. Former Catholic auxiliary bishop of Split-Makarska. Several interviews. Unpublished.

Svete, Zdenko. Yugoslav ambassador to the Holy See (1980–1984) and chairman of Croatia's Commission for Relations with Religious Communities (1985–1990). Several interviews, Split, 1989, 1990, and Zagreb, 1991. Quoted in the column "Religion and politics." *Nedjeljna Dalmacija*,

Unković, Vitomir. Former chief secretary general of Commission for Relations with Religious communities of the Executive Council of the Sabor of the Socialist Republic of Croatia. Quoted in *Nedjeljna Dalmacija*,

Vincetić, Luka. Catholic writer, parish priest in Trnava, Croatia. Two interviews, 1990 and 1991. Unpublished.

Vrcan, Srdjan. Sociologist of religion. Several interviews. Quoted in the column "Religion and politics." *Nedjeljna Dalmacija*,

Žanić, Pave. Bishop of Mostar-Trebinje, Bosnia-Herzegovina (retired). Several interviews. *Nedjeljna Dalmacija, Herzegovina*, 1990 and 1991.

English-Language Monographs and Articles

Alexander, Stella. *Church and State in Yugoslavia since 1945*. London: Cambridge University Press, 1979.

Andrić, Ivo. *The Development of Spiritual Life in Bosnia under the Influence of Turkish Rule*. Edited and translated by Želimir Juričić and Hohn F. Loud. Durham, NC: Duke University Press, 1990.

Armstrong, John A. *Nations before Nationalism*. Chapel Hill: University of North Carolina Press, 1982.

Artemije (Radosavljević), Bishop of Raška-Prizren. "Remarks by the Bishop Artemije at the Current Issues Briefing 15 September 1998." *Current Issues*. Washington, DC: United States Institute of Peace, 1998.

Banac, Ivo. "The Dissolution of Yugoslav Historiography." In *Beyond Yugoslavia: Politics, Economics and Culture in a Shattered Community*. Edited by Sabrina P. Ramet and Ljubisa S. Adamovich. Boulder, CO: Westview Press, 1995.

———. *The National Question in Yugoslavia—Origins, History, Politics*. Ithaca, NY: Cornell University Press, 1984.

Belčovski, Jovan. *Historical Bases for Autocephaly of the Macedonian Orthodox Church*. Skopje: Makedonskata knjiga, 1990.

Bellah, Robert N., and Phillip E. Hammond. *Varieties of Civil Religion*. San Francisco: Harper and Row, 1980.

Berger, Peter L. "Secularism in Retreat." *National Interest* (winter 1996–97).

———, ed. *The Desecularization of the World: Resurgent Religion and World Politics*. Washington, DC: Ethics and Public Policy Center,

Beyer, Richard, J. *Medjugorje Day by Day* (Notre Dame, IN: Ave Maria Press, 1993).

Boban, Ljubo. "Jasenovac and the Manipulation of History." *East European Politics and Societies* 4, 3 (1990).

Bulajić, Milan. *The Role of the Vatican in the Breakup of the Yugoslav State: The Mission of the Vatican in the Independent State of Croatia: Ustashi Crimes of Genocide*. Belgrade: Ministry of Information of the Republic of Serbia, 1993.

The Crime of Genocide—A Plea for Ratification of the Genocide Pact. Chicago: Serbian National Defense Council of America, 1951.

Dedijer, Vladimir. *The Yugoslav Auschwitz and the Vatican: The Croatian Massacre of the Serbs During World War II.* Documents selected and compiled by Vladimir Dedijer. Translated by Harvey L. Kendall. Buffalo, NY: Prometheus Books, 1992.

Denitch, Bogdan D. "Religion and Social Change in Yugoslavia." In *Religion and Atheism in the U.S.S.R. and Eastern Europe.* Edited by Bohdan R. Bociurkiw, John W. Strong, and Jean K. Laux. Toronto: University of Toronto Press, 1975.

Djilas, Milovan. *Wartime.* Translated by Michael B. Petrovich. New York: Harcourt Brace Jovanovich, 1977.

Doder, Dusko. *The Yugoslavs.* New York: Random House, 1978.

El-Sadat, Anwar. *Those I Have Known.* New York: Continuum, 1984.

Esposito, John L. "Religion and Global Affairs: Political Challenges." In *Symposium: The Impact of Religion on Global Affairs, SAIS Review.* Washington, DC: Paul H. Nitze School of Advanced International Studies (summer–fall 1998).

Esposito, John L., and Michael Watson. *Religion and Global Order.* Cardiff University of Wales Press, 2000.

Hobsbawm, Eric, J. *Nations and Nationalism since 1780: Programme, Myth, Reality.* Cambridge, UK: Cambridge University Press, 1990.

Huntington, Samuel P. *The Clash of Civilizations and the Remaking of World Order.* New York: Simon and Schuster, 1996.

———. *Religion and the Third Wave: Democratization in the Late Twentieth Century.* Norman: University of Oklahoma Press, 1991.

Hussein, Hashim M. D. *Malaysian Tigers in Bosnia.* Kuala Lumpur: Berita, 1996.

Izetbegović, Alija. *The Islamic Declaration: A Programme for the Islamization of the Muslim Peoples.* Sarajevo: published by the author, 1990.

Johnston, Douglas, and Cynthia Sampson, eds. *Religion: The Missing Dimension of Statecraft,* New York: Oxford University Press, 1994.

Kohn, Hans. *Nationalism: Its Meaning and History.* Malabar, FL: Krieger, 1965.

———. *Pan-Slavism: Its History and Ideology.* Notre Dame, IN: University of Notre Dame Press, 1953.

Kurdulija, Strahinja. *Atlas of the Ustasha Genocide of the Serbs 1941–1945.* Belgrade: Europublic, 1994.

Lane, Chrystel. *The Rites of Rulers: Ritual in Industrial Society—The Soviet Case.* Cambridge, UK: Cambridge University Press, 1981.

Lydall, Harold. *Yugoslav Socialism: Theory and Practice.* New York: Oxford University Press, 1984.

Manhattan, Avro. *The Vatican's Holocaust: The Sensational Account of the Most Horrifying Religious Massacre of the Twentieth Century.* Springfield, MO: Ozark Books, 1986.

Marriot, J. A. R. *The Eastern Question: An Historical Study in European Diplomacy.* Oxford: Clarendon Press, 1918.

Mojzes, Paul, ed. *Religion and the War in Bosnia.* Atlanta, GA: Scholar Press, 1998.

———. *Religious Liberty in Eastern Europe and USSR—Before and After the Great Transformation.* Boulder, CO: East European Monographs, 1992.

———, ed. *Religion and the War in Bosnia.* Atlanta, GA: Scholar Press, 1998.

Mosse, George L. *The Nationalization of the Masses: Political Symbolism and Mass*

Movements in Germany from the Napoleonic Wars through the Third Reich.
Ithaca, NY: Cornell University Press, 1975.

Niebuhr, Reinhold. *The Nature and Destiny of Man*, vol. 1, *Humane Nature*. Lousville, KY: Westminster John Knox Press, 1996.

Omrčanin, Ivo. "Forced Conversions of Croatians to the Serbian Faith in History." Paper presented to the Third World Congress for Soviet and East European Studies, October 30–November 4, 1985, (Washington, DC: Samizdat, 1985).

Pavlovich, Paul. *The History of the Serbian Orthodox Church*. Toronto: Serbian Heritage Books, 1989.

———. Perica, Vjekoslav. "The Catholic Church and the Making of the Croatian Nation, 1970–1984." *East European Society and Politics* 14, 3 (fall 2000).

———. *Deadline Doomsday? Yugoslav Religious Organizations in Conflict, 1981–1997*. Washington, DC: United States Institute of Peace Grant Program, 1998. Summary in *Contributions to the Study of Peacemaking*, vol. 6, edited by Anne-Marie Smith (Washington, DC: United States Institute of Peace, December 1999).

———. "Interfaith Dialogue versus Recent Hatred: Serbian Orthodoxy and Croatian Catholicism from the Second Vatican Council to the Yugoslav Wars of the 1990s." *Religion, State and Society*, 29, 1 (March 2001).

———. "Religious Revival and Ethnic Mobilization in Communist Yugoslavia, 1965–1991: A History of the Yugoslav Religious Question from the Reform Era to Civil War." Ph.D. diss., University of Minnesota, Minneapolis, 1998.

Petrovich, Michael B. *A History of Modern Serbia: 1804–1918*. New York: Harcourt Brace Jovanovich, 1976.

Radu, Michael. "The Burden of Eastern Orthodoxy." In *Religion in World Affairs*, 283:300. *Orbis* 42, 2 (spring 1998).

Ramet, Sabrina P. *Balkan Babel: The Disintegration of Yugoslavia from the Death of Tito to the Ethnic War*. 2nd ed. Boulder, CO: Westview Press, 1996.

———. *Balkan Babel: Politics, Culture, and Religion in Yugoslavia*. Boulder, CO: Westview Press, 1992.

———. *Nationalism and Federalism in Yugoslavia: 1962–1991*. 2nd ed. Bloomington: Indiana University Press, 1992.

———. *Nihil Obstat: Religion, Politics, and Social Change in East-Central Europe and Russia*. Durham, NC: Duke University Press, 1998.

Ramet, Sabrina P., and Ljubisa S. Adamovich, eds. *Beyond Yugoslavia: Politics, Economics and Culture in a Shattered Community*. Boulder, CO: Westview Press, 1995.

Ramet, Sabrina P., and Donald W. Treadgold. *Render unto Caesar: The Religious Sphere in World Politics*. Washington, DC: American University Press, 1995.

Reaction to Events in Kosovo. No. G74. Camberley, UK: Conflict Studies Research Center of the Royal Military Academy Sandhurst, June 1999.

Reimer, James A., ed. *The Influence of the Frankfurt School on Contemporary Theology: Critical Theory and the Future of Religion*. Lewiston, NY: Mellen Press, 1992.

Religion and the Future of International Relations in Bosnia-Herzegovina and the Former Yugoslavia: A Conference Involving Members of the Local Religious Communities and Overseas Observers," Central European University, Budapest, Hungary, October 12–14, 1997. (Chairmen's Report). Washington, DC: United States Institute of Peace, 29 October 1997.

Roksandić, Drago. "Religious Tolerance and Division in the Krajina: The Croatian

Serbs of the Habsburg Military Border." In *Christianity and Islam in Southeastern Europe*. Occasional paper no. 47. Woodrow Wilson Center for East European Studies, January 1997.

Rullmann, Hans P. *Assassinations Commissioned by Belgrade: Documentation about the Belgrade Murder Apparatus*. Translated from the German by Zdenka Palić-Kušan. Hamburg: Ost-Dienst, 1981.

Rusinow, Dennison. *The Yugoslav Experiment 1948–1974*. Berkeley: University of California Press, 1977.

Samardžić, Radovan. *Religious Communities in Yugoslavia*. Belgrade: Jugoslavenski Pregled, 1981.

Spasojević, Svetislav. *The Communists and I: The Serbian Patriarch German and the Communists*. Translated by Todor Mika and Steven Scott. Grayslake, IL: Free Serbian Orthodox Diocese of the United States of America and Canada, 1991.

Stark, Rodney, and William S. Bainbridge. *The Future of Religion: Secularization, Revival and Cult Formation*. Berkeley: University of California Press, 1985.

Tillich, Paul. *The Encounter of Religions and Quasi-Religions*. Edited by Terence Thomas. Lewiston, NY: Mellen Press, 1990.

Tudjman, Franjo. *Horrors of War: Historical Reality and Philosophy*. Translated by Katarina Mijatović. New York: Evans, 1996.

Velimirovic, Nicholas. *Religion and Nationality in Serbia*. London: Nisbet, 1915.

Voegelin, Erich. *Political Religions*. Translated by T. J. Di Napoli and E. S. Easterly II. Lewiston, NY: Edwin Mellen Press, 1986.

Vrcan, Srdjan. "Religion and Churches and the Post-Yugoslav War." In *Religion and Nationalism*, edited by John Coleman and Tomka Mikols. London: SCM Press, 1995.

———. "Religion, Nation and Class in Contemporary Yugoslavia." In *The Influence of the Frankfurt School on Contemporary Theology: Critical Theory and the Future of Religion*, edited by James A. Reimer. Lewiston, NY: Mellen Press, 1992.

Wilkinson, Sir J. Gardner. *Dalmatia and Montenegro*. Vol. 1–2. London: John Murray, 1848.

Yugoslavia: History, Peoples and Administration. Vols. 1–3 of *Geographical Handbook, Series B.R. 493A*. London: British Admiralty Naval Intelligence Division, October 1944.

Yugoslavia's Way: Programme of the League of Communists of Yugoslavia. Translated by S. Pribichevich. New York, 1958.

Literature in Serbo-Croatian, Serbian, Croatian, and Bosnian

Adresar Katoličke crkve u SFRJ. Zagreb: Kršćanska sadašnjost, 1986.

Almanah jugoslavenskog sporta. Belgrade: Savez za fizičku kulturu Jugoslavije, 1977–1990.

Almanah—Srbi i pravoslavlje u Dalmaciji i Dubrovniku. Zagreb: Savez udruženja srpskog pravoslavnog sveštenstva u SR Hrvatskoj 1971.

Bahtijarević, Štefica. *Religijska situacija na području zagrebačke regije*. Zagreb: Institut za društvena istraživanja Sveučilišta u Zagrebu, 1985.

———, and Branko Bošnjak, eds. *Religija i društvo*. Zagreb: Center za idejno-teorijski rad Gradskog komiteta SKH, 1987.

Batelja, Juraj, and Celestin Tomić, eds. *Propovijedi, govori i poruke zagrebačkog nadbiskupa kardinala Alojzija Stepinca 1941–1946*. Zagreb: AGM, 1996.

"Biskupska konferencija Jugoslavije: Prilog BKJ rasparavi o aktualnim promjenama Ustava SFRJ u svijetlu kršćanske etike." *AKSA* 42, 10 October 1987, p. 909.

Boban, Ljubo. *Kontroverze iz povijesti Jugoslavije.* Vols. 1–3. Zagreb: Školska knjiga, 1987; 1989; 1990.

Bogdanović, Dimitrije. *Knjiga o Kosovu.* Belgrade: Knijiževne novine, 1990.

Bošković, Milo. *Antijugoslavenska fašistička emigracija.* Belgrade: Sloboda, 1980.

Branimirova godina—Od Rima do Nina. Zadar: Odbor za proslavu Branimirove godine, 1980.

Bratić, Radoslav, ed. *Pavle, Patrijarh srpski: Molitve i molbe, besede, razgovori, propovedi, pisma i izjave.* 2nd ed. Belgrade: BIGZ, 1997.

Bulajić, Milan. *Misija Vatikana u Nezavisnoj Dr žavi Hrvatskoj: "Politika Stepinac" razbijanja jugoslavenske dr žavi i pokatoličavanja pravoslavnih Srba po cijenu genocida: stvaranje "Civitas Dei" i "Antemurale Christianitatis."* 2 vols. Belgrade: Politika, 1992.

Čalić, Dušan, and Ljubo Boban, eds. *Narodnooslobodilačka borba i socijalistička revolucija u Hrvatskoj 1944 godine.* Zagreb: JAZU, 1976.

Ćebić, Petar. *Ekumenizam i vjerska tolerancija u Jugoslaviji.* Belgrade: NIRO Mladost, 1988.

Ćimić, Esad. *Metodologijski doseg istraživanja unutar sociologije religije u Hrvatskoj.* Zagreb: IDIS, 1991.

Crkva 1991—Kalendar Srpske pravoslavne patrijarsije za prostu 1991 godinu: 1941– 1991 Nezaceljene rane na telu Srpske crkve. Belgrade: Sveti Arhijerejski Sinod, July 1990.

Dan Velikog Zavjeta. Split: Crkva u svijetu, 1997.

Dedijer, Vladimir. *Novi prilozi za biografiju Josipa Broza Tita.* Vols. 1–3. Rijeka: Liburnija, 1980–84.

———. *Vatikan i Jasenovac: dokumenti.* Belgrade: IRO Rad, 1987.

———, and Antun Miletić. *Genocid nad Muslimanima 1941–1945: zbornik dokumenata i svedo čenja.* Sarajevo: Svijetlost, 1990.

Djilas, Milovan. *Druženje s Titom.* Harrow, UK: Aleksa Djilas, 1980.

———, and Nadežda Gaće. *Bošnjak Adil Zulfikarpašić.* 3rd ed. Zurich: Bošnjacki institut, 1995.

Djordjević, Dragoljub. *Beg of Crkve.* Niš: Gradina, 1984.

———, *Povratak svetog.* Niš: Gradina, 1994.

Djordjević, Mirko. *Znaci vremena.* Belgrade: Janus, 1998.

Djurić, Veljko D. *Prekrštavanje Srba u Nezavisnoj Dr žavi Hrvatskoj: prilozi za istoriju verskog genocida.* Belgrade: Alfa, 1991.

———. *Ustaše i pravoslavlje: Hrvatska Pravoslavna crkva.* Novi Beograd: Beletra, 1989.

Dokumenti o protunarodnom radu i zlo činima jednog dijela katoličkog klera. Zagreb: Vlada Narodne Republike Hrvatske, 1946.

Draganović, Krunoslav, and Josip Buturac. *Poviest crkve u Hrvatskoj.* Zagreb: Hrvatsko književo društvo svetog Jeronima, 1944.

Dugandžija, Nikola. *Božja djeca—Religioznost u malim vjerskim zajednicama (uz zagrebačko istraživanje).* Zagreb: Republička konferencija Saveza socijalističke omladine Hrvatske and Institut za društvena istraživanja Sveučilišta u Zagrebu, 1990.

———. *Jugoslavenstvo.* Beograd: NIRO Mladost, 1985.

———. *Religija i nacija.* Zagreb: Centar za kulturnu djelatnost, 1983.

———. *Svjetovna religija.* Belgrade: Mladost, 1980.

Ekmečić, Milorad. "Jugoslavenski krst, križ i polumese." Series of 13 articles. *Borba*, February–March 1990.

———. *Stvaranje Jugoslavije 1790–1918*. Vols. 1–3. Belgrade: Prosveta, 1989.

ENM (Bishop Nikodim Milaš). *Pravoslavna Dalmacija*. Novi Sad: Knjižarnica A. Pajevića, 1901; reissued in Belgrade, 1989.

Franić, Frane. *Bit ćete mi svjedoci. Zbirka božićnih, korizmenih i uskrsnih propovijedi, poruka i poslanica, 1954–1988*. Split: Crkva u svijetu, 1996.

———. *Konkretno društvo-samoupravni socijalizam—identifikacija u ljubavi, a ne u ideologiji*. Split: Crkva u svijetu, February 1988.

———. *Putovi dijaloga*. Split: Crkva u svijetu, 1973.

Frid, Zlatko, ed. *Vjerske zajednice u Jugoslaviji*—Religious communities in Yugoslavia—Historical Survey, Legal Status, the Church in Socialism, Ecumenism, Dialogue between Marxists and Christians. Zagreb, 1971.

Gatin, Nenad, et al. *Starohrvatska sakralna arhitektura*. Zagreb: Nakladni zavod Matice Hrvatske; Kršćanska sadašnjost, 1982.

Gavrilović, Žarko. *Na braniku vere i nacije*. Belgrade: IZ Patrijaršije, 1986.

Glišić, Milomir. *Odnos mladih prema religiji*. Gornji Milanovac: Dečije novine, 1982.

Grbić, Risto. "O crkvenim finansijama." In *Srpska Crkva na istorijskoj prekretnici*. Belgrade: Pravoslavlje, 1969.

Gross, Mirjana. "Liberalizam i klerikalizam u hrvatskoj povijesti (19. i početak 20. stoljeća)." *Naše teme* 31, 6–7 (1987).

Grubišić, Ivan, et al. *Religija i Sloboda: Prilog socioreligijskoj karti Hrvatske*. Split: Institut za primjenjena društvena istraživanja, 1993.

Grujić, Radoslav M. *Pravoslavna srpska crkva*. Kragujevac: Svetlost-Kalenić, 1989.

Hvala Sarajevo: poruke zahvalnosti gradu i zemlji domaćinu XIV zimskih olimpijskih igara. Sarajevo: Organizacioni komitet XIV zimskih olimpijskih igara, July 1984.

"Istina o naoružavanju terorističkih formacija HDZ u Hrvatskoj." *Narodna Armija*, special issue, 26 January 1991.

Jelić-Butić, Fikreta. *Četnici u Hrvatskoj, 1941–1945*. Zagreb: Globus, 1986.

———. *Ustaše i Nezavisna Država Hrvatska*. Zagreb: Liber, 1977.

Jerotić, Vladeta. *Vera i nacija*. 2nd ed. Belgrade: Tersit, 1995.

Jevtić, Atanasije. *Od Kosova do Jadovna*. Belgrade: Sfairos, 1984.

———. *Stradanja Srba na Kosovu i Metohiji od 1941 do 1990*. Priština: Jedinstvo, 1990.

———. *Velikomučenicki Jasenovac, ustaška tvornica smrti: dokumenti i svedo čenja*. Valjevo: Glas crkve; Belgrade: Sfairos, 1990.

Jevtic, Atanasije, et al., eds. *Zadužbine Kosova: spomenici i znamenja srpskog naroda*. Prizren: Eparhija Raško-Prizrenska i Bogoslovski fakukultet, 1987.

Jevtić, Miroljub. *Od Islamske deklaracije do verskog rata u Bosnia i Herzegovini*. Belgrade: Filip Višnjić, 1993.

Jukić, Jakov. "Teorije ideologizacije i sekularizacije." In *Religija i sloboda—Prilog socioreligijskoj karti Hrvatske*, edited by Ivan Grubišić et al. Split: Institut za primjenjena društvena istraživanja—Centar Split, 1993.

Jurišić, Karlo. "Ranije pokrštenje Hrvata i problem nedostatka arheoloških spomenika." In *"Počeci hrvatskog kršćanskog i društvenog života od VII do kraja IX stoljeća"; Radovi drugog medjunarodnog simpozija o hrvatskoj crkvenoj i društvenoj povijesti*. Split: Nadbiskupija Splitsko-Makarska, 1990.

Karamatić, Marko, ed. *Znanstveni skup "Rat u Bosni i Hercegovini: uzroci, posljedice, perspektive."* Sarajevo: Samobor: Franjevačka teologija, 1993.

Katolička Crkva i Hrvati izvan domovine. Zagreb: Kršćanska sadašnjost, 1980.

Kočović, Bogoljub. *Žrtve drugog svetskog rata u Jugoslaviji.* London: Veritas Foundation Press, 1985.

Kolarić, Juraj. *Pravoslavni.* Zagreb: Veritas, 1985.

Kovačević, Sreten. *Hronologija antijugoslavenskog terorizma 1960–1980.* Belgrade: ISRO Privredno finansijski vodič, 1981.

Krestić, Vasilije Dj., *Through Genocide to a Greater Croatia.* Belgrade: BIGZ, 1998.

Krišto, Jure. "Katolička crkva i Nezavisna Država Hrvatska." Series of essays. *Hrvatski obzor,* April–May 1997.

———. *Prešućena povijest: Katolička crkva u hrvatskoj politici 1850–1918.* Zagreb: Hrvatska Sveučilišna naklada, 1994.

Kustić, Živko. *Stepinac.* Zagreb: Studio Promotion, 1991.

Mileusnić, Slobodan. *Sveti Srbi.* Kragujevac: Kalenić, 1989.

———, ed. *Duhovni genocid: pregled porušenih, oštećenih i obesvećenih crkava, manastira i drugih crkvenih objekata u ratu 1991–1993.* Belgrade: Muzej Srpske pravoslavne crkve with Privredne vesti "Europublic," 1994.

Miljanović, Mitar. "Srpska pravoslavna crkva i nacionalno pitanje." *Glas Crkve.* no. 1, January 1991.

Mišović, Milo. *Srpska crkva i konkordatska kriza.* Belgrade: Sloboda, 1983.

Mužić, Ivan. *Katolička crkva u Kraljevini Jugoslaviji. Politički i pravni aspekti konkordata izmedju Svete Stolice i Kraljevine Jugoslavije.* Split: Crkva u svijetu, 1978.

Nikolić, Vinko, ed. *Stepinac mu je ime: zbornik uspomena, svjedočanstava i dokumenata.* Zagreb: Kršćanska sadašnjost, 1991.

Novak, Viktor. *Magnum crimen—Pola vijeka klerikalizma u Hrvatskoj.* Belgrade: Nova Knjiga, 1986.

Omerbašić, Ševko. "Religijska politika." *Mirotvorni Izazov,* no. 13 (winter 1995–96).

Opći šematizam Katoličke crkve u Jugoslaviji. Sarajevo: Vrhbosanska Archdiocese, 1939.

Opći šematizam Katoličke crkve u Jugoslaviji. Zagreb: Kršćanska sadašnjost, 1975.

Perić, Ratko. *Ekumenske nade i tjeskobe.* Mostar: Crkva na kamenu and Biskupijski Ordinarijat, 1993.

Perica, Vjekoslav. "Dva spomenika jedne ere: Političke konotacije izgradnje pravoslavne crkve i katoličke konkatedrale u Splitu, 1971–1991." *Časopis za suvremenu povijest* 31, 1, 1999.

———. "Vjera i politika." Weekly column. *Nedjeljna Dalmacija,* 1988–1991.

Peričić, Eduard, and Antun Škvorčević, eds. *Trinaest stoljeća kršćanstva u Hrvata, monografija Nacionalnog Euharistijskog kongresa—NEK 84.* Zagreb: BKJ, 1988.

Pešić, Branko. *Godine hrama Svetog Save.* Beograd: M. komunikacije, 1995.

Pešić, Vesna. "O krivičnom delu silovanja: Uporedna analiza sa SFRJ, užu Srbiju, Kosovo i Vojvodinu." In *Kosovski čvor: drešiti ili seći?* Belgrade: Chronos, 1990.

Petešić, Ćiril. *Katoličko sve ćenstvo u NOB-u 1941–1945.* Zagreb: Vjesnikova Press agencija, 1982.

———. *Što se dogadja u Katoličkoj crkvi u Hrvatskoj?* Zagreb: Stvarnost, 1972.

Popović, Justin. *Pravoslavna crkva i ekumenizam.* Salonika: Hilandar, 1974.

Popović, Justin (Otac Justin). *Istina o Srpskoj pravoslavnoj crkvi u komunističkoj Jugoslaviji.* Belgrade: Ćelije Monastery, 1990.

"Predlog Srpskog crkveno-nacionalnog programa." *Glas Crkve,* 28 June 1989.

Ranković, Ljubomir, Radovan Bigović, and Mitar Milovanović, eds. *Vladika Nikolaj: izabrana dela. Knjiga XII.* Valjevo: Glas Crkve, 1997.

Raspeto Kosovo: Uništene i oskrnavljene Srpske pravoslavne crkve na Kosovo i Metohiji, Jun–Avgust 1999. Prizren: Raška-Prizren Diocese, 1999.

Reljić, Slobodan. "Crkva, država, civilno društvo." *NIN*, no. 2476, 11 June 1998.

———. "German Djorić: Crveni patrijarh ili Gandi sa Balkana." Series of four essays. *NIN*, 31 August–21 September 1990.

———. "Obnovljena religija." *NIN*, no. 2574, 27 April 2000.

Šagi-Bunić, Tomislav. *Crkva i domovina*. Zagreb: Kršćanska sadašnjost, 1970.

———. "Nitko ne može biti bog povijesti." Interview. *Nedjeljna Dalmacija*, 24 June 1990.

———. "Sadašnji trenutak dijaloga izmedju katolika i komunista u Jugoslaviji." 17 essays. In *Glas koncila*, Zagreb, February–August 1972.

———. *Tematizacija religije u Programu SKJ*. Zagreb: Kulturni radnik, no. 3 (1988).

Samardžić, Radovan. "Religija u političkim sukobima u Jugoslaviji." *Vojno delo*, nos. 4–5, 1992.

Simić, Sima. *Prekrštavanje Srba za vrijeme drugog svetskog rata*. Belgrade: Kultura, 1990.

Šimundža, Drago, ed. *Godina velikoga zavjeta*. Split: Crkva u svijetu, 1977.

Sindik, Dušan, ed. *Sećanja Jevreja na logor Jasenovac*. Belgrade: Savez jevrejskih opština Jugoslavije, 1985.

Slijepčević, Djoko. *Istorija Srpske Pravoslavne Crkve*. Vols. 1–3. Munich: Ostrog, 1976–1978.

Špeletić, Krešo, ed. *Tito i sport*. Zagreb: Stvarnost, 1979.

Spomenica Ilmije. Sarajevo: Udruženje Islamskih vjerskih službenika, 1971.

Spomenica Udruženja pravoslavnih sveštenika Jugoslavije 1941–1945. Belgrade: Udruženje pravoslavnih sveštenika Jugoslavije, 1960.

Srpska pravoslavna crkva 1219–1969. Spomenica o 750-godišnjici autokefalnosti. Belgrade: Sveti Arhijerejski Sinod, 1969.

Stošić, Ljiljana. "Srpski crkveni spomenici u Makedoniji 1282–1690." *Velika Srbija* 2, 1 (1990).

"Strahinja Maletić: XX vek u tridesetak slika." *NIN*, no. 2570, 30 March 2000.

Titova Štafeta—Štafeta mladosti. 5th ed. Belgrade: Muzej 25th Maj, 1981.

Titu: poruke, želje, zaveti, 4 Januar–14 Maj 1980. Belgrade: Borba, 1981.

Turčinović, Josip. *Katolička crkva u južnoslavenskim zemljama*. Zagreb: Kršćanska sadašnjost, 1973.

Unković, Vitomir. "Pregled odnosa funkcionera Katoličke crkve prema socijalizmu." *Ideje Drugog vatikanskog koncila*. Zagreb: IDIS, 1976.

Ustav Republike Hrvatske. 9th ed. Zagreb: Informator, 1995.

Večan pomen: Jasenovac: mjesto natopljeno krvlju nevinih 1941/1985/1991—(Eternal Memory—Jasenovac, the Place Soaked in the Blood of Innocents, with Summaries in English—On the fiftieth Anniversary of Martyred Jesenovac and of the seventh Anniversary of the Consecration of the New Church of the Nativity of St. John the Baptist—Memorial Church Jasenovac. Belgrade: Holy Synod of the Serbian Orthodox Church, 1990.

Velimirović, Bishop Nikolaj. "Konkordatska borba 1937 godine." In *Vladika Nikolaj: izabrana dela. Knjiga XII*, edited by Ljubomir Ranković, Radovan Bigović, and Mitar Milovanović. Valjevo: Glas Crkve, 1997.

Vereš, Tomo. *Filozofsko-teološki dijalog s Marksom*. Zagreb: Filozofsko-teološki institut Družbe Isusove, 1973.

Vincetić, Luka. "Hrvatski katolicizam i srpska politika—Otvoreno pismo Preds-

jedniku BKJ, zagrebačkom nadbiskupu kardinalu Franji Kuhariću i Biskup-
skoj Konferenciji Jugoslavije." *OKO*, 16–30 November 1989.

———. "Otvoreno pismo ocu Atanasiju Jevtiću." *Danas*, 13 August 1991.

Vrcan, Srdjan, et al. *Položaj, svest iponašanje mlade generacije Jugoslavije*. Zagreb:
IDIS, 1986.

Zakon o pravnom položaju vjerskih zajednica Socijalističke Republike Hrvatske. Zagreb:
Narodne Novine, 11 April 1978.

Žerjavić, Vladimir. *Opsesije i megalomanije oko Jasenovca i Blajburga: gubici stanovništva Jugoslavije u Drugom svjetskom ratu*. Zagreb: Globus, 1992.

———. *Population Losses in Yugoslavia, 1941–1945*. Zagreb: Dom and Svijet, 1997.

Živković, Gordana, ed. *Čovek i crkva u vrtlogu krize: šta nam nudi pravoslavlje danas?*.
Niš: Gradina, 1993.

Živković, Ilija, ed. *Ranjena Crkva u Hrvatskoj—uništavanje sakralnih objekata u
Hrvatskoj 1991–1995*. Zagreb: Hrvatski Informativni centar, 1996.

———. *Raspeta Crkva u Bosni i Hercegovini—uništavanje katoličkih sakralnih objekata u Bosni i Hercegovini 1991–1996*. Zagreb: Hrvatski Informativni centar,
1998.

Zorica, Slavko. "Dalmatinske teme i dileme" (Dalmatia's Themes and Dilemmas).
Pravoslavlje, 15 April 1988.

Literature in Other Languages

Bizilj, Ljerka. *Cerkev v policijskih arhivih*. Ljubljana: Cankarjeva Založba, 1990.

Cannata, Francesco Maria. "Mosca-Belgrado: L'Asse Ecclesiastico Antioccidentale." *LIMES*, no. 1/2000, June 2000.

Dimevski, Slavko. *Istorija na Makedonskata pravoslavna crkva*. Skopje: Makedonska
knjiga, 1989.

Garde, Paul. *Vie et mort de la Yougoslavie*. Paris: Fayard, 1994.

"Gli Stati-Mafia: Criminalità e potere a cavallo dell' Adriatico—I pericoli per
L'Italia." *LIMES*—Quaderno Speciale, May 2000.

Gorymov, M. M. *Russkie doborvoltsy v Bosnii, 1992–1995 gg*. Moscow: Vestnik,
1997.

Hory, Ladislaus. *Der Kroatische Ustascha-Staat, 1941–1945*. Stuttgart: Deutsche
Verlags-Anstalt, 1964.

Manoschek, Walter. *Serbien ist Judefrei: militarische Besatzungpolitik und Judenvernichtung in Serbien 1941/42*. Munich: R Oldenbourg, 1993.

Mattei, Giampaolo. *Il cardinale Alojzije Stepinac: una vita eroica nella testimonianza
di quanti con lui sono stati vittime della persecuzione nella Jugoslavia comunista*.
Vatican City: L'Osservatore romano, 1999.

Melčić, Dunja, ed. *Der Jugoslawien-Krieg: Handbuch zu Vorgeschichte, Verlauf und
Konsequenzen*. Wiesbaden: Westdeutscher Verlag, 1999.

Omrčanin, Ivo. *Diplomatische und politische Geschichte Kroatiens*. Washington, DC:
Ivor Press, 1990.

Rastello, Luca. "La Vergine Strategica: Medjugorje come fulcro del nazionalismo
Croato." *LIMES*, no. 1/2000, June 2000.

Rivelli, Marco Aurelio. *L'arcivescovo del genocidio:monsignor Stepinac, il Vaticano e
la dittatura ustascia in Croazia, 1941–1944*. Milan: Kaos, 1999.

Roter, Zdenko. *Katoliška cerkev in država v Jugoslaviji 1945–1973*. Ljubljana: Cankarjeva Založba, 1976.

Snegarov, Ivan. *Istoriia an Okhridskata arkhieskopiia-patriarshiia.* Vol. 2. 2nd ed. Sofiia: Akademichno izdatelstvo "Prof. Marin Drinov," 1995.

Shtylla, Valter. *Monumente kulture ne Kosove.* Tirane: Butimet Toena, 1998.

Turczynski, Emanuel. *Konfession und Nation: Zur Fruhgeschichte der serbischen und rumanischen Nationsbildung.* Düsseldorf: Padagogischer Verlag Schwann, 1976.

Velev, Ilija. *Pregled na srednovekovni crkvi i manastiri vo Makedonija.* Skopje: Naša knjiga, 1990.

Newspapers and Periodicals

AKSA. Zagreb.

Borba. Daily. Belgrade.

Crkva u svijetu. Monthly review of theology. Split.

Duga. Weekly. Belgrade.

Feral Tribune. Weekly. Split.

Glas Crkve. Šabac-Valjevo Diocese, Valjevo, Serbia.

Glas Knocila—Katolički tjednik. Zagreb.

Glasnik Srpske pravoslavne crkve. Belgrade.

Glasnik Vrhovnog Islamskog Starješinstva. Bimonthly. Sarajevo.

Književne novine. Belgrade, Association of Writers of Serbia.

LIMES. Italian Journal of Geopolitics. Rome.

MI—list katoličke mlade ži. Zagreb.

Monitor. Weekly. Podgorica, Montenegro.

Nacional. Weekly. Zagreb.

Naša Borba. Daily. Belgrade.

Nedjeljna Dalmacija. Weekly. Split.

NIN—Nedeljne informativne novine. Weekly. Belgrade.

Novi list. Rijeka, Croatia.

Osservatore romano. Vatican City.

Politika. Daily. Belgrade.

Pravoslavlje—novine Srpske patrijaršije (Newspaper of the Serbian patriarchate). Belgrade.

Preporod—Islamske informativne novine. Sarajevo.

Radio Free Europe/Radio Liberty. News agency. Washington, DC.

Relazioni religiose. Monthly bulletin. Trieste, Italy.

Religija, politika, društvo. Bimonthly bulletin. TANJUG, Belgrade.

Republika. Biweekly. Belgrade.

Slobodna Dalmacija. Daily. Split.

Službene vijesti Biskupske konferencije Jugoslavije. Zagreb.

Vesnik. Monthly newsletter. Association of Orthodox Clergy of Yugoslavia, Belgrade.

Vijesnik. Daily. Zagreb.

Vijesnik biskupije splitske i makarske. Office of the Archibsop, Split.

Vijesnik nadbiskupije splitsko-makarske. Office of the Archbishop, Split. 1982–1991.

INDEX

Abdić, Fikret, 143
Active Islamic Youth, 170
Ajvatovica ("Little haj"), 86
Alexei II, Patriarch, 159, 203
Algeria, 80
Amfilohije (Radović), Metropolitan,
143–144, 154, 158, 173–175
Andjelović, Petar, 179
Andrić, Ivo, 117, 234
Anti-fascist Assembly of the People's
Liberation of Macedonia
(ASNOM), 47, 103, 154, 154
n.110. *See also* Prokhor Pčinjski
Anti-fascist Council of the People's
Liberation of Yugoslavia
(AVNOJ), 103
Antifascist nationalism, 22, 107
Anti-Yugoslav émigré organizations,
28–30, 35, 39, 41, 48, 14, 188
carry out terrorism, 28–29, 28
nn.45–48, 29 n.50, 62, 62 n.33,
201
clergy members of, 29, 29 nn.50–
51
Apparitions at Medjugorje, 109–122,
171–173, 208
and Bosnian War 120, 122, 171
and Croatian enclave in
Herzegovina 171–172, 172 n.35
and global anticommunism 110,
114–116
history of Marian apparitions,113–
117

popularity in the United States, 112–
113, 121–122, 172–173, 172
n.36, 173 n.38
Serbian Church's reaction to, 120–
121
Vatican's management of, 113, 113
n. 25, 115, 118, 120, 172
Arkan, Željko Ražnatović, 141, 153,
207
Artemije (Radosavljević), Bishop, 181,
183 n.75, 204–205, 205 nn.72–
74
Atanasije (Jevtić), Archimandrite
Bishop, 144, 144 n.58, 146, 204
his anti-western and antiecumenical attitudes, 33, 202–203
and Jasenovac, 147 n. 76, 151, 151
n. 92
and Kosovo issue, 124–125, 127
Atheism, 35, 38, 63, 71–72, 101–102,
132, 196
Auschwitz, 149, 150–151
Avramov, Smilja, 151

Badurina, Srećko, Bishop, 179
Bajrami, Jetiš, Mufti, 145 n.68
Baković, Anto, 141
Baptist Church, 13, 36, 40 n.112,
239, 239 n.54. *See also* Religious
peacemaking.
Barbarić, Slavko, 111
Barišić, Marin, Archbishop, 195, 197,
199

Basara, Svetozar, 157–158
Bečković, Matija, 127, 127 n.31
Behmen Omer, 87
Beljo, Ante, 141
Bishops' Conference of Bosnia and
  Herzegovina, 192
Bishops' Conference of Yugoslavia
  (BKJ), 10–11, 37, 40, 134, 163,
  163 n.168
Bleiburg, 26, 29–30, 30 n.56, 168
Bogdanović, Dimitrije, 33–34, 125
Bogetić, Antun, Bishop, 209
Bogović, Mile, Bishop, 195
Bosnian Franciscans, 117, 179, 221
Bozanić, Josip, Archbishop, 177
Brotherhood and unity, 94–95, 99–
  102, 130, 148, 206–210, 224–
  226
  attacked by religious leaders, 106,
    106, n.93, 150
  as civil religion 104–106, 106 n.
    94, 148
  religious roots of the idea, 101,
    224–225
Bulajić, Milan, 161, 163, 167 n.8

Catalonia, 113–114
Catechism (Religious instruction), 41,
  42, 42 n.127, 192
Catholic Action, 19, 110
Catholic-Orthodox relations, 15–16,
  19, 32–34, 34 n.75, 64, 66, 68–
  69, 72–73, 130, 145, 148, 151–
  152, 156–157, 164, 185
Census data, 6 nn.18–20, 7 n.32, 40
  n.115
Cerić, Mustafa, Reis-ul-ulema, 81–
  82, 85, 142 n.49, 169, 181–
  182
Četniks, 22, 30, 33, 34, 48, 150
Checchini, Michele, 137
Chechnya, 169
Christian-Marxist dialogue, 31
Church in the Croat People, 10, 216
Church of Jesus Christ of Latter-Day
  Saints, 14–15
Church-State relations
  church finances and state funding
    of religious activities, 35–37, 40,
    40 nn.112–113, 81, 140, 140
    n.40, 190

commissions for relations with
  religious communities. See
  Commissions for religious affairs
under communism, 26, 35–39, 68
  n.4, 133–134, 137–139
in interwar kingdom, 17–20
in successor states, 168–175, 189–
  190, 200, 205
Čičak, Ivan Zvonimir, 57
Ćimić, Esad, 75–76
Clerical associations, 48–49, 74
Commissions for religious affairs, 78,
  133–134, 134 n.6
Communist atrocities, 26, 97, 189
Communist Party. See League of
  Communists.
Communist persecution of clergy, 26–
  27, 61, 72, 136
Community of St. Egidio, 164, 240,
  240 n.57. See also Religious
  peacemaking; Vatican
Concordat crisis, 17–18, 20
Ćosić, Dobrica, 43, 107, 123–124
Ćosić, Krešimir, 15
Croatian Bishops' Conference, 190,
  194, 198
Croatian Catholicism, 9–11, 42, 163
  Croatian Church abroad, 40–42
  and Croatian national identity, 10,
    21, 62
  and Croatian National Movement
    57–59, 61–63
  and Independent State of Croatia
    24–25, 147, 151, 155
  supports HDZ party 140–142, 193–
    194, 197–198, 202
Croatian Catholic Lay Movement. See
  Catholic Action
Croatian community of Herzegovina-
  Bosnia, 191, 198
Croatian Democratic Community
  (HDZ), 140–141, 187, 190–192
Croatian Orthodox Church, 151
Croatian Revolutionary Brotherhood
  (HRB), 30. See also Anti-Yugoslav
  émigré organizations
Croatian War for the Fatherland, 197,
  199, 207
Czestochowa, 60, 113. See also
  Apparitions at Medjugorje;
  Poland

Dečani monastery, 125, 127, 181, 202
Dedeić, Miraš, 175. *See also*
    Montenegrin Orthodox Church
Dedijer, Vladimir, 97, 100–101
Dervish orders, 14, 84. *See also*
    Djemali Shehu
Destruction of places of worship, 3
    nn.1–5, 4 n. 6, 166, 202–204
Dimevski, Slavko, 47
Djemali, Shehu, 79–80
Djilas, Milovan, 26, 49, 96, 225
Djordjević, Dragoljub, 220
Djordjević, Mirko, 220, 222, 240
Djujić, Momčilo, 23
Doder, Dusko, 4, 41, 78
Dole, Robert, 203
Draganović, Krunoslav, 25, 29, 35
Dragičević, Ivan, 109 n.1, 172. *See
    also* Apparitions at Medjugorje
Dragojlović, Dragan, 129–130
Drašković, Vuk, 124
Duka, Tomislav, 141
Duraković, Nijaz, 76
Dušanić, Svetozar, 158

Ecumenism, 15–16, 31–34, 32 n.66,
    33 n.72, 154–156, 180
Ekmečić, Milorad, 8
Elections of 1990, 140–143, 142 n.47
El-Sadat, Anwar, 99, 108
Ethnic cleansing, 22, 166. *See also*
    Genocide; Holocaust
European Union (EU), 198, 235, 237,
    242–243
Evangelical Church, 13, 40 n.112

Fatima miracle, 114–116, 119. *See
    also* Apparitions at Medjugorje
Filipović, Muhamed, 170
Finci, Jacob, 221
Forcible conversions, 24, 151–152,
    155
Franić, Frane, archbishop of Split-
    Makarska, 62–63
    and Croatian National Movement,
    57–58, 58 n.9
    his views on Yugoslav socialism,
    31, 136–137, 137 nn.21–22
    and interfaith dialogue, 32, 34
    and Medjugorje apparitions, 111,
    119–120

role in Great Novena, 57–59, 67
    supports Tudjman and HDZ, 194
Frid, Zlatko, 59, 62

Gandhi, Indira, 91
Gavrilo (Dožić), Patriarch, 23
Gavrilović, Žarko, 124
Genocide, 29, 124–125, 147, 149,
    151, 157, 167–168
Germanus (Djorić), Patriarch 39, 50,
    127
    conducts Church's foreign policy,
    52–53
    his views on World War II and
    Croatian Catholicism, 149, 152,
    157
    his views on the role of Islam in
    Yugoslavia, 145, 145 n.67
    and Kosovo, 123, 125
    and Macedonian Orthodox Church,
    46–47, 147 n.21, 46
    proposes partition of Yugoslavia,
    158, 158 n.123
    and Yugoslav socialism, 51–52, 106
    n.93
Gomirje monastery, 52
Gračanica church, 44, 125, 202
Great Novena, 21, 63–68, 109, 150.
    See also Church in the Croat
    People, National Eucharistic
    Congress
Greece, 33, 52, 173
Grmič, Vekoslav, 31
Grubišić, Ivan, 193, 196, 219

Hadžiabdić, Naim, Reis ul ulema, 81
Hilandar monastery, 9, 52, 129–130,
    173
Holocaust, 147, 150, 168, 177, 196
    n. 40, 199–200

Independent State of Croatia, 21,
    24–25, 27, 147, 151, 157, 187,
    189
Indonesia, 170
Inquisition, 157, 157 n.129
Inter-Confessional Petition, 137
Interfaith Council of Bosnia-
    Herzegovina 181, 185, 236. *See
    also* Religious peacemaking
Interfaith dialogue. *See* Ecumenism

Yugoslavs (by nationality), 101–102, 207, 207 nn.84–85

Žanić, Pave, Bishop, 121, 147–148
Žića monastery, 6–7, 51–52

Žitomislić monastery, 121
Zovko, Jozo, 111–112, 111 n.13, 122. *See also* Apparitions at Medjugorje
Zulfikarpašić, Adil, 87–88, 142